DATE DUE		

Voices in Family Psychology

Voices in Family Psychology

1

edited by

Florence W. Kaslow

SAGE PUBLICATIONS
The International Professional Publishers
Newbury Park London New Delhi

For information address:

SAGE Publications, Inc.
2111 West Hillcrest Drive
Newbury Park, California 91320

SAGE Publications Ltd.
28 Banner Street
London EC1Y 8QE
England

SAGE Publications India Pvt. Ltd.
M-32 Market
Greater Kailash I
New Delhi 110 048 India

Printed in the United States of America

Library of Congress Cataloging-in-Publication Data

Voices in family psychology / edited by Florence W. Kaslow.
p. cm.
Includes bibliographical references.
ISBN 0-8039-3336-3 (v. 1). — ISBN 0-8039-3794-6 (v. 2)
1. Family psychotherapy. I. Kaslow, Florence Whiteman.
[DNLM: 1. Family Therapy. WM 430.5.F2 V889]
RC488.5.V65 1990
616.89'156—dc20
DNLM/DLC
for Library of Congress

90-8281
CIP

FIRST PRINTING, 1990

Sage Production Editor: Susan McElroy

Contents

Foreword

SANDRA B. COLEMAN

There are rare and special moments in growing up when we experience a unique surge of pride in our parents or our siblings, a feeling that makes us want to shout to the entire universe, "That's *my* Mom, (Dad, sister, brother)." Similarly, what I want to do now, having just completed reading the final manuscript for *Voices in Family Psychology,* is raise my voice and yell, "These family psychologists are my colleagues! Aren't they brilliant, creative, thoughtful, and simply marvelous?" With such an enthusiastic response how can I even begin to write an objective, unimpassioned opening to a contribution that is bound to be a bookshelf treasure? I suppose, however, that I must momentarily "unpuff" my chest and exchange my affective response for a more cognitive one which, though certainly more sober, will still be imbued with an upbeat hum.

The two volumes of *Voices in Family Psychology* present a multilevel range of information. Although each chapter offers a personal and professional chronicle of each contributing family psychologist's life, taken together the volumes offer an historical account of the field of family psychology as well as the contributions that have been conceived and developed as a consequence of our work. The result is a massive compendium that is heavily weighted with knowledge. A one word descriptor is *impressive*!

Interconnecting themes pervade the chapters providing the reader with an enriching experience that transcends each individual biography. It is obvious that family psychologists are diverse and individualistic yet they share many common basic roots. The theoretical underpinnings that provided our early nurturance are largely derived from individual psychoanalytic and behavioral schools of thought. As we developed ourselves we grew into the more diverse realms of the structural/strategic and systemic schools of family therapy, while many of us are now "fellows" in more integrative theoretical models. Another common theme is that family psychologists are still dedicated to their original training in traditional psychology and thus honor the Boulder Model in maintaining a scientist-practitioner stance. The family psychologists represented here impart an attitude of openness and flexibility that has allowed each one to create either an instrument, a methodological approach to treatment, a major research study, or a novel project. Clearly, none of us has been content to merely practice family therapy. Each one of us has presented multiple offerings to the field and there is no indication that, regardless of age or number of years of being in the profession, anyone is winding down. There is an unrelenting sense of energy that pervades each chapter and it is my guess that the reader is in serious danger of being infected by the zealousness that pervades these pages.

It is interesting that family psychologists represent so much diversity. From linguistics to genocide to cults, addiction, forensics, divorce, fatherhood, and gender – there is an endless list of topics and issues that we address. Although one could undoubtedly find prolificacy and divergency among many other groups of family therapists, we whose origins are in psychology appear to have a uniqueness identifying us as a somewhat different breed. This is the scientific attitude that is embedded in our foundation in classical psychology. It is the commitment to research, to scrutiny and assessment, that forever questioning attitude that says, "Show me," "Prove it," "Replicate it," "Refine it . . ." For anyone who promotes a heterogeneous profession called "Family Therapy" a sound reading of *Voices* should demonstrate the value of having traditional psychology underpinnings. The educational benefits of such a competency-laden background are brilliantly made obvious here.

Aside from the shouting, when I finished reading all the manuscripts my tendency to respond to stimuli with graphic representations was piqued. All I wanted to do was draw genograms of "us." I kept seeing family psychologists as having networks of interconnecting genograms that stood parallel to the idiosyncratic blood-related personal genogram of each contributing author. We have genograms that connect us to our theoretical parents, some that fasten us together by topical themes and interests and there are other genograms that link us to our personal experiences of marriage, divorce, childrearing, and often, remarriage. Finally, perhaps one of the most powerful genograms I see is the one that connects us to our dreams, for as an optimistic lot we all believe in a future world for family psychologists – a world that is far more expansive than the present one in which we all grew up. And that chorus of expressive hope should form a stereophonic circle around Florrie Kaslow who choreographed the opportunity for us to share our lives and our knowledge by harmonically raising our "voices."

Preface

FLORENCE W. KASLOW

In August 1987, when I began preparing my Presidential Address for presentation at the membership meeting of the Division of Family Psychology (number 43) of the American Psychological Association (APA), I anguished over what I might have to say that was new, different, and—I hoped—significant. While I was on the plane to New York, the fearsome lightning outside finally ignited a spark inside my thoughts. What flashed into consciousness were such questions as: (1) Why had the treatises on the history of family therapy (including my own) chronicled the field *as if* the contributions of the major pioneers to the field of family therapy came mainly from male psychiatrists (Ackerman, Bowen, Boszormenyi-Nagy, Jackson, Lidz, Minuchin, Whitaker, and Wynne—among others) and female social workers (namely, Satir)? (2) Why was the significant work of psychologists unsung or underplayed? (3) Why when psychologists and psychiatrists coauthored books and chapters did psychologists' names almost always come second? (4) Did the psychologists' grounding in research mean that, as a group, we wanted a data base to undergird the reliability and validity of our hypothesis, theories, and techniques before going public in writing and speaking with global statements that imply "I say it, therefore it is so"? (5) Had we almost voluntarily avoided the limelight accorded the "gurus" because of the lack of "provability" of some of the operating assumptions and/or some personality factors more characteristic of psychologists? For me, these were provocative and disturbing questions that had to do with identity and power issues.

Like many others who entered the family field in the later 1960s and early 1970s, I found the activity and excitement was in the interdisciplinary nature of the evolving "specialization" of marital and family therapy. APA, like other national one discipline organizations, was not receptive to a practice that legitimated treating several members of the same family conjointly. The American Association for Marriage Counseling (AAMC), founded in 1942, and renamed the American Association for Marital and Family Therapy (AAMFT) in 1978, beckoned to all mental health and pastoral counseling professionals interested in family theory, dynamics, and treatment—regardless of discipline of origin or degree. It offered a forum for dialogue and education, the comraderie was easy and open, and the organization spawned a fine journal in 1974 (now the *Journal of Marital and Family Therapy*).

In 1977 a second interdisciplinary organization emerged—the American Family Therapy Association (AFTA). Its founders' vision was that it would remain relatively small (up to 1,000 members, which it has) and be geared to experienced teachers, trainers, researchers, and highly skilled clinicians. Like many of the other contributing authors of *Voices in Family Psychology,* I have been and remain an active member of both organizations and have derived wonderful benefits and friendships in each. I too went through years of focusing on the similarities between family therapists of all professional backgrounds and seeking to obliterate the differences. For I was and remain "loyal" to my extended family therapy family; it is a very rich and meaningful aspect of my professional heritage.

Yet something was troublesome. What this was remained baffling until a group of people who belonged to the Academy of Psychologists in Marital, Sex and Family Therapy began to work toward the formation of the Division of Family Psychology in the early 1980s. All were periodically disturbed by the loss of their identity as psychologists for this is also a vital part of our inheritance; it is the other family from which we are descendants.

With this significant development and the accompanying recognition within the larger field of psychology that it heralded, we could proudly claim and feel part of both professional families of origin. I respect each tradition and want to remain connected to both as do many of my family psychologist colleagues. We also want to proclaim our shared identity.

Thus it seemed essential for me to utilize the forum of the Presidential Address to highlight the contributions of psychologists to the colorful tapestry known as the family field. I quickly made a list of those whose contributions immediately crowded into consciousness. They were all individuals whose work I was familiar with through the literature; I also was fortunate to know all of them personally from my involvement in professional organizations, through our mutual service on journal boards, and/or from our writing chapters for each other's books. My speech contained allusions to and a brief summation of main contributions of the following prominent family psychologists:

- James Alexander
- Carolyn Attneave
- John Bell
- Arthur Bodin
- Israel Charny
- Sandra Coleman
- Paul Dell
- Charles Figley
- James Framo
- Harry Goolishian
- Alan Gurman
- Chris Hatcher
- Neil Jacobson
- Diane and Sam Kirschner
- David Kniskern
- Luciano L'Abate
- Kitty LaPerriere
- Howard Liddle
- Rachel Hare Mustin
- Augustus (Gus) Napier
- William (Bill) Nichols
- David Olson
- William Pinsof
- Margaret Singer
- M. Duncan (Duke) Stanton
- Lenore Walker
- Gerald Zuk

The presentation was greeted with an enthusiastic response. One of the first reactions from the audience was "This will no doubt become the basis for Florrie's next book." And, at that moment, through a groundswell consensus of support, it did.

Almost all of those present who had been mentioned agreed to write chapters. They also recommended others who merited inclusion and I realized there were others I had overlooked in my first list. Many indicated that they thought such a book was long overdue and would be destined to become a major textbook in graduate and professional schools, family institutes, and an important historical reference book for use by family practitioners.

In my letters of invitation to potential contributing authors, I tried to be as inclusive as possible. Unfortunately, many of those whose voices should be included here were already overcommitted. I deeply regret that their significant work is not part of these volumes and want them to know they are missed. No doubt there were some involuntarily omissions: to those eminent individuals—my apologies.

My goal was to provide a comprehensive volume on family psychology, spanning the four generations of the field's existence, from the experiential and evolutionary vantage point of those who have created, enlivened, and enriched the research, theory, and practice in the extant literature. Each author was asked to follow the same "outline" so that there would be a consistency in the flow of the chapters. As becomes obvious, the majority of the authors are innovators; conformity is not typically a personality trait they exhibit. Some departed from the guidelines to, as usual, "do their own thing."

Some found it difficult to share aspects of their personal heritage and odyssey. The format and content of each turns out to be consistent with the authors' theoretical preference and therapy style; it is told in their most resonating voice.

The majority of authors conveyed that the experience of writing for this book was unique—compelling, reflective, illuminating, and sometimes very distressing. Many reported struggling with how to write in the first person and cite mostly their own work without sounding extremely narcissistic. Most had never before attempted anything this autobiographical and personally revealing. Some felt very stirred up and went back into treatment. Others encountered unexpected defenses. All reported that the request to pull the threads of their personal heritage and professional work together provided a fine opportunity for review and integration as well as the thinking through of directions for the 1990s.

Because in the family field we are concerned about progression through the generations, the legacies bestowed, the intergenerational transmissions, indebtedness, and loyalties, it seemed important to try to group the authors according to the generation in which they first made their contribution. Thus this became the guiding rationale of the organizational structure. Because in the growth of our profession, developments—including the entry of new leaders—have occurred with great rapidity, we are not using the classic definition of a generation as twenty years. My selection of the cut-off years (pre-1969, 1969-1976, 1977-1982, and 1983 into the future) was perhaps somewhat arbitrary, but these seemed congruent with the evolution that has transpired in the field.

Each author was given the dates and section description headings and asked to place himself or herself in this historical context. The main determinant of where someone fit was when he or she first became known through publications and presentations beyond his/her local community. As the book evolved, there has been some reshuffling to have professional peers grouped together. There is certainly some overlap: some of the authors span all four generations; most have made substantial contributions through at least two of the generations. One's generational alignment is not necessarily related to chronological age. There are some who became family psychologists after spending years in other careers; others made their debut on the national scene quite young. Within each part of the book, the chapters are organized alphabetically by the first author's last name.

Each volume has an Epilogue. That for Volume 2 attempts to tease out *themes and patterns,* to dispel some of the popular myths in the field, to draw some *conclusions,* and to make some prognostications about the next decade.

This book is a testament to the work of several dozen leading theoreticians, researchers, teacher/trainers, and clinicians who classify themselves under the broad rubric of family psychology. Family therapy is one of several activities we engage in; it is not the totality of what we do. Our roots are diverse. The authors travelled many paths en route to the self-definition of family psychologist—including but not limited to social psychology, experimental psychology, child clinical psychology, educational or school psychology, and family sociology. All are multitalented, ingenious, tenacious, exceedingly bright, and successful. My sincerest appreciation to each of these busy "V.I.P.'s" for taking time out to be a contributing author to these volumes.

Sincere appreciation is also expressed to Terry Hendrix at Sage Publications who eagerly accepted the book for publication when I first approached him about it. Because Sage is publishing Division 43's *Journal of Family Psychology,* it seemed a fitting connection. To Scott Ripple at Sage who awaited receipt of all parts of this massive volume, my thanks for your patience and support.

And most of all, thanks to our families of origin that gave us the gift of life, to our families of creation with whom we intimately share our adult years, to our professional families who share our trials and triumphs, and to our patients and students who keep our work vital and "on track."

Florence W. Kaslow
West Palm Beach, Florida
May 1989

PART I

THE FIRST GENERATION: PIONEERS AND RENEGADES PRE-1969

This part is a recapitulation and recognition of the first generation of family psychologists. All of these contributors began publishing before *1968*; most were by then already teaching and training others. All are still quite active as psychologists and are well known as theorists, researchers, clinicians, organizational leaders, authors and editors, journal board members and/or teachers, trainers, and supervisors. They share expertise in these manifold functions with colleagues in the other three generations also—as becomes obvious in later chapters.

Each was a courageous trail blazer. They had the temerity to challenge the existing psychotherapeutic establishment and experiment with new ways of conceptualizing and treating families. Many had their roots in psychoanalytic/psychodynamic therapy and found it accounted for some but not all of what they needed to know. Several decades later this remains equally true: Their brilliance, audacity, and confidence in their ability to continue pushing beyond the boundaries previously set propels them into new terrain. Many have become valued and revered mentors to their colleagues and students.

1

A Maverick Finds an Identity

CAROLYN L. ATTNEAVE

It is difficult to condense more than 65 years of the trends and events that result in professional identification for anyone. The questions biographers and editors ask make life seem so much more simple and direct than it ever really turns out to be. This is particularly so for mavericks like me who spent much of that time unclaimed and unbranded, however strong a personal identity was always at the core of being.

ROOTEDNESS IN FAMILY OF ORIGIN

Most family therapists acknowledge the strong effects and influence of their family of origin, and could write the full amount allowed in this chapter on just that subject. I can only hint at it here, and hope that it will lead to understanding, for I have a double heritage. My mother's family was Delaware Indian, with an oral history reaching back to before European contact and a documented one since then. Perhaps fittingly enough that first contact was with the Swedish, who for a brief period explored and settled the area between Chesapeake Bay and Long Island Sound that was Delaware territory.

In my father's family two streams merged. His mother emigrated as a teenager from Sweden in the 1880s and soon married. Grandfather Lewis came to Texas around the turn of the century and forbade any questions about whence he came or why. Since my paternal grandmother was deaf at the time

I knew her in the 1920s, there was no chance to know her history or adventures either—though there was much affection between us. Since this lack of communication developed after my father was grown, Swedish patterns were subtly transmitted.

From these paternal grandparents and aunts and uncles, I learned much of a way of life that valued books and reading, concerts, plays, and good things to eat that to me were exotic—like strawberries with *cream* and sugar on sliced tomatoes! Grandfather Lewis was a railroad man, a conductor and later railroad company executive, with strong convictions about individual rights and responsibilities shared by most of those who started life anew in Texas and became successful.

Mother was born in 1900 in Indian Territory later known as Oklahoma. She was the third of three sisters, the oldest of whom died when she was about four years old. A brother was born when Mother was five years of age.

Grandfather Adams was a Tribal Chairman, and often chuckled about being taken to Washington, DC, to be photographed by the Smithsonian and introduced to the President and other government officials. His brother, Richard C. Adams, spent most of his adult life in Washington, ferreting out the documentation that eventually established the successful basis for the settlement of tribal land claims against the United States. He and "Uncle Will" Rogers were mythical characters of my childhood, for we never met them in person.

At various times during my elementary school years I lived with my maternal grandparents, a well-known American Indian custom. Sometimes one or both of my cousins, boys 18 months and 3 years older than I, were also there, teaching me to be a younger sister of brothers. When at home with my parents I was the older sister of a brother nearly seven years younger. At my grandparents' home, there was also a great-grandfather who lived to be well over 100 and of whom I have vivid memories of times we spent together, fishing, scraping apple pulp because neither of us had front teeth to bite into them, and visiting the Mexican families who lived on our ranches, in either Texas or New Mexico.

Mother and Dad had one year of college before the outbreak of World War I, and married when Dad finally got home from the Navy in 1919. I was born in El Paso, Texas, but by the time I was two years old, the family had started out on its nomadic journey as Dad climbed upward from "rough neck" in the oil field to his eventual position at retirement in the home office of Standard Oil of California in the Division of Marketing Training. In between he probably held almost every job in the sales and service side of the oil company—from pumping gas to driving trucks to managing plants. He didn't talk much or often but did read aloud, and shared books and magazine articles and poetry when I began reading for myself earlier than I can remember.

Mother's family had moved from Indian Territory to Texas when she was about 11 years old, and she and her sister spent some time in private boarding schools. "Does the white man think boarding schools are a good idea? Then where does he send his children?" asked Grandfather. His girls then had something of an Ivy League education until Mother's senior year in high school. Grandfather made El Paso a center of his activities, often contracting in Mexico on road and canal building because there he "passed for a Yanqui." Much of his profit subsidized his brother's research and helped the tribe back in Oklahoma.

From this family I absorbed an Indian perspective on life and the world. Particularly I recall being taught the interrelated nature of all things, from rocks and trees to insects and fish. I was also saturated with a deep respect for roles and personalities of animals, and also plants, and a need to understand all kinds of people and how they related to one another.

I remember, too, being taught by example to prioritize opportunities and experiences and use of time. For instance, schools and books were steadily available, and lessons could always be made up by a little work. There might be only one day, however, to see the circus unload 30 miles away, with a chance to actually touch and feed an elephant! Or, equally important, this morning might be one's best chance to see the sun rise at the equinox and learn how all the roads and section lines oriented to it. I remember staying home to watch the butterflies emerge from their chrysalis and to find the first wild flowers—or comfort a friend, help with the harvest, or squish mud with our feet to make adobe bricks. Nothing was ever neglected, even routine chores, but the timing fit the occasions, not the clock and the calendar of the more mechanical outside world.

I took indoor plumbing and street cars for granted in the cities my parents lived in, but on the ranch with my grandparents we walked behind mules, pumped water by hand, ground our corn, and bathed in the family washtubs on Saturdays. We swept the beaten clay floors with a sprinkling of water, which made the adobe houses deliciously cool!

Such shifts in living between families never disturbed me, probably because *in tribal societies one belongs to all the relatives, including extended clans and tribal groups when with them. One always knows who one's biological parents are, but parental roles are shared much more widely, and children have much greater security, both in reality and in their own sense of being loved and appreciated.* It's something more "civilized" societies could learn with a good deal of profit (Attneave, 1969a, 1969b, 1977, 1982).

This inner security stood me in good stead during my nomadic childhood and beyond. In my 30s I realized that I had never lived in any place longer than two years in my whole life—unless you count the Stanford campus where I was an intermittent resident for 10 years of graduate school! No wonder even today I have trouble answering the social question, "Where are you from?" I attended uncounted elementary schools in California, New Mexico, and Texas and four high schools in three-and-a-half years, graduating from the last one before my sixteenth birthday and leaving for college a month later.

I used to think that this restlessness must have stemmed mainly from the Indian heritage, but as I recently began discovering my Swedish cousins and the family history of that branch, I find them born or growing up in much the same way—from southern Sweden to Germany, Japan, and even nearby in the northwestern United States. Sometimes I am wistful as other adult friends show me how they keep in touch with grade school and high school friends—but on the other hand, I learned and explored each new place adventurously and certainly felt secure. The Delaware grey-green eyes and lighter complexions probably saved me from much prejudice, and while we always knew our identity, my brother and I enjoyed our "camouflage", like being able to wander through the woods unheard and unnoticed. Unless the subject was thrust upon us, we just didn't mention our heritage to others—and in those days there were no benefits, educational or otherwise, if one lived off a reservation.

College was almost a problem. I had taken it for granted that I would go, but the family had only enough money for one of us. My mother felt strongly that my brother would need it most, since he would have to support a family. (Perhaps that gave them a few more years to accumulate the needed savings?) I was awarded a scholarship to Occidental College near Los Angeles, however, and was promised a job to pay for board and room. With relief for all, I was off on my own, never to return as a regular member of the family again.

PROFESSIONAL HERITAGE

The nomadism persisted through the undergraduate years, usually because I had to earn my own way but sometimes also to explore possibilities of various twists and turns of choosing a career. I managed to graduate in four years with a B.A. in English and minors in Drama and Art, but it took four colleges to do it. Later I joshingly collected on a bet with one of the registrars about settling down when I completed the second B.A. because within the next three years I had added not only Stanford but Smith College in Northampton, Massachusetts, and the Coast Guard Academy in New London, Connecticut!

Undergraduate Meanderings

All these colleges had something to contribute to my own total integration, but space forbids following some of the byways. Certainly when I began college I had no real idea that a field of study called "psychology" existed, and indeed none of the undergraduate schools offered a major in the field. I was among the privileged 30 who took the first course Occidental ever offered in psychology as a part of my minor in philosophy. I recall little of it except my first introduction to the Normal Curve as a way of describing human characteristics from length of toes to distribution of test scores. The instructor was an experimental psychologist, and skipped developmental and mental health sections of his subject. It was a fascinating but esoteric field. I felt the same way about many of the carefully teased out conclusions in perceptual psychology later. It was nice to quantify them and know how it was done, but most of them were principles that I later learned in a more practical setting at art school.

Probably the most direct thread to later work was in the weekly discussion meetings with those he was advising by Benjamin Stelter, head of the English Department. There we learned to look at human motivations and emotions, especially in reaction and interaction with events in their own contexts. It was much like the views inbibed from my Indian grandfather, but now given depth and breadth through the historical panorama. Stelter, who at one time had successfully sponsored more Rhodes Scholars than anyone else in the United States, urged all of us to be omnivorous in collecting knowledge. "Everything is grist for the mill of understanding literature" was his theme. I recall winning a prize he offered one semester for getting a top grade for the same term paper submitted independently to the most classes. Mine was accepted by the departments of English, Logic, History, and Biology. As I recall, the topic had to do with the impact of evolutionary thought and theory.

When student aid funds were cut, I left Occidental and tried a year at Yuba Junior College. It was a long commute through the Central Valley of California on a student-organized school bus that picked up and delivered rural students, starting before dawn and returning sometimes as late as 10 p.m. My idea was to gain some business skills, but typing, shorthand, and bookkeeping seemed repetitious and boring. I took some art courses to preserve my sanity and turned the skills I had learned on my job as technical director for the Drama Department at Occidental into income, designing and executing sets for the junior college and local theater groups.

The Art Department and some of the sets I had designed produced a surprise scholarship to the College of Arts and Crafts in Oakland. By staying with an aunt and continuing my theater work around the San Francisco Bay area, I had a delightful time. But the other students took themselves so seriously as artists that even the faculty couldn't convince me to stay. I recall that, when we were all doing abstractions, I merely enjoyed playing with the form and color while the other students dramatically declaimed they were expressing themselves emotionally. I watched them interpret my canvases the same way and probably got my first glimpse of how projective tests worked. I decided art school wasn't the place for me. With the promise of a job in the Federal Theater at the World's Fair on Treasure Island as soon as I got a degree, I entered Chico State and completed my first B.A. in English and Art within a year.

At Chico I rediscovered psychology, with electives in child development and testing children. Isa D. Reid, Ph.D., was a friend of Maude Merril and had helped in the standardization of the 1939 Stanford Binet. From her I realized that there were people interested in how children grew and thought, not just in turning them into proper adults. She taught us to administer and score individual tests, usually retesting youngsters she had herself tested a few years before. Once we had done the testing accurately we were given the files to read, checking on the growth of the children in all dimensions, socially and physically as well as intellectually. We observed them and related our findings to their past history and present social context in order to make a sensible report that would be useful to teachers, parents, and any others who worked with them. She was a strict taskmistress, but it was a fascinating challenge.

When the funds were withdrawn from the Federal Theater in a political swipe at Eleanor Roosevelt and F.D.R.'s New Deal, I was at first devastated. Not only was that job gone, but there were no others in the spots I had hoped to find them. All the Federal Theater's experienced crews were also out of work. Many people had told me that all college women ought to get a teaching credential as an insurance policy until they got married or *if* something catastrophic happened. That idea finally made sense.

I totaled up how long it would take me to earn a certificate to teach high school English (which required an M.A.). Another possibility was to go back and collect the undergraduate courses for an Elementary Credential. It seemed a clear choice. I liked the younger children and I recalled the courses with Dr. Reid, which would both count. At Chico I was able to put together a program for the credential; it took another year and a summer session. I continued my theater work and assisted Harlan Adams, who headed the Speech and Drama Department.

Graduate School Interspersed with Related Work

I began teaching sixth grade in San Carlos, California, with a magnificent contract of $1,800 for nine months. In 1940 this was more than the usual beginning teacher's salary because I undertook to work with the problem children in Therapeutic Dramatics. True to my earlier experience, I felt strongly that I could not understand why these children misbehaved—nor how to teach those in my regular class—unless I knew what they thought and what their life outside school was like. Several times a week I visited their homes and families. I learned their hobbies, interests, difficulties at home, parents' ideas and occupations, and, especially, how they got along with their brothers and sisters. Sometimes the children's behaviors in school were merely ones carried on as acceptable or expected at home, but sometimes they worried the parents, too. Having these contexts I could devise entries into the intellectual world of school that connected with what the children already knew and then take them into the next steps. In the "Dramatics Club" we improvised plays and sketches around the behavioral problems the kids were having. Both they and I cast individuals in exaggerations and complementaries of their usual life roles and helped them learn in these sketches how their behaviors affected others. Interpretations were made through the guise of directing their acting and everyone participated in the feedback and discussion. The story lines were fantasy, but the characters and their problems were right out of home, school, and neighborhood. These plays were well received, but the biggest gains were in the children's control over their own behavior.

The Superintendent of Schools, Clark Robinson, was encouraging his faculty to take graduate work at Stanford. He introduced me to Paul Hanna, the international leader in developing community-based schools, who became my mentor in the early years at Stanford.

I found myself in exciting academic seminars, team-taught and interdisciplinary, so that I worked under Hilgard (Psychology) and I.J. Quillen (Educational Sociology) as well as Hanna. This was 1941-1942, and in that summer we designed the schools for the Japanese relocation centers. We interviewed the Japanese people themselves and then built a proposal that used their own resources and worked toward their goals and conceptions of a good education rather than imposing a completely external curriculum. Some of us even made fairly accurate predictions, based on our relationships with the administrators of the "camps," identifying programs that would be successful and those where riots might occur.

Military Service—SPARS

By Christmas of 1942, I felt an urge to be more involved in the war effort itself, and inquired about the possibility of joining the WAVES after school was out. It just happened that recruiting was on for the initiation of the SPARS (Coast Guard) with pressure to form the first class in January. I quickly resigned my school position and became the youngest officer commissioned in the U.S. Coast Guard as well as a member of the first class of women to enter the Coast Guard Academy in New London, Connecticut.

Those years were exciting and busy. They enlarged my life experiences and gave me access to more various subcultures, including the very wealthy in Palm Beach, Washington, DC "cave dwellers", who had always lived in the nation's capital, the clannish "conches" who inhabited the

Florida Keys, and the adolescent and young adult enlisted women and the world of the military. Like working in canneries, the theater, and other odd jobs I had held, these experiences added much to a later ability to work with all kinds of people, but there was nothing with a direct line to eventually becoming a psychologist.

At the end of the war I declined an opportunity to remain as a regular Coast Guard officer and also said goodbye to the dream of pursuing a career as a professor of English Literature. I had arranged to attend Oxford on the GI Bill, but Oxford then decided not to admit women who already had a bachelor's degree and I had two! It was back to Stanford to reformulate goals and work my way back into civilian life.

Return to Graduate School

Completing a Master's in Elementary School Administration in 1947, I took a position as Assistant Superintendent of Ventura School for Girls, a state institution for delinquent women aged 16 to 21. Nominally I was responsible for education and training, but the superintendent often left me in full charge of several hundred young women, their housemothers in the various cottages, and other support staff.

My predecessor had never moved outside her quarters unaccompanied by one or more Dobermans; nevertheless, she had been stabbed, in spite of her fears and precautions. I had a Siamese cat on a leash instead. Very early in my term I observed how taking him on visits to a disturbed cottage or a screaming girl in detention provided something alive and safe, from whom the girls would receive affection and to whom they often expressed their grief and sadness. The cat's presence was calming and often prevented tensions escalating into riots. The rate of recidivism seemed to be related not so much to the character of most of the girls as it was to the complete separation of the mandated curriculum from the reality of the culture and neighborhoods to which they returned. But I didn't know how to prove it, or make major changes.

There was a clinical psychologist available, but most of her work was shrouded in confidentiality and legality. Her efforts were entirely assessment and, ironically, I was not considered qualified by her to share her findings. Since undergraduate days, this was my first glimpse of psychology as a possible profession of its own, and I wasn't sure I liked it. It did seem, however, that such skills could be useful in a broader application.

After a bit more than half a year, I returned to Stanford to complete a Ph.D. By then I was convinced that while elementary school teacher preparation included much exposure to developmental theory and other aids in understanding pupils, this was not enough. Many times teachers in the classrooms could use a consultation with the child psychologist. Best of all there should be counselors in the elementary as well as secondary schools. At that time, the late 1940s, there were no such positions anywhere in public schools.

To prepare myself to create such a role, I needed credentials in counseling, and my degree plan included all the available ones for both high school and rehabilitation counseling. To secure the needed skills with children, I turned to the Psychology Department. The Stanford child clinical program was headed by Maude Merril-James. Through my earlier work, I was proficient and knowledgeable in the use of the Stanford-Binet; after monitoring a couple of administrations and scorings, she waived all requirements for the testing of children. We respectfully differed about moving beyond scores to try to integrate the child's history and context when interpreting them. She felt that the purpose of testing was to obtain objective data for other professionals to use. For those times, this was the classic definition of what a clinical psychologist could and should do. Freed of testing laboratory requirements, I took as much learning theory, perception, and developmental psychology as was offered. I supported myself by occasional jobs and as a teaching assistant in Educational Sociology and Education Psychology.

PROFESSIONAL ZEITGEIST

The atmosphere of the graduate school at Stanford retained its multidisciplinary approach in the sciences particularly. Among the most fascinating ways of participating in this zeitgeist was via a series of seminars held in faculty homes around the then very new ideas of a general systems theory. Invited students joined with faculty from Psychology, Engineering, Medicine, Physics, and Anthropology. We read and discussed the first presentations (often prepublication) of Norbert Weiner (1948, 1950), W. R. Ashby (1956), L. von Bertalanffy (1949a, 1949b), W. Koehler (1938), and G. Bateson and J. Ruesch (1951) among others. Just as "Unified Field Theory" was the goal of the "hard sciences" of the 1980s, these concepts cut across social and traditional sciences with the concepts of information processing, feedback, and oscillations as models for both animate and inanimate behaviors and change. The goal of general systems theorists was (and still is) a parallel means of unifying the explanations and abstract descriptions of social, biological, and mechanical actions and reactions.

The emphasis in these seminars was on the construction of theory and testing it in both the laboratory and in observations in the normal world. The many fields of interest allowed comparisons and ideas from diverse perspectives to be examined and inevitably carried back to the clinic, as well as the laboratory, for further development.[1]

While decades later a new generation of therapists discovered the power of systems theory as a scientific justification for an already established field of family therapy, in the late 1940s the clinical focus was very much on the individual. Indeed, at that time I was more intrigued by the merging of efforts at achieving scientific elegance for the worldview I had been taught as a child by my Delaware Indian grandfather. I still remember his quiet smile when I would describe a seminar discussion, followed by a matching observation of his own or from the traditional wisdom of his tribe. This recognition across worlds was often repeated in working with elders and leaders of many tribes as different from each other as Navajo, Ojibway, Sioux, and Kwakiutl.

Individual teachers of psychotherapy at Stanford had less tolerance for varied viewpoints. With my "double major" in counseling based in the School of Education and Clinical Psychology, I purposely played it very safe for my dissertation topic (Attneave, 1952). The study of occupational prestige was acceptable to all as having potential information to contribute, especially in understanding client aspirations and motivations, and it would not offend any of the then-current schools of thought about psychotherapy.

There was considerable benefit in being able to move between clinical work in psychology, which, in addition to its foundation built on testing, also had a dynamic therapeutic orientation. In rehabilitation counseling there was a very eclectic approach with an emphasis on cognitive learning and stimulating both adaptability and problem-solving attitudes. The school counseling faculty were enthusiastic about Carl Rogers and his reflective, accepting approach. Among ourselves as doctoral students we often compared these varied perspectives and viewpoints. In classes, however, we had to remember which instructors would react negatively to terms such as *transference, unconditional positive regard,* or *positive reinforcement.* At that time (the 1940s), Carl Rogers was the only therapist who was willing to make films and audio transcripts of his cases as they happened. Therapists of other schools who relied on logical defenses of their convictions could become quite emotional if students seemed to be leaning toward someone else's theories. Perhaps this tendency has residuals in the various "schools" of family therapy today, as well as in the struggles between biochemical-, behavioral-, and Freudian-based therapies.

Internship

My internship, which ran parallel to the wrestling with theories of systems, was a more obviously prophetic link to my later activities. It was unique in its emphasis on families.

Thomas Aikin and his wife had had long and distinguished careers as educators. They had decided to form a private agency, Consultants to Parents, to provide services not ordinarily available. While clinics and special schools were available for developmentally handicapped and emotionally disturbed children, these agencies often had little knowledge or even awareness of other resources. They seldom knew how to help with the needs of the family. The Aikins hoped to coordinate a tailor-made program of treatment, rehabilitation, and education for these children and their families.

Each child needed a comprehensive evaluation, by psychological tests and through careful observation. These were my tasks. The written reports had to be accurate and jargon-free so that the parents could use them; they also had to be helpful to any clinic or other facility to which the children might be referred. I often became aware of very real differences in behavior when the child was in the presence of one or both parents, compared to times alone with me. This was not the focus of Consultants to Parents, but they were among the first to use a child psychologist to help families as a whole.

From these early experiences, I retained several seeds that became incorporated in my later work. One was a later realization of the *real usefulness of having parents behind a one-way mirror while I was testing a child.* We could then discuss our mutual observations of the child's behavior in terms of their own experience of it. Later I found that with a cotherapist, one member of the clinical team could usefully sit behind the mirror with the parents while another worked in play therapy with an individual child, or interacted with a sibling system. Still other times, *real shifts in family therapy could be made by leaving the sibling system a task and sitting behind the mirror with the parents in order that they and I might experience their rivalries and their ways of relating when adults were not present.*

I found that clear, descriptive psychological reports could be used by parents and other involved personnel in a meaningful way. Obsession with scores, labels, and diagnoses were sometimes necessary for bureaucratic reasons, but such value-laden judgments didn't really increase understanding the child's problem. This was undoubtedly reinforced later by being in the audience when the town of Oxford, Mississippi, saw themselves playing themselves, warts and all, in William Faulkner's film, *Intruder in the Dust* (Faulkner, 1948, 1949). Since Faulkner wrote honestly and objectively about his own community, including both friends and enemies, no one resented him or his work.

Marriage and Beginning a Family of My Own

Getting to know Faulkner and his people was one of the direct benefits of my marriage in 1947 to Fred Attneave III, a fellow student in the doctoral psychology program. A native of Mississippi, Fred is an experimental psychologist, interested in perception; he completed his dissertation as I finished collecting the data for mine. His work included developing a better method for scaling the way people make perceptual judgments about shapes, weights, form, and color. Mine used social perceptions to show that these followed the same general laws as sensory perception and also to demonstrate the impact of socioeconomic experiences on the accuracy of one's specific judgments. This dissertation got written between babies and the coveted degree became official the week the second child was born.

There were seven good years before the divergence between the experimental frame of mind and the developmental/clinical one became too great to be bridged. That, among other things, led to our separation and divorce. Once again I found myself needing to support myself, this time with two young dependent children.

Beginning a Full-Time Professional Career

During 1956-1957, the first year back on my own, I was Director of Student Personnel at Texas State College for Women in Denton. Much about the position was ideal, with its involvement in student life and activities that often included both children as well. I taught one class in mental health to seniors and was responsible for testing and classifying students and handling a multitude of problems, from those of seriously disturbed students to dealing with stray dogs. However, the administrative nature of the position meant many night hours and more times away from Dorothy, age 5, and Philip, age 3, than seemed good for us as a single-parent family.

Meanwhile, another Stanford psychology classmate surfaced as head of Psychology at Texas Technological College in Lubbock, Texas. Sylvan Kaplan had very good bait with which to lure me away. He had already established the only graduate program in psychology for blind graduate students, most of whom were interested in becoming rehabilitation counselors. At this time he wanted to build a second specialty that would include blind children. Collaborating with the Home Economics Child and Family Relations Department and using their preschool facilities, he proposed a diagnostic and educational center for children with sensory handicaps and physical disability problems. He had already recruited a multidisciplinary staff and I was delighted to join them, in 1958, with a joint appointment in Human Development in both Psychology and Home Economics.

Politics, however, again played fatally with my career plans. Scarcely was the ink dry on the contracts than Texas Tech was placed on the blacklist by the AAUP for summarily dismissing a tenure-track professor who was supposed to have been part of this project. It seems he wrote a paper about integrating blind and sighted children in the same classroom. One of the very conservative college trustees saw the word *integration* and immediately decided the Psychology Department was advocating racial integration, to which he was violently opposed. Further, the trustee discovered that the speech and hearing instruments for the preschool program were procured under a federal grant which required a pledge of no racial discrimination in the facility where they were to be used. That equipment sat in a boxcar for more than a year and eventually was returned to the federal government unopened.

I stayed on at Texas Tech, developing a private practice working with families and children, as well as consulting to elementary schools. I taught undergraduate child development and a variety of courses in the Rehabilitation Counseling program. I specialized in counseling techniques, but I recall most vividly the challenge of introductory statistics taught to 12 graduate students, none of whom could see the blackboard!

Probably my greatest professional learning came through working with Bill Daughterman, a classmate of both my brother's and Jay Haley's. A deep and lasting friendship grew between our families. Bill was blind and received his pre-Stanford education at state schools for the blind and other special facilities as well as from tutors and special readers. He had then gone to Kansas, where he developed close relations with some of the Menninger Staff and came to Texas Tech as an excellent clinician and counselor. Above all, I learned from him to *listen* and to observe clients and students with *all* my senses.

During these years in Lubbock I only published one brief article (Attneave, 1958). It amuses me now to realize that in a peripheral way it involved families. Faced with 100 or more students in child development, I needed some way for them to develop skills in objectively observing and recording samples of children's behavior. It occurred to me that the newly available television could provide a common sample and a realistic situation in "real time" for all of us. I required a written report of an assigned segment of such programs as "Leave It to Beaver" as a regular part of the classwork. Lively discussions as to whether the youngsters on TV acted in ways the text said they should followed. It seemed to me a healthy expansion of examples of school behaviors provided in their required readings.

Although I was dimly aware of the problem of "publish or perish," my personal priorities were centered on my family. When colleagues boasted of their publications, I thought of Cordelia in *King Lear* who, when her sisters flattered their father with lavish gifts, presented him with her children instead of jewels! I did try to get some kind of grant to free me to develop my ideas about families and children. However, comments with the rejections indicated that they were not appropriate activities for psychology or were merely dreams from an idealist insulated from the real world in an ivy-covered tower of academia.

Away from Academia into Full-Time Clinical Work

After four or five years it seemed time to move on to doing my own kind of work, focusing on children and families, although I still knew of no real precedent for it. In 1962 I discovered that the state of Oklahoma had vested all outpatient mental health authority in its Public Health Department. County health departments were setting up community guidance clinics with a priority set upon working with children and "those who impacted on children's lives." The charge and responsibilities were in many ways a flexible and appropriate definition of what I wanted and the family moved to begin what was in many ways a most satisfying period.

Shawnee, Oklahoma, was the headquarters for my work, growing out to eventually include two of the four counties between Oklahoma City and Tulsa, with initial efforts and planning for the other two. For a time I was the only full-time clinical psychologist and mental health resource in this region, which was 100 miles by 100 miles in a rough square.

Within these counties, my team of coworkers included the public health officer, who was an M.D. and who served as a family physician to the poor and indigent families and in emergencies to anyone who needed it. Under him, and as my colleagues, were the public health nurses, dedicated women who made house calls down dirt roads and served as school nurses. They were excellent case finders and information resources on children referred for help. They knew the families well and usually the other people important in their lives as well. There was also a dentist, who often noticed more than normal anxiety or fright in his young patients and afforded me opportunities to observe children and parents in easy and informal ways in his office, which often made formal offers of help or referral much easier than it would have been if I had been a stranger.

Community Involvement and Building Staff

When other specialized services were needed, I looked for a way to build them out of the community: social workers were available in the Welfare and Children's Services departments and in the Bureau of Indian Affairs. The county judge served as Juvenile Court judge and also as head of "Lunacy Court," dreadfully named, but the only mechanism for procuring aid from state institutions for the mentally ill and retarded. School board members, administrators, and teachers came in as clients seeking help and often became resources themselves.

In building a staff, only disciplines and personnel not represented in the rural communities and county seats were recruited. For instance, many schools had access to a bachelor level speech therapist, so we added one to our staff with an M.A. to consult with school staffs and take on some of the more specialized problems. There were some classes for the retarded in a private facility, but recognition of learning disabilities was just emerging. Often the school classroom teacher needed help in understanding and coping with both the retarded and the children with learning disabilities who were placed in the regular classroom. We hired Mary Bowers, a fine, experienced special education teacher, who also had training in diagnostic testing. She acted as a consultant directly to the teachers in developing curriculum materials and teaching techniques adapted to the general classroom and specifically tailored for the special child who needed them. A psychiatric consultant was secured for a half day each week.

All cases began with a family and health history, which often meant involving the family physician. It is intriguing to notice that at the end of my tenure two of these general practitioners were taking time off to complete psychiatric residencies.

Although 40 percent of the population was American Indian, only about 5 percent of the children referred in the early days were from this group. I was sure bridges could be built between the two populations and began making my way back into the Indian world, where I found real acceptance and a feeling of being at home even though none of the seven tribes in my "catchment area" were Delaware. Within a few years' time the proportional representation of our caseloads matched the demographic distribution of the region: racially, economically, and in almost all other characteristics. It was all a matter of determining the context in which the child lived, as well as that of the school and other aspects of the community. Then one worked to mutually solve the problems, whether they were misunderstandings, deep differences in values, or any of the other bases for human difficulties.

While this sounds like a rosy picture, it was not always so simple. I recall one schizophrenic teenager who would have had to wait two years for one of the 16 beds available for children and youth in the state hospital system. By mobilizing the network of her family, the small crossroads community where she lived, and the school teachers and pupils, it was possible to evolve a protective environment that took care of her when she was out of contact with reality and fostered her strengths when she was "ordinary" (normal). In another case, the network mobilized included a smaller cluster of family members, their clergyman, and the staff of a special medical facility in Tulsa for two adolescent incest victims, both now happily married with families of their own. The county judge found this approach so useful, especially the creation of networks of caretakers and community personnel, that he began initiating it in his cases of difficult custody decisions and planning for delinquent youth.

During this time I began to know and consult with Povl Toussieng, M.D., who headed the Child Psychiatry Program at the University of Oklahoma Medical School. He invited me to lecture at Grand Rounds and on other occasions, especially on understanding American Indian patients. The local pediatricians sent me for special training in the psychoemotional and neurological problems of children at Yeshiva University in New York City and later accepted my preliminary neurological screenings as guides for their own work-ups and referrals.

Outside of very limited groups away from Oklahoma (Attneave, 1969a, 1969b), however, other professionals did not seem to think what I tried to say was worth listening to or publishing. The chief criticism was that I had no status in academia. Certainly my ideas of working with families as a unit, rather than just with children, seemed strange. The practical results, however, within my region were proving family interventions practical, effective, and sound.

It was into this context that a copy of *Family Process,* mailed out by Jay Haley to increase subscriptions, appeared on my desk. I read it in a state of shock! Here was a professional journal that was filled with interdisciplinary material, and all focused on working with families as a reputable clinical and professional activity. There was even a name for all this—Family Therapy!

Philadelphia: The Child Guidance Clinic

When my children moved to Oregon to live with their father and attend high school, I had the freedom to consider a move east to investigate the family therapy movement. The Philadelphia Child Guidance Clinic was looking for a psychologist and I interviewed Minuchin and Haley. We were mutually pleased by the idea of my joining their staff. With a few months to make sure that the program in Oklahoma would continue without me, I was off to join the staff of the Philadelphia Child Guidance Clinic.

The two-year period in Philadelphia, fall 1968 to spring 1970, was an intense learning and exploring time. Rittenhouse Square, once a stronghold of early Philadelphia descendants, was now the gathering place for hippies. There were changes in other areas, too, especially an expansion in black neighborhoods. The Child Guidance Clinic was located in South Philadelphia. A large proportion of its clientele were troubled black families and youngsters; many others came from working class ethnic populations. Of the cases I was assigned, very few were from middle- and upper-class, stable income families.

There was culture shock in moving from a rural to an urban setting and to a new culture in the northern black community. I quickly realized that I needed to develop "street smarts" to know the difference between how one would solve the problems of a rebellious 12-year-old, depending on whether his mother was fearful of realistic threats to his/her safety or fantasizing and overprotective. I decided to find a place to live within the black community and to shop where they did, go to one of their churches and generally experience their world. My efforts were accepted and I became a recognized part of this social group.

Less intensively, I also made real contact with the Puerto Rican community through a neighborhood grocery store that imported from the island and where Spanish was spoken more often than English. I also became familiar with the Italian street market, the Jewish garment district, and Irish pubs, but never really penetrated those groups as deeply. As a mature single person I was freer to do this self-education outside of working hours than were most of the professional staff.

Among the professional community, I also set about becoming as widely acquainted as possible. Jay Haley used to tease me about "collecting family therapists", something he himself had spent years doing earlier in his own career (Haley & Hoffman, 1967). There was one unexpected problem: other family therapists and their agency or institutional affiliations seemed to be competitive in establishing their "empires." Exchanging consultations about clientele who moved from one to another was not a regular practice. However, I found it could be done. Ivan Boszormenyi-Nagy, Jim Framo, Alfred Freidman, David Rothschild, and Braulio Montalvo were all in the area. Nathan Ackerman and Carl Whitaker, among others, visited Philadelphia to consult and present their own work. I made contact with and learned as much I could from them all and found their similarities and differences fascinating. Regardless of their theories, and they all had potent ones, their actual work reflected their own backgrounds and experiences, often without their realizing how different their perspectives were from one another.

Thanks to Jay Haley, I became acquainted with Ross Speck and his initial work creating urban networks around individuals and families in crisis. I recall challenging him about his use of tribal metaphors when he had not himself experienced living and working with American Indians (Attneave, 1969a; Speck, 1969). We became friends, colleagues, and coauthors during my second year in Philadelphia and completed our book, *Family Networks* (Speck & Attneave, 1974), by working together over long weekends after I moved to the Boston area. Expanding the unit of interaction from the immediate nuclear family to include friends, neighbors, and professionals willing to involve themselves in designing ways of helping one another was a familiar concept for me. Ross Speck provided some vocabulary and theoretical basis for talking about it. Implementing it in urban settings complemented my previously rural experience.

Boston: The Massachusetts Department of Mental Health

In the spring of 1969 I encountered the Boston Family Institute staff of Fred and Bunny Duhl and David Cantor. Fred Duhl recruited me for a position as Field Director (actually a kind of "Executive Officer" or full-time Second in Command) for a Labor Department contract to train disadvantaged persons as employees of the state mental health system. While the contract did not call for it, we anticipated the coming movement of institutional patients to community facilities. Instead of losing the expertise of experienced institutional staffs, we were able to include training for the current staff of state hospitals and schools for the retarded in the same programs. We aimed at preparing as many people as possible for work in community-based agencies and mental health centers being planned by the Department of Mental Health.

I worked with the staffs of about five state hospitals, two institutions for the retarded, and three embryo community mental health centers. There were varying degrees of success, but on the whole, if Massachusetts had continued being able to transfer funds from large institutions into community-based ones, there would have been an outstanding improvement in its services to those in need of mental health care and their families. However, the tragic lack of real political understanding and support for the changes, in Massachusetts and throughout the country, has led to the emergence of the very difficult phenomena of "bag ladies" and other homeless mentally ill.

Private Practice, Teaching, and Consulting in Boston

During my entire time in Boston (1969-1975), I maintained a small private practice in family therapy, supervision and consultation. As part of this activity I saw a number of families, usually in their own homes. I had become a Teaching Fellow of the Boston Family Institute (BFI) soon after arrival. At that time BFI expanded from serving as an in-service training unit at Boston State Hospital and began accepting as trainees professionals in the Boston metropolitan area. I also offered independent seminars focusing on the therapists' own families of origin and procreation. These and other seminar course topics were sponsored by the Society for Family Therapy and Research and by the Professional School for Psychologists organized by the Massachusetts Psychological Association. Such activities permitted me to keep my clinical skills alive and growing even when my formal positions were more oriented to administration and research.

American Indian Mental Health Research

My major affiliation changed in 1972, as the Massachusetts Department of Mental Health contract with the Department of Labor was completed. For a number of years, I had met with the American Psychiatric Association Task Force on American Indian Mental Health. This task force proposed and received a grant to survey and evaluate the mental health services to American Indians offered by the Indian Health Services (IHS), a branch of the U.S. Public Health Service. Morton Beiser, M.D., who chaired the task force, was also on the faculty of the Department of Social Psychiatry of the Harvard School of Public Health, which became the base for conducting the IHS evaluation. I was appointed to this same department of the Harvard School of Public Health, first as a Research Associate and later promoted to Lecturer. My responsibilities included visiting more than 50 American Indian reservations, as well the professional and administrative staffs of IHS and its mental health services units.

The model used called for self-evaluation of each area's mental health programs in which local goals were made specific. I visited and described the two best programs as selected by the IHS area, the two least successful programs, and at least one, sometimes two, average programs. The final report for each area included the history and geography of that region, a description of the various tribal cultures, both historically and in contemporary settings, and a description of the programs visited (Attneave & Beiser, 1975-1976). The main thrusts of this project were to increase awareness of the accomplishments of mental health services to stimulate a healthy growth and partnership with the tribal people they served. This has continued over the years in consulting relationships and is still being followed in collaboration with many tribes and service units in the United States and in Canada.

Society of American Indian Psychologists

There were many serendipitous results of these countrywide travels and contacts. One of note was the eventual formation of the Society of American Indian Psychologists (SAIP). In the 1960s very few American Indian psychologists were known. As I traveled I met five, along with many more American Indian persons who aspired to such a career or were students progressing toward it. An informal network of American Indian Psychologists emerged in which we exchanged news and encouraged one another. Those with degrees began actively mentoring and providing emotional support for those trying to enter this profession. By the time the National Institute of Mental Health and the American Psychological Association (APA) were ready to organize formal avenues of participation for minorities, there was a sufficient number of American Indian psychologists to maintain representation and active participation.[2]

Harvard School of Public Health

My base for all these activities was the Harvard School of Public Health, in the Department of Social Psychiatry headed by Alexander Leighton. Dr. Leighton was finishing up a 25-year study of "Stirling County," a pseudonym for a very real region in Nova Scotia. His research included the epidemiology of mental health problems and some very intensive following of the relationship of catastrophic events in the lives of many people to their ability to cope, as well as their development of symptoms requiring psychiatric treatment. A large team had worked with him over the years and several were part of this department faculty.

Morton Beiser, under whom I worked, was one of these and his experience in relating social contexts to both mental health and illness, not only in Canada but also in Senegal, was invaluable in the American Indian project. The Beiser family became an adopted one for me and we have enjoyed many collaborations and adventures over the ensuing years.

None of these tasks were specifically family therapy-oriented, yet there was a rich acceptance of the need for work with families and communities as part of the emphasis on various stages of prevention that is part of the basic orientation of public health as contrasted with the general practice of medicine. I was given glimpses of the wider scope of national and international planning of programs and the applications of concepts that had previously seemed to me more location specific. I also became involved on a national and international level in professional organizations such as the General Systems Society, American Orthopsychiatric Association (ORTHO), APA, The National Institute for Mental Health, the World Federation for Mental Health, and the Association for Indian Affairs. I continued to be active in Psychiatric Outpatient Centers of America, of which I became the first woman president. My position at Harvard fostered the associations that led to my being involved later with two White House conferences on the family, a special panel for the Commission on Mental Health, and a presidential appointment to the Advisory Commission on Women's Equity in Education.

More directly concerned with family therapy was my involvement in the chartering board that organized and established the American Family Therapy Association (AFTA) and with the American Board of Family Psychology, which under the auspices of the Academy of Family Psychology established a diplomate in marriage, family, and sex therapy specialties.

In all these activities, and especially at the Harvard School of Public Health, I deeply appreciated receptiveness to my conviction that indigenous and tribal people had much to contribute in the way of mental health and understanding a variety of viable family structures and role divisions (Attneave, 1974a, 1977, 1982). Sharing these ideas with John Spiegel, M.D., led me to exploring island cultures in the South Pacific as well as many other adventures illustrating how value orientations affect human interpersonal transactions. Similar contact with Norman and Betty Paul and their work with survivors of the World War II Holocaust led me to insights about the endemic depression and alcoholism among American Indian populations. These ideas are now being tested and found valuable by many American Indian and Alaska Native groups who are seeking to heal the depressions of those affected by violence, both currently and in their family histories of surviving massacres and oppression three or more generations back (personal communications, 1988).

The research on the American Indian mental health services strengthened this conviction and demonstrated a very real need for an accessible, indexed bibliography of American Indian mental health (see below). NIMH funded such a project, from a grant written while I was at Harvard. Academia and experience had finally become blended into acceptability!

On the Move Again – The University of Washington

Fate again took a turn, however, as Alexander Leighton reached retirement age. All of the faculty and research staff decided to seek other positions. Like a seed pod popped open, we scattered in all directions. Morton Beiser and I hoped to find appointments in the same place, but he returned to Canada to the Department of Psychiatry at the University of British Columbia and I became Director of American Indian Studies and Professor of Psychology at the University of Washington in Seattle, a three-hour drive away.

During my two years as Director of American Indian Studies (1975-1977), I did very little teaching, although I helped staff the cases accepted for student-supervised practice in the Psychological Services Clinic. My Psychology Department responsibilities focused on the development of an Indian mental health bibliography (Attneave & Kelso, 1977; Kelso & Attneave, 1981).

The American Indian Studies faculty were persons of American Indian identity who had joint appointments in various Arts and Sciences departments: Art, Law, Communications, Economics, and Anthropology. The School of Education had a parallel program for specialists preparing American Indians as teachers, and the School of Medicine supported a number of American Indian students each year. The Indian Studies faculty, together with the Dean of Arts and Sciences, evolved a system of rotating the chair among the Indian faculty, which worked well for a while. Finally under another dean, it was transferred to the Department of Anthropology as a special section. This enabled American Indian Studies to retain its identity when budget cuts amalgamated the Black, Asian, and Chicano Studies programs under an umbrella of "Ethnic Studies."

Full-Time in Psychology and Family Therapy

Meanwhile, I became involved full-time in the Clinical Psychology program. At first there was little interest or support for family therapy, but Martha Perry, Ph.D., who was first head of Child Clinical Training and later of the total clinical program, made work with families a requirement for the child clinical majors. This opened the door in the Psychology Department to offering graduate seminars in family therapy.

Several schools at the University of Washington other than Arts and Sciences had an interest in the field and offered at least an introductory course in such varied settings as educational counseling, social work, psychosocial nursing, and psychiatry. A little informal work made it easy to plan so that none of us duplicated one another's activities. Students could elect courses from the various other disciplines to develop a comprehensive background in family therapy theory and some limited practice experience. With Johan Verhulst, M.D., a Belgian psychiatrist also with a Ph.D. in psychology, Carl Fellner and John Childs, both psychiatrists who had trained or worked with Carl Whitaker, and later Julia Heiman, Ph.D., a psychologist with international status in marital and sex therapy, we organized the Interpersonal Clinic as a part of the Medical School faculty at Harborview Community Mental Health Center. There we saw couples, families, and occasionally networks as we trained medical school residents, psychology interns, and, occasionally, other well-qualified advanced graduate students.

My seminars became very interdisciplinary and were the final preparation before trainees could participate in the Interpersonal Clinic for students in nonmedical graduate programs. I could offer a full year of work, alternating years for a while between a seminar in Social Network Theory and one in Ethnicity and Family Therapy. In 1981-1982, all these various disciplines of faculty were just on the verge of applying for accreditation as a special graduate program through the Association of Marriage and Family Therapy (AAMFT) and academic channels. The University and Washington State as a whole experienced a budget crunch and had to reduce the number of faculty. Instead of applying criteria for dismissal across the board, the University decided to remove whole separate programs from the university offerings. Those of us in the family field stuck to the protective coloration of our own departmental appointments and so survived to continue informal collaboration.

Sabbatical Year: Coeducation at St. Vincent College

After completing seven years as a full-time faculty member, I was given a National Science Foundation Visiting Professorship for Women to enable me to have a sabbatical year in 1982-1983. The purpose of the professorship was to study the transition of a small liberal arts college in western Pennsylvania from 146 years as an all-male institution to coeducational status. For many years prior to this, I had been a fairly regular visitor to St. Vincent College and its sponsoring Archabbey, the first Benedictine monastery in North America. I had given several lectures there on family and presented a number of short courses and workshops for students and adults from the surrounding region. This had enabled me to collect baseline data before the sabbatical. I continued data collection, using senior psychology majors, and as a participant observer served as a member of the faculty during the initial year of coeducation. I have continued the relationship and collected data spanning the transition years of coeducation, which are being analyzed as a follow-up to the original report (Attneave, 1983). I considered this an ideal opportunity to study cultural change in a well-defined community and how it can be accomplished smoothly.

As the teaching part of that year, I team-taught a variation of the seminar in Ethnicity and Family to upper-division students, partnered by Douglas Nowicki, OSB, Ph.D., a traditional analytically oriented child psychologist. Dr. Nowicki was head of the Psychology Department and knew the students well. Our theoretical differences and biases made it a lively and interesting course. It was challenging to teach concepts divorced from professional application. I also taught pastoral counseling in the only graduate department, the Seminary. Obviously, a sensitivity to family roles and process seemed to me important to include. One of the courses was very pragmatic, as the men in it were all serving their diaconate, an internship in local parishes before final ordination, and were frequently encountering family situations. St. Vincent became a second home after 18 months in residence, and I visit at least once a year.

I returned to the University of Washington campus and taught my obligatory year before taking another brief leave to rehabilitate myself from surgery to replace joints destroyed by arthritis that had seriously limited my mobility. After another year and a half following that adventure, I retired in 1987, teaching part-time for a while, but now free of such constraints and obligations.

EPILOGUE

As I come full circle, then, to my present status as Emeritus Professor, I have found that this, too, is a big adventure. I have been freed to actually be lazy, reading omnivorously not just in the professional literature, but also fantasy, science fiction, and mystery stories by the dozens. I have time to cultivate my own garden, both literally and figuratively by devoting time to local community work. This latter is a real challenge because, as an ordinary citizen, I have no professional status but am challenged to try to apply my insights and knowledge from within the group itself. In many ways it is a real test of my long-held concepts and skills, especially in the local parish, which is only slowly adapting to the participation of lay persons, let alone women, in its significant operations.

I am still in contact with the professional community through a widespread set of networks. My telephone calls and visitors over the last year include not only consultation visits with leaders of the American Indian community up and down the West Coast from Alaska to Los Angeles and easterly across the Plains, the Southwest, and Canada, but visits and conferences on a national and international scale concerning family therapy and social networks, with a special emphasis on Scandinavia. Every few months there are visits from leaders in Norway and Sweden and contact by phone and letters from all over the United States and from places on the globe as widely separated as the Arctic and Australia, or Europe and South Africa or China. In 1988 I presented formal addresses under the sponsorship of the American Academy of Psychoanalysis and the American Orthopsychiatric Association (Ortho) as well as one local workshop organized by the University of Washington Extension to initiate dialogue between Jungian and family therapists.

Influence from Personal Family Life

Several personal questions are often asked of family therapists. One has to do with the history of one's own family and its influence on one's work. I have sketched some of the generalizations of my American Indian heritage from my family of origin. In the family of procreation, my two children and I have remained in contact and visit as often as geography and our own commitments permit, for fun as well as support in times of crisis. The particular experiences of single parenting and custody shifts have of course influenced my work with other families. The thrust of these experiences has not been to fix my sights on any one solution to such problems, but to reaffirm the innate adaptability of human beings. Undoubtedly it has increased my capacity to empathize with others in similar predicaments.

There is no space in this chapter to detail the other families into which I and one or both of my children have been informally adopted and with whom there has been tremendous sharing over the years. Memories are vivid of celebrations of Passover and bar mitzvahs; of christenings and confirmations; weddings and funerals; of naming ceremonies, potlatches, giveaways, healing ceremonies, and powwows; of graduations, ordinations, and all manner of anniversaries. Without sharing these lives in addition to my own biological family experiences, certainly my practice of family therapy would seem in retrospect to have been impoverished. As these families enrich my own life, they also have supplemented and complemented the theoretical development of the professional work.

Personal Therapy

A second group of relevant questions focuses on the experience of personal therapy. I have sought help of this kind, sometimes with benefit and sometimes not. The first occasion was mystifying but positive. On one occasion, returning to Stanford after an exhaustive interlude of work, I was referred to a then little-known therapist named Milton Erickson. It was a profitable several months, but the details are beyond recall. I had forgotten it entirely until Jay Haley's book, *Uncommon Therapy* (1973), described Erickson. The period when I consulted him was that in which I was also learning about various schools of therapy. The most vivid recollection I have of Erickson was that he, not the patient, stretched out on a couch during our sessions!

At the time of the disintegration of the marriage, there was no marital therapy available except a short-term consultation with a legal service. The lawyer saw each of us privately and separately, and his only contribution was to refer us to a single law firm to arrange an uncontested divorce. The court accepted the recommendation of no alimony, but did award child support "to make up the difference between a woman's potential earnings and a man's." That token amount was deeply appreciated when it made music lessons and other similar opportunities possible. It was certainly a modern point of view, almost a radical one for domestic courts in the 1950s.

During the first few years after the divorce both children showed distress about having a single parent, which was in those days uncommon. I consulted two different child psychiatrists. The first was of the school of thought that blamed mothers for their young children's problems. He caused me considerable anguish before a pediatrician established that a genetic anomaly caused one child's frequent illnesses. With effective treatment regimens, the distress in the family was relieved.

The second psychiatrist was far more supportive in helping all of us to reach insights into our feelings and behaviors. He was also the only medical person other than dentists ever to offer the professional courtesy of reduced fees. The financial savings were considerable and the boost to my self-esteem to be treated as a colleague is still appreciated.

I had the opportunity for supervision in my family work from Harry Aponte at the Philadelphia Child Guidance Clinic and from David Kantor and Bunny Duhl in Boston. All three were case-oriented rather than involving me in any positive therapy. Following their example, I try to keep the same distinction in my own supervisory activities. I make referrals, and try to support without interfering in a trainee's own therapy with someone else. When students or former students are accepted for therapy, the reverse also applies, of course. Case material—particularly problems of countertransference—may arise, but actual supervision of the case and techniques of acting on insights developed in therapy are delegated back to the responsible supervisor.

Whose "Brand" Do I Wear?

Many people, especially in the more recent generations of family therapists, ask, "To which school of family therapists do you belong?" To graduate students I'm inclined to answer "my own" and suggest they do some research. For prospective clients who inquire, I use the opportunity to explore what concepts they have picked up from media and popular literature, and particularly how they conceptualize their needs. From this discussion we can then mutually decide if they think I can help or if a referral to a specifically focused therapist would be a better match.

I asked a number of colleagues where they would fit me into the bewildering proliferation of subclassifications of the family field. The results were nearly unanimous in mentioning "network intervention—but that's only part of what you do." "Integrative" and "eclectic" also had a high percentage of mentions. A few puzzled over the label "systems" but discarded it because it has been preempted by a particular group of family therapists who employ a narrow and concrete definition. If I were to carry the "systems" label the result would probably be mutual embarrassment, somewhat like a rancher with a herd of Hereford cattle who found a Texas Longhorn in their midst!

This lack of belonging to anyone's herd is characteristic of a maverick, which for the benefit of non-Westerners is a term applied to unbranded cattle ranging freely. Historically any rancher who rounded up a maverick could apply *his* brand and incorporate the creature into his herd. Mavericks several years old didn't like being fenced in, however, and frequently resumed their independent ways. So far, no school of family therapy has claimed me, although many find elements in common.

If I have to find a "brand," it seems that the best label would be "eclectic." That term is viable only if there is some underlying method of prioritizing one's selection of techniques and concepts to apply in varied situations. For this task I return to my roots in *general systems* and offer this theory. It is described in Attneave (1974b). Since that publication is hard to find I will summarize it briefly.

The wide variety of human behaviors can be divided into four classifications as follows:

1. *The physical systems.* Chemical interactions, the common physiological systems of circulation, digestion and nutrition, hormonal, perspiration, elimination, structural musculoskeletal, and sensory. These are the primary fields of medicine, including biochemical, surgical, physiological, and prosthetic interventions.
2. *The emotional/cognitive systems.* These systems represent the mental life of people as they perceive and contemplate their environment. Emotions are the recognition of changes in the physical body in response to some aspect of the

environment. Cognitive systems abstract these, and also sensory explorations of the environment, and organize information. These are the primary focus of both dynamic (Freudian, Jungian, Adlerian) and behavior modification techniques of interventions, as well as many other forms of psychotherapy.

3. *Social systems.* These are based on the interactions of people in dyads, triads, and larger groups. Intimate relationships that continue from conception over the lifetime of individuals (in one form or another) are the province of most family therapy. However, significant relationships also occur outside the biologically defined family in both lifelong and shorter term or intermittent states of activation. Group therapies, support groups, culturally based therapies, and social network interventions include these other social contexts in varying ways.
4. *Systems of values.* These systems, often referred to as "mystic systems," make the fourth classification. Here one finds religious practices and principles, moral and ethical assumptions, value orientations, and loyalties to ethnic and cultural traditions. Pastoral counseling and the healing and teachings of gurus, shamans, and Zen masters are examples of therapists who consciously include this classification in their normal practice. Although often not identified by either practitioners or their clientele, most therapists make assumptions within this classification, even if only to attempt to omit it as "nonscientific."

These four types of systems coexist. All are equal to one another, but may become organized hierarchically in particular contexts, for temporally limited periods. In times of stress, this hierarchical organization becomes more rigid, and if prolonged the smooth interchanges and balancing feedback among systems become interrupted and distorted. It is at this point that clients (patients) present themselves or are referred.

As an eclectic therapist I spend time initially exploring all of these systems to determine both the origins and the current focal points of distress. The eclectic therapist can then select appropriate therapeutic interventions and either work with the sequence of the systems involved, or make appropriate referrals to specialists.

Over a lifetime I have had an opportunity to learn from specialists in each of these four classifications of human behavior; this has led toward an appreciation of the strengths and the limits of many specific types or schools of therapeutic activity. It seems to me that most outstanding therapists, particularly in family work, have similar wide competence but choose to orient themselves toward those skills with which they are most proficient. None of us are so talented, or so wise, as to be masters of them all. My own choices are to help people understand and integrate across these groupings, with a major focus on the social and value systems, as appropriate in the stages of the life cycle. The selection and implementation of any intervention is effective to the degree that it grows out of the context of the client family so that they have a different experience, which allows them to shift their perceptions, understandings, and, especially, behavior. Theory and labels are useful to me, perhaps, but the experiential learning itself is often therapeutic enough.

Where Is Family Psychology Going?

I see a real decline, at least on the West Coast, in interest in, or support for, academic training in clinical work in general, let alone family therapy. Clinical programs don't allow time to develop clinical skills in their graduate students before trying to hothouse them into statistically linear and correlational experiments and controls. This model has served experimental psychology well, but clinical work is different in its complexity and focus. One has to be pretty rugged to manage to master both the art and the science involved in the time allowed for a profession, even if that time is measured in years.

Economically, clinicians have adapted to the withdrawal of federal funds by courting insurance payments, only to find that these often prohibit reimbursement for any but individual treatment. A few health maintenance programs have discovered long-range benefits of the family approach, but not enough to support the field. In many places the result is that family psychology becomes available only to those able to pay for it—or from the professional affluent enough to donate services.

Psychiatrists are suffering similar pressures to conform to a model of biochemical treatment, but some valiantly continue to demonstrate the need for accompanying psychoemotional and social therapy and have a longer tradition of this behind them. Social workers have gradually gained status as therapists and have had from the beginning a family and community orientation. Clinical nursing is also finding its way toward recognizing the importance of families, especially in psychosocial nursing, which includes the former category of psychiatric nursing, along with application to pediatrics, women's clinics, oncology, and other more traditional nursing specialties.

Family therapy-oriented psychologists can view these other fields as competition, or as providing interesting and enriching colleagues with skills and concepts to share. Certainly the two national organizations of family therapists, AFTA and AAMFT, and the one international one, IFTA, are eclectic in the disciplines of members and choice of officers and leaders.

Within psychology itself there are hopeful signs of recognition. One was the development of a Diplomate in Family Psychology, by its own board and the Academy of Family Psychology; now, in 1990, details have been worked out for family psychology to become a specialty under the American Board of Professional Psychology. This recognition will define and establish status and legitimacy for family, marriage, and sex therapy. Good leadership should ensure continuation of APA's Division of Family Psychology.

With energies fragmented in all these directions, many family psychologists choose to find a niche to settle into rather than fight for the status of guru with followers. Perhaps this is healthy, as a stage of growth for a profession. The lures of power and prestige are strong, but they may not be the measure of effective adaptation to our changing contexts in constructive ways.

After all, not all of us are cut out to be media stars. In the past three decades the field has been established as a legitimate form of therapeutic endeavor. At this time we do not need lots of comet-like innovators, training devotees to specific techniques, jargon, or special models. Family therapy in psychology and elsewhere needs many of us, doing our own bit, sharing as best we can, until the world's context and our skills and experience are in appropriate conjunction. Perhaps, if I have a final thought to share, it is a verse from an old folk song that probably originated with the American Shakers. It recurs as a theme in my own reflections about life and career:

When true simplicity is gained,
To bow and to bend we shall not be ashamed.
Life may spin us with all its might,
But by twisting and turning we come down right,
And find in the center a garden of delight.

It's a gift to be simple; it's a gift to be free.
It's a gift to be found just where we ought to be!

NOTES

1. Gregory Bateson was one of those excited by the possibility that in this way some of his insights from anthropology might have usefulness in solving the riddles of the behavior and thought processes of mental patients. It was not until after I left Stanford that he recruited Jay Haley and John Weakland to test some of these ideas, with the resulting contribution of the theory of the "double bind" (Bateson, Jackson, & Weakland, 1956). (See also Bateson, 1972, 1979).

2. The Society of American Indian Psychologists (SAIP) meets during each APA annual convention and current information about members can be secured from the National Center for American Indian and Alaska Native Mental Health, 4200 East Ninth Ave., Denver, CO 80262.

REFERENCES

Ashby, W. R. (1956). Self regulation and prerequisite variety. *Introduction to cybernetics* (Chapter 11). New York: John Wiley.

Attneave, C. (1952). *Occupational prestige: An experimental evaluation of its correlates.* Doctoral dissertation, Stanford University, California.

Attneave, C. (1958). TV as a laboratory for developmental psychology. *American psychologist.* Washington, DC: American Psychological Association.

Attneave, C. (1969a). Outpatient services to American Indian patients, *POCA PRESS, 6,* 8-12. (Morristown, New Jersey: Psychiatric Outpatient Clinics of America.)

Attneave, C. (1969b). *Outpatient psychiatry from a social learning perspective.* Mexico City: Institute de Nerologica. (In both Spanish and English).

Attneave, C. (1969c). Intervention in tribal settings and urban social networks. *Family Process, 8,* 192-210.

Attneave, C. (1974a). Medicine men and psychiatrists in the Indian Health Service. *Psychiatric Annals, 9*(4), 49-55.

Attneave, C. (1974b). Therapeutic synergy. *Proceedings General Systems Society.* Arlington, VA.

Attneave, C. with A. Tulipan & E. Kingstone (Eds.) (1974b). *Beyond clinic walls.* University: University of Alabama Press.

Attneave, C. (1975, Revised 1977). *Family network map.* Self-published but distributed by Boston Family Institute, 315 Dartmouth Street, Boston, MA.

Attneave, C. (1977). The wasted strengths of Indian families. In S. Unger (Ed.), *The destruction of American Indian families.* New York: Association on American Indian Affairs.

Attneave, C. (1982). American Indian Families: Immigrants in their own homeland. In M. McGoldrick, J. Pearce, & J. Giordano (Eds.), *Ethnicity and family therapy.* New York: Guilford.

Attneave, C. (1983). *St. Vincent College in transition: Coeducation* [Grant Report no. PRM-8212011]. Washington, DC: National Science Foundation.

Attneave, C., & Beiser, M. (1975). *Service networks and patterns of mental health utilization.* (Eight volumes: *Alaska area; Aberdeen area; Albuquerque area; Billings area; Navajo area; Oklahoma area; Phoenix area; Portland area*). Rockville, MD: Indian Health Service.

Attneave, C., & Beiser, M. (1976). *Service networks and patterns of utilization of mental health services: Summary and recommendations.* Rockville, MD: Indian Health Service.

Attneave, C., & Ensign, T. (1983). *Revised Value Orientation Scale: Standardization and results* [Report no. PRM-8212011]. Washington, DC: National Science Foundation.

Attneave, C., & Kelso, D. (1977). *American Indian mental health annotated bibliography. Volume 1* [Grant no. 7-R01-28198]. Parkville, MD: National Institute of Mental Health.

Bateson, G. (1942). Regularities and differences in national character. In G. Watson (Ed.), *Civilian morale.* Boston: Houghton Mifflin. (See also Bateson, 1972.)

Bateson, G. (1972). *Steps to an ecology of mind. Collected essays in anthropology, psychiatry, evolution and epistemology.* New York: Chandler. Paperback edition, New York: Ballantine.

Bateson, G. (1979). *Mind and nature: A necessary unity.* New York: E. P. Dutton.

Bateson, G., Jackson, D. D., & Weakland, J. (1956). Toward a theory of schizophrenia. *Behavioral Science, 1,* 251-264.

Bateson, G., & Ruesch, J. (1951). *Communication: The social matrix of psychiatry.* New York: W. W. Norton.

Faulkner, W. (1948). *Intruder in the dust.* New York: Random House.

Faulkner, W. (1949). *Intruder in the dust* [Film]. Filmed on location, Oxford, Mississippi, MGM.

Haley, J. (1973). *Uncommon therapy: The psychiatric techniques of Milton H. Erickson.* New York: W. W. Norton.

Haley, J., & Hoffman, L. (1967). *Techniques of family therapy.* San Francisco: Basic Books.

Kelso, D., & Attneave, C. (1981). *Bibliography of North American Indian mental health.* Westport, CT: Greenwood. *Note:* Collection and indexing has continued and is now part of the work of the Center for American Indian Mental Health, Department of Psychiatry,

University of Colorado Medical School, Denver. Contact them for inquiries to the Computerized Cumulative Bibliography.

Koehler, W. (1938). Open and closed systems. In *The place of values in the world of fact* (pp. 314-325). London: Liverwright.

Minuchin, S., Montalvo, B., Guerney, B. G., Jr., Rasman, B. L., & Schumer, F. (1967). *Families of the slums: An exploration of their structure and treatment.* New York: Basic Books.

Personal Communications. (1988). Leonord Duhl, Ric Iolino, Candy Fleming, Theresa La-Framboise, and David Bullis have within the last few months told me of how the leaders in Alaska of a native health corporation, the Mescalero Apache and Flathead tribes, Medicine Lake in Canada, and Seattle and other urban Indian centers have all found the relationship to traumatic historical events a real link to depression and alcoholism in Indian families. ACOA seems to be moving in this direction.

Speck, R. (1969). Network therapy: A developing concept. *Family Process, 8*(2), 182-191.

Speck, R., & Attneave, C. (1972). *Family networks: Retribalization and healing.* New York and London: Pantheon. (Foreign editions in Spanish, Japanese, Swedish, Dutch, German, and in English from London.)

Speck, R., & Attneave, C. (1974). *Family networks: Retribalization and healing* (#V-131, paper). New York: Vintage. (Foreign editions in Spanish, Japanese, Swedish, Dutch, German, and in English from London.)

von Bertalanffy, L. (1949a). Open systems in physics and biology. *Nature.*

von Bertalanffy, L. (1949b). The theory of open systems in physics and biology. *Science, III,* 23-29.

Weiner, N. (1948). *Cybernetics.* New York: Houghton Mifflin.

Weiner, N. (1950). *The human use of human beings.* Boston: Houghton Mifflin.

2

Coming of Age in the New World of Family Systems

ARTHUR M. BODIN

ORIGINS OF INTEREST

I could say that my interest in the family field dated from volunteering one day a week in the summer of 1963 to assist Paul Watzlawick in quantifying the "Blame" section of the MRI Structured Family Interview. It was clinched by the excitement of meeting Don Jackson, Virginia Satir, Jay Haley, John Weakland, Jules Riskin, and Gregory Bateson that summer at the Mental Research Institute (although Gregory Bateson worked with, but not as part of, the MRI).

Watching some family therapy sessions conducted by Jerry Rose and other MRI staff members added a vivid third dimension to the exciting conceptual papers I was reading from the first four years of MRI's history.

This still falls short of explaining how I was first drawn to Palo Alto in that summer of 1963. I had heard that the Palo Alto Veterans Administration Hospital was sponsoring some of the most exciting work in clinical psychology at the time. I also knew that the MRI was developing a new way of looking at concepts that Thomas Szasz (1961) attacked in his article and book, *The Myth of Mental Illness,* and Don Jackson (1964) examined in *Myths of Madness*. There was also the original double-bind paper by Bateson, Jackson, Haley, and Weakland (1956) that I selected for presentation to a graduate psychology class the year before. And still, none of these sources extend far enough beneath the surface to their roots in my family of origin.

Returning from a summer at MRI, I succeeded in persuading the Director of Clinical Training at the State University of New York at Buffalo (SUNY/Buffalo), Marvin Feldman, to offer that school's first course in family therapy in 1963. To this endeavor Feldman brought his experiences fresh from a year at the Tavistock Clinic. I then persuaded the graduate department to sponsor its first doctoral dissertation (mine) using methods drawn from social psychology to study families. I compared these as "natural" (what sociologists call "traditioned") groups, having a shared history and an expectation of a continuing future together, with "ad hoc" groups, having neither shared pasts nor expected futures together.

Professor W. Edgar Vinacke had recently arrived at SUNY/Buffalo from the University of Hawaii, where he had created with his graduate students considerable literature on coalition formation in ad hoc triads. I wanted him to be my dissertation chair and I presented two possible areas of interest: word association or families. "You'd like to do your dissertation on one of these two topics," he reflected, puffing a long time on his pipe. Finally, looking directly at me, he asked, "Which do you *really* want to study?" Though I had been ambivalent for weeks, it took me less than a second to reply, "Families." This single direct question clarified my interests for years to come. Sudden clarity? Yes. Surprising? No.

Generational Comparisons Generate Curiosity

For as long as I could remember, families had fascinated me. Perhaps my interest had been heightened by growing up without brothers or sisters, although my father had two sisters, both younger, and my mother had eight brothers, seven older. I was impressed with how diluted their own pressures sounded: the intensity of interest in each child was discontinuous and spread among many rather than fixed on one. When conflicts arose between my parents, I could sometimes feel the temptation and always the taboo about siding with either of them. Having lived within such a cycle of temptation and taboo about triangulation, it is hardly surprising that I was interested in coalition formation and other forms of conflict management and resolution.

The stories my parents told me about their own growing up were incredibly rich with details of lively interaction among siblings and between parents and some combination of children. I marveled at how complex and continuous the family interaction was in their childhoods. My interest in understanding how differently my mother, my father, and I had experienced life in our families of origin led me to write down the numbers of relationships in families with various numbers of people. I later learned that this chart constituted a mathematical model called "Pascal's Triangle."(See Table 2.1.)

More specifically, for a single person there is only the relationship with one's self. In a husband-wife situation there are three relationships: each to

Table 2.1 Number of Relationships and Family or Group Size (Combinations of *n* Members Taken *m* at a Time)

	Individuals	Dyads	Triads	Foursomes	Fivesomes	Sixsomes	Sevensomes	Eightsomes	Ninesomes	Tensomes	Elevensomes	Twelvesomes	Grand Total
n \ *m*	1	2	3	4	5	6	7	8	9	10	11	12	
1	1												1
2	2	1											3
3	3	3	1										7
4	4	6	4	1									15
5	5	10	10	5	1								31
6	6	15	20	15	6	1							63
7	7	21	35	35	21	7	1						127
8	8	28	56	70	56	28	8	1					255
9	9	36	84	126	126	84	36	9	1				511
10	10	45	120	210	252	210	120	45	10	1			1023
11	11	55	165	330	462	462	330	165	55	11	1		2047
12	12	66	220	495	792	924	792	495	220	66	12	1	4095

NOTE: There is an interesting relationship that would enable you to reconstruct this table without memorizing anything but the relationship. Specifically, each number higher than one is the sum of the number directly above it + the number to the left of that number directly above. Moreover, the grand total for a family of a given size is one more than twice the grand total for a family with one member less.

him- or herself, plus the dyadic relationship. In a two-parent, one-child situation there are three individuals relating to themselves, three dyadic relationships, and one triadic relationship for a total of seven. In a family of *n* members there will be *n* monadic relationships and *n* relationships from which only one person is missing, as well as one relationship involving the total group. The number of relationships (*R*) in a family of size *n* is readily apparent:

$$R = 2^n - 1$$

Having one child increases the number of relationships from 3 to 7; adding another child boosts it to 15. The dilution referred to is quantifiable in terms of the number of dyads in a family: 3 in my family of origin, 10 in my father's family of origin, and 55 in my mother's family of origin. The dilution is even more dramatic if all possible relationships are considered: 7 in my family of origin, 31 in my father's family of origin, and 2,047 in my mother's family of origin. These "relationships" refer to *combinations*; the situation becomes even more complex if permutations are taken into account to reflect each person's view of each of the relationships. In my mother's family, with its morass of relationships, it is no wonder that the dilution of attention to any one child and the alliance of children against parental intensity permitted the brothers to get a laugh by answering their parents in ways that would have been unthinkable in my home. For example, when my maternal grandmother would ask one of her sons, "What time are you getting home?" she would receive this reply flung over a shoulder by him walking out the door: "Half-past!"

A Family Interaction Dissertation

It was hardly a coincidence that my dissertation (Bodin, 1966) focused on coalition, disagreement, and compromise in family triads. I subsequently reported: (Bodin, 1969a)

> Traditional small-group research has rarely dealt with actual families and family experimentation has barely begun to capitalize on the techniques of traditional small-group research. To help bridge this gap, a set of samples was selected so as to include both *ad hoc* triads of strangers and actual family triads. Moreover, the methods were drawn both from traditional small-group research and from recent family experimentation.
>
> The 36 families investigated were of the following three types: (1) father, mother, and delinquent son; (2) father, mother, and nondelinquent son; and (3) father, mother, and nondelinquent son, each from a different family and all

total strangers to one another prior to the experiment. These three triad types were called, respectively, *problem, normal,* and *synthetic* family triads. . . .

The major hypotheses were: (1) the *authenticity hypothesis,* predicting differences between synthetic families and authentic families, and (2) the *normality hypothesis,* predicting differences between problem and normal families. . . .

[The negotiable game the families played as part of the study yielded a record of bargaining and coalition behavior under three power patterns but] failed to support the hypotheses, except in specific respects, e.g., the normal families in comparison with the problem families showed: (1) less tendency to "go it alone," (2) more tendency to "share and share alike," and (3) more tendency for fathers to show benevolence by forming coalitions even when all-powerful.

However, the questionnaire results [from 60 "unrevealed difference" items on six common family concerns] conclusively supported both hypotheses. Findings supporting the authenticity hypothesis include: (1) consistently higher overall and parental agreement in real than in artificial families, (2) greater maternal compromise in synthetic than in normal families, and (3) more efficient joint decision-making in actual than in artificial families. Findings supporting the normality hypothesis include: (1) greater father-son agreement in normal than in problem families, (2) greater maternal influence in normal than in problem families, and (3) more perceptual distortion by mothers—overrating their husbands and underrating themselves—in normal than in problem families.

Neither task supported the flexibility hypothesis that normal families would show less rigidity than problem families.

A cross-situational comparison revealed that sons lost status from the game to the questionnaire, which had greater family import.

In sum . . . there is evidence that task relevance is important in determining behavioral differences among family types. In this case, the questionnaire appeared to be superior to the game. Additional distinctions among family types rest on differences in individual roles (mothers showing the most distinctive behavior) and also in family rules (synthetic families functioning least efficiently, probably because they lost time developing interaction norms akin to those already evolved by real families). (Bodin, 1969a, pp. 125-127)[1]

Homeostasis: Criticisms and Advantages

Because I attempted to measure homeostasis in my dissertation, I also discussed criticisms of the concept (Bodin, 1966), some based on an inaccurate understanding of the concept in its original biological context. One crucial caution follows:

The first objection to applying the concept of homeostasis to families is that it is a corruption of the doctrine of homeostasis to invoke it as an explanatory principle in psychology. Maze (1953) has espoused this point of view in criti-

> cizing a previous review of this subject by Fletcher (1942). Maze's (1953, p. 406) caution was couched in the following eloquent terms: "The mere existence of the word provides another opportunity for us to give up the tiresome research for those mechanisms which actually produce the effect in question, the constancy, and simply to attribute its production to the activity of a vaguely conceived and therefore very accommodating force named 'homeostasis' " (p. 406).[2]
>
> He noted that Fletcher had extended Cannon's . . . conception of homeostasis [Cannon, 1926], conferring upon it a causal connotation not present in the original. Agreeing with Maze's objection, Toch and Hastorf (1955) rescued the concept of homeostasis for psychology by distinguishing between its descriptive and explanatory uses. They suggested that only the latter uses entail the dangers of a *deus ex machina,* implying that psychological theorists will be on safer ground if they shun pseudo-solutions by restricting "homeostasis" to its descriptive usage. (Bodin, 1966, p. 202)

Though homeostasis has been the subject of many articles since 1966, I often feel the critiques are based on underestimating the awareness of family psychologists that homeostasis has long been appreciated as a useful *descriptive,* not *explanatory,* concept.

The Influence of Individual Psychotherapy

During three years of psychoanalysis when I was in my early twenties, I worked on a number of concerns, including conflicting feelings about a girlfriend and about some aspects of our relationship. Though I knew well that such a request was unorthodox and probably unacceptable, I attempted to persuade the analyst to have some sessions with my girlfriend either alone, with me, or both. Of course he refused, but the idea seemed very natural to me, though it had not yet received much publicity. This was several years before the founding of MRI and its development of family therapy training sequences beyond the sporadic in-service family therapy training then available at a few mental health facilities.

MY EARLY YEARS AT MRI

In 1964 I attended a conference of family therapy trainers at the Eastern Pennsylvania Psychiatric Institute in Philadelphia. There I met Don Jackson and Jay Haley again, and also Nathan Ackerman, Murray Bowen, Lyman Wynne, Norman Paul, Andrew Ferber, and Ivan Boszormenyi-Nagy, among others. At a dinner meeting during the conference Norman Paul proposed the formation of an American Family Therapy Association. Don Jackson, Nathan Ackerman, and Lyman Wynne all rose to counsel against such a move. They said their psychoanalytic training and experience with that field led them to hope that the family field would not prematurely stultify ideas and stunt its own growth through creating a machinery for imposing orthodoxy, which they seemed to feel had happened in American psychoanalysis. They also expressed the sentiment that such a national organization would be tempted to erect barriers against entering the field and would become the gatekeeper, perhaps further inhibiting the richness which a multiprofessional, multidisciplinary field could otherwise enjoy. AFTA did not form until many years later. In its annual meetings, AFTA seems so far to have resisted some, though perhaps not all, of the temptations foreseen by its prenatal oracles!

At this same meeting Don Jackson firmed up with me an arrangement for coming to work at MRI as a follow-up to an invitation I had received from Jay Haley earlier that year. On my arrival at MRI in 1965, as was his custom with new staff members, Don invited me to write a paper with him, on "Paradoxical Communication and the Marital Paradox" (Jackson & Bodin, 1968).

I had many fascinating experiences in those early days at MRI. There was a considerable spectrum of opinion within the Institute, ranging from Virginia Satir's view emphasizing interactional *and* intrapsychic concepts, to Jay Haley's not always transparent views couched in such statements as, "Perhaps there is no such thing as the individual and we are all points in space/time!" (He was unfazed by such questions as, "Then who just said that?") I devised a brief scale of 20-some items which staff members volunteered to take, knowing it was designed to discern where they fell on a continuum from the most intrapsychic to the most interactional positions at the Institute. Not surprisingly, it was Don Jackson who scored right in the middle, a position altogether befitting the director of an organization of highly individualistic pioneers.[3]

Conjoint Family Therapy: Its Place in the Universe

In writing a chapter for W. Edgar Vinacke's *Readings in General Psychology,* I summarized the place of family therapy:

> An especially significant function of family therapy for psychologists attuned to the sociotherapeutic shift is its location at the interface between social and clinical psychology. Both fields are relevant to present practices and future developments in family therapy, and both may gain by their relationship to a host of theoretical and practical concerns which can be studied within the context of family therapy. In fact, Weakland (1962) suggests the use of family therapy as a research arena. This strategy would augment our knowledge of *ad hoc* groups of strangers by fostering systematic investigation of the most important of all actual "traditioned" groups. Family therapy thus might well prove invalu-

> able as a vital bridge between social and clinical psychology. As the locus of our attention shifts from making inferences about what goes on within the individual to actually *observing* what goes on between people, several fundamental changes in our thinking must follow. The very nature of our questions will change. . . . Some cherished concepts of causality must also change as *interpersonal* actions are increasingly viewed as the contexts in which *intrapersonal* phenomena emerge. (Bodin, 1968b, p. 229)[4]

Conjoint Family Assessment: A Paradigm Awaiting Discovery

Along came an invitation to write a chapter on "Conjoint Family Assessment: An Evolving Field" (Bodin, 1968a) for Volume I of a series initiated by Paul McReynolds, *Advances in Psychological Assessment*. In this chapter I pointed out that our current assessment techniques were designed mainly for use with individuals rather than with families. I attempted to define a new category of assessment techniques appropriate to concepts and methods of conjoint family therapy:

> This category is distinguished by evaluation of interaction patterns of whole and partial families as *systems,* requiring simultaneous focus on two or more family members in terms of their transactions. Designed to parallel what goes on in conjoint family therapy, this new concept of the test situation emphasizes interpersonal factors even more than intrapsychic factors—though in relation to these. The aim is to find out not only how the individuals characteristically respond to certain kinds of stimuli, but also what types of stimuli these family members characteristically present to one another, and in response to what. Thus, the family members are viewed as participants in interaction sequences that cannot be understood in purely individual terms, because such event chains cannot occur in isolated individuals. . . .
>
> One reason why this extrapolation is impossible is that a salient feature of many families is the range and intensity of disparities that bar any integrated picture based on simple summation or comparison of individual points of view. Another factor making such extrapolation a futile exercise is the emergent quality of unpredictable uniqueness in family interaction or, for that matter, in any interpersonal interaction. Indeed, this quality constitutes the defining characteristic of conjoint family therapy, the advent of which necessitates the development of a new kind of assessment analogous to the situation existing in conjoint family therapy. It is extremely difficult to predict family interaction from results of individual testing because the subject's responses are so largely determined by his relationship with the tester. The test results may therefore reflect the tester-subject relationship to an indeterminate degree, thus actually obscuring analysis of family interaction. It is better to obtain family interaction data in the first place. (pp. 223-224)[5]

Later in that chapter I describe some conjoint approaches, both subjective and objective: In the former category, the "rigged" conflicts of Goodrich and Boomer (1963), the Family Interaction Apperception Test (FIAT) (Elbert, Rosman, Minuchin, & Guerney, 1964), structured family interviews, and a particularly promising technique called "the Marbles Test."[6]

Family Life-Space Diagrams

A quick technique for obtaining rich data on family relationships was devised by my combining two old ideas: life-space diagrams and Venn diagrams. Data are clinically useful and can be quantified in theoretically meaningful form. Having the family compare its members' drawings illuminates certain intrapsychic and interpersonal strains and strengths. Venn diagrams are modified by using rectangles instead of circles to facilitate drawing and measuring.

Family members are positioned to prevent plagiarizing and are cautioned if the need arises. The following detailed instructions may bypass imagination as a limiting factor in producing rich material.

> Now that I've given you a pen and some paper, please put your name at the top left of each page and the date at the top right, and at the top center please write the title "Reality" on the first page and "Wish" on the second. (Pause) Now I'd like you each to draw two special diagrams of your family. What's special about these diagrams is that they don't require any artistic skills. Simply show each person in the family as a rectangle. [This term is explained further in whatever detail proves necessary. Any questions about whom to include are answered with, "That's up to you." Some flexibility may be in order if feelings run strong that such others as grandparents or pets are crucial to include.]
>
> The rectangles can be perfectly square, or long and thin, or anything in between. They can be standing up on end the tall way, or lying down on edge the flat way, or tilted at any slanted angle. You can make them any size and any place on the paper. They can be separate, touching, partly overlapping, completely overlapping, or enclosed, one within another. Your rectangles can all look alike, or some of them can be different, or all of them can be different. Once you have all the rectangles on the page, please label them so we can all tell who's who when we look at them later. In the first diagram please show your family relationships as you actually experience them these days, and in the second one, how you wish them to be. Do you have any questions?

Some possible intra-individual variables are the size, shape, orientation, and location of each rectangle, as well as the number included, and who. Possible inter-individual variables are distance between rectangles, differentiation, coalition, originality, and scatter. Some comparisons that might be made are intra-individual Reality versus Wish and Pre versus Post, as well as inter-individual Reality versus Wish and Pre versus Post.

After presenting an overview of conjoint family assessment and conjoint family therapy, I described some actual as well as possible applications of videotape in training family therapists (Bodin, 1969c) and compiled a brief guide to the family therapy training literature (Bodin, 1969b). Next, I reviewed the family therapy training and study opportunities in the San Francisco Bay Area (Bodin, 1971a) and summarized some points learned and questions stimulated by the training program conducted at MRI since 1959 by Virginia Satir, turned over to Fred Ford in the 1966-1967 period. The training made use of techniques and teaching aids such as: (1) audio tapes, (2) videotapes, (3) observation, (4) specific assessment and therapeutic techniques, (5) research activities, (6) interactional techniques within the training group, (7) demonstrations, (8) simulated families, (9) supervisory teams, and (10) consultation.

MRI FAMILY THERAPY TRAINING FEEDBACK

From alumni of the nine-month Intensive Family Therapy Training Program I obtained some potentially useful feedback:

> Alumni were questioned concerning how they coped with resistances beyond ordinary institutional inertia encountered in trying to increase acceptance of family therapy concepts, and/or practices, in other work settings. . . . The answers may be illuminating for others trying to gain acceptance of family therapy in their work settings: (1) Go slowly in making changes, balance the new with the old. Be explicit about your beliefs but don't oversell. (2) Get the right administrators. Fit into agency needs and philosophy; impress them by being clear and concise, but never assaultive. (3) Work toward alteration in training institutions; residents should be exposed to family therapy; push for staff training, but discourage expectations of thorough learning from a few demonstrations. (4) Invite therapists to observe, first talking to them to make them realize that other current methods are not being attacked; that they do not have to throw away much in the family therapy approach, but there is room for what they already know. (5) Make known that family therapy is valuable, pick a case where conventional therapy is not making headway and then persist with family therapy long enough to demonstrate its value. Nothing is more effective than positive results in gaining acceptance for the family therapy approach. (6) Work through in-service training for counselors, ministers, parents, personnel department heads. . . .

> A number of important training issues have been brought into focus, though not completely resolved, by the experience at MRI. Those remaining unresolved are questions of balance, involving optimizing the "mix" of several values so that integration may be appropriate to the particular course. Ideological issues include the balance between interpersonal and intrapsychic points of view, action and insight-oriented interventions, the . . . [specific] viewpoint of one pioneer and an eclectic spectrum of views. Pedagogical issues include the balance between theory and practice, studying and treating families, pre-structuring and evolving the course with trainee participation in decisions, personal style, lecture and discussion, observation and doing, substantive feedback by video- and audio tape, and unaided observer feedback; supervision by the teacher and outside consultation; task-centered teaching and supervision and trainee-centered teaching and supervision, with personal and perhaps therapeutic elements. Training needs include more knowledge of when to see which subgroups within a family, a new interactional vocabulary, earlier and more continuous teaching of family therapy, audio and videotape libraries, co-teachers, more knowledge on therapist selection of families, and balancing brief therapy of several families and extensive therapy of one family. (Bodin, 1971b, pp. 169-170)[7]

Going Beyond Talk

With Andy Ferber I explored "How To Go Beyond the Use of Language" (Bodin & Ferber, 1972), describing some family therapy applications of (1) the telephone, (2) writing, (3) bibliotherapy, (4) poetry, (5) humor, (6) audio tape recordings, (7) music, (8) body sculpture, (9) role playing, (10) theater games, (11) psychodrama, (12) sociodrama, (13) diagrams, (14) family history charts, (15) genograms, (16) photographs, and (17) home movies.

Exploring Brief Therapy

During the first six years of MRI's Brief Therapy Center, founded in 1967 with Dick Fisch and John Weakland as Director and Associate Director, respectively, along with Jay Haley, Paul Watzlawick, and myself, we observed each other at work and discussed what we had seen immediately afterward and again several days later. We tried to find out why in the observation room we had often said we would favor a particular next intervention which, in fact, the therapist in the room with the patient then initiated within the next moment or two! We reasoned that our common thinking must stem from some shared premises, and we set out to discover them. They included:

1. taking symptoms seriously as targets for change;
2. viewing problems mainly as situational difficulties between people and systems;

3. regarding such problems as stemming mainly from attempts to adapt to some life change;
4. seeing normal transitional steps or ordinary life difficulties as the main events leading to such problems;
5. seeing both denial and exaggeration as coping strategies likely to escalate "difficulties" into "problems";
6. noting that the exacerbation of a difficulty into a problem often results from a positive feedback loop in which the attempted "solution" has caused the intensification of a difficulty into an official problem;
7. viewing long-standing problems not as "chronicity" but as a possible opportunity to interrupt a repetitive coping strategy which may be maintaining the difficulty and exacerbating it into a problem, often providing exceptional opportunities for motivating the patient, who is tired of the suffering and eager enough for change to try something different;
8. viewing problem resolution as requiring interruption of vicious positive feedback circles with newly substituted behavior patterns;
9. substituting counter-intuitive actions rather than continuing longer and harder with attempted solutions guided by what everyone knows is "right" and "logical";
10. shifting, often in an opposite direction from the patient's attempted solution. (Such shifts are usually toward a more modest and clearly stated goal, which we refer to as "thinking small," to make it much more difficult for the patient to claim or believe that the goal is beyond reach. The extreme instance of "thinking small" is to ask for no change at all until some careful observations have been made by the patient.); and
11. basing our approach on direct observation of what is happening in the system, how it maintains its patterns, and how they may be altered most effectively, rather than asking "why" questions, which promote a focus on individual motivation and self-justification rather than on systemic interaction and mutual influence.

A key point made by Weakland, Fisch, Watzlawick, & Bodin (1974, p. 147) is that "The presenting problem offers, in one package, what the patient is ready to work on, a concentrated manifestation of whatever is wrong, and a concrete index of any progress made."

MRI'S FIRST TWENTY YEARS

Summarizing MRI's first two decades is no small task. As Alan Gurman has noted on the basis of his tally, MRI was the single leading source of articles published in the two main family therapy journals during each of the first two decades of the field. Nevertheless, I reviewed a number of projects and points of view at MRI in a chapter for the *Handbook of Family Therapy* (Gurman & Kniskern, 1981), to which I intentionally gave a pluralistic title—"The interactional view: Family therapy approaches of the Mental Research Institute" (Bodin, 1981).

Family Therapy: An Overview

At the invitation of the American Psychiatric Association Commission on Psychiatric Therapies, chaired by Toksoz B. Karasu, I contributed the chapter on "Family Therapy" for their two-part work, *The Psychiatric Therapies*. I reviewed the historical background, the spectrum of structures, theoretical and philosophical issues, family and therapist parameters, indications and limitations, ethical and professional issues, and financial and legal issues, concluding with comments on some tasks and trends (Bodin, 1984).

Family therapy publications proliferate (Broderick & Schrader, 1981) but gives only a hint of the humanitarian impact of this field. If *psychotherapy* is concerned with the ability to work and love, then *family therapy* is particularly concerned with love. Many family therapy patients feel it makes sense to participate in a type of therapy that provides a window for direct observation of how they and their loved ones interact. In addition, they appreciate a forum for reviewing and resolving differences, but with their loved ones actually present and participating rather than remaining outside the immediate process, as in individual therapy.

The Emergency Treatment Center: Outreach to Families in Their Community Context

When John Elderkin Bell became the Director of MRI about 1969, he developed the idea of extending the family focus still further. He suggested looking at the family and its members in relation to work settings, schools, churches, social welfare agencies, the criminal justice system, hospitals, clubs, and other public and private organizations in which family members function concurrently with their family functioning. Bell suggested that MRI staff members scan the spectrum of possibilities he sketched as a heuristic map for developing new interests and projects. I considered developing a project involving families and schools or families and law enforcement (these interests, of course, having nothing to do with my mother's having been a teacher and my father an attorney!). I was well aware, however, from the teaching experiences of both my mother and my wife that it would be extremely difficult to introduce changes into any public education system. Consequently, as an alternative, in 1969 I turned my attention to some local police departments. I rode with more than six dozen police in seven different departments, and developed a course in Police-Community Relations. Though many topics were of interest – some of special concern for civil peace during the tumultuous Vietnam protest years – my interests naturally converged on the intersection of police work and family psychology: family fight calls to the police, known as "415-F's," or domestic disturbance calls.

Diana Everstine, who also had worked with police, heard of my work and approached me to serve on her dissertation committee. While a doctoral student at the California School of Professional Psychology in San Francisco, she had conceived the idea of a Mobile Emergency Team, a concept that I had also known was needed, since a friend on the Oakland Police Department had been teasing me by asking, "Where are you guys at 3:00 a.m. when we really need you?" Over the next two years, Diana Everstine, her husband Louis, and I developed and implemented a three-person Mobile Emergency Team for the City of Mountain View.

The model was very successful, and in 1975 we were awarded a Santa Clara County contract and some California Innovative Programs' funding to establish the Emergency Treatment Center (ETC). Responding to telephone calls to 292-HELP, it provides 24-hour, 7-day-a-week mobile service to almost 900,000 people in the western two-thirds of Santa Clara County. We intervene in any situation involving a child. Most commonly these are the "status offenses" of running away, truancy, or being beyond parental control; they are also drug and alcohol abuse, child abuse and molestation, suicide attempts, rape, panic about divorce or parental death, gang conflicts, and any other problems involving minors.

Referrals come to us from a dozen police departments, the probation department, the schools, other agencies, other professionals, and the public at large. Now in its 16th year, the Emergency Treatment Center has become a United Way agency in Santa Clara County. In its first year it provided services in ten cities to 340 families, 129 headed by a single parent and 69 others with a divorce and remarriage. Eight cases involved threatened or attempted homicide, 38 cases involved attempted suicide by adolescents, and 23 cases involved rape, assault, incest, or molestation. The volume has increased since ETC's first publication (Everstine, Bodin, & Everstine, 1977) and much experience has since been gained in dealing with family crises, summarized in the book *People in Crisis* by D. Everstine and L. Everstine (1983). Though affiliated with MRI, ETC has its own Clinical Director, Diana Everstine, and its own Board of Directors, of which I am President. Funding comes from fees, an annual county contract, the United Way, some foundation grants, and our own fundraising efforts.

Approaches to Divorce: Counseling, Evaluation, and Mediation

In 1979, having extended my family interests into the forensic areas of divorce counseling, custody evaluation, and divorce mediation, I went to North Carolina to attend a one-week workshop with O. J. Coogler (the founder of the divorce mediation movement), John Haynes, Larry Gaughn, and Linda Girdner. I have taught more than two dozen Divorce Mediation workshops since then to mental health and Conciliation Court personnel and attorneys. I developed a list of "Suggestions for Talking with Your Child(ren) about Divorce" (Bodin, 1982), a "Planning Form for Child's Contact with Each Parent" (Bodin, 1985), and a "Parental Activity Worksheet" (Bodin, 1988) to help parents make realistic custody plans.

A Family Tradition of Interest in Family Interaction

My own wife and children have influenced my work in so many ways that only a few can be recounted here. I feel extremely fortunate in having been able to draw upon my family life as an invaluable source of understanding in some facets of my professional life. I have gained an appreciation of how tremendously important something can seem to one person while seeming minor to another. Another realization concerns how vital it is to family harmony to decrease the discontent by whittling away at details rather than expecting one incredible flash of insight or understanding to resolve everything in one fell swoop.

Another appreciation I have gained from my family of creation is how tremendously different children can be—if only through their genetic endowment. My son, for example, has always been comfortable with his things strewn casually around his room. My daughter, on the other hand, has always arranged her things in an orderly fashion without any prodding from my wife or me and without any particularly neater example on my wife's part over mine, since we both have about the same comfort level with clutter. Yet another realization useful in my practice is that two parents with different sibling rivalry experiences as children—or lack of such experiences—may have very different reactions to sibling rivalry of *their* children.

A particularly vivid spectrum of understanding has been colored in for me by the four stages of my wife's career to date. Before we had children Miriam taught full-time. Then, until they were in elementary school, she stayed home. She got her Early Childhood Education credential and, until they were in junior high school, worked half-time as Assistant Director of a parent co-op nursery. When she felt eager to move on, I gave her a copy of *What Color is Your Parachute?*, and she invented a career to utilize her education background in new ways, as an independent educational consultant. Miriam found one other person doing what she had in mind and worked as an apprentice to her for more than a year, working directly with parents and children about educational decisions. For the past 12 years, she has been identifying options and making recommendations based on personal interviews and reports from a variety of mental health professionals. She has traveled widely, gaining first-hand knowledge of the staff, program, facilities, and students at more than 500 schools throughout the country. As a result, I have experienced marriage with my wife not working outside the home, working part-time, and working full-time, first as an employee and then in independent practice. This variety has taught me something about how women are developing themselves and their careers and about the importance of synchronous changing by the mate in order to maintain connubial coordination. I am deeply impressed by how occupational development powers personal growth. Also, I find it extremely gratifying that Miriam's transition to independent practice has deepened our understanding of each other's work.

Perhaps the most family-focused publication I've had the pleasure of working on was one I wrote with my daughter, then in 4th grade, titled "The Topsy-Turviness of Mrs. Piggle Wiggle" (Bodin & Bodin, 1977). My daughter had noticed the paradoxical effects of "Mrs. Piggle Wiggle's" presenting everything upside down and backward to children, evoking easy compliance rather than stubborn resistance.[8]

DEVELOPMENT AND DEFINITION

To my brief summary of the family therapy field as of 1983 I would add only a few thoughts. During the past half decade, the family field has seen another important development. The Academy of Psychologists in Marital, Sex and Family Therapy, with a history of more than 25 years, became increasingly active and focused through the leadership of Daniel Araoz. Its efforts, coupled with those of the American Board of Family Psychology (ABFamP), chartered in 1981, prepared the way for the American Psychological Association to establish Division 43, the Division of Family Psychology. Through this development a great many psychologists deeply involved in family work feel that at last they have a "home" within the American Psychological Association (APA) as well as a bulletin, *The Family Psychologist,* and a journal, the *Journal of Family Psychology.*

The Division of Family Psychology is still defining itself and its mission. In 1990 the Board of Directors adopted the following mission statement: "Family psychology integrates the understanding of individuals, couples, families, and their wider contexts. The division of Family Psychology seeks to promote human welfare through the development, dissemination, and application of knowledge about the dynamics, structure, and functioning of families." Our membership flier reflects the breadth of our field along the following lines:

> Family Psychology applies and integrates systems contexts in such areas as: family theory, research, assessment, training, supervision, and therapy; premarital, marital, and divorce and remarriage counseling; drug and alcohol abuse; forensic family psychology; divorce mediation; child, spouse, and elder abuse; governmental policy and the family; pediatric and geriatric family psychology; the family and work, education, health, and illness; and family violence.

This definition can be broadened by including remarriage families, substance-abuse families, and a host of other special family populations.

Informally, our Division defines the field of family psychology still more broadly, as reflected by the current list of its Service Committees, including: (1) Aging and Ageism, (2) AIDS: Families and Larger Systems, (3) Continuing Education, (4) Diagnosis and Classification, (5) Education and Training, (6) Ethical Concerns, (7) Family Abuse Concerns, (8) Gender Concerns, (9) History and Archives, (10) Hospital-Family Practice, (11) Hostage Families, (12) Legislation and Social Policy, (13) Marketing and Public Advocacy, (14) Mediation, Children and Law, (15) Minority and Ethnic Concerns, (16) Research, and (17) School-Family Practice.

COMING OF AGE

Through this odyssey I have come of age professionally in the new world of family therapy as it first emerged and later differentiated further through establishment of APA's Division of Family Psychology. I am proud to have served on APA's Council of Representatives when it established the Division of Family Psychology, and to have served in 1988 as the Division's fourth president.

Coming of age is a prelude to the generative stage. It is gratifying to have been present to participate in the birth and formative years of this field along with Larry Vogel and Richard Mikesell as the last presidents of the predecessor "Academy," and George Nixon as the first president of Division 43. I believe the Division of Family Psychology offers much to its members. It carries the promise of an even wider impact on other psychologists by introducing systems thinking throughout APA.

GROWTH OF FAMILY PSYCHOLOGY LITERATURE

In 1990 I searched APA's PsycINFO data base for those references containing the terms "marriage," "marital," or "family" *and* "therapy," "assessment," "measurement," "evaluation," or "treatment." Collapsing the data into five-year periods spanning the two decades beginning with the first year of the data base, 1967, the totals show almost a six-fold increase:

- 1,146 references from 1967-1971
- 2,177 references from 1972-1976
- 2,976 references from 1977-1981
- 6,699 references from 1982-1986

These figures speak for themselves. In addition, one recent issue of *Contemporary Psychology* (September, 1988) contains reviews of four books with some form of the word "family" in the title, plus one with that word in the review title. I hope the activities of our Division, with its committee work, convention programs, and publications, furthers the quality of family psychology literature as well its quantity.

This is an era of expansion, excitement, and enthusiasm for the family field. Through and beyond our Division members I believe the field of family psychology will continue to define and develop ideas and interventions of increasing benefit to the science and profession of psychology and to the public we serve.

THE FAMILY FIELD: SOME TASKS AND TRENDS

My earlier look into the future of family therapy (Bodin, 1984) still seems pertinent. The future of family therapy will probably reflect the future of families. In this country, divorce and remarriage have become more common, and people are living longer. Thus, divorce therapy, custody evaluation, divorce mediation, and the treatment of families formed by remarriage are of great importance, along with the therapy of elders and their families.

Several additional areas within the family therapy field are becoming ripe for research. These include: (a) the effects of different epistemological assumptions on the process and outcome of therapy; (b) the efficacy and impact of different approaches to evaluating families; and (c) the range and variety of individual cognition, emotion, and behavior and of interpersonal interaction in "normal," "healthy," or at least nonlabeled families. Another type of research need concerns the method rather than the focus of investigation. Specifically, the family field has lacked longitudinal research, perhaps because it requires a steady stream of determined investigators as well as an exceptionally stable institutional support structure within which to organize and sustain such studies. Longitudinal research is sorely needed to answer myriad questions about family therapy approaches across the spectrum of individual and family disturbances and about the long-range development of normal families and their individual members.

It is apparent that the family field is shifting from the polarized positions of its pioneers. Many among the new generation of family therapists are able to assimilate and integrate various positions without sacrificing the coherence of their approach. Thus, as the family field matures, its new practitioners seem more eclectic, reflecting the courage to appreciate and apply a broad spectrum of available theories and techniques. (Bodin, 1984, p. 475)

NOTES

1. From *Research in Family Interaction* (pp. 125-127) by W. D. Winter and A. J. Ferreira (Eds.). Palo Alto, CA: Science & Behavior Books. Copyright 1969 by Science and Behavior Books. Reprinted by permission.

2. From "On Some Corruptions of the Doctrine of Homeostasis" by J. R. Maze, 1953, *Psychological Review, 60,* p. 406. Copyright 1953 by American Psychological Association. Reprinted by permission.

3. Another fascinating and repeated experience was seeing Virginia and Don (Mom and Pop) get mad at each other, often over what seemed to me to be differences in their style or momentary degree of overtness in the exercise of power, though both showed mastery of a range in this regard. Virginia would say, "I'll bet he'll send me flowers tomorrow." Don would send her flowers the next day. Virginia would try to act disgruntled. The incident would pass. I couldn't help remembering how mystifying it had been to me in childhood that my mother loved receiving flowers; at about age 17 I grasped that it was precisely that the flowers would soon be gone, leaving nothing but the thought that prompted their giving and the elation of receiving them, that made them so precious.

4. From *Readings in Introductory Psychology* (p. 228) by W. E. Vinacke (Ed.). New York: American Book Co. Copyright 1968 by American Book Co. Reprinted by permission.

5. From *Advances in Psychological Assessment* (pp. 223-224) by P. McReynolds (Ed.). Palo Alto, CA: Science & Behavior Books. Copyright 1968 by Science & Behavior Books. Reprinted by permission.

6. The Marbles Test, originated in Argentina and reported by Usandivaras, Grimson, Hammond, Issaharoff, and Romanos (1967), requires only a set of marbles and a board on which to set them. The dimensions recommended were 12×12 holes for couples, 15×15 for families of three, and 20×20 for larger families. The family members are each given about 20 marbles, one color per person. The instructions are simply to place the marbles on the board so as to make a design. Among the observable variables are: points of contact between marbles of various colors,

inclusion and noninclusion in clusters, and porosity or open space within clusters. This test is truly quick, quantifiable, highly palatable, and interactional. It yields a picture of such factors as how some family members cluster together or isolate themselves, and how much freedom there is to be playful and communicative in the process.

7. From Public Health Service. (1971). *Project Summaries of Experiments in Mental Health Training* (HSM Publication No. 72-9046). Washington, DC: U.S. Government Printing Office. Reprinted by permission.

8. Laura's early interest in language and interaction seems to have surfaced again in her college senior thesis, titled: " 'What is a Lizard?': The Role of Collaborative Interaction in One Child's Acquisition of Semantic Category Hierarchies."

9. From *The Psychiatric Therapies: Part II. The Psychosocial Therapies* (p. 475) by The American Psychiatric Association Commission on Psychiatric Therapies. Washington, DC: American Psychiatric Association. Copyright 1984 by American Psychiatric Association. Reprinted by permission.

REFERENCES

Bateson, G., Jackson, D. D., Haley, J., & Weakland, J. (1956). Toward a theory of schizophrenia. *Behavioral Science, 1,* 251-264.

Bodin, A. M. (1966). Family interaction, coalition, disagreement, and compromise in problem, normal, and synthetic family triads. *Dissertation Abstracts International, 28*(3B), 1184. (University Microfilms No. 6607960)

Bodin, A. M. (1968a). Conjoint family assessment. In P. McReynolds (Ed.), *Advances in psychological assessment,* (Vol. 1.). Palo Alto, CA: Science & Behavior Books.

Bodin, A. M. (1968b). Conjoint family therapy. In W. E. Vinacke (Ed.), *Readings in general psychology* (pp. 219-231). New York: American Book.

Bodin, A. M. (1969a). Family interaction: A social-clinical study of synthetic, normal, and problem family triads. In W. D. Winter & A. J. Ferreira (Eds.), *Research in family interaction* (pp. 125-127). Palo Alto, CA: Science & Behavior Books.

Bodin, A. M. (1969b). Family therapy training literature: A brief guide. *Family Process, 8,* 272-279.

Bodin, A. M. (1969c). Videotape applications in training family therapists. *Journal of Nervous and Mental Disease, 148,* 251-261.

Bodin, A. M. (1971a). A review of family therapy, training and study in the San Francisco Bay Area. *Family Process, 10,* 111-121.

Bodin, A. M. (1971b). Training in conjoint family therapy. In *Project summaries of experiments in mental health training.* Public Health Service Publication No. 2157. Washington, DC: Government Printing Office.

Bodin, A. M. (1981). The interactional view: Family therapy approaches of the Mental Research Institute. In A. Gurman & D. Kniskern (Eds.), *Handbook of family therapy* (pp. 267-309). New York: Brunner/Mazel.

Bodin, A. M. (1982). Suggestions for talking with your child(ren) about divorce. In P. A. Keller & L. G. Ritt (Eds.), *Innovations in clinical practice: A source book* (Vol. 1, p. 384). Sarasota, FL: Professional Resource Exchange, Inc.

Bodin, A. M. (1984). Family therapy. In The American Psychiatric Association Commission on Psychiatric Therapies (Eds.), *The psychiatric therapies: Part II. The Psychosocial Therapies* (pp. 441-481). Washington, DC: American Psychiatric Association.

Bodin, A. M. (1985). Planning form for child's contact with each parent. In *Mediate your divorce: A guide to cooperative custody, property, and support agreements* (p. 202). Englewood Cliffs, NJ: Prentice-Hall.

Bodin, A. M. (1988). Parental activity worksheet. In C. E. Sherman, *Practical divorce solutions: California edition* (pp. 95-96). Occidental, CA: Nolo Press.

Bodin, A. M., & Bodin, L. J. (1977). The topsy-turviness of Mrs. Piggle Wiggle: Its symbolic significance. *Family Process, 16,* 117-118.

Bodin, A. M., & Ferber, A. (1972). How to go beyond the use of language. In A. Ferber, M. Mendelsohn, & A. Napier (Eds.), *The book of family therapy* (pp. 272-317). New York: Science House.

Broderick, C. B., & Schrader, S. S. (1981). The history of professional marriage and family therapy. In A. Gurman & D. Kniskern (Eds.), *Handbook of family therapy* (pp. 5-35). New York: Brunner/Mazel.

Cannon, W. B. (1926). Physiological regulation of normal states: Some tentative postulates concerning biological homeostatics. In *Jubilee* (Vol. 4, pp. 91-93). Paris: Charles Richet.

Elbert, S., Rosman, B., Minuchin, S., & Guerney, B. (1964, March). *A method for the clinical study of family interaction.* Paper presented at the American Orthopsychiatric Association, Chicago.

Everstine, D., Bodin, A. M., & Everstine, L. (1977). A mobile service for police crisis calls. *Family Process, 16*(3), 281-292.

Everstine, D., & Everstine, L. (1983). *People in crisis.* New York: Brunner/Mazel.

Fletcher, J. M. (1942). Homeostasis as an explanatory principle in psychology. *Psychological Review, 49,* 80-87.

Goodrich, D. W., & Boomer, D. S. (1963). Experimental assessment of modes of conflict resolution. *Family Process, 2,* 15-24.

Gurman, A. S., & Kniskern, D. P. (Eds.). (1981). *Handbook of family therapy.* New York: Brunner/Mazel.

Jackson, D. D. (1964). *Myths of madness.* New York: Macmillan.

Jackson, D. D., & Bodin, A. M. (1968). Paradoxical communication and the marital paradox. In S. Rosenbaum & I. Alger (Eds.), *The marriage relationship: Psychoanalytic perspectives* (pp. 3-20). Palo Alto, CA: Science & Behavior Books.

Maze, J. R. (1953). On some corruptions of the doctrine of homeostasis. *Psychological Review, 60,* 405-412.

Szasz, T. S. (1961). *The myth of mental illness.* New York: Hoeber-Harper.

Toch, H. H., & Hastorf, A. H. (1955). Homeostasis in psychology. *Psychiatry, 18,* 81-91.

Usandivaras, R., Grimson, W., Hammond, H., Issaharoff, E., & Romanos, D. (1967). The marbles test. *Archives of General Psychiatry, 17,* 111-118.

Weakland, J. H. (1962). Family therapy as a research arena. *Family Process, 1,* 63-68.

Weakland, J. H., Fisch, R., Watzlawick, P., & Bodin, A. M. (1974). Brief therapy: Focused problem resolution. *Family Process, 13,* 141-168.

3

Marital Therapy and Genocide: A Love of Life Story

ISRAEL W. CHARNY

At cocktail parties years ago I used to quip that my professional specialties were *marital therapy and genocide.* It drew a quick smile and interest in the subject of marriage, but rarely any conversation about genocide. In recent years the remark seems to me to be irreverent.

For a variety of personal reasons, my life-long fascination with psychology has led me both to a delightful (and playful) intrigue with family interaction, and especially the mysteries of marriage, and to trying to understand more of how human beings can be so incredibly anti-other humans on the levels of community and society, culminating in the most dread destructiveness of all, genocide.

For me, all levels of human behavior are necessarily related through the "living fact" that it is we same human beings who are operating on each of these levels. On the level of idea development, I have always felt an instinctive distaste for any idea position that takes a single focus, such as individual psychodynamics, and insists that this is the whole truth, the only truth, and forbids discourse with other levels of experience such as couple therapy or family therapy. It continues to sadden and anger me that so many of my colleagues choose to go with whatever idolatry—psychoanalysis, structural family therapy, short-term treatment—ad infinitum and actively denigrate and dismiss the significance of all other ideas without seeing the multilevel nature of reality. It similarly saddens me that the great majority of my colleagues in family therapy don't fully understand, or make an effort to understand, that the larger societal system in which people are discriminated against and abused, up to and including being murdered en masse, are very much the proper study of all of us, including systems thinkers in family therapy. It gives me personal pleasure to be a family therapist, and to enjoy my major subspecialty of treating couples, but I cannot forget how many people and couples were treated as chimney smoke and atomic waste earlier in this century. Looking toward the future I am painfully aware than one atomic bomb can easily put an end to associations of marriage and family therapy.

I "love" all psychotherapy because it gives me an image of us as human beings more capable of feeling alive, safe, free to be what we may be, enjoying a fun-of-being with other human beings in the process of our treks on this earth. I am for every mode of psychotherapy and every way of thinking about human beings that frees individuals to be authentic and at home with the different parts of their personality, but I also insist that a person must be constructive (nondestructive) with other human beings (Charny, 1986a); I am for every idea and model for organizing societal experiences that protect the freedom of every people (racial/religious/ethnic/national) to experience their identity, within an international framework in which each people is obligated to respect every other people. My version of family therapy is that it begins with the "family" of objects and ideas in my own individual head, goes on to the network of very real intimate relationships I have with my personal loved ones, and then to my participation in our larger family of man with whom I and all of us share a single planet. (I cannot conceive, for example, that I would be ready to treat a family for its inner system of relationships while ignoring the fact that the wage earner of the family is an arms merchant selling his wares wherever commercial gain beckons.)

Pain and Loss Early On In My Family of Origin

The deepest, most impressive lesson about the multilevel organization of human existence that I ever had was through the cancer illness and death of my mother. She took ill when I was six years of age and died when I was fourteen years old. Because I was very lucky to have loved her—she was a sweet and caring person, wonderfully intelligent and skillful in languages—I grieved and hated very deeply her illness and death. I learned that she had been done in by an alien force within her that utilized every possible form of espionage and sabotage to kill her. Obviously the "Nazi" who killed my mother—the cancer killer—was evil, and my unquestioned task was to try to contribute toward defeating and killing such evil, and thus over time evolved much of my efforts to study genocide, "the human cancer" (Charny, 1982), which destroys millions of innocent people (Charny, 1985a).

Like other caring children who want to undo the tragedy that has befallen a beloved mother and who wish to magically discover the cure for her illness and heal her after all, I set out on a voyage to do battle with her enemy, yet in the process I was forced into a whole series of disconcerting discoveries. For one thing, my inner mind reported back to me all too frequent thoughts and desires of my own that were distinctly similar, in fact identical to those of the accursed enemy, which meant that the evil that I was fighting was also present in me! Even the seemingly open and shut story of my good mother underwent troublesome transformations as I was thrust into new knowledge of my rage at her for having been so good that she was incapacitated in life and had left me all alone. In my mind, I could have killed her for leaving me, which made me feel guilty that maybe in real life I was the one responsible for her death and not the mysterious illness that had destroyed her. All this meant a serious crisis of faith for me, for here I was embarking on a profession whose intention and code is to *help* human beings, and I was undertaking a serious commitment to study the worst evils that human beings can do to others not only in the family but in genocidal events such as the Holocaust. Maybe I was working at these good things because I was trying to atone or undo my own increasingly discernible evil.

Even my clinical work betrayed me. I was chief psychologist at a children's psychiatric hospital and, in attempting to do therapy with autistic children, I found that I hated them bitterly. Years later I came to understand that the parts of me that were being ripped open by the autistic children were not only mine but also transference-evocations that replicated the unconscious intentions to annihilate these children that they had suffered in the genesis of their autistic condition. (See Charny, 1980b, for a detailed narrative of treatment of two autistic children, where the guiding theoretical principle was to help the parents release the child from being an object of their unconscious desires to annihilate him or her.)

There were also other uncomfortable realizations that I had to face, such as that in many ways I felt too weak and vulnerable, and another reason I wanted to study violence and evil was in order to become stronger like the very people I was fighting against. Also there was an ugly competitive part of me that wanted to annihilate people who stood in my way. It took me many years to come to the conviction that my goal in fighting violence against life was valid, and there is a basic integrity in me that really respects life and is sincerely committed to fighting against unnecessary destruction of life.

BEGINNING FAMILY THERAPY

While completing my Ph.D. in clinical psychology at the University of Rochester, I became a school psychologist for the Rochester Public School system. Here my most interesting assignment was in an interdisciplinary team of a day-treatment program for psychotic and severely acting out children. There were no inpatient facilities for children in the area at that time; our hard-worked unit for ten children, in an empty wing of a sprawling old school building, was at the frontier of confrontation with these severe problems.

Our treatment model necessarily was a traditional one of individual psychotherapy for the child accompanied by parent counseling, both linked as well as we could to one another, and to what we sensed was the child's related process in the educational/group work sequence (Charny, 1959). We learned as we worked and improvised in response to unfolding developments and crises. The most dramatic lesson I had in family psychology involved one severely acting out youngster whom I was treating in individual therapy. After many months of intense struggle in play therapy real changes began to be evident in the child's everyday behavior. At that point, the child's mother—there was no father in the family picture—took ill with what was reported to be a difficult but not critical illness that required her hospitalization. She called for me from her hospital bed to come to see her and, to my utter amazement, stated explicitly that unless I stopped influencing her child to change as I had been doing, she would die! Two weeks later she was dead.

Personal Therapy

In 1958, I moved to Philadelphia. The occasion was my having been accepted as a student at a psychoanalytic institute, a dream I had had for many years. It was not an accredited institute of the American Psychoanalytic Association, but nonetheless it was an organized program that included physicians and psychologists, and I was excited. My agenda also included a definite intention to undergo a second psychoanalytic therapy after I had terminated my first experience as an analysand in Rochester with a full-scale admission that I had wanted to have intercourse with my mother and feared that my father would do you know what, so that I would have a proper excuse to leave that therapy. The experience had been very helpful for me in clarifying the intense anxiety I had suffered during graduate school, but I sensed it was way off the mark of the character issues with which I needed help. After all the preparations had been made, including my securing work in Philadelphia at the institution where I was to begin doing family therapy two years later, I went to visit the director of the Institute. He lived in an absolutely beautiful home on Philadelphia's gracious "Main Line," and young professional me, on the verge of breaking out of graduate school poverty, was thoroughly taken by the promise of an esthetic and gracious life to come. Nonetheless, I emerged from that interview with a decision to postpone my attendance. My instinct told me something was wrong, even very much so.[1]

I never did attend the Institute. After moving to Philadelphia, I went in to psychoanalysis privately with a student of Leon Saul (1972), the "radical" psychoanalyst who dared to propose that analysis could be conducted far less than five times a week, and who insisted that the central issue in most therapy is a person's hostility and not their oedipal instincts. This analysis freed me to encounter wells of rage in myself, to accept the essence of the emotion and the power of life in it, but also to be responsible for pacing and limiting my anger, and integrating it with constructive intentions and loving.

In the meantime, I had gone on to my post as chief psychologist at Oakbourne Hospital, a residential treatment center for severely disturbed children that was an outpost of the Philadelphia Child Guidance Clinic, and which shared a joint training program for postdoctoral fellows in clinical psychology and residents in child psychiatry. It was a brave and even excellent hospital and we dared to risk and explore new methods of therapy, including an experiment with "isolation treatment," or severe sensory deprivation, as the context for facilitating psychotherapy of the child (Cohen, Charny, & Lembke, 1963).

Our team was thoroughly committed to family-oriented treatment, but in the traditional context. The children were seen in individual therapy either by the psychologist (me) or the psychiatrist director of the hospital, Richard L. Cohen; the parents were seen by the chief social worker, Pernilla Lembke, or another social worker. Under the circumstances of hospitalization the weekly visits of the family to the child took on enormous importance, and it was our policy to focus on the interaction in the visit in the social work treatment of the parents. We all sensed that profound dramas were unfolding before our eyes.

One week the chief social worker came in with a serious concern; in the course of one such visit, the child had begun speaking to her. Her question was whether we, the children's therapists, would agree to her communicating with them! About the same time a major problem had developed for the social work staff who were unable to handle the increasing workload of conducting intake interviews with the many families applying for admission along with treating parents of ongoing child patients. It was the director's decision that he and I would relieve some of the load by undertaking some of the intake interviews with parents—a traditional social work function. Thus now we created the very "unkosher" situation where our social workers were actually talking to children, and we vaunted child psychotherapists were actually talking to parents.

It was into this untenable context that our director brought word of a soon-to-be published paper by Don Jackson (1959) describing the new maverick approach of family therapy. Under Dick Cohen's able direction the decision was taken that we were going to go all the way and treat children and parents simultaneously! My first case was that of an autistic child in a family of no less than 13 members. I got an instant lesson in flexibility about not insisting on seeing the whole family every time. My second case involved a psychotic child who, prior to hospitalization, had been in outpatient therapy for four years. His therapist had reported that he had not spoken at any time save once, when the few words he said caught the therapist so by surprise that he never discerned what they were. The child fought severely against coming to the first family session. I was asked to come and help bring him from his hospital quarters; he tore my shirt in the scuffle. But once he got into the family treatment room, the child started talking and never stopped! Within a few short sessions, before my unbelieving eyes, his parents who had appeared all along as an appropriately concerned "nice couple" were into a severe marital crisis, the mother was in a major depressed suicidal crisis, the child was obviously better, and I was into the beginning of my lifelong romance with family therapy. I was very lucky to be launched experientially into family therapy very early (Charny, 1962).

I suffered/loved four years at Oakbourne Hospital; absorbed in the intensity of treating psychotic kids and their families, and the intensity of being part of a staff that processed relationships with one another authentically as the nexus within which our treatment work took place. It was at once deeply anxiety-provoking and profoundly stimulating of growth. During this time I enjoyed some of the finest supervision I was ever to have, based on what was happening inside of *me* in my treatment work and not based on a discussion of what was happening with *them* (Charny, 1986d).

Eventually, my work at this very special hospital had to come to an end. The years of emotional intensity were beginning to get in the way of other aspects of my development; I felt that it was time to stop "living and breathing" unconscious processes day and night, and that I wanted to feel freer to devote more of my energy to participating in "normal" social and community activities. There was also a gnawing professional problem that precluded my staying on longer in a setting where, although I was growing, I could never aspire to become the leader, because I was not a psychiatrist.[2] It was time for a new initiative to express some aspect of my yearnings for leadership.

GUIDANCE CONSULTANTS – A PSYCHOLOGICAL GROUP PRACTICE

I undertook a leap into the unknown world of full-time private practice in a group practice I created under the name "Guidance Consultants—A Psychological Group Practice" in Paoli, Pennsylvania, a suburb at the end of Philadelphia's "Main Line." At that time in the Philadelphia area there were a number of clinical psychologists who had developed part-time practices, but to my knowledge only one other clinical psychologist had taken the plunge into full-time private practice (Samuel Granick). So I was entering into basically uncharted territory, as well as innovating a group practice.

We employed a wide range of techniques: conjoint family therapy, individual therapy for children, individual therapy for either or both of the parents, group therapy for one or both of the parents. I wrote about combining individual and family therapy (Charny, 1966) and created a series of questionnaires for patients combining individual and family data (Charny, 1969b). The staff of therapists included psychologists, social workers, and psychoeducational therapists, each working at the treatment tasks that were consistent with their profession's historical tradition but also in whatever modes of therapy fit their natural talent, without any artificial restrictions. The psychoeducational therapists were educators who undertook not only to teach skills to children with learning problems, but to treat the emotional blockages that were making it difficult for that child to learn. Thus a reading lesson was also an engagement of the yearnings and fantasies that intruded on the child's ability to read, or the rage that was obscuring the child's ability to see, or any of the dynamics that can make a child "blind" to the world of letters and symbols. Psychoeducational sessions were also related to the family therapy, and interactions between parents and children in tutoring sessions were utilized in vivo as a basis for working with the parents on how they could expect more of the child.

In the cases of the two autistic children that I have already described from this period (Charny, 1980b) the division of roles and therapies went something like this: conjoint family therapy with me, often together with the psychoeducational therapist; mother-child sessions with the psychoeducational therapist, often with me joining them; depth individual psychotherapy for the child with the psychoeducational therapist; psychoanalytic therapy for the mother with me; psychodynamically-oriented therapy for the father with the social worker; marital therapy with the social worker; and remedial educational work for the child in a series of summer camp and special school settings.

In the early years it made my head spin with anxiety to think through how to tailor a treatment plan for a given family. There were no rules or "pharmaceutical guides," but it seemed clear to me that there were many ways of evoking and restructuring the experiential capacity of a person and a family. I was excited by the juxtaposition of individual and family therapy techniques, but when it came time to take my ABPP exams in clinical psychology and I presented a case I had treated in this way, I encountered a wall of suspicious eyes, and I failed. I decided to take the examination over again the following year and to present another case that I had also treated in a combination of individual, couple, and group therapy as if it were only a case of individual therapy; now (1965) I had no problem in passing.

TEACHING THE VIOLENCE OF THE HOLOCAUST: THE PSYCHOLOGY OF AGGRESSION AND NONVIOLENCE

Somewhere around 1965, I heard myself asking deep inside of myself, "How could human beings be so evil to one another as they were in the Holocaust?" I wrote Israel's memorial authority for the Holocaust, Yad Vashem, to ask if they could direct me to bibliographic resources on the psychology of the Holocaust. The brief polite reply I received that regretfully they had no material on the subject whatsoever was a paradoxical trigger of my desire to seek new knowledge.

I proceeded to organize an interdisciplinary study group of professionals. We included a philosopher and novelist who has since become one of the famous writers of our generation; a director of theater, who has gone on to be an outstanding creative educator; a Quaker psychiatrist who taught us fascinatingly how the denial of natural passions of anger and hostility in *good*-souled Friends would drive some of these good people into psychotic conditions; educators; and psychologists. At each meeting, one member of the group would present a paper seeking to understand an aspect of the puzzle of the sources and structures of human destructiveness. We became "PAN: Group for the Research of the Psychology of Aggression and Non-Violence." In 1968 I published my first paper on teaching about the Holocaust as an opportunity to teach nonviolence "to potential future aggressors and victims" (Charny, 1968).

To learn more about human aggression and destructiveness, I studied certain topics of aggression and destructiveness in individuals and families (Charny, 1967, 1971a, 1973b). One topic to which I devoted myself was the subject of marital love and hate. My theory was that here was an important natural laboratory for the study of the unwitting sources of human destructiveness involving only two people, where the beginnings of the relationship were generally optimal in that most couples intended to befriend/love each other and build a cooperative "society," but before long, so many were tearing each other apart.

Not that this was my only reason for studying marital love and hate. For one thing, I was predestined to specialize in marital therapy from age one in my life when my parents decided that mother would take my older brother and me to Palestine and father would stay behind in the United States. Father visited us during two of the summers, and then we were reunited in New York when I was age four. Within a year of that happy family reunion, I became witness to the most difficult tensions and fights between my parents, and within two years I saw the beginnings of the dread illness in my mother that was to kill her. A second very personal reason for my interest in marriage was that by now I was past the ten-year mark of my first marriage, which was full of the stresses of love and hate, and which I had known in my own heart even before marrying was destined to end in a divorce (which finally took place after twenty-four years of that marriage!).

In 1969, I had an article published in *Family Process* entitled "Marital Love and Hate" (Charny, 1969a). It stirred an incredible range of interest from all over the United States, from professional colleagues and from people in all walks of life, including the media. I transformed the article into a book by the same name; it was published by Macmillan and then reissued in paperback (Charny, 1972d).

Another project that I undertook was the development of a new model for newscasting of violent events so that they would not constitute subliminal messages of acceptance and even celebration of the unending violences of everyday life in American society (Charny, 1972c). I also went to work on developing a model for the use of violence in fictional television programs. The latter brought me into contact with several major networks and eventually I received an intoxicating offer from CBS to be their consultant. Before the contract papers were signed, I was informed that the plan was vetoed by a network VP because employment of me and use of my model would have constituted an obligation to monitor and reduce violence in their programs; they were not prepared to do this.

I became active in the American Orthopsychiatric Association, and over a succession of years held posts as chairperson of the "Ortho" Task Force on the Quality of Life, and then its Task Force on Mental Health Aspects of Aggression, Violence and War. Over several annual programs we created a series of sessions that undertook to struggle with the perplexity of human destructiveness, including sessions devoted, perhaps for the first time, to the study of genocide as a process. A few years later the thematic thrust of these sessions led to an edited book, *Strategies Against Violence* (Charny, 1978).

MOVING TO ISRAEL IN 1973

During all these years I was preparing for a dream I had harbored "all my life." I often quip that my decision to move to Israel in 1973 was based entirely on my strong-minded independence and free will, and of course didn't have much to do with the fact that I had been given my first name long before the dream of a Jewish state had come true, that I had been brought to Palestine at age one where I grew up with Hebrew as my first tongue, or that my father continued to speak Hebrew with us children when our family was reunited in New York.

In 1962, when I set up full-time group private practice, I told myself that it would be for ten years, and then I would move to Israel. In fact, I created a chart that I kept faithfully over the years to show the age projections of everyone in our family, including each of our three children as they were born, and our first and beloved dog. When the ten-year time beckoned in 1972, I found myself terrified and fell back on the handy excuse that promotion of *Marital Love and Hate* was going strong (I was appearing on television all over) and I needed to give it another year. I remember in the Fall of 1973 feeling weak and trembly when I realized it was time for the decision and that if I put it off one more time I might never fulfill my dream-imperative. In genuine terror, I committed myself to the move.

We arrived in the Land of Milk and Honey in July 1973 to our own home, which had been built for us in the preceding year. It was at once so familiar and so strange. What a strange people I was now a part of! Our fellow Jews, the Israelis, whom of course I had known in various contexts including our repeated visits to Israel for many years, were alternately warm and helpful in ways that I did not recognize in the pseudopolitenesses of my America, yet simultaneously rude; worse: nasty; worse: elitist, humiliating, and fight-seeking (virtually everybody in Israel is into neighbor-wars, for example). No less a shock to me, then and now, is how getting simple administrative/operational things done in Israel, whether banking, paying taxes, making telephone calls, organizing secretarial work in a public institution, or getting repairs done, is a nightmare of inefficiencies, bungling, and insults, this in a society that is also characterized by outstanding originality, innovation, last-minute flexibility, an ability to make do with limited resources, and a hunger to penetrate the frontiers of new knowledge and development in one field after another. It takes years of living in Israel to understand the ins and outs of its white and black markets of legal and less than legal economies, Israelis' brightness and stupidity, warmth and abusiveness, high ethical values and arrogant involvement with power.

The first part-time positions I accepted were as a consultant to the Kibbutz Child and Family Clinic, a large multiclinic system under the direction of Mordecai Kaffman (1963, 1985), which was one of the first places to introduce family therapy into Israel, and as a teacher in a two-year family therapy training program for social workers (under the direction of Dror Wertheimer at the Institute of Continuing Education of the Ministry of Welfare, the first organized professional training program in family therapy in the country—Wertheimer, 1978). Ten years later the latter was to flow into the development of the first university programs in family therapy, first postgraduate and then graduate as well, which I established and today direct at the Bob Shapell School of Social Work at Tel Aviv University. I was pleased to be in contact with two major "indigenous" populations of Israel, the vaunted socialist-agricultural communities of the kibbutzim, and the welfare clientele of the poor and various ethnic and socioeconomic minorities, while at the same time beginning my own private practice with the usual upper-middle and upper-class clientele.

I was curious to know who my new colleague-therapists were, and to this day I am still touched by the paradox of what I learned. A fair number of therapists did not have anything of the training let alone academic degrees that had become the minimum credentialing requirements in my United States. Many of them had gathered many years of clinical experience, but lacked basic clinical and dynamic knowledge of emotional and mental disorders. A kind of naive sincerity prevailed of talking with patients about what was going on in their minds and hearts that was not related to organized knowledge of psychopathology and psychodynamics. What simultaneously warmed me and dismayed me was that, person for person, these Israeli therapists were superior to their American counterparts in their authenticity and caring, the uncontrived natural ways in which they went about their work, hence the sincerity of their empathy, involvement, and certainly their natural identification with their patients as members of a common community. Overall, the results of treatment seemed to me far better, and the length and intensity of treatment far less, under these blessed circumstances of therapists who really felt more for and with their patients. I could not help but see how often in American practice a kind of invisible glass wall separated therapists and patients as they played their roles in a choreography of "as-if-caring."

What fun to be in a pioneering country. It was like starting all over again in various aspects of professional life. There was no family therapy association in Israel. In 1975, a small American psychological group that was devoted to family therapy elected to hold a meeting in Tel Aviv for the usual reasons of tax-deductible conferences in wonderful faraway places. However, as the appointed date neared, the principal organizers found themselves unable to make the trip and called on a couple who had recently emigrated to Israel, Yocheved and Ephraim Howard, to take over organization of the meeting to which approximately 50 American psychologists would be arriving. Yocheved and Ephraim recruited several of us who were involved in family therapy and together we constituted a local organizing committee. Nobody knew how to create a mailing list at that time, so shortly beforehand we simply placed an advertisement in local newspapers that on such and such dates there would be a professional conference on family therapy. The meeting room that had been rented could hold up to 300 people, but on the appointed day, many more than that number turned up, and, given characteristic Israeli predilections, fists were soon flying over the insufficient seats. An exciting family therapy conference was had by all, and for us in Israel the handwriting on the wall was clear: A committee was convened shortly thereafter to create the Israel Association of Marital and Family Therapy and Family Life Education. This group asked me to serve as president during the period of organization; then, after we formally launched the association in 1977, I continued as its first president until 1979, with Yocheved Howard as our indefatigable executive secretary.

DEVELOPING THE FIRST UNIVERSITY PROGRAMS IN FAMILY THERAPY IN ISRAEL

Our family therapy association flourished. Our international conferences were very successful. National conferences were celebrated with full attendances. Local branches developed in our three major cities. At the universities, a variety of courses in family therapy began to appear. I was asked to draw up plans for a continuing education program in family therapy at our university, and in 1984 the Postgraduate Interdisciplinary Training Program in Family Therapy came into being at the Bob Shapell School of Social Work at Tel Aviv University. My one absolute requirement was that the program be interdisciplinary in student body as well as faculty. The program is based on an eclectic philosophy that emphasizes the therapist's use of self, beginning with the awareness that each of us is drawn to and by certain therapeutic tools and modalities more than others, and these natural proclivities should *not* be translated into beliefs or claims that these techniques are intrinsically superior to all others, but they are ways in which *we* feel more confident and effective.[3]

At this writing, our third class is completing training, our fourth class is completing its first year, and we are making preparations for applications from the fifth class, altogether a total of some 125 students. The success of the program led to a paradoxical situation where graduate students interested in family therapy complained more and more that they were getting inferior training. As of the fall of 1987, a specialization in family therapy was developed in the Masters program. This program, and with it unfolding opportunities in the future for doctoral studies, also means a shot in the arm for research in marital and family therapy.[4] With regard to this aspect of my work, for years I thought it was my obligation to supervise any reasonable-sounding idea that students would propose, and the result had been boredom, avoidance, cynicism, and often a poor job. It took me many years until I came to the conclusion that I should only supervise dissertations on subjects of genuine interest to me, where in a basic sense I am collaborating with the student. Since then I have been enjoying myself much more.

At this writing, there is a growing group of students who are completing dissertations based on the "Existential/Dialectical Model of Marital Interaction and Functioning," which I developed over many years (Charny, 1980a, 1986c). The first dissertation completed on this subject (Arnon, 1984) grew out of a year-long tutorial in which the student, an experienced therapist, and I explored together the development of the model. In her dissertation she was able to show that training in the use of the profile helped therapists to develop a clearer view of their marital therapy cases. One student has since studied the effects of a stroke on the quality of a marriage (Machlin & Charny, in preparation); another has studied changes in marital functioning following couple therapy undertaken at the time of mid-life crisis (Kirschner & Charny, in preparation); a new dissertation is underway about the marital interaction of children of Holocaust survivors (Erel & Charny, in preparation); and another student is at work on creating a paper-and-pencil questionnaire based on the model (Assianelli & Charny, in preparation). Other family therapy studies in preparation or on the drawing boards include a study of the effects of being family therapists on therapists' lives (see Charny, 1983b); a systems analysis of affairs; a study of intergenerational intervention in couple therapy; and a study of the responses of one parent to another who is manifestly persecuting, rejecting, or intruding on the emotional identity and needs of a child (see Charny, 1972b).

HOLOCAUST AND GENOCIDE STUDIES ALONGSIDE FAMILY THERAPY

On some occasions I have real professional/personal pleasure in having the two major parts of my professional self invited to speak up as parts of a single whole. Some years ago, a dear colleague in Norway, Hans Holm, who had been editor for some years of *Fokus på Familien,* the Norwegian journal of family therapy, invited me to do a several-day workshop on the theme, "Aggression and Violence in Therapy and Human Relationships: A Dialectical Approach." In 1985 AAMFT gave me several lovely honors: electing me in its first group of International Fellows (along with Arnon Bentovim and Rosemary Wiffen from England, Maurizio Andolfi from Italy, and Helm Stierlin from Germany); anointing me a "Master." I did a live marital interview and consultation (which is now part of the Master's Video Series [Charny, 1985b]) in a session chaired by Florence Kaslow.[5] I presented a plenary on existential/dialectical marital therapy; but what delighted me no less was being "allowed" to present a small workshop on the contribution of social sciences to understanding genocide.

It always saddens me that so many of my professional "buddies" who really do enjoy my presence and collaboration get a glazed look in their eyes when the subject of my work on genocide and human destructiveness comes up. My major book published in 1982, *How Can We Commit the Unthinkable?: Genocide, the Human Cancer* (Charny, 1982), has been reviewed far and wide with high praise for the most part, but not that much in family therapy circles. There has been no review that I know of that has related to the material that I worked on about "the family life of human beings who are to be the genociders," where I attempt to develop a series of transitional meanings among studies of the individual, family psychology, and phenomena on the societal level.

Considering the fact that I grew up on pure individual psychoanalysis where interpretations of societal or large-scale phenomena, if attempted at all, were simply exaggerated extensions of individual psychodynamic concepts, I am proud that I work at moving back and forth between different levels, being careful not to fall into traps of pure reductionism or positing equivalent phenomena at different levels of behavioral organization. But I do look for transitional continuities across levels such as the psychology of self-defense in marriage and in national experiences, how aggressions escalate in family life and in intergroup relations, or how scapegoating, dehumanization, projection, and sacrificing operate with terrible consequences on all levels of human interaction (Charny, 1972a, 1973a, 1980d, 1982, 1986a, 1988d; Fromer & Charny, in preparation).

In thinking about the "minds" of peoples and nations, I originated an idea for what I called a *Genocide Early Warning System,* which I developed over many years of collaborative research with my colleague, clinical psychologist Chanan Rapaport, then director of Israel's largest social science think tank, the Henrietta Szold National Institute for Research in the Behavioral Sciences in Jerusalem (Charny & Rapaport, 1977, 1980; Charny, 1981, 1982, 1988a, 1988b, 1988c). The purpose of the early warning system is first and foremost to "yell loudly" as information about mass murder develops, for it has been characteristic of virtually all cases of genocide in our twentieth century that the world mostly chooses not to know what is happening until the dead are long buried. The early warning system model also intends to develop long-range views of whether or not given societies will head toward state-authorized mass murder of target peoples.

The underlying structure of our early warning system model is based on a conceptualization of basic human psychological processes that all people and all societies must deal with in one way or another, and which are subject to run-away processes or exaggerated defenses that, even unwittingly, lead to destructiveness. For example, all peoples need to make discriminations of possible dangers to their survival, and in the course of making such judgments it is common for each people to project onto another a threat to its survival. In the name of that projection, in other words in the name of self-defense, a people are likely to convince themselves that the threat of their destruction justifies their striking out preemptively to destroy their enemy.

A number of graduate students have joined me in studying various aspects of human evil, such as a study of the readiness of student professionals in medicine, psychology, and social work to agree to follow fictional government orders to reduce treatment resources for seriously indigent and hopeless cases under conditions of severe economic shortages, and ultimately, as conditions worsen, to plan and execute euthanasia of such patients. We have studied the readiness of the student professionals to cooperate with a forced removal of Arabs from Israel to neighboring lands (Fromer & Charny, in preparation). Another study concerns the extent to which Israelis are prepared to ignore or even cooperate with fictional regimes that are persecuting a minority people when the relationship with that government is variously beneficial to Israel's political, economic, or defense needs, or when there is a danger to the Jewish community within that nation (Sarid & Charny, in preparation). Following the Holocaust and everything that it tells us about human behavior and nature, let alone Milgram's (1974) brilliant experiment and other social science studies that have begun to document the knowledge of human destructiveness, is there any doubt about what the results of such studies will be? I feel very strongly that we need to map and remap the subject from dozens of angles until we will have created a firm psychology of evil and destructiveness.

In 1979 I undertook to convene a first International Conference on the Holocaust and Genocide to take place in Tel Aviv in 1982. Elie Wiesel accepted my invitation to become president of the Conference, and we worked together very closely. Neither of us had any reason to expect that before long we would be seriously divided in our responses to a haunting moral issue. The cause célèbre developed around the planned participation of some six papers (out of several hundred) on the Armenian genocide at the hands of the Turkish government earlier in 1915-1923. The Turkish government has a firm and long-standing policy of opposing any mention of those events and insists that there was no genocide of the Armenians (Charny, 1986b). It made the strongest representations to the Israeli government, and to a variety of world and American Jewish organizations, including threats that certain Jews would be at risk of losing their lives unless the Armenian subject was censored from the Conference. In response to this danger to Jewish lives, the government of Israel requested that we remove the Armenians from the Conference. Both Elie Wiesel and I, independently, and unhesitatingly, said no. Then the Israeli government called for the Conference to close down entirely. Ostensibly the government offered funds to move the Conference to another venue somewhere else in the world at a later date. Elie Wiesel agreed to cancel the Conference, but I refused.

The Conference became a case study in the handling of pressures against one victim people to deny the rights of another victim people for reasons of realpolitik, and a case study of the efforts of no less than two governments to control academic and scholarly pursuits (Charny, 1983c, 1986e). We were the objects of intense international scrutiny including some six stories in the *New York Times*. For me personally, the whole experience was an exhilarating ordeal. Among other mundane things, it was all happening at a time in my life when I was newly divorced and about to move into a new home with my new bride. There was a period of several months when I had to carry the Conference's financial obligations from my own pocket until replacement monies came in from people and organizations who admired our work. But I was delighted to find out about myself that at no point did I hesitate to do what I felt was right, and I look back upon the whole saga with great pride and pleasure.

Elie Wiesel sent me a "Dear Dr. . . ." letter after the Conference severing all relationships, but a year later we embraced once again and have continued to work together. Not only has he been a brilliant spiritual leader in memory of the Holocaust, but his linkage of Auschwitz with Hiroshima and Nagasaki, and his warnings about the future of all mankind, make him a dearly needed leader on behalf of the holiness of all human life. And that is what I feel the strongest about, as a Jew, person, therapist, and scholar of the Holocaust and genocide.

THE INSTITUTE ON THE HOLOCAUST AND GENOCIDE

I have continued as executive director of the Institute on the Holocaust and Genocide. According to the bylaws of this nonprofit organization, I am not allowed to receive any salary or remuneration whatsoever for my work. We issue an international newsletter that I edit called the *Internet on the Holocaust and Genocide,* which I vowed would remain a brief, readable newsletter-type publication that people would read in their bedrooms and bathrooms rather than discard. The goals of the Institute are to bring together different peoples as well as different professions in an interdisciplinary process to study the nature of genocide, and especially the development of means for the possible prevention of genocide and mass murder.

We initiate and support scholarly projects. In 1988 we published a volume of authoritative scholarly summaries of the knowledge base in various areas of the study of genocide, accompanied by critical annotated bibliographies (Charny, 1988a). A volume of papers from the Conference in 1982 that we published earlier has earned strong reviews (Charny, 1984). We ourselves initiate a certain number of research projects. Dan Bar-On, a Fellow of the Institute, has recently completed a brilliant and courageous study of the children of victimizers in the Holocaust in Germany (Bar-On & Charny, in press). We did a small study of people who came to see Claude Lanzmann's monumental movie *Shoah* in Tel Aviv in which we asked these Jewish-Israeli viewers how they felt about an incident when Israeli soldiers murdered some 49 Arab civilians in cold blood back in 1956 (Charny & Fromer, in press). We are now moving toward a follow-up study of some sixty-nine scholars who signed prominent advertisements in the *New York Times* and elsewhere that in effect supported Turkish allegations that there never was a genocide of the Armenians.

Occasionally, there have been observations that some scholars of the Holocaust and genocide have suffered psychological consequences because of their work. But I have found the study of Holocaust and genocide has also added to my deep appreciation of life and even unabashed intentions to enjoy life a great deal as I continue doing the little I can to combat this horrendous evil. One of my most recent publications is in the form of an imaginary playlet that has Hitler, Stalin, Pol Pot, Idi Amin, and Talaat coming together to consult an international law firm – Satan, Whore, and Conformist – as to how they might continue in their grand work without having to be concerned about growing efforts to create legal machinery against genocide (Charny, 1987b).

LOOKING BACK AND AHEAD

I have had the pleasure of being part of so many new initiatives. I recognize that I really like creating new ideas and structures. In my professional life, I am proud of a relative firstness of being in full-time private practice back in 1962, and developing one of the first psychological group practices; delighted at my role in being among the founders of the Israel Family Therapy Association and both its founding and first president; pleased to have organized and to be the director of the first university postgraduate interdisciplinary program in family therapy in Israel, and recently to have added development and direction of the first graduate program in family therapy; I am glad about my initiative and leadership in creating the first International Conference on the Holocaust and Genocide and in the continuing work under my directorship of the Institute on the Holocaust and Genocide.

Throughout, my professional and personal wellspring has been in the practice of psychotherapy. The privilege of encountering truth straight on, meeting with the complexity and mystery of the way we are, each in ourselves and then in the fabrics of our relationships with one another, more than fascinates me. The therapeutic process washes over me like a roaring waterfall that fills me with smiling wonderment and awe. To be in touch with something of our human beauty, genius, and warmth quiets and comforts me; at the same time to be in touch with our human ugliness, madness, and evil enrages, frightens, and humbles me.

As I near my sixties—I am terrified of the numbers of my older age—I feel better than I ever have in my life, but I have dreams and awareness of death for myself and others that are more vivid and sadder than before. I sense/believe that I have a good number of "whammies" (a baseball word for the number of hits a player believes are left in his bat) left in me. In family therapy, I am pregnant with what I hope will be a meaningful book on marital therapy (1986c, 1987a), and a continuing series of researches on the mystery of what happens when couples together create their unique system. In my work on the Holocaust and genocide, I am fascinated about continuing what I am calling studies of evil.

I am delighted to see young people grow into being interesting and capable adults, and so apparently I am going to enjoy that aspect of being older and seeing the young ones become strong, even though I also fear the jealousy in me. I look forward prayerfully to years of more relaxed but still active retirement, and the good old tradition of travel, especially with the person I enjoy being with so much, my wife (and colleague family therapist), Judy.

As for marriage and family therapy, we are growing into a powerful professional group because we obviously tap major truths about peoples' needs and inevitable difficulties in living in connection and intimacy (Charny, 1980a). I hope, but am not at all convinced, that we will grow up more and get past the horror of any therapist or group of therapists insisting that they work in the one and right way, and that other therapeutic techniques are inferior to theirs (Charny, 1974, 1983a). I believe that the future of the art *and* science of family therapy will be based on our understanding more and more how effective therapy is a function of the interaction among diagnosis of the individuals and family unit who are to be treated, the selection of specific treatment tools that the therapist makes based on a combination of scientific knowledge of the strengths and weaknesses of different techniques and the therapist's knowledge of his or her natural skills, and the therapist's use of self as a genuine participant in the therapeutic transaction. There are now more statements in the literature calling for integrated models of family therapy; one of the most persuasive is by the editor of this book who has written about a diaclectic model (Kaslow, 1981).

I also hope that family therapy remains fresh and friendly, removing barriers among professionals and inviting the playful and humorous in us even as we go about our serious business.

NOTES

1. My judgment about the Institute's director was sadly confirmed in later years, first by the appearance of a terrible book (I have written my share of mediocre things but I trust none deserve to be described as terrible), and then a few years later he eloped to another continent where shortly thereafter he committed suicide.

2. Some years later when the physical entity of Oakbourne Hospital had closed down and was incorporated as an inpatient unit at the new quarters of the Philadelphia Child Guidance Clinic, the nonpsychiatrist who had been the head teacher at Oakbourne became the director of the inpatient unit, but that was something we couldn't conceive of in our wildest dreams in those days.

3. We teach that the design of any therapy is a function of an interactive "equation" of the needs of the patients (including diagnostic considerations, patient resources, and sociocultural backgrounds) × (times) the specific therapeutic tools and techniques chosen by the therapist (based on the natural skill repertoire of the therapist and on empirical and intuitive knowledge of the appropriateness of certain tools for the case) × (times) the therapist's use of self (in addition to the choice of techniques, the whole range of the therapist's best and shadowy worst personal qualities and idiomatic style).

4. This program is based on a European model where the requirement for the doctorate is "only" a dissertation, whereas the larger program of graduate courses and seminars that is part of doctoral programs in the United States is included in the Masters program.

5. I have enjoyed a variety of signal professional experiences with Florence Kaslow over the years including participating in the editorial board of *Journal of Marital and Family Therapy* during the breakthrough period of its growth under her direction.

REFERENCES

Arnon, Y. (1984). *A tool for the assessment of the marital relationship.* Master's thesis, School of Social Work, Tel Aviv University.

Assianelli, S., & Charny, I. W. (in preparation). *Development of a questionnaire for couples to assess marital functioning and interaction based on an existential/dialectical mode.*

Bar-On, D., & Charny, I. W. (in press). How do children of perpetrators of the Holocaust cope with their conscience and maintain their "moral self"? (Hebrew). *Israel Quarterly of Psychology.*

Bar-On, D., & Charny, I. W. (in press). *The logic of moral argumentation of children of the Nazi era in Germany.*

Charny, I. W. (1959). Communication between psychotherapist and teacher in treatment of the severely disturbed child. *Mental Hygiene, 43,* 40-47. Reprinted in *Afakim,* 1959, *13,* 264-268 (Hebrew), and in H. Holt (Ed.), *Educating emotionally disturbed children.* New York: Holt, Rinehart & Winston, 1969, pp. 413-421.

Charny, I. W. (1962). Family interviews in redefining a "sick" child's role in the family problem. *Psychological Reports, 10,* 577-578.

Charny, I. W. (1963). Regression and reorganization in the "isolation treatment" of children: A clinical contribution to sensory deprivation research. *Journal of Child Psychology and Psychiatry, 4,* 47-60.

Charny, I. W. (1966). Integrated individual and family psychotherapy. *Family Process, 5,* 179-198. Excerpt reprinted in C. E. Schaefer & J. Briemeister (Eds.), *Family therapy techniques for problem behaviors of children and teenagers.* San Francisco: Jossey-Bass, 1984, pp. 55-57.

Charny, I. W. (1967). The psychotherapist as teacher of an ethic of nonviolence. *Voices: The Art and Science of Psychotherapy, 3,* 57-66.

Charny, I. W. (1968). Teaching the violence of the Holocaust: A challenge to educating potential future oppressors and victims for nonviolence. *Jewish Education, 38,* 15-24.

Charny, I. W. (1969a). Marital love and hate. *Family Process, 8,* 1-24. See book 1972d. Excerpts from article and book reprinted in K. C. Kammeyer (Ed.), *Confronting the issues: Sex roles, marriage and the family.* Boston: Allyn & Bacon, 1973, pp. 303-313; S. R. Steinmetz & M. A. Straus (Eds.), *Violence in the family.* New York: Dodd, Mead, 1974, pp. 52-58; E. A. Powers & M. W. Lees (Eds.), *Process in relationship.* St. Paul, MN: West, 1976, pp. 117-140; J. Burke (Ed.), Reader, School of Social Work, Adelphi University. Lexington, MA: Ginn, 1980; M. A. Lamanna & A. Riedmann, *Marriages and families: Making changes throughout the life cycle.* Belmont, CA: Wadsworth, 1981, pp. 306-307; M. Edelstein (Ed.), *Personality development and the dynamics of human behavior.* Reader, School of Social Work, Adelphi University. Lexington, MA: Ginn, 1983, pp. 50-68.

Charny, I. W. (1969b). *Individual and family developmental review. Manual & booklet of history forms: I. Counseling objectives. II. Family developmental history. III. Personal developmental history. IV. Child developmental history.* Los Angeles, CA: Western Psychological Services.

Charny, I. W. (1971a). Normal man as a genocider: We need a psychology of *normal* man as genocider, accomplice or indifferent bystander to mass killing of man. *Voices: The Art and Science of Psychotherapy, 7,* (2), 68-79.

Charny, I. W. (1972a). Injustice and betrayal as natural experience in family life. *Psychotherapy: Theory, Research and Practice, 9,* 86-91.

Charny, I. W. (1972b). Parental intervention with one another on behalf of their child: A breaking-through tool for preventing emotional disturbance. *Journal Contemporary Psychotherapy, 5,* 19-29.

Charny, I. W. (1972c). We need a *human* language for reporting the tragedies of current violent events: Towards a model for the content, tone and dramatic mood of the broadcaster reporting the news of human violence. *International Journal of Group Tensions, 2,* (3), 52-62.

Charny, I. W. (1972d). *Marital love and hate.* New York: Macmillan. Paperback, New York: Lancer, 1973.

Charny, I. W. (1973a). And Abraham went to slay Isaac: A parable of killer, victim and bystander in the family of man. *Journal of Ecumenical Studies, 4,* (3), 304-318.

Charny, I. W. (1973b). How can psychotherapy contribute to a cultural press for peace? *Voices: The Art and Science of Psychotherapy, 4,* (3), 304-318.

Charny, I. W. (1974). The new psychotherapies and encounters of the seventies: Progress or fads? *The Humanist* (2-part series, May-June, July-August). Reprinted in *Reflections, 10,* Merck, Sharp & Dohme, 1975 (2-parts: 21-31, 3-17); I. D. Welch, G. A. Tate, & F. Richards (Eds.), *Humanistic psychology: A sourcebook.* New York: Prometheus, 1978, pp. 117-140.

Charny, I. W. (Ed.). (1978). *Strategies against violence: Design for nonviolent change.* Boulder, CO: Westview.

Charny, I. W. (1980a). Why are so many (if not really all) people and families disturbed? *Journal of Marriage & Family Therapy, 6,* (1), 37-47.

Charny, I. W. (1980b). Recovery of two (largely) autistic children through renunciation of maternal destructiveness in integrated individual and family therapy. In L. R. Wolberg & M. L. Aronson (Eds.), *Group and family therapy 1980* (pp. 250-281). New York: Brunner/Mazel.

Charny, I. W. (1980d). A contribution to the psychology of genocide: Sacrificing others to the death we fear ourselves. In Y. Dinstein (Ed.), *Israel yearbook of human rights* (Vol. 10, pp. 139-154). Tel Aviv: Faculty of Law, Tel Aviv University.

Charny, I. W. (1981). A computer information system for major violations of human rights. In C. D. Spielberger, I. G. Sarason, & N. A. Milgram (Eds.), *Stress and anxiety* (Vol. 8, pp. 423-430). Washington, DC: Hemisphere.

Charny, I. W. (1982). *How can we commit the unthinkable?: Genocide, the human cancer.* In collaboration with C. Rapaport. Foreword by Elie Wiesel. Boulder, CO: Westview. Paperback (with title change: *Genocide the human cancer: How can we commit the unthinkable?*), New York: William Morrow (Hearst Professional Books), 1983.

Charny, I. W. (1983a). Structuralism, paradoxical intervention and existentialism: The current philosophy and politics of family therapy. In L. R. Wolberg & M. L. Aronson (Eds.), *Group and family therapy 1982* (pp. 200-215). New York: Brunner/Mazel.

Charny, I. W. (1983b). The personal and family mental health of the family therapist. In F. Kaslow (Ed.), *The international book of family therapy* (pp. 41-55). New York: Brunner/Mazel.

Charny, I. W. (1983c). The Turks, Armenians and Jews. In I. W. Charny & S. Davidson (Eds.), *The book of the International Conference on the Holocaust and Genocide. Book One: The conference program and crisis* (pp. 269-315). Tel Aviv: Institute of the International Conference on the Holocaust and Genocide.

Charny, I. W. (Ed.), (1984). *Towards the understanding and prevention of genocide* [Selected presentations at the International Conference on the Holocaust and Genocide]. Boulder, CO: Westview; London: Bowker.

Charny, I. W. (1985a). Genocide: The ultimate human rights problem. *Social Education: Special Issue on Human Rights* (Washington, DC: National Council for Social Studies), *49,* (6), 448-452. Reprinted in *Social Science Record,* 1987, *24,* (2), 4-7; *Social Issues Resource Series: Human Rights,* 1986, *2,* article no. 57.

Charny, I. W. (1985b). *Live therapy-consultation to a couple and their therapist* [Videotape]. In the "Master Therapist Series." Produced and distributed by the American Association of Marriage and Family Therapy.

Charny, I. W. (1986a). Genocide and mass destruction: Doing harm to others as a missing dimension in psychopathology. *Psychiatry, 49,* (2), 144-157.

Charny, I. W. (1986b). Templates for denial of a known genocide: A manual. *Internet on the Holocaust and Genocide,* issue 7, p. 3.

Charny, I. W. (1986c). An existential/dialectical model for analyzing marital functioning and interaction. *Family Process, 25,* (4), 571-590.

Charny, I. W. (1986d). What do therapists worry about?: A tool for experiential supervision. In F. Kaslow (Ed.), *Supervision and training: Models, dilemmas and challenges* (pp. 17-28). New York: Haworth. Reprinted from *The clinical supervisor.*

Charny, I. W. (1986e). One is either for life or not. Preface to R. C. Hovannisian (Ed.), *The Armenian genocide in perspective* (pp. 5-7). New Brunswick, NJ: Transaction Books.

Charny, I. W. (1987a). "Marital trap analysis"—Incompetence, complementarity and success traps: Identifying potential future dysfunctions based on a couple's current collusive agreements. *Contemporary Family Therapy, 9,* (3), 163-180.

Charny, I. W. (1987b). How to avoid (legally) convictions for crimes of genocide (a one-act reading). *Social Science Record, 24,* (2), 89-93. Reprinted in *California courier,* April 24, 1988.

Charny, I. W. (Ed.). (1988a). *Genocide: A critical bibliographic review.* London: Mansell Publishing; New York: Facts on File.

Charny, I. W. (1988b). The study of genocide as a process. In I. W. Charny (Ed.), *Genocide: A critical bibliographic review* (pp. 1-19). London: Mansell Publishing; New York: Facts on File.

Charny, I. W. (1988c). Intervention and prevention of genocide. In I. W. Charny (Ed.), *Genocide: A critical bibliographic review* (pp. 20-38). London: Mansell Publishing; New York: Facts on File.

Charny, I. W. (1988d). Understanding the psychology of genocidal destructiveness. In I. W. Charny (Ed.), *Genocide: A critical bibliographic review* (pp. 191-208). London: Mansell Publishing; New York: Facts on File.

Charny, I. W., & Fromer, D. (in press). "And you shall destroy the evil in your midst": The Holocaust at the hands of everyday human beings. In A. Barnea (Ed.), *Life after the Holocaust* (Educational text for high school studies – Hebrew).

Charny, I. W., & Fromer, D. (in press). *A study of attitudes of viewers of the film "Shoah" towards an incident of mass murder by Jews (Kfar Kassem, 1956).*

Charny, I. W., & Rapaport, C. (1977). *A genocide early warning system: Establishing a data bank for events of genocide and other major violations of human rights.* Jerusalem: Szold National Institute for Research in the Behavioral Sciences [mimeo].

Charny, I. W., & Rapaport, C. (1980). A genocide early warning system. *The Whole Earth Papers,* 14, 28-35. (New Jersey: Global Education Associates).

Cohen, R. L., Charny, I. W., & Lembke, P. (1963). Parental expectations as a force in treatment: The identification of unconscious parental projections onto the children's psychiatric hospital. *Archives General Psychiatry, 4,* 471-478.

Erel, D., & Charny, I. W. (in preparation). Marital interaction of children of Holocaust survivors: The intergenerational transmission of grave post-traumatic memories and concerns.

Fromer, D., & Charny, I. W. (in preparation). The readiness of student professionals to agree and participate in selections of a target population for "special treatment," forced migration, or euthanasia.

Jackson, D. D. (1959). Family interaction, family homeostasis, and some implications for conjoint family psychotherapy. In J. H. Masserman (Ed.), *Individual and familial dynamics* (pp. 122-141). New York: Grune & Stratton.

Kaffman, M. (1963). Short-term family therapy. *Family Process,* 21, 216-234.

Kaffman, M. (1985). Twenty years of family therapy in Israel: A personal journey. *Family Process, 24,* 113-127.

Kaslow, F. W. (1981). A diaclectic approach to family therapy and practice: Selectivity and synthesis. *Journal of Marital and Family Therapy, 7* (3), 345-351.

Kirschner, P., & Charny, I. W. (in preparation). *Changes in marital functioning and interaction following treatment of couples in mid-life crisis.*

Machlin, R., & Charny, I. W. (in preparation). *Changes in marital functioning and interaction of couples following stroke.*

Milgram, S. (1974). *Obedience to authority.* New York: Harper & Row.

Sarid, O., & Charny, I. W. (in preparation). *Attitudes of Jewish Israelis to (fictional) minority groups: Values versus pragmatism.*

Saul, L. J. (1972). *Psychodynamically based psychotherapy.* New York: Science House.

Wertheimer, D. (1978). Family therapy training in Israel. *Journal of Marriage and Family Counseling, 4,* 83-90.

4

Understanding the Therapeutic Process: From Individuals and Families to Systems in Language

HAROLD A. GOOLISHIAN
HARLENE ANDERSON

Preparing the material for this chapter has been a reminder of the many random forces that have shaped the complexity of our history, our narrative—a reminder that we continue to grow and change in our thinking, and yet somehow remain the same. This is true of the nearly forty years of professional practice, thinking, and research that we present in these pages. Where it all began is difficult to pinpoint; what future twists and turns our narrative will take are unpredictable. What is significant on this journey are the conversations we have had along the way. These are conversations with friends, colleagues, families, patients, ourselves, and even with strangers. The conversations are also in the books and papers we read and the presentations we hear. Our history has been a procession of multiple, simultaneous, and sequential conversations. Although we have shared in many conversations, our work together over the past fifteen years also reflects those conversations not coexperienced. Over time, however, they have all touched, interconnected, and influenced our work. Most important of all these conversations are those we have had with our students; these more than the others made us think. They made us invent new understanding, new theory, and new practice. They made us ask different questions of our work. We will focus on the implications these conversations have had for us, how they have forced us on a new, unique, and somewhat anthropocentric adventure. It is our students, past and future, who require us to have a continuing, conscious shift of focus. But, first, we will begin with what each of us brought to our ongoing work together.

PRESENTING OURSELVES

Harold Goolishian: Early Experience and Curiosities

I am usually called Harry. My career did not begin as a student in psychology or family therapy; family therapy had not been invented yet. I tried a few other ideas first. My childhood and adolescence had been spent in the south end of urban Boston. This area of the city was a melting pot of races, cultures, and social classes and my family was a microcosm of this cultural mix. My father was from Armenia and my mother claimed an Irish and English heritage. Adolescence was interrupted by World War II. I served more than four years with the U.S. Marine Corps in the Pacific Islands. Beginning my service as a young man of seventeen, these were crucial years for my personal and professional growth. During the war my exposure to multiple cultures and civilizations completed the process of awareness begun in childhood. This was an openness and sensitivity to, and curiosity about, the awesomely diverse ways in which humankind organizes behavior around the myths and rites that are considered our history and heritage. These experiences left me with a keen awareness, and some confusion, about the many different ways in which people manage their ordinary problems and dilemmas. I did not realize the impact these experiences had on me. I did not foresee the continuing influence they would have on my professional growth.

During the war I took a correspondence course in Psychology. A general introductory text by Woodworth (1940) was used. I remember being captivated by the material. Yet this academic psychology left unanswered my curiosity and interest with the many different ways of behaving, thinking, and feeling that I had observed. I was unaware of what had happened to me but had to keep trying to understand these differences. I could not then be, and I still have not been, freed of this fascination.

I began my student years in 1946 at Boston University as a pre-law major dedicated to making my mark as one of Boston's greatest lawyers. My experience convinced me that the practice of law required a thorough grounding in psychology, sociology, and anthropology, so I loaded up on social science courses. Unknowingly I was still struggling to understand and incorporate those many differences in acting, thinking, and believing that I had observed in my fellow Marines, the Islanders, and the many people from other countries that I had become friends with over the war years, as well as my childhood friends and neighbors. I respected these differences, and even tried to mimic them in naive anthropological attempts to understand them. I was fascinated by these impressions and puzzled by the questions they posed. Near the end of my undergraduate studies, I took a required course in statistics; the effects of this puzzling mathematical knowledge derailed my thinking. I was amazed that such ordering of data was doable. It seemed as if it were actually possible to study and understand human behavior through rigorous statistical research. I no longer needed the crude and naive anthropological methodologies that I had previously used. This shift in focus led to a change in major. I enrolled in graduate school with a goal of becoming a researcher in human behavior.

I began graduate school in 1948 at Michigan State University. It was then Michigan State College of Agriculture and the Applied Sciences. I began as a learning theorist with Dr. Ray Denny, a recent graduate of Iowa (under Spence) as my mentor. I would have continued on as a research psychologist and Hullian theorist, as I was quite taken by the apparent simplicity and completeness of learning theory, had it not been for my wife's allergies. The addition of rat dandruff to our relationship was a serious threat to her health and the continuation of our still new marriage. I again shifted focus and changed my major to clinical psychology and was accepted as a Veterans Administration supported intern.

In 1950, a general dissatisfaction with the narrowness of the graduate program at Michigan State prompted several colleagues and myself to leave and finish our degrees at the newly formed University of Houston, Psychology Department. Several of our Michigan professors had been recruited into the new department; the possibilities of being part of this new program were exciting.

I enrolled at Houston in the fall of 1950, and began my requisite clinical training at the University of Texas Medical School in Galveston. In 1952 I completed my dissertation, *A Factor Analysis of Psychometric and Behavioral Data,* and I joined the faculty of the Department of Neurology and Psychiatry as an instructor. I retired in 1981 as a Professor, Department of Psychiatry and Behavioral Sciences. In addition to my present work at the Galveston Family Institute, I hold Professorships in Family Medicine at Baylor College of Medicine, in Psychiatry at the University of Texas Health Sciences Center, Houston, and in the Graduate Departments of several Universities.

Retirement for me meant the freedom to work full-time on the building of the Galveston Family Institute and the academic freedom to do therapy, think, teach, and write without the full-time constraints of a university. And now the rest of the story.

Harlene Anderson: Something Did Not Fit

I am a fourth generation Texan of Swedish and German descent and fit the stereotypical profile of many family therapists. I grew up in a middle-class family and in an insulated environment. My parents owned their own business, as many of our relatives did, and worked in it together. My parents, however, had an unusual sensitivity to the misfortunes of others and to others as unique individuals rather than as lumps of ethnic, cultural, or religious beings. I believe that this pioneer heritage, this sensitivity, and the collaborative spirit of a family-owned business have influenced the path I have taken within the psychology and family therapy fields.

Like many family therapists of my generation I stumbled into the field through circumstance and pursued it through practical experience, collaboration, and self-directed learning. During the heyday of the War on Poverty and the beginnings of the community mental health movement I chose a career that would help mankind, and believed that undergraduate training in psychology—however unimaginative—would prepare me for this work. I completed my undergraduate studies at the University of Houston in 1964. However, I soon learned that, while the programs I worked in presented a host of opportunities to test my newly gained skills, I was continually frustrated when I attempted to translate what I had read in books to the situations in which I worked. Many times psychological theory did not fit with the people or situations that I encountered.

Still motivated by the naive belief that credentials equal competency, I simultaneously entered graduate school and began work at the first community mental health center in Texas. My graduate student status insured that I would be shuffled from one service area to another: inpatient, day hospital, neighborhood clinic, school, and the patient's home. In all situations I was constantly astonished at the differences in clients' appearance and behavior in the hospital versus their appearance and behavior in their homes; at how the mother I met in the kitchen was not the mother the patient described in group therapy; and how the patient I saw at the neighborhood clinic was not the one described in the chart. Also, I observed that many professionals became active participants in their clients' and families' everyday lives. To my mind something did not fit, but it would not be until later that I would make sense of these observations.

This mental health center experience began to stir in me a sensitivity to the importance inherent in notions such as context, multiple realities, myths, families, and respect. These observations still influence me and continue to demonstrate the limits of both "individual" and "family" thinking and the limits of the mental health field in general. I experienced first hand that what begins as a creative and novel idea can easily become a stagnant and traditional program or approach.

I received an MA in psychology from the University of Houston in 1968. In 1970, I joined the Pediatric Department at the University of Texas Medical

Branch in Galveston as a staff member of another War on Poverty "showcase" program. This was a multidisciplinary program for children and youth from low-income, disadvantaged families; it followed a traditional child guidance model. Each discipline separately performed their service and reported at weekly staff meetings. Although a lot of effort was expended to provide high quality comprehensive health services, I soon felt again that something did not fit. The clients here, like in the other programs that I had worked, represented a different reality than the program.

I met Harry when I first joined the Pediatric Department and began to hear rumors that he and his colleagues in the Psychiatry Department were doing some exciting things with families. Harry had a reputation for being creative and following theoretical paths tangential to established thinking. These personal qualities coupled with rumored success in therapy with families intrigued me, and to learn more I began attending his course on family therapy. Immediately I felt a sense of fit and was soon immersed in this new family therapy field. I read and re-read all of the early writings in the field. I observed Harry with families whenever possible and, at first haltingly, I tried to duplicate his work with my clients. The next year I again signed up for the course and was continually intrigued and sometimes frustrated that every time I thought "Now I've got it" Harry would change what he was doing in the clinic and what he was saying in the classroom. Looking back, however, it was this fluid characteristic that attracted me to family therapy.

I transferred to the Psychiatry Department, drawn by the collaborative spirit and the permissive atmosphere of the Department and the opportunity to work with Harry more intensively. We soon found that there were many similarities in our experiences and thoughts about our clinical and training work. It is this similarity that has been our strongest bond and it has kept us working and studying together since. We fit.

In addition to my efforts at the medical school and later at the Galveston Family Institute, I spent five years in Boston, Massachusetts, where I did consultation and training in family therapy and was a faculty member of the Family Institute of Cambridge. In 1984 I received a doctorate in Psychology from the Union Graduate School. Throughout this period, Harry and I maintained our collaborative work and writing through my commuting to Houston and through our computer modems. The combination of working simultaneously in a familiar context and in new ones provided a unique opportunity for many conversations and a cross-fertilization of ideas that have significantly influenced my recent thinking and work.

THE JOURNEY

Looking Back:
The Early Medical School Years

Family therapy in Galveston was pioneered during the early 1950s at the University of Texas Medical Branch within the Department of Neurology and Psychiatry. The Department was primarily a clinical psychiatric treatment center almost totally limited to hospitalization, combined with various physical and psychopharmacological therapies. The origin of family therapy was similar to that in other centers. There was a growing dissatisfaction with the capacity of current psychotherapeutic and psychoanalytic theory and technology to inform a way to work with the difficult psychotic and adolescent populations we were treating.

It is surprising that family therapy flourished in such a setting. Looking back, however, there were two significant catalysts: isolation and benign neglect. Geographically, Galveston is a barrier reef island in the Gulf of Mexico fifty miles from Houston. Intellectually, Galveston is an island as well. Its isolation has encouraged two contradictory tendencies that bear on our development as family psychologists: the first, a tendency to withdraw and interact exclusively with an intimate group of colleagues; the second, to reach out to gain the interactive stimulation necessary for intellectual growth. Galveston's isolation contributed a context for us and for our clients that influenced our use of time, distance, and difference as key elements in the new concepts and approaches we were developing. Possibly had we been on either of the other two coasts we would not have had that liberty to think. We would have been at risk of being swept up in the massive movements and allegiances that developed in the burgeoning fields of psychology and family therapy.

Coupled with this isolation, a bountiful neglect in the academic setting permitted us to fill voids. Because the medical school served as a state outpatient and inpatient facility, it offered a never-ending referral base of clients from a variety of socioeconomic backgrounds, cultural groups, ages, and geographic areas who presented diverse problems. Impoverished, multiproblem families, juvenile delinquents, chronic schizophrenics, and other difficult populations pushed us to have a constant awareness of their unique needs and situations, and therefore, to constantly question our work context and our theory when they did not fit. Because we were eager to work with those clients that others preferred not to "treat," we were left alone. The medical school also offered us the advantage of working with and training a variety of health professionals including health science students, nurses, psychologists, physicians, medical students, and allied health students. The department was "clinical" and we could assume all the teaching we could handle. It was a combination of these experiences that fed our curious minds and impelled us to constantly revise our theory and practice.

A process had begun in 1952 that has not yet stopped. We were challenged to deal with multiple systems and to work with multiple realities because our referral sources were varied and often continued to be involved in the client's treatment. We learned to think differently about the "ownership" of patients. Our patients were the clients of the medical school, not our "private clients." This perspective lifted the economic constraints of private-practice settings and permitted our capacity to vary format, style, and approach. This economic freedom coupled with an early abandonment of the traditional view of confidentiality and the private, closed context of therapy allowed us the freedom to think in terms of cotherapists and teams of therapists sharing concurrent responsibility for treatment. Thus, early on, we were not limited to one active therapist in the therapy room with others relegated to inactive listening supervisory roles. By 1955 the team had become the therapist. The value of teams is well established now, but then these ideas about team practice represented a radical break with traditional psychotherapy methods.

We did not appreciate the advantage of this bountiful neglect until the family therapy program was shut down in the late 1970s. A change in department chairperson and administration resulted in the implementation of a restrictive "medical model" that led to the development of the Galveston Family Institute independent of the medical school.

Abandoning the Tradition: The Evolution of Multiple Impact Therapy

Back in the early 1950s, our group in Galveston became very frustrated with the lack of resources to work with the delinquent, acting-out, troubled adolescents who had been diagnosed as schizophrenic, neurotic, and personality disordered. In 1952, with the support and encouragement of the Hogg Foundation for Mental Health, we created a research and clinical effort known as the Youth Development Project (Goolishian, 1962; Smith, 1956, 1959); Goolishian was the director.

Our original frustration began in 1952 and arose from the dilemma presented by the ineffectiveness of psychodynamic therapy in working with the adolescent population the clinic was to serve. We knew that adolescents could not be managed in psychotherapy because of their inability to form the transference neurosis necessary for successful treatment. We experimented with seeing families. The Project ultimately evolved into an interdisciplinary team whose mission was to develop and study a "brief family therapy" approach to working with troubled adolescents. This struggling effort to work collaboratively with disturbed young people gave rise to the development of the nontraditional Multiple Impact Therapy (popularly known as MIT) research program. The original MIT team was staffed by Robert MacGregor, Agnes Ritchie, Eugene McDanald, Frank Schuster, and Harold Goolishian. Somewhat later in 1959 Alberto Serrano joined the group. These early efforts are described in the book *Multiple Impact Therapy with Families* (MacGregor et al., 1964) and in several papers (Goolishian, 1962; Ritchie, 1960; Serrano, McDanald, Goolishian, MacGregor, & Ritchie, 1962). This project was funded in 1957 by the United States Public Health Service and was one of the earliest federally supported research projects in Family Therapy.

Originally, the treatment at the Youth Development Project was based on a traditional child guidance clinic model. The psychiatrist or psychologist saw the child and the social worker saw the parents (usually the mother). Because confidentiality was a strong theoretical and ethical issue, dialogue between disciplines was difficult and only occurred through charts and weekly case staffings.

The staff's dilemma intensified in these conferences as each therapist in reporting on the therapeutic progress of his or her client seemed to colleagues as if he or she was describing the same patient but one with a *different* family, *different* family dynamics, *different* etiology, *different* problem definition, and *different* treatment strategy. Staff struggles ensued when members perceived the ineffectiveness of the treatment as a result of their colleagues' inability to work effectively with the patient. There was even occasional talk of colleague incompetence. Heated talk and debate ensued around different explanations about the process of "change" and "no change" in therapy. It became painfully evident that the interactions of the members of the therapy team paralleled the patterns and themes of the core family struggle. It was as if the therapists through their various positions had "inherited," or had come to mirror, the core family struggle.

This process became a major impetus in the group's movement from thinking in terms of individuals and individual characteristics toward thinking about family systems. These exchanges, in an almost imperceptible manner, led us to think of therapy systems encompassing family, therapists, referral sources, and other broader systems persons.

In the early phases of this work the team (then MacGregor, Ritchie, Schuster, and Goolishian) noted that client change was enhanced by two conditions: (1) families in crisis, a state of disequilibrium, were very amenable to change and, (2) adolescent development offered natural access to rapid therapeutic change. They also observed that with the momentum of adolescent growth, change could occur in a brief period of time and with minimum intervention. It was also noted that traditional treatment was often hampered by time, distance, and economics. These observations led to three major theoretical assumptions (MacGregor et al. 1964):

> 1. Recognizable patterns of parental interaction are apt to produce and maintain in dynamic equilibrium specific forms of developmental arrest in offspring which issue in various types of behavioral maladjustment in adolescence. (p. xvi)
>
> 2. Certain types of interactions of the team with itself and the family in crisis may serve as model behavior with which the family may identify in its problem-solving efforts. (p. xvi)
>
> 3. Certain messages of respect from the team to the family concerning the family's predicament and capacity for change may have favorable impact on the family's self-evaluative and self-revisory functions (family self-rehabilitative processes). (p. xvii)

These basic premises led to the development of multiple changes in clinical practice and theory. The team attempted to interrupt the "unhealthy" family patterns by participating in family communications to model "healthy" interpersonal interaction. Our notions of pathology were changing. For example, we perceived that a child was at risk for developmental arrest and dysfunctional behavior if at any time in the child's development one or another of the parents related to the child in a fashion more appropriate to the adult relationship. The nature of the pathology and symptom development were thought to be related to the psycho-sexual-social developmental stage in which the generational violation occurred.

Like most other early family therapists, we understood families in traditional terms. The father was conceptualized as the provider and leader of the household. The mother was described as having a nurturing role. The children had their own responsibilities and boundaries based on age and sex. The primary therapeutic objective was to reestablish clear boundaries between the various generations and to put the authority for the family back in the parents' hands, and thereby establish a healthier family balance or homeostasis.

Teams were formed to work with the adolescent, the family, and any other system relevant to the problem. Referring professionals as well as other helping professionals (e.g., physicians, ministers, school and social agency staff) already involved or likely to become involved with the family were considered critical to the success of the therapy. The teams met with the family and the relevant others in multiple simultaneous and sequential sessions over a two-to-three day period and used as many hours as needed. A consultant to the team observed the sessions from behind a one-way mirror and primarily intervened at the team level through scheduled and spontaneous team conferences initiated by either the consultant or the therapy team.

An important premise of this early work was that therapy should be an evolutionary process, blending therapist, team, family, and broader system data in a manner tailored to the particular family and problem. The group designed a structured format to guide the therapy toward this end by meeting with the consultant in a "briefing session" to familiarize themselves with the case material, to formulate an opinion, and to plan the initial interview. Next the team met with the whole family and relevant others to work toward the objectives agreed upon in the briefing session, while the consultant observed the meeting behind a one-way mirror. This meeting was followed by a team/consultant conference to review the session and to plan the next step. At this point, individual team members typically met concurrently with subsystems such as individual family members, parents, siblings, or relevant community members. Later sessions included either the whole family, combinations of its members, or individual members. Team members were free to participate in any interview. Gregory Bateson, who was a consultant to the project, described these serial overlapping interviews as "cross-monitoring" (MacGregor et al., 1964, p. 191). Each step in therapy (e.g., who to see) evolved out of the team/consultant conferences. These decisions were based on the teams' evolving plan regarding intermediary objectives and overall goals, strategies for reaching those objectives and goals, and assessments of the family's response to the therapy. There was a one-half day six week follow-up.

The research project was a resounding success. Follow-up at 6 and 18 months revealed major change in over 75% of the adolescents and their families (MacGregor et al., 1964).

Questioning Unquestioned Therapy Values

By the mid-1960s, key therapy concepts and structures had evolved out of the original MIT project. Many of these are quite similar to concepts that are now considered central to thinking in systemic family therapy. More important, however, is that these MIT innovations questioned many previously held therapy values and liberated us from our inherited theoretical assumptions and approaches to therapy. Among these innovations were the use of (a) the concept of the family in the context of a referral process, (b) one-way mirrors and observation, (c) therapy teams, (d) consultants working with a "live" therapy process, (e) team and team/consultant briefing and planning sessions and within-session breaks, (f) initial formulations, (g) client feedback to help guide the therapy, (h) thinking in terms of therapy and problem systems, (i) the notion of therapy as a coevolutionary process, (j) homework assignments, (k) teams and consultants in a live therapy training context, (l) team and family and team/family process, (m) the membership of all helping professionals in the problem system, and (n) time and distance as critical elements of therapy.

Therapy was considered an evolving process and a converging of family/therapists strengths. The therapy process was circular in that there was a continuing recalibration of therapist, consultant, and team behavior in response to the family as well as to each other. The team always prefaced MITs with an initial formulation, now more popularly known as an hypothesis (Selvini Palazzoli, Boscolo, Cecchin, & Prata, 1978, 1980). These formulations, and all strategies and goals, were continually refined and changed based on the feedback from the family and its members. As with current systemic thought, the team was "more interested in having the family entertain the idea that there are solutions than in advancing any particular remedy" (MacGregor et al., 1964, p. 188).

Families were viewed as possessing the capacity for change and as capable of finding the solutions for their own problems. Great effort was devoted to respecting the family's and its individual members' realities or what the MIT team called *"communicating respect for each family members' point of view or protecting family members from losing face."* Because teams wanted to maximize cooperation and minimize the opportunity for resistance to develop, there was an emphasis on what today is known as positive connotation (Boscolo, Cecchin, Hoffman, & Penn, 1987; Selvini Palazzoli et al., 1978, 1980). Although the MIT team did not openly describe it as such then, they were working from a premise that resistance is an interactional phenomenon. The group was clear in its understanding that an open team with internal integrity was essential to therapeutic interaction.

Team process was considered critical to client change. The consultant's interventions were primarily at the team level, as in the Milan systemic method (Boscolo et al., 1987). That is, the consultant aimed to create a context for therapist flexibility and creativity, and thus introduced information or perturbations at the team level rather than at the family level. The MIT team was not yet thinking of differences (multiple views of team or family) as described by Bateson (1976) as "news of a difference," but rather, as a way of modeling "healthy differences" for the families.

Although the entire therapy was considered as a continuous intervention, the team made more explicit interventions in the form of "homework assignments" given at the lunch breaks, the end of each day, and at the end of the last day to be carried back to the home situation. All assignments were carefully planned to precisely fit the uniqueness of each family's dynamics.

From a theoretical perspective the original MIT work resembled, and was in some respects a forerunner to, many current positions in the family therapy field today. A developmental approach was considered sufficient to explain "family pathology." As indicated earlier, symptoms were considered to be related to the developmental stage in which a generational violation occurred.

This led to the major thrust of the MIT treatment, to restore family boundaries. The similarities between this position and later structural family therapy (Minuchin, 1974) are quite obvious. The MIT team of MacGregor, Ritchie, Schuster, Goolishian, and Serrano had visited Minuchin and his colleagues at the Wiltwyck School for Boys and had demonstrated the MIT approach to that group in 1957. In a report to the NIMH this clinical research team reported the use of an adapted MIT program in their family work with delinquent adolescents (MacGregor et al., 1964, p. 245).

The MIT team, however, was not comfortable for long with organizational and structural descriptions of families and moved beyond them as they wrestled with their increasing dissatisfactions with this recently developed theory and practice.

BEYOND MIT

The outcome of the MIT work was the formation of a nontraditional psychotherapeutic format and discontinuous change in our thinking that made it impossible to return to the usual methods of clinical practice and theory. A more responsive paradigm was demanded to understand the therapeutic process more richly. Thus the most significant outcome of the MIT work was the paradigmatic shift in our thinking.

A period of professional and personal isolation and loneliness followed the completion of this clinical research project. The team members went their separate ways: Ritchie, McDanald, and Goolishian remained at the Medical School, MacGregor went to Chicago, and Schuster and Serrano moved to El Paso and San Antonio respectively. This break up of the intense and intimate clinical and research relationship developed during the MIT study created a professional despondency that was almost intolerable. The broader professional context, organized psychology, did not offer an appropriate platform to deal with family and systemic approaches, nor with the many other dramatic changes in our thinking and practice.

In 1969 George Pulliam, a social worker, joined the Division of Child and Adolescent Psychiatry. This was an academic division that developed as a result of the early family therapy research. The combination of George and Harry sparked a renewed energy in the department. MIT's were frequently conducted and became a major vehicle for training. We did not, however, continue to practice MIT solely in its original form. Instead, we continued to question and elaborate our current theory and clinical practice. Concurrently, videotaping was used as a major tool for supervision with trainees. Although presentations had been made of MIT work since as early as 1957, we had been limited to audio tapes and live viewing. The expanded use of videotaping proved invaluable in our teaching and other presentations.

Soon others became key members of the core team. Paul Dell, who had been a psychology intern and then a family therapy fellow, joined the faculty. Harlene, who had been in the Pediatric Department and had participated in the early family movement, became a key member. Although others joined the group for periods of time, Harry, George, Harlene, and Paul became the stable working team that continued and expanded the training at the medical school.

A CONTINUOUS SEARCH FOR THEORY

The mid- to late 1970s continued to be productive for us. As we continued to teach, to practice, and to understand and explain our work, we struggled with the popular explanatory concepts of homeostasis, positive and negative feedback, and second cybernetics. Writers such as Hoffman (1971); Hoffman and Long (1969); Speer (1970); Watzlawick, Weakland, and Fisch (1974); and Weakland, Fisch, Watzlawick, and Bodin (1974) offered hope of release from the constraints of homeostasis, negative feedback, and symptom functionality as explanations for problems. During this period the direction of our thinking was significantly influenced by Humberto Maturana (1975, 1978), Ilya Prigogine (1976), and Francisco Varela (1976). It was in 1977 that we learned of Nobel Laureate Prigogine's study of the thermodynamics of nonequilibrium systems and Maturana and Varela's theories of autopoiesis and structure determined systems. We read their work with great excitement and intuitively knew that their conceptions fit with the way we viewed families, systems, and change. This fit was described by Dell and Goolishian (1981).

We simultaneously struggled with what we later called a "co-created reality" (Anderson, Goolishian, Pulliam, & Winderman, 1986; Anderson, Goolishian, & Winderman, 1986). This notion developed out of our efforts to describe to trainees the interaction between client and therapist and what we were doing clinically. One of the most difficult concepts for our trainees to grasp was the discursive process between the client and the therapist, the conversation that takes place in the consultation room. The trainees always emphasized the skills and techniques as the important aspects of doing therapy (e.g., end of session interventions, reframes, homework assignments) while we struggled to emphasize the process of therapy (e.g., the phenomena of moving within and with the client's reality, client's language, therapist positioning). We began to talk about this process in terms of a *co-created reality, a therapeutic reality* that is *co-constructed by client and therapist and in which they both participate, share, and develop meaning.* We believed then, as we do now, that it is the slow and careful development of a co-created reality in narrative that provides the context and the space for change. This represented a shift from understanding therapy as a series of strategic interventions (the therapist changing the client or the client's reality) to the conclusion that the only person in the room that the therapist is able to change is the therapist.

THE GALVESTON FAMILY INSTITUTE: THE FORMATIVE PERIOD

During this energized period of thinking, teaching, and practice there was a major philosophic and leadership change in our academic home. In 1977, a new chairman was appointed. All "nonpsychiatric" and "nonmedical" therapies and teaching programs (such as family therapy) were downgraded. The department no longer provided the benign and bountiful neglect historically important to our flexibility and development. This administrative change made it impossible for us to continue our modification of ideas and practices. We could no longer meet the needs of our clinical research because of mounting pressures to meet the traditions of the medical institution and the fitting of clients to clinical programs. This has left us curious about the process through which universities are able to stifle and cut off creative thinking.

Because we thought that we had something to offer, and because of our deep commitment to enjoy, pursue, and nurture our ideas and work, our group formed, in 1977, the Galveston Family Institute, a not for profit educational and research institution (Anderson, Goolishian, Pulliam, & Winderman, 1986). Harlene left the medical school to steer the Institute during its formative years. Soon to retire from the medical school, Harry continued full-time there and donated many hours to the Institute's endeavors. What we accomplished was to organize our work, our teaching, and our research outside of, and free from, the growing constraints of the changing university medical center. However, we organized the Institute on the familiar and workable university model. We took those traditions with us that had proven essential to our training and practice: faculty and staff had no private practices, positions were salaried, and moneys from contracts, clinical services, and training went to the organization rather than to individuals. Maintaining these elements provided a structure with multiple advantages that maximized the opportunity for colleague interaction in the clinical (cotherapists, consultants, teams) and training domains (team teaching). We considered this structure essential to the recursive process of the development of new ideas and treatment techniques. It is this model that we believe has largely contributed to our ability to provide quality training, a high degree of flexibility in our clinical work, and the continued evolution of clinical theory.

The Institute faculty and staff formed a tight colleague community that increasingly developed a reputation as an "island" and "renegade" group, but for different reasons than before. The "founding" faculty were Goolishian, Anderson, Pulliam, and Dell. Lee Winderman and Rob Horowitz were our first postdoctoral psychology fellows. Lee stayed on as a faculty member and is now in private practice in Houston. We openly challenged the wider family therapy community in terms of the politics of establishing a training Institute because *we refused to design a training program to fit the requirements of any accrediting agency.* We considered being eclectic as a sign of muddled thinking and treasured our focused specificity. We even questioned the very concept of family therapy itself. This rigorous position, and our advocacy for our work, rather paradoxically, has fostered a climate that has permitted and forced many discontinuous changes in our thinking, teaching and research. These changes have led us away from current structural and social science thinking to the world of language, and the interpretive sciences.

CURRENT THINKING AND DIRECTIONS

Linguistic Systems: Hermeneutics, Narrative, and Meaning

Over the last few years we have begun a major shift away from the foundational theories of social science that inform most theories of psychotherapy. Most psychotherapies (individual, marital, group, or family) are based on the sociological and scientific paradigms that view reality as empirically objective. Within this position is the embedded assumption that the scientist is merely a passive observer of events, that is, events are external in their meaning and independent of the observer. Therapy foundational concepts such as stability, homeostasis, lack of change, fixation, and differentiation, as well as prevailing theories of pathology and treatment reflect this observer-independent bias. Because of this bias, the theories become normative in nature. This is true regardless of our general position with reference to individual versus family therapy.

For example, social theoreticians, like Talcott Parsons, have long been intrigued by the question of order, stability, and permanence patterns (1951, 1954, 1960, 1964). For Parsons, just as for family therapists, the concepts of homeostasis and teleologically driven patterns of growth are central to understanding human systems. Family therapists have assumed a Parsonian-like

(Anderson, Goolishian, Pulliam, & Winderman, 1986) description of the individual, the family, and the larger system as sociocultural systems, that is, social systems are viewed as cybernetically layered. Each system is constrained by the system immediately above it. The individual is constrained by the family, the family by the larger system, and the larger system by the society. Thus for the individual theorist psychosis and neurosis are conceptualized as defects in the psychic system. For the family theorist, the defect resulting in psychosis and neurosis is seen to be in the family system. Goolishian (1985) described such a layered sociocultural view as an "onion theory" of social systems.

More recent developments in the systemic therapies have attempted to develop an alternative conceptual framework that bypasses the linear use of power, control, and hierarchies in therapeutic practice. This new thinking began to be evident when Bateson criticized the use of the Double Bind theory (1976) as a theory of schizophrenia and suggested that the use of concepts of power and control were epistemologically flawed. We have been greatly influenced by the shift in the social sciences and philosophy toward a reinvolvement with the cognitive, perceptual, and discursive. The thinking emanating from this shift has the promise of liberating us from the constraints of our earlier epistemologies. We have been increasingly impressed with the limitations of the physical, cybernetic, biological, and sociological epistemologies that inform our clinical field.

The basic limitation in these scientific epistemologies is, in fact, their very scientism. This scientism leaves the social scientist unable to conceptualize the humans studied as subjects embedded in cultural practices and in conversation with each other. It prevents us from seeing our subjects and clients as people who think and construe, understand and misunderstand, interpret and guess, have agency and intention (Taylor, 1985). It fails to recognize that we reflect on the meanings we produce with each other. We are attempting to move away from: (1) the constraints of biological models of the cell that place major emphasis on simple survival and nutritional status, (2) physical models that emphasize the objective status of things in the world independent of the preinterpreted act of observing, and (3) cybernetic models that emphasize control and control theory. We see little utility in the increasingly popular cognitive models that define humans as simple *information processing machines* as opposed to *information generating phenomena.*

In making this theoretical shift we find ourselves increasingly committed to joining the current intellectual debates regarding the impossibility of using scientism for the understanding of human beings. We believe that the field of therapy is rapidly moving toward a more hermeneutic and interpretive position regarding the data of the field. This is a view that emphasizes "meanings" as created and experienced by individuals in conversation with one another.

This position does not rely on decontextualized facts. Rather, it insists on the inseparability of fact, value, detail, context, observation, and theory. We are more interested in *local* explanation than in universal or general explanations. By local we mean the actual dialogue that takes place in the ordinary situations of daily conversation rather than emphasizing the universal, and other broad, community understanding.

We have developed a number of ideas that move our understanding and explanations of therapy into the arena of shifting systems that exist only in the vagaries of discourse, language, and conversation. Our current operating position draws from the sciences of interpretation and hermeneutics and drives our understanding of therapy and pathology from the epistemological domains of social structure and biology, to the domains of semantics and narrative. This position leans heavily on the assumption that human action takes place in a reality that is created through social construction and dialogue (Anderson, 1984; Anderson, Goolishian, Pulliam, & Winderman, 1986; Anderson, Goolishian, & Winderman, 1986; Anderson & Goolishian, 1988; Goolishian & Anderson, 1987). This leads us to believe that we live, and we understand our living, through the socially constructed realities that give meaning and organization to our experience. This is a world of human language and discourse. We have discussed these ideas about systems of meaning under the rubric of *problem-determined systems, problem-organizing dis-solving systems,* and *language systems* (Anderson & Goolishian, 1985, 1988; Anderson, Goolishian, Pulliam, & Winderman, 1986; Anderson, Goolishian, & Winderman, 1986; Goolishian & Anderson, 1981, 1987). This shifting of labels represents a shifting of ideas as well as a fear of labeling.

Foundational Premises

Our current operating position is predicated on the following foundational premises:

1. Human systems are language-generating and, simultaneously, meaning-generating systems. Communication and discourse define social organization; that is, a sociocultural system is the product of social communication, rather than communication being a product of structural organization. All human systems are linguistic or communicative systems and are best described by participants rather than by outside "objective" observers or test instruments. *The therapeutic system is such a linguistic system.*

2. Meaning and understanding are socially and intersubjectively constructed. Intersubjective refers to an evolving state of affairs in which two or more people agree (understand) that they are experiencing the same event in the same way. It is impossible to know (understand) what another person is experiencing, we can only attempt to understand what it is they say about it. Meaning and understanding involve this intersubjective experience of under-

standing. It is understood that agreement is always fragile and continually open to renegotiation and dispute. We do not arrive at or have meaning and understanding until we take communicative action, i.e., engage in some meaning-generating discourse or dialogue within the system for which the communication has relevance. *A therapeutic system is a system for which the communication has a relevance specific to itself.*

3. Any system in therapy has coalesced around some "problem." The system will be engaged in evolving language and meaning specific to itself, to its organization and to its discipline-solution around "the problem." In this sense, the therapy system is distinguished by the co-created meaning, "the problem," rather than a social structure that distinguishes "the problem." *The therapeutic system is a problem-organizing, problem-dis-solving system.* The problem system may, or may not, be marked by the boundaries of family. Any assemblage of communicating persons may comprise the problem system, and this includes the professional attempting psychotherapy.

4. Therapy is a linguistic event that takes place in what we call a therapeutic conversation. The therapeutic conversation is a mutual search and exploration through dialogue, a two-way exchange, a criss-crossing of ideas in which new meanings are continually evolving toward the "dis-solving" of problems and thus the dissolving of the therapy system and hence the *problem-organizing problem-dis-solving system. Change is the evolution of new meaning through dialogue.*

5. The role of the therapist is that of a master conversational artist—an architect of the dialogical process—whose expertise is in the arena of *creating a space for* and *facilitating* a dialogical conversation. *The therapist is a participant-observer and a participant-facilitator of the therapeutic conversation.*

6. The therapist exercises this therapeutic art through the use of *therapeutic questions* that facilitate the development of conversational space and the dialogical process. *The therapist becomes an expert in asking questions from a position of "not knowing" rather than asking questions that demand specific answers.* To do otherwise is to close experience. In asking questions from a position of *"not knowing"* the therapist participates in the co-creation of new realities that emerge from the evolution of new personal narratives and, therefore, change in individual and social organization.

7. Problems are nothing more than operations that stem from our human narratives in such a way that they diminish our sense of agency and personal liberation. Problems are concerned or alarmed objection to a state of affairs for which we are unable to define competent action (agency) for ourselves. In this sense, *problems are no more than alarmed objection, and they exist in language.* This view is opposed to the family therapy concept of structural pathology. *All problems are unique to the narrative context from which they*

derive their meaning. There are no commonalities across problems that can be understood, independent of this narrative context.

8. Change in therapy is the result of the *creation of a new narrative,* and therefore the *opening of opportunity for new agency.* The transformational power of narrative rests in its capacity to re-relate the events of our lives in the context of new and different meaning. *In this manner co-created narrative history must remain coherent with memories and events. Simultaneously these narratives permit a new meaning that is mediated through the different logic of the changing narrative.* We live in and through the narrative identities that we develop in conversation with each other. *Therapy is simply the expertise to participate in this process.*

These premises combine to inform a therapy that reflects a move from a hierarchical to a horizontal, egalitarian, and collaborative effort. They permit and inform a therapist position freed from having objective knowledge to the therapist as a co-participant in the co-creation of new therapeutic realities. It has become possible within this thinking to move from a therapy that is interventionist and that relies on the strategic skill of the therapist, to a therapy that is mutual and that relies on the expertise and integrity of our clients. It is a set of constructs that permits us to move from a therapy based on concepts of pathology and disease to a therapy that is simply dialogical and semantic in nature. This theory of therapy emphasizes the socially created narratives that define our identities and that are central in organizing and coordinating our mutual social behavior.

IN SUMMARY

Family psychology and family therapy have provided an exciting and, at times, frightening journey for nearly forty years. Each of us started from an original interest in psychodynamic and psychoanalytic theory and we quickly moved to family therapy and now on to semantic models. This has not been an easy shift. The territory is uncharted, and there has always been a considerable professional loneliness and isolation. Issues of propriety and ethics, such as patient confidentiality and the fragility of the therapeutic relationship were always there, and always troublesome. Later, and at our more cynical moments, we have thought that if we, and others, had been truly traditionally "ethical" there might not have been such a phenomena as family therapy.

And now these many years later, we think that the credit for our persistence in changing our ideas goes to our students. Fortunately, education and the sharing of ideas have always been central in our work. Not only did we have responsibilities for young psychologists and other health workers, but we also played a major role in professional organizations and their various activities.

There were officerships and committee work in state and national associations and we participated in the organizing of national and regional professional conferences, workshops, and other presentations. The number of students has been huge, and they all asked questions. We were continually faced with the problem of not having adequate answers and explanations. We could not abandon the compelling need to examine our assumptions. Without the naive wisdom of students, this evolution in our thinking most likely would not have occurred. In their *not-knowing,* they knew exactly what questions to ask. Perhaps our contribution to this process was simply our willingness to change. Our educational philosophy has always been that one cannot teach therapy. All that is possible is to provide a context in which therapy can be learned. It was in this context that questions could be asked that permitted us the dialogue and conversation necessary to our teaching and changing.

In retrospect, we are sometimes amazed at how similar our current work with individuals and families, now based on our thoughts about problem systems that exist in language and meaning, is to our earlier move from individual work to family work. Many of our original concepts and descriptions are similar to, or are the seeds of, that which we do today, and yet, in this similarity, so totally different. Early in the 1950s at the Youth Development Project and in the MIT research there were teams, observation rooms, ongoing consultation, client input into the consultative process, and the inclusion of more than just family members. Today we understand these issues quite differently and this different understanding makes them very different phenomena. Our narratives for understanding have changed, and thus our histories and our realities have changed.

As we contemplate this paradoxical similarity and difference, we also ask ourselves, "What have been the chief contributions of the family therapy and family psychology movements?" Our answer does not include the usual references to family dynamics, family pathology, family therapy techniques, the power of the family, or other such concepts. For us, the chief contributions have been in the role of the family therapy movement in the process of provoking change. The family movement has driven us to change our clinical theories and our clinical practices. Through the theories of family therapy we were able to challenge seriously the limitations of available therapeutic technologies. More importantly, we broke free from the growing constraints and the decreasing usefulness of psychodynamic theory. This contribution and challenge continues. We are moving away from the scientism of traditional psychology to the sciences of hermeneutics, narrative, and discourse. These changes could not have taken place without the strength of the family movement and the way in which it provided the original theoretical opening and opportunity to seriously question our theories. None of this could have been accomplished, nor would our theoretical restlessness continue today, without the family of family therapists.

In saying these things we do not intend to denigrate or minimize the importance of "family." Quite the contrary, we emphasize the extraordinary importance of those with whom we share our lives. It is in our families and our intimacies that we participate in the creation of the narratives that define us. We are often reminded of our similarity with Freud, who is reported to have said (Erickson, 1953) that the measure of mental health is "working and loving." Working and loving could not be possible without the social intercourse and conversation that take place in the shared living of work and family. There is little that is possible for a person to do in life outside of working and loving. Our families are important to us. What we are doing is challenging the notion of "family" as constituted by the normative concepts of social role and structure. The concept of family therapy based on these concepts of role and structure limits our clinical work to issues of disease, pathology, and therapist expertise in interventionist actions.

In the place of these concepts we are suggesting the effective power of language, dialogue, and the social construction of meaning. We do not exist, in a human fashion, independent of the narratives we weave with those with whom we work and love. This is our essence. Our families and our intimacies are not formed out of the mute and faceless anonymity of social structure. We are who we are in the live world of conversational exchange with others. The narratives that relate to our vocabulary of self descriptions are a result of *local conversational exchange.* This mostly occurs in our family and other close living. This semantic and narrative view of human self and human agency may result in the fields of psychotherapy returning to an ancient concept; a concept that invokes the power of the "talking cure."

It is this direction that we predict will occupy the debates and discussions of family psychologists and family theorists over the next generation. This movement from a world understood in terms of structure to a world always in process will have far reaching implications for us. It is our view that a social theory based in the biological metaphor of survival and stability, or based in the physical metaphor of structure, interaction, predictability, and measurement, or based on the metaphor of cybernetics and control is simply not adequate. We are suggesting a shift to an epistemology of the semantic and narrative. This move will place the social sciences and family theory within the domain of the interpretive sciences. In taking this direction we can remove the limitations of the subject/object dichotomy that now distances us from what we do.

Perhaps all we have accomplished over this forty year journey is a slow evolution from *the science of the understood,* understood through objective observation and measurement, to *the science of understanding,* understanding through conversation and dialogue. If this is true, the next forty years could be an even greater adventure.

REFERENCES

Anderson, H. (1984). *The new epistemology in family therapy: Implications for training family therapists.* Doctoral dissertation, University Microfilms No. 85-00, 784.

Anderson, H., & Goolishian, H. (1985). Systems consultation to agencies dealing with domestic violence. In L. Wynne, S. McDaniel, & T. Weber (Eds.), *The family therapist as consultant.* New York: Guilford.

Anderson, H., & Goolishian, H. (1988). Human systems as linguistic systems: Preliminary and evolving ideas about the implications for clinical theory. *Family Process.*

Anderson, H., Goolishian, H., Pulliam, G., & Winderman, L. (1986). The Galveston Family Institute: Some personal and historical perspectives. In D. Efron (Ed.), *Journeys: Expansions of the strategic and systemic therapies.* New York: Brunner/Mazel.

Anderson, H., Goolishian, H., & Winderman, L. (1986). Problem determined systems: Towards transformation in family therapy. *Journal of Strategic and Systemic Therapies, 5,* 1-14.

Bateson, G. (1972). *Steps to an ecology of the mind.* New York: Ballantine.

Bateson, G. (1976). Forward. In C. Sluzki & D. Ransom (Eds.), *Double bind: The foundation of the communicational approach to the family.* New York: Grune & Stratton.

Boscolo, L., Cecchin, G., Hoffman, L., & Penn, P. (1987). *Milan systemic therapy: Conversations in practice.* New York: Basic Books.

Dell, P. F., & Goolishian, H. (1981). Order through fluctuation: An evolutionary epistemology for human systems. *Australian Journal of Family Therapy, 2,* 175-184.

Erickson, E. H. (1953). Growth and crises of the healthy personality. In C. Kluckhohn & H. A. Murray (Eds.), *Personality in nature, society, and culture.* New York: Alfred Knopf.

Freud, S. (1953). Quoted in E. H. Erickson, Growth and crisis in the healthy personality. In C. Kluckholn & H. Murray (Eds.), *Personality in nature, society and culture.* New York: Knopf.

Gergen, K. (1985a). The social constructionist movement in modern psychology. *American Psychologist, 40,* 266-275.

Gergen, K. (1985b). Social constructionist theory: Context and implications. In K. Gergen & K. Davis (Eds.), *The social construction of the person.* New York: Springer.

Goolishian, H. (1962). A brief psychotherapy program for disturbed adolescents. *American Journal of Orthopsychiatry, 32,* 142-148.

Goolishian, H. (1985). *Beyond family therapy: Some implications from systems theory.* Invited address presented at the annual meeting of the American Psychological Association, Division 43, San Francisco, CA.

Goolishian, H., & Anderson, H. (1981). Including non-blood related persons in treatment: Who is the family to be treated. In A. Gurman (Ed.), *Questions and answers in family therapy.* New York: Bruner/Mazel.

Goolishian, H., & Anderson, H. (1987). Language systems and therapy: An evolving idea. *Journal of Psychotherapy, 24*(3S), 529-538.

Hoffman, L. (1971). Deviation amplifying processes in natural groups. In J. Haley (Ed.), *Changing families: A family therapy reader.* New York: Grune & Stratton.

Hoffman, L. (1981). *Foundations of family therapy: A conceptual framework for systems theory.* New York: Basic Books.

Hoffman, L., & Long, L. (1969). A systems dilemma. *Family Process, 8,* 211-234.

MacGregor, R., Ritchie, A., Serrano, A., Schuster, F., McDanald, E., & Goolishian, H. (1964). *Multiple impact therapy with families.* New York: McGraw-Hill.

Maturana, H. (1975). The organization of the living: A theory of the living organization. *International Journal of Man-Machine Studies, 7,* 313-332.

Maturana, H. (1978). Biology of language: The epistemology of reality. In G. A. Miller & E. Lenneberg (Eds.), *Psychology and biology of language and thought.* New York: Academic Press.

Maturana, H., & Varela, F. (1987). *The tree of knowledge: The biological roots of understanding.* Boston, MA: New Science Library, Shambhala Publications.

Minuchin, S. (1974). *Families and family therapy.* Cambridge, MA: Harvard University Press.

Parsons, T. (1951). *The social system.* New York: Free Press.

Parsons, T. (1954). *Essays in sociological theory* (Rev. Ed.). New York: Free Press.

Parsons, T. (1960). *Structure and process in modern societies.* New York: Free Press.

Parsons, T. (1964). A functional theory of change. In A. Etzioni & E. Etzioni (Eds.), *Social change.* New York: Basic Books.

Prigogine, I. (1976). Order through fluctuation: Self-organization and social system. In E. Jantsch & C. Waddington (Eds.), *Evolution and consciousness: Human systems in transition.* Reading, MA: Addison-Wesley.

Ritchie, A. (1960). Multiple impact therapy: An experiment. *Social Work, 5,* 16-21.

Selvini Palazzoli, M., Boscolo, L., Cecchin, G., & Prata, G. (1978). *Paradox and counterparadox.* New York: Jason Aronson.

Selvini Palazzoli, M., Boscolo, L., Cecchin, G., & Prata, G. (1980). Hypothesizing, circularity and neutrality: Three guidelines for the conductor of the session. *Family Process, 19,* 3-12.

Serrano, A., McDanald, E., Goolishian, H., MacGregor, R., & Ritchie, A. (1962). Adolescent maladjustment and family dynamics. *American Journal of Psychiatry, 118*(10), 897-901.

Smith, B. K. (1956). *A quarter for growing up.* Austin, TX: The Hogg Foundation for Mental Health.

Smith, B. K. (1959). *A family grows.* Austin, TX: The Hogg Foundation for Mental Health.

Speer, D. C. (1970). Family systems: Morphostasis or morphogenesis, or is homeostasis enough? *Family Process, 9,* 259-278.

Taylor, C. (1985). *Human agency and language.* Cambridge, UK: Cambridge University Press.

Varela, F. (1976). Not one, not two. *Co-Evolution Quarterly, 10,* 62-67.

Watzlawick, P., Weakland, J., & Fisch, R. (1974). *Change: Principles of problem resolution.* New York: W. W. Norton.

Weakland, J., Fisch, R., Watzlawick, P., & Bodin, A. (1974). A brief therapy: Focused problem resolution. *Family Process, 13,* 141-168.

Woodworth, R. S. (1940). *Psychology.* New York: H. Holt and Company.

5

Creating Therapeutic and Growth-Inducing Family Systems: Personal Moorings, Landmarks, and Guiding Stars

BERNARD G. GUERNEY, JR.

BECOMING A FAMILY PSYCHOLOGIST

Roots in Family of Origin

I came in with the Great Depression. I hope to go out with a bit less of it. As was not unusual during that time, I was an only child. Fortunately, I grew up in the upper floor of a house also occupied by my aunt and uncle and their three children. In this extended-family environment I therefore was not without sibling-like experiences. My general impression of family psychologists and therapists is that they have enjoyed their family backgrounds and feel they have derived strength from them. My feelings are like that as well.

While a graduate student, and drawing upon my experiences as an intern, I conceived family therapy at a time when I didn't know anyone else had done so. And today I believe that the prevailing model of therapy—whether individual or family—is outmoded. So I guess I should be considered something of an iconoclast. If I am, I come by it honestly for that is one of the ways I would characterize my late father. He was a person with ideas quite independent of the prevailing *zeitgeist*. For example, although he was extremely permissive with me, there was one activity at which he drew the line. In fact, although there must have been one or two others, it is the only thing I can remember being expressly forbidden to do. I was forbidden to join a "militaristic" organization—the Boy Scouts. (It was typical of his permissive attitude that, although I was not allowed to join it, I was allowed to be a guest participant whenever the occasion presented itself, which was not infrequently.)

Although he never went to college and had to earn his living for the most part in nonintellectual pursuits, my father was a book lover, a well-known secondhand bookstore owner, a published short-story writer, and a translator and scholar of Russian literature. He was the first to translate Russian classics to English directly from Russian, and edited a number of critically acclaimed anthologies of Russian literature. He might spend a day in the library tracking down, say, a picture of a particular Russian coin to translate its description properly. I spent many a pleasurable day with him at the New York City Public Library. I also remember—accurately, I hope—a little calligraphic sign he made and kept pinned to a shelf on his desk where he would see it whenever he lifted his head: *"Ancora impara,"* Greek for "still learning." So, in addition to a healthy disrespect for authority, he imparted to me a great respect for learning and scholarship. Evaluation of my workshops almost always include comments crediting me with being warm, accepting, and caring. If so, I come by these traits honestly also, because they are the primary adjectives that I would use to describe my late mother. Trying to enhance these qualities in as many families as possible constitutes my life's work.

Professional Heritage — Theoretical and Clinical Underpinnings

I consider myself very fortunate that in my professionally formative years I was exposed to each of the major schools of psychotherapy. My undergraduate training as a major in psychology at Brooklyn College was extremely intensive, and predominantly Freudian. The professor I remember most vividly, however, was the experimental psychologist Herman Witkin, who gave his students a deep understanding and appreciation for experimental psychology. His advice to students was to take as many clinical practicum courses and get as much supervision as you can while you are still in school because supervised clinical training would be difficult to come by afterward, whereas factual knowledge and theory could be learned more easily from books, with no feedback from an instructor. With due credit, I have passed this idea on to many another student since then.

At Pennsylvania State University, where I received an M.S. and Ph.D. in clinical psychology, I was fortunate to have Dr. William U. Snyder (a former student of Carl Rogers) as my major psychotherapeutic and research mentor, and also to have been supervised by Dr. Leon Gorlow, who was a Rogerian group and individual therapist. (I remain in touch with both of them, just as many of my students do, and I hope will continue to do, with me.) As I had developed a deep respect for Freudian theory in my undergraduate years, I similarly developed a deep respect for Rogerian theory and methods during my graduate years. Once again I was lucky to have an excellent mentor in experimental design and statistics, Dr. William S. Ray. He emphasized understanding the reasons for various designs and overall strategies of experimental research rather than formal statistical esoterics, and for that I will be forever grateful. I also am grateful to Dr. George Guthrie, from whom I learned how to get what could be gotten from projective testing techniques while maintaining a healthy skepticism about the exaggerated claims, overelaborations, and the overconfidence to which projective tests often are subject.

At Penn State I also acquired a great pride in being a psychologist—for example, Dr. Snyder urged us to use "Dr." in front of our names at all times, saying that "Ph.D.s were doctors when physicians were still barbers," urged us to refer to medical men as "physicians," and encouraged us to favor the term *client* over *patient* wherever reasonable.

I am also appreciative of Penn State because it was there that I met Louise Fisher, my future wife and mother of our three beloved children. In 1951 on our first day of graduate school I met her and proposed to her. It took me over a year to persuade her to accept. We were married shortly before we went on our internship.

Dual careerism was quite uncommon in those days and we were concerned about finding a place where we could intern together. We also had additional requirements that were unusual; we wished to work in a setting that emphasized the treatment of children. We hoped to be able to work in an APA-approved setting that was not dominated by psychiatry and medicine. Surprisingly, as early as 1953 we were able to find a setting that allowed us to meet all of these criteria. The Wichita Guidance Center was one of the earliest mental health facilities directed by a psychologist. He was Dr. Joseph Brewer, who proved to be an excellent person under whom to train, as also were Drs. Salvatore Russo, Harold Bessel, and Glen Roberts. Here we were fortunate to be exposed to yet another major school of psychotherapeutic theory: We were supervised by a psychiatrist, Dr. Austin Adams, who was trained at the William Alanson White Institute and supervised us according to the interpersonal theories of Harry Stack Sullivan.

After interning, we returned to Penn State to do our dissertations, and recognized that another advantage to having Dr. Snyder as a mentor was that he was a pioneer in advocating joint experimental research in psychotherapy. He encouraged research in which a group of doctoral students doing separate dissertations gathered data on a common core of clients in an integrated design that could be far more comprehensive than any one student could manage alone. Thus with Donald Ford and Jeff Ashby, my wife and I were able to do one of the early experimental comparisons of treatment outcomes while at the same time studying client, therapist, and process variables independently and in a way that related each variable to the others and to outcome (Ashby, Ford, Guerney, & Guerney, 1957). This experience provided the foundation for much of my research in later years.

Our training at Penn State imbued my wife and me with a great respect for what learning theory and research might be able to contribute to understanding and improving psychotherapy. We, therefore, paid real heed to some of the early studies of behavior modification (e.g., Gordon Paul's research and the kind of research that later was pulled together by Krasner and Ullmann, 1965). In our postgraduate years, such research led us to educate ourselves through readings and workshops in the methods of behavior modification. (For similar reasons, I became and remain a charter member of the Association for the Advancement of Behavior Therapy.)

Each of the major schools of psychotherapy—psychodynamic, humanistic, behavioral, and interpersonal—has had a significant and lasting influence on my development as a family psychologist/therapist. Although I recognize that there are certain points at which the theories conflict, I always have been unwilling to let go of the great truths in each one. I consider the major schools of therapy, in the main, complementary rather than incompatible. This view led me to develop an approach to family therapy, *Relationship Enhancement* (or RE), that draws on what I consider to be the special strengths of each while rejecting what I view as the weaker aspects of each when these parts are incompatible with the stronger features of another therapy (B. Guerney, 1983). Many professionals consider RE to be a "communications" approach, while others consider it "client centered" and still others classify it as "behavioral." It is "communications" and "client centered" and "behavioral," but it also is psychodynamic and interpersonal. Thus I categorize RE as an *integrated* approach. Some professionals consider RE not to be "systemic." I would define a systemic family therapy as one that deliberately seeks and directly instigates changes in the rules, the pattern of organization, and the nature of the interpersonal interactions existing in a family. To me, *systemic* does not imply that psychological changes within individual family members at emotional, cognitive, and behavioral levels may not also be attended to and promoted directly. In RE therapies, we seek changes in all of these areas and at all these levels in a coordinated way.

Pathways Chosen—
Professional Life Cycle Development and Choices

My clinical observations during internship were what made me into a family psychologist and systems-thinking psychologist. At that time, the notion that members of the same family should be seen for therapy by the same therapist—let alone be seen *together*—was unthinkable. Yet my observations caused me to believe that there were probably more and greater problems caused by *not* seeing parents and children together. The nonacceptance of therapeutic recommendations and the dropout rate led me to believe that no matter how skillful and tactful the clinicians, parents perceived the process of being separated from their children's treatment as a demeaning and psychologically threatening experience.

It was as if a parent was being told, "You fouled up on your child, so we will put your child under the influence of a good parent (the therapist). And because you messed up, something must be wrong with you too, so we will put you in therapy. When your child is better and your head has been straightened out, we will then allow you to come back together again." I thought this implicit message had a great deal to do with explaining why many parents did not follow the recommendation to enter therapy. I also observed that many children were withdrawn from therapy by their parents just as a strong therapeutic relationship was becoming evident. It seemed to me that rivalry with the therapist and feeling demeaned and second-best as parents might be responsible for this phenomenon. Another dropout point seemed to be when there was some temporary and minor acting-out on the part of the child. It appeared impossible for the parents to comprehend that this might be a desirable phase that the child had to go through on the way to uncovering and mastering certain feelings. Instead, parents often saw this as a sign that therapy was failing and withdrew the child. Thus still another way in which the separation of parent and child in the treatment process seemed to be creating problems was the impossibility, despite great efforts at trying to do so, of getting the parents to understand the process/dynamics of the child's treatment when the parents were not themselves an intimate part of that treatment process.

The whole system of treatment seemed based on the idea that the parents were at fault. Although clinicians were as tactful as could be, all of their behaviors seemed to be saying to parents, "We have to find out what you are doing wrong and get you to correct it." I came to believe that this created defensiveness and resistance, making the treatment process more difficult than it needed to be.

In contrast, I viewed most parents as extremely eager to do well by their children and willing to make every effort but simply not knowing how to go about it. This was not to say that they did not have emotional blocks, nor that their poor parenting did not stem from faulty handling of emotions, poor self-concepts, and so forth. But I thought that these difficulties could be faced best and overcome most expeditiously if parents were looked upon as *allies* in the treatment process rather than (however discreetly) the ones at fault.

I also observed that during lunch-hour discussions a therapist who saw the husband in marital therapy would often get into an argument with the therapist who was seeing the wife. This suggested to me that each therapist was suffering from lack of perspective, which could best be obtained by the same therapist seeing both husband and wife. The thought was quick to follow that, at least some of the time, the goal of helping them resolve misunderstandings and conflicts would be served best by having them discuss their differences *together* with the therapist.

So, I left my internship with the idea of putting to work the notions that parents and children (or married couples) should be seen together at the same therapeutic sessions, at least some of the time, and that insofar as possible they should be treated as partners or allies of the therapist.

I had no opportunity to try out these ideas when returning to Penn State to complete my course work and dissertation, nor afterward when I spent a year at Lafayette Clinic in Detroit. In 1957 I joined the clinical psychology graduate program at Rutgers University and reestablished, in a new location and with new training objectives, the Psychological Clinic of Rutgers University (which had been started as one of the first psychological clinics in the nation by Dr. Henry Starr and then directed for many years by his wife, Dr. Anna Starr).

My wife and I began to explore the possibilities of a family therapy in which parents were included in the child's play-therapy sessions, with the therapy largely based on the observations and experiences of these joint sessions. My earlier exposure to Sullivanian interpersonal theory was now reinvigorated by the publication of Timothy Leary's *Interpersonal Diagnosis of Personality* (1957). I remember vividly the meeting my graduate student advisee, Jack Shannon, and I had with Leary when he was at Harvard (before his notoriety in areas other than psychology) as we planned research (Shannon & Guerney, 1973) to test Leary's theory. Interpersonal theory as developed by Leary seemed to me, then and now, to be a wonderful system for studying and understanding family dynamics and family therapy (B. Guerney & L. Guerney, 1961).

Starting in the late 1950s, my wife and I explored the many possible combinations and permutations for conducting joint marital/family therapy sessions (B. Guerney & L. Guerney, 1964). I began writing grant applications to conduct research on the system of family therapy that we termed *filial therapy* (B. Guerney, 1983), and which we now call *child relationship enhancement* family therapy.

NIMH grants first allowed us to do a pilot study and then a large-scale three-year assessment of the effectiveness of filial therapy with emotionally disturbed children. Drs. Lillian Stover, Michael Andronico, and Mary O'Connell were of great assistance in conducting this project, as was our psychiatric consultant, Dr. Jay Fidler. The research showed that parents could learn quickly and well to perform the key therapeutic behaviors of a child-centered play therapist (Stover & Guerney, 1967). We were able to demonstrate that the acceptance rates of referrals to enter treatment and the stay rate of people in this form of therapy were many, many times greater than those reported in the literature for traditional treatments (B. Guerney & Stover, 1971). The therapy proved to be extremely effective: The reduction in symptomatology for the children was quite dramatic, the improvement in psychosocial adjustment was striking, and the failure rate quite low (B. Guerney & Stover, 1971). Later studies demonstrated that these effects began to occur quickly (Sywulak, 1977), that they contrasted sharply with change rates for a control group of normal children (Oxman, 1971) and that normalcy levels obtained by the children were maintained for over three years (Sensué, 1981). It also was demonstrated in later studies that gains in filial therapy could not be attributed to coming in for treatment (Sywulak, 1977). And, although not tested directly, a number of findings made it appear likely that gains were not due to placebo effects, thank-you effects, or the like (B. Guerney & Stover, 1971; Sywulak, 1977). Even taken alone, the original three-year study demonstrated that a family approach to treatment and the inclusion of family members (parents) as allies in the treatment process was an extremely effective mode of treatment.

That research demonstrated that it was possible to take a pathogenic family system and change it into a therapeutic and growth-maintaining family system. Family members could become the *psychotherapeutic agents* of the family therapist.

We pondered: if this family member could become the therapist's psychotherapeutic agent, why not others—such as paraprofessionals, teachers, friends, and other nonfamily intimates? George Albee's (1959, 1968) and Nicholas Hobbs's (1964) views on the need to leverage professional help inspired many toward that goal. Frank Reissman's (1965) *helper-therapy principle,* that helping others also can be of great benefit to the helper, stands out in my mind because it so well conceptualized a phenomenon we observed continually in our own work. My search of the literature resulted in an edited volume, *Psychotherapeutic Agents: New Roles for Parents, Teachers, and Paraprofessionals* (Guerney, 1969). Later, to my amazement and chagrin, I learned that—apparently because of the strangeness of the concept involved—some professionals thought the book was about *drugs* (from confusion with psychotropic agents?). Apparently, little attention is paid to subtitles.[1]

Eventually, a good bit of work along the lines of this broadened concept of psychotherapeutic agents was conducted using RE skills and methods. For example, work with paraprofessionals (Avery, 1978), teachers (B. Guerney & Flumen, 1970; B. Guerney & Merriam, 1972; Merriam & Guerney, 1973), foster parents (L. Guerney, 1974), friends (Ridley, Avery, Dent, & Harrell, 1981), and intimates (Most & Guerney, 1983; Ridley & Bain, 1983; Ridley,

Jorgensen, Morgan, & Avery, 1982; Waldo, 1987b) showed them capable of assisting others to attain better levels of adjustment and interpersonal functioning.

By the time *Psychotherapeutic Agents* was published, our ideas on the medical versus educational models had been formulated, and my wife, Gary Stollak, and I began to write articles on the subject (B. Guerney, L. Guerney, & Stollak, 1971; B. Guerney, Stollak, & L. Guerney, 1970). In 1972, to promote the educational model I started the not-for-profit organization IDEALS (Institute for the Development of Emotional And Life Skills). Its mission was to promote the idea that psychological, emotional, and interpersonal problems, including those involving strong emotional and cognitive sets that originally had been fixed under early family pressure, usually could be best treated by training clients in psychosocial skills. Several members of the current IDEALS board—which consists of Drs. Michael Andronico, Charles Figley, Eric Hatch, and Mary O'Connell—have served the organization faithfully since its inception.

To my disappointment, IDEALS was unable to raise the resources to play a significant role in advancing the educational model. The educational model fared well on its own, however, and has become an active competitor in every aspect of mental health. Now, many psychotherapists teach people how to change their personalities and emotions in all sorts of ways through psychosocial skill training. Clients are taught how to achieve (or delay) orgasm, to inhibit aggression, to be more assertive, to end long-standing addictions, and to control their physiology (e.g., tension and blood pressure). This psychosocial skills-training mental health revolution has advanced so far now that some young therapists seem unaware that such things were ever treated through traditional medical-model psychotherapies! There is even an interdisciplinary professional association devoted exclusively to the furtherance of psychosocial skill training—the Interpersonal Skill Training and Research Association (ISTARA).[2] Consequently, in more recent years IDEALS has focused entirely on training practicing professionals in RE methods.

THE LARGER PROFESSIONAL MILIEU

While I was in graduate school, I was not aware of anyone doing family therapy. A few years after my graduation in 1956, Ackerman (1958) published *Psychodynamics of Family Life* and I discovered that John Bell, a clinical psychologist, had written an article on family group therapy as early as 1953 (Bell, 1953). Later I found his monograph on family therapy (Bell, 1961) both inspiring and illuminating. I also attended what must have been one of the earliest workshops on family therapy, conducted in New York City by John Bell.

In the 1960s I had a graduate student at Rutgers University who was aware of another therapist in New York who was starting a research project on family treatment with delinquent adolescents at the Wiltwyck School for Boys. That student, Braulio Montalvo, put me in touch with Salvador Minuchin, the director of the project, and for several years I commuted weekly to Harlem (where the major part of that research was conducted) and to Minuchin's home in Manhattan (where key staff members collaborated on writing). My main role was in the research aspects of the project; with Bernice Rosman, Shirley Elbert, Montalvo, and Minuchin, I helped to develop research measures including the Family Task and the projective Family Interaction Apperception Test (FIAT). I also developed a system for studying therapist-family and among-family interactions that reflected changes in interaction patterns from early to late stages of therapy. These clinical/research instruments were reported in the book on the project (Minuchin, Montalvo, Guerney, Rosman, & Schumer, 1967). Deservedly, the main impact of that work resided not in the research, but in Minuchin's seminal thoughts about family therapy. During the project I observed therapy sessions and developed a deep appreciation for Minuchin's clinical acumen and completely charming interpersonal style.

BEING IDENTIFIED AS A FAMILY PSYCHOLOGIST

Focus and Major Concerns

Despite my admiration for Minuchin's therapeutic skills, his approach was not consonant with my beliefs about how to work with the family system to bring about change in the most sure, efficient, and durable manner. To my mind these objectives would not be achieved best by following the medical model that Minuchin (and other mainstream schools of family therapy) followed. In order to make parents feel they were allies of the family therapist and to remove the threat to self-image and self-esteem embodied in diagnostically oriented therapies, I was following the educational model in the type of family therapy I was developing. Briefly contrasting the key elements of the medical and educational models will help to clarify the differences between RE and the currently predominant approaches to family therapy.

Before drawing the contrasts it is necessary to point out that the medical model is not synonymous with the disease model. Moreover, either the medical or the educational model may be used to implement any type of therapeutic approach—whether, for example, psychodynamic treatment or behavior modification. Therapists with inclinations toward one school of therapeutic thought initially may be more inclined to think along educational lines than followers of other schools. Such predilections account for the fact that there are many more programs of an educational nature based on behavior modification than on Freudian theory. But the latter does not go unrepresented in the educational paradigm (e.g., transactional analysis). No criticism is intended of the medical model as it may be used in the biochemical treatment of people suffering from actual illnesses that involve mental/interpersonal symptomatology, such as schizophrenia and bipolar depression. But wherever *psycho*therapy is used (which includes all of family therapy) I view the educational model as a competitor to the medical model, and a superior one.

The key difference between the two is that in the medical model therapists *use* their skills to make changes in the psyche and behavioral patterns (including family-system behaviors) of clients. In contrast, therapists following the educational model seek to *transfer* to their clients those particular aspects of therapeutic, intrapsychic, and interpersonal knowledge and skills that the clients need in order to improve, thereby empowering the clients to take charge of their own lives.

The two models may be contrasted by taking a five-point conceptual/procedural paradigm of the medical model, and contrasting it with the comparable paradigm of the educational model. In discussing the medical model, I'm not talking about actual use of medicine, but rather analogs to medical concepts/procedures as they are used by individually- or family-oriented therapists. The contrasts are deliberately sharpened.

First, the medical-model therapist tends to think of clients as sick or maladjusted, and mentally places them like the physically sick or deformed in a category somewhat different than normal people (e.g., different than the therapist or the therapist's family): "They" are not like "us." This often serves to justify behavior toward clients that clearly would not be permissible with "normal" people such as one's own family, colleagues, or friends – paradoxical instructions, for example.

In contrast, the clinician following the educational model tends to view clients as wishing to attain goals not currently being accomplished. Therefore, these persons are in need of instruction as to "how to" do so. (This does *not* exclude people who are forced into treatment rather than volunteering for it.)

Second, family therapists following the medical model seek to identify the dynamic, the structure, or the pattern – analogous to microbes or scar tissue – causing the maladjustment. The therapist sees a need to *diagnose* the family, to place it in a diagnostic category such as "triangulated," "enmeshed," or "disengaged." Only in this manner will the therapist know what to correct and how to correct it. It is assumed that once the noxious structural or functional defects are removed the healthy pattern will emerge, just as the body cures itself when a pathogen is countered by antibiotics or when a broken bone is splinted.

The contrasting concept within the educational model is one of *value and goal clarification:* helping the family members to clarify and to decide upon the goals that they might pursue in order to satisfy their individual, collective, and interactional psychosocial ambitions. Some goals initially may be phrased in negative terms—including the removal of any symptoms—but every negative goal has a positive goal on its flip side. Similarly, every positive goal has a negative one. The side one chooses to focus upon in therapy effects every aspect of the treatment process. In contrast to the medical model, there is no assumption in the psychoeducational approach to therapy that if you find and eliminate an obstruction to proper functioning, proper functioning will emerge. Rather, it is assumed that clients usually should be actively taught how to think and behave in order to meet their goals when they have not been able to do so in the past.

Third, within the medical model, once the diagnostic picture is decided upon the therapist decides what *prescriptions* to give to the family (or what manipulations or reinforcements must be conducted) to bring about the necessary changes. As in medicine, it is not important that the family therapist share much with the client about exactly how and why the prescription will work. Nor is it any more important to the therapist that the family members understand the true reasons the prescriptions was given than it is to the physician that the patient understand how a drug does its work. In this model, each case is viewed diagnostically as a unique problem and the combinations and permutations of maladies and prescriptions tend toward the infinite. As Tolstoy (1933) observed in the opening passage of *Anna Karenina,* each unhappy family is unhappy in its own way.

In the educational model, the concept replacing prescription is *program selection.* Here one seeks to accomplish positive goals by instituting new, positive patterns. Attained and secured, these displace conflicting and previously dominant negative patterns. The therapist need not know in advance—or ever—what the negative patterns were. Rather than identifying and removing negative patterns directly and assuming desirable patterns will follow automatically, it is assumed that if you can put incompatible desirable patterns in place reliably, the negative ones are extinguished.

Happy families, as Tolstoy also observed, tend to be alike. And because they seek happiness, their goals also tend to be alike. I believe all families within this culture (and perhaps universally) wish for a family environment in which they can feel secure, appreciated, loved, and loving. So one can seek to find a program that offers to help the family attain these objectives. There probably always will be people and families who need a unique program, just as there are some students who cannot be accommodated by the usual scholastic curriculum, but the vast majority of the troubled families today making use of family therapy probably would fit quite well within a standard curriculum of a few dozen programs in a School for Living (B. Guerney, 1982). These would include programs to help families move through the stages of child development, societal steps (e.g., school entrance, marriage, retirement), and the stages of the family life cycle. Remedial programs (therapeutic ones) are necessary only for those who failed to learn how to deal effectively with their self- and other-related cognitions and emotions at the appropriate developmental stages.

Because the educational model deals with a moderate number of psychosocial goals, it is possible to take a programmatic approach to therapy. Therapists can make use of programs and materials developed by others much as teachers use syllabi, texts, and audiovisual aids. Hence, as others continue to develop and refine programs geared to specific goals, therapists will find that they need to design unique programs less frequently. Rather, the therapist selects a program, already developed and tested, in accord with the needs of the individual or family (such as smoking cessation/alcohol abstinence, relaxation, orgasm frequency, ejaculation control, conflict resolution, cooperation, child rearing, or dealing with the terrible twos).

Fourth, within the medical model the next phase is that of *treatment.* Again, the patient or family need understand little about the treatment process and essentially need only do what they are told. Their understanding of how the "medicine" works is not essential, and some even regard this as undesirable; in fact, many physicians don't warn their patients about possible side effects lest the patient then imagine them. Many family therapists likewise seem to feel prescriptions will work best if the family is not informed of the way in which they work. The diagnostic-prescriptive skill of the therapist counts for nearly everything, the clients' understanding and skill counts for little. Ideally, they need undergo no struggle to express, understand, learn, or master. As long they do what they are told, the desired cure will follow.

In the educational model the phase corresponding to treatment is *teaching* or *skill-training.* In this model the family members' role (very young children excepted) involves a conscious, effortful, collaborative attempt to understand fully and to master skillfully what they have agreed to learn and to practice. The family members are asked to expose themselves to the risk of failing to perform well. Such education also gives them the opportunity to enjoy the great feelings that arise from successful task mastering.

Fifth, within the medical model, when the process has been successful one speaks of *cure.* What this means is that the offending pattern (e.g., enmeshment or triangulation) has been removed and, therefore, the individual or family has been restored to a normal state. The process is essentially a subtractive one. The individual or family restores itself to health because the therapist has been able to eliminate the pathogen.

In the educational model the state achieved is viewed as one of *goal attainment.* The family members have acquired new sets of attitudes and skills that restructure the operative rules of the family system. They fully understand what has happened and why. Consequently, they can bring those skills consciously into play in a wide variety of family and nonfamily situations to accomplish new goals as they may arise in future stages of the life and family cycles. The process is essentially an additive one wherein the individual or family has acquired skills (and their associated attitudes) that the vast majority of normal individuals and families, at this stage of cultural development, do not possess.

It's a family therapy based mainly on the educational model that we've been developing for the last few decades. Although not originally thought of in this present-day terminology, its objective almost from the beginning has been not simply to remove pathology from the family system, but to create a *therapeutic family system.* The goal is to empower family members to serve as psychotherapeutic agents for one another. Training kin who are in constant residence to be therapeutic agents is likely to be a far more effective strategy than one in which a therapist acts alone (Guerney, 1964).

Empirical Bases of the Educational Model

Belief in the scientist-practitioner model cautioned us to feel compelled, however strong our clinical enthusiasm, to seek data on RE therapies derived from group comparisons with reasonably large samples. We built gradually toward controlled comparisons of this type of treatment model with waiting-control, own-control, and eventually alternate-treatment-control groups. We waited until we had reasonably strong evidence of efficacy before moving on from child-oriented family therapy to marital therapy (originally called "conjugal" RE) and to parent-adolescent family therapy.

Moving from young children to older children and from dyads to larger family units, and to smaller units as well (i.e., doing RE family therapy when only one family member is willing to come for therapy), involved adding many new skills, therapeutic techniques, and procedures. When we worked with adolescents and adults, we were able to make the therapeutic process one which promoted even more equity and mutuality among family members. But the basic lessons learned, about how to teach family members to create a therapeutic family system, carried over quite well from age group to age group, and up from dyads to larger family units and down to individuals who undertake the task of changing their families. Studies comparing RE to controls and to alternate treatments continued to offer strong support of the efficacy of RE when couples and adolescents were included in what then became the "RE family" of family therapies (L. Guerney & B. Guerney, 1985).

Once a therapeutic paradigm for a particular population—parents with young children, adolescents together with their parents, couples, singles—was developed, colleagues and I developed problem prevention/enrichment programs for each (e.g., B. Guerney, 1977, 1988; L. Guerney, 1978, 1988; Preston & Guerney, 1983; Vogelsong, 1978). As I view it, the skills families need to prevent intrapsychic and family-system problems from developing are essentially the same skills that troubled families need to overcome their problems. It is a matter of when families learn them—before or after trouble strikes. Eventually, children may be able to pick up such skills by the modeling of their parents, in which case many of the nonbiochemically caused mental health problems we know today should diminish greatly. But as yet the vast majority of parents, at least in this country, don't have these skills. So, through social modeling, children are often learning ways of behaving that are incompatible with the goals to which they (and their parents) aspire.

Such family aspirations, I believe, are for a sense of security, companionship, trust, loyalty, fairness, understanding, respect, and a sense of loving and being loved. I believe that the skills taught in RE facilitate such basic family goals.

Purposes and Acceptance of RE Family Therapies

A summary of the *purposes* of the knowledge/skills/attitudes acquired in RE might be useful at this point. Family members learn skills that facilitate some or all of the following: self-understanding; self-expression; understanding others' perspectives/feelings (empathy, compassion); helping others to feel understood, respected, and valued; understanding key child-development milestones, the appropriate exercise of control and authority with children; problem/conflict resolution; the ability to teach skills to others; effecting desired changes in oneself and assisting others to make changes that they have agreed to make; priority setting so as to select and apply those attitudes and skills that best further one's most important goals in a given situation; bringing a set of learned skills to bear in as many situations and places as is appropriate; and keeping skills sharp and ready for use when they are needed. Not all of the skills in the program are taught to all families. For example, parenting skills are not needed by a childless couple.

Being recognized as a family therapist came early; the contributions of my colleagues and I were recognized fully by David Olson (1970) in the first major review of family therapy. Nevertheless, RE family therapies have remained largely outside the mainstream, as I discussed with Nicholas Aradi (1985):

ARADI: Why hasn't RE made greater inroads in the family therapy field?

GUERNEY: It is not due, in my judgment, to the effectiveness of the approach. It has been found to be extremely effective with substance abuse, spouse abuse, and other marital and family problems. . . . Why hasn't it spread? First, some practical reasons. I have not operated out of a strong training base. Penn State has a very strong family program in general, but only a couple of graduates each year have emphasized marriage and family therapy. Rather, the great majority go on to teaching and research in human development and family studies, which *is* the program's title and major thrust. That has meant not putting many people out in the field who really know about RE and who can spread it on the basis of their primary training. I think you can make up for that if you are a good organizer, marketer, and have charisma—qualities that help spread a method. I don't have much strength in those areas. The same is true for the kinds of writing that I've mainly done; it's been mainly hard research: not very charismatic. . . . But, also, I think RE hasn't spread because RE is a very strange animal to most people in the field.

ARADI: That's curious. I never thought of RE as strange. It seems so straightforward and accessible.

GUERNEY: It follows the educational, skill training model. . . . You . . . [build, educate, and train] people in the strengths they can then use to fix those wrongs (and other problems that come along later in time) while striving to accomplish positive goals. That is not the way most therapists think. They are very problem oriented and concerned with figuring out what they need to do on the basis of symptoms and what is *wrong* with the family. . . .

[Many people] find it difficult to believe that symptoms can be eliminated better, and structural or other problems can be solved more efficiently and effectively when the family members tackle them themselves, with the therapist focusing mainly on teaching them positive skills and strengths to equip them to do so. Once our couples or families learn the basic skills, they solve many of their problems *between* therapy sessions. . . . If family therapists know about RE at all, they know it has been used for prevention and enrichment. So, I think perhaps they must mentally classify it there and say to themselves, "It couldn't be real therapy. That's not for me."

ARADI: Some of the criticism made about RE is that it is individualistic. That is, it looks at one piece of the system—an individual, or maybe a dyad—but doesn't take into account the context in which the individual functions. How would you respond to people who say the RE is not a systemic or transactional model of therapy?

GUERNEY: The way I would define using a systemic approach is that you deal with the interaction between the parts. . . . And, there is no approach that is more a systems approach than RE, if you accept that definition.

> Another thing to think about in relation to systems is the part-whole relationship . . . when you change a system, i.e., the pattern of interaction among a set of parts—the way in which parts function thereafter will be different than before. Likewise, when you change a part, the way in which the system functions thereafter will be different. The dangers to avoid in therapy are those of changing individual parts in a way that will cause the system to shake itself apart, and to avoid changing the system in such a way that certain parts will be isolated or cut off from the system. Therefore, whether a family therapy approach will prove successful for a family over the long term depends on its using therapeutic procedures that will change both the system's functioning and the individual parts' functioning *simultaneously in an integrated way*. . . . I think RE does that beautifully. And it does it so well because all the procedures used are aimed at achieving this sort of integrated, reciprocal parts/whole change.

If the rapid increase in the number of workshops I am being asked to conduct and the number of professionals who are requesting to know about training and certification in RE therapies are any guide, the situation is now changing. One probable reason is that meta-analytic research has shown that compared to other methods, RE demonstrates very strong improvement effects (Giblin, Sprenkle, & Sheehan, 1985). Another is that certain views that RE has represented in the past are now becoming accepted more widely. Such views include seeing individual and intrapsychic change on the one hand and family therapy on the other not only as theoretically compatible but as synergistic. Within the RE framework, emotions and cognitions (which are essentially intrapsychic) and behaviors (which are essentially interpersonal and interactional) all are viewed as equally important for creating therapeutic change (L. Guerney & B. Guerney, 1987). Such integration between what is usually thought of as individual change and what is thought of as systemic change now is gaining acceptance. Also gaining in acceptance is the idea that it is desirable and possible to integrate schools of therapy that heretofore had been considered incompatible. This works for greater acceptance of RE therapies because they integrate, in a consciously selective way, aspects of all of the major schools of psychotherapy and place them within a systemic framework.

The integration of marital therapy and enrichment, long identified with RE, now is beginning to be recognized (B. Guerney, Brock, & Coufal, 1986). Also the word *educational*—as in "psychoeducational"[3]—has become much more acceptable recently, thanks largely to the work of Carol Anderson (1983). Luber and Anderson, in fact, provided early recognition of the applicability of RE to schizophrenics and other inpatients and their families by inviting a chapter on this topic (Vogelsong, Guerney, & Guerney, 1983) for the book *Family Intervention with Psychiatric Patients.* Also, other old hands at making significant use of the educational model (Barton & Alexander, 1981; Jacobson, 1977; Patterson, 1976; Patterson, Reid, Jones, & Conger, 1975) have been successful recently in penetrating the mainstream, perhaps also making it easier for RE to do so.

Finally, done appropriately, RE can be used alongside some other approaches to family therapy; this too should aid in the acceptance of RE therapies. Thus RE may now be entering the mainstream, or at least becoming a noteworthy side stream, of the family therapy movement.

WHITHER THE FUTURE?

Personal Goals

If a man's reach should exceed his grasp, then I am in clover. My grasping ability always seemed pitifully inadequate to me. Now the years remaining may not be much more than could be counted on fingers and toes. It doesn't look like I'm going to close the gap; in fact, the gap seems to get bigger by the day. So I try to take some measure of comfort from Durkheim's advice: When you are on a journey and the end keeps getting farther and farther away, realize that the real end is the journey.[4]

My "reach" includes the hope of further elaborating upon RE's integration of the theoretical formulations and clinical methods of the major schools of psychotherapy as those pertain to marital/family therapy; doing more work on integrating individual and family therapy; and integrating all of this within a type of systems framework that has easily visible implications for conducting family therapy. I think the systems perspective that offers the greatest hope of accomplishing the last-mentioned goal is that of Donald Ford (1987; Ford & Ford, 1987), and I hope that I may be able to collaborate with him in this effort.

I want to see as much research as possible done on RE. Hence, I intend to continue my custom of happily providing informal consultation to graduate students and others doing therapy/problem-prevention/enrichment research elsewhere as well as at Penn State. In addition, my personal goals include conducting a limited amount of one-on-one training, including long-distance training via audiotape and videotape for those who might be interested in eventually becoming IDEALS faculty members or establishing RE centers or institutes.[5]

Another goal is to provide more therapists with a firsthand knowledge of the nature of RE therapy. Thus, through IDEALS, I'm planning to conduct therapy demonstrations for agencies or consortiums of agencies that might like to witness this type of therapy in their own community with a case representative of their own client population. I hope that some such demonstrations can be two-day marathons, which would be interspersed with group discussion. That way, observers could see aspects of various stages of RE therapy.

Crisis intervention and ultrashort-term RE marital/family therapy are other areas in which I would like to do writing and research in the coming decade. After touting the educational model so loudly, it's a bit embarrassing to say that RE therapy also can be and is used within the medical-model framework. That is, therapists can *use* their RE skills to solve a family's problems, rather than *imparting* the skills to the family to allow them to solve their problems themselves. This is done only when a crisis demands immediate solution (with no opportunity to first train the family in RE skills), or when it is necessary to try to solve major problems in less than 10 hours. RE techniques have been developed for these situations, yet have been written about only very briefly or not at all.

Another objective is to do more research and/or writing concerning certain marital/family RE formats that I believe to be very useful but which have not yet been explored extensively. Perhaps the most important and generally useful of these would be the front-loaded format in which clients are taught the basic RE skills in six hours of therapy scheduled within the first week or, at most, two weeks. In this way clients can acquire the skills quickly and be ready to tackle severe problems by the second or the third week.

Another format I would like to explore more actively for RE therapy is the marathon (Rappaport, 1976). Marathons have the advantage of providing for great emotional intensity and the potential for allowing serious problems to be resolved very quickly, and are attractive for both therapist and client. The problem (aside from getting reimbursed from insurance companies) with the usual one- or two-day marathon approach as it usually is applied is that it doesn't permit easily training the family in generalization/transfer skills. Lack of such training sharply raises the risk that the family will not continue to use the skills when it enters new stages of the family life cycle and new problems and conflicts arise. A marathon format in which the family spends one full day (or perhaps two full days) followed by an additional two or three full days spread out with an increasingly greater number of weeks intervening between the later sessions might overcome the problem. Although such a format seems best suited for use with a family that has a member who is an inpatient or is in long-term residential care, I think it also holds promise for any family experiencing unusual time pressures for resolving their problems. In addition, I would like to combine this format with telephone booster procedures of proven efficacy (B. Guerney, Vogelsong, & Coufal, 1983).

I'd also like to facilitate research on what we've termed "unilateral" RE, wherein only one family member is willing to come in for family therapy and takes on the task of learning to transform the family system single-handedly. I'd like to see this research done both in individual and group unilateral formats.

I plan to be of help to anyone interested in encouraging empirical and, if feasible, controlled research on RE with a wide variety of other clinical populations in much the same way that has already been done with wife batterers (B. Guerney, Waldo, & Firestone, 1987; Waldo, 1986, 1987a), drug addicts (Cadigan, 1980), and delinquents (B. Guerney, Vogelsong, & Glynn, 1977). For example, I'd like to see research done on alcoholics, a population for which clinical experience and pilot research has indicated a high success rate for RE (Matter, McAllister, & Guerney, 1984; Waldo & Guerney, 1983). RE also has been employed and judged clinically fruitful as a form of group therapy for chronic schizophrenics (H. Malone, personal communication, 1983) and for mixed-diagnosis groups of inpatients (P. Cousins, personal communication, 1988). This, too, is an area in which I plan to encourage others to conduct more clinical and empirical investigations. Examples of other clinical groups where study seems warranted include those who are depressed, phobic, or suffering from anxiety. Yet another area in which I would like to encourage controlled RE research would be with special populations of a different sort. A few examples: single-parent families, blended families, teenage parents, runaways, and families of adult criminals on probation.

I hope to write a new how-to-do-it book for RE therapy as a supplement to the original one (B. Guerney, 1977). With Michael Waldo, I've begun planning an edited volume describing how RE has been employed in various settings with various populations.

Where Is the Field Headed?

I hope and predict that in the 1990s there will be a greater integration of the fields of therapy, problem prevention, and enrichment. I think more family professionals will come to see these areas as separate aspects of the larger, more important question: How do we produce positive changes and prevent negative developments within individuals by improving their family systems? I hope to see the overarching concept of *family empowerment* used to help blend the fields of family therapy, problem prevention, and enrichment. I'm hopeful that therapists will be more willing to think about problem prevention and enrichment as a potential part of their areas of expertise and as things that they, as therapists, perhaps are equipped better than anyone else to offer to the public (B. Guerney, Brock, & Coufal, 1986).

I think my biases are not distorting my vision when I observe that the psychosocial skill training movement has made great strides in the area of individual therapy and is making inroads in the family therapy field (Levant, 1986). I believe that the growth of psychosocial skill training family therapies will accelerate in the 1990s.

I have long proposed (B. Guerney, 1977, 1982) that for those who are not biochemically ill, the "school for living" should replace hospitals and community mental-health centers as the major institutional format for helping emotional troubled people. I predict that whatever they may be called, there will be a significant growth of such institutions before the turn of the century.

My fervent hope is that programs designed to prevent family problems and to enrich and strengthen family life will take firm root and spread throughout the nation in elementary and high schools. I think some real progress will be made in this area in the 1990s. If the experience others and I have had in conducting RE-related programs in elementary and high schools (Avery, Rider, & Haynes-Clements, 1981; B. Guerney & L. Guerney, 1981; B. Guerney, L. Guerney, & Sebes, 1984; B. Guerney, Stover, & Andronico, 1967; C. Hatch, 1983; E. Hatch, 1973; Haynes & Avery, 1979; Rocks, 1980) can be of assistance to any reader, my colleagues and I would be delighted to provide it.

I think the coming decade will see a growing integration between psychosocial skill training and self-support groups. I hope that it will become common for support group members to receive training in psychosocial skills in order to increase the potency of their mutual support. This is happening locally with RE in church groups. I think family psychologists are in a particularly good position to collaborate with support groups and to offer them such training.

I also envisage that more psychotherapists who now work with individuals experiencing "intrapsychic problems," and who don't wish to do family therapy per se, will nevertheless bring members of the client's family—whether or not they have anything to do with creating or maintaining the client's problem—into the therapeutic process in order to help the therapist help the client. That is, more family members will be looked upon as potential therapeutic agents. I hope that family psychologists will play a large consulting role to psychotherapists in facilitating this process.

EPILOGUE

I have derived great satisfaction from seeing family therapy grow from something that was "crazy" to something that in the course of only a few decades has won such widespread recognition as something of value. Having been able to contribute to that development, as small as that contribution may have been, has been most gratifying. More important, working in the area has enabled me to become friends with a wide array of exceptionally able, warm, and giving people. Some have been part of an intimate circle of students and colleagues who contributed much heart, time, and talent to the growth of RE.[6] Others are part of a wider circle of the larger-than-life people—many of them prominent in the field—who have been friendly, supportive, and gracious.[7] What a wonderful family to add to my also wonderful birth and immediate families.

NOTES

1. This was a lesson from which I failed to profit fully. The publisher of *Relationship Enhancement: Skill Training Programs of Therapy, Problem-Prevention, and Enrichment* (1977) left the subtitle off the cover without my knowledge; probably because of the word *enhancement*, many professionals assumed that RE was an enrichment method rather than—instead of in addition to—a therapeutic method.

2. Those interested in ISTARA may contact Dr. Luciano L'Abate, Department of Psychology, University Plaza, Atlanta, GA 30345.

3. In the late 1960s, we considered the term *psychoeducational* to describe the educational model but did not use it because I discovered it was associated with remedial education of the more scholastic kind and there was already a journal by that name. Recently, the term has come into usage and the double meaning seems no handicap.

4. Carlfried Graf Durkheim, as paraphrased by Joseph Campbell in Bill Moyer's *Myth* series on PBS.

5. The current heads of these centers deserve mention: Peter Cousins, Ph.D. (Houston, TX), Barry Ginsberg, Ph.D. (Doylestown, PA), Gary Hartley, Ed.D. (Charlottesville, VA), Mary O'Connell, Ed.D. (New Brunswick, NJ), Craig Pierce, M.A., M.C.C. (Albuquerque, NM), and Laurie Johnson, M.Co. (Cartersville, GA).

6. Those not already mentioned for their specific contributions or publications include: Nicholas Armenti, Karen Blaisure, Michael Caccavella, Cleo Campbell, Jan Cavanaugh, Louise Clempner, Jerry D. Collins, David Eardley, Austin Ely, Clifford Essman, David Factor, Joyce Fonash, Mary Frazier, Mark Ginsberg, Roy Grando, Lois Greenberg, Gary Gruber, Nelson Hanawalt, Jan Harrell, Peter Horner, Robert Howard, Randall Jessee, Joanne Kempher, Judy Lay, Ethan Levine, David Mandelbaum, Earl Merritt, Patricia Morello, Ardalene Nease, Ronald Nease, Joanne Preston, Thomas Rocks, Debbie Saidla, Weldon Sams, Cynthia Schellenbach, Steven Schlein, Maryhelen Snyder, Cricket Steinweg, Gary Stollak, Jake Thiessen, Evelyn Roberts Thomas, Risë Van Fleet, James Van Horn, Robert Weiman, John Williams, Glen Wolfgang, and Patricia Yoder.

7. Those not already mentioned include: William Bukoski, Charles Cole, Preston Dyer, Donald Freedheim, Donald Ford, Allen E. Ivey, Neil Jacobson, Luciano L'Abate, Ronald Levant, David and Vera Mace, Joseph Matarazzo, David Olson, Jacqueline Sallade, Douglas Sprenkle, and Richard Wells.

REFERENCES

Albee, G. (1959). *Mental health manpower needs.* New York: Basic Books.

Albee, G. W. (1968). Models, myths, and manpower. *American Psychologist, 23,* 168-180.

Anderson, C. (1983). A psychoeducational program for families of patients with schizophrenia. In W. R. McFarlane (Ed.), *Family therapy in schizophrenia.* New York: Guilford.

Aradi, N. S. (1985). Interaction and relationship: An interview with Bernard Guerney, Jr. *The Purdue Family Therapist, 2*(1), 1-2.

Ashby, J. D., Ford, D. H., Guerney, B. G., Jr., & Guerney, L. F. (1957). Effects on clients of a reflection and a leading type of psychotherapy. *Psychological Monographs, 71*(24).

Avery, A. W. (1978). Communication skills training for paraprofessional helpers. *American Journal of Community Psychology, 6,* 583-592.

Avery, A. W., Rider, K., & Haynes-Clements, L. A. (1981). Communication skills training for adolescents: A five-month follow-up. *Adolescence, 16,* 289-298.

Barton, C., & Alexander, J. F. (1981). Functional family therapy. In A. S. Gurman & D. P. Kniskern (Eds.), *Handbook of family therapy.* New York: Brunner/Mazel.

Bell, J. E. (1953). Family group therapy as a treatment method. *American Psychologist, 8,* 515.

Bell, J. E. (1961). *Family group therapy.* (Public health monograph No. 64.) Washington, DC: Government Printing Office.

Cadigan, J. D. (1980). *RETEACH program and project: Relationship enhancement in a therapeutic environment as clients head out.* Unpublished doctoral dissertation, Pennsylvania State University.

Ford, D. H. (1987). *Humans as self-constructing living systems: A developmental perspective on behavior and personality.* Hillsdale, NJ: Lawrence Erlbaum.

Ford, M. E., & Ford, D. H. (Eds.). (1987). *Humans as self-constructing living systems: Putting the framework to work.* Hillsdale, NJ: Lawrence Erlbaum.

Giblin, P., Sprenkle, D. H., & Sheehan, R. (1985). Enrichment outcome research: A meta-analysis of premarital, marital, and family interventions. *Journal of Marital and Family Therapy, 11*(3), 257-271.

Guerney, B. G., Jr. (1964). Filial therapy: Description and rationale. *Journal of Consulting Psychology, 4*(28), 303-310.

Guerney, B. G., Jr. (Ed.). (1969). *Psychotherapeutic agents: New roles for nonprofessionals, parents, and teachers.* New York: Holt, Rinehart & Winston.

Guerney, B. G., Jr. (1977). *Relationship enhancement: Skill training programs for therapy, problem prevention, and enrichment.* San Francisco: Jossey-Bass.

Guerney, B. G., Jr. (1982). Establishing a school for living cooperative: A proposal. In N. Stinnett et al. (Eds.), *Building family strengths* (Vol. 4, pp. 277-290). Lincoln: University of Nebraska Press.

Guerney, B. G., Jr. (1983). Marital and family relationship enhancement therapy. In P. Keller & L. Ritt (Eds.), *Innovations in clinical practice: A source book* (Vol. III, pp. 40-53). Sarasota, FL: Professional Resource Exchange.

Guerney, B. G., Jr. (1988). Family relationship enhancement: A skill training approach. In L. A. Bond & B. M. Wagner (Eds.), *Families in transition: Primary prevention programs that work.* Newbury Park, CA: Sage.

Guerney, B. G., Jr., Brock, G., & Coufal, J. (1986). Integrating marital therapy and enrichment: The relationship enhancement approach. In N. Jacobson & A. Gurman (Eds.), *Clinical handbook of marital therapy* (pp. 151-172). New York: Guilford.

Guerney, B. G., Jr., Coufal, J., & Vogelsong, E. (1981). Relationship enhancement versus a traditional approach to therapeutic/preventative/enrichment parent-adolescent program. *Journal of Consulting and Clinical Psychology, 49,* 927-939.

Guerney, B. G., Jr., & Flumen, A. B. (1970). Teachers as psychotherapeutic agents for withdrawn children. *Journal of School Psychology, 8*(2), 107-113.

Guerney, B. G., Jr., & Guerney, L. F. (1961). Analysis of interpersonal relationships as an aid to understanding family dynamics: A case report. *Journal of Clinical Psychology, 17*(3), 225-228.

Guerney, B. G., Jr., & Guerney, L. F. (1964). Choices in initiating family therapy. *Psychotherapy: Theory, Research, and Practice, 1*(3), 119-123.

Guerney, B. G., Jr., & Guerney, L. F. (1981). Family life education as intervention. *Family Relations, 3*(4), 591-598.

Guerney, B. G., Jr., Guerney, L. F., & Sebes, J. M. (1984). Promoting family wellness through the educational system. In D. R. Mace (Ed.), *Prevention in family services: Family wellness* (pp. 214-230). Beverly Hills, CA: Sage.

Guerney, B. G., Jr., Guerney, L. F., & Stollak, G. E. (1971). The potential advantages of changing from a medical to an educational model in practicing psychology. *Interpersonal Development, 2*(4), 238-246.

Guerney, B. G., Jr., & Merriam, M. L. (1972). Toward a democratic elementary school classroom. *Elementary School Journal, 72,* 372-383.

Guerney, B. G., Jr., Stollak, G. E., & Guerney, L. (1970). A format for a new model of psychological practice: Or, how to escape a zombie. *The Counseling Psychologist, 2*(2), 97-104.

Guerney, B. G., Jr., Stollak, G. E., & Guerney, L. (1971). The practicing psychologist as educator—An alternative to the medical practitioner model. *Professional Psychology, 2*(3), 276-282.

Guerney, B. G., Jr., & Stover, L. (1971). *Filial therapy: Final report on MH 1826401* [Mimeograph]. State College, PA.

Guerney, B. G., Jr., Stover, L., & Andronico, M. P. (1967). On educating the disadvantaged parent to motivate children for learning: A filial approach. *Community Mental Health Journal, 3,* 66-72.

Guerney, B. G., Jr., Vogelsong, E. L., & Coufal, J. (1983). Relationship enhancement versus a traditional treatment: Follow-up and booster effects. In D. Olson & B. Miller (Eds.), *Family studies review yearbook* (Vol. 1, pp. 738-756). Beverly Hills, CA: Sage.

Guerney, B. G., Jr., Vogelsong, E. L., & Glynn, S. (1977). *Evaluation of the family counseling unit of the Cambria County Probation Bureau* [Mimeographed, 45 pages]. IDEALS, P.O. Box 391, State College, PA 16804.

Guerney, B. G., Jr., Waldo, M., & Firestone, L. (1987). Wife battering: A theoretical construct and case report. *The American Journal of Family Therapy, 15*(1), 34-43.

Guerney, L. F. (1974). *The training of foster parent trainers.* The Pennsylvania State University, in cooperation with the Pennsylvania Department of Public Welfare.

Guerney, L. F. (1978). *Parenting: A skills training manual.* IDEALS, P.O. Box 391, State College, PA 16804.

Guerney, L. F. (1983). Introduction to filial therapy. In P. Keller & L. Ritt (Eds.), *Innovations in clinical practice: A source book* (Vol. II, pp. 26-39). Sarasota, FL: Professional Resource Exchange.

Guerney, L. F. (1987). *Parenting: A manual for trainers.* IDEALS, P.O. Box 391, State College, PA 16804.

Guerney, L. F., & Guerney, B. G., Jr. (1985). The relationship enhancement family of family therapies. In L. L'Abate & M. A. Milan (Eds.), *Handbook of social skills training and research* (pp. 506-524). New York: John Wiley.

Guerney, L. F., & Guerney, B. G. Jr. (1987). Integrating child and family therapy. *Psychotherapy, 24,* 609-614.

Hatch, C. L. (1983). *Training parents of underachieving black elementary students in communication, child management, and tutoring skills utilizing community paraprofessionals.* Unpublished doctoral dissertation, Pennsylvania State University.

Hatch, E. (1973). *An empirical study of a teacher training program in empathic responsiveness and democratic decision making.* Unpublished doctoral dissertation, Pennsylvania State University.

Haynes, L. A., & Avery, A. W. (1979). Training adolescents in self-disclosure and empathy skills. *Journal of Counseling Psychology, 26*(6), 526-530.

Hobbs, N. (1964). Mental health's third revolution. *American Journal of Orthopsychiatry, 34*(5), 822-833.

Jacobson, N. (1977). Training couples to solve their marital problems. *International Journal of Family Counseling, 5*(1), 23-31.

Krasner, L., & Ullmann, L. P. (1965). *Research in behavior modification.* New York: Holt, Rinehart & Winston.

Leary, T. (1957). *Interpersonal diagnosis of personality.* New York: Ronald Press.

Levant, R. F. (Ed.). (1986). *Psychoeducational approaches to family therapy and counseling.* New York: Springer.

Matter, M., McAllister, W., & Guerney, B. G., Jr. (1984). Relationship enhancement for the recovering couple: Working with the intangible. *Focus on Family and Chemical Dependency, 7*(5), 21-23 & 40.

Merriam, L., & Guerney, B. G., Jr. (1973). Creating a democratic elementary school classroom: A pilot-training program involving teachers, administrators, and parents. *Contemporary Education, 45*(1), 34-42.

Minuchin, S., Montalvo, B., Guerney, B. G., Jr., Rosman, B., & Schumer, F. (1967). *Families of the slums: An exploration of their structure and treatment.* New York: Basic Books.

Most, R. K., & Guerney, B. G. Jr. (1983). An empirical evaluation for training leaders for premarital relationship enhancement. *Family Relations, 32*(2), 239-251.

Olson, D. (1970). Marital and family therapy: Integrative review and critique. *Journal of Marriage and the Family,* 32, 501-538.

Oxman, L. (1971). *The effectiveness of filial therapy: A controlled study.* Unpublished doctoral dissertation, Rutgers University.

Patterson, G. R. (1976). Parents and teachers as change agents: A social learning approach. In H. L. David (Ed.), *Treating relationships.* Lake Mills, IA: Graphic Publishing.

Patterson, G. R., Reid, J. B., Jones, R. R., & Conger, R. E. (1975). *A social learning approach to family intervention: Families with aggressive children* (Vol. I). Eugene, OR: Castalia.

Preston, J., & Guerney, B. G., Jr. (1983). *Relationship enhancement skill training.* [Photocopy, 600 pp.] State College, PA.

Rappaport, A. F. (1976). The conjugal relationship enhancement program. In D. H. Olson (Ed.), *Treating relationships* (pp. 41-46). Lake Mills, IA: Graphic Publishing.

Reissman, F. (1965). The "helper" therapy principle. *Social Work, 10*(2), 27-32.

Ridley, C. A., Avery, A. W., Dent, J., & Harrell, J. (1981). The effects of relationship enhancement and problem solving programs on perceived heterosexual competence. *Family Therapy, 8,* 60-66.

Ridley, C. A., & Bain, A. N. (1983). The effects of premarital relationship enhancement program on self-disclosure. *Family Therapy, 10*(1), 13-84.

Ridley, C. A., Jorgensen, S. R., Morgan, A. C., & Avery, A. W. (1982). Relationship enhancement with premarital couples: An assessment of effects on relationship quality. *American Journal of Family Therapy, 10,* 42-48.

Rocks, T. (1980). *The effectiveness of communication skills training with underachieving, low-communicating secondary school students and their teachers.* Unpublished doctoral dissertation, Pennsylvania State University.

Sensué, M. E. (1981). *Filial therapy follow-up study: Effects on parental acceptance and child adjustment.* Unpublished doctoral dissertation, Pennsylvania State University.

Shannon, J., & Guerney, B. G., Jr. (1973). Interpersonal effects of interpersonal behavior. *Journal of Personality and Social Psychology, 26*(2), 219-225.

Stover, L., & Guerney, B. G., Jr. (1967). The efficacy of training procedures for mothers in filial therapy. *Psychotherapy: Theory, Research, and Practice, 4*(3), 110-115.

Sywulak, A. E. (1977). *The effect of filial therapy on parenting acceptance and child adjustment.* Unpublished doctoral dissertation, Pennsylvania State University.

Sywulak, A. E. (1984, November). Creating a whole atmosphere in a group home for retarded adolescents. *Academic Psychology Bulletin, 6,* 325-326.

Tolstoy, L. (1933). *Anna Karenina* (Vol. I & II, C. Garnett, Trans., B. G. Guerney, Ed.). Moscow: State Publishing House for Fiction and Poetry.

Vogelsong, E. L. (1978). Relationship enhancement training for children. *Elementary School Guidance and Counseling, 12*(4), 272-279.

Vogelsong, E., Guerney, B. G., Jr., & Guerney, L. F. (1983). Relationship enhancement therapy with inpatients and their families. In R. Luber & C. Anderson (Eds.), *Family intervention with psychiatric patients* (pp. 48-68). New York: Human Sciences Press.

Waldo, M. (1986). Group counseling for military personnel who battered their wives. *Journal for Specialists in Group Work, 3*(2), 132-138.

Waldo, M. (1987a). Also victims: Understanding and treating men arrested for spouse abuse. *Journal of Counseling and Development,* (65), 385-388.

Waldo, M. (1987b). Primary prevention in university residence halls: Paraprofessional-led relationship enhancement training for college roommates. *Journal of Counseling and Development.* Manuscript submitted for publication.

Waldo, M., & Guerney, B. G., Jr. (1983). Marital relationship enhancement therapy in the treatment of alcoholism. *Journal of Marital and Family Therapy, 9*(3), 321-323.

6

Reconciling Personal and Professional Priorities

LUCIANO L'ABATE

PREPROFESSIONAL ROOTS

Coming to this country as an exchange student at 20 years of age from Florence, Italy, to Tabor College, Hillsboro, Kansas—an institution supported by the Mennonite Brethren Church—was quite a cultural shock. My first real teacher of psychology was P. E. Schellenberg, a Minnesota Ph.D. who was also the president of the college. He introduced me to the nondirectivism of Rogers, who outside of Freud was then (1949-50) the major challenging theorist-therapist available (in Hillsboro, Kansas). After graduation I moved on to Wichita University (now State University) for an M.A., where I came into close contact with the two best teachers I have ever had: Nicholas Pronko and David Herman. They were both "interbehaviorists," students and followers of J. R. Kantor (Pronko, 1980). Kantor preceded systems thinking in psychology by postulating behavior as the outcome of interpersonal events, as relationships between people and people and between people and things. Unfortunately, Kantor has not been as influential and recognized in psychology as he deserves to be. Pronko was a challenging teacher, introducing me to the critical works of Korzybsky (1948; "The map is not the territory") and general semantics (Chase, 1938; Rapaport, 1950, 1954), Dewey and Bentley (1949) as well as to linguistics (Carroll, 1953, 1964) and philosophy of science. Herman provided me with a very substantial and solid knowledge base that served me well at Duke University, where I went for my Ph.D. in psychology. He also supervised my first counseling cases using wire recordings. The Wichita Child Guidance Clinic served as a first practicum introduction to play therapy and one-way mirrors under the supervision of Salvatore Russo.

At Duke, the inevitable influence of learning theory was pervasive. In my Ph.D. dissertation on paired-associates learning and manifest anxiety, I found (L'Abate, 1956) the unexpected importance of gender differences in experiencing and expressing anxiety. At that time gender differences were believed to be either spurious, irrelevant, or suspicious, and my separating of two ANCOVAs for males and females was received with less than auspicious reactions from my dissertation mentor, Gregory A. Kimble.

After I received the Ph.D. degree, I received a NIMH research grant while I worked as a part-time instructor at East Carolina College (now University) and full-time psychologist in the Pitt County Health Department. This research yielded a replication of the same gender differences found in my dissertation. These gender differences in the experience and expression of anxiety were also replicated in children (i.e., girls tend to experience and express certain unpleasant feelings, while boys tend to deny them). We shall come back to this point later.

Beginning of the Conflict

This introduction leads into the major perceived split that seems to plague some clinical psychologists. How can one contend with and reconcile: (1) wanting to behave flexibly, compassionately, and caringly, and to individualize one's approach to the needs of clients (children and their parents), with (2) one's training as a rigorous "scientist"?

In my first job as a child clinical psychologist in the Pitt County Health Department, a social worker—as traditionally done—would interview the parents of a referred child, the psychologist (that was me) would evaluate the child, and the psychiatrist would administer medication and take on the most severe cases. Because the clinic's structure was rather informal, I was able to see children in play therapy and interview their parents separately. After two years in Greenville, I went to Michael Reese Hospital in Chicago on a USPHS postdoctoral fellowship in child psychotherapy under Roy Grinker and Sheldon Korchin, who also (among others) supervised me. There and then, of course, only individuals were seen; I was not allowed to see any families (I asked, but I was told to deal with the "introjects"). The split between clinician and researcher became even greater: On the one hand, I had to digest all of the untested and untestable psychoanalytic lore. On the other, I continued to pursue research on paired-associates learning and manifest anxiety, as a (semi-)rigorous researcher.

This split between the clinician and researcher parts of me continued throughout my tenure in the psychiatry department of Washington University in St. Louis, where (in the psychology department), Jane Loevinger had become a model of a researcher whose work had direct clinical applications. The need to reconcile being helpful with being maximally effective and rigorous became more and more acute with increasing family and professional pressures. The need to make every minute count was at the very core of the dilemma: How can one help as many people as possible with a minimum expenditure of one's time and energy? This has remained a continuous struggle for me.

Helping psychiatrists, pediatricians, and neurologists make their treatment decisions from psychodiagnostic evaluations, however, produced a great deal of dissatisfaction—not only about the inefficiency and costs of the total process, but also about the whole business of politics in a psychiatry department where psychologists were relegated to the role of second-class citizens by being kept in technical, diagnostics-only positions. Cutting corners would not do (like administering just MMPIs, or restricting evaluations to a few scales from each test). The more referrals that were received from psychiatrists, the greater the frustration. Clearly, there was no way to meet ever-increasing needs for evaluation from many referring sources, nor to meet the personal needs to: (1) combine practice with research, (2) combine evaluation with therapy, and (3) to be responsible for the entire process of intervention, including pre- and posttest, *after* therapeutic interventions. In addition, no one else seemed concerned about spending a whole day and more to evaluate one single patient.

The Laboratory Method

A resolution to the foregoing dilemmas was realized toward the end of my tenure at Washington University: St. Louis Children's Hospital asked me to evaluate 50 children with a $6,000.00 budget. This was a chance, a challenge, and an opportunity to meet some of the needs just stated. I was able to start a diagnostic laboratory in the Children's Hospital using part-time volunteers, whom I trained to administer simple tests like the Draw-A-Person, Peabody, Benton, and Sentence Completion; a half-time graduate student administered the WISC (or Stanford-Binet) and Rorschach. To guarantee uniformity and quality of evaluation, I created batteries by age that would evaluate each child according to intellectual, emotional, organic, and educational functioning. The graduate student and volunteers would administer and score these batteries. I was responsible for writing up reports and consulting with referring sources.

This was the beginning of breaking away from traditionally costly and time-consuming diagnostic and therapeutic practices. In the laboratory method (L'Abate, 1968a, 1968b, 1973, in preparation) the psychologist assumes supervisory and professional responsibility, interpreting and writing up reports of the psychological evaluation from data collected by paraprofessionals or technicians. In this way, one can maintain an individualized approach to the specific needs of each client and collect data for research purposes.

When I started the laboratory method in clinical psychology, I was warned of various dire consequences, both personal and professional. Therefore, I wrote up the whole approach and sent it (1963) to the Professional Practices Committee of the American Psychological Association. They reassured me that what I was doing was not only ethical under the existing guidelines, but that they also felt it was praiseworthy. Since then I have not had any worry about my work with the laboratory method, provided it was responsibly ethical, professionally useful, therapeutically helpful, and personally gratifying.

Although my psychology colleagues were worried about using this approach, pediatricians and pediatric neurologists appreciated it. At the time (1963), I had estimated that a complete psychodiagnostic evaluation by a Ph.D. would cost approximately $120.00. With this approach I was able to bring down the cost of each evaluation to $34.00 *without cutting corners* (i.e., no short versions or shortened tests). From 50 children in the first year, this laboratory—still in existence—has been able to evaluate upward of 20,000 children to date, using a full-time staff of one psychologist-director and two psychometricians.

Consequently, my major focus in the last quarter of a century has been to bridge the gap between myself as a practicing clinician, and as an aspiring scientist through *the laboratory method.* I continually address the question: How can one help individuals, couples, and families attend to their specific, really ideographic needs, and at the same time collect data as if one were a research scientist in the laboratory rather than in a professional office? Since 1963 I have been committed to working with people face-to-face and indirectly through intermediaries, both professionals and paraprofessionals.

After moving to Atlanta from St. Louis (1964), I extended the laboratory approach to: (1) evaluation of couples and families (L'Abate & Wagner, 1988); (2) monitored play therapy with children (L'Abate, 1979); (3) structured enrichment with functional and semifunctional couples and families *at risk* in primary prevention programs (L'Abate, 1977, 1983, 1987; L'Abate & Rupp, 1981; L'Abate & Weinstein, 1987; L'Abate & Young, 1987); (4) workbooks in secondary prevention with individuals, couples, and families *in need* of some help, but not in such critical distress as to want therapy (L'Abate & Cox, in press); and (5) tertiary prevention, or family therapy with families *in crisis,* using systematically written homework assignments (L'Abate, 1986).

Once methodological independence was established through the laboratory method, it was easy for me to develop a theoretical independence that led to an upward spiral of different practices. This led to different thinking, which in turn was conducive to changing existing practices, and so forth. Emphasis on theory and method brought about the realization that both can be completely independent of each other except for inferential jumps; related indirectly; or directly related, whereby theory is derived from method and vice-versa (L'Abate, 1990; L'Abate & Bryson, in press). Thus, ideas emerged in isolation from other theorists—in opposition to established dogmas and practices—and in concert with clients, my wife, collaborators, and students.

Expanding Horizons—The Family Factor

After a short stint at Emory University in Child Psychiatry (1964-1965), the move to Georgia State University brought contacts with humanistically oriented colleagues, who introduced me to the work and influence of Virginia Satir, George Bach, Eric Berne, the Gouldings, and the human potential movement of that time (1966-1969). In the meantime, also at GSU, the second application (diagnostic evaluation being the first) of the laboratory method took place through the construction of an experimental playroom that monitored automatically most—if not all—of the aggressive and constructive play of children referred for evaluation and therapy. Each child was evaluated before and after fifteen hours of weekly play therapy sessions. The outcome of this research was very clear (L'Abate, 1979): IQ scores predicted, at a high level of significance, constructive (in a positive direction) and aggressive (in a negative direction) play in children. Improvement in these childrens' behavior outside of the playroom was slow, however, because we were not paying attention to the rest of the family. More effective and efficient ways to help children and their families had to be found.

To get more training and credentials in family therapy, I attended workshops and conferences with leaders such as Fred and Bunny Duhl, Andy Ferber, Jim Framo, Jay Haley, Murray Bowen, and many others. As a result of these experiences, the Child (now Family) Clinic at GSU began rejecting referrals for just testing children, asking families instead to come in all together as standard operating procedure.

FAMILY THERAPY TRAINING: SYSTEM THEORIES AND CLINICAL MENTORS

In the past, clinical training for many therapists has consisted of receiving supervision from Rogerian nondirectivists, as well from psychoanalytically or behaviorally oriented supervisors. Those who affected me the most were the flexibly eclectic ones, like Louis Cohen and Oscar Parsons at Duke and Sheldon Korchin at Michael Reese. Although throughout graduate school I had been affected greatly by the works of pioneers in general systems theory (Reusch & Bateson, 1951; von Bertalanffy, 1968), this new ideology—as seductive and exciting as it was then—has become for me another dogma. The antireductionistic and antiempirical stance taken by most of its exponents and followers I find unacceptable. Without research of some kind, no critical and corrective feedback is possible to improve our clinical practices. This shortcoming is one of the many difficulties in the psychoanalytic and humanistic schools (L'Abate, 1990). Reductionism and verifiability, although disparaged by systems theorists and practitioners, constitute the very essence of being a family *psychologist* rather than a family therapist.

Personal Therapy

I denied my need for therapy until my middle-age crisis, when I moved (1965) from the psychiatry department at Emory University in Atlanta to Georgia State University under less-than-happy circumstances. That particular individual therapy experience was strictly supportive, crisis-oriented, and of short duration. Later, my wife and I went into marital therapy after ten years of marriage. We started initially with an existential therapist, who had been a student of Carl Whitaker. He reassured us of our inherent worth and competence, and hit us where we needed it the most: in how we experienced and expressed our feelings and emotions. He succeeded in breaking down most of the intellectual defenses that each of us had built around ourselves and our marriage. Nonetheless, things between us were not getting any better—because, I think, that therapist failed to provide us with the structure we needed then—and we terminated.

Eventually, during the time of our greatest crisis, the greatest therapeutic help came from a totally unexpected source, Dan MacDougald. He is a lovably eccentric, unorthodox lawyer who has dedicated himself to treating criminals using a system of written homework assignments derived from his interpretation of biblical, physiological, and pseudopsychological principles. He was the only "therapist" who could take on both of us and tell us directly, directively, and rather exactly where our thinking was screwed up. His original emphasis on written homework assignments was, years later, incorporated into my therapeutic approach (L'Abate, 1986; L'Abate, 1990; L'Abate & Cox, in press).

Professional Zeitgeist

Being isolated as a family therapist and wanting very much to keep my identification as a psychologist led me into setting up a complete training program (L'Abate, 1983, 1985, 1987) in family psychology, emphasizing those very aspects that were left out of traditional family therapy training: (1) theory construction and consideration of individual personality development in the family (L'Abate, 1976, 1986; L'Abate & Bryson, in press); (2) emphasis on theory testing, through objective evaluations of couples and families (L'Abate, 1987; L'Abate & Wagner, 1988); (c) preventive work with functional and semifunctional families (L'Abate, 1990; L'Abate & Weinstein, 1987; L'Abate & Young, 1987), and (d) systematic family therapy (L'Abate, 1986).

Spirit of Creativity and Inquiry: Being Identified as a Family Psychologist

The more I created, the more open I became to new and different ideas. Finally, I was able to see systems thinking at best as a misguided metaphor or just an ideology, and at worst as a cult and—perhaps—the worst intellectual fraud perpetuated on an entire profession that has taken it as dogma and transformed it into various cultic practices. I realize that this is a scathing, provocative indictment, but I do not see that this theory has added one iota of empirical evidence to support and validate itself. I did not arrive at such an incendiary conclusion irresponsibly, or without fear and trepidation (L'Abate, 1987, 1990). I feel, however, that beating around the bush on this issue will only perpetuate a way of thinking that I consider destructive of families and of professionals alike, and I intend to fight the dangerous and deleterious effects of this ideology.

I receive a great deal of sustenance from my students and from the families I see. My private practice is my laboratory. My students help me verify some of my ideas and put them into practice (L'Abate & Wagner, 1988). Thus, I have created a triangular, ever-growing spiral. My teaching affects my writing, which in turn is affected by my clinical practice. Each of these three activities feeds into the other, allowing each to grow.

PATHWAYS CHOSEN: DEVELOPMENT AND SELECTION OF PROFESSIONAL LIFE CYCLE

Blind Alleys, Nonproductive Hunches and Endeavors

It is fortunate that I cannot remember many nonproductive hunches and endeavors, unless one were to look at my early incursion into paired-associated learning as such. I do not. I learned from every possible detour or "mistake" I made. I try to waste as little time as possible in investments that do not pay off. To make anything work for me, it has to (1) save time and energy, (2) represent an advancement, either theoretical or clinical, that I can be comfortable with, pleased and proud of, and (3) serve as a foundation for further work for me or for my students, or both.

Productive Undertakings in Research and Practice

Eventually, to comprehend the various approaches in family therapy (Hansen & L'Abate, 1982), I integrated them into models that helped me make theoretical and therapeutic sense of families (L'Abate, 1986). In the last few years, I have been able to accumulate a substantial body of writings that represent four areas of interest: (1) theory construction and testing (Hansen & L'Abate, 1982; L'Abate, 1976, 1983, 1985, 1986, 1987; L'Abate & Bryson, in press; L'Abate & Wagner, 1988); (2) primary prevention with functional and/or semifunctional families at risk (L'Abate, 1977, 1990; L'Abate & L'Abate, 1977; L'Abate & Milan, 1985; L'Abate & Rupp, 1981; L'Abate & Weinstein, 1987; L'Abate & Young, 1987); (3) secondary prevention with individuals and families in need (L'Abate, 1990; L'Abate & Cox, in press); and (4) crisis intervention and therapy (L'Abate, 1986; L'Abate & Cox, in press; L'Abate, Ganahl, & Hansen, 1986; L'Abate & McHenry, 1983; Weeks & L'Abate, 1982).

The ultimate culmination of the laboratory method can be found in programmed therapy (L'Abate & Cox, in press). I am convinced, after 30-plus years of working with many troubled individuals and their families, that they can be helped by using therapeutic *writing* as preparation for therapy, an alternative to therapy, or an addition to the verbal, face-to-face, or even nonverbal therapies. This process implies that as a therapist I can work *at a distance* without face-to-face contact with clients, decreasing costs, increasing therapeutic efficiency, and enabling me to help many more people than I could otherwise.

The medium of the written word, whether open-ended (diaries or journals), focused ("Write about your depression at prearranged times"), or programmed (written homework assignments to deal with crises, or individualized workbooks) has been completely untapped by the therapeutic establishment. I see the purpose of programmed workbooks (L'Abate, 1990; L'Abate & Cox, in press) in secondary prevention as opening new research vistas. For instance, I can now work with "normal" college students or prison populations. It is possible also to work at a distance with missionary and military families, who often cannot be helped because of distance and frequent relocations without an approach such as programmed therapy.

Workbooks for me represent the front line of intervention in secondary prevention along cost-effective, mass-produced lines (L'Abate & Cox, in press). I already have published workbooks to deal with depression, negotiation, and intimacy in couples (L'Abate, 1986). With my coworkers, I have written workbooks for impulsivity in acting-out individuals, as well as for anxiety in acting-in individuals, polarizations in couples, and building and improving relationships. We are extending this approach for use with people who have various addictions (L'Abate, Farrar, & Serritella, in press).

Seeking Congruence and Cohesiveness

Reconciliation of conflictual demands means finding greater personal and professional consistency and cohesiveness between myself as a person, as a husband, as a father, and as a professional. Within me as a person, I have struggled to define myself as being as helpful as I can be to my wife and to my children. Within the professional me, I had to recognize the struggle between various roles: Am I a diagnostician or a therapist? A researcher or a clinician? A preventer or a therapist? These have been the dimensions of internal conflict that I was able to lay to rest once I found ways of reconciling these struggles, first methodologically and then theoretically, evaluatively, and interventionally.

Finally I had to conclude that there is little one can do to improve styles or techniques of individual therapists. I could, however, give myself and others better conceptual and clinical tools. What started as a strictly theoretical endeavor (L'Abate, 1976, 1983, 1986) became a full-fledged program of research, linking evaluation with interventions at primary, secondary, and tertiary prevention levels (L'Abate, 1985, 1986, 1987). The primary characteristics of this framework from the very outset were to be reductionistic and verifiable, unlike most concepts current in the family therapy field.

REDUCTIONISM IN THEORY CONSTRUCTION

The theoretical framework is relatively simple. It consists of two assumptions, space and time. They, in turn, subsume two different and orthogonal dimensions defined by two polarities: approach-avoidance and discharge-delay (see Figure 6.1). These fundamental dimensions give rise over time to the development (L'Abate, 1976, 1986; L'Abate & Bryson, in press) of two basic sets of abilities: the ability to love and the ability to negotiate. The ability to love is made up by being able to be emotionally available to oneself and others through: (1) the attribution of importance to self and to loved ones (partner, child, lover, parent, etc.), and (2) briefly, love itself is expressed through: (a) caring, (b) seeing the good, (c) forgiveness, and (d) intimacy, or sharing of hurts and fears of being hurt (L'Abate, 1983, 1986).

From the attribution of importance, it is possible to elaborate a four-part classification of: (1) *Selfulness* or *Full Self* ("I am important, you are important"; which interpersonally translates itself into "I win, you win"); (2) *Selfishness,* ("I am important, you are not"; "I win, you lose"); (3) *Selflessness,* ("you are important, I am not"; "you win, I lose"); and (4) *No Self* ("I am not important, neither are you"; "I lose, you lose"). From this classification we (L'Abate & Bryson, in press) have derived extensions to gender differences and psychopathology such that about 25% of both men and women are socialized for Selfulness; 40% of men are socialized for Selfishness and 10% for Selflessness; 40% of women are socialized for Selflessness and 10% for Selfishness; and the remaining 25%, both men and women, are socialized for No Self. At first blush this framework would appear similar to transactional analysis (TA); however, I owe my intellectual debt more to Foa' & Foa' (1974) than to TA. As far as intimacy is concerned, my single-factor definition (i.e., the sharing of hurts and fears of being hurt) is quite different from many other multifactor definitions (L'Abate, 1983).

The ability to negotiate is a multiplicative function of:

1. the structure of negotiation, as made up by division or allocation of
   (a) authority-responsibility,
   (b) orchestration-instrumentation decisions, and
   (c) resources negotiated (i.e., information, services, possessions, and money); times
2. negotiation potential, as made up of
   (a) style or level of functioning at the time, as defined by the ARC model (Abusive-apathetic, Reactive-repetitive, and Creative-conductive);
   (b) level of competence, as defined by the ERAAwC model (Emotionality, Rationality, Activity, Awareness, and Context); and
   (c) Priorities, which can be
      (i) intra- or extrafamilial (self, marriage, children, parents/siblings-in-law, work, friends, and leisure),
      (ii) attachments, beliefs, and commitments (the ABC model), and
      (iii) modalities of exchange (*being, doing,* and *having*).

The last three modalities of exchange are borrowed and derived from Foa' and Foa's (1974) resource-exchange theory in social psychology. They postulated six classes of exchange possible between and among people: love and status (together as *being* here), information and services (*doing*), and possessions and money (*having*). Recently, Hewitt and I (L'Abate & Hewitt, 1988) have extended the same framework to sex and sexuality.

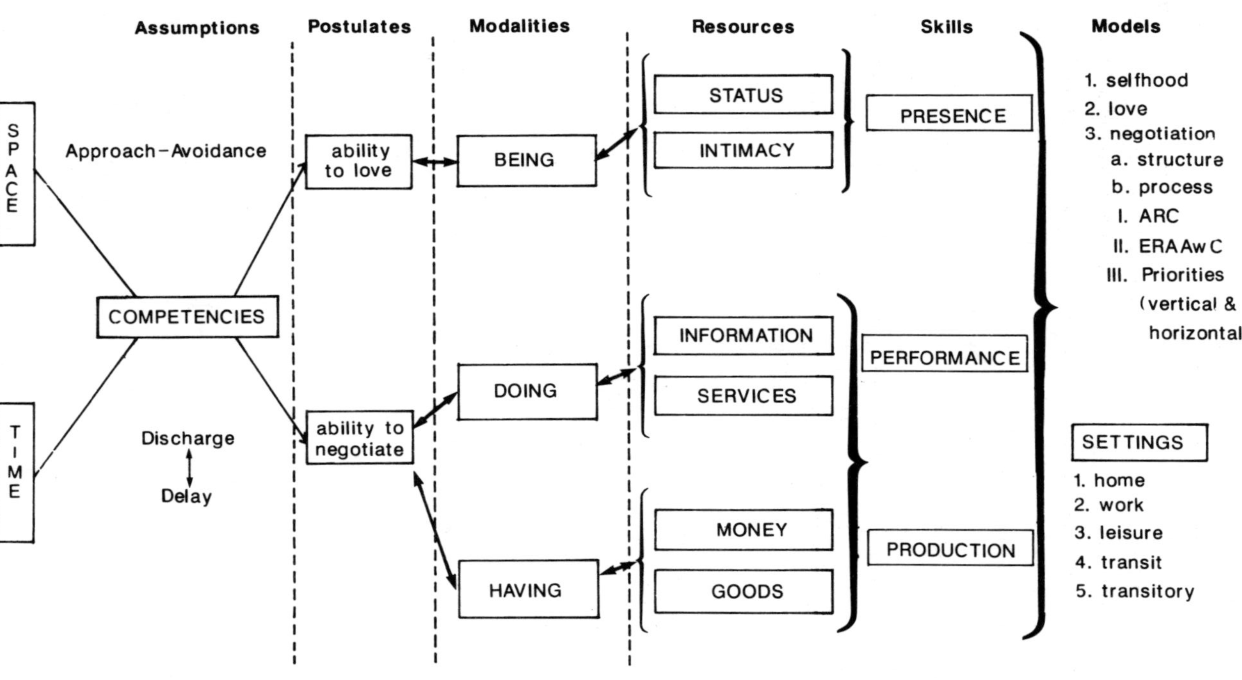

Figure 6.1. A Developmental Theory of Interpersonal Competence

Special Colleagues and Collaborators

One of the major satisfactions of my last 20 years has been to practice together with my wife, Bess L. L'Abate (L'Abate & L'Abate, 1977). She has been the major source of corrective, caringly creative challenge; unendingly mutual chagrin; and inevitably critical conflict that has sharpened my wits, clarified my thinking, reinforced my assets, and decreased my liabilities. I doubt whether I would have been able to produce as much and as well without her constant presence, her unrelenting reality testing, and her Greek-given oracular qualities of doom and gloom that have forced me to assume a more positive stance in many endeavors.

My students have been my major source of dialogue, inspiration, and motivation. Among 30-plus students that I have helped in their quest for the Ph.D. during the last 18 years, there are many who have become collaborators and colleagues and who are now outstanding contributors to the field, such as Joseph Frey, Gary Ganahl, Edgar Jessee, Wayne Jones, Sherry McHenry, Michael O'Shea, Victor Wagner, Gerald Weeks, Steven Weinstein, and Robert Wildman II. By selecting these few I do not want to slight many others who are now active, busy, and successful practitioners around the country. Ever since I started as a supervisor in my first job, by a very subtle process (unbeknownst to me) I have attracted very competent students. I am very proud of each of them.

I have also been very lucky in finding many collaborators among faculty members inside my department at GSU (Ray Craddick, Earl C. Brown, Gregory Jurkovic, Michael Milan) and outside of it (Dennis A. Bagarozzi, Leonard Curtis, James Hansen, Doris Hewitt, Richard Sauber, and many others). For the last 10 years, I have profited a great deal by my association as consultant of the Cross Keys Counseling Center, where I see families I would not see in my private practice. All of these associations have produced a process of working together that has been very affirmational and important for me, personally and professionally.

Areas of Satisfaction

The major area of satisfaction is testing a hunch or hypothesis, developing means and methods of testing, and finding out whether the hunch is valid, invalid, or somewhere in between. Empirical verification of theoretical hypotheses is for me the most exciting of all pursuits. Creating new ways of intervening in helping people is just as important for me, especially when I am aware that my thinking is supported by some empirical evidence, rather than the word or influence of a guru. Seeing actual behavior follow isomorphically from theory is also very satisfying. Leisure-time pursuits such as reading, playing cards, traveling, and until recently playing tennis have been major areas of satisfaction that prevent professional burnout.

Concerns, Dilemmas, and Challenges

After settling the struggles between clinician and researcher, the next major struggle—which took many years to resolve—was one of identity. Am I a family therapist or am I a family psychologist? The more I saw writings and colleagues that denied and, in some cases, regretted their background as psychologists, the more I became convinced that I was, am, and choose to remain primarily a family psychologist. Once this primary identification was established, a few things began to happen. I rejected systems theory as being abstractly general and vague, empirically sterile and essentially undemonstrable, and too separate from psychology as a science and as a profession to be attractive or useful. I believe that a great many (not all) family transactions, despite their undeniably emergent quality, can be derived reductionistically from different psychological disciplines. For instance, from developmental psychology, family psychology can be reduced to concepts such as:

1. development throughout the individual, marital, and family life cycles;
2. attachment, which can be extended from parent-child relationships to intimate, adult relationships (marriage, friendships, etc.);
3. dependency and its derivative stages of childhood, denial of dependence, or independence in adolescence, autonomous interdependence in adulthood, and old-age dependency;
4. distance between intimates, deriving from cultural training regarding body image to interpersonal fusion, diffusion, and confusion, producing victories (functionalities) and defeats (dysfunctionalities) among intimates (L'Abate, 1985, 1986; L'Abate & Bryson, in press);
5. transmission of behavior from parents to children, and from children through siblings and extended families assuming a continuum of likeness (L'Abate, 1976; L'Abate & Bryson, in press) postulating six different categories: from *symbiotic* ("I am you," "I cannot live without you") and *autistic* ("I am not") at the two extremes, to *sameness* ("I am like you") or *oppositeness* ("I am or want to be the opposite of you") toward the middle, *and similarity* or *differentness* ("I am somewhat like you, but I am also different from you.") in between; and
6. this continuum of likeness is postulated as being at the basis of styles in intimate relationships (the ARC model), competences (the ERAAwC model), and priorities (described earlier).

In personality theory, personality can be broken down into three distinct areas of competence (L'Abate & Bryson, in press): (a) *being* or presence, (b) *doing* or performance, and (c) *having* or production. Situations can be broken down into distinct, sometimes overlapping settings: home, work, leisure, and transit (commuting from one setting to another, including transitory settings, such as shopping places or bars, barbershops, or beauty salons). Thus, personality development becomes understood as a function of specific Competency × Setting interactions, which are more particularistic and contextual than any vague and unspecified Personality × Situation interaction.

In addition, the concept of individual differences—difficult to account for on the basis of systems theory—can be reduced also to the paramount importance of gender differences, producing very relevant conflicts and tensions that have characterized the battle of the sexes for centuries. These gender differences are especially relevant in stress theory, where emotion-focused (mostly in women) versus problem-focused (mostly in men) coping strategies have produced a model of family coping derived from stress theory based on monadic psychology (L'Abate, in press).

VERIFIABILITY IN THEORY TESTING

Verification of the theory has taken place along two major lines of endeavor: diagnostic-evaluative and interventional. The first line proceeds along two different but overlapping directions: (1) to measure outcomes of intervention, and the creations of paper-and-pencil, self-report tests derived from the models in the theory, as well as picture tests for entire families (L'Abate & Wagner, 1988); and (2) to measure process during interventions through content analyses of therapy transcripts.

The second line of verification, through interventions, occurs in three different ways: structured enrichment programs derived from the models with nonclinical families in primary prevention (L'Abate & Weinstein, 1987; L'Abate & Young, 1987); theory-derived and theory-independent workbooks in secondary prevention (L'Abate, 1990); and (c) systematic homework assignments for individuals, couples, and families, some of which are derived from theoretical models (L'Abate, 1986, 1987; L'Abate & Cox, in press). Thus, the theory can be verified in five different ways.

Current Involvements and Projects

I am now involved in finishing two research projects designed to evaluate: (1) the effectiveness of workbooks in comparison to role-playing and traditional lectures in psychology of adjustment classes; and (2) the relative influence of face-to-face contact versus the effects of written therapeutic feedback, using programmed workbooks as cost-effective, mass-produced ways of helping undergraduates—and, in the future (it is hoped), high school students— at risk for dropping out, acting out, and suicide (L'Abate & Cox, in press). I plan to make therapeutic applications through workbooks the "swan song" of my life's work utilizing the laboratory method.

Linkages, Networking, and Integration

Outside of publishers and publications, working with students and families, and occasional workshops and conferences I find very little time to connect with many people, except friends. If there is any connection it is through the written word. I see my work as fitting into the context of justification (i.e., empirical verification), deterministic pragmatism, demonstrable specificity, and explicitly practical applications. I hope that what I am proposing in the laboratory method and in programmed therapy has the potential to help many people for much less money than has been possible until now. I also hope my theoretical efforts will be tested, not only by me or my students, but especially by others outside of my laboratory.

Whither the Future?

There is nowhere for family psychology to go but up. I hope that family psychology will be able to: (1) break away from the theoretical shackles and blinders of systems theory; (2) avoid the currently irresponsible clinical practices of family therapy, where no routine objective evaluation is taking place; (3) depend more on psychological theories based on empirical evidence rather than on wishful or magical thinking and guru-like mystification; and (4) develop through *critical* thinking.

Personally, I want to muster enough evidence to finish my magnum opus on the laboratory method in clinical psychology (L'Abate, in preparation) after I retire from GSU in 1990. I hope by then to have amassed sufficient evidence to convince others to practice also (not exclusively) "long distance" through intermediaries or through the written, programmed word. I have tried to avoid mutually exclusive practices all my life. I can be a caring therapist (with my wife's and other's help) as well as a reasonably rigorous researcher (again, with help). I can be a diagnostician as well as a therapist. I can work as a preventer as well as a crisis reducer. I can discover (invent?) new ideas as well as test them for their validity. I can even use and enjoy systems ideology, provided I keep in mind that it is just a metaphor and not a theory.

Epilogue and Conclusion

Since 1970, when a lot of things happened in the field of mental health, family therapy, and many precursors of psychoeducational and supposedly preventive efforts, a great deal of excitement has been generated by breaking away from traditional mental health practices. Starting with the laboratory method, and deriving through it theoretical models of personality development in the family has been very exciting. Verifications of these theoretical models and of practical methods of intervening with families also have been exciting pursuits during the last 20 years. There is nothing in front of us in family psychology but upward progress and continued excitement.

REFERENCES

Carroll, J. B. (1953). *The study of language: A survey of linguistics and related disciplines in America.* Cambridge, MA: Harvard University Press.

Carroll, J. B. (1964). *Language and thought.* Englewood Cliffs, NJ: Prentice-Hall.

Chase, S. (1938). *The tyranny of words.* New York: Harcourt Brace Jovanovich

Dewey, J., & Bentley, A. F. (1949). *Knowing and the known.* Boston: Beacon.

Foa', U., & Foa', E. (1974). *Societal structures of the mind.* Springfield, IL: Charles C Thomas.

Hansen, J. C., & L'Abate, L. (1982). *Approaches to family therapy.* New York: Macmillan.

Korzybski, A. (1948). *Science and sanity: An introduction to non-Aristotelian systems and general semantics.* Lakeville, CT: International Non-Aristotelian Library Publishing Company.

L'Abate, L. (1956). Transfer and manifest anxiety in paired-associate learning. *Psychological Reports, 2,* 119-126.

L'Abate, L. (1964). *Principles of clinical psychology.* New York: Grune & Stratton.

L'Abate, L. (1968a). The laboratory method as an alternative to existing mental health models. *American Journal of Orthopsychiatry, 38,* 286-287.

L'Abate, L. (1968b). The laboratory method in clinical psychology: An attempt at innovation. *The Clinical Psychologist, 21,* 183-184.

L'Abate, L. (1973). The laboratory method in clinical child psychology: Three applications. *Journal of Clinical Child Psychology, 2,* 8-10.

L'Abate, L. (1976). *Understanding and helping the individual in the family.* New York: Grune & Stratton.

L'Abate, L. (1977). *Enrichment: Structured interventions with couples, families, and groups.* Washington, DC: University Press of America.

L'Abate, L. (1979). Aggression and construction in children's monitored playtherapy. *Journal of Counseling and Psychotherapy, 2,* 137-158.

L'Abate, L. (1983). *Family psychology: Theory, therapy, and training.* Lanham, MD: University Press of America.

L'Abate, L. (Ed.) (1985). *Handbook of family psychology and therapy. (Volumes 1 & 2).* Homewood, IL: Dorsey Press.

L'Abate, L. (1986). *Systematic family therapy.* New York: Brunner/Mazel.

L'Abate, L. (1987). *Family psychology II: Theory, therapy, enrichment, and training.* Lanham, MD: University Press of America.

L'Abate, L. (in press). A family model of coping. In B. N. Carpenter (Ed.), *Personal coping: Theory, research, and applications.* Elmsford, NY: Pergamon.

L'Abate, L. (1990). *Building family competence: Primary and secondary prevention strategies.* Newbury Park, CA: Sage.

L'Abate, L. (in preparation). *The laboratory method in clinical psychology.*

L'Abate, L., & Bagarozzi, D. A. (in press). *Sourcebook of marriage and family evaluation.* New York: Brunner/Mazel.

L'Abate, L., & Bryson, C. H. (in press). *A theory of personality development.* New York: Brunner/Mazel.

L'Abate, L., & Cox, J. (in press). *Programmed therapy: Self-administered interventions with individuals, couples, and families.* Pacific Grove, CA: Brooks/Cole.

L'Abate, L., & Curtis, L. (1975). *Teaching the exceptional child.* Philadelphia, PA: W. B. Saunders.

L'Abate, L., Farrar, J., & Serritella, D. (in press). *Handbook of differential treatment of addictions.* Newton, MA: Allyn & Bacon.

L'Abate, L., Ganahl, G., & Hansen, J. C. (1986). *Methods of family therapy.* Englewood Cliffs, NJ: Prentice-Hall.

L'Abate, L., & Hewitt, D. (1988). Toward a classification of sex and sexual behavior. *Journal of Sex and Marital Therapy, 14*, 29-39.

L'Abate, L., & L'Abate, B. L. (1977). *How to avoid divorce: Help for troubled marriages.* Atlanta, GA: John Knox.

L'Abate, L., & McHenry, S. (1983). *Handbook of marital interventions.* New York: Grune & Stratton.

L'Abate, L., & Milan, M. (Eds.). (1985). *Handbook of social skills training and research.* New York: John Wiley.

L'Abate, L., & Rupp, G. (1981). *Enrichment: Skill training for family life.* Washington, DC: University Press of America.

L'Abate, L., Schuham, T., & Schneewind, K. (in press). *Family psychology and psychopathology.* Englewood Cliffs, NJ: Prentice-Hall.

L'Abate, L., & Wagner, V. (1988). Testing a theory of developmental competence in the family. *American Journal of Family Therapy, 16*, 23-35.

L'Abate, L., & Weinstein, S. (1987). *Structured enrichment programs for couples and families.* New York: Brunner/Mazel.

L'Abate, L., & Young, L. (1987). *Casebook of structured enrichment programs for couples and families.* New York: Brunner/Mazel.

Pronko, N. H. (1980). *Psychology from the standpoint of an interbehaviorist.* Monterey, CA: Brooks/Cole.

Rapaport, A. (1950). *Science and the goals of man: A study in semantic orientation.* New York: Harper.

Rapaport, A. (1954). *Operational philosophy: Integrating knowledge and action.* New York: Harper.

Ruesch, J., & Bateson, G. (1951). *Communication: The social matrix of psychiatry.* New York: W. W. Norton.

Sauber, S. R., L'Abate, L., & Weeks, G. R. (1985). *Family therapy: Basic concepts and terms.* Rockville, MD: Aspen Systems.

von Bertalanffy, L. (1968). *General systems theory: Foundations, development, applications.* New York: George Braziller.

Weeks, G. R., & L'Abate, L. (1982). *Paradoxical psychotherapy: Theory and practice with individuals, couples, and families.* New York: Brunner/Mazel.

7

Team Family Methods in the Public Sector

ROBERT MACGREGOR

Team Family Methods (TFM) grew out of Multiple Impact Therapy with Families (MIT) (MacGregor et al., 1964) and enhanced the service to the public sector. The goals of the method are to free up natural growth processes, helping people accept what they are and can be rather than what is implied in the language of *change.* Our therapeutic ingredient is respect. Understanding the family and larger system dynamics of what has led to difficulties helps the problem behavior make sense to team and family. Diagnosed in the identified patient as functioning at a particular level of developmental arrest, the statement of the problem must include the strength of the family system and the extent of its closed-system functioning. Treatment planning then may include utilization of family support systems such as churches, youth service agencies, and geriatric services as well as a recommendation for family, individual, and group psychotherapy.

BECOMING A FAMILY PSYCHOLOGIST

Roots in Family of Origin

Coming from a family of teachers, and being myself a teacher, I found that psychology offered me the multidimensional route from which my contribution has grown. But it was not from my family alone; it was always a team.

Teamwork may have come from my mother, a professor of physical education. She also had been part of a champion tennis-doubles team in western Pennsylvania. My father, both a mechanical and a chemical engineer, died when I was age 9. We moved from Wheeling, West Virginia, to the home of his sisters in Bay City, Michigan. They were principals of two neighboring grade schools. As the youngest with three older sisters, I was in Aunt Helen's grade school, one sister was in junior high, and one went to the family alma mater (the University of Michigan), joining our oldest sister. My mother, meanwhile, gained training to become a receptionist at a hospital in East Cleveland, Ohio, where I finished junior high and my next sister was in high school. We returned to Bay City, where my mother was an administrator with a social agency. My sister and I finished high school and left for the University of Michigan at Ann Arbor. With the help of my mother's sister—director of the Children's Library in Detroit—I had learned to do library work for pay both in high school and in college. In the summers of 1938 and 1939, my uncle in Cleveland put me to work as a dining-room cashier on a huge side-wheel cruise ship that ran weekly round trips from Buffalo to Chicago via Mackinac Island. That's where I learned the skill necessary to wait tables in sorority houses. What I really learned was that if I paid a fair share of my college expenses, I became a part of the team that determined the direction of my education.

Professional Heritage

My B.A. degree was completed in 1941; I was an interdepartmental social science major and obtained a Michigan teacher's certificate. But the children with whom I did practice teaching were so tough personally that I returned to graduate school in the guidance and personnel sequence and received an M.A. in 1942, just in time to be drafted into the Army. I completed my internship in clinical psychology at Station Hospital, Camp Davis, North Carolina.

My interest in the public sector is in part a result of my continuing identity as an educator as well as a clinical psychologist. The group-approach interest had been influenced by my summer, 1941, internship in group therapy with Fritz Redl, Ph.D. (Redl, 1942) at the University of Michigan Fresh Air Camp for juvenile delinquent preadolescents. With Dr. Redl, William Morse, Ed.D., and Alvin Zander, Ph.D. under the direction of Vice President Howard Y. McClusky, we developed the extramural service of the University of Michigan. In my part-time faculty position, my task in 1941 was to teach Mental Hygiene of Adolescence in small towns around the state and, while there, enhance community organization. We would develop a community calendar so that instead of competing for meeting dates, the clubs and organizations developed a collaborative schedule to deal with overlapping and overlooking. From this, I learned that in better communication with each other, these organizations can become available as family support systems—an idea that is a vital part of Team Family Methods in the public sector.

Pathways Chosen

Understanding of the public sector and bureaucracies was enhanced by my clinical psychology internship in the Army during World War II and later as director of psychotherapy in the psychology unit of the VA Mental Hygiene Clinic, Washington, DC. There, in the late 1940s, working with psychiatrists Jerome D. Frank, Harold F. Searles, Jarl Dyrud, and Eugene C. McDanald in collaboration with the Washington School of Psychiatry, we did some research, the results of which were published (Powdermaker & Frank, 1953). The research yielded a typology of group participants that I verified by using Ralph K. White's *Value Analysis* (1951) in my doctoral dissertation, *A Factoral Study of Verbal Content Associated with Several Types of Group Behavior* (MacGregor, 1954), at New York University. These became understood more clearly according to levels of developmental arrest as my wife, a developmentally oriented child psychologist (M. Clin. Psych., Univ. of Michigan), joined me in training at the Washington School of Psychiatry in 1950. I traveled to New York on weekends to complete my Ph.D. at NYU in 1954, the same year I was awarded the Certificate in Applied Psychiatry for Psychologists from the Washington School of Psychiatry.

BEING IDENTIFIED AS A FAMILY PSYCHOLOGIST

The interpersonal and developmental thinking of Harry Stack Sullivan, M.D., senior faculty member of the Washington School (Sullivan, 1953), and my own personal analysis at the school have shaped my contribution to the method. My practice in the VA Clinic increasingly included having patients bring family members to participate in treatment. This interest in family dynamics led Eugene McDanald to invite me to join him in the faculty of neurology and psychiatry at the University of Texas Medical Branch in Galveston, Texas, in 1956. There, I was research director of the Youth Development Project and received federal funding and funding from The Hogg Foundation for Mental Health. Harold A. Goolishian, Ph.D., was project codirector and director of the Division of Psychology. An outcome of this collaboration was publication of *Multiple Impact Therapy with Families* (MacGregor et al., 1964). Alberto C. Serrano, M.D., then an instructor, particularly contributed to relating the division-of-functions view of family interaction to the developmental schema.

From our experience in group therapy we had learned that although patients are often too defensive when confronted, they can listen and understand as they hear their problems discussed between one therapist and another group member. Thus, we developed a team-family group situation that is an open system, not made up of just the hospital staff but also including someone the client knows and trusts as well as other needed specialists. The problems are defined as levels of family-wide developmental arrest, and the goal is freeing up of natural growth processes. The value systems seemed similar to those by which we had diagnosed the VA group members and have since become translatable into DSMIII terms. For example, the "Self-Righteous Moralist" with a developmental arrest at the Childish level (MIT "Autocrats" Type B) may be diagnosed as Obsessive Compulsive Disorder (300.30). As various members of the team notice that the presenting problem makes sense in terms of the family situation in which the nominal patient lives, the therapeutic ingredient of respect has impact. Family history, not just the here and now, becomes a useful basis for understanding (MacGregor, 1970).

An example from our 1964 MIT book (pp. 188-189) should illuminate these concepts.

Listening With a Difference

> Each member of the therapy team understands and hears a little differently what is said and unsaid. When these differences of opinion are openly discussed in the family's presence, and do not lead to an impasse or to hurt feelings among team members, the family may learn how to have differences among its members. From the acceptability of competing suggestions the family observes that there may be several ways to diminish or resolve the family difficulties. The team is more interested in having the family entertain the idea that there *are* solutions than in advancing any particular remedy.
>
> In a number of multiple-therapist sessions, sessions in which two or three therapists met with one or more members of the family, the various therapists held differing opinions about such recurring problems as a weekly allowance, use of the family car, responsibility for dishwashing, lawn-mowing, and other chores. Such differences of opinion among team members usually concerned specific issues about the family present at the time, but occasionally referred to differences in over-all philosophy and attitude about child rearing. . . .
>
> This freedom to disagree was a living demonstration of differences of opinion without loss of mutual respect.

Even back then we enjoyed arguing. We were a multidisciplinary team to enhance the training of psychiatrists. Agnes Ritchie was the team's social worker. The outside team member was more difficult to recruit at the medical school but the value of such participation was impressive. Often we had the hospital chaplain represent the family's pastor. As probation officers were to be involved with juveniles after discharge, we found it useful for their training, and for easier continuity, to have them participate in family sessions for discharge planning. I was invited to various juvenile probation officer training sites to teach the method and began to understand that there were other human-service workers, often paid by the taxpayers, who would be involved on the case and who, therefore, should be included in the team. This represented the growth and shift from MIT to TFM in the public sector.

In a presentation at this stage in our growth—focusing particularly on juvenile offenders—at the American Psychological Association Convention in Philadelphia, September, 1963, Kalman Gyarfas, M.D., superintendent of the State of Illinois Mental Health Center serving the entire Chicago area, recognized that the method could relieve his staff, as individuals, of having to pretend competence beyond their discipline. The idea that the convener of the team brings in those with the expertise needed for the case, such as a vocational rehabilitation specialist, made a great deal of sense to him. I welcomed Dr. Gyarfas's invitation to come to Chicago to put the method to work in the public sector.

In Illinois, as a psychologist at a mental health center in a program with interns, I was able to spread knowledge of the method to other psychologists by having interns make presentations of their experience at regional meetings of psychological associations and group psychotherapy societies. I had been program chair of the Southwestern Psychological Association meeting and of the Southwestern Group Psychotherapy Society; thus, when I came to Illinois, I quickly was put to work in that capacity with the Illinois Group Psychotherapy Society, for which I subsequently served twice as president (1971 and 1983).

Psychology interns and clinical pastoral interns traveled with me, in 1968 through 1975, to clinics around the state of Illinois. Downstate visits were monthly for me, but sometimes the students returned weekly to state-aided clinics interested in continuing to use the method. It was particularly in the poor areas of Chicago that we found the privacy of the doctor's office was trusted better when the patient was accompanied by an advocate. Students and staff from other clinics considering the method, sitting apart from the family and team, were welcomed by the clients. The one-way mirrors in our clinics and hospitals were used less and less because, without them, the clients could see how many concerned people were really on their cases. Families were assured that those sitting in the outer circle would give their ideas to the team after the session; however, if something seen as not useful occurred, an observer could approach the team. This was especially helpful in black communities, where their ethnic identity was represented clearly either on the team or in the consultant group.

The method starts with the selection of the team. Sometimes matters such as tension between a Department of Children and Family Services worker and a public welfare worker, stimulated by certain family members "bad-mouthing" one to the other, can be reduced by the convener of the team conferring with them together the day before a team-and-family meeting. The Team Family Method starts with the *opening team conference* in which the convener assures the members that their areas of expertise and previous relationships with the client will be supported. They discuss tentative diagnosis and treatment plans. The meeting must be brief, as the family in the waiting room might attribute a long wait to collusion in a closed system. Next, comes the *opening team-family conference* wherein the family joins the team in the inner circle and the convener reviews his or her understanding of how this get-together was arranged. The convener invites team and family to say how they persuaded each other to come. The team dialogue reflects the open system. We can quickly get down to important matters, as there is plenty of evidence that the client is not without advocates.

As the issues take shape in less than an hour, the team will call for *separate sessions* by generation or sex according to the current diagnostic impressions. The separate session with the children may reinforce the generation boundary, as they come to understand their parents may be discussing matters related to their marriage. Parents may fear that, in separate sessions with the younger generation, team members might pressure the youth(s) to reveal family secrets. The team members present handle this by engaging in a discussion, in the presence of the children, of the issues as they understood them in the opening team-family conference, respecting the children as consultants whose contributions will improve the team's usefulness. The children and team develop an agenda to take back to the closing team-family conference in about three quarters of an hour. Toward the end of the separate session with the younger generation, one of the team members present leaves them to carry their message to the parents in an *overlapping conference.* The other therapists with the children promise to bring them to the closing session in about 15 minutes.

Entering the separate session with the parents, the overlapping therapist first listens to issues as the team with the parents reviews them, thereby helping the parents hear how they were understood. The overlapping therapist then relates that to the viewpoint of the youth (e.g., "Oh, they said you'd talk about that, and it's something you could talk about at church; what they're really worried about is, Sister is pregnant!").

When the youth rejoin from their separate session to the *closing team-family conference,* their overlapping therapist first reports to them what he or she tried to communicate on their behalf. Now that so much that was withheld collusively from awareness is prominent in all their minds, the closing conference includes suggesting that they live with these new realizations for a few days and then return for another session.

Other additional therapies—such as vocational training, group therapy sessions for some youth, marital therapy, and individual therapy—also may be arranged. If the first session was held at a mental hospital as a part of discharge planning, the next session may be at a community clinic with some hospital staff there to entrust the family to the clinic and insure continuity of care. When divorce and other extrusion of family members has weakened the family system, often a church Sunday-school area is used as the next site as part of ongoing training in team family methods for church and community agency personnel. It is easier for some patients to go there than to a mental health center, and utilizing this type of setting enhances the possibility of family support from churches and community agencies.

We learned that it is the "feeling of belongingness" needed by youngsters from broken homes that pushes them to join street gangs. With this clear, the task becomes to help develop community alternatives to gangs. In their concern for alienation as a "disease" of the 1980s, the Team Family Methods Association (TFMA) held an all-day series of workshops at the University of Illinois Chicago campus ("*G*oing *A*fter *N*ew *G*oals, A Creative Approach to the Gang Phenomenon") in May, 1985, with the participation of the Gang Education Team of the Archdiocese, county probation officers, the Chicago Police Department, community organizations, and former gang members with their parents. Previous procedures were revised. Placing a friendly adult in the midst of a gang as a role model had only strengthened the gangs. Graduate students, however, were able to route some gang members toward rehabilitation. Schools, through PTAs, have involved businesses that offer belongingness and self-confidence in the workplace, a recommendation that also came from the gang-member group at the May meeting. Spiritual needs expressed in gang symbols and graffiti alerted churches to offer a plan of belonging and spiritual satisfaction. Corporations and private donors responded through the Archdiocese. We were able to report progress in a panel TFMA presentation ("Alternatives to Gang Violence") at the American Orthopsychiatric Association conference in 1986.

The Team Family Methods Association started with people who had observed the method or participated in sessions at the request of a convener. The successful application of the method in Texas, Minnesota, Iowa, Arizona, California, and Illinois is reflected in the membership. The resource directory initially included nonmembers knowledgeable in the method; those who were new participants or observers were sent a free issue of the quarterly newsletter. My wife and I are permanent honorary board members.

It is the networking of TFMA that has assured continuous collaboration between agencies. Written linkage agreements that spell out the arrangements necessary to assure confidentiality and consent have become a basis for acceptablity of families being a part of training. This includes the videotaping of some sessions. The association's directory makes names of participants readily available.

When a probation officer convenes a team, it may be the welfare worker assigned to the family's public-housing project who will help monitor the progress. It may be that there is a recommendation of the team's psychologist from a state-aided mental health clinic that the youth participate in group therapy at the clinic, augmented perhaps by a vocational rehabilitation program that needs monitoring. In the work of convening other professionals, the respect and affirmation of their expertise is part of the cohesive yet open system model. The members of the team accept their share of the division of functions while recognizing which one is to be the coordinator. As in the continuity-of-care concept, that function may change as the identified patient graduates from group psychotherapy to occupational therapy.

In TFMA quarterly meetings, instead of participants experiencing competition concerning techniques or their epistemology (as the literature indicates is happening in family therapy), there is a growth-enhancing sharing process. These meetings include workshops on stress management, holistic process, conflict management, and the structural and strategic methods many of the participants have learned by taking courses in local family-therapy institutes. The group long has been accustomed to the principle that growth comes through sharing, teaching, and putting to work what seems useful.

In San Antonio, Alberto C. Serrano developed ongoing relationships between public schools, the Community Guidance Center, other agencies, and the pediatric and psychiatric services of the local branch of the University of Texas Medical School from 1968 until the mid-1980s. Despite his departure to become medical director of the Philadelphia Child Guidance Center in 1985, these relationships have endured and made continuity of care available, particularly to the Spanish-speaking population. When Dr. Serrano made a presentation of this to a TFMA conference in Minneapolis in 1975, it had a profound effect on the networking of services in Minnesota. This has also been my experience as I taught the method in the State Training School for Boys in Eldora, Iowa, with the participation of public school staff and juvenile officers from Des Moines, and at the Family Crisis Intervention Program, Clark County, Washington (Anderson et al., 1979).

Networking the resources and use of a method that helps open a closed system and free up natural growth processes by respecting the family history are understood better when we agree that the treatment plan is based on diagnosis. The convener of the team is usually a person trained in the diagnostic system of developmental arrest, or he or she may select a psychologist also able to plan treatment appropriate to the levels of developmental arrest and to help the other team members appreciate the way the family diagnosis and that of the identified patient can be expressed in more conventional terms such as DSM III-R nomenclature (American Psychiatric Association, 1987).

Under stress, a living system withdraws the sensitive aspects of itself that ordinarily might respond to input that nurtures its "growing edge". For example, a child's teacher wants to help, but the family unwittingly conspires to disqualify the teacher ("She can't understand us Catholics"). The longer the system is closed, the more it must operate on obsolete information. Each part of the system then continues repetitively to perform its role. The developmental arrest in a system that is thus feeding off itself loses energy and excludes growth, and as energy runs down some parts get extruded just as failure to nourish a houseplant causes leaves to turn yellow and drop off. Youths may seek growth in gangs or be extruded to residential placement.

In our approach, we have worked with and classified four types of families. Each has a different way of fostering developmental arrest, and the definition of each type yields a treatment strategy specific to the family problem as well as the method for opening the closed system discussed.

Family Type A. With the nominal patient presenting behavior like the Narcissistic Personality Disorder (DSM III-R 301.81), more generally referred to as "the schizoid ones", these families are defined more specifically as "presenting infantile functioning in a nominal patient chronologically beyond childhood". Their orientation to power often is expressed through misplaced concreteness, whereby they carry out to the letter the request of another, a way of keeping the other responsible. They have no interest in learning limits and have access to fantasy to keep their security in relationships. The Type A family provides the kind of symbiotic relationships that a child needs to let fantasy dominate reality.

The function of the marriage seems to be to provide support to a man or woman still tied to the family of origin. The support is not used to emancipate but to endorse the prior relationship. The new wife wants him in his family context, sometimes because his network looks as if it could provide for her; sometimes her network looks as if it could keep her absorbed so he could have the children. The poor differentiation of self and function is represented occasionally by the inability of the father to relinquish mothering functions to his wife. Or he seems to be a family pet that the girl can relate to until she has a baby of her own.

Family therapy for the Type A family has to do with helping the parent who is most at the mercy of the child find self-affirmation elsewhere in the adult community through job training, perhaps, while the other parent monitors the child's entry into day school. The mother can give the child more when that parent receives more strength from elsewhere (e.g., on the job), even though she may be with the child less. Although it is not always a practical goal to make the family romance come out "right" in the Type A family, often the development of an independent basis for self-esteem in one spouse makes that one able to love and affirm the other.

Family Type B. The family that presents primary arrest in development at the childish level exhibits as its problem a member oblivious to authority, the "Autocrat." This appears to be a preoedipal power orientation that differentiates between parents not on the basis of sex but in terms of which has the most benefits to hand out. In Ferenczi's (1950) terms, it is a poor resolution of the problem of infantile omnipotence—the child trusts only what he or she can command.

The marriage in such a family may have been an effort on the part of the man to gain power among his peers by winning the kind of girl they favored. From her standpoint, this affirmation from peers was also welcome. In the early months, fear of exposure of their lack of vocation for marriage may have been relieved by the way each could continue associating with common or separate groups. Childbearing, however, often reduces these contacts as the mother increasingly is occupied with the child. This sort of father, however, seems to "heave a sigh of relief" that she is so engaged, turning his wife over to the child and returning to more isophile satisfactions with cronies.

Now, with the mother left to the mercy of the child for gratifying her tenderness needs, the child realizes early on that nothing matters as much to her as he or she does. It appears there is little opportunity to recognize the seniority and importance of the father in the mother's life. The mother needs the child too much to let him or her grow, and the father owes him or her too much to control the child. The child has little chance to find out what it does not control. In many ways, he or she is treated as if not strong enough to take "no" for an answer. With signals of both strength and weakness, the child collusively joins in not putting any potencies to the test.

It is the disenchantment with the symbiosis that fixes the arrest in development. These mothers are very vulnerable to the attitude of peers. When the feedback from the neighborhood is that the child is arrogant, the balloon of fantasy is broken. Often for a mother, it is broken by her becoming tired of the lonely hours of child attending, when peer recognition was the real object of the marriage. The child senses the extruding forces and responds with unrelenting vigilance. Now a prisoner of this world, without resource to fantasy, he or she must watch everyone for handles to manipulate, trusting no one, not asking for favors, but pressing small claims. If you don't like him or her, he or she takes credit for having won your displeasure.

Again, the therapeutic strategy has to do with making the family romance come out right. The team affirms that the man has something to offer his wife, and that the task is but that of winning her away from the child. Her tendency to count only on the power that comes from being a mother, and thereby to exploit the child, has a history that can be respected. We affirm her ability to let her husband know how to win her, perhaps offering for him the excuse that he is "shy" to make respectable sense out of a previous defensive posture. We make known our confidence that the youth's difficulty in accepting changes will diminish as the couple firmly and affectionately let the child know he or she is indeed strong, strong enough to "take *no* for an answer".

Family Type C. This family often presents a youth arrested at the juvenile level, the "Intimidated One". This is a juvenile in Sullivan's (1953) sense of the age of competition and compromise, intimidated in Erikson's (1963) sense of fear of showing the capacity to take initiative. This is the youngster most clearly representing the Oedipus complex. The youth diminishes his competence in the presence of the parent of the same sex at the time that parents seeks to affirm their own adulthood by watching the child for achievements that represent parental influence. It is weakness as much as power that the son has seen in the father. He has been there when his mother's passive-aggressive ways led the father to extend his leadership to ridiculous extremes. There is little clarity in the father's image, and whatever presence there is often is shrouded in temper. Not to upstage the father or more demanding siblings, this youth seeks a share of nurture by exposing inadequacy, tics, tricks, and habits rather than by rebellion or arrogance. Yearning for recognition from the same-sex parent, but intimidated by authority, he or she becomes a compulsive pleaser, with but not of the group, and ready to do the bully's bidding in hopes of being accepted as "one of the gang."

The function of the marriage in this type of family has to do with the way two people negotiate with each other in a conventional-appearing relationship. Both come to it with exaggerated ideas of performance required in marriage. Both may have feared that single life would have confirmed to the world their presumed inferiority. The wife may have been attracted by the man's readiness to make decisions about what they did on dates. Femininity for her then became, in part, a matter of assuring the male that he will decide. This assurance of no competition in the area that he presumes to be his weakest is tempting to him. In marriage, he finds himself overextended, invited to bear alone responsibility for decisions beyond his competence, but unable to relinquish that aspect of the role. The couple need each other in many ways that are obscured by their mutual participation in denial of dependency. The husband's remote position is negotiated by disqualifying himself from aspects of family life behind a facade that gives him an appearance of individuality, often expressed in macho-type behavior.

I have shown elsewhere (MacGregor, 1969) that in all types of families each sibling knows the parents so differently that each may be said to have a different family constellation. Where one child shares the burden of rearing the family scapegoat, another may owe him or her for the freedom from too much supervision. It appears to be the threat to the marriage itself that contributes to the intimidation in Type C families. The scarcity theme abounds. The mother declares that the love she must give the two does not leave enough for the third. There is no question as to who is in the leadership position; the father is a tyrant not allowed to abdicate. Although dividing up work is the spoken expectation, disqualifying oneself from doing work is the pattern the children learn. Rather than a "conflictual family", from the team's vantage we see collusion to hide fear of intimacy and to make a facade of strength.

In therapy the effort is to help the parents see that although they came by their need to hide from each other honestly, they can now recommend themselves to each other and to their children. History is used, for example, to show the mother in her husband's presence that the idea of manhood handed him was what a boy could hear in the locker room. We remind him that boys who "had something going for them" were not talking; it was the pretender who passed along the excessively aggressive distortion of manhood from which he correctly disqualified himself. If mother can bring out parallel distortions from her growing up, father can without injury to his pride relinquish the now-respected facade. Strategy in psychotherapy includes much that is customary in child guidance work with children.

Family Type D. Such a family may present with a youth arrested at the preadolescent level, the "Rebel." This is the youngster who seems to campaign for the privileges of young adulthood, but who always wins more supervision. Fascinated with authority, the youth breaks rules to win its firm hand. When singled out for study, he or she becomes obscure, diffusing his or her identity into the group. The courage to support an individual identity seems fraught with fears of too much, too soon.

The function of the marriage in this family type has to do typically with the doubts about herself of a woman who perhaps had a failure in a previous affair or marriage. This time, she took no chances and proceeded to find herself a man she could manage – a "mama's boy", perhaps. He, on the other hand, may have had serious doubts about his ability to negotiate his way in the world, and was attracted by her executive talent. The courtship revealed her attention to what others see of his image, and that she seemed to ask little for herself. He entrusted himself to her management. His career became, in a way, her project. Her considerable community activity is done not in her own, but in the family's name. The way she recruits the children into participation unwittingly gives them a message of some kind of weakness in father ("Don't bother your father with that, he has to be available for his work").

The daughter sees in the mother colorless drudgery with which it is hard to identify, while father is more accessible. Alone "on a pedestal" in the front room, seemingly a privileged character, he is available to her plea. The generation barrier is threatened ("Mother doesn't talk to and understand me the way you do. . . . All the other girls have these dresses for the dance. . . ."). Father has, of course, been deprived of the needed data, and from his isolated position does sees not the error of judging mother and daughter as equal petitioners before him. In these families, the threat to the generation and sexual boundaries leads to rebellious behavior that requests control, and to prolonged identity diffusion that may lead the youngsters out of the home to runaway pads.

Therapeutic strategy has to do with shoring up the generation barrier. When the daughter can see that her mother comes first (ahead of herself) with father, then the father can with tenderness affirm her growing young womanhood, and the youth can dare to show the competence and individuality that leads to being known as a person. Including the school counselor who called attention to problem behavior as a member of the team that meets with the family for treatment planning might help to keep the system open when exposure to only the mental health specialist might be experienced as a threat that could increase defensiveness.

WHITHER THE FUTURE?

Spreading the Team Family Method by working with hospitals, youth service agencies, and churches is the wave of the future. Inservice training in hospitals, particularly for the nursing staff, has helped with the acceptability of the method currently with Forest PsychCare Hospital in Des Plaines, Illinois. In assuring aftercare and parental acceptance of the work, nurses who have lived with the identified patient can with empathy share the similarity of their experience with family members who otherwise may feel self-blaming for the symptomatic behavior. This confirms the teaching procedures we have developed in state hospitals. Hospital chaplains have been particularly effective in discharge planning so that the family will have team-family sessions in the receiving mental health clinic, rather than just continuation of recommended medication.

As a psychologist, I have enjoyed the interdisciplinary experience of my career in the public sector. It has enhanced the respect for our profession, particularly by the emphasis on respecting the area of expertise of each participant rather than developing rivalry between professionals. When I was teaching the method in doctoral programs at DePaul University (1970-73), St. Xavier Graduate Program (1977-78), and Forest Institute of Professional Psychology (1979-88), each of the students was assigned to apply the theoretical position of a different school of family therapy by representing that view on the team in role-played family therapy sessions, both in their write-up of the sessions, and in a postsession classroom critique. Although the languages differed, they seemed to fit well into freeing up natural growth processes – even if, for example, the cybernetic model was as mechanical as feedback from the thermostat on the wall.

EPILOGUE

The certification and licensing statutes guarantee quality at the supervisory level, but do not exclude from the Team Family Method the participation of vocational rehabilitation specialists, clergy, or relevant persons from the school system, right down to the volunteer school crossing guard. It would help if some of our associations would put less emphasis on certification and more on the family dynamics of the closed-system functioning of agencies and of schools of thought. The Team Family Method has reduced the elite emphasis in the growing field in the process of making the service available to all. Psychologists can be attuned particularly to the efficiency with which juvenile probation officers can handle their cases better with the perspective of this method. For the public sector, this means fewer referrals to other agencies and more efficient use of the taxpayers' money.

For me, the growing interest in the Team Family Method of clinics, hospitals, and agencies means that I will enjoy more time on the road lecturing and consulting with organizations interested in putting the method to work.

REFERENCES

American Psychiatric Association. (1987). *American Psychiatric Association diagnostic and statistical manual of mental disorders* (3rd ed., rev.). Washington, DC: American Psychiatric Association.

Anderson, R. S., Dagoloff, M. L., Roy, R., Swarts, G., Howard, B. A., & Godfrey, J. A. (1979). *Family crisis intervention program of Clark County, Washington.* New York: Basic Books.

Erikson, E. H. (1963). *Childhood and society.* New York: W. W. Norton.

Ferenczi, S. (1950). Stages in the development of the sense of reality. In *Sex in psychoanalysis.* New York: Basic Books.

MacGregor, R. (1954). *A factoral study of the verbal content associated with several types of group behavior.* Ann Arbor, MI: University Microfilms, Document 9317.

MacGregor, R. (1969). The family constellation from the standpoint of various siblings. In O. Pollack & A. S. Friedman (Eds.), *Family interaction and female delinquency.* Palo Alto, CA: Science & Behavior Books.

MacGregor, R. (1970). Group and family therapy: Moving into the present and letting go of the past. *International Journal of Group Psychotherapy, 20,* 494-515.

MacGregor, R., Ritchie, A. M., Serrano, A. C., Schuster, F. P., Jr., McDanald, E. C., Jr., & Goolishian, H. A. (1964). *Multiple impact therapy with families.* New York: McGraw-Hill.

Powdermaker, F. B., & Frank, J. D. (1953). *Group psychotherapy studies in methodology of research and therapy.* Cambridge, MA: Harvard University Press.

Redl, F. (1942). Group emotion and leadership. *Psychiatry, 5,* 573-596.

Sullivan, H. S. (1953). *The interpersonal theory of psychiatry.* New York: W. W. Norton.

White, R. K. (1951). *Value analysis: The nature and use of the method.* New York: Society for the Psychological Study of Social Issues.

8

Tear Down the Fences: Build Up the Families

WILLIAM C. NICHOLS

The gate was removed first. Then the workmen took down the cyclone fence, rolled it up, and removed the posts. As I stood on the front steps of the administration building of the state mental hospital where I was training and watched the barrier between the hospital and outside world being removed, I did not fully realize the extent of the revolution that was occurring. That came a little later.

At approximately the same time the fence went down, the two padded cells at a private hospital where I worked on weekends as a psychiatric aide became obsolete and were turned into a surgical unit. This was in the mid-1950s. Behind the changes was the advent of the major tranquilizing drugs—the Thorazine revolution, I came to call it. Padded cells and fences no longer were required or used automatically and routinely.

Reading the state hospital records, I was struck by the fact that a patient would recover, be released, and be back in four, five, or six months. We were operating with a revolving-door policy. The conclusion seemed obvious that we were sending patients back to the same "sick" families and "sick" social situation that sent them to the hospital originally. We could get them back on their feet, functional enough to get out of the hospital, but that was not adequate. We had to do something about the families and the settings, the contexts out of which they came. Could we change the families and the social settings enough so that many of them did not have to become disturbed in the first place or, if they did, could stay out of the hospital after treatment?

I spent a subsequent year working in a state institution for the mentally retarded, where we would get some residents to the point that they might be able to function outside the institution. Community placement possibilities were lacking, and their families often were so devastated by the identified patients' problems that they were not able to help.

Somebody told me that dealing with the social setting was called *ecological psychology*. I read the books by Barker and his associates (Barker & Barker, 1951; Barker & Wright, 1954) but found their quantitative approach too focused on counting and classifying and too far removed from the world of genuine, human everyday behavior to offer practical, immediate possibilities for coping with the issues I was seeing. Those developments, of course, preceded the 1960s and the community mental health legislation that would have people treated in the community rather than in large mental hospitals, and the later deinstitutionalization emphasis with its often tragic consequences from "dumping" mental patients into unprepared communities.

GETTING TO THE FENCE CRISIS AND BEYOND

There were other things that brought me to a concern with family and psychology. Born six months before the Great Depression began in 1929, I spent the early years in three- and even four-generational households, growing up in both a nuclear family and in a large extended-family system. My acquaintance with death came at age six when my remarkable great-grandfather, whose bedroom was next to mine, died at age 83. Sundays and holidays frequently involved a gathering of the extended family at my grandparents' home as my aunts and their families came for dinner. My parenting was spread among several adults, including my biological parents and my paternal grandparents. What I later found in cultural anthropology about family organization, child rearing, and personality formation made instant sense.

Drastic changes from our stable living in Fayette, Alabama, occurred when I was in the first grade and my father began work that caused frequent and unpredictable moves as he was transferred from one construction site to another. In the first four grades I made 12 school changes and lived in eight different towns and two states, sometimes returning to Fayette between moves. In new places I soon learned about pecking orders (often having to fight during the first days either on the playground or when waylaid on the way home from school); forming and leaving relationships; loneliness; friendship; competitiveness; and adaptation.

These experiences also accelerated a process of introspection and identity questioning for me. Parenthetically, I find it fascinating that similar questions to many I was raising within myself during elementary school days as an

Anglo-Saxon Protestant male in the Deep South were being asked by a Jewish female contemporary in New York (see Duhl, 1983). My personal, existential concerns of childhood and their young adult versions led to a strong interest in personality theory. How do we get to be like we are? How did I turn out with such different questions, perceptions, and interests from the people around me? How do some persons come through some circumstances relatively unscathed, while others are done in by them?

After the sixth and seventh grades, I never again lived with my intact nuclear family for more than a summer. I stayed in Fayette with my grandparents at my own request in order to participate in athletics while my parents and sister moved to my father's work. At my grandparents' home I often shared a room with older cousins. Staying with our parents alone gave my sister some reason to feel that she was an only child. Our parents separated while I was in college, and a decade or so later legally ended a marriage that evidently had never been satisfying.

Given this background it is not difficult to understand why I have spent so much time grappling with personality theory and marital interaction and therapy, and why I began to look for a psychology doctoral program with a family focus. Such a program was not available in 1957; I would have to put together a program of my own. Columbia University had, a helpful professor suggested, the best family program in the country, and I could do a postdoctoral year at the Merrill-Palmer Institute in Detroit. Merrill-Palmer offered innovative marital and family clinical work as well as excellent training in individual psychotherapy. With the professor's help in getting to Columbia, that was the path I took.

Columbia's program essentially was based on dynamic and social psychology and family studies. I was able to get some supervision in individual and marital therapy to add to what I had secured earlier. After receiving my doctorate in 1960, I became an assistant professor in the University of Alabama system in Birmingham. Following three years of university teaching, I received a National Science Foundation fellowship for a summer of graduate study in anthropology at the University of Colorado and then went to Detroit in 1963-64 for the long-anticipated postdoctoral year. The Merrill-Palmer internship drastically altered my career. Challenged by an intensive training program, I saw vast new possibilities for working therapeutically with a spectrum of patients. More than that, I began to learn what I could do and how to develop the skills to implement my ideas for working with individuals, couples, and families. Challenge and supportive supervision combined to provide the opportunity for me to make tremendous leaps forward that year as a clinician and in my attempts to integrate theoretical and practical concepts.

A month after completing the postdoctoral training and returning to the university ranks, I was invited to join the Merrill-Palmer faculty. "When?" was my response. At the end of the academic year in June, 1965, I returned to Merrill-Palmer as a member of the counseling and psychotherapy faculty, specializing in marital therapy. It was a time and place of tremendous intellectual ferment, where we were part of the significant struggle to gain a place for nonmedical therapists. It was not easy to do the marital and family therapy that we insisted on doing at Merrill-Palmer and in our private practices in the midst of an exceedingly conservative psychoanalytic climate.

From 1965-69 at Merrill-Palmer and for three subsequent years at the Advanced Behavioral Science Center (a private foundation in Michigan where our core psychotherapy faculty went from the institute) I trained postdoctoral therapists from psychology, psychiatry, social work, and other fields in individual, marital, and family therapy. Starting with a dynamic base and adapting a traditional child guidance model, we worked with problems ranging from individual developmental issues to difficulties experienced by families with severely emotionally disturbed preschool children. I spent part of those years in private practice as a psychologist and marital and family therapist and part of one of them as a half-time visiting lecturer in the family area at Eastern Michigan University. By 1973 I was engaged in private practice full-time and heavily involved in editing, organizational, and community activities.

The opportunity to work with doctoral students and shape a family-therapy doctoral program took me to the Florida State University in Tallahassee as professor of home and family life in 1973. I was there for three years, putting my ideas for educating and training family therapists into effect in an interdivisional doctoral program in marriage and the family. Working with the students both academically and clinically was highly gratifying, even though conducting an interdepartmental program was not free of frustration for faculty or students. Together, we demonstrated the positive effects of fostering colleagueship rather than competition among doctoral students and the tendency of students generally to rise to the level of performance expected of them. All of the students accepted into the program during my FSU years completed their doctorate and most have become solid family-therapy professionals as teachers, clinicians, and administrators.

Rank, tenure, and satisfaction were not enough to keep me at Florida State when my wife, Alice, and I discovered that the arrival of double-digit inflation as our three children were entering college and graduate school was creating a huge, growing deficit in family finances. Consequently, it was back to Michigan in 1976, where I returned to private practice for 11 more years. For more than half of those years I was an adjunct professor of psychology at the University of Detroit, teaching individual, marital, and family therapy to master's and doctoral students. I also commuted to Wisconsin part-time one fall while serving as a visiting professor of family therapy at the University of Wisconsin-Stout. Consultation and supervision at clinics in the Detroit and Grand Rapids areas provided additional opportunities for continuing to teach and sharpen my ideas.

In December, 1987, I became executive director of the Governor's Constituency for Children in Tallahassee, where we moved in order to assume responsibility for an elderly parent. At the time of this writing, I am in the private arena as an organizational consultant on governance, family policy, and human systems. I do some private practice, edit a journal (*Contemporary Family Therapy*), edit the *Family Therapy News* for the American Association for Marriage and Family Therapy, and am writing articles and books.

MY MAJOR ANCHOR AND FULFILLMENT

My relationship with Alice Mancill has been the anchor and major source of satisfaction and stability for me since we met in 1952. Trying to extend not only support to our three children – Camille, Bill (William Mancill, not junior), and David – but also freedom to develop their own personhood in a setting with two idiosyncratic parents has meant that our family life has never been dull. Somehow, all of us survived their teenage years in the horrendous 1960s and 1970s (not without scars for all), and emerged with deep ties of respect, love, and enjoyment in our family and for one another. In recent years we have moved into new friendship and colleague relationships with three unique young persons.

The therapy part of my professional career has remained at the office. We structured other parts of my work and Alice's work/family roles so that the children could see us at work and sometimes participate in our vocational and professional activities as they wished to. Alice, who took only three years to complete a bachelor's degree and earn a Phi Beta Kappa key, has carried her own authority and identity locally and nationally with my professional groups as well as in circles of her own. We have made joint decisions to do some vocational/professional things and to refrain from others. Alice has both tolerated my workaholism supportively and demanded that I keep it under reasonable control. For more than a decade some of our vocational interests and talents have meshed nicely and we have worked together in organizations and on publications.

DR. SPOCK WASN'T ALL WRONG: TRUST YOURSELF

Some of my psychologist colleagues describe themselves as psychologists who do family therapy—emphasizing that they are not family therapists, but that they do family therapy. I respect their position and think that I understand its ramifications: One's professional and perhaps personal identity is attached firmly to roots in a particular discipline, with all that is implied in terms of education; training; intellectual, emotional, and professional security; and having a clear and consistent reference group.

My stance is quite different: I am a clinical psychologist *and* a family therapist. I paid the price to secure education, training, and credentials in both disciplines. I also pay the intellectual and emotional price—and sometimes the practical one—of being both, and of being willing to acknowledge that psychology and family therapy are sometimes overlapping but are always essentially different bodies of knowledge. Fundamentally, my commitment is to the bodies of knowledge and to families more than it is to being a psychologist or a family therapist.

Although I recognize the political importance of labels and pressure groups and enjoy professional comradeship and personal relationships as much as most, I have neither a "lodge brother" nor a true-believer mentality. I need not be in agreement with my contemporaries or have consensual validation about theoretical orientation, professional stance, or personal work. Therefore, I have resisted the advice and admonitions in a widely used textbook on personality theories to immerse oneself in a single theory and then to learn others. I have either too little passion or too much sense to be a true believer, and I am either too stubborn or value my intellectual and personal integrity too much to follow a guru. Rather, I have tried to take the issues and observations that appear to me and deal with them, making my own synthesis (Nichols, 1988d; Nichols & Everett, 1986). I ask that students identify as much as they can with my way of learning and of ethically regarding and respecting the people with whom they work. Of course, there is a paradox here: When you teach someone to think for themselves, you have to be prepared for them to make their own mistakes, to disagree with you, and to make choices and decisions different from yours. Trying to teach and encourage students to think for themselves does not leave much room for seeking personal followers. As clear as this seems, it is not always easy to accept emotionally. I can understand why many professionals need disciples, but for myself, anything less than insisting that students and colleagues be their own persons is not honest. I also recognize the paradoxes in that statement.

Age gradually is diminishing my tendency to be as casually iconoclastic as I once was. Rather than bluntly pointing out that "the king has no clothes on," as I was wont to do when I spotted what I considered phoniness earlier in my career, I am much more willing and able now simply (and quietly) to not join in the charade. One does not have to challenge directly. The implications of learning theory are persuasive that the appropriate way to extinguish a behavior is to refuse to reward it; the overrated and overstated is likely to collapse or simply fade from the scene in due time if ignored.

Groucho Marx's retort of "Why?" to the party cry "The show must go on!" reportedly got him thrown out of the club for his impertinence. That's one way to do things. Another, of course, is simply to refuse to join in the hoopla or to leave the party quietly. The latter is a nonreward to the inanity and is stronger in many instances than a direct challenge. My intent these days is to take a middle-ground approach and make my statements clearly and firmly, then let others do what they will.

A NON-MASLOVIAN HIERARCHY AND OTHER VALUES

Along my developmental path there evolved a hierarchy of values consisting of emphasizing first the personhood of the professional, then the knowledge base of family, and finally (for the clinical practitioner) the techniques of therapy. The personhood of the professional in terms of clinical practitioners refers to a concern with the integrity of the therapist, with his or her character and human qualities. The same qualities are needed in researchers and teachers, as a Cyril Burt case (Hernshaw, 1979) tragically illustrates.

Personal therapy has been a part of my own preparation, including a mandatory year during the Merrill-Palmer internship (Nichols, 1968a). For our postdoctoral interns at Merrill-Palmer and the ABSC foundation, personal psychotherapy was part of the package in the training model that was used. At Florida State I arranged for therapy to be available for my students. There have never been struggles over whether they "had to have therapy"; our major difficulties have concerned its funding.

I want my students to be bright, kind, and tough-minded, able to ask themselves tough questions and to be good researchers in a practical, clinical sense as well as in the usual sense of academic researcher. Ethical behavior is essential, and ethically questionable behavior—including failure to treat clients in a responsible manner—is not tolerated.

Under "knowledge base," I include the implication that anyone claiming expertise in the family area (whether as researcher, teacher, clinician, or combination thereof) must be grounded fundamentally in substantive knowledge of family structure, process, and dynamics. Family specialists must be that, not specialists in some other substantive body of knowledge who transfer their techniques or extrapolate to family from another knowledge base. Conceptual tools from other disciplines are helpful, but they are not the same as having a substantive knowledge of family and conceptual tools for researching and evaluating family and working with families.

Therapeutic techniques are last in the lineup. My approach has been to try to help students turn into lifelong learners, about families and about themselves, who devise their own treatment techniques. I have repeatedly told students:

> I don't teach techniques as such, and I don't teach them in isolation but only in relation to a particular case and a particular situation. In supervision I may teach a thousand techniques. Techniques are developed out of the needs of the persons and situations that face you in the clinical setting. To oversimplify only a little, there are two major approaches: fitting the persons to the therapy, or fitting the therapy to the persons. The initial and the ongoing assessments that you do should determine what is needed and what makes the most sense with a given case.

Assessment of the personalities and the problems with which they are faced in clinical situations, therefore, is crucial. Interventions are tailored to what is discovered in such assessments, to the needs of the clients, and from the abilities of the clinician.

I urge students to observe, and to reflect on what they observe. I have used the metaphor of splitting off part of one's mind and running it like a computer to reflect and analyze what's happening and what it means; with another part, stay available to interact directly with the people. My students are expected to try to have sound bases for their actions and to reflect on the reasons that they have made "intuitive" interventions. It is not responsible behavior to do something "because it seemed like a good idea" or because they observed the technique at a workshop and liked it.

My psychology training was not gained in a traditional fashion, something that currently prevents me from obtaining state licensure where I reside because my doctorate was not from "an APA-approved program." My predoctoral, doctoral, and postdoctoral preparation contained the substantive content and clinical training that I wanted and was sufficient to earn licensure in Michigan where I practiced for 20 years. It also was deemed acceptable for credentialing as a diplomate in clinical psychology from the American Board of Professional Psychology (ABPP) and engaging in extensive organizational activity, including offices and honors, with state psychological and other societies. Would I do it the same way again? Probably, because I learned important things that were not available in conventional psychology programs.

My predoctoral education and training included a heavy exposure to dynamic psychology—starting with Sigmund Freud—that was reinforced in doctoral and postdoctoral work. Significantly, it also contained an introduction to the work of Harry Stack Sullivan, an influence that continues to affect my thinking. I worked with teachers and colleagues who used systems theory intuitively before von Bertalanffy (1968) was discovered by psychologists.

From the beginning I struggled to juggle what I learned from psychoanalysis with what I learned from sociology, social theory, anthropology, and observation of human behavior and interaction. I did a lot of psychoanalytically oriented treatment until it became evident that an intrapsychic emphasis alone had severe drawbacks. Eventually, the emphasis in my treatment shifted until most of my clinical work involved marital and family interventions and occasional individual therapy. Individual therapy and working on imbedded intrapsychic conflicts have a role, but only if they are considered in light of the social context and events in which they were imbedded and are maintained. The most appropriate descriptive label for my approach probably is "the individual in context." The concern about losing sight of the individual through preoccupation with systems that I expressed more than a decade ago (Nichols, 1978) still prevails.

SYNTHESIZING: A CIRCULAR PROCESS WITH INCOMPLETENESS

The integrative, synthesizing approach that guides my career is a middle-of-the-road orientation. In it, one pulls in every piece of worthwhile information available and compares it with the existing theoretical framework and knowledge base, using one's best critical abilities to determine what is worth pulling in and one's best analytical abilities to determine how it fits and what is to be discarded, retained, or modified. One must be ready to live with ambiguity, because there are sound observations and findings from varied sources that do not fit together smoothly. The result will be the retention of two or more pieces of information that are contradictory in some cases, but that are valid each in their own right. This is the "lumps in the oatmeal" theoretical or knowledge-base phenomenon that I have referred to elsewhere (Nichols & Everett, 1986).

This model requires flexibility. As one is trying to gather new information and form new hypotheses, one holds a knowledge base and operating hypothesis both firmly and tentatively, just as many of us do in clinical assessment and treatment. One proceeds with them as guides and underpinnings as confidently as possible but remains ready to discard old data and hypotheses when they become outmoded, obsolete, or fail to explain what is transpiring.

A reason that I have always liked the work of Sullivan, is that he continually synthesized findings of other fields with materials from his clinical work, and grappled with understanding and changing the social environment until his death. Sullivan drew on the worlds of social science, anthropology, linguistics, social psychology, sociology, and other disciplines associated with human behavior for understanding. His catholic emphasis and persistent endeavors to integrate findings provided an intellectual and professional model that I found compatible with my striving to make sense out of what I encountered in work and life and synthesizing that with what others discover by their methods of observation, research, and reflection.

My approach to learning involves researching and studying something until there are "no squishy areas." This means continuing until the same references begin showing up repeatedly in a literature search or until the same points begin to recur in continuing observations. In the precomputer days of the 1960s, I spent five years running down the history of the fields of classical marriage counseling and marital therapy. By the time I put the material into a bibliography I was reasonably certain that I had not missed many significant references in the English language.

MAJOR CONTRIBUTIONS

My work has been done in a variety of settings and under several different rubrics. Family, psychotherapy, personality, marital and family therapy, clinical psychology, forensic psychology, writing, editing, teaching, clinical practice, and extensive organizational and other practical pursuits have been among my interests and pursuits.

Marital Therapy

There was not much marital therapy around in 1960 when I completed graduate school. Most of what was available—such as that stemming from the work of Oberndorf (1934, 1938), Mittelman (1944, 1948), and Martin and Bird (1953; Bird & Martin, 1956)—was based on psychoanalytic theory and relied heavily on making insight-driven intrapsychic changes in individuals. Still ahead for the most part were serious attempts to take the individual and the marital system into account simultaneously in therapy.

Essentially, a dichotomy in thinking existed: Either one assumed that marital difficulties stemmed from some form of individual problems and that the treatment of choice was individual psychotherapy (an "individual-only" approach), or that marital difficulties could be dealt with by means of a relatively superficial form of marriage counseling (a "relationship-only" approach) (Nichols, 1973; Nichols & Everett, 1986). One worked only with individuals *or* with relationships. There was still a lot of tiptoeing around psychoanalytic taboos regarding transference and countertransference concerns, and some continuing reluctance to breach the traditional medical/psychiatric hegemony over psychotherapy.

By 1966 I was well into the process of struggling to develop an integrative marital therapy that stood between psychodynamic and systems approaches, although the psychodynamic side was still uppermost. The emphasis on the "individual in context" slowly began to come into balance so that what I appreciated about marital choice and marital interaction from nonclinical sources could be merged into clinical understanding. The early emphasis on neurotic interaction (Eisenstein, 1956) had to be modified and melded with more "normal" explanations for behaviors. Individually oriented object relations (e.g., Blanck & Blanck, 1968) that lacked an adequate theory of interaction were replaced with my continuing modifications and applications of the object-relations theory of Fairbairn (1952, 1963) and Dicks (1963, 1964, 1967).

Other additions were made along the way. Learning theory, which works well in some instances but not in others, was added to the ongoing integrative approach (Nichols & Everett, 1986). The middle to late 1970s were occupied partly with bringing my marital therapy more solidly into a mainstream family-therapy framework and further operationalizing clinically a "streams and tributaries" multigenerational, developmental approach that I had been teaching since graduate-school days (Nichols, 1988d, p. 10). This included a considerable expansion of multigenerational interviewing and family-of-origin sessions (Nichols, 1985a).

Intergenerational relations and the adaptation of individuals, couples, and families in a changing context are continuing concerns. This can be seen in the theme of comprehending substantive issues as they relate to development and connecting them to family and marital interaction. That theme was reflected in an early paper on psychotherapy with teenagers (Nichols & Rutledge, 1965) and in subsequent papers on divorce adjustment and children of divorce (Nichols, 1977b, 1984b, 1985b, 1986a; Nichols & Everett, 1986), stepfamilies (Nichols, 1980b), and family violence (Nichols, 1986b). The clearest contemporary statement of my marital-therapy approach can be found in *Marital therapy: An integrative approach* (Nichols, 1988d).

Education and Training Endeavors

I was privileged to teach and supervise postdoctoral clinicians a quarter-century ago in an innovative program with creative colleagues at an important early developmental period in the family-therapy field. Our Merrill-Palmer and subsequent private-foundation settings and times provided the opportunity for me to develop an emphasis on professional socialization and the shaping of a professional orientation on the part of students/trainees while helping them acquire substantive knowledge and master clinical skills.

In addition to whatever differences I have made in the careers of several score students/trainees, one of my main thrusts in education and training includes a model integrating substantive knowledge and clinical training in an articulated curriculum that has been adopted widely, generally without the adoptors knowing the original source (Nichols, 1988c). My predictable criticism of much training in family therapy today is that it is training of students to follow mentors and gurus, and not education of students to develop their own ways of thinking and acting based on a sound theoretical and clinical foundation.

Accreditation

Conceptualizing and implementing accreditation of educational and training programs in family therapy stands as a major contribution. In 1974 I started the hard work of converting an intraorganizational pattern of approving programs for American Association of Marriage and Family Counselors membership purposes into an accrediting program and body serving the broader field of family therapy. This included constructing the first set of standards, the major outlines and some details of which are still in use; writing the first manual on MFT accreditation (Nichols, 1974c); establishing procedures and securing the accreditation of programs; and demonstrating in 1978 to the United States Office of Education, then in the Department of Health and Rehabilitative Services, that there was a new and separate academic discipline of marital and family therapy; and in conjunction with others, notably attorney Steven L. Engelberg, gaining recognition of the accreditating body – now the Commission on Accreditation for Marriage and Family Therapy Education of the renamed American Association for Marriage and Family Therapy – by the commissioner of education, an event that caused an observing psychiatrist/family therapist to exclaim, "This is historic! For the first time ever family therapy has been officially recognized!"

Organizational

Organizational structures and resources sometimes provide the only vehicle to advance certain kinds of issues and interests. That certainly was the case in the developing family field. In 1960, there were only two family-focused organizations in the United States that seemed to offer any promise of advancing family therapy. In terms of substantive knowledge and educational endeavors, the National Council on Family Relations (NCFR) was available. I began to participate in its meetings, offering several early papers to NCFR audiences. I served on the organization's board of directors for 12 years.

Clinically, the most relevant organization in the 1960s was the tiny group of elitists who comprised what is today the 17,000-member American Association for Marriage and Family Therapy. Four degrees and postdoctoral training got me in the door in 1964 as the equivalent of today's student member. By 1969 I was heavily into organizational activity, serving my first term on the board of directors, and taking on a series of professional responsibilities that still continue.

My key organizational contributions include having served as president of both the AAMFT and the NCFR and conceptualizing and giving leadership or support to several major developments in each, including conceiving and helping to launch a research institute in the AAMFT; helping to create an international section and supporting the development of state affiliates in the NCFR; and working cooperatively to bridge gaps among several national family and family-therapy organizations, including founding the Coalition of Family Organizations (COFO) in Washington in 1977 during my NCFR presidency. My efforts to bring rapprochement between the family-studies field represented by the NCFR and the marital and family therapy area represented by the AAMFT resulted primarily in one joint annual meeting in St. Louis in 1974 and their collaborative work in COFO.

Moving the AAMFT headquarters to Washington and the center of political power in the United States during my presidency of that organization marked a change in the AAMFT and in family therapy's political and public policy involvement. Leading the AAMFT to adopt membership requirements based on education in substantive marital and family, family therapy, and professional areas, as well as on extensive supervised clinical experience, and restructuring the AAMFT to deal with becoming a large-scale membership organization were major goals that we met during my AAMFT presidential term. My participation in several other significant groups such as the American Family Therapy Association (charter member), International Family Therapy Association (charter member), and the Family Psychology Division of the American Psychological Association has been limited.

Organizational contributions at the state level have included serving as cofounder and president of an early, major state marital and family therapy association in Michigan and later helping to merge it into the national AAMFT structure. I worked for several years to advance both state marital and family therapy and state psychology and enhance cooperation between the two groups. Psychology organizational work included the presidency of the Michigan Society of Licensed Psychologists, executive committee membership in the Michigan Psychological Association, charter membership in the Michigan Society of Forensic Psychology, and seven years as an officer of a highly effective political action committee, the Psychologists' Task Force.

Legislation/Licensure

Contributions here include pioneering work in the area of model legislation for state regulation of marital and family therapists, such as writing the first legislative handbook (Nichols, 1974b) in the field, constructing model legislation that was adapted to the needs of several states, and providing testimony or consultation in more than a dozen states. Related activity includes giving leadership to a Michigan regulatory board during eight years of service (seven as chair).

Journals and Editing

My founding and serving as first editor of what is now the *Journal of Marital and Family Therapy* was an important happening. Starting the journal occurred in a simple way. In 1973 I was issued a casual challenge to "give the AAMFC the journal it's been wanting for 20 years." Following a preliminary meeting with the board of directors, the board gave the go-ahead to a firm proposal in early 1974. Late that fall, volume one, number one (dated 1975) was ready for distribution with lead articles by Jay Haley and James Framo. For political reasons, its title (*Journal of Marriage and Family Therapy*) reflected the organization's name. Fortunately, within a few years my successor as editor, Florence Kaslow, was able to get the journal appropriately renamed. Altogether with the *JMFT,* the *Family Coordinator,* and (currently) *Contemporary Family Therapy,* I have edited family-field journals for a dozen years and served on the editorial boards of five other journals including the new *Journal of Family Psychology.* In 1986 I became editor of the *Family Therapy News,* a 17,000-circulation professional newspaper sponsored by the AAMFT.

Writing

My family psychology publications began in 1965. Thaxton and L'Abate (1982) identified my work as being among the most frequently cited in the family therapy field in the 1970's decade.

No One Is an Island:
Special Colleagues and Collaborators

I owe a debt to many colleagues. Aaron L. Rutledge, Ph.D., opened some doors of professional opportunity for me in the 1960s at Merrill-Palmer and, more importantly, shoved the horizons of treatment possibilities back almost infinitely. His vision, creativity, and audacity helped me to break shackles of intellectual limitation. Also, I am indebted to Laura Singer-Magdoff, Ed.D., one of my instructors and supervisors at Columbia University and later a colleague in organizational struggles. I continue to learn from her efforts to make dynamic psychology less esoteric and more practical in couples interaction and treatment.

There have been several other colleagues with whom I have worked through the years; the most significant colleagueship has been with Gertrude Zemon-Gass, Ph.D. We shared offices, cases, clinical and professional problems, and ideas for 20 short years; no week went by that I did not learn something from her – and contribute a few ideas in return. We did collaborative treatment and occasional four-way interviews, sharing cases with a complete sense of regard and respect for the integrity of the other. Despite differences in age, gender, and ethnic and cultural backgrounds we think so much alike in many ways that it is comfortable and scary at the same time. We also think differently in some ways: Her piercing insights often give me something to try to relate to what I already know, or to put into practical operation. Her perceptions about human need and the rightness of the time for offering interventions were the impetus behind my pioneering work in adjustment to divorce education in 1967-68 and "problems of a second marriage" educational endeavors nearly a decade later. The similarities and differences in thinking as well as sharing a common pool of values also have made it easy to do collaborative writing.

PROFESSIONAL SATISFACTIONS

Some of the major professional satisfactions from my family psychology endeavors include: seeing all the students who entered a graduate program secure their doctorates and not having a single one try to be a replica of me; helping young and middle-aged authors break into print; working with clients and seeing results, learning as I advanced through the years that most of the time I was getting better at helping them; having a larger part of the family-therapy field begin to come around to emphasizing the individual as well as the system, and seeing integrative efforts become a more visible part of the scene; experiencing the thrill of succeeding in establishing and gaining recognition for accreditation in the family-therapy field; and watching my family and family-therapy efforts in Washington bear fruit.

FITTING INTO THE SCHEME OF THINGS

There has been a consistent theme throughout my work: understanding and dealing with the individual in context. For me, in terms of comprehension and analysis, human personality breaks down into inside and outside dimensions. How does one maintain an adequate fit between inside oneself and outside oneself? How can we better understand and foster developmentally the crucial and delicate balance between dependency and independency needs of human beings?

Personality in both its "normal" and "abnormal" aspects is a continuing concern. What sustains personality in normal and extreme conditions? Bettelheim's (1958) work based on his 1938 concentration-camp experience and reports by others (e.g., Schein, 1958) on brainwashing in Korea in the early 1950s offered some help and posed further questions about how personality can be torn down and individuals can adapt.

What enables some persons to survive and even thrive in hostile or at least nonsupportive environments? What are the discernible factors, if we can find any, in the development of creativity and intellectual curiosity in one family member? How does a youngster born in a log cabin decide to become a mathematician and end up with a Ph.D. from the country's major mathematics department when there was no apparent supporting context for his curiosity and ambition? How do families and the surrounding ecosystem produce an engineer who becomes President of the United States and a beer-drinking brother who is described as "a good ole boy" and "cracker-barrel smart?"

As we live in relationships, how do we form the important, especially the intimate, relationships of our lives? A significant part of my interest is still concerned with the marital relationship and with understanding and expanding the kinds of object-relations approaches pioneered by Fairbairn (1952, 1963) and Dicks (1963, 1964, 1967). How do the object relationships of the developing infant/child and those of the parents fit and interact to fulfill what Parsons and Bales (1955) called the irreducible functions of the nuclear family: the primary socialization of the young and the stabilization of adult personality?

Struggling with these issues and with the still-unresolved issue of "context" will occupy part of my attention in the forthcoming years. We have not made much progress in dealing with the context issue, despite important work in ecological family psychology. As I have worked as a child and family advocate I have been both impressed and depressed with the lack of community and social support for individuals and families, for human beings. Support is needed not only by families for their individual members, but also by the social setting for the families and for the individuals as individuals in the social setting.

Where many of the practical and organizational things that I have worked on in the psychology and family fields over nearly three decades fit into the larger scheme remains to be seen, the outcome depending on what happens in the future.

WHITHER THE FUTURE, AND ASSOCIATED THOUGHTS

Unlike many questions in the family field, I believe the question of why psychologists are heralded less than other groups in the family field has some straightforward answers. Traditionally, psychologists have been trained and educated to study the individual; the individual is the primary substantive and theoretical base of psychology. One obvious area of some exception is social psychology, an interstitial area between the individual and society and an area shared and claimed by both sociology and psychology.

Clinical psychology's traditional rootage in assessment was, of course, focused on the individual. When the first major books on family assessment were put together (e.g., Straus, 1969), they included some instruments by psychologists, but most family measurement tools were developed by sociologists. Even today there are significant shortcomings associated with the employment of some widely used assessment instruments with marital couples because they are individually oriented tests and include no theory of marital interaction. Using such instruments with two individuals and comparing the outcomes is an additive approach that can generally be expected to yield a different outcome than assessment with an instrument based on human relatedness and interaction and applied to partners simultaneously (Willi, 1984).

Psychologists often have attempted to make extrapolations from individual or group theory and therapy to marital and family interaction and therapy. The family is a group with some features in common with other groups, as well as some crucial differences. It has a history of its own, a culture of its own derived and filtered from the larger culture, and a set of permanent relationships based on genetics and "blood" ties and modified by the additions and subtractions—the accessions and losses—of members by marriage and divorce or death.

The gestalt of a family is significantly different because of its shared history, blood relationships, and the roles ascribed to it by the society from that of artificially formed groups, no matter how much meaning and influence other kinds of primary groups may hold or exert on individuals. The family is the foremost of primary groups, both in terms of primacy in time and the depth and meaning of influence on its members. It is also very different as a whole from the sum of its individual members' characteristics.

True, psychologists have studied groups as well as individuals, but such study has tended to be from the perspective of an individually based orientation or, occasionally, from the viewpoint of group-dynamics perspectives based on research with nonfamily groups.

Traditionally, psychologists who have done research on marital and family topics have not persisted in their research and tied it to existing knowledge and theory building. For example, when Goodman (1973) studied research publications on marriage counseling in the early 1970s, she found that "for most of the authors, their publication represented only a limited excursion into the field rather than a central concern with furthering knowledge" (p. 114).

When I was testifying before a special panel assembled by the U.S. Office of Education in 1978 on the question of whether "marriage and family counseling/therapy was an amalgam of social work, social psychology, and pastoral counseling or a discipline in its own right" and therefore worthy of being recognized for academic accreditation, an American Psychological Association representative testified that it was simply an advanced specialization in clinical psychology. How this was so was never described or demonstrated.

Conversely, citation and demonstration of the specific and extensive substantive content taught in articulated curricula in existing marital and family therapy graduate programs was sufficient to convince the special interdisciplinary panel composed of a family sociologist, a psychology professor, and an education professor that a distinct academic body of marital and family therapy knowledge existed.

The kind of limited view of family, and the obvious loyalty bind that requires that one must be a psychologist first and foremost, provide those who would be family psychologists with a significant handicap to the pursuit of their ambitions. Adding a family-therapy track in a traditional psychology department (as in more than a score of psychology programs during the 1980s), is not likely to ease the problem for graduates. I think that a split will continue to exist in the professional identity of individuals following such tracks, and that most are likely to experience strong informal pressure to pay heed to the rewards and sanctions of their mother discipline.

If there is a bridging area between the family field and the field of psychology, it probably is the area of social psychology. When I started teaching social psychology nearly three decades ago, I made personality theory the central concept, the backbone or organizing principle. Following the implications of this "individual in context" approach provides some potential for constructing a sound and productive family psychology, *if* we give adequate attention to the family and group side of the equation.

The kind of family psychology that I have in mind is one in which the substance of group life—specifically family group life—is as much of the education of the psychologist as the substance of psychology of the individual. Family psychologists must stand squarely in both fields, family and psychology, in order to form a family psychology of the kind I think would be most solid. They must be both family specialists and psychology specialists.

REFERENCES

Barker, R. B., & Barker, L. S. (1951). *One boy's day: A specimen record of behavior.* New York: Harper.

Barker, R. B., & Wright, H. F. (1954). *Midwest and its children: The psychological ecology of an American town.* Evanston, IL: Row, Peterson.

Bettelheim, B. (1958). Individual and mass behavior in extreme situations. In E. E. Maccoby, T. M. Newcomb, & E. L. Hartley (Eds.), *Readings in social psychology (3rd ed.)* (pp. 300-310). New York: Holt, Rinehart & Winston.

Bird, H. W., & Martin, P. A. (1956). Countertransference in the psychotherapy of marital partners. *Psychiatry, 16,* 353-360.

Blanck, R., & Blanck, G. (1968). *Marriage and personal development.* New York: Columbia University Press.

Dicks, H. V. (1963). Object relations and marital studies. *British Journal of Medical Psychology, 36,* 125-129.

Dicks, H. V. (1964). Concepts of marital diagnosis and therapy as developed at the Tavistock family psychiatric units, London, England. In E. M. Nash, L. Jessner, & D. W. Abse (Eds.), *Marriage counseling in medical practice* (pp. 255-275). Chapel Hill: University of North Carolina Press.

Dicks, H. V. (1967). *Marital tensions.* New York: Basic Books.

Duhl, B. (1983). *From the inside out and other metaphors.* New York: Brunner/Mazel.

Eisenstein, V. (Ed.) (1956). *Neurotic interaction in marriage.* New York: Basic Books.

Fairbairn, W. R. D. (1952). *Psycho-analytic studies of the personality.* New York: Basic Books.

Fairbairn, W. R. D. (1963). Synopsis of an object-relations theory of the personality. *International Journal of Psycho-Analysis, 44,* 224-225.

Goodman, E. S. (1973). Marriage counseling as science: Some research considerations. *Family Coordinator, 22,* 111-116.

Hernshaw, L. S. (1979). *Cyril Burt, psychologist.* London: Hodder & Stoughton.

Martin, P. A., & Bird, H. W. (1953). An approach to the psychotherapy of marriage partners. *Psychiatry, 16,* 123-127.

Mittelman, B. (1944). Complementary neurotic reactions in intimate relationships. *Psychoanalytic Quarterly, 13,* 479-491.

Mittelman, B. (1948). The concurrent analysis of married couples. *Psychoanalytic Quarterly, 17,* 182-197.

Nichols, W. C. (1968a). Personal psychotherapy for the marital therapist. *Family Coordinator, 17,* 83-88.

Nichols, W. C. (1968b). Work and family life: A male dilemma (Plenary address). *Annual Meeting Proceedings: National Council on Family Relations.* New Orleans.

Nichols, W. C. (1969). Family problems in upgrading the hardcore. *Family Coordinator, 18,* 999-106. (With G. Zemon-Gass & A. L. Rutledge)

Nichols, W. C. (1973). The field of marriage counseling: A brief overview. *Family Coordinator, 22,* 3-13.

Nichols, W. C. (Ed.) (1974a). *Marriage and family therapy.* Minneapolis: National Council on Family Relations.

Nichols, W. C. (1974b). *Marriage and family counseling: A legislative handbook.* Claremont, CA: American Association of Marriage and Family Counselors.

Nichols, W. C. (1974c). *Marriage and family counseling: A manual on legislation.* Claremont, CA: American Association of Marriage and Family Counselors.

Nichols, W. C. (1975a). Sexuality in the midst of change. *Osteopathic Physician, 44*(9), 52-57.

Nichols, W. C. (1975b). "Take me along" – A marital syndrome. *Journal of Marriage and Family Counseling, 1,* 209-217. (With G. Zemon-Gass)

Nichols, W. C. (1977a). Counseling the childless couple. In R. F. Stahmann & W. J. Hiebert (Eds.), *Counseling in marital and sexual problems,* 2nd ed. (pp. 134-145). Baltimore: Williams and Wilkins.

Nichols, W. C. (1977b). Divorce and remarriage education. *Journal of Divorce, 1,* 153-161.

Nichols, W. C. (1977c). An end to the double standard. *Osteopathic Physician, 46*(1), 80-89.

Nichols, W. C. (1978). The marriage relationship. *Family Coordinator, 27,* 185-191.

Nichols, W. C. (1979a). Accreditation in marital and family therapy. *Journal of Marital and Family Therapy, 5*(3), 95-100. (With V. Smith)

Nichols, W. C. (1979b). Doctoral programs in marital and family therapy. *Journal of Marital and Family Therapy, 5*(3), 23-28.

Nichols, W. C. (1979c). Education of marriage and family therapists: Some trends and implications. *Journal of Marital and Family Therapy, 5*(1), 19-28.

Nichols, W. C. (1979d). Notes and Comments, AAMFT: AFTA. *Family Process, 18,* 99-101.

Nichols, W. C. (1980a). Marriage counseling. *The encyclopedia americana* (International ed., p. 192). New York: Americana.

Nichols, W. C. (1980b). Stepfamilies: A growing family challenge. In L. R. Wolberg & M. L. Aronson (Eds.), *Group and family therapy 1980* (pp. 335-356). New York: Brunner/Mazel.

Nichols, W. C. (1980c). Therapy for divorcing clergy: Implications from research. *Journal of Divorce, 4(1),* 83-94. (With K. & I. Hutchison)

Nichols, W. C. (1982). Preserving traditional families: The myth, the reality, the need. *Conciliation Courts Review, 20*(2), 55-61.

Nichols, W. C. (1984a). Foreward (and contributor of items). In V. D. Foley & C. A. Everett (Eds.). *Family therapy glossary.* Washington, DC: American Association for Marriage and Family Therapy.

Nichols, W. C. (1984b). Therapeutic needs of children in family system reorganization. *Journal of Divorce, 7*(4), 23-44.

Nichols, W. C. (1985a). A differentiating couple: Some transgenerational issues in marital therapy. In A. S. Gurman (Ed.), *Casebook of marital therapy* (pp. 199-228). New York: Guilford.

Nichols, W. C. (1985b). Family therapy with children of divorce. *Journal of Psychotherapy and the Family, 1*(2), 55-68.

Nichols, W. C. (1986a). Sibling subsystem therapy in family system reorganization. *Journal of Divorce, 9*(3), 13-31.

Nichols, W. C. (1986b). Understanding family violence: An orientation for family therapists. *Contemporary Family Therapy, 8,* 188-207.

Nichols, W. C. (1987). Boredom in marital therapy: A clinician's reflections. *The Psychotherapy Patient, 3,* 137-146.

Nichols, W. C. (1988a). The family systems approach. In C. R. Figley (Ed.), *Stress and the family: Family treatment innovations* (Vol. III). New York: Brunner/Mazel.

Nichols, W. C. (1988b). Gaslighting: A marital syndrome. *Contemporary Family Therapy, 8,* 188-207 (with G. Z. Grass).

Nichols, W. C. (1988c). An integrative psychodynamics and systems approach. In H. A. Liddle, D. C. Breunlin, & R. C. Schwartz (Eds.), *Handbook of family therapy training and supervision* (pp. 110-127). New York: Guilford.

Nichols, W. C. (1988d). *Marital therapy: An integrative approach.* New York: Guilford.

Nichols, W. C. (1988e). Polarized couples: Behind the facade. In J. F. Crosby (Ed.), *When one wants out and the other doesn't: Doing therapy with polarized couples.* New York: Brunner/Mazel.

Nichols, W. C., & Everett, C. A. (1986). *Systematic family therapy: An integrative approach.* New York: Guilford.

Nichols, W. C., & Rutledge, A. L. (1965). Psychotherapy with teenagers. *Journal of Marriage and the Family, 27,* 166-170.

Oberndorf, C. P. (1934). Folie a deux. *International Journal of Psychoanalysis, 15,* 14-24.

Oberndorf, C. P. (1938). Psychoanalysis of married couples. *Psychoanalytic Review, 25,* 453-475.

Parsons, T., & Bales, R. F. (1955). *The family, socialization and interaction process.* Glencoe, IL: Free Press.

Schein, E. H. (1958). The Chinese program of indoctrination for prisoners of war: A study of attempted "brainwashing." In E. E. Maccoby, T. M. Newcomb, & E. L. Hartley (Eds.), *Readings in social psychology, 3rd ed.* (pp. 311-344). New York: Holt, Rinehart & Winston.

Straus, M. A. (1969). *Family measurement techniques: Abstracts of published instruments, 1935-1965.* Minneapolis: University of Minnesota Press.

Thaxton, L., & L'Abate, L. (1982). The "second wave" and the second generation: Characteristics of new leaders in family therapy. *Family Process, 21,* 359-362.

von Bertalanffy, L. (1968). *General systems theory: Foundations, development, applications.* New York: George Braziller.

Willi, J. (1984). *Dynamics of couples therapy.* New York: Jason Aronson.

9

People and Paths Along the Way: A Trek Through Words and Images

MARGARET THALER SINGER

There have been many people and many paths along the way to my career in studying families. It all began when I was age 10 and began to notice the conversational skills of certain of my relatives. In wonderful ways they could recount happenings from their past. I cannot recall any adults who were silent at family dinners. I best recall Sunday afternoons in the summers. The heat and humidity hung low and children were glad to just sit and listen. There were winter evenings when it was too cold to do much except sit and talk.

The winters were spent in Denver, Colorado (where I was born July 29, 1921), and the summers in New Albany, Indiana, and nearby Louisville, Kentucky. My mother had moved west, and was working as a legal secretary for an elderly judge when she met my father. My father has returned from France and World War I, and remained in the Army Engineer Corps as a sergeant for a few years. He went to work for the United States Mint and eventually became chief operating engineer there. My mother left office life to work very hard running a small ranch at the outskirts of Denver raising chickens and asparagus and cooking and tending to transient "hired help."

I was an only child in my parents' home during the school year, but spent most of my summers in the Louisville area with my maternal grandparents and my mother's siblings and extensive Irish Catholic family. There were third, fourth, and fifth cousins around and one knew the family tree well. My mother's family had tales of family life in Ireland, and of the New World where many immigrated after a potato famine, some entering through the port of Baltimore and going to New Orleans and others getting to the Louisville area. My paternal grandfather was of German background from Bavaria, and my paternal grandmother was Irish Catholic. My father's parents had died before I was born, but my father passed on tales of his family life in Aspen, Rifle, and Cripple Creek, Colorado, as gold and silver mining rose and waned and cattle and sheep raisers warred for grazing land. As a very small child I recall meeting Baby Doe Tabor and elderly survivors of a long-gone West, including women who had "packed a gun" because of being the daughter of a U.S. marshal or other extenuating circumstances in a much wilder West. In the winters I heard of the long ago West, in the summers of Ireland and the long ago South.

The stories allowed me to "see" from word pictures a recreation of earlier family events. Some tales went back several generations and told of long-gone men, women, children, and places. Some were sad stories, but even with the saddest tales there was humor, determination, and hope. Resignation was not the end product.

When I asked my mother why certain members of her family were so fascinating, why some were such fun to be around, she replied that they were "great raconteurs," and she then took off recounting tales about them. I got the idea, even though I could not spell the word for some time. The great raconteurs were good people; they could talk; they told what had happened; they were not "making things up"; and they ended their tales in ways that allowed another person to join in the conversation. Indeed their acclaim and the joy they produced, even in telling about funerals and sad things, grew from their skill in describing people and how things seemed at events, and encouraging others to join the conversation. The only license to embroider lay in taking a humorous perspective on whatever had the slightest possibility of containing elements of humor.

It took me years to put into words what the tacit rules of humor were, even though I had been able to imitate what I heard. Eventually I caught on to how to search for the incongruities that exist in situations and how to make those appear humorous, and I learned to prize visualizable humor. Hostility and humiliation were not part of the kinds of humor and tale recounting that got one points in these family circles.

I wanted to learn to participate in interactions like the raconteurs did. I did not make it a serious study until the summer when I was 12 years of age, and resolved that I was going to "practice talking". Because I was used to practicing the cello many hours a day, practicing talking was no big deal. A person just worked at an art. So I did. I never fully achieved the skill, the liveliness and fey rapidity that the best of them had, but I worked at it. I must have caught on to at least some of the basic unspoken rules, because I have been able to pass on some talk and humor skills to my children—a son who early on showed a talent for "raconteuring" and uses the skills in journalism and public-relations work, and a daughter who is a medical student with talents in talk and humor as well as an interest in science.

In the fall I returned to my parents's home in Colorado more artful at conversations, fun, and humor. As some teenagers then became movie connoisseurs, I became a connoisseur of conversations. I internally rated the tales I heard my father and his friends tell of their childhood in the mining camps and the "old-timers" they recalled, and I heard them redo World War I, the battlefields of France, life on Gibraltar, and postwar army posts.

In junior high school I decided that writing was as much fun as conversation. I practiced the cello and began to write humorous essays. I discovered a friend who played the flute aspired as I did to become a scriptwriter for Jack Benny. His radio programs were visualizable to levels that almost no other radio humor attained, and the content was similar to what was approved style in my family—visualizable humor and fun found in the incongruities of situations. I recall the summer I was thirteen; my friend and I laughed and wrote. We could recite Jack Benny programs. We knew we needed to practice writing as we practiced the cello and flute. When people ask me today: Did you send scripts to Jack Benny? I know they never "practiced."

There was something fabulously beautiful and inspiring about hearing your teacher play cello passages with soul and near perfection. Master musicians could make the cello sing. So master wordsmiths could create pictures with words. I can still see Jack Benny in bed ill at a ski resort. The nurse approaches him as an increasing clack, clack, clack occurs; they bicker a bit, and as her voice recedes into the distance the same clacking sound recedes. Jack Benny yells to her: "Take off those skis." The picture was made.

In college (University of Denver, B.A., 1943, M.A., 1945, Ph.D., 1952) I majored in speech for a bachelor's degree and in speech pathology for a master's degree and participated in intercollegiate debate, oratory, and extemporaneous speech before going to graduate school to complete a doctoral degree in clinical psychology. My mentors were debate coaches and speech teachers and my favorite courses were logic and propaganda analysis (World War II was occurring and colored all of life).

University of Colorado School of Medicine

Early in 1945 I went to work as a psychologist at the University of Colorado School of Medicine Department of Psychiatry. There my mentor was Dr. John Benjamin, a true scholar and Socratic-method teacher who taught me the intricacies of diagnosis, the Rorschach, and interviewing. Dr. E. W. Busse gave me my first research position. Dr. Franklin G. Ebaugh made diagnosis a crucial step in planning and daily reminded all who worked for him of the history of psychiatry and his mentors by conducting staff conferences in a large classroom that had a huge life-history outline painted on the wall to remind all that a patient's history was important, and to remind viewers of the great names in psychiatry.

Therapy

While still in Colorado, I was counseled by senior staff friends that if one aspired to succeed in the psychology-psychiatry world of the future, it would behoove one to go into psychoanalysis. Of the few available analysts in Denver at the time, the most senior and scholarly, Dr. John Benjamin, was a personal friend and my Rorschach tutor of many years. That left a small list of analysts each of whom I had met professionally. All but one I considered markedly depressed. The one vital and cheerful person was Dr. Jule Eisenbud. I told him how I had selected him, and we settled in for an eighteen-month period. My analysis ended when I left Denver to become a senior psychologist in the Laboratory of Psychology at the Walter Reed Army Institute of Research in Washington, DC.

Immediately prior to my deciding to seek my fortune outside of Denver, I attended one of those indescribable employee-reward nights. I sat and watched one capable woman after another, most named Miss Something, march up and receive a 10-year pin, even 20- and 25-year pins for service to the medical school. I had been working about eight years there. I saw the writing on the wall, in bright neon letters—if you stay on, you will join that long gray line. I did not see the opportunities there that I wanted. Immediately I wrote three letters, enclosing a curriculum vitae: one to Dr. Frieda Fromm-Reichman at Chestnut Lodge, one each to the chief psychologists at NIMH and at Walter Reed Army Hospital. I wanted to live in Washington, DC, be in a clinical psychiatry research unit, and I liked what I knew of Harry Stack Sullivan's work, its impact on the Washington School of Psychiatry with its social interaction view of behavior. All three letters ended up with Dr. David McKay Rioch, director of neuropsychiatry at what was soon to be called the Walter Reed Army Institute of Research. He invited me to an interview and included a government travel order. I went and the job at Walter Reed was beyond what I had dreamed of finding.

Walter Reed Army Institute of Research

At the Walter Reed Army Institute of Research I became a senior psychologist in the Laboratory of Psychology and initially was the only female professional in the unit. There I worked for Dr. Rioch, a man who knew lots about everything, and was able to lead junior staff into becoming avid and careful researchers. He was a traveling troubadour of science; he knew what every scientist of renown was working on and in sharing this information implied how it might relate to our own work. The men with whom I worked and collaborators at other institutions brought backgrounds and contributions in psychiatric, psychological, and physiological research that were remarkable. The contacts and work with these men made major contributions to my life. Drs. Rioch, Morton F. Reiser, Edgar H. Schein, Harold B. Williams, John Mason, Louis J. West, Robert J. Lifton, Herbert Weiner, I. Arthur Mirsky, Ardie Lubin, and Douglas Price were each then making and continued to make major contributions to the behavioral sciences.

Working with them allowed me to learn an enthusiasm and spirit about research. It helped me to continue to value the need for and power of good clinical observations. I came to respect the creativity of sharing, clarifying, and wording clinical observations so that they could form the basis of more narrow and controlled observations. Without good clinical observations about human behavior, and without sensitive speculation about what impact upon each person others' human and social situations had, laboratory experiments in the behavioral sciences can be sterile.

There is excitement in sharing clinical observations, and an artistic pleasure in putting agreed-upon observations into words on paper. The experience of achieving with another person what I came to term the "the third product"—the final evolved written report—is a real social pleasure. When two persons write separate observations and interpretations and eventually pool and integrate these findings, they produce a third product together that is better than either of the two original products. Mutual respect combined with knowledge of the reasoning of science and a willingness to work hard permeated the Water Reed group. It was multidisciplinary. Each person brought special expertise to the study of how environments, human interactions, and words influenced health, illness, and coping with stress.

The research ranged from studying prisoners of war from the Korean conflict to studying sleep deprivation, predicting who might develop peptic ulcers under stress, studying doctor-patient interactions, and biochemical and behavioral states in precardiac and chest surgery patients. My contributions centered around attempting to see what, if any, connections could be found between various analyses of language styles, contents, and social behavior and measures of biochemical or other criteria (Price, Thaler, & Mason, 1957; Schein & Singer, 1962; Schein, Singer, & Cooley, 1961; Singer, 1974; Singer & Schein, 1958; Strassman, Thaler, & Schein, 1956; Thaler, Reiser, & Weiner, 1957; Weiner, Singer, & Reiser, 1962; Weiner, Thaler, Reiser, & Mirsky, 1957). Growing out of this work and my participation in studies of stress, both at Walter Reed and later, I later was elected the first woman and the first psychologist to be president of the American Psychosomatic Society.

Lyman Wynne, NIMH, Bethesda, Rochester, and Berkeley

My next work propelled me into family research. Dr. David Hamburg and Dr. Lyman Wynne came to visit me after my husband (a biophysicist who had been working at the Naval Ordinance Lab near Washington) and I moved to Berkeley. They invited me to work in an unusual way—to work in Berkeley on material gathered at NIMH in Bethesda. I joined the National Institute of Mental Health's Adult Psychiatry Branch Family Studies program, working on a long-distance basis. I was in Berkeley and Lyman Wynne was in Bethesda. From 1959 through 1973, Lyman Wynne and I collaborated on family studies growing out of the NIMH setting; in 1973 he moved to the University of Rochester School of Medicine and we continued our work long distance. I lived and worked in Berkeley and made many trips to Bethesda or Rochester. Out of this research relationship grew the many studies on family communication that Lyman Wynne and I did along with colleagues, such as Margaret Toohey. For 30 years we have been able to do research without living in the same town. A few of our many publications on a variety of topics are: Doane et al. (1982); Jones et al. (1984); Loveland, Singer, and Wynne (1963); Schuldberg, Singer, and Wynne (1990); Singer (1967, 1977b, 1978a, 1978b, 1978c); Singer and Wynne (1963, 1965a, 1965b, 1966, 1985); Wynne and Singer (1963a, 1963b); Wynne, Singer, and Toohey (1976a); Wynne, Singer, Bartko, and Toohey (1976b).

Lyman Wynne and I began our collaboration with an intense interest in how one person shares attention with others and tries to communicate with them. We have been interested particularly in studying the sharing of attention and meaning within families. The rationale is that families can be viewed as systems, and that the styles of communication within families are part of the family-system properties. It has been within this framework of studying families that our particular use of the Rorschach and other projective devices has been designed. We also have applied the same principles to devising scoring manuals for use with the Thematic Apperception Test, the Object Sorting Test, and Proverb Interpretation (see references in Singer, 1977b).

Verbal behavior samples were gathered from family members and analyzed with the intention of studying the impact of a person's conversational style on others. To do so, a shift was made from using Rorschach responses and other behaviors primarily to infer intrapsychic phenomena to using them to conceptualize the probable impacts or effects of the person upon others who must deal with him or her in intimate, ongoing relationships.

To this end, we have used psychological assessment techniques in ways that appear close to traditional approaches, yet diverge from them in important respects. At first glance we may seem to be taking only a slight change in perspective for our interpretations, but in actuality we proposed and followed a rather major reorientation regarding the analysis of Rorschach responses and other verbal behavior. We used the Rorschach and other standardly administered assessment devices not in the traditional way, with primary emphasis upon the revelation of an individual's intrapsychic experiences, but with an emphasis upon identifying, formalizing, and interpreting the *impact* of his or her verbal communication upon others.

It has seemed to me that my youthful interest in what made certain members of my own family good raconteurs and what distinguished them from others has come to fruition. An early interest in how words created pictures in my mind has been relevant to my work on family communication.

SHARING FOCI OF ATTENTION AND MEANING: VISUALIZABLENESS

Lyman Wynne and I made the assumption that the Rorschach task is an analog to those many occurrences in daily life in which two individuals attempt to establish a consensually shared view of reality. During a viewing and discussing of reality, one person offers a focus of attention, labels what he or she sees, and offers this interpretation to the other. In turn the second person then responds to the offered focus of attention in some way. The Rorschach offers a relatively standardized starting point for sampling to what extent attentional foci and meaning are shared mutually during such a verbal transaction.

In this section I am drawing heavily upon several articles and refer the reader to those detailed examples of how families containing normal young adult offspring and neurotic, borderline, and both remitting and nonremitting schizophrenics have been studied. We have always emphasized in our work that we assume both innate and experiential factors are codeterminants of behavior (Singer & Wynne, 1965a, 1965b; Wynne, Singer, Bartko, & Toohey, 1976; Singer, 1977b). We have studied each family member as an individual, the parents as a couple, and the family as a group communicating over the Rorschach task. Manuals exist for scoring communication deviances in the individual, spouse, and family Rorschachs and other standard task situations.

We were especially interested in what links, if any, might exist between the thought disorders of schizophrenic young adults and the communication styles of their parents. A good deal of research that attempted to find some concordance between the psychiatric diagnosis of parents and their offspring had been inconclusive. Over the years we analyzed the recorded and transcribed verbal transactions of parents (1) as they individually talked with a tester over projective and other psychological test material; (2) as the parents talked together as a couple with a research interviewer; (3) as the parents transacted together with their children in test situations, without staff present; and (4) as parents, offspring, and staff met in family therapy sessions. In this research the focus has been on the formal, stylistic features that characterize communication, especially on how parents focus their own attention and how they go about sharing meaning. We have been interested primarily in studying how parents communicate and relate to other persons, and for the present have relegated to a secondary position the study of the content of their transactions (Wynne & Singer, 1963a, 1963b; Wynne, Singer, Bartko, & Toohey, 1976; and references in Singer, 1977b).

On both theoretical and empirical grounds we believe that the particular forms or styles in which attention is established are an enduring feature of family transactions and make formative contributions to the ego structure of the growing child. We find that in families containing a young adult schizophrenic offspring both parents tend to have frequent difficulties in establishing a focus of attention and sharing meaning. Communication in these families is especially disturbed at the attention level (i.e., where are we looking?) whereas in the families of borderline, neurotic, and normal individuals communication disorders are more prominent later on, after an attentional focus has been shared by two or more persons.

We have used the Rorschach procedure to study families because it is a situation in which one person tells another person what an ambiguous scene looks like. This person must try to direct the other person's attention and thoughts so that his or her ideas are conveyed to a listener. This is a prototype of those typical and frequent interchanges between parents and children in which a parent says what something looks like and tries to explain a bit further about the idea. Such acts are repeated in various forms over the years within families. Each of us talks daily with other persons in similar encounters in which we express an opinion and later try to elaborate upon it.

In the Rorschach task as we have used it, whether the blots are viewed by an individual, a spousal pair, or a family, a person is asked to say aloud what he or she thinks each blot looks like. These words can be regarded as the outward, visible products of his attentional processes. First, the respondent has to join the focus offered by the tester who has proposed the task; then he or she is supposed to attend to the images and ideas that come to awareness in his or her own mind and to select appropriate ones to express aloud to the tester. Thus this person's spoken words reflect the orderliness, or lack of it, of attentional processes as they are used at that moment in a verbal transaction with another person. It is assumed that those attentional and communicational features detectable in the Rorschach task are structural, that is, quasi-stable stylistic attributes. It is assumed further that these samples of attention and language in this particular task are representative of how a person deploys attention and uses language in similar labeling and descriptive exchanges with other persons. In our scoring manual, various communication deviances are cited that we feel reduce the visualizableness of verbal communication and disrupt a listener's attention; that is, for a number of reasons a listener cannot piece together the words offered by a speaker to form a coherent, consistent picture or frame of reference in his or her head based upon the remarks of the speaker (Singer, 1967; Singer & Wynne, 1966, 1985).

We have characterized the bewildered moments listeners can experience as they hear deviant communication into a series of simple questions. Each of the six groups of communication deviance categories scored on the Rorschach are clustered around a central question which that group of communication deviances is likely to generate in listeners. We word them as follows:

Disruptions of the task and the relationship with the tester: The items labeled disruptions cause a listener to think: *What are we talking about? I am losing track.*

Task set and commitment problems: The impact of the items scored under this heading is to cause a listener to wonder: *Does the speaker really mean what he or she is saying? Will he or she hold onto this idea? Is the speaker taking responsibility for this idea? Is he or she really engaged in the task?*

Referent problems: Here the listener hears things worded in ways that cause him or her to ponder: *What is being talking about?* From what the speaker says, the listener can not be sure he or she is sharing the same points of reference.

Language anomalies: Here are grouped items that class those instances in which a speaker's wording causes a listener to wonder: *Did I really hear that? Did I get that right?*

Reasoning problems: Items classed under this title cause a listener to think: *I believe I know what the speaker thinks, but how can I deal with it?*

Indefinite and cryptic comments: The response here is: *What does the speaker mean?* (This may be an extreme form of referent problem).

Keeping these types of questions in mind we help raters to remain transactionally oriented. We feel that the Rorschach responses, or any other verbal material, can be used to assess the possible impact of one person's remarks upon the thought processes of another. We find, however, that a manual needs to be modified for each type of transaction (Rorschach, TAT, Object Sorting, Proverbs, How Did You Meet, family discussions, etc.).

The Visualizability of Language

The extent to which one person's spoken words create visual images in another person's mind may be the most central basis for understanding what the speaker says; that is, grasping meaning seems highly dependent upon the person's words building pictures in another person's mind. The greatness of authors may hinge upon the haunting impact of the world their words build in a reader's mind. For example, Charles Dickens is regarded as unmatched for his power to portray the society of his day. His words vividly create in the reader's mind the scene, the person he is describing, and the emotional tone of his character. Common, everyday conversation is not expected to reach the almost photographic resolution of Dicken's words, but there seems to be an enduring need for certain levels of visualizability.

A speaker can repair imagery, coherence, and reasoning through various means. As a person listens, he or she expects that the words will permit him or her to visualize that to which the speaker refers. The listener expects to be able to build up certain relationships among objects, events, ideas, and persons mentioned by the speaker. We reason that when a speaker violates the expectancies that words will be used with their usual meanings and that reasoning will follow everyday laws of logic, the listener becomes baffled and bewildered to varying degrees, and feels that he or she has lost contact with the speaker. When a listener hears the speaker dropping in bits of incomplete ideas, using words in private ways, reasoning oddly, losing the focus of the message, shifting the task set without saying so, or doing other idiosyncratic things, the listener feels lost and unable to build up a coherent mental image of what is being described. Because the speaker has strayed too far from expected patterns, the listener cannot build up a sensible, reliable mind's-eye view of what is under discussion. The communication deviances to which we allude are not simple violations of grammar, or untutored usage, but rather are idiosyncratic utterances that impair the sharing of attention and the flow of meaning between persons.

After a long series of studies in which we established and others' work confirmed that the parents of schizophrenics, in contrast to other parent groups, had a predictable propensity to blur and impair meaning and attention, we returned to exploring two aspects of our initial major vantage point. We had hypothesized that samples of parental communication gathered under standard conditions could be analyzed for its (a) pathogenic impact (communication deviances), (b) symptomatic implications (Thought Disorder Index), and (c) competence-enhancing features.

These three domains of parenting can be studied, we hypothesized, by inspecting in orderly ways the verbal communication of parents. That is, the samples of parental communication (whether from each parent alone with a tester, together as a spousal pair, or as parents with their children) can be studied to ask three questions: How relatively *symptomatic* (thought disordered to non-thought disordered, using the TDI or Thought Disorder Index) is this communication from this parent? How relatively *pathogenic* is this parent's communication (communication deviance, or CD, scoring)? How competence-enhancing (CE, competence-enhancing scoring criteria) is this parent's communication? (Schuldberg, Singer, & Wynne, 1990).

Thus, we and other colleagues have analyzed the verbal behavior of parents from these three perspectives. (Schuldberg, Singer, & Wynne, 1990). In this work we proposed that certain features of parental communication as sampled using the Rorschach task as the standard manner of securing samples could be scored and quantified. Jones et al. (1984) studied a set of healthy transactional behaviors occurring in the three-person context of the consensus Rorschach procedure (Loveland, Singer, & Wynne, 1963; Singer, 1968). We have hypothesized that competence-enhancing (CE) features in parental communication could presumptively facilitate healthy child development and may counteract biological and social risk factors. To summarize that research, a set of scoring categories was developed and applied to Rorschach communication from both parents of a series of 10-year-old boys, children at risk for future development of mental disorders because a parent in each family had been hospitalized for a mental disorder.

> These categories of healthy parental functioning were compared with test indices of parental mental health and psychopathology and related to independently obtained teacher and peer ratings of the children. On the individual Rorschach, parents of well-adjusted children tend to engage in such behaviors as making a clear transition to each new percept, identifying the location of what is seen spontaneously, reporting percepts with positive affective connotations, engaging attention by addressing the tester directly, describing how to look at the blot in order to share their percepts, explaining responses fully in the inquiry, and giving responses freely, without urging from the tester. These positive, healthy attentional and affective features of parental communication occur independently of measures of parental psychopathology. Two of the Competence-Enhancing communication measures rate healthy counterparts of Communication Deviance; others add significantly to Communication Deviance in predicting offspring adjustment. The results indicate that Competence-Enhancing, pathogenic, and symptomatic communication are separate domains of parenting (Schuldberg, Singer, & Wynne, 1990).

OTHER PATHS

In the early 1970s, many families were losing members into some of the cultic and new-age groups. Upon investigation I found that there were updated versions of thought-reform programs being brought to bear on myriad young adults and others in these groups. Along the way I was a court-appointed examiner of Patricia Hearst along with my colleague from the end of the Korean War, Louis J. West, M.D. (now at UCLA as psychiatry department chairman). We were appointed because of our early work on the thought-reform programs seen in China in the early 1950s and variants used on prisoners of war in Korea. I have published a number of articles on cults and their impact on families and individuals (Singer, 1978b, 1979, 1986, 1987; West & Singer, 1980). With Professor Richard Ofshe I have brought the conceptualization of thought reform up to date (Ofshe & Singer, 1986). I have concluded that families, couples, and groups—including cults—can be judged by determining whether they focus on development of the individual member or on preservation of the system itself. Systems that are *member-focused* attempt to enhance the autonomy and growth of the individual members; the system is open to internal changes in order to prepare the members for interacting in responsible ways in broader systems. A *preservation-focused* system has a world view committed to the enhancement and preservation of the system itself (Singer, 1988). My work in the area of how language is used to either influence persons toward autonomy or toward being deployable agents of the system has led to my being an expert witness in many legal cases (Singer & Nievod, 1987b).

The Next Decade

My work in family studies, in thought reform and influence, and in psychosomatic medicine has led me to believe that the next decade will be one in which attention will be directed to group interaction, influence, how controls are established, and how modeling of behavior occurs. Much more focus on social interaction, modeling of behavior, and group process in family studies may be in the offing.

The Connections Along the Pathways

In my work over the years in analyzing communication, it often has seemed as if I had the opportunity in my professional work to study what had always interested me—why when some persons spoke, their language was so visualizable that I could "see" what they were talking about. Thus, it is as if the pleasure of my childhood in hearing tales told in which I could see what the words told has been and continues to be present in the work I do. And somehow I always have that underlying sense of fun and humor that I learned from my mother, combined with the desire that words make pictures, that caused me to want to write humorous essays and to appreciate Jack Benny radio programs. It also allowed me to have some of the most delightful moments of laughter shared with all the persons with whom I have worked over the years. Some of my jobs have centered on analyzing speech from some very sad situations, yet being able to laugh in those moments of appreciating the awfulness of the context in which those speakers spoke.

As I guide beginning therapists, I warn them that if they cannot visualize what the client is referring to, if they cannot see what a couple or family is talking about in a visualizable way, they need to slow the process down and get some words that build pictures for them. Without those word pictures, how can they help anyone map out where they have been or where they are going? Words must be used like food and water, for survival.

Life is complicated enough without allowing someone to use words in a beclouding and baffling way. One cannot be understood if one's words do not allow another to see what has happened. We cannot help another person along the path if we do not use words that convey what we see.

To my parents, to all those wondrous wordsmiths along the path, I want to say thank you for all the pictures and all the excitement of being allowed to "see" someone else's world. I want to thank everyone who is so vividly in my mind as I write this; thank you for allowing the wondrous humor that only words seen in incongruous contexts can create.

As a person with both an Irish and German heritage and a love for words, let me end by quoting Ludwig Wittgenstein: "Everything that can be thought of at all can be thought of clearly. Everything that can be said can be said clearly." And, may I add, if this happens we share word pictures. These word pictures are the way in which we connect with others or fail to connect. Parents connect with their children with word pictures that probably make the bonds which connect after the first early bonds and enable a baby to move into being a human rather than a mere organism. If this does not occur, the words of parents get them and their children off on side paths and we find humans painfully trying to reach one another while stumbling about in the brambles. When one gets lost in the word-brambles there is no sense of connection and no laughter, and no shared pictures to allow another to follow along a path that has been found, and to feel the warmth of humor. Without humor how can perspective be found? Without clear word pictures how can a shared world be felt?

REFERENCES

Doane, J. A., Jones, J. E., Fisher, L., Ritzler, B., Singer, M. T., & Wynne, L. C. (1982). Parental communication deviance as a predictor of competence in children at risk for adult psychiatric disorder. *Family Process, 21,* 211-223.

Jones, J. E., Wynne, L. C., Al-Khayal, M., Doane, J., Ritzler, B., Singer, M. T., & Fisher, L. (1984). Predicting current school competence of high risk children with a composite cross-situational measure of parental communication. In N. Watt, E. J. Anthony, L. C. Wynne, & J. Rolf, (Eds.) *Children at risk for schizophrenia: A longitudinal perspective* (pp. 393-398). New York: Cambridge University Press.

Loveland, N. T., Singer, M. T., & Wynne, L. C. (1963). The family Rorschach: A new method of studying family interaction. *Family Process, 2,* 187-215.

Ofshe, R., & Singer, M. T. (1986). Attacks on peripheral versus central elements of self and the impact of thought reforming techniques: Review and analysis. *Cultic Studies Journal. 3,* 3-24.

Price, D., Thaler, M., & Mason, J. W. (1957). Studies of preoperative emotional states and adrenal cortical activity in cardiac and pulmonary surgery patients. *Archives of Neurology and Psychiatry, 77,* 646-656.

Schein, E. H., Singer, M. T., & Cooley, W. E. (1961). *A psychological follow-up of former prisoners of war of the Chinese communists: Part II. Results of psychological tests.* Cambridge: MIT Press.

Schein, E. H., & Singer, M. T. (1962). Follow-up intelligence test data on prisoners repatriated from North Korea. *Psychological Reports, 11,* 193-194.

Schuldberg, D., Singer, M. T., & Wynne, L. C. (1990). Competence-enhancing communication by parents of high risk children. *Journal of Family Psychology, 3,* 255-272.

Singer, M. T. (1967). Family transactions and schizophrenia: I. Recent research findings. In J. Romano (Ed.), *Origins of schizophrenia* (pp. 147-164). Amsterdam, Holland: Excerpta Medica International Congress Series, No. 151.

Singer, M. T. (1968). The concensus Rorschach and family transactions. *Journal of Projective Techniques, 32,* 348-351.

Singer, M. T. (1974). Engagement-involvement: A central phenomenon in psychophysiological research. (Presidential address). *Psychosomatic Medicine, 36,* 1-17.

Singer, M. T. (1977a). Psychological dimensions in psychosomatic patients. *Psychotherapy and Psychosomatics, 28,* 13-27.

Singer, M. T. (1977b). The Rorschach as a transaction. In M. A. Rickers-Ovsiankina (Ed.), *Rorschach psychology* (pp. 455-485). Huntington, NY: Robert E. Krieger.

Singer, M. T. (1978a). Communication disorders and the families of schizophrenics. In L. C. Wynne, R. L. Cromwell, & S. Matthysse (Eds.). *The nature of schizophrenia: New approaches to research and treatment* (pp. 499-511). New York: John Wiley.

Singer, M. T. (1978b). Therapy with ex-cult members. *Journal of the National Association of Private Psychiatric Hospitals.* 9(4), 14-18.

Singer, M. T. (1978c). Attentional processes in verbal behavior. In L. C. Wynne, R. L. Cromwell, & S. Matthysse (Eds.). *The nature of schizophrenia: New approaches to research and treatment* (pp. 329-336). New York: John Wiley.

Singer, M. T. (1979). Coming out of the cults. *Psychology Today, 12,* January, 72-82.

Singer, M. T. (1986). Consultation with families of cultists. In L. C. Wynne, T. Weber, & S. McDaniel (Eds.). *The family therapist as consultant* (pp. 270-283). New York: Guilford.

Singer, M. T. (1987). Group psychodynamics. In R. Berkow (Ed.), *Merck manual* (pp. 1467-1471). Rahway, NJ: Merck Sharp and Dohme Research Laboratories.

Singer, M. T. (1988, August). *Systems: Similarities and differences across several settings.* Invited address, American Psychological Association Meeting, Atlanta, Georgia.

Singer, M. T., & Nievod, A. (1987). Consulting and testifying in court. In B. Weiner & A. Hess (Eds.), *Handbook of forensic psychology* (pp. 529-554). New York: John Wiley.

Singer, M. T., & Schein, E. H. (1958). Projective test responses of prisoners of war following repatriation. *Psychiatry, 21,* 375-385.

Singer, M. T., & Wynne, L. C. (1963). Differentiating characteristics of the parents of childhood schizophrenics, childhood neurotics and young adult schizophrenics. *American Journal of Psychiatry, 120,* 234-243.

Singer, M. T., & Wynne, L. C. (1965a). Thought disorder and family relations of schizophrenics: III. Methodology using projective techniques. *Archives of General Psychiatry, 12,* 187-200.

Singer, M. T., & Wynne, L. C. (1965b). Thought disorder and family relations of schizophrenics: IV. Results and implications. *Archives of General Psychiatry, 12,* 201-212.

Singer, M. T., & Wynne, L. C. (1966). Principles for scoring communication defects and deviances in parents of schizophrenics: Rorschach and TAT scoring manuals. *Psychiatry, 29,* 260-288.

Singer, M. T., & Wynne, L. C. (1985). Schizophrenics, families and communication disorders. In R. Cancro (Ed.), *Research in the schizophrenic disorders: The Stanley R. Dean award lectures,* Volume I (pp. 231-249). New York: Spectrum.

Strassman, H. B., Thaler, M., & Schein, E. H. (1956). A prisoner of war syndrome: Apathy as a reaction to severe stress. *American Journal of Psychiatry, 112,* 998-1003.

Thaler, M., Reiser, M. F., & Weiner, H. (1957). An exploration of the doctor-patient relationship through projective techniques: Their use in psychosomatic illness. *Psychosomatic Medicine, 19,* 228-239.

Weiner, H., Singer, M. T., & Reiser, M. F. (1962). Cardiovascular responses and their physiological correlates: A study in healthy young adults and patients with peptic ulcer and hypertension. *Psychosomatic Medicine 24,* 447-498.

Weiner, H., Thaler, M., Reiser, M. F., & Mirsky, I. A. (1957). Etiology of duodenal ulcer: Relation of specific psychological characteristics to rate of gastric secretion (serum pepsinogen). *Psychosomatic Medicine, 19,* 1-10.

West, L. J., & Singer, M. T. (1980). Cults, quacks, and nonprofessional therapies. In H. I. Kaplan, A. M. Freedman, & B. J. Sadock (Eds.). *Comprehensive textbook of psychiatry III* (pp. 3245-3258). Baltimore: Williams and Wilkins.

Wynne, L. C., & Singer, M. T. (1963a). Thought disorder and family relations of schizophrenics: I. A research strategy. *Archives of General Psychiatry, 9,* 191-198.

Wynne, L. C., & Singer, M. T. (1963b). Thought disorder and family relations of schizophrenics: II. A classification of forms of thinking. *Archives of General Psychiatry, 9,* 199-206.

Wynne, L. C., Singer, M. T., & Toohey, M. L. (1976). Communication of the adoptive parents of schizophrenics. In J. Jorstad & E. Ugelstad (Eds.). *Schizophrenia 75: Psychotherapy, family studies and research.* (pp. 413-451). Oslo, Norway: Universitets forlaget.

Wynne, L. C., Singer, M. T., Bartko, J., & Toohey, M. L. (1976). Schizophrenics and their families: Research on parental communication (A revised form of the Sir Geoffrey Vickers Lecture). In J. M. Tanner (Ed.), *Developments in psychiatric research* (pp. 254-286). Sevenoaks, Kent, England: Hodder & Stoughton.

PART II

THE SECOND GENERATION: INNOVATORS AND EXPANDERS 1969-1976

The contributors grouped as the second generation share many characteristics used to describe the first generation included in Part I. Some of them were entirely trained in psychodynamic and experiential theory and therapy; others were grounded in learning theory and behavior therapy, systems theory and structural/strategic interventions. Most are solidly trained researchers who are known for both their basic and applied research. All have incorporated the general persona, so highly valued in psychology, of the scientist/practitioner. Each is a generalist with special interests and proficiencies. Each has become well known and well respected. Some are fearlessly outspoken and have tread where others dare not enter; others convey their messages with more silver-tongued delivery. At this stage in their development, all continue to innovate; most are well into integrating from seemingly diverse theoretical schools and areas of practice. There is not a conformist among them. In their chapters they valiantly share their journeys—the triumphs and set-backs alike. Like those in the first generation, most have become mentors and role models for students, supervisees and those who flock to their workshops.

10

Functional Family Therapy: A Relationship and Process

JAMES F. ALEXANDER
COLE BARTON

I (J.A.) would like to begin with a few introductory remarks. The first is a note of appreciation for being in this book. To be considered among the colleagues that appear on these pages is a great, great honor. Second, I'd like to explain the style of the chapter. Although two authors are listed, the chapter will be presented in the voice of the first author, Jim Alexander, who has been the most visible progenitor of the Functional Family Therapy (FFT) model. The chapter is being coauthored because the model, and all its accomplishments, have always involved the input of many people. Among these, Cole Barton has been the person with the greatest continuity of participation, and the one who most often has been able to see and articulate what has been going on when it seemed I didn't have a clue! In mapping out many parts of this chapter, Cole has been of great assistance, just as he has helped shaped the model and the lives of many colleagues and clients. At the outset I want to thank him, and all the other mentors, colleagues, and students who have meant and given so much to me.

OVERVIEW

The Functional Family Therapy approach to intervention is brief, effective, efficient, and well researched. Its origins include very special people, several diverse clinical traditions, and several academically based conceptual frameworks. Its goals are straightforward and fairly modest: to allow all family members to grow, be happy, and be effective in their family relationships. The model has been controversial (e.g., Myers Avis, 1985), lauded as uniquely effective (e.g., Gendreau & Ross, 1980), and sometimes considered a major model of family intervention (e.g., Todd & Stanton, 1983). There is no doubt that the approach is almost uniquely effective with one particular type of family: conflicted and often multiproblem, not well motivated, with at-risk and often acting-out adolescents (e.g., Alexander & Parsons, 1973; Barton, Alexander, Waldron, Turner, & Warburton, 1985; Gordon, Arbuthnot, & McGreen, 1983; Klein, Alexander, & Parsons, 1976). The model's success, in relatively few sessions, with this type of family is a result of several important features, including the strong emphasis on several distinct phases of intervention (Alexander & Parsons, 1982; Alexander, Barton, Waldron, & Mas, 1983), and the fact that the model does not require that any family member change his or her basic interdependency or connectedness needs with respect with any other family member. Those needs, along with other basic values such as religious-nonreligious and openness-closedness with others, are accepted as they exist at intake. The therapist helps all family members express their needs in new ways that are more effective and positive, and that respect and meet the needs of others. FFT insists that family therapy can be a win-win situation—an attitude which is very helpful but not common in the type of difficult families we have tended to treat in the past.

INFLUENCE OF THE PREPROFESSIONAL YEARS

The integrative nature of Functional Family Therapy (FFT) parallels my development as a family psychologist, and is apparent at several levels: the gender and interpersonal style of my mentors, the conceptual models and disciplines upon which the work is based, and the different realities (i.e., science and theory, clinical practice, training) in which I and the model operate. Most of these elements have been represented in professional publications and presentations. Not present in the literature are descriptions of the people and experiences that have shaped, perhaps as much as anything else, what we are about. These people and experiences constitute an important part of this chapter.

Family of Origin

Not one of my publications mentions my family of origin, much less relates my family to my professional work. I simply haven't felt comfortable sharing this information, and had planned to continue this tradition, with some sort of excuse, in this chapter. Part of me has always felt (hoped?) that others' understanding of my professional work could be based exclusively on my reflecting sensitivity, responsible scholarship, and rigor—things that make up good clinical work and good science. To be honest, I had not particularly wanted to share the pain that has been part of why I am here. I see value, however, in offering a bit of information (though hesitantly) about my family of origin as an introduction to your understanding Jim Alexander as a family psychologist, and to Functional Family Therapy (FFT) as a conceptual and intervention model.

My mother was attractive, very smart (graduated high school at age 15, musical director of a local radio station at age 16), very talented, and a professional woman most of her life. As a professional she placed considerable emphasis on interpersonal relationships, and great value in warmth and a soft approach to influencing others. Not only did this influence my own developing style as a professional, but it can be seen in the emphasis on therapist warmth and relational skills in the Functional Family Therapy model (Alexander & Parsons, 1982; Alexander, Barton, Schiavo, & Parsons, 1976).

Because of my closeness with my mother, it is not surprising that my first major clinical mentor (Josephine Morse) and my first major family therapy supervisor (Lucy Rau Ferguson) were women. This strand has continued throughout my professional development, up to and including the individual (Florence Kaslow) who has had the most to do with my involvement with, and ultimately the presidency of, Division 43 (Family Psychology) of APA. Although nowadays it is fairly commonplace for competent women to be in combined supervisory (i.e., power) and supportive roles, such was not the case 40 years ago. I can thank my mother for letting me experience such a situation during my early years, thereby helping me to be able to seek out and grow from these experiences with such special women later on.

Unfortunately (or perhaps fortunately, depending on what you think of the outcome), not all of my family of origin experiences were so positive. Along with Mom's brilliance, or perhaps because of it considering how her family and culture treated such women, she (and I, as "#1 son") experienced the painful breakup of her four marriages and of several other relationships, as well as her struggles with alcohol, manipulativeness, and major physical problems. I never was permitted to live with or even communicate with my own dad, but I did have to endure two alcoholic stepfathers, physical abuse, and being kidnapped by an abusive uncle as part of a custody battle.

These experiences provided a deep—and for a long time not well-articulated—basis for many of the elements of the Functional Family Therapy model. In particular, my awareness of the vulnerability of children in a problematic family context has led to a treatment approach that emphasizes immediate therapeutic impact using techniques that help even unmotivated family members to engage in the family therapy process (e.g., see Morris,

Alexander, & Waldron, 1988). Simply put, I could not stand to work in a field that would treat only the individual at-risk youth when their family experiences were so much a part of the context. At the same time, I could not allow these kids to be vulnerable to forms of family therapy that depended upon sufficient parental motivation in order for the kids to be helped. Children need to be protected and helped even *before* the alcoholic parent is dry, even *before* the parents' marriage is "fixed," even *before* the economic and other environmental realities can be made more supportive, and even *before* a parent's neurosis can be resolved. This commitment to enhancing parent involvement can be seen in an early evaluation of the FFT model with delinquents from two-parent families (Alexander & Parsons, 1973). Although in other treatment programs the rate of involvement for both parents in two-parent families had been barely over 30%, the FFT program was able to increase the participation of both parents to 97%. Further, compared to other programs, FFT produced a 50% to 70% reduction in recidivism in the youths and their siblings at follow-up periods that extended up to three years.

Pathways Chosen

Part of my family's chaotic lifestyle included 20 moves across seven states by the time I entered high school. In retrospect, it comes as no surprise that by the time I entered Duke University I planned a career in the Navy as an engineer—just a "wee bit" of a need for order and security!

It took only one year for me to figure out (via failing grades and enough beer to float Duke University) that I wanted to become a helping professional rather than an engineer. Yet even as an undergraduate psychiatric attendant in the Duke University Medical Center, I realized that helping people change required more than the warmth, caring, and relationship skills that I had earlier thought would be sufficient. Watching the (seemingly brilliant) ward psychiatrists and psychologists made it seem that a conceptual model was necessary; a model rooted in science and theory and translated into coherent clinical technique. A career in psychology seemed to hold the greatest promise for integration of structure and rigor, yet at the same time warmth and relationship skills.

EVOLUTION INTO A FAMILY PSYCHOLOGIST

Early Professional Experiences and Conceptual Models

Michigan State University offered outstanding graduate training in individual relational approaches to therapy with psychologist mentors such as Bill Kell, Bill Mueller, and Al Rabin. The limitations of an individual model of treatment for children in an outpatient setting (e.g., see Alexander, 1967), however, soon became apparent to me. MSU professors offered an alternative in the then very new arena of family therapy. The encouragement of Art Seagull, the intense and enriching supervision in early family therapy models by Lucy Rau Ferguson, and the challenging style of Gary Stollack combined with Eysenck's (1961) criticisms led me to the nascent behavioral family and systems models.

As I developed professionally my family of origin issues continued to be expressed. Whereas the majority of my early clinical experiences were relationally oriented and directly influenced by female psychologists, the early academic and conceptual aspects of FFT were considerably more technically and theoretically oriented, and influenced by male clinical theorists/scientists such as Jay Haley, Salvador Minuchin, and Gerald Patterson. At the same time, and in a manner that in retrospect seemed appropriate for someone with my life experiences with father figures, I maintained considerable independence, to the extent that I declined an invitation to join the Philadelphia Child Guidance Center staff as a young professional in the early 1970s.

Instead I chose to continue in relative isolation from the emergent leaders in the family therapy field so as not to be too identified with any particular family theory ideology. I remained (from 1968 on) in the relatively young and blossoming University of Utah Department of Psychology, which provided input from developments in such areas as social learning, neuropsychology, social attribution, cognition and information processing, group and interpersonal processes, and interaction methodology and statistics. As a result, FFT has emerged as an integrative model, combining a strong relational emphasis and a well-developed structural/technical component. The model encompasses a scientific emphasis contributed by my academic colleagues, a rich clinical base emphasized by colleagues and enriched by my students, and a strong commitment to improvement based on feedback from all of these sources.

Early Integration Attempts

What has now become labeled the Functional Family Therapy Model was initially labeled "Systems-Behavioral" (Alexander & Parsons, 1973). The behavioral component of the model incorporates the strong empirical commitment of behaviorism, and reflects that tradition in its clear articulation of treatment goals, the application of technology to achieve those goals, and scrutiny of the processes and outcomes involved. The strategic aspects of treatment were derived from systems principles that had been articulated at the time (e.g., Haley, 1963). Systems principles provided a means for understanding apparently contradictory and irrational aspects of family behavior that didn't seem to follow behavioral principles as they then were being delineated.

A coincidental but ultimately very meaningful context in which the model was developed derived from the early treatment populations involved. Whereas the behavioral principles that were being translated into "behavioral parent training" seemed both appealing and effective (e.g., see Patterson, 1965), the translation of such principles into working with delinquent families met with failure. Most then-popular behavioral techniques relied heavily upon control by the "social engineers," as is the case with such techniques as token economies and parent contingency management. In delinquent families, however, overt parental control often was absent and even seemed developmentally inappropriate. Instead, a framework needed to evolve in which parents continued to retain control, but not based on as clearly a complimentary one-up position as is developmentally appropriate with younger children (Alexander, Coles, & Schiavo, 1984). The concept of control as proposed by Haley (1963) suggested an alternative framework that presumably could be used more effectively with families of delinquents and other kinds of acting-out youth.

Despite this conceptual appeal, the translation of systems principles into clinical technology seemed at best magical. As a young professional with training responsibilities in a department of psychology I found it difficult to think in terms of "manualizing" the systems approaches being proposed. As a result, I felt it important to develop a framework which integrated the perspectives of the systemic model, yet retained the flavor and sometimes the specific technology of behaviorism. This integration resulted in the highly successful empirical demonstrations of treatment impact on family process (e.g., Parsons & Alexander, 1973) and outcome (e.g., Alexander & Parsons, 1973; Klein et al., 1976; Barton et al., 1985).

The Maturing Influences

The period from the mid-1970s to the early 1980s was an exciting and dramatic period in the evolution of the systems and behavioral models independently, and in the Functional Family Therapy model that derived so much from both. Minuchin's book (1974) provided conceptual clarity and visual representation of structure, which made it much easier to train family therapists and research the family therapy process. At the same time, from a social learning perspective, Patterson and Reid (1970) proposed the reciprocity-and-coercion hypothesis that identifies acting-out children as both "victims and architects." This concept, an extension of the linear causality model, represented a major conceptual change. It placed responsibility for deviant behavior in a very different context—the reciprocal participation of parent and child, a context that is more consistent with the precepts of systems therapy approaches.

Unfortunately, the larger political and economic context of clinical intervention required that family therapy pioneers emphasize marketing of family therapy more than research in family therapy. As a result, systems-based family therapy models experienced a dramatic increase in popularity and utilization, but the empirical basis for family therapy techniques seemed to be more restricted to developments in the behavioral field.

As a second-generation model, FFT was able to capitalize on the inroads made by the pioneers in order to maintain an ongoing research program as a source of input into the evolving family therapy models (e.g., Alexander, 1973; Alexander & Parsons, 1973; Parsons & Alexander, 1973). Additional approaches to understanding human behavior also were beginning to be recognized and incorporated into the evolving FFT model (Barton & Alexander, 1981). In particular, the social cognition and information processing models being developed in psychology were translating into an increased attention to the contribution of the individual in the family context, and the nature of the cognitive processes that seemed to influence these contributions over and above those of other family members. Further, the transactional perspective being developed by Irwin Altman, Ph.D.—who was my department chair, mentor, and friend—represented an overarching integrative focus that reminded researchers and clinicians to incorporate time and the concept of change into the basic definitions of behavior patterns (Altman & Rogoff, 1987).

Contributions of the Cultural Context

Another coincidental but major factor in the development of the FFT model consisted of the social/cultural context in which the model was being developed. In particular, early treatment populations in Utah generally included 60% members of the Church of Jesus Christ of Latter-Day Saints, or Mormons. The values of this population regarding family structure were in many respects dramatically different from my own and most of the other earlier contributors to the FFT model. These value differences, which included a suspicion of therapeutic involvement with helping professionals outside of the theological structure of the Mormon church, could have translated into high dropout rates and low family participation. Therefore, issues of dealing with different and at times conflicting value systems needed to be addressed quickly and effectively. Further, because the population of youth were so vulnerable, and existed in a context of high family conflict with poor treatment outcomes, we could not afford to engage in a lengthy treatment process which overtly or covertly attempted to force family members to adopt a different value system.

As a result, FFT developed into a high-impact, short-term approach that dealt directly with resistance issues by helping all family members feel accepted and legitimized. In the process of developing a model in which contradictory value systems between the family and therapist could coexist, this principle expanded to helping families in which the conflicting value systems were intrafamilial. Great emphasis was placed on mutual respect and adaptive coexistence despite contradictory value systems. To attain this goal, the model depended heavily on a "matching-to-sample" philosophy (Parsons & Alexander, 1973). This philosophy allows for a variety of family structures and value systems to be seen as adaptive, and recognizes that one set of ubiquitous ideals need not be applied to all families. Going further, this philosophy suggests, for example, that a nonsymptomatic and happily adaptive Mormon family may be different in many important ways from a happy, adaptive single-parent Jewish family in California, or from an adaptive "traditional" Midwestern family in which one parent is much more religious than the other parent. This philosophy also allowed us to work successfully with lesbian couples, single-father families, and a variety of blended families, all of which seem far removed from the infamous "all-American ideal." With its insistence on acceptance of diverse value systems and structures, FFT has been suited particularly well to deal with such varieties of clinical contexts in ways that enhance motivation and decrease therapy dropout rates.

THE FUNCTIONAL FAMILY THERAPY FAMILY: INTERPERSONAL CONTEXTS

The evolution of ideas and techniques that constitute FFT has occurred through collaboration with others; FFT is clearly an interpersonal phenomenon. In traditional terms, I have been the visible figurehead, but FFT is a mosaic that represents the contribution of numerous colleagues. Most of these colleagues initially had the role of student, but in reality they acted as a source of growth (and sometimes the very essence) of every aspect of FFT. This growth occurred in particular at the University of Utah in two contexts: the family therapy clinic and the research group. The rest of the chapter will often use the word *we,* reflecting the direct input of various collaborators.

The Family Therapy Clinic

When the University of Utah Psychology Department moved into its new building in 1972, we made certain that adequate clinic space was available with the facilities allowing for live observation, videotaping capability, and communication between supervisor-observers and clinicians. The use of these elements was stimulated by my indirect and direct observation of the Philadelphia Child Guidance Clinic staff in the early days of Minuchin, Haley, Rosman, Montalvo, Aponte, and others in the early 1970s.

These capabilities and the format of training were important to the development of the model. Historically, trainees experienced didactic classroom training, followed by translations into role playing, seeing experienced FFT therapists use the model, and then experiencing live supervision while working with families. Frequently trainees have raised questions that reflected what was articulated poorly about the model, particularly in regard to how to assess family functioning and the timing of interventions. At other junctures the realities of the clinical context determined what aspects of FFT were part of the underlying principles of the therapy, versus what aspects of performing FFT were distinctive attributes of a particular therapist. On still other occasions, the behavior of families highlighted in dramatic fashion which aspects of the model worked and which did not.

Moreover, the clinic has maintained an ethic of having trainees *and* trainers "put it on the line" by working in front of colleagues. In addition, trainees have been expected to debrief at the end of each of their sessions with supervisors, to formulate a plan for the next session, and to review videotapes of their work in order to understand their impact as well as to determine what they have missed. This in-the-trenches flavor has meant that the model has been tested repeatedly in realistic and meaningful clinical contexts, and has been subjected to extraordinary scrutiny. This scrutiny has been enhanced by the fact that many trainees also were participating in research on process and outcome aspects of the model.

The Research Group Context

The research group periodically also has included faculty colleagues and practitioners with interests in families, process research, psychotherapy research, and statistical or methodological issues. This group has shared an investment and sophistication associated with review and familiarity with the published literature on FFT and other family therapies, with thematic interests in social psychological models of interpersonal processes, gender issues in psychology and family therapy, and behavior therapies. There has been a strong group norm for presenters and participants to be able to critique research on methodological and statistical grounds as well as clinical utility.

Understandably, this has resulted in presentations with a high degree of investment and energy. The group has recognized the need for social-emotional as well as technical support of the presenter, and has provided such support willingly. Thus, in both process and content, the group has meta-communicated the importance of responsible scientist-practitioner professional development.

In addition, the group has reiterated the trite systems notion that "the whole is greater than the sum of the parts." Participation and observation have made most of the members better researchers, and probably most of them are better clinicians for having experienced an empirical scrutiny of clinical concepts in the research area. This is part and parcel of the essence of family psychology, and has epitomized the long tradition of FFT.

In both the clinical and research arenas we have emphasized an open flow and exchange of ideas. We have valued and attempted to model professional commitment, ethics, and honest self-evaluation. After beginning as junior trainess, students have progressed into more senior supervisory roles in both clinical and research activities, and have taken advantage of opportunities to participate in publications, write grants, and train other professionals. For example, our earliest training tape was created by Robin Malouf as part of a Ph.D. preliminary examination project.

Outcome Research

The original outcome study research was conducted with Bruce Parsons and involved the rarely attained—but methodologically desirable—random assignment to comparative treatments. Reprinted numerous times, the data deriving from this project did much to legitimize family intervention as a sound and professionally responsible form of treatment at a time when few such empirical demonstrations were available. Subsequent replications (e.g., Barton et al., 1985) have focused on a more seriously delinquent population, with families at risk for having children removed from the home, and with status delinquents seeing less professionally advanced therapists. The results of these evaluations demonstrated both satisfactory cost benefits associated with applying FFT, and that the model was successful when delinquents had committed serious crimes and had been incarcerated in a reform school, although the absolute level of success was considerably lower. Taken together, the data from these outcome studies formed a crucial foundation for the legitimacy of FFT. Though family therapy was emerging as a popular clinical approach, in the political zeitgeist of the 1970s there were very few empirical demonstrations of the advantages of conjoint methods of intervention. Community decision makers and the research-oriented professional community found the FFT outcome data to be sufficiently provocative and persuasive to warrant training workshops and implementations of family-based programs not only in Utah, but to some extent in a variety of contexts nationwide (e.g., see Gordon, Arbuthnot, Gustafson, & McGreen, 1988).

MECHANISMS OF FFT

Given the success in forging links between behavioral methods and the abstractions of systems theories, our research and clinical supervision groups experienced considerable discussion about what was "really going on." Several studies from within the FFT group have suggested that there are several ingredients to FFT that are also crucial determinants of the success of the treatment model.

As a first example, a study of successful and unsuccessful FFT cases was undertaken (Alexander et al., 1976). Raters, supervisors, and family members agreed which cases were the failures and successes in the sample, and actual (blind) process ratings of the behavior of families in therapy confirmed these appraisals. Supervisors and peers rated therapists on a host of dimensions, and data analyses revealed that the attributes of therapists which were rated constituted two skill classes: *relationship* and *structuring*. *Relationship* skills are akin to those postulated by humanistically oriented therapists, as well as some interpretive behavior akin to practices of "relabeling" or "reframing." *Structuring* skills reflect the ability of therapists to model and to direct families overtly to change their behaviors.

These data were surprising and ran counter to the trend toward attributing change in clients to the potency of therapy manipulations. Indeed, these data are consistent with the conclusion that the skills of therapists, given similar commitment to and aptitude for the technology of FFT, were crucial determinants of the impact of therapy.

Recognizing the potency of these data and concerned about the feminist issues of the day, Janet Warburton argued that one important class of therapeutic characteristics (i.e., gender) was being ignored by me and other senior FFT trainers. In the first of a series of studies on gender effects, her data demonstrated that male and female therapists emit and elicit very different kinds and sequences of behaviors from parents. Further, there seemed to be some biases operating against female therapists as reflected in family members' (in particular, fathers') willingness to direct aversive communications to them. This line of research has been carried on to the present day by Sue Hayden, Haydee Mas (Mas, Alexander, & Barton, 1985), Nanci Klein, Alice Newberry (Newberry & Alexander, 1987), and Norm Liddle.

Although the issue of the importance of therapist style and personality as variables in service delivery had its origins in the clinic and the literature (Beavers & Kaslow, 1981; Kaslow, 1977; Truax & Mitchell, 1971), the evidence that supported these assertions came from the counterintuitive but heuristic research findings. In the absence of empirical evidence, the issues of therapist relationship skills and the volatile topic of sex roles could have been debated ad nauseam. Thus, not only did students bring important heuristic issues to the group for discussion and clinical supervision, but they pushed the legitimacy of these concerns with persuasive empirical evidence.

Statistical Approaches to FFT Phenomena

The psychology department at the University of Utah has long been a fertile environment for creative and rigorous statistical training. Charles Turner and Don Hartmann have taught generations of students to appreciate the importance of statistical rigor in assaying evidence, and in their teaching and consultation have shown most members of the FFT group how informed use of statistics can benefit clinical researchers' ability to ask the right questions.

The therapist-characteristics data (Alexander et al., 1976) are a case in point. The multiple-regression analytic strategy allowed the group to ask questions about which variables seemed to be related meaningfully to each other, and which were relatively more important in predicting clinical outcomes. More recently, Turner and Hartmann facilitated FFT's expertise as to how sources of statistical dependency (e.g., in ANOVA analyses) in fact capture the phenomena of interest for family therapy researchers, as to how the Multivariate Analysis of Variance is a creative and constructive way to examine relationships between people as to the advantages to examining multiple dependent measures as a set, and how Path Analysis methods help us understand the importance and sequencing of events that predict a clinical outcome.

These statistical developments have been important to the development of the FFT model in several ways. Traditionally there has been pessimism about researchers' ability to study family therapy because of limitations of traditional statistical methods. It often is presumed that such statistics are only appropriate to tightly controlled laboratory experiments. The experience of the FFT group, however, has been to discover that statistics are quantitative metaphors which can reveal relationships and patterns in the data that would otherwise elude detection and, moreover, test the significance of these patterns. These statistics frequently have made it possible to ask meaningful questions about families and the process of therapy that could not be measured directly (see Alexander & Barton, 1980).

FFT IN THE PRESENT: THE INDIVIDUAL IN THE FAMILY CONTEXT

Though early disseminations of FFT efficacy generated enthusiasm because of the model's success with a difficult population, the focus on behavioral and systemic variables left readers with the task of intuiting how actually to perform in the behavior change process. Trainees could recognize the aptitudes of talented therapists, yet had a difficult time figuring out how to perform in a similarly effective manner because they had to "read between the lines" of manuscripts in order to infer the reasoning behind maneuvers. One trainee (Mark Ward) likened the experience to playing golf: One gets a scorecard, a layout of the course, rules for counting strokes, and a list of acceptable clubs; however, one does not get a guide for how or in which settings to use the different clubs. Thus, although FFT originators were able to perform effectively and directly train others to do so (Barton et al., 1985), disseminating the model was constrained considerably by our inability to delineate and help others to know how and when to say things to promote good relationship skills and motivate families to change. Although systems transactions were conceptualized as the explanatory mechanisms (e.g., see Alexander, 1973), clinically it seemed that individuals—or individuals in combination—were the agents for both positive change or its converse, resistance. Thus, in the early 1970s the individual family member reemerged as an analytic unit in our systems-behavioral model, although this unit was never conceptualized independently of the dyadic and larger contexts in which the individual interacted (Barton & Alexander, 1981). This extension of the model continued our tradition of input from new conceptual developments in other areas of psychology, in this case social cognition, attribution theory, information processing, and schema theory. The greatest impetus for this development, however, derived from our need to better understand the mechanisms of change in therapy and in particular to articulate and understand the bases of resistance to change. Again, because the model so frequently was applied to very at-risk populations in which low motivation, high dropout rates, and at times very destructive activities were quite characteristic, we felt we simply could not afford to allow resistance issues to be played out over a longer time frame, because other models that typically involve a longer time frame with this population seemed to be characterized by high dropout rates and disappointing outcomes (e.g., see Alexander & Parsons, 1973).

Maladaptive Attributions

In examining the maladaptive system-maintaining activities of individual family members, Cole Barton recognized that attribution theories in social psychology served as metaphors to explain why people persisted in blaming styles, how family members' attributions would create a consistency between problematic feelings and perceptions of family members, and most importantly how these combinations of events would logically lead family members to behave in maladaptive ways. In observing the techniques of early FFT progenitors (e.g., Jim Alexander and Bruce Parsons), Cole noticed that they used language that blamed no one, and typically attempted to structure a perceptual reality in which all family members were identified as having benign, or at least nonmalevolent, intentions with respect to each other. These observations were consistent with the emerging literature on reframing, relabeling, paradoxes, and positive connotation; these maneuvers seemed to represent linguistic means to change attributions in the direction of benign and interpersonally based—rather than blaming and individualistic—explanations.

FFT research group discussions of these phenomena led to a series of studies (e.g., Barton, Alexander, & Turner, 1988; Morris et al., 1988) of how attributions are a crucial part of FFT. This line of work represents both the past, present, and future of considerable clinical and research focus in FFT. To date our research has confirmed that the net effect of reattributions can be to attenuate the family's aversive dialogue, an important setting event for overcoming resistance and preparing for change. Nevertheless, the research also demonstrated that these reattributions are not generalized easily from one to another family topic, nor is it easy to demonstrate successful development of uniform reattributions that will apply successfully to all families (e.g., Alexander, Barton, Mas, & Waldron, 1989). In other words, although relabeling is seen as an important precursor to long-term change (Alexander & Parsons, 1982; Barton & Alexander, 1981; Morris et al., 1988), these attributions that prepare families for change are fragile and cannot by themselves correct limitations in families' communication repertoires. Behavior change technology is still necessary, and fitting behavior-change techniques to the unique patterns and individuals in each family represents a major focus of FFT. The concept of interpersonal functions represents the organizing principle for this focus.

Interpersonal Functions: Dyadic Interdependency Patterns

Consistent with the framework articulated so well by Haley (e.g., 1976), FFT also conceptualizes symptoms as relational definitional attempts. In particular, FFT asserts that symptoms—in fact, all behavioral patterns—create a certain pattern of relatedness, albeit sometimes maladaptive and painful, between two or more people. In particular, the characteristic patterns that transpire between individuals were seen as the best "fit" each individual could attain with respect to their needs for a certain level of interdependency in each dyadic relationship. Some patterns create high degrees of interdependency (e.g., enmeshment or contact/merging), some create relatively low levels of interdependency (e.g., disengagement or distance/autonomy), and some seem to reflect a chaotic and/or ambivalent mixture of both (come here-go away, or midpointing). Understanding these relational processes helped us also to understand the patterns of resistance that we were experiencing in our first decade of applying systems-behavioral principles to the families we were seeing. In particular, it became clear that resistance was directly a function of the degree to which the new behavior patterns we proposed violated the relational interdependency needs being expressed in the problematic interactions. Because these resistance patterns appeared in the form of dropout or lengthier treatment, as the decade of the 1980s emerged this became an increasing problem as public agencies had fewer and fewer resources to expend on this high-risk population. Insurance companies were beginning to place increasing constraints on the length of services that could be provided, particularly on an outpatient basis, to these youths.

As a result, FFT expanded its earlier stated principle of respecting the basic and divergent value configurations of different families and family members, and added the principle of respecting the existing interdependency needs of each family member. Rather than attempting to initiate behavior change patterns that overtly violated individuals' relational needs, FFT adopted as its guiding principle the importance of substituting interdependency needs for the currently operating maladaptive expressions. Thus, a therapeutic task is to legitimize and help each family member to express his or her interdependency needs, but to do so in ways that are adaptive and facilitative to the happiness and growth of each family member, even when the interdependency needs of the members are different (e.g., "I can feel closer, and not abandoned, by your distance needs if you will ask for distance overtly and let me know that rather than leaving, you are just 'regrouping.' At the same time, you don't need to feel overwhelmed by, and rejecting of, my need for closeness because now you feel you can legitimately get some distance when the relationship begins to feel too intense. You can then come closer when you feel more able.").

The concept of interpersonal functions, or relatedness needs, represents the point of intersection between the individual and the larger system. As such it always has been exciting but difficult to simplify, and extremely effective in guiding change technology (e.g., Barton & Alexander, 1981) but controversial (e.g., Myers Avis, 1985). So it remains to this day, constituting a conceptual and technical issue that needs additional clarification. Using this concept, FFT has been impressive in its demonstrated short and long (e.g., up to three years) impact. It has been evaluated as the unique empirically verified treatment of choice for acting-out delinquent families (e.g., Gendreau & Ross, 1983). Because the model is so clear in its assertions regarding what to change and what *not* to change in therapy, however, the basic concepts must and will continue to receive scrutiny from us and (it is hoped) others. Those who have developed FFT over the years hope this same attitude, including careful process and outcome evaluation, will characterize the rest of the work in family psychology and family therapy. This reflects a value system that always has guided my work, and brought me into the field of family psychology in the first place.

FFT IN THE FUTURE

Because FFT always has been much more of a process than a completed model, in many ways we anticipate the future will look much like the past as new conceptual, statistical, and technical aspects of the field are integrated. We see the immediate future characterized mostly by extensions rather than by major developments in the nature of the model. For example, a number of colleagues are having considerable success in extending the framework and many of the techniques developed with at-risk adolescent families into new populations and syndromes such as a marital framework for alcohol treatment (e.g., Jill Sanders), eating disorders with preadolescent and adolescent youth (e.g., Janet Warburton), more traditional marriage/couples issues (e.g., Randy Phelps), various aspects of behavioral medicine including improving medical compliance (e.g., Cole Barton, Jim Alexander), and reunified families of previously missing and exploited children (e.g., Cole Barton, Chris Hatcher).

New statistical and conceptual models also have allowed younger FFT researchers (e.g., Norm Liddle, Alice Newberry) to extend our previous process research on the mechanisms of change in therapy, as well as more integrative theory development with respect to individual-system links (e.g., Jann DeWitt). This latter work demonstrates the richness of the history of input into model development that always has characterized FFT, reflecting in this case very recent developments in information processing approaches to self-concept, self-schema theory, and traditional FFT concepts such as interpersonal functions.

These developments reflect not only a richness of the model and the traditions that have contributed to it, but also a richness of the people involved who have been developing and extending the model. FFT is a relationship—a relationship between many intellectual, scientific, and clinical traditions, a relationship between clinicians and researchers in which both contribute to each other, a relationship between students and mentors that again enriches both, and a relationship among the many wonderful students, colleagues, and mentors whom I have been blessed with the opportunity to know and share. Not only do I thank all of you for the past, but I continue to look forward to the future as I, and the model, continue to grow.

REFERENCES

Alexander, J. F. (1967). The therapist as a model—and as himself. *Psychology, Theory, Research, and Practice, 4,* 164-165.

Alexander, J. F. (1973). Defensive and supportive communications in normal and deviant families. *Journal of Consulting and Clinical Psychology, 40,* 223-231.

Alexander, J. F., & Barton, C. (1980). Intervention with delinquents and their families: Clinical, methodological, and conceptual issues. In J. Vincent (Ed.), *Advances in family intervention, assessment and theory.* Greenwich, CT: JAI Press.

Alexander, J. F., Barton, C., Schiavo, R. S., & Parsons, B. V. (1976). Behavioral intervention with families of delinquents: Therapist characteristics and outcome. *Journal of Consulting and Clinical Psychology, 44*(4), 656-664.

Alexander, J. F., Barton, C., Waldron, H., & Mas, C. H. (1983). Beyond the technology of family therapy: The anatomy of intervention model. In K. D. Craig & R. J. McMahon (Eds.), *Advances in clinical behavior therapy.* New York: Brunner/Mazel.

Alexander, J. F., Barton, C., Mas, C. H., & Waldron, H. B. (1989). The minimizing of blaming attributions and behaviors in delinquent families. *Journal of Consulting and Clinical Psychology, 57*(1), 19-24.

Alexander, J. F., Coles, J. L., & Schiavo, R. S. (1984). Parents as leaders of adolescents: A developmental model. In G. Rowe, J. DeFrain, H. Lingren, R. MacDonald, N. Stinnett, S. Van Zandt, & R. Williams (Eds.), *Family strengths 5: Continuity and diversity.* Newton, MA: Education Development Center, Inc., and University of Nebraska-Lincoln.

Alexander, J. F., & Parsons, B. V. (1973). Short term behavioral intervention with delinquent families: Impact on family process and recidivism. *Journal of Abnormal Psychology, 81*(3), 219-225.

Alexander, J. F., & Parsons, B. V. (1982). *Functional family therapy: Principles and procedures.* Carmel, CA: Brooks/Cole.

Alexander, J. F., Warburton, J., Waldron, H., & Mas, C. H. (1985). The misuse of functional family therapy: A non-sexist rejoinder. *Journal of Marital and Family Therapy, 11*(2), 139-144.

Altman, I., & Rogoff, B. (1987). World views in psychology: Trait, interactional, organismic and transactional perspectives. In D. Stokols & I. Altman (Eds.), *Handbook of environmental psychology.* New York: John Wiley.

Barton, C., & Alexander, J. F. (1981). Functional family therapy. In A. S. Gurman & D. P. Kniskern (Eds.), *Handbook of family therapy.* New York: Brunner/Mazel.

Barton, C., Alexander, J. F., & Turner, C. (1988). Defensive communications in normal and delinquent families. *Journal of Family Psychology, 1,* 390-405.

Barton, C., Alexander, J. F., Waldron, H., Turner, C. W., & Warburton, J. (1985). Generalizing treatment effects of functional family fherapy: Three replications. *American Journal of Family Therapy, 13*(3), 16-26.

Beavers, W. R., & Kaslow, F. W. (1981). The anatomy of hope. *Journal of Marital and Family Therapy, 4,* 119-126.

Eysenck, H. J. (1961). The effects of psychotherapy. In H. J. Eysenck (Ed.), *Handbook of abnormal psychology* (pp. 697-725). New York: Basic Books.

Gendreau, P., & Ross, R. R. (1980). Effective correctional treatment: Bibliography for cynics. In R. R. Ross & P. Gendreau (Eds.), *Effective correctional treatment.* Toronto: Butterworths.

Gordon, D. A., Arbuthnot, J., Gustafson, K. E., & McGreen, P. (1988). Home base behavioral-systems family therapy with disadvantaged juvenile delinquents. *The American Journal of Family Therapy, 16*(3), 243-253.

Gordon, D. A., Arbuthnot, J., & McGreen, P. (1983, October). *Short-term family therapy and school consultation with court-referred delinquents.* Paper presented at the Society of Police and Criminal Psychology, Cincinnati, OH.

Haley, J. (1963). *Strategies of psychotherapy.* New York: Grune & Stratton.

Kaslow, F. W. (1977). On the nature of empathy. *Intellect, 2,* 273-277.

Klein, N. C., Alexander, J. F., & Parsons, B. V. (1976). Impact of family systems intervention on recidivism and sibling delinquency: A model of primary prevention and program evaluation. *Journal of Consulting and Clinical Psychology, 45*(3), 469-474.

Mas, C. H., Alexander, J. F., & Barton, C. (1985). Modes of expression in family therapy: A process study of roles and gender. *Journal of Marital and Family Therapy, 11*(4), 411-415.

Minuchin, S. (1974). *Families and family therapy.* Cambridge, MA: Harvard University Press.

Morris, S., Alexander, J. F., & Waldron, H. (1988). Functional family therapy: Issues in clinical practice. In I. R. H. Falloon (Ed.), *Handbook of behavioral family therapy* (pp. 109-127). New York: Guilford.

Myers Avis, J. (1985). The politics of functional family therapy: A feminist critique. *Journal of Marital and Family Therapy, 11*(2), 127-138.

Newberry, A. M., & Alexander, J. F. (1987, November). *A therapy process study of roles and gender.* Poster session presented to the annual convention of the Association for the Advancement of Behavior Therapy, Boston, MA.

Parsons, B. V., & Alexander, J. F. (1973). Short term family intervention: A therapy outcome study. *Journal of Consulting and Clinical Psychology, 41*(2), 195-201.

Patterson, G. R. (1965). An application of conditioning techniques to the control of a hyperactive child. In L. Ullmann & L. Krasner (Eds.), *Case studies in behavior modification* (pp. 370-375). New York: Holt, Rinehart & Winston.

Patterson, G. R., & Reid, J. B. (1970). Reciprocity and coercion: Two facets of social systems. In C. Neuringer & J. Michael (Eds.), *Behavior modification in clinical psychology* (pp. 133-177). New York: Appleton-Century-Crofts.

Todd, T. C., & Stanton, M. D. (1983). Research on marital and family therapy: Answers, issues, and recommendations for the future. In B. B. Wolman & G. Stricker (Eds.), *Handbook of family and marital therapy.* New York: Plenum.

Truax, C. B., & Mitchell, K. M. (1971). Research on certain therapist interpersonal skills in relation to process and outcome. In A. E. Bergin & S. L. Garfield (Eds.), *Handbook of psychotherapy and behavior change.* New York: John Wiley.

11

Zen and the Art and Science of Being a Family Psychologist

SANDRA B. COLEMAN

ROOTS OF MY BECOMING – THE PERSONAL

"I will become the first woman president of the United States." I made this decision at the age of six as I walked my rather lengthy route to school. Alone on this walk, which I took morning, noon, and after school, I began an early pattern that was to permeate my life – alone with nature my ideas take form. Here I was at six years old already knowing that a leadership role was, for me, essential.

Such young feminist thinking arose in the culture of the Second World War and as I ponder it now, it seems rather remarkable. The early zeal for achievement is understandable, considering that I am a first-born daughter, the first grandchild on my mother's side, and one of the few female grandchildren in my father's very large family. Also significant is the fact that I "came from" two very bright, educated parents. The feminist thinking does not immediately seem to derive from any family context as my parents had a fairly traditional marriage, although I do recall my father always helping with the dinner dishes. We were a "model" (later to be reframed as "pseudo-mutual") family from all external and even some internal viewpoints and, on the surface, my childhood was content, secure, and loving.

Leadership was reinforced in school when I was repeatedly given timed reading and math tests and "pitted" against the top male student in my class. He, the leading male academic, and I, the leading female, were asked to race through these tests to see who could outdo the other. Sometimes he would win and other times I would. He became a prominent medical specialist, no doubt having been influenced by our early competitive matches.

My feminist leanings were supported by being given the role of Susan B. Anthony in the major 6th-grade class play of the year. Later, in high school, I stood on a high table behind a screen where in a long gold sequined gown I portrayed the Statue of Liberty. Clearly all these events influenced my belief that my destiny was not limited by gender.

At 16 years of age I wanted to become a surgeon, but after my father's sudden death from a coronary during my first semester at the University of Michigan, the family leadership role became my major priority. This, according to my mother, was the legacy my father bestowed upon me. Seven months after my father died my mother underwent surgery for a benign meningioma on the optic nerve. She was 42 years old at the time; my father had died at age 45. At age 18 I began to think that one's life span was indeed very limited. This belief was particularly cogent as I had already experienced many family deaths. When I was nine years old, my maternal grandfather died, followed by my paternal grandfather's death a few years later.

My maternal grandmother, my all-time favorite relative, died when I was about 11 or 12 years of age. She had come to live with us and a short time later suffered a cerebral hemorrhage. I found her on our sun deck where she lay paralyzed and trapped in the screen door. She died in our home approximately one month later. The following year my mother's older sister and only living sibling died suddenly of a brain tumor. The effect of all these deaths on my mother was profound. She had also lost a brother, the eldest child in her family of origin, when he was 23 years old. He was a law student and an outstanding athlete. Until the night before my first marriage I thought he had hemorrhaged to death as a result of a tonsillectomy. The truth was that he had tuberculosis, but that was a much-guarded family secret divulged on the eve of my marriage because my mother thought I was now "old enough to know the truth."

The pressure of becoming the head of the family was too much for me and after transfering to an Eastern college for one semester after my father's death, I left school and took a hospital-based course in medical technology. I then escaped into an early marriage with my former high school boyfriend and in 1955, in my fifth month of pregnancy, finished first in my class. My daughter was born 11 months after my wedding and by the age of 23, I had added two sons. I immersed myself in my three babies, all born within three years and five months, and denied the problems in my marriage. I also ignored my former lofty goals. After all, this was the late 1950s and all of the popular girls quit college and exchanged "A"s for diapers.

After my youngest was born, I began to sense a need for something more than having the most adorable, well-behaved babies and the best recipe for chocolate cake in the neighborhood. I took a volunteer course and, on my weekly one-day retreat from motherhood, I worked as a lab technician in a nearby state hospital. What happened as a result of that experience was as serendipitous as my career that followed.

In the midst of a growing awareness that my marriage was ultimately destined for failure, I began to find the patients at the state hospital far more interesting than their blood cells. Because these were the days before pop psychology flooded the book market, I knew almost nothing about the field to which I found myself drawn. I gradually moved out of the laboratory and began working with the art therapist. Here were the beginnings of my interest in projective material. Within a short time I began an academic pursuit of knowledge that started with a few courses and ended nearly 10 years later when, in January 1973, I was awarded my Ph.D. My early idea of pursuing psychology courses just for the sake of learning was soon invaded by that old mechanism that sought the lead. It did not take long to know that without a doctorate my future would be limited.

My years as a student were accompanied by a divorce from my first husband and a few years of single parenthood in the changing culture of the sixties. Although I was almost destitute financially, I was enriched and exhilarated by being on campus in the midst of the women's movement and that of Black power. These experiences changed my already avant garde views of life even more. I also shared a great deal with my now school-age children, promising them that I would complete college before they entered. Less than one year before my daughter's graduation from high school I did just that.

In 1967, at the beginning of my graduate program and without the help of current knowledge about remarried families, I delved into my own second marriage, thus entering another form of family living. This included natural father visits, former in-law visits, a new spouse and his very definite ideas about family life, his parents and sister and their attitudes and values, and the recurring problems of my mother who was left disabled from the second round of surgery on her tumor-ridden brain. Also, there were intermittent calls from my younger sister, who lived in the Southwest with her physician husband, their three children, and a merry-go-round of complex problems, most of them psychological in nature.

During those difficult years the wonderful camping trips that my husband, Jim, and I took with the children and our dog and cat provided the palliative thread from my childhood. Often while Jim and the crew were swimming or hiking, I sat in the woods and studied or wrote. My best grades and most creative papers always resulted from my connection with nature. Somehow the fertility of the soil and the protectiveness of the trees were my source of healing life's complexities and producing original thought. Even now as I look out the window of my wooded hideaway, deeply isolated with my German Shepherd and blue-eyed Birman cat beside me, I feel the contact with my past, knowing that where I was is where I am and all that I will write on the pages to follow is as related to my outdoor connection as it is to any of the professional experiences that I will describe.

ROOTS OF MY BECOMING – THE PROFESSIONAL

The pattern of setting a conscious goal only to find it altered by serendipitous disruptions leading somewhere else is the major theme marking my career. During my graduate school years I majored in child development with a concentration on childhood psychopathology; my goal was ultimately to do neonatal research. I believed very strongly that early identification of developmental problems was essential in preventing children from becoming dysfunctional. Despite my interest in the early stages of life, however, my doctoral dissertation focused on cognitive deterioration at the end of life (Coleman, 1973).

My interest in childhood psychopathology was actualized during graduate school by several years of work in the late 1960s and early 1970s as a staff psychologist at a psychiatric hospital for severely disturbed children and adolescents. It was here, among children with Early Infantile Autism and Childhood Schizophrenia, that I first became a family psychologist. It is perhaps rare that one can actually point to that moment in time when a change occurs but my experience was such that I will never forget it.

I had been working as a traditional child therapist. My training was heavily rooted in psychodynamic theory with every stage of Freud's postulations about early development clearly demonstrated in the therapy playroom. How easy it was to see the anal stage documented when a schizophrenic child fashioned feces out of clay. For some time I had been working with Marla, a mute, schizophrenic 12-year-old. We were using the doll house and putting the miniature dolls to sleep. Marla vehemently reacted with guttural, "*No*"s every time I placed the parents in the same bed or even in twin beds. In a rage, Marla would toss the mother doll into another room. My initial thought was that she was particularly angry at her mother, for according to the prevailing concept of the schizophrenagenic mother (Fromm-Reichmann, 1959), this made sense. However, I also had another idea to test.

During the sixties and seventies, child therapy was traditionally considered the domain of the child psychiatrist or child psychologist, while the social worker took charge of the parents. This was the model in which I was trained and few questioned the rationale behind this. Thus, it was not unusual that throughout Marla's hospitalization a social worker was responsible for her parents and older brother. The latter had been diagnosed as an ambulatory schizophrenic, who functioned marginally at best. Neither Marla nor I were included in the biweekly "family" sessions. Repeatedly I begged the social worker to let us come to a session and finally, because his cotherapist was going on maternity leave, he agreed that I could temporarily take her place. He had some skepticism about my bringing Marla, but agreed that on a few occasions it was acceptable.

After two sessions together, the social worker was called to a meeting when Marla's family had already arrived for their scheduled therapy. I was told to see them briefly, explain his absence and reschedule for the following week. This was the opportunity I was seeking and I was not about to lose it. After a few moments of the usual initial greetings, I asked, "How long has it been since you and Mr. T. have slept in the same bedroom?" The response was amazing! Mrs. T. cast a furtive glance at her husband and then asked, "How do you know that?" I said, "Your daughter told me." Quickly, Mr. T. retorted, "But she doesn't speak!" When the social worker returned after this very unusual session he was shocked to learn that although he had treated this family for 2½ years, only the "silent" and absent member knew the degree to which the marriage had deteriorated. (The T's further revealed that they had not had any sexual contact for almost a dozen years, perhaps even since Marla's conception.) This was my first leap toward becoming a family psychologist.

Shortly after Marla taught me about the importance of families, I entered formal family therapy training at Eastern Pennsylvania Psychiatric Institute (EPPI) in Philadelphia. In 1969, this was one of the nation's leading family training centers. The family that became my primary "live" case during the next two years was one whose "IP" was an 11-year-old boy who had regressed to a prenatal stage of development. After almost a year of hospitalization in a major children's hospital and endless testing for rare physical diseases, "Lonny" had become a bedridden, tube-fed patient at the psychiatric hospital where I worked.

In order for me to be the family therapist for this case, the unit director required that I also see Lonny[1] in individual therapy several times a week. As I think about my early clinical training years, both Marla, who was mute, and Lonny, who never uttered a sound for the first three years of therapy, and their families, remain as indelible images teaching me more about human development and how family systems interact than I ever learned anywhere.

My early training derived from von Bertalanffy's (1968) original work on systems theory. Thus, from the beginning, I learned to think about interactions within systems. Along with the systems framework was an emphasis on communication theory, although the psychodynamic gleanings of many of the early family therapists were still evident. I was fortunate, however, to be able to grasp the profound importance of "thinking" systems and, although I never had any super-powerful mentors, I did draw a mass of information from all my training experiences that allowed me to develop my own paradigm in which I integrated all of the years of academic learning about individual psychosocial, psychosexual, and cognitive development with my clinical training in systems theory.

BEING A FAMILY PSYCHOLOGIST

The Research Years

Background

For my doctoral dissertation (Coleman, 1973) I personally designed and conducted individual interviews with 100 women, ages 19 to 94 years of age. The entire dissertation period went quickly and when I passed my oral examination only six months after submitting my original dissertation proposal, I knew that I wanted to include research in my future career.

When my first position as a research associate became extraordinarily unrewarding, I interviewed for what I thought was another research job, this time in a therapeutic community (T.C.) for recovering drug addicts. The year was 1972 and the drug problem was beginning to gain national attention as well as federal funding support. At a follow-up meeting I asked about the program's research interests. I was stunned by the response, "What research?"

Here again was that haunting pattern of my life. What I thought was an interview for a research position turned out to be one for a director. The T.C. wanted to establish a family therapy unit; my background and training suggested that I was the most qualified candidate. Although initially disappointed, an unknown magnetic pull or "chemistry" dictated that I accept this challenge. I was unaware that by doing so I was setting a pace for the next decade of my professional career.

From today's vantage point, it may be difficult to understand how the field of addiction could be so unattractive to professionals. But in the early 1970s the major figures in command of drug and alcohol treatment were recovering folk, themselves. Professionals were suspect and unwanted persona. It was probably almost a year before the paraprofessional staff accidentally learned that I was a "doctor." In the Philadelphia area, M. Duncan ("Duke") Stanton from the Philadelphia Child Guidance Clinic and I were two of the rare professionals who were clinically involved in the drug abuse field. There were a few others in the region who were doing statistical trackings and other nonclinical research, but Duke and I were in the trenches working with and studying the lives of addict families.

As I worked with addict family after addict family, an amazing repetitive pattern became apparent. These families had had a most unusual number of early, unexpected, and sudden deaths, traumatic losses, and family separations. These experiences, which often had occurred many years previously, were right on the surface. All I had to do was lightly tap this area and an enormous flood of unresolved sadness was released. Most interesting was the discovery that the long-deceased member was frequently enshrined by the family as if she or he were a saint to be kept alive and worshipped. It was not unusual to find the deceased's room left untouched, his/her clothes still hanging in the closet as if tomorrow she or he would return and resume life without breaking stride.

Additional evidence for the obsessive involvement with death was derived from the preadolescent groups that I ran for the younger siblings of the recovering addicts. Although these youngsters were also in family therapy, they rarely seemed to get enough attention because so much was focused on their elder brothers and sisters. As a means of implementing a prevention program I saw 18 siblings in weekly group therapy during a two-year period. Here again, the most persistent, recurring theme was that of death (Coleman, 1978, 1979a).

It was clear to me that along with these unresolved losses and separations there was an absence of a belief system or sense of religiosity that allowed healing to take place. This left a void that obviously contributed to the lack of resolution. Further, the fear of death or bodily harm was so great that one commonly found these families living in terror. The anticipation and preoccupation with death seemed to result in an uncanny counterphobic pattern. These families and their chemically dependent children repeatedly immersed themselves in death-defying behaviors, most clearly represented by their slow suicidal flirtation with drugs.

My interest in research was activated when I launched a preliminary study to see if my clinical observations were factually supported. My initial pilot study of 25 addict families (Coleman, 1975) revealed that the patterns of grief I had noticed were unquestionably present. There was also a high incidence of alcoholism among family members as well as repeated separations from the family, particularly during periods of childhood. Often this was found in the addicts' parents' history, underscoring an intergenerational transmission of this peculiar pattern.

Major Research Period

During the next 10 years of my career my efforts went toward writing articles and presenting my clinical discoveries at professional meetings throughout the country. I began to build an intergenerational theory of addiction. Whenever I recall this period of my work I become gripped with a special kind of reverence for the families, because in addition to sharing their turbulent histories, these people were perhaps more appreciative of the interest and time I spent with them than any other group of people I have ever treated. They were especially loyal and committed to therapy, which allowed the research studies that followed to evolve from a very solid, trusting core. They contributed much to my work and to my own personal growth as a family psychologist.

Although I originally came to the drug field hoping to do research, I wound up in a clinical position. As my observations of the addict family became overwhelmingly acute, however, my need to do research took priority. My attempt to conduct serious research at the drug program was blocked by an advisory board and an administration that were not supportive. Thus, my choice was obvious—abandon my research goals or leave. My resignation was a painful decision, as I was incredibly connected to both the staff and the recovering addicts and their families. It was also difficult to separate from the environment where I had gained such vital knowledge. Nor was it easy to leave the physical surroundings of the therapeutic community on an old, wooded estate in Bucks County just a few miles from my home. For four years I had worked in a converted carriage house from which I could see the magnificent tree-filled rolling hills exhibiting the external signs of the changing seasons in almost perfect tandem with the families' struggles for internal change. The influence of nature on my creative thinking was remarkable. I sometimes wonder if my right brain would have functioned as well if I had seen the same families in the city's concrete jungle.

When I left the drug program—except for my private practice, which was always secondary—I felt bewildered and disoriented. I now had no connection with a professional institution. I was comforted, however, by the support that my departure received from some of the other drug program staff who resigned in protest.[2] My supporters wished to impart a message: the lack of interest in significant research was a naive and irresponsible decision and no one with real commitment to the field could comfortably remain employed by a facility with such questionable values.

Despite my sense of loss, I immersed myself in addressing the theoretical issues associated with my earlier pilot study of the addict families (Coleman, 1975). I became preoccupied with this along with trying to increase my private practice income when suddenly my thematic karma presented itself once more. The Center for Family Research at George Washington University Medical School needed a project director to conduct a research project on drug abuse and the family. Don Davis, a family psychiatrist, had been searching for someone to assume the responsibility of developing research to determine what was happening across the country to the families of recovering addicts. Don and I immediately connected and I became responsible for this major national study funded by the National Institute on Drug Abuse (NIDA) (Coleman, 1976; Coleman & Davis, 1978).

This was in the mid-1970s and funds from the National Institute on Drug Abuse (NIDA) were amazingly adequate. Essential to a study like this was a large travel budget and this project had sufficient funding for both travel and my utilization of a very high level national task force.[3] If ever there were days of pomp and circumstance in the world of research—this was such a time.

From the question about the families of drug addicts in treatment emerged a massive study (Coleman, 1976, 1979b; Coleman & Davis, 1978; Coleman & Kaplan, 1978; Coleman & Stanton, 1978) that in its first stage encompassed a national sample of 2,012 drug treatment centers. The second phase of this research consisted of designing and mailing a lengthy questionnaire (Coleman, 1976) to those programs that in some way involved families ($N = 500$). There was also a separate questionnaire (Coleman, 1976) for the therapists who were doing the family treatment. In the final aspect of the study I made site visits to a geographical cross-section of programs representing the most comprehensive family work.

This last phase was the most fascinating. In a five-month period I traveled 26,000 miles and visited treatment centers all across our country. From the small Mormon-dominated, homespun program on the fringes of Salt Lake City, Utah, to a world-renowned program in Minnesota, I learned about attitudes and values regarding the roles families play in the acquisition and rehabilitation processes of drug abuse. I saw probably one of the finest family-oriented programs anywhere in the world in the "backwoods" region of Mandan, North Dakota. Here a Swedish psychiatrist had established a heroin- and alcohol-recovery program ("Heartview") many years previously where families were *required* to move physically into one of the apartments. I also drove 800 miles across the Navajo Nation and talked to Native American family counselors who, in the midst of rural desolation and extreme poverty, were studying about Minuchin and structural family therapy (Coleman, 1979b).

This study was conducted during the most significant period of my career from the standpoint of pure learning. Other than during graduate school, there was never a time when so much information permeated my being. I learned about drug treatment and families but I also learned about our country from a perspective quite unlike that of a tourist. Each site visit included at least one other task force member because I wanted the research data deriving from the structured interviews with the family therapy staff to be as objective as possible. Each member of the task force made a special contribution and I appreciated the unique opportunity to work and travel with them.

This work produced the first systematic study on the role of family therapy in the drug rehabilitation field. The most significant finding was that drug treatment agencies and their staffs were committed enough to make a major contribution to a project solely interested in family therapy with drug abusers. This suggested that working with these families was now a relevant treatment.

The consistent finding that pervaded the results was that there were relationships between the degree of heroin abuse and both the extent to which family therapists were trained and the degree to which an agency actually used family therapy as a major treatment. More specifically, this research demonstrated that low-opiate groups got more family therapy, a more advanced or more adequately trained family therapist, and an agency that fostered family therapy as a central mode of rehabilitating the addict (Coleman & Davis, 1978; Coleman & Stanton, 1978). These data did not imply that those abusing heroin were *less* in need of family therapy, only that those who received it were in programs that were more likely to include families.

At the same time that I was immersed in this research I also began to participate in many national task force efforts for the National Institute on Drug Abuse (NIDA). I served for four years on a NIDA research review committee (Epidemiology and Prevention Subcommittee of the Drug Abuse Epidemiology, Prevention and Services Research Branch). In addition, I continued to expand my own theory about drug addict families and the intergenerational effects of repetitive patterns of loss in their lives (Coleman, 1979b, 1980a, 1980b, 1981b; Coleman & Stanton, 1978). Many of my earlier papers and presentations were beginning to flow into a relatively cogent conceptualization and it was clearly time to move beyond mere clinical speculation.

My first grant application to conduct a retrospective study of death and addiction met with review committee interest but with some skepticism about studying the issues of death. The early and mid-seventies were still nourished by a generation looking for the "highs" of life, and the gloominess of research on death issues was considered perhaps too ethereal for scientific study. It took several years before that attitude changed. My experience in wanting to study death and loss was similar to many other experiences in my life when I would set a goal that was unattainable due to the cultural or educational milieu at the time. My interests often seem to arise prematurely, only to become "popular" after I've turned to something else. This was true for my early interest in neonatal psychology, which just a few years later became a very solid area of study. After my dissertation work with adult women I had attempted to find a way to integrate adult development into academics. At that time there was an occasional, rare general course in adult development, but adult psychology was not a serious track of study. The same was true of my initial attempts to gain support for looking at death and addiction. Fortunately, however, my perseverance produced success and thus I was able to conduct a fascinating research study on life cycle and loss in the addict family (Coleman, 1982, in preparation-b; Coleman, Kaplan, & Downing, 1986).

This research examined the function of heroin addiction as a family-learned method of coping with death, separation, and loss across the life cycle. Heroin addicts, psychiatric outpatients, and normal students were given an extensive interview and test battery to determine the incidence of loss of family members and significant others. Because the impact of death is often overcome through religious rituals, this study also investigated the subjects' perceptions of the families' religious values and orientation to life's meaning and purpose. Results indicated that the incidence of death differed significantly across groups and that addicts had a distinct orientation to death, were more suicidal, and had more premature and bizarre death experiences. During childhood they had more family separations, and they tended to develop a distinct pattern of continuously separating from and returning to their families. They were also less likely to have a clearly defined purpose in life. A subset of parents from each group was also interviewed and tested, and these results supported the theory of the *intergenerational transmission of behavior* (Coleman, 1982; Coleman et al., 1986).

THE EVOLUTION OF A NEW FOCUS OF FAMILY PSYCHOLOGY

My serendipitous pattern of not finding something when I looked for it, but instead having something else unexpectedly occur, continued. Again, this happened as I was in the midst of the loss study. As Director of Research at Achievement through Counseling and Treatment (ACT), an inner-city drug program in Philadelphia, I had remained free of clinical responsibilities. However, the clinic's medical director begged me to see a family as a demonstration model for staff drug counselors who at this time knew very little about family therapy. The family had many complex and rigidified problems and although they did well in many ways, later when I examined the outcome I realized that the case was, in fact, a failure.

For years I had wondered about the remarkable synchronization between families and therapists that was displayed in video sessions at workshops and professional meetings. Often I questioned the seemingly miraculous successes that resulted from seemingly brilliant interventions. I wondered so often, don't family therapists ever fail?

My book, *Failures in Family Therapy* (Coleman, 1985), resulted from this questioning. Although it was initially difficult to launch an effort that would expose our frailties, when Carl Whitaker offered his support by agreeing to write a chapter, others enthusiastically followed. There was no attempt to extend invitations according to formal academic discipline, yet family psychologists were among the major contributors to *Failures in Family Therapy*.[4] I shall always be especially grateful to the contributing authors for their willingness to examine a most difficult and, for some of us, painful clinical experience.

The writing and editing of this book brought to a close the middle years of my career. Although there were many other articles, workshops, presentations, journal board memberships, and national professional involvements that took place during the decade from the mid-1970s to the mid-1980s, my research and "*Failures*" remain the highlights of the period. Along with these special projects were many friendships and colleagueships associated with my work making each effort particularly significant and meaningful both professionally and personally. Thus, it is unquestionably accurate to call this phase my "Enrichment Period."

CURRENT FOCUS

The "Team"

As was my custom, during the final months of completing my last research project and the development of the *Failures* book, my next professional change was already in process. Again, without any direct conscious plan, Family Guidance Center, Inc., was conceived. Private practice was something that I had always done on a part-time basis; I had never wanted a full-time practice. After the research funding cutbacks under Ronald Reagan's administration, however, I became weary of the "approved, not funded" status of my grant proposals. Clearly, the kind of family life-cycle research in which I had been engaged was not high priority. It was also not high priority for me to be a director of an empty department, for, without funding, I could not support a research staff. I had to find something else.

Given my lifelong theme of leadership, I needed to create a structure that I could lead—Family Guidance Center, Inc., was the result. A small private setting would permit me to combine my clinical, research, or writing and training interests. When I discovered an environment in a colonial Williamsburg building on the banks of the Delaware River I knew that here I could blend my professional energy with my love of nature. I was now ready to move toward my next professional stage of life.

The past eight years have been an integration of all that I previously experienced and accomplished. But beyond the maintenance of my old interests, I am now finding room to develop new ideas and shape future trends.

Despite my initial state of mourning for my large research projects and national involvement in the drug field, I have discovered a different kind of excitement. The joy I feel comes from the creative system in which I am working. Here there is an unusual sense of kinship and colleagueship among a small group of professionals committed to a high standard of innovative clinical work. One of our most challenging projects is our reflecting team, which developed more than six years ago when we started doing Milan systemic therapy. Despite our enthusiasm about this approach, after a few years we forced ourselves to assess, redefine, and change the project in order to achieve a more successful outcome (Coleman, 1987, in preparation-a). We are currently engaged in a comprehensive six-year follow-up of the entire sample of families treated by the team.

Each year student interest in our work increases; we now have an increasing number of participating doctoral students as well as an attorney in training and a clinical psychology/law psychologist. Because so few graduate programs or private clinical practices are able to use a reflecting team, our work is a special attraction. I wonder if this development is another of the unplanned events portending a future trend.

Gender Issues

As mentioned, my feminist leanings are deeply rooted in childhood experiences. Thus, it is not unusual that throughout my career I have manifested a special interest in women. Because I was one of the first young single mothers to return to the campus in the 1960s, I consider myself a grass roots pioneer in the feminist movement. I know how terribly frightening it can be to move into a male-dominated academic system with little more than the armor provided by Betty Friedan's *The Feminine Mystique* (1963) under one's arm.[5]

Throughout my career I have encouraged women to fight the oppression of sexism, to believe in themselves, and to overcome obstacles that stand in the way of their growth. My work with women's therapy groups is a consistent part of my clinical practice and repeatedly I share the delight of women who are able to shed their trappings and grab their dreams.

Since its inception in 1981, Family Guidance Center has fostered a series of ongoing women's programs. These groups have been overwhelmingly successful, serving as a significant backdrop for women who have made astounding life changes (for example, one former clerk in a large steno pool is now a licensed stock broker on the New York Exchange; a former homemaker is currently a pediatric resident). It is always particularly rewarding to be part of such a growth process.

Three years ago I developed a group called "Women and Spirituality." The members have all moved beyond traditional therapy and have well-honed skills in problem solving. In this group we talk about the "spiritual" issues that surround a woman's mystique. We work with meditation and Eastern philosophical methods of reaching within ourselves to grasp our goddesses. Again, the Center provides a posttherapy opportunity for women who wish to continue their special journey.

During the 1970s, when I worked almost exclusively in the field of addiction, I led groups for women who were mothers or wives of addicts; often they were chemically dependent themselves. At this time the drug field was not kindly disposed to female alcoholics or addicts and there were no role models like Betty Ford or Elizabeth Taylor and no national advocates for women. My involvement with helping these women change and give up their addictive behaviors for more meaningful self-expression was a step toward helping them develop more adequate roles in their families. On the level of professional psychology, I wrote and spoke at many national conferences about the demeaning position of women addicts and alcoholics (Coleman, 1980c, 1981a).

In the 1980s I have enjoyed participating in the Women's Colloquium, a group of women who held two major meetings at Stonehenge, a charming Connecticut inn. The colloquium, led by Monica McGoldrick, Fromma Walsh, and Carol Anderson, focused on women's contributions to the field of family systems. These meetings offered a relatively small group of invited women to share their work and seminal ideas.

My involvement with women on a national level has led to my recent completion of research on the role of gender in family therapy training institutes (Coleman, 1988; Coleman, Avis-Myers, & Turin, in press). This study derived from the Women's Task Force of the American Family Therapy Association (AFTA). The purpose of the research was to determine what, if any, attention family therapy training programs give to gender issues. More specifically, the study sought to determine if the subject of gender is part of the required student curriculum.

Results of this study are disappointing. It appears that despite all the efforts of the feminist movement and the incisive contributions made by women in the family therapy field (Goldner, 1985) little attention is given to gender by even the most sophisticated and "best" training institutes. Very few programs have any formalized means of teaching trainees about the importance of gender; rarely are there any required or recommended readings on gender. In most situations such issues are included only as they emerge in class discussions or in supervision. The most frequently cited reason for not including the issue of gender in the curriculum is the difficulty of integrating it into the major theoretical models. For me this effort represents the inception of more in-depth work yet to come.

WHITHER THE FUTURE?

As the field of family psychology approaches the end of the century, major questions must focus on both the microcosmic as well as the macrocosmic issues that surround our very existence. No longer do I ponder so much about what intervention works best. Not that I believe that this is irrelevant, but I think that the dilemmas we face in family psychology far exceed what I once considered to be most compelling.

Microcosmic Level

On the level of the microcosm, which for most family psychologists is their exclusive clinical interface, there are significant questions to be answered. Many of them derive from what is most generally unique to psychologists—the research arena. Here, we who have been trained in traditional Ph.D. programs are research specialists with the skills to establish a data base for a field of therapy that is still groping for its scientific roots. Some of the most salient issues the field needs to confront are presented in Wynne's recent publication (1988) on the controversies and recommendations in family therapy research. Perhaps most relevant to my point of view are Reiss's (1988) ideas regarding the need for more adequate theory construction that is free of the conceptual language of specific schools.

I believe that in my research with drug addict families I attempted to accomplish what Reiss suggests. I wanted to develop a theory about people across their life cycles, identifying who was in the system when each baby was born and what biopsychosocial events surrounded each person from birth to death. More specific to my interests were how family members coped during a traumatic event and what particular belief system facilitated their struggle. My intensive structured questionnaire (Coleman, 1982) contributed much toward establishing a solid base of such information. This instrument and its accompanying investigation support a theory of loss and addiction that is gender-free and conceptually adaptable to any school of family therapy.

Another important need in our field is to better identify and understand how change occurs in families. This point is also made by Reiss (1988). At present I doubt that any of us know whether a family changes as a result of therapy or something that happens outside of professional intervention. In my opinion, what we need to discover is how a family promoted change or solved a problem *prior* to the event that led to therapy. If we could determine how a family has changed itself over time, we could learn more about the family's idiosyncratic perceptions and thus create a better "fit" between our interventions and the family's own belief system and adaptive style. I am currently trying to develop a brief instrument to be taken prior to or during the first therapy session to measure how in the past the family has achieved mastery over problems. This instrument could delineate the family's own problem-solving methods and reinforce its sense of competency. By using the family as the "experts" from the beginning of our contact with them, we are saying that we respect their personal resources and do not view them as passive perpetrators or victims of dysfunctional behavior. I have difficulty with our narcissistic views of ourselves and our therapies as major facilitators of change, for in thinking this way we sometimes overlook the family's own assets, thus often rendering them impotent.

In my attempt to do a microanalysis of family therapy failure I concluded my book (Coleman, 1985) with an "epistemology of failure." One of my earlier concerns is still associated with what I call "problems of mind." Just

> how we perceive our work and what we think about our thoughts of a particular family – the metaperceptions of who the family is, what it can or cannot do, what it is and what it might become. . . . How we 'know' the family to be is our initial source of potential success or failure. Thus, our primary error may be one of perception, of mind. (p. 374)

We humans are limited by our vision and our language, by our previous experiences and how we place new ones in former frameworks, i.e., Bateson's (1979) process of "abduction."

As I previously suggested (Coleman, 1985),

> the therapist, in order to facilitate change, needs to adjust a three-way visual lens in order to see epistemological errors from inside the family, inside himself or herself, and the interaction between them. (p. 379)

We do not know what we do not know and our conceptual blindspots often lead us to a treacherous therapeutic precipice. I believe that all too often we are stuck with the limitations of not only Western mind but perhaps even more – universal mind.

Macrocosmic Level

On the macrocosmic level, family psychologists must face more extensive contemporary dilemmas. Our work with families must include much understanding from *within* their personal life spaces. We must also reach into the greater ecostructure that surrounds today's family. The effects of our cultural environment are far more complex than at any previous time. The very concept of family has dramatically changed; so many children are receiving primary care from nannies, day-care programs, and a host of other surrogate parents. The long-term effects of being raised by a single parent or growing up in a joint custody arrangement are as yet undetermined. Certainly family life-styles emerging from an era of fast foods and "latchkey kids" vastly alter our traditional concept of what constitutes "normal" or abnormal family life.

Along with changes within the family, there is an infinite number of environmental hazards. How much human beings will be disrupted by pollution, acid rain, AIDS, and a plethora of cancer-producing agents is unknown. While the potential of a nuclear holocaust frightens some of us, the unknown causes of hundreds of dead seals and dolphins being washed ashore and the pollution of so many of our waterways pose insidious, far-reaching problems to all of us. Just how these environmental conditions will penetrate family life is unpredictable. However, family psychologists must allow their assessment and treatment of families to encompass not only traumas such as incest, drugs, and divorce, but also the dysfunctions unfortunately imposed by a perturbed society.

The Transpersonal Level

One day, about a dozen years ago, while riding my horse alone on a country trail, I felt myself move into a state of serenity that I had not previously experienced. This feeling of oneness with my environment or "cosmic unity" was percipitated by my relationship with an animal. I realize that my most profound moments of psychological and spiritual integration have come through my relationships with nonhuman beings.

My book *Failures* (Coleman, 1985) was written with my German Shepherd at my side. On most days my two Shepherds accompany me on my daily meditative walks through wooded trails and if I arrive at the Center without any canine or feline cotherapists, my families in treatment often threaten to abandon therapy. As one woman retorted recently, "I hope you don't mind, but you know Jeffrey (her husband) comes here as much for the dogs as he does for his therapy!"

My relationship with nonhumans and the academic path that has evolved from our coexistence has taught me about things that we in family psychology don't often learn from our studies. Also, my exploration into Eastern thought has guided me in appreciating that our Western psychological theories and their associated interventions don't always provide enough of the information we seek. For example, Ian Wray, a clinical psychologist and member of the

Western Buddhist Order, acknowledges the psychological parallels between Buddhism and psychotherapy but also underscores their differences (Wray, 1986). According to Wray,

> psychotherapy aims to establish emotional health, with the overcoming of psychological problems and the cure of neurosis, whilst Buddhism aims to go much further than this, with the attainment of emotional health being but the first stage in its path of human development. Psychotherapy is based upon the intellectual traditions of the West, whilst Buddhism claims to be based upon a Wisdom which transcends the intellect. (p. 156)

Wray (1986, p. 165) further suggests that Western schools of psychotherapy, despite their theoretical differences, are generally legitimized by their scientific influences. In contrast, the many varieties of Buddhism are all connected by the concept of *prajna* or "transcendental wisdom," which is not ". . . merely an intellectual quality. . . ." "Prajna is as much Compassion as Wisdom, and requires loving kindness as a prerequisite." In this sense, psychotherapy as practiced in Western family psychology is merely the first stage of spiritual development. If one moves beyond the state achieved via traditional therapy, it is possible to reach a state of "mindfulness," which is gained through the practice of meditation and leads to a higher form of spiritual development.

In my work with families, my dog, Quinto, exhibits a mindfulness that is amazingly spiritual in the true Buddhist sense. Without the clutter of theories to dictate his approach, he moves toward family members with an uncanny perception of who they are and what they need. Recently he entered an initial session of a family presenting with Gina, their suicidal 14-year-old daughter. He circled the family in his usual fashion, then moved swiftly to his toy box and again circled the family, this time with his favorite stuffed animal, "Puppy," dangling from his mouth. After a few seconds he sat in front of the father, silently honoring his power but without permitting him to take "Puppy" from the secure spot held by very firm incisors. Once more Quinto circled the family and this time he paused in front of the suicidal girl. Without hesitation he gently released "Puppy" onto her lap. She was astonished and had difficulty hiding her pleasure in being so special. I reinforced this by telling her how rare it was for him to ever give "Puppy" to anyone. (What I didn't tell her was that Quinto only gives a toy to someone in dire need, otherwise toys are used as mere "joining" techniques and are never given up.) Each week thereafter, Dad was honored first but "Puppy" was placed in Gina's lap. Ultimately, after another suicidal gesture, Gina was hospitalized and I recommended that the family continue their treatment at the hospital also.

Three months later they asked to return to see me in preparation for Gina's imminent homecoming. We had three sessions before their daughter's discharge. In each of the three sessions Quinto repeated his former pattern by honoring the father first. It was a complete surprise to all when he purposely dropped "Puppy" in the lap of Gina's younger brother who I had suggested some months before would become the next "problem" if the family didn't make some necessary changes. But perhaps the most fascinating behavior occurred when Gina returned. Within seconds of her arrival, Quinto, with "Puppy" in tow, ran past her brother and placed the tattered toy in her lap. I think her mouth is still agape!

Although many might question the limits of a dog's ability to "know" in the sense of "languaging" (Maturana, 1988), my observations tell me that Quinto intuits the interior of the family and in his canine mindfulness transcends the barriers of Western psychology demonstrating over and over that

> The more you talk and think about it,
> The further astray you wander from the truth.
> Stop talking and thinking
> And there is nothing that you will not be able to know.
>
> UNKNOWN AUTHOR (p. 163)

At one time, any metaphysical reference was viewed as bordering on witchcraft. We now may be approaching an age, however, when the revolutionary views of quantum physics validate the scientific significance of studying the nature of existence. Surely the notions that all natural phenomena are creations of mind and do not necessarily represent reality stands in marked contrast to the mechanistic Newtonian model. Sheldrake's (1981) concept of "morphogenetic fields" forming as a result of influences of past organisms, which then further influence *behavior* of the same species due to connections across time and space has particular relevance to intergenerational family work. Sheldrake goes further, however, and applies this concept to nonliving things, such as crystals. Scientists like Capra (1975) and Wilbur (1977, 1982) see profound connections between modern physics and the study of consciousness. This revolutionary way of thinking is reflected in Grof's (1975, 1985; Grof & Grof, 1980) work, and has influenced his definition of the transpersonal level of experience in which consciousness is extended ". . . beyond the usual ego boundaries and beyond the limitations of time and space" (Grof, 1985, p. 155).

To further discuss these exciting yet complex insights of the new paradigm emerging from physical, behavioral, and transcendental religious sciences goes beyond the present task. But as family psychologists probe the works of Maturana (1978; Maturana & Varela, 1987) and others in the newest camp called "constructivism," they might also venture into the writings of thinkers such as Capra, Sheldrake, Wilbur, and Grof, for it well may be that the new discoveries from the highly respected physical sciences will guide us toward a greater expansiveness in understanding families and the processes through which we, the family psychologists, help them heal.

EPILOGUE

My contributions to the field are difficult to assess personally. At times it seems that much of what I have accomplished is disconnected and perhaps too serendipitous. However, I ultimately trust my inner guiding mechanism, for my overall range of interests and contributions are indeed connected by a fine but very strongly interwoven thread. When therapy does not succeed, when families cannot overcome their addictions, when gender issues are overlooked, I always want to know, "What was missing?" Thus, I suppose one might view my efforts as a search for what is missing, and in this sense I believe that what I have found is not as significant as the process of exploration I have undertaken.

Alan Watts (1975) was interested in the "Way of Wisdom" and believed that man became caught in his own trap by trying to gain control over nature. Bateson (1979), too, saw the "myth of power." According to Buddhism, true understanding only derives from emptiness. When we as family psychologists can open our minds to the family's own void as well as to the emptiness of our own cleverly constructed interventions, we may then be able to grasp the intimate meaning of the family's struggle.

Even in this advanced age of family therapy, we do not see it all, and what we miss may well be the "difference that makes the difference." We still have too many blind spots and too much partisanism in our field. To see more we have to be wary of too much conceptual thinking; it is said by Zen masters that when one is talking about moving one has not yet begun to move.

> If you take pride in your attainment or become discouraged because of your idealistic effort, your practice will confine you by a thick wall.
>
> A ZEN PARABLE

NOTES

1. Lonny, as a consequence of nine years of intensive family and individual therapy, ultimately "regained" his life. After more than three years at the hospital, although still mute he returned home to his family. He was gradually weaned from homebound education to public school and graduated from a major university with a high cumulative average. Currently he is living independently, earns a high salary, and holds a responsible position in a scientific field for a large international corporation. A more adequate description of the intensive therapy involving Lonny and his family goes far beyond the present chapter. I hope to soon complete the termination project that Lonny and I began to write together (Coleman, in preparation-c).

2. Two of those who resigned were colleagues and program directors who had been there longer than I. John McBrearty was a full professor at Temple University and was responsible for all the statistics that the T.C. needed to compile annually to secure federal and local funding; without John the program could be in a serious economic position. John was a sounding board for my research and was always there to listen and contribute to my ideas. John, too, gave up a great deal, for the contacts with staff and the recovering addicts were a rewarding contrast to his academic pursuits. My other long-term friend and colleague, Larry Huntzberry, was the director of the residential program. He was perhaps the most significant clinical person on staff, with the ability to relate to the needs of the addict inpatient along with his/her traumatized family. At that time Larry had not yet completed his doctoral work, had a wife and young son, and was really in no position to give up his job. His resignation left him in a precarious financial position with only his private practice for support.

3. My task force included several family psychologists, such as Jim Alexander (see Chapter 10), Jack Friedman, Terry Levy, Alexa Panio, M. Duncan Stanton (see Chapter 19), and David Wellisch.

4. It is interesting to note that more psychologists than any other group agreed to struggle with the task proposed by the book. The psychologist authors were Margaret Baggett, Sandra Coleman, Paul Dell, Ilda Fischer, Robert Jay Green, Alan Gurman, Neil Jacobson, Florence Kaslow, Luciano L'Abate, Howard Liddle, and Paul Watzlawick.

5. Despite my many years of success, it is hard to forget that in 1966, as an undergraduate senior, I was told by an adviser that I shouldn't worry about grades or graduate school because after all ". . . you are a single parent and a mother. When you graduate you will have enough education to teach school so why worry about continuing . . . ?" I recall thanking this professor kindly and then dashing home to hasten the completion of my applications to graduate school.

REFERENCES

Bateson, G. (1979). *Mind and nature: A necessary unity.* New York: Dalton.

Capra, F. (1975). *The tao of physics.* Berkeley: Shambhala.

Coleman, S. B. (1973). *The effect of aging on Piaget's developmental stages: A study of cognitive decline.* Doctoral dissertation. Temple University, Philadelphia.

Coleman, S. B. (1975). *Death as a social agent in addict families.* Paper presented at the 83rd Annual Convention of the American Psychological Association, Chicago, IL.

Coleman, S. B. (1976, December). *Final Report: A national study of family therapy in the field of drug abuse.* Prepared for the Behavioral and Social Science Branch; National Institute on Drug Abuse. Grant No. 3H81-DA-01478-0151.

Coleman, S. B. (1978). Sib group therapy: A prevention program for siblings from drug-addicted families. *The International Journal of Addictions, 13*(1), 115-127.

Coleman, S. B. (1979a). Siblings in session. In E. Kaufman & P. N. Kaufman (Eds.), *Family therapy of drug and alcohol abuse* (pp. 131-143). New York: Gardner Press.

Coleman, S. B. (1979b). Cross cultural approaches in treating drug addict families. *Journal of Drug Education, 9*(4), 293-299.

Coleman, S. B. (1980a). Incomplete mourning and addict family transactions: A theory for understanding heroin abuse. In D. Lettieri (Ed.), *Theories on drug abuse* (pp. 83-89, 315-318). Publication of the Division of Research, Social Science Branch, National Institute on Drug Abuse.

Coleman, S. B. (1980b). The family trajectory: A circular journey to drug abuse. In B. G. Ellis (Ed.), *Drug abuse from the family perspective* (pp. 18-31). Washington, DC: U.S. Department of Health and Human Services, Public Health Services, Alcohol, Drug Abuse, and Mental Health Administration, National Institute on Drug Abuse.

Coleman, S. B. (1980c). Women and addiction: Theoretical problems and clinical solutions. In National Drug Abuse Center's (Ed.), *Handbook of family therapy training* (pp. 1-17).

Coleman, S. B. (1981a). An endangered species: The female as addict or member of an addict family. *Journal of Marital and Family Therapy, 7*(2), 171-180.

Coleman, S. B. (1981b). Incomplete mourning in substance abusing families: Theory, research and practice. In L. Wolberg & M. Aronson (Eds.), *Group and family therapy—An overview* (pp. 269-283). New York: Brunner/Mazel.

Coleman, S. B. (1982, April). *Final report: Heroin—A family coping strategy for death and loss.* Prepared for the Psychological Services Branch, Division of Research, National Institute on Drug Abuse. U.S. Department of Health and Human Services.

Coleman, S. B. (1985). *Failures in family therapy.* New York: Guilford.

Coleman, S. B. (1987, September). Milan in Bucks County. *Networker.* pp. 43-47.

Coleman, S. B. (1988). *The role of gender in family therapy training.* Report submitted to American Family Therapy Association.

Coleman, S. B. (in preparation-a). *A view of Milan from the other side of the mirror.* Manuscript in preparation.

Coleman, S. B. (in preparation-b). *From pins to needles: Parent's handbook on preventing drug abuse.* Manuscript in preparation.

Coleman, S. B. (in preparation-c). *Whisper me my life.* Manuscript in preparation.

Coleman, S. B., Avis-Myers, & Turin, M. (in press). *Whither goest gender: A study of the role of gender in family therapy training institutes.* Manuscript submitted for publication.

Coleman, S. B., & Davis, D. I. (1978). Family therapy and drug abuse: A national survey. *Family Process, 17*(1), 21-29.

Coleman, S. B., & Kaplan. J. D. (1978). A profile of family therapists in the drug abuse field. *American Journal of Drug and Alcohol Abuse, 5*(4), 171-178.

Coleman, S. B., Kaplan, J. D., & Downing, R. W. (1982). *Coleman family background questionnaire.* Copyright Registration Number TXu 258-477.

Coleman, S. B., Kaplan, J. D., & Downing, R. W. (1986). Life cycle and loss—The spiritual vacuum of heroin addiction. *Family Process, 25*(1), 5-23.

Coleman, S. B., & Stanton, M. D. (1978). An index for measuring agency involvement in family therapy. *Family Process, 17*(3), 479-483.

Friedan, B. (1963). *The feminine mystique.* New York: Dell.

Fromm-Reichmann, F. (1959). Notes on the mother's role in the family group. In D. M. Bullard & E. V. Weigart (Eds.), *Psychoanalysis and psychotherapy: Selected papers of Frieda Fromm-Reichmann.* Chicago: University of Chicago Press.

Goldner, V. (1985). Feminism and family therapy. *Family Process, 24*(1), 31-47.

Grof, S. (1975). *Realms of the human unconscious: Observations from LSD research.* New York: Viking Press.

Grof, S. (1985). *Beyond the brain.* New York: State University of New York Press.

Grof, S., & Grof, C. (1980). *Beyond death.* London: Thames & Hudson.

Maturana, H. R. (1978). Biology of language: The epistemiology of reality. In G. A. Miller & E. Lenneberg (Eds.), *Psychology and biology of language and thought.* New York: Academic Press.

Maturana, H. R. (1988). Private communication at conference at Horsham Clinic, Philadelphia, PA.

Maturana, H. R., & Varela, F. J. (1987). *The tree of knowledge: The biological roots of understanding.* Boston: New Science Library.

Reiss, D. (1988). Theoretical versus tactical inferences: On how to do family psychotherapy research without dying of boredom. In L. Wynne (Ed.), *The state of the art in family therapy research: Controversies and recommendations* (pp. 34-45). New York: Family Process Press.

Sheldrake, R. (1981). *A new science of life: The hypothesis of formative causation.* Los Angeles: J. P. Tarcher.

Stanton, M. D., & Coleman, S. B. (1980). The participatory aspects of indirect self-destructive behavior: The addict family as a model. In N. Farberow (Ed.), *The many faces of suicide: Indirect self-destructive behavior* (pp. 187-203). New York: McGraw-Hill.

Unknown Author. (1988). *Mountain record of Zen talks.* Boston: Shambhala.

von Bertalanffy, L. (1968). *General systems theory.* New York: George Braziller.

Watts, A. (1975). *Tao: The watercourse way.* New York: Pantheon.

Wilbur, K. (1977). *The spectrum of consciousness.* Wheaton, IL: Theosophical Publishing House.

Wilbur, K. (1982). *The holographic paradigm and other paradoxes: Exploring the leading edge of science.* Boulder, CO: Shambhala.

Wray, I. (1986). Buddhism and psychotherapy: A Buddhist perspective. In S. Claxton (Ed.), *Beyond Therapy* (pp. 155-172). London: Wisdom.

Wynne, L. (1988). *The state of the art in family therapy research: Controversies and recommendations.* New York: Family Process Press.

12

Integrating the Life of an Integrative Family Psychologist

ALAN S. GURMAN

BECOMING A FAMILY PSYCHOLOGIST

A Boston Boy

I really never have taken enough time to read nonprofessional books. So I am indebted to a patient of mine who, about a year ago, encouraged me to read *Boston Boy,* a memoir of the great political analyst and jazz critic, Nat Hentoff. Nothing I've read in 20 years has helped me feel as connected to my past. Not because of my interest in jazz, which is nil, but because of Hentoff's loving description of both the joy and the pain of a Jewish Bostonian's boyhood and adolescence. Hentoff's Jewish Boston was the Roxbury section of the city in the 1930s and 1940s, while mine was the Dorchester-Mattapan area of the 1950s and 1960s. My only sib was 7½ years my senior, so we chummed around together very little, and I had such persistent anxiety about facing parental (read: paternal) criticism that I stayed away from home as much as possible. My peers became my world long before adolescence. It was an interesting lot: When we formed a social and athletic club at the local YMHA in junior high, we bypassed all the usual club names ("Sabres," "Knights," and so on) and chose one more befitting our desire to present ourselves to the world as different from other 12-year-old boys and, especially, smarter. We called ourselves the "Aardvarks" (we were convinced that fewer than 5% of adolescents knew what an aardvark was). My friends were very achievement-oriented and very competitive (in athletics, in grades, in out-punning each other, and in our use of sarcastic humor). I don't know if my friends had any influence on my becoming a psychologist, but they certainly had an enormous influence on my entering some kind of profession.

My other common bond with Hentoff was that we both attended Boston Latin School (also attended by virtually all my close friends), the oldest (dating from 1635) high school (and junior high) in the United States. I doubt that six years of translating Cicero, Homer, et al. had any influence on my becoming either a psychologist or a family therapist, but going to "BLS" probably did. If appreciating differences is a requirement of being a good family therapist, then my first "practicum" was life at BLS. My neighborhood was populated almost entirely by Jewish and Irish families, whereas at BLS (which was what is nowadays called a "magnet" school, drawing students from every corner of the city), my classmates were also Italian, Greek, Black, WASP, Chinese, Hungarian, French Canadian, Polish, and Hispanic. I think this six-year implosion of ethnic, racial, and religious diversity contributed to my becoming an integratively oriented therapist (Budman & Gurman, 1988; Gurman, 1981) who has a hard time believing that there are "right" ways of being or doing almost anything.

At Latin School, you either succeeded, or you left (admission was competitive and everyone went on to college). At each year's first assembly of seventh graders, our principal would say, "Look to the left of you, look to the right. Six years from now, two thirds of you won't be here!" He wasn't kidding . . . I was almost counted among the two thirds.

I usually got rather high grades in social studies, English, and foreign languages, but mathematics and the sciences were nearly the academic death of me. Having been urged by my father (a very successful mechanical engineer) to enroll in the "advanced science" program, starting in seventh grade, I "chose" my adolescent acting-out symptom in a most familial way: Because I found it very difficult to please my father, I proceeded to flunk almost every course related to his field. Not very subtle, I admit. In the years between 1957 and 1963 there was no family therapy, so my symptoms continued unabated, going into remission just in the nick of time (my senior year).

My father, who was more competent at more things than any one person has a right to be, made it clear to me, my brother, and my mother that there was always another way to look at things, i.e., his way. I'm certain that I've introjected and "reframed" his rather critical stance as a rationale for keeping myself open to many points of view (e.g., about psychotherapy). My intrapsychic compromise with my scientist father became to earn a reputation in the family field as a research-oriented psychologist, but, stubborn all the way, to do it *my* way: by writing a great deal, rather than by producing a lot of original research. I had been the sports coeditor of my high school magazine, and writing had always come naturally to me (as well as to my brother, for many years a high school English teacher, and now an ecological science (!) writer). Writing also allowed me to express myself without being interrupted, not something I could do often in my family. The other wonderful thing about writing, I discovered, was that even if people hated what you published, only *you* could criticize yourself *while* you wrote!

Psychology: An Arranged Marriage That Has Lasted

Perhaps my choice of psychology as a profession wasn't "arranged," but it certainly was overdetermined. As a college freshman at Boston University, enrolled in the College of Liberal Arts, I had to declare a tentative major field, if only so that the college could assign me to an academic adviser. As one might predict, I immediately crossed off all scientific departments, soon followed by fields I knew nothing about (e.g., economics), and I was left with a short list: psychology, sociology, or anthropology. The latter two sounded intriguing, but I, like most 18-year-olds, was unfamiliar with them, so they, too, got "X"d out. In truth, I had wanted to be an English major, to become a creative writer, but at that time I had no idea of wanting to teach at the college level, and was much too practical a person who thought that "making it" as a writer was about as likely as making it as a folk singer (my ego-ideal). When I had narrowed my list of possible majors to just a few, I suddenly recalled that as a high school sophomore I had read my brother's copy of *A Primer of Freudian Psychology* (Hall, 1954) and enjoyed it. Voila! A psychologist I was to be! Of course, my immediate conscious awareness of the basis for choosing my major was mostly a rationalization. I became a psychologist to understand myself better (so I could feel I was more in charge of my life), and I became a family psychologist to understand my family (not to "save them," as the usual line goes).

Fortunately, I actually enjoyed my college courses in psychology and other social sciences, though I continued to fill my elective time with courses in modern literature. As my senior year approached, my psychology adviser told me I'd never gain admission to any of the graduate schools that interested me, and counseled me to apply to a very low-grade alternative. In my usual rebelliously persistent, stubborn way, I set out to prove him wrong, was admitted to Columbia University in 1967, and earned my Ph.D. in less than four years.

At first, graduate school was not very exciting for me, but as the courses became more clinical, my enthusiasm exploded. I went to Columbia (Teachers College; TC) because it was by far the most prestigious program that accepted me; I knew little about the program. Unlike most programs in the New York metropolitan area, which were heavily, oppressively psychoanalytic, TC's was fervently eclectic, with an almost universally first-rate faculty. Behavior therapists, Sullivanians, "Tavi" (Tavistock) groupers, community psychologists, pro-projective testers, and anti-projective testers—they were all there.

My wife, Gerri, was also there, starting in my second year. Having met in my sophomore year of college, we were married after she graduated. I recall one day during my senior year worrying about whether I would get into graduate school. "Of course you will—you're going to be famous someday," she reassured me. Always self-critical, I thought that surely she must have poor judgment. But her support and encouragement were what sustained me through graduate school.

The atmosphere in the program was one of mutual respect for differences, and encouragement of students to think seriously about a wide range of possibilities—a perfect personality match for me. The frosting on my graduate school cake was the privilege of working with Allen Bergin, one of the premier psychotherapy researchers in the world, for my dissertation. He not only fostered my autonomy and showed respect for my ideas at every turn, but also went to bat for me in my efforts to carry out a relatively unorthodox dissertation research study, the theoretically and clinically most interesting parts of which involved the intensive study of single cases of psychotherapy (Gurman, 1973a, 1973b).

In graduate school, behavior therapy especially appealed to me (though my dissertation focused on the then "in" area of therapists' "relationship skills,"—empathy, warmth, and genuineness), no doubt because of my respect for the person who taught in that area, Allen Bergin (before he became my dissertation adviser). While psychotherapy research definitely had become the core of my professional identity, other rewarding experiences came my way as well. My first clinical experience was in a specially arranged field practicum in a suburban New Jersey high school, leading a therapy group of male underachievers. Did I ever know something about *that*! My urge to write was unstoppable, so, on my own and for no course credit, I wrote and published one of my first journal articles, interestingly (given where my career was to lead) titled, "The Role of the Family in Underachievement" (Gurman, 1970)! I had never met the families of any of the student patients in my group, but I thought I understood what the families of underachievers were about, anyway. What chutzpah!

My predoctoral internship was the equivalent in hours of a two-year internship, at various Veterans Administration Hospitals in New York (Westchester County, Long Island, and Brooklyn) and in Connecticut; these included an outpatient clinic, a general medical and surgical hospital, and two inpatient psychiatric facilities. I also learned a fair amount about behavior therapy and individual psychodynamic therapy in the VA system, and had some very talented supervisors. I also learned that the largest health care delivery system in the world basically acted as though families didn't exist.

My only attempt at marital therapy in the VA system was with a couple in which the wife was terrified of her husband's anger and violent outbursts (she herself was a "service-connected" veteran, as was her husband, otherwise I probably would never have been allowed to meet with her without her husband being present). Her husband was a New York City fireman whose career had come to an abrupt halt as the result of a back injury suffered on duty. For this, he hated the world, and his wife was no exception. When really worked up, she told me, he would do such intimidating things as ripping kitchen cabinets off the wall. In the second session I discovered that her husband was 6′4″ tall and tipped the scales at about 225: solid muscle. Though basically I was still a behavior therapist, naively out to change the world, I intuitively retreated to a more reflective, "Rogerian" style with this man. That session was my "clinical experience" in family therapy until I moved to the Department of Psychiatry at the University of Wisconsin Medical School in Madison in 1971 for a postdoctoral clinical psychology fellowship. (At Columbia, I did take the one course offered on marriage counseling. At that time, marriage counseling certainly was, as Manus [1966] described it, "a technique in search of a theory.")

In Madison, I became a family therapist. No, not because Carl Whitaker was there, although I was in his seminars for two years. Carl and I didn't exactly operate the same way, and I was probably one of the few trainees in the Department who never did cotherapy with him.[1]

I "discovered" family therapy through my interest in psychotherapy research. In 1972, in the Department Library, I came across *Family Process* for the first time. I noticed an article, "The Results of Family Therapy" (Wells, Dilkes, & Trivelli, 1972), which I read with great interest, as I had never before seen or heard of any outcome research having to do with family therapy. As I read Wells et al., I immediately recognized that there were quite a few family therapy outcome studies which they had not included in their review. (In graduate school, I had written a paper on group marital therapy that was later published [Gurman, 1971].) At first, I decided to write a "commentary" on the Wells et al. paper, filling in the gaps in their literature review. But my "commentary" soon expanded into what became the first comprehensive review of outcome research in marital therapy (Gurman, 1973a). Though I had now written reasonably eloquently about marital therapy *research,* I had almost no idea of what marital (or family) *therapy* was all about. I set out to see what these folks were doing and read very widely from whatever sources I could lay my hands on. Along the way, I simply started to *do* family therapy, learning it the hard way, by self-instruction. I couldn't have had a better, or worse, supervisor.[2]

Following Variously Colored Brick Roads

As I noted earlier, I, like most psychologists, was trained first in general psychology, then clinical psychology, before becoming a "family psychologist." If others entered the field through the back door, e.g., forming peer study or supervision groups, then I entered through the basement of treatment research. Beyond writing a couple of articles on marriage and the family as a graduate student, my first genuine venture into the field was the writing of my article, "The Effects and Effectiveness of Marital Therapy" (Gurman, 1973a). This publication was to be the start of a writing career leading to a reputation, as Jacobson and Weiss (1978) referred to me, as one of the "chroniclers of and gatekeepers" for the field, or as Taggart (1978) dubbed me, the "curator and connoisseur of the relationship between family therapy and psychotherapy research" (p. 109).

During the first few years after graduate school, my clinical theoretical orientation was still clearly behavioral-social learning, and my marital therapy work followed suit. But, as I thought about my behavioral work with couples, in terms of my effectiveness and the kinds of assumptions about people, relationships, and change, I questioned more and more. (Also, my wife Gerri's caring assaults on my obsessive-compulsiveness led me to be more open in my thinking about therapy.) Not that I dismissed behavioral strategies and techniques, which are dominant in my clinical work to this day. My questioning about the *meanings* of, and implicit messages and values behind, what I was doing as a behavioral therapist led to a presentation of a critique of behavioral marital therapy (BMT) at the annual meeting of the Association for the Advancement of Behavior Therapy in 1975. I became a member of the loyal opposition. That paper, revised with Roger Knudson (Gurman & Knudson, 1978), then a psychology trainee in our department, became the first of a four-part exchange (some called it a polemic quartet) in *Family Process* on BMT.[3]

My having written about marital therapy treatment research and having published one of the first textbooks on marital therapy (Gurman & Rice, 1975) probably were factors in my being invited to be the main critic and discussant at what was to become an historical professional conference on marital therapy. In 1977, Tom Paolino and Barbara McCrady of the Butler Hospital/Brown University Medical School organized a most exciting conference in which proponents of the major "schools" of marital therapy (e.g., psychoanalytic – Carol Nadelson; behavioral – Bob Weiss; strategic – Carlos Sluzki; general systems – Peter Steinglass) presented their theories and clinical methods. My task, guaranteed to endear me to each of my presenter colleagues, was to offer a critique of *all* their points of view! Despite my trepidation, my presentation was well received, and the book that the conference organizers put together from the meeting (Paolino & McCrady, 1978) had a major impact on the field.

The major impact on *me* from writing that chapter was that in doing it, I had done an extraordinary amount of reading and learned a great deal. This equipped me to begin to develop some of my own ideas about an integrative model of marital therapy (Gurman, 1981, 1985). It also emboldened me to begin to take on the most daring project of my professional life to that time. With Dave Kniskern, who had been a predoctoral psychology trainee in the Wisconsin Psychiatry Department a couple of years earlier, but whom I thought of as a peer early on, I would try to put together the best family therapy textbook available. This was a most risky and challenging venture. While Dave and I had some standing in the field by 1979, probably we were rather naively bold to believe that truly major figures in the field would be willing to write chapters for the book we were proposing. Our naivete was fortunate, because the result was the *Handbook of Family Therapy* (Gurman & Kniskern, 1981a). It wasn't our "names" that persuaded those colleagues to join us in that project, but rather, the need in the field for what we were attempting. We got into some risky business in the *Handbook* by writing quite extensive "Editors' Notes" on each of the chapters. In those notes, we not only made comparative observations and comments, but, at times rather forthrightly expressed disagreement with the view of an author, identified widely cherished beliefs about therapy that had little or no empirical basis, and so on. Most readers (especially students) loved our "Editors' Notes." A few of our authors did not; yet in every case our "Notes" led to useful and enjoyable correspondence and conversations. The *Handbook* is still one of my most cherished professional accomplishments, and Dave Kniskern and I are preparing its second edition.

Then, in 1980, Florence Kaslow was nearing the end of her tenure as the second Editor of the *Journal of Marital and Family Therapy*. I decided to apply for the Editor-electship. Only now, as I near the end of my second and final term as Editor of *JMFT,* do I begin to appreciate fully the enormous honor and responsibility I have carried for eight years. A family therapy colleague recently described the editorship of *JMFT* as "the single most influential position in the field" (along with the editorship of *Family Process,* I assume he meant). I am generally not an actively (consciously?) political person, so I'm sure I have denied some important "political" aspects of decisions I have made and actions I have taken as the *JMFT* Editor. Still, I am quite conscious of having worked diligently to establish the *Journal* as a true "omnibus" journal, owing its intellectual and clinical allegiances to an orientation of open-mindedness, multipartiality, and quality.

It is fascinating to me how often people in this field (and every other one, and everywhere else in life) project their fears onto each other. One (obviously "political") definite aim I had in editing the *Journal* was to make clinically relevant research more prominent than it had been in any of the (two dozen or so) family therapy journals, but to do so while maintaining a clear balance among research, training, clinical, and theoretical contributions. Even though I annually documented, in my "Editor's Report," the rate of acceptance of articles of each type, and research articles never dominated the picture numerically (nor exceeded the proportion in other major family therapy journals), a few colleagues in the field disparagingly decried the "fact" that the *Journal* had become a "research journal." It has been a disappointment to me that some mental health professionals have gotten so anxious about research and the challenge of empirical accountability that they have distorted reality in this situation. It is also quite ironic that I am viewed by some as some kind of unreal-world researcher, as I haven't actually conducted any research in several years, spend about two days a week doing psychotherapy, and devote most of my university time to seminar teaching and clinical supervision. With thanks to Twain, "Reports of my research activities have been greatly exaggerated!"

CONSOLIDATING AN IDENTITY AS A FAMILY PSYCHOLOGIST

Such exaggerated reports, however, have not exactly been fabricated. Certainly, my earliest contributions to the fields of family therapy and family psychology were in the realm of research, and I published the first comprehensive review of outcome research on marital therapy (Gurman, 1973a) and the first comprehensive, integrative review of marital and family therapy (Gurman & Kniskern, 1978a, 1978b, 1981b). There were, and still are, several dominant matters that interested and concerned me, dating back to graduate school days: (1) how effective are the major "schools" of marital and family therapy compared to no treatment?; (2) in general, are some "schools" more effective than others?; (3) are some "schools" more effective than others for specific types of problems?; (4) do patients/families ever worsen as a result of marital/family therapy, and, if so, what predicts such deterioration?; and, (5) what are the universal, or common, factors in effective marital/family therapy?

In all of this, my overriding aim has been to try to bridge the usual gaps between research and practice, between researchers and clinicians. Thus, I have written extensively on both what implications from research may be derived for clinical practice (e.g., Gurman & Kniskern, 1978a, 1978b, 1978c, 1981b) and ways in which clinically relevant thinking needs to be brought to bear on research endeavors (e.g., Gurman, 1971; Gurman, Kniskern, & Pinsof, 1986; Gurman & Knudson, 1978). Here, I will summarize the major findings of these several analyses of family therapy outcome research. The interested reader is referred, inter alia, especially to Gurman and Kniskern (1978a, 1978b, 1981b) and Gurman et al. (1986) for documentation and elaboration of these working conclusions about the current state of empirical research findings in the field.

1. Nonbehavioral marital and family therapies produce beneficial outcomes in about two-thirds of cases, and their effects are superior to no treatment.
2. When both spouses are conjointly involved in therapy in the face of marital problems, there is a greater chance of positive outcome than when only one spouse is treated.
3. The developmental level of the identified patient (e.g., child/adolescent/adult) shows no reliable effect on treatment outcomes.
4. Positive results of both nonbehavioral and behavioral marital and family therapies typically occur in treatment of short duration, that is, up to 20 sessions.
5. Marital and family therapies at times may be associated with both individual (identified patient) and relationship deterioration.
6. A therapist "style" of providing little structuring of early treatment sessions and confrontation of highly affective material may be reliably associated with observed deterioration effects and is clearly more deterioration-promoting than a style of stimulating interaction and giving support.
7. Family therapy is probably as effective as and possibly more effective than many commonly offered (usually individual) treatments for problems directly attributable to family conflict.
8. There is no empirical support for superiority of cotherapy compared with marital or family therapy conducted by a single therapist.
9. A reasonable mastery of technical skills may be sufficient for preventing worsening or for maintaining pretreatment family functioning, but more refined therapist relationship skills seem necessary to yield genuinely positive outcomes.
10. Certain family variables (for example, identified patient diagnosis, quality of family interaction, and family constellation) exert unreliable effects on clinical outcomes.

Dave Kniskern, Bill Pinsof, and I have also examined the research evidence on the efficacy of the various marital and family therapy methods for well-defined clinical problems and disorders, and have suggested the following tentative conclusions:

1. Of the 15 major family and marital therapy approaches, 6 have shown at least moderately positive evidence of efficacy with at least one clinical disorder or problem.
2. With the arguable exception of Psychodynamic Therapy, all the methods with at least moderately positive evidence of efficacy for some problems are highly directive in nature.
3. There are four disorders (schizophrenia, substance abuse, juvenile delinquency, and marital discord) for which we now have at least moderately positive evidence of the efficacy of more than one method of family treatments.
4. There are seven disorders for which at least moderately positive evidence exists that at least one method is effective.
5. Outcome research of any sort has been conducted on fewer than one quarter of the possible combinations of family therapy methods and clinical problems/diagnoses.
6. Evidence of at least probable effectiveness has been demonstrated for only about 10% of these combinations.
7. Unfortunately, the size of treatment effects of specific marital and family therapies, or of these therapies as a whole, has not yet been systematically and comprehensively evaluated.

To summarize: When family therapy treatment methods have been tested rigorously, significantly positive and, at times, extremely impressive, outcomes have been documented.

Creating a Flexible Clinical Map

Consonant with my conviction that there are "truths" in every method of clinical practice, as well as "universals" that are common to effective psychotherapy of every kind, I have worked over the last decade to derive a flexible clinical map for psychotherapy, one that incorporates our profession's various understandings of what motivates human behavior and how human behavior is most effectively and efficiently changed. In doing so, I have attempted to resolve apparent incompatibilities among the theoretical propositions of several dominant "pure" theories of therapy, to show that these can, in fact, exist, not only in harmony, but also in synergy. Moreover, I have worked to demonstrate that many well-accepted and widely used techniques and strategies in therapy make perfectly good conceptual and clinical sense within theoretical frameworks far afield of the traditions within which they were born.

My writings on such an approach to integrative psychotherapy have, thus far, focused on marital therapy (e.g., Gurman, 1985) and individual therapy (Budman & Gurman, 1988). Here, I will summarize the core of my thinking about Integrative Marital Therapy (IMT) (Gurman, 1978, 1980, 1981, 1982, 1985).

IMT is committed to three major premises. First, it is argued that any effective psychotherapy requires a broad basis for adequately describing and explaining human behavior. Second, in IMT it is held that a focus on either intrapersonal factors alone *or* interpersonal factors alone is not only arbitrary, but also represents a distortion of social psychological reality. Finally, it is believed within IMT that truly "systemic" thinking in clinical practice requires the therapist to consider not only cognitive, affective, and behavioral aspects of human experience, but biochemical and cultural/social as well.

At a practical level, IMT also assumes that effective psychotherapeutic intervention at one apparent level of the organization of human experience inevitably effects change at other levels. Thus, there is no inherent tension in utilizing discernibly different therapeutic methods for different types of clinical problems, though most clinical practice in IMT does not rest on the application of "pure" singular treatment methods (e.g., the intervention emphasis in a case could be "structural," but incorporate specific "behavioral" instruction, interpretation of family members' motivations, and so on).

IMT does not, however, randomly mix and match. Rather, it borrows systematically from those clinical schools of thought that seem to me to have particularly powerful explanatory power in regard to different levels of intimate relating, and which provide a basis for generating concrete, reliable, and teachable clinical interventions. The "schools" from which IMT predominantly draws are Object Relations Theory, Social Learning Theory, and General Systems Theory.

This approach offers an integrative framework for the understanding of marital attraction, conflict, and satisfaction and provides the basis for the actual conduct of couples therapy. As a particular organization of self-regulated social behavior, marriage is seen as best understood, for clinical purposes, in terms of the implicit "rules" of what behavior is allowed and what is disallowed. Conflict arises, then, and continues when "rules" are violated that are central to each partner's sense of self. These relational rules begin with both the conscious and unconscious expectations of, and anxieties about, intimate relating that are brought to the relationship by each partner. The patterned regularities of marriage, then, do not evolve randomly or only from repetitive interactions but also from a subtle interplay of the implicit relationship rules of each individual (Sager, 1981).

The mutual regulation of marital behavior is a function of the needs and efforts of each partner to shape the other to stay within, or get within, the limits of behavior allowed by that person's "rules," what I have called "implicit behavior modification." That is, people unwittingly (and wittingly as well) reinforce and extinguish behavior in their mates that is allowed and disallowed, respectively, according to their own internal expectations of a marital partner, and do likewise in response to the behavior of their mates that is allowed and disallowed according to the internal "rules" of how one needs to "see" one's self. Defenses, then, operate in order to avoid "seeing" behavior that is inconsistent with one's internalized image of one's ideal mate and/or with one's requirements for maintaining a consistent view of one's self. It is the utopian and anxiety-based expectations that people bring to marriage that sensitize them to slight deviations from these relational "rules," which, when they occur, increase the amplitude and frequency of counter-control maneuvers.

Now, this discussion might seem to suggest that marriage is a state of existence worthy of being avoided by any sensible person. Quite to the contrary, the processes described above, often referred to derisively as "collusion," in fact represent, in part, attempted solutions of individual difficulties. That is, not only is it true that marriage is potentially healing of past wounds, but also that people who stay in (even many of the most conflicted) marriage(s), do so for just such reasons.

This having been said, two essential principles of IMT become understandable: First, because people shape each other's personalities, marital therapy can lead to "individual" change. Second, behavior change can change the inner schemata both of one's self and of one's behavior.

The aims, in general, of IMT, then, are

1. to interrupt and modify the couple's self- and other-protective collusive processes so that each partner may be "exposed," in the safety of the therapeutic experience, to anxiety-arousing aspects of self and of the partner;
2. to identify and clarify the links between individual experience (conscious thoughts, preconscious "automatic thoughts," conditioned affective responses, and so on) and the marital interaction;
3. to create therapeutic tasks that both challenge the couple's reflexive, rule-governed problematic behavior and allow in new information about each partner in order to restructure self-perceptions and perceptions of the partner; and
4. to teach interpersonal relationship skills (e.g., problem-solving, conflict resolution, and communication skills), as needed, if they are missing from each partner's repertoire; or, if these essential skills are not "used" in the marriage, but can be seen in each person's interactions with people other than their spouse, the goal is to remove the blocks to their appearance in the marriage.

To these ends, the integrative therapist calls upon specific interventions from a variety of therapeutic traditions, e.g., interpretation to enhance both interpersonal and intrapersonal insight (psychodynamic); training in communication and problem-solving skills, behavior rehearsal, and modeling (behavioral); cognitive restructuring and self-control methods (cognitive); enactment and task assignment (structural/strategic); and paradoxical techniques such as prescribing symptoms and reframing (systemic). These varied techniques are called upon not from the eclectic therapist's stance of "doing whatever works," but from the integrative perspective in which each of these particular operations, and others, is seen to be fully consistent with the integrative conceptualization of marital conflict and distress, and to foster the integrative goals of more accurate self-perception and perception of one's partner and the adoption of alternative styles of intimate relating that are both personally more adaptive and relationship-enhancing.

Collaboration and Friendship

Among enhancing relationships, my first truly influential colleague in psychology was Allen Bergin at Columbia. After my wife, no one has so profoundly and positively affected my career, not so much in terms of its direction or content, as in terms of encouragement, support, and, probably, having more faith in my abilities than I myself had.

My first real professional collaborator was Andy Razin, also a Columbia Ph.D. psychologist, who later earned his M.D. and took psychiatric residency training. Andy and I have been close friends since the second grade, coedited the sports section of our high school magazine, and later coedited a well-known book on psychotherapy research (Gurman & Razin, 1977).

Since coming to Wisconsin, my closest day-to-day colleague has been Dave Rice, with whom I teach every week and with whom I published an early marital therapy anthology (Gurman & Rice, 1975) and a few empirical pieces on therapists' theoretical orientations (see Rice, Chapter 18, this volume).

Except for Dave, I have never been especially connected to my faculty colleagues at Wisconsin for professional enrichment and learning, but rather have cast the line of my most important professional network rather far from Madison. I have collaborated closely on what I consider to have been important projects with Neil Jacobson (Jacobson & Gurman, 1986) and Bill Pinsof (Gurman et al, 1986) (both family therapists), and with Simon Budman (not a family therapist) (Budman & Gurman, 1988). My most consistent and productive collaboration has been with Dave Kniskern (see References). For me, collaboration with a colleague on a project that is truly important to me does not work unless my relationship with that person extends beyond our immediately shared task; I have never taken on any significant professional project with someone I did not consider a close friend.

WHITHER THE FUTURE?

In thinking about the next decade of the field of family psychology, I find it most difficult to separate out my sense of where family *psychology* is going as distinct from where family *therapy* is going, and where clinical psychology is going. The relatively newly demarcated boundary of "family psychology," it seems to me, thus far has been largely riding on the coattails of family therapy, except in one area and that is, not unpredictably, treatment research. Because the entire field of family therapy, it also seems to me, has grown enormously more respectful of and interested in clinical research in the last decade, such inclinations will probably not distinguish family psychologists, as a group, from other mental health professionals dedicated to the study and treatment of the family. Indeed, it is well known that few Ph.D. clinical psychologists publish or do research beyond graduate school, and I see no basis to predict that this will change. At the same time, it is very likely that the major pool of potential clinical family researchers will continue to be found in clinical psychology rather than in other mental health professions.

The valuable empirical work on family therapy, which I am certain clinical psychologists will continue to generate, will inevitably have a strong and positive impact on the field of family therapy. The more challenging task in this domain, I believe, will involve the degree to which systems-oriented psychologists will succeed at influencing the educational and training curriculum in what I believe will continue to be their true "home field," i.e., clinical psychology. Frankly, I am not very optimistic on this score: I predict that, at most, in the next several years, a dozen widely respected clinical programs will come to be known as clearly oriented toward a systemic perspective on clinical matters, while many will continue to retain a token family person on their faculties. "Family psychology," then, will basically remain what it is today, a professional interest group with strongly held beliefs, but not a profession.

And that may be the good news, not the bad. I think I am among a minority of family psychologists who continue to support the fundamental value of the lion's share of what is taught in most clinical psychology graduate school programs. For example, I continue to advocate the importance of family psychologists (or family therapists or family social workers, and so on) learning a good deal about such traditional areas as individual psychopathology, individual developmental and personality theory, and individual (especially cognitive-behavioral and psychodynamic) psychotherapy. I am suspect of family therapists (whether in psychology or not) who have never been trained in such matters, because I have difficulty believing that, as a group, they can do effective family therapy without such a background.

Moreover, because I predict that clinical integration will be the major conceptual challenge of the nineties (as I had earlier called it "The Challenge of the 80s" [Gurman, 1980]), I do not find it possible for advances in this realm to occur in the field of family psychology unless young psychologists receive a solid grounding in most of the traditionally valued areas of clinical psychology (though I do think we could misplace all our Rorschach cards and never be worse off for having done so). Likewise, the continuing refinement of brief psychotherapy, with individuals as well as with couples and families, is essential to the survival of the practice of psychotherapy, and "the basics" of our field must not be ignored therein (Budman & Gurman, 1988). Family psychologists must first be psychologists.

NOTES

1. A couple of years later, after I had joined the faculty in Psychiatry, Dave Rice (see Chapter 18, this volume) and I tried to lead a seminar together with Carl and Dave Keith. Dave Rice's and my ideas about therapy were so different from theirs that I thought we must have come from different planets. Our attempt at a collaborative seminar was never repeated.

2. Getting to be competent by self-instruction hasn't been limited to family therapy. Four years ago, I began to be a soccer coach of my then eight-year-old's neighborhood team. I'd never even seen a soccer game until two years earlier. Now, of course, in my "spare time," I've started to write a book on coaching soccer.

3. The exchange (Gurman & Kniskern, 1978c; Gurman & Knudson, 1978; Gurman, Knudson, & Kniskern, 1978; Jacobson & Weiss, 1978) was sufficiently heated that it led most who read it to assume that Neil Jacobson and I must despise each other. It has been quite a surprise to many, then, to discover that Neil and I have become good friends, and can even cooperate well enough to coedit a book (Jacobson & Gurman, 1986).

REFERENCES

Budman, S., & Gurman, A. S. (1988). *Theory and practice of brief therapy.* New York: Guilford.

Gurman, A. S. (1970). The role of the family in underachievement. *Journal of School Psychology, 8,* 48-53.

Gurman, A. S. (1971). Group marital therapy: Clinical and empirical implications for outcome research. *International Journal of Group Psychotherapy, 21,* 174-189.

Gurman, A. S. (1973a). The effects and effectiveness of marital therapy: A review of outcome research. *Family Process, 12,* 145-170.

Gurman, A. S. (1973b). Instability of therapeutic conditions in psychotherapy. *Journal of Counseling Psychology, 20,* 16-24.

Gurman, A. S. (1973c). Effects of therapist and patient mood on the therapeutic functioning of high- and low-facilitative therapists. *Journal of Consulting and Clinical Psychology, 40,* 48-58.

Gurman, A. S. (1978). Contemporary marital therapies: A critique and comparative analysis of psychoanalytic, behavioral and systems theory approaches. In T. J. Paolino & B. S. McCrady (Eds.), *Marriage and marital therapy.* New York: Brunner/Mazel.

Gurman, A. S. (1980). Behavioral marriage therapy in the 1980's: The challenge of integration. *American Journal of Family Therapy, 8,* 86-96.

Gurman, A. S. (1981). Integrative marital therapy: Toward the development of an interpersonal approach. In S. Budman (Ed.), *Forms of brief therapy.* New York: Guilford.

Gurman, A. S. (1982). Using paradox in psychodynamic marital therapy. *American Journal of Family Therapy, 10*(1), 72-74.

Gurman, A. S. (1985). Tradition and transition: A rural marriage in crisis. In A. S. Gurman (Ed.), *Casebook of marital therapy.* New York: Guilford.

Gurman, A. S., & Kniskern, D. P. (1978a). Research on marital and family therapy: Progress, perspective and prospect. In S. Garfield & A. Bergin (Eds.), *Handbook of psychotherapy and behavior change* (2nd ed.). New York: John Wiley.

Gurman, A. S., & Kniskern, D. P. (1978b). Deterioration in marital and family therapy: Empirical, clinical and conceptual issues. *Family Process, 17,* 3-20.

Gurman, A. S., & Kniskern, D. P. (1978c). Behavioral marriage therapy: II. Empirical perspective. *Family Process, 17,* 139-148.

Gurman, A. S., & Kniskern, D. P. (Eds.) (1981a). *Handbook of family therapy.* New York: Brunner/Mazel.

Gurman, A. S., & Kniskern, D. P. (1981b). Family therapy research: Knowns and unknowns. In A. Gurman & D. Kniskern (Eds.), *Handbook of family therapy.* New York: Brunner/Mazel.

Gurman, A. S., Kniskern, D. P., & Pinsof, W. M. (1986). Research on the process and outcome of marital and family therapy. In S. Garfield & A. Bergin (Eds.), *Handbook of psychotherapy and behavior change* (3rd ed.). New York: John Wiley.

Gurman, A. S., & Knudson, R. M. (1978). Behavioral marriage therapy: I. A psychodynamic-systems analysis and critique. *Family Process, 17,* 121-138.

Gurman, A. S., Knudson, R. M., & Kniskern, D. P. (1978). Behavioral marriage therapy: IV. Take two aspirin and call us in the morning. *Family Process, 17,* 165-180.

Gurman, A. S., & Razin, A. M. (Eds.). (1977). *Effective psychotherapy: A handbook of research.* Elmsford, NY: Pergamon.

Gurman, A. S., & Rice, D. G. (Eds.). (1975). *Couples in conflict: New directions in marital therapy.* New York: Jason Aronson.

Hall, C. S. (1954). *A primer of Freudian psychology.* New York: Mentor Books.

Hentoff, N. (1986). *Boston boy: A memoir.* Boston: Faber and Faber.

Jacobson, N. S., & Gurman, A. S. (Eds.) (1986). *Clinical handbook of marital therapy.* New York: Guilford.

Jacobson, N. S., & Weiss, R. L. (1978). Behavioral marriage therapy: III. The contents of Gurman et al. may be hazardous to our health. *Family Process, 17,* 149-164.

Manus, G. I. (1966). Marriage counseling: A technique in search of a theory. *Journal of Marriage and the Family, 28,* 449-453.

Paolino, T., & McCrady, B. S. (Eds.) (1978). *Marriage and marital therapy.* New York: Brunner/Mazel.

Sager, C. J. (1981). Couples contracts and marital therapy. In A. Gurman & D. Kniskern (Eds.), *Handbook of family therapy.* New York: Brunner/Mazel.

Taggart, M. (1978). Abstracts. *Journal of Marriage and Family Counseling, 4,* 109.

Wells, R. A., Dilkes, T., & Trivelli, N. (1972). The results of family therapy: A critical review of the literature. *Family Process, 7,* 189-207.

13

Developing Family Environments with Families

DALE L. JOHNSON

FAMILY INFLUENCES

I was born in a house my father built, at least partly, in Sanish, North Dakota, across the Missouri River from an Indian reservation, at the end of the Soo Line Railroad, and one of the last of the true frontier towns in America. It now lies under Lake Sakakawea.

The priority of family was impressed on me early as my parents, Kenneth Johnson and Mildred Christensen, sister Pat, and I lived surrounded by grandparents, aunts, uncles, and 28 cousins.

As a small boy I spent my days riding my horse in the hills, trapping along the Missouri, skiing, skating, and taking full advantage of the almost limitless freedom granted by my parents. Although Sanish was devastated by the Depression, with a drought, and by grasshoppers, and we had little money, with a mother who was a gifted teacher (she retired this year at age 86), a father whose humor and sociability made every day special, and a house full of teachers and relatives who lived with us for various lengths of time, life for a small boy was exciting.

I had a remarkable degree of autonomy. Even as a very young child I was free to come and go as I wished. Only the Missouri River itself was out of bounds. I was rarely punished. Good behavior was expected and minor slips were tolerated. It was a rough place to live and many of the local adolescents were involved in delinquent behavior. If we had stayed on there I might have joined them.

A sense of social responsibility was extended to the larger society through the actions of my grandfather, Lars Christensen, an immigrant from Denmark, a homesteader, and one of the founders of the Nonpartisan League, the populist movement that was depicted in the movie *Northern Lights.* Discussion among the relatives was often political and the theme was of the interplay between social and individual responsibilities. My mother and my family emphasized the former, my father and his family, the latter. In either case, it was clear that if you were unhappy with the state of affairs, you should set out to change it and not expect change to take place because others will rush in to help out. Much later, a year in Norway (1973-1974) reminded me that this ethic was solidly rooted in the Scandinavian worldview and had been transplanted with little change to the Dakotas.

My childhood years were as nearly ideal as I can imagine. In particular, the family environment was secure, loving, intellectually stimulating, and, much of the time, uproariously funny.

EDUCATIONAL INFLUENCES

My early elementary years were spent in the Sanish school with its rich mixture of various Anglo and American Indian children and an exciting meld of cultures. When I was 10 years of age my family moved to another small town in North Dakota, away from my beloved hills, but to a better job for my father, managing and eventually owning a hardware and farm implement store.

My high school, the Benson County Agricultural Training School, had 125 students in 4 grades, and my senior class had only 24 students. There were so few students and so many things to be done that every one had to play many roles. Everyone was responsible, no one was left out, and we were all obligated to one another. Academically, it was not a strong school, but there was a tough and creative English teacher who made us write and a teacher of agriculture who introduced us to statistical design and drilled us in practice sessions with Robert's Rules of Order. He said the world runs through meetings and we should be prepared to make these meetings as effective as possible.

From high school I went to the University of North Dakota in 1947. Although UND provided a rich experience, I was an inconsistent scholar. My initial major was pre-medicine, because, among other reasons, I had been fascinated by the life of the medical researcher in Sinclair Lewis's *Arrowsmith* (1925), but I had little interest in the premedical curriculum. Journalism was of interest as I was doing well financially as a part-time photographer and the life-style seemed exciting. But in my junior year I discovered psychology and anthropology and knew that I had found what I wanted. Although I was accepted for medical school, I chose psychology, and have had no regrets. UND also provided a rich social experience (it was something of a party school), gave me the chance to gratify another passion, basketball, and advanced my political development from a conservative republican to a liberal democrat. Most important of all, the UND experience brought me to Carmen Acosta, my wife of 36 years. There was little accident in that meeting: I discovered her, was fascinated by her even before we had met, asked a cousin to introduce us, and set out to woo her. The success of that project was the most important in my life.

I chose Kansas for my graduate work in 1951 because according to the catalog it appeared to offer the psychoanalytic orientation I thought I wanted. It also offered the opportunity to be trained at the Menninger Institute. On arrival I discovered that Roger Barker had come in as chairman and had swept the place clean of psychoanalytic influence. He had repopulated the faculty with Lewinians and gestalters: Fritz Heider, Martin Scheerer, Erik Wright, Herb Wright, Al Baldwin, Lee Meyerson, Tony Smith, Bert Kaplan, Anni Frankl, and Ed Wike. We were immersed in the work of Goldstein (1939), Koffka (1935), Kohler (1947), Lewin (1951), Piaget (1953, 1954), Werner (1948), and Wertheimer (1945). Having come from a behaviorist school and seeking psychoanalytic insights, I was stunned to hear Scheerer in his first lecture tell us that the major sources of error in American psychology were behaviorism and psychoanalysis.

The faculty were in no sense dogmatic and loved academic argument. They believed that students needed to have an understanding of all major points of view and so brought in as visiting professors Austin Des Lauriers (1962), Paul Bergman, Joseph Nuttin (1953), Sigmund Gundle (psychoanalyst), and Jack Michael (behaviorist).

Today there are few gestalters or Lewinians, but on the other hand, much of contemporary psychology is based on ideas that have sprung from those sources. Information processing in cognitive psychology, ecological psychology, the idea of understanding environmental forces, holistic approaches – all began there.

My work with Meyerson (Barker, Meyerson, Wright, & Gonick, 1953) profoundly affected my understanding of the impact of physical illness upon behavior and he, more than anyone else, taught me how to think like a psychologist.

Then John Chotlos entered the scene and I learned to be skeptical of psychological theories and methods. Chotlos introduced a loyal group of students to the intellectual pleasures of existential/phenomenological philosophy and psychology. He led a seminar entitled "Some problems in clinical psychology" which continued for four years. This seminar emphasized the importance of understanding direct experience. I did my dissertation with Chotlos on the moral judgment of schizophrenics.

I think Scheerer was right about psychoanalysis. Although I was in contact with psychoanalytic thinking over the years, and briefly in analytic treatment (four sessions for migraine headaches that were treated successfully later with ergotamine tartrate), I now find it to be of no value as a psychotherapy, as a theory of development, or as a guide to understanding the behavior of individuals or groups. I think it has retarded the progress of science and contributed a mythology of human behavior that has been injurious to the seriously mentally ill, to women, and to families. The Golsteinian (1939) organismic alternative offered by Scheerer (1954), along with Chotlos's phenomenology, Barkerian ecology, and the Piagetian view of development have seemed to me much more satisfactory and scientifically sound sources of theoretical reference.

OPPORTUNITIES AND OTHER INFLUENCES

Cross-Cultural

My boyhood interest in cultural issues was reinforced by marrying Carmen, who had studied in Mexico and had strong interests in the research area. In graduate school Lee Meyerson provided us with an opportunity to spend a summer studying the social situation of the blind among the Mazahua of central Mexico.

We spent four summers working with Bert Kaplan in his study of the use of native categories for classifying mental disorder with the Navajo (Kaplan & Johnson, 1964). Later, Carmen and I did similar research with the Sioux in the Dakotas (Johnson & Johnson, 1965). We also helped the Olympic Mental Center plan its delivery of services for Indians of western Washington. We recommended that the center take advantage of indigenous resources and develop a flexible outreach system involving community-visiting psychiatric nurses.

There was other field research in Mexico, Guatemala, and Norway (Johnson, Teigen, & Davila, 1983) and in all of this we brought the children, and often a grandparent, along. There were the hazards of illness (one child developed malaria in Guatemala), but we deemed the advantages of sharing interesting experiences to be greater than the possible risks.

The cross-cultural work taught me that Pike's idea of emic (the view of the culture itself) is as important as the etic (the generalist, universalist view) approach to understanding cultures. Although of course impressed with cultural differences, I have also been struck by the great within-culture differences that exist and with the basic similarities of people everywhere. I cannot accept explanations of any human behavior as simply "cultural" and prefer to understand the individuals within the cultural context.

Small Group Research

After graduate school I joined the Veterans Administration Hospital in Houston in 1957 and worked with seriously mentally ill patients on an acute admitting ward. In 1960 I became the director of the new Human Interaction Training Laboratory (HITL) for psychiatric patients. The HITL was designed by Bob Morton and based on training principles developed by Robert Blake and Jane Mouton for management training (Rothaus, Morton, Johnson, Cleveland, & Lyle, 1963). All patient groups were self-directed and time limited. Staff provided social skills training and participants recorded their impressions of their group interactions and made use of the feedback this provided. Relations between staff and participants were highly democratic and much was made of taking responsibility for one's actions. Groups were also held responsible for the actions of their members. Men in the program had a variety of psychiatric problems, chiefly anxiety, depression, and addictive disorders, and they were encouraged to place their difficulties in a "problems in living" context. Ideas of illness or therapy were minimized. Program goals were to reduce symptoms by enhancing social sensitivity, social skills, an internal locus of control, and an experimental attitude toward problem-solving (Carlson, Johnson, & Hanson, 1981). The research carried out with 2,000 men in 200 groups was typical of much of the group dynamics research on small groups that grew out of a Lewinian orientation (Lewin, 1951). Our evaluation research found the program to be at least as effective as conventional group psychotherapy programs and with considerably less cost (Johnson, Hanson, Rothaus, Morton, & Lyle, 1965).

I found the opportunity to join training groups as a participant and as a trainer essential for my own development and much more important than personal psychotherapy.

CURRENT INTERESTS

By interest, training, and the shaping of occupational requirements I am a developmental and clinical psychologist. Through a combination of choice and chance I have been involved for the past two decades in two different, but related, ways of working with families. Each has involved research, intervention, and political advocacy.

As a developmentalist, my interests were initially on the socialization of the child. This concern meant that I was as much interested in the environment in which the child developed as in the child's developmental response to these environmental circumstances. Like many psychologists of the 1960s, I was also interested in how the environment promoted or deterred the optimal development of the child, and as a clinical psychologist I felt that one must intervene to improve the chances for optimal development. It has also seemed obvious to me that environmental influences do not have a one-time effect, nor that early experience has an unalterable determining influence on the life course of development. Development is transactional: One is influenced by the environment and influences that environment throughout the life span.

Writing this paper has provoked reflection about my projects. I use the term *projects* in two of its meanings; as a program of organized effort, and in the Sartrean existential sense as a projecting of oneself into the world and creating a future, a being-in-the-world (Sartre, 1956). I have had to ask to what extent my past experiences have structured or even determined present work, and to what extent this work has been shaped by choices made on the basis of expected or hoped for outcomes. There is also, of course, the role of mere chance.

Poverty Families

From the HITL I went across the bayou in 1964 to the University of Houston to teach developmental and clinical psychology. Soon, however, I was department chairman (1966-1972) and I became occupied with administrative duties. These administrative concerns led me into work with families in a way that I did not expect. Late in 1968, Paul Dokecki and I applied for and received funds to start a Parent-Child Center (PCC). We were soon (1970) able to convert that project into a Parent-Child Development Center (PCDC), one of three PCCs selected by the Office of Economic Opportunity, under Mary Robinson's direction, to become research and development centers. Robinson believed that early childhood education programs for children of poverty had not done well because they began too late in the child's life and did not provide for continuity of effects. Her proposal was to begin within the first three years of the child's life and to work with parents as well as children to provide continuity. One would have to change environments in order to have lasting effects. As the most important environment for nearly all infants and young children is the family, however defined, it would be necessary to influence family behavior. Our charge was to develop such a program with very low income minority families and to provide them with a wide range of services. The basic goal was to improve the school performance of the children, but we set as a general goal that the program should optimize child competence.

This was a challenge for which my background was well suited. Although I had virtually no earlier experience with families, I thought that my involvement with cultural issues, small groups, and program development and evaluation could be put to good use.

The Parent-Child Development Center (PCDC), a parent-child education program designed specifically for low-income Mexican-American families, the result of these concerns, has been almost as effective as we planned it to be, and more efficacious than I ever expected. At the end of the program, when children were three years of age, the program mothers, compared with control mothers, were more affectionate, used more praise and less criticism, and were more encouraging of their children's verbalizations. Their homes were more stimulating as educational environments (Andrews et al., 1982; Johnson, 1975). At follow-ups in the preschool and elementary years, and in junior high school, the program children were doing better in school and had fewer behavior problems (Johnson & Breckenridge, 1982; Johnson & Walker, 1986; Johnson & Walker, 1987). The program was not only effective in improving the children's school success, it was also virtually unique as a vehicle for the primary prevention of behavior problems and was cited by the American Psychological Association on prevention as "exemplary" (Johnson, 1988).

Two years ago, I became the director of an extensive evaluation of a project similar to the PCDC. Avance is a two-year parent education program in San Antonio, directed by Gloria Rodriguez, that also works with Mexican-American families. As in the PCDC, much emphasis is put on parent education, but it differs in that the second year is directed at helping mothers earn their high school equivalency credentials and in improving their vocational skills so they can move into better jobs.

Families of the Seriously Mentally Ill

My second introduction to the area of families was prompted by necessity. The oldest of our three children, a son, developed schizophrenia in 1972 when he was 19 years of age. Although he was a remarkably able child, we had become greatly concerned about his use of marijuana, LSD, and possibly PCP in high school, but he said he had quit drugs. He completed school near the top of his class, was elected vice president of a large student body, and went on to an Ivy League university in 1971. My wife and I discovered that adequate treatment facilities were not available, with or without insurance, and as parents of a person with schizophrenia we were isolated by our son's mental health helpers. None of our son's various helpers ever invited us for an interview, we had to initiate conferences, and one psychiatrist accused us of having caused our son's mental illness.

This experience of living with schizophrenia has thrown me back into work with the seriously mentally ill and their families. Our family's experience with the mental health system, whether the system of private or public psychiatry, was shocking, appalling, and endlessly frustrating. Individual practitioners of all types tended to be caring, if lacking in skills, but the system was not designed for serious mental illness. We feared that our son was one more mentally ill person who would simply "fall through the cracks" and that he would spend his life in an institution, among the homeless, or perhaps at best isolated in a back room of our home. Not inclined to be passive, in 1980 we found other families who felt as we did and organized a group called Citizens for Human Development. We set out to change the system in Houston and Texas. Two years later we discovered that an organization called the National Alliance for the Mentally Ill (NAMI) had been formed in 1979 and we joined. I was elected to the NAMI board and served as a vice president. Carmen is president of the Texas Alliance for the Mentally Ill. We have appreciated the fact that NAMI is made up of families, the clients themselves, and friends of the mentally ill. We also have supported NAMI's going beyond mutual support to education and advocacy. As an organization, it is as important to the mentally ill and their families as my grandfather's Nonpartisan League was to his fellow farmers. Both organizations were formed to change social systems that were not responsive to those who were involved in them.

Before long I was cochair of NAMI's Curriculum and Training committee, which is made up largely of mental health professionals who are also educators and who have some kind of family involvement with serious mental illness. The committee's purpose is to influence the way the mentally ill and their families are treated by professionals. Through writing books and journal articles, presenting grand rounds, making presentations at conventions, consulting with accrediting groups, and doing workshops, the committee has had some success. As each state develops its own Curriculum and Training Committee there should be an even greater impact on how professionals work with the mentally ill and their families. My own contribution to this work has been in studying the experience of living with a mentally ill person on family members (Johnson, 1987b; 1990). In my own work and in reviewing the literature on the experience of living with mental illness I have found that families are indeed burdened. The experience is associated with such heightened levels of anxiety, depression, and psychosocial dysfunction that these families must be considered as a population at risk. In addition, they are burdened economically. Families are bothered by positive symptoms such as hallucination, delusions, and disturbed thinking, but equally troubled by the negative symptoms, anhedonia and lack of motivation. Researchers have focused almost exclusively on parents of the mentally ill. Other relatives who are also affected by living with mental illness—siblings, children of the mentally ill, and spouses—have been virtually neglected. Finally, it is clear that as the mentally ill person recovers, the experience of burden lightens.

The Curriculum and Training Committee has had some success in changing the views of professionals toward the mentally ill and their families. There is, however, much work to be done. Families of the mentally ill are still heavily burdened and too often abused. It is a task for researchers to find ways to relieve the pressures and prevent abuse. It is also essential that we know more about the consequences of living with mental illness for all family members, including such understudied groups as siblings, adult children of the mentally ill, and spouses. There are other questions for research: What is the role of the family in treating mental illness? How can professionals best work with families? Why do families give up and why don't they give up? What are the cultural variations in family experience?

Common Features

These two lines of work with families are less distinct than they may seem. They have in common that each group has been underserved and each presents serious service delivery problems. Furthermore, interventions for each often have been inappropriate and families have been derogated and depreciated. Finally, successful ways of intervening could not be developed until certain problems had been solved.

Families of both types have told professionals that what they want is information, access to resources, instruction on how to help their family member, training in how to cope with stress, and the respect of professionals who help them. They have rejected the idea that they are deficient as family providers (the once popular idea that low-income families are culturally deficient is repugnant), or that their lives are pathological (families of the mentally ill do not agree that mental illness is a product of pathological family interactions). These families have not asked for therapy for their family problems. Their goals are to help their children do well in school and take solid places in society and to overcome the handicaps of poverty and social discrimination (low-income families) or mental illness and stigma (families of the mentally ill).

My involvement with these two lines of interest undoubtedly reflects my own values and beliefs and these are more apparent retrospectively than they were prior to the actions taken. *These include being against interpretation and for description, being against controlling families and for offering them opportunities, and being against deciding for families and for working with them to make decisions that are grounded in their own best interests as they perceive them to be.*

As a professor I teach a graduate course on working with the families of the mentally ill. After several sessions in reviewing pertinent literature and moving toward an understanding of the community context of providing services for the mentally ill, we work together with families at St. Joseph Hospital.

DIRECTIONS FOR THE FIELD

Interest in the family seems to be increasing. Schorr (1988) has pointed out that the American family is in great trouble, and that the consequences for children are deplorable. Furthermore, she points out in the title of her book that solutions are *Within Our Reach,* that is, we already know how to alleviate many of these problems.

Applied psychology has turned away from its preoccupation with the treatment of symptoms arising from early repressed conflicts and turned toward what is called cognitive-behavioral psychology with its here-and-now orientation, concern with thoughts, and emphasis on action. Because so much of this new direction is based soundly on research, and the effectiveness of interventions that have emerged has been demonstrated, it can be expected to continue. The general line of theory and application can also be expected to have an effect on research on family interventions.

Psychologists seem to be increasingly aware of the need to work with environments, not just individuals. This concern has been articulated by such developmental psychologists as Bronfenbrenner (1979) and Garbarino (1982), but clinicians have been slow to grasp the implications of an ecological approach. Of course, there are exceptions, as in the work of Lusterman (1988). Briefly, in working with families, the first step is to analyze the life circumstances, the situation, or context of individual families; identify the major problems; describe the resources that are available; and find the blocks to attaining individual and family goals. Essential in this process is that the professional pay close attention to what family members want for themselves and for others in their family. It is also essential that attention be given to what the family needs to reach its goals. In this assessment, the professional should place heavy emphasis on research-based knowledge. Then, the family's stated wants and the professional's assessment of needs are examined together for coherence and compatibility. The process of blending these two sources of information is an interactive, or transactive, one, with each being modified and amplified by the other. The process requires a true collaborative interaction between the family members and the professionals in designing services that are mutually satisfactory. In the past this process has been neglected in favor of the authority of the professionals, and families have suffered mistreatment and neglect.

For families of poverty, the PCDC model was developed on the basis of this interaction of family wants and research-based definitions of needs, and the result has been encouraging. Avance is a newer application of this method, and goes an important step further in taking into account the importance of the parent's development not just as a parent, but as a person in his or her own right.

For families of the mentally ill, the question of needs has been answered, at least in part, by an interesting series of studies on interventions with families. The work of Leff and Vaughn (1981) in England; Falloon, Boyd, and McGill (1984) in southern California; and Anderson, Reiss, and Hogarty (1986) in Pittsburgh has demonstrated that the relapse rate for persons with schizophrenia can be reduced from about 40% with medication and supportive care in the nine months following hospitalization to about 10% in the same period of time with family management training, medication, and supportive care. These are highly significant effects. These new family programs stand in contrast to the conventional systemic or strategic family therapy, which has been proclaimed the therapy of choice for schizophrenics and their families for years (Haley, 1987), but for which there is still no evidence of effectiveness (Terkelsen, 1983).

The new family psychoeducational or family management programs will probably be extended to other clinical areas. In a sense, this has already happened in working with children with attention deficit disorders and their families (Barkley, 1981). Other likely problem areas are affective disorders, borderline personality disorders, substance abuse, and child abuse. It seems likely that as the new family methods are evaluated, their effectiveness will encourage widespread adoption. In time, they may be regarded as the first choice for interventions with more traditional psychotherapies, including family therapy, being reserved for special problems.

It seems to me that psychologists cannot accept the notion that empirical research on family intervention procedures is not possible. Of course, all problems that can be posed cannot be dealt with through empirical research procedures. Phenomenologists know that. But one can recast problems, remember the original request for help or family goals, and carry out research on how effective procedures are in reaching these goals. This has been done by the Parent-Child Development Center researchers (Andrews et al., 1982) and by the family management program researchers mentioned. Unvalidated claims such as those made by Haley (1987) are unacceptable.

PLANS

Completion of a book on the Houston Parent-Child Development Center is long overdue and has high priority among my plans. Next I want to do a book on psychosocial rehabilitation for families and professionals. Other writing plans are farther down the line.

The opportunity to evaluate the Avance program has made it possible to take advantage of developments in knowledge about family environments since the PCDC evaluation was designed. In particular, I now think it is imperative that the affective characteristics of the child's family environment be considered, and this aspect has been included in our current work. Undoubtedly, my work will continue to play on the environment/person interaction. I will also continue to develop service delivery methods and in doing this work to reframe how one thinks about those families that professionals find difficult. My inclination is that we shouldn't think of "resistant families," but think of ineffective delivery systems or of not being aware of what families understand that they want and need. The reframing process rests on a foundation of respect for the family.

SUMMARY

The two major family projects with which I have been involved for the past 20 years, work with families of poverty through the Houston Parent-Child Development Center and Avance and families of the seriously mentally ill, appear rather different but actually have much in common. Most of my research has been with families as makers and managers of environments for the development of family members.

It is clear to me that one must work with families, recognizing their special circumstances and being guided by what they want at least as much as by what we as professionals believe they need. The autonomous, self-generative aspects of the family must have priority and should be fostered. As we know from the research of Bandura (1982), Seligman (1975), and others, a sense of self-efficacy is vital for the development of self-esteem and the ability to function without burdening depression. My concern has been that families of poverty and of the seriously mentally ill are already burdened by forces to a great extent beyond their control. As a researcher and practitioner I would like to find ways to lighten these burdens and develop family strengths to cope better with the remaining exigencies.

REFERENCES

Anderson, C. M., Reiss, D. J., & Hogarty, G. E. (1986). *Schizophrenia in the family: A practitioner's guide to psychoeducation and management.* New York: Guilford.

Andrews, S. R., Blumenthal, J. B., Johnson, D. L., Kahn, A. J., Ferguson, C. J., Lasater, T. M., Malone, P. E., & Wallace, D. B. (1982). The skills of mothering: A study of Parent Child Development Centers. *Monographs of the Society for Research in Child Development, 47*(6, Serial No. 198).

Bandura, A. (1982). Self-efficacy mechanism in human agency. *American Psychologist, 37,* 122-147.

Barker, R. G., Meyerson, L., Wright, B. A., & Gonick, M. R. (1953). *Adjustment to physical handicap and illness* (2nd ed.). New York: Social Science Research Council Bulletin Series.

Barkley, R. A. (1981). *Hyperactive children: A handbook for diagnosis and treatment.* New York: Guilford.

Bronfenbrenner, U. (1979). *The ecology of human development.* Cambridge, MA: Harvard University Press.

Carlson, R. M., Johnson, D. L., & Hanson, P. G. (1981). Social sensitivity and self-awareness in group psychotherapy. *Small Group Behavior, 12,* 183-194.

Des Lauriers, A. M. (1962). *The experience of reality in childhood schizophrenia.* New York: International Universities Press.

Falloon, I. R. H., Boyd, J. L., & McGill, C. W. (1984). *Family care of schizophrenia: A problem-solving approach to the treatment of mental illness.* New York: Guilford.

Garbarino, J. (1982). *Children and families in the social environment.* Hawthorne, NY: Aldine de Gruyter.

Goldstein, K. (1939). *The organism.* New York: American Book.

Haley, J. (1987, December). Schizophrenics deserve family therapy, not dangerous drugs and management. *Family Therapy News.*

Heider, F. (1958). *The psychology of interpersonal relations.* New York: John Wiley.

Johnson, D. L. (1975). The development of a program for parent-child education among Mexican-Americans in Texas. In B. Z. Friedlander, G. M. Sterritt, & G. E. Kirk (Eds.), *Exceptional infant* (Vol. 3, pp. 374-398). New York: Brunner/Mazel.

Johnson, D. L. (1984). The needs of the chronically mentally ill: As seen by the consumer. In M. Mirabi (Ed.), *The chronically mentally ill: Research and services.* New York: SP Medical and Scientific Books.

Johnson, D. L. (1987a). Effective primary prevention of behavior problems in Mexican-American children. In R. Rodriguez & M. T. Coleman (Eds.), *Mental health issues of the Mexican origin population in Texas.* Austin: Hogg Foundation.

Johnson, D. L. (1987b). Professional family collaboration. In A. Hatfield (Ed.), *Families of the mentally ill: Meeting the challenges.* San Francisco: Jossey-Bass.

Johnson, D. L. (1988). Primary prevention of behavior problems in young children: The Houston Parent-Child Development Center. In R. H. Price, E. L. Cowen, R. P. Lorion, & J. Ramos-McKay (Eds.), *14 ounces of prevention: A casebook for practitioners.* Washington, DC: American Psychological Association Press.

Johnson, D. L. (In press). The family's experience of living with mental illness. In H. Lefley & D. L. Johnson (Eds.), *Mental health professionals and families of the mentally ill.* Washington, DC: American Psychiatric Association Press.

Johnson, D. L., & Breckenridge, J. N. (1982). The Houston Parent-Child Development Center and the primary prevention of behavior problems in young children. *American Journal of Community Psychology, 10,* 305-316.

Johnson, D. L., Hanson, P. G., Rothaus, P., Morton, R. B., & Lyle, F. A. (1965). Human relations training for psychiatric patients: A follow-up study. *Journal of Social Psychiatry, 11,* 188-196.

Johnson, D. L., & Johnson, C. A. (1965). Totally discouraged: Depressive syndrome of the Dakota Sioux. *Transcultural Psychiatric Research, 2,* 141-143.

Johnson, D. L., Teigen, K., & Davila, R. (1983). Anxiety and social restriction as experienced by children in Mexico, Norway and the United States. *Journal of Cross-Cultural Psychology, 14*, 439-454.

Johnson, D. L., & Walker, T. (1986, April). *A follow-up evaluation of the Houston Parent-Child Development Center: School performance.* Paper presented at the annual meeting of the American Educational Research Association, Chicago.

Johnson, D. L., & Walker, T. (1987). The primary prevention of behavior problems in Mexican-American children. *American Journal of Community Psychology, 15,* 375-385.

Kaplan, B., & Johnson, D. L. (1964). The social meaning of Navaho psychopathology and psychotherapy. In A. Kiev (Ed.), *Magic, faith and healing* (pp. 203-229). New York: Free Press.

Koffka, K. (1935). *Principles of gestalt psychology.* New York: Harcourt Brace.

Kohler, W. (1974). *Gestalt psychology.* New York: Liverwright.

Leff, J. P., & Vaughn, C. E. (1981). The role of maintenance therapy and relatives' expressed emotion in relapse of schizophrenia: A two-year follow-up. *British Journal of Psychiatry, 139,* 102-104.

Lewin, K. (1951). *Field theory in social sciences.* New York: Harper.

Lewis, S. (1925). *Arrowsmith.* New York: Harcourt.

Lusterman, D.-D. (1988). Family therapy and schools: An ecosystemic approach. *Family therapy today, 3*(7), 1-3.

Nuttin, J. (1953). *Psychoanalysis and personality.* New York: Sheed & Ward.

Piaget, J. (1953). *The moral judgment of the child.* Glencoe, IL: Free Press.

Piaget, J. (1954). *The construction of reality in the child.* New York: Basic Books.

Rothaus, P., Morton, R. B., Johnson, D. L., Cleveland, S. E., & Lyle, F. A. (1963). Human relations training for psychiatric patients. *Archives of General Psychiatry, 8,* 572-581.

Sartre, J. P. (1956). *Being and nothingness.* New York: Philosophical Library.

Scheerer, M. (1954). Cognitive theory. In G. Lindzey (Ed.), *Handbook of social psychology* (pp. 91-143). New York: Addison-Wesley.

Schorr, L. (1988). *Within our reach: Breaking the cycle of disadvantage.* Garden City, NY: Doubleday.

Seligman, M. E. P. (1975). *Helplessness: On depression, development and death.* San Francisco: Freeman.

Terkelsen, K. G. (1983). Schizophrenia and the family: Adverse effects of family therapy. *Family Process, 22,* 191-201.

Werner, H. (1948). *Comparative psychology of mental development.* New York: International Universities Press.

Wertheimer, K. (1945). *Productive thinking.* New York: Harper.

14

A Multifaceted Family Psychology Potpourri

FLORENCE W. KASLOW

PERSONAL HERITAGE

Philadelphia was the city in which I made my debut as the second daughter of Rose and Irving Whiteman. Each had come to the United States separately on ships jammed with passengers emigrating from Russia to escape anti-Semitic programs and military conscription. They arrived in the first decade of the twentieth century; both were still in their formative early childhood years. Each of their families settled in the Jewish immigrant area of North Philadelphia. Grateful to have landed safely in the land of the free and eager to leave behind the persecution and totalitarianism of Eastern Europe, they embraced the ideology of democracy and set about getting settled in, earning a living, and becoming acculturated without losing their Jewish identity or Yiddish language proficiency. The deeply ingrained values of their heritage, particularly the pursuit of and reverence for knowledge and social justice, were perpetuated from and through their generation to my sister and me and our numerous cousins. These have remained basic tenets in my life that I have also endeavored to instill in my children.

My dad was one of 12 children who survived the rigors of life in Russia and the trip to the United States. My paternal grandfather was a well-respected Orthodox Rabbi who assumed a leadership role in the ghetto-style community in which they settled with other Jewish immigrants from Poland, Hungary, Lithuania, and the Ukraine. My paternal grandmother kept a kosher home and my Dad and his siblings were raised in a traditional, religiously observant home and community. My grandmother was respected for her mathematical wizardry and her fine memory as well as her ability to raise a huge family on a terribly meager budget.

My Dad was the seventh in line, with five brothers and six sisters. All of the men and several of the women were extremely brilliant—they became poets, writers, philosophers, historians, linguists, and businessmen and -women. All of the children completed high school and became American citizens. Most became fluent in English, adding this to their other languages. I remember as a teenager being impressed with my Dad's and my uncle's fluency in speaking and cross-translating in about six languages. My parents and grandparents often spoke Yiddish in front of us—partly as a way of communicating adult messages to which we were not supposed to be privy and partly to entice us to acquire some proficiency in their "mother tongue." Fortunately, I had an easy affinity for languages, and in addition to Yiddish, went on to learn Spanish and the usual smattering of high school French and German—all of which have facilitated my guest-lecturing around the world and my continuing appreciation for one's heightened ability to communicate more sensitively in the languages of one's audience. I continue to attempt to expand my linguistic skills with every trip I make.

My Dad acquired fluency in English and developed an extensive speaking vocabulary; fortunately, this was part of the legacy he transmitted to me. A person who venerated education and being well informed about politics and current affairs, his limited formal education and total lack of prior financial resources led my Dad to spend his working years, well into his seventies, as a grocer. How clearly I remember my early childhood years of living in a house attached to my parents' "Mom and Pop"-style corner grocery store. For years in the post-Depression era they worked from 7 a.m. to midnight—seven days a week—"to make ends meet." There was always food but never any luxuries. We grew up without a family car. When my parents' financial situation improved slightly, Dad got a job in someone else's store so Mom wouldn't also slave so hard and we moved into a "row house" in a better neighborhood, not attached to a store. Now that Sundays were free, we made a weekly pilgrimage—by trolley car and subway—to visit grandparents, as maintaining family bonds was essential. So was contributing financially or with food, clothing, or shelter to any member of the extended family who needed it. Dad was quiet, self-contained, unemotional, hard working, exacting, and strict. Yet he was always there for me—physically present and expressing his concern and interest by nonverbally demanding that I do my best and excel in academic pursuits. I learned in first grade that anything less than all A's was not acceptable, and being eager to please, this is what I strove for. Later when my high school grades showed an occasional B (chemistry, physics) his displeasure fed into my feelings of inadequacy. Along with acquisition of knowledge, tangible signs of achievement such as top grades, awards, and graduating with distinction and honors were to be sought and prized; these were proof of the realization of the American dream.

Only in the past two decades have I realized that his desire was for me to fulfill his unrealized ambition; therefore it was unstable and, for me, always constituted a tremendous pressure to excel and be productive. From the time my first book was published (Kaslow, 1972b), the query was always, "When will your next one be done?" My parents collected my books, which I of course gave them as presents; what saddened me is they proudly showed them to friends and relatives—but never read them.

If the intellectual, academic, and politically attuned aspects of my life were fostered by my Dad, the emotional, creative, fun-loving, and mischievous qualities were nurtured by my vivacious and warm Mom. She worked extremely hard and believed there wasn't anything that had to be done that she couldn't learn to do and master for her family. Energetic, lively, and optimistic, Mom made friends easily and sought to expand her horizons and ours. Within our limited financial resources, she exposed us to the world of music and dance at the local recreation center and encouraged our activities. Because I was usually the smallest in the chorus line and I exhibited some talent as a tap dancer, from age 3½ on, my niche became front row, center stage. Dance became my channel of expression, an outlet for my plentiful energy, and a wonderful medium for getting attention and compliments. My parents apparently believed old Eastern European superstitions that if you compliment a child or exhibit pride in your good fortune, trouble will befall you—perhaps an envious neighbor would cast an "evil eye" (Foulks, Freeman, Kaslow, & Madow, 1977). They also believed praise led to conceit; therefore, they attempted to motivate through criticism and admonishments to try harder and do better.

I loved the physical release and creativity of dance, the esprit de corps of rehearsals, and the excitement of performances. Dance became a core theme in my identity. My sister, Cicely, and I became a dance team during our adolescence and became part of a USO troupe. Since we had never had the opportunity to go away to summer camp, USO tours offered an early taste of growing up. When we performed at Veterans Administration hospitals, we saw directly the horrors wrought by war and the havoc brought into the lives of returning servicemen and their families. Perhaps my later interest in military families (Kaslow & Ridenour, 1984) and in global peace partially emanated from my experiences during those USO tours when I was so vulnerable and impressionable. By this time, ballet and modern dance classes had been added to the schedule. Dance and theater remain to this day an important aspect of my total life.

My Mom was the only daughter in a family with four sons. She was the second from the youngest and in her growing up years, strove mightily to keep up with her brothers and to be competent in any task she undertook or that was thrust upon her. When she was about 10 years old, her beloved father died; she missed him incredibly for years and no one ever fully filled this gap for her. Her mother was gregarious, charming, and delightful and remarried several more times—only to again be widowed each time. Both my maternal grandmother and my mom exuded warmth, sincere concern for others, and a natural intuitiveness. Many attributed "psychic powers" to them; to the extent that I've ever witnessed mental telepathy—my mom possessed it. She always wanted to "be somebody" and sought perfection in all that she did. From my mom I seem to have "inherited" and/or acquired my joie de vivre, high energy, sociability, resourcefulness, tenacity, and intuitiveness. In a way I derived the best of what each of my parents had to offer. Along with this went the challenge of being programmed to achieve and succeed—in order not to hurt or disappoint them.

EARLY COLLEGE AND WORK HISTORY: CONTRIBUTORY ELEMENTS TO CAREER CHOICE

My parents believed daughters should go to work as secretaries upon completion of high school and contribute to the family income. We were expected to live at home until we married and be proper, conservative young ladies. My sister pleaded to go to college and finally they scraped enough money together to send her as a commuting student to inexpensive Temple University. She withdrew to get married after her freshman year. Two years later, when I graduated from high school, they were adamant about my going to work immediately as all the relatives and they believed I would do as my sister had done and they would only be wasting scarce resources. As I had begun working at 12 years of age in a relative's office, and by 16 years of age had been a sales girl, file clerk, and bookkeeper, I decided I'd work my way through college, if that were the only way. During my freshman year I held two jobs. I was barely 16 years old; 90% of my classmates were World War II veterans going to college on the G.I. Bill and were much older and quite worldly. I felt overwhelmed and decided to take some time off and work to save money toward future tuition. I acquired secretarial skills and worked at the Philadelphia Fellowship Commission and Jewish Community Relations Council. I became convinced that I wanted to become a helping professional and that concepts of religious freedom, equality, and humanitarianism were important values.

At 18 years of age I returned as a high sophomore to Temple University (having taken evening courses during my working hiatus). I quickly was noticed by the Dean of Women and received a scholarship based on merit and need from the Women's University Club. This time I only needed to have one job to cover the rest of my expenses. I lived at home throughout my undergraduate years. This was essential financially; and, indeed, my parents would not countenance a young, single daughter living any place else.

I majored in Sociology, minored in Psychology, and graduated with distinction. This time 'round I enjoyed everything about college—classes, studying, dating, and organizational life. My extracurricular activities were plentiful. Among the most valued were the opportunities I had as a junior and senior to serve on the staff for Temple's Freshman Camp orientation and to be a participant at Shawnee International Leadership Training Institute. As a young adult, I finally got to summer camp, and was catapulted into international student activities and the doctrine of "one world." I thoroughly enjoyed both experiences. Clearly they influenced future choices.

I felt fortunate to be the first one in my family of origin to be able to go to and complete college. I was the second girl in my Dad's extended family and the first person in my Mother's family to do so. Everyone was surprised and some found it incomprehensible that I had graduated, received many honors, and also had an active social life. In some ways, I "danced my way through college"—occasionally performing in nightclubs to earn money. I taught Israeli folk dancing at Hillel Foundation and traded Latin and other social dancing lessons with men I dated in exchange for driving lessons. It had become very clear that innovativeness, negotiation, and trade-offs definitely were essential to my survival and to making life interesting.

MY FIRST "PROFESSIONAL" POSITION

Upon graduation, I worked for a short time as the Assistant Regional Director of the Philadelphia B'nai Brith Youth Organization. Here I learned a great deal about the adolescent stage of the life cycle, about group dynamics and peer group interaction, and about organization development and mass programming. I was the staff member assigned to work with the A.Z.A. Boys Leadership Council, their basketball league, and the adult male advisers group.

Despite some initial trepidation on my part about working with the boys' activities and some uncertainty on theirs about the new, young female staff person assigned to work with them, it went very well. I came to understand adolescent boys better and to respect the kind of caring and sophisticated men who become boys' club (in this instance, chapter) advisers. The skill I acquired then in understanding group dynamics and doing group work made the transition to later becoming a group therapist relatively easy. Similarly, it was essential to become conversant with organizational structure and functioning. These two aspects combined became part of the foundation for my entry—15 years later—into management consultation work and still undergirds my more recent endeavors (since 1986) in the arena of family business consultation.

ON TO GRADUATE SCHOOL AND A WHOLE NEW WORLD

Although I thoroughly enjoyed my position and status, I had realized during my senior year that I wanted and needed to go to graduate school and so I had sent in several applications. I knew my parents found the idea alien and unaffordable. Therefore, with encouragement and guidance from several professors and university administrators, I had applied for fellowships. Since the idea of going long enough to earn a doctoral degree seemed grandiose and beyond my reach, I decided to enter a School of Social Work and get a "terminal master's." Ohio State offered what I then considered a generous fellowship—tuition plus a $100-a-month living stipend. When I announced to my parents that I had applied for graduate school and had been awarded a fellowship, they expressed amazement and a new respect for my determination. They voiced concern that all of my friends were getting married and starting families and that I might lessen my chances for marriage if I delayed it for too long and/or overwhelmed potential husbands with being more educated than they were. Many friends, relatives, and professors expressed similar sentiments; this was a popular view in the mid-1950s. Even my male therapist, a psychoanalyst with whom I had originally entered treatment around career planning, cautioned me about becoming too independent and hard to handle. Chauvinism was more overt then, but not persuasive enough to diminish my determination.

When I departed for Columbus and my first living-away-from-home experience (of more than a month's duration), my parents exhibited mixed emotions of pride and concern—their "baby" was leaving home—probably never to return, except as a visitor.

To this day I believe in the validity of warm and enduring family ties and loyalties. I do not label close relationships as "enmeshed" or "overprotective" unless they hamper the quest for individuation and autonomy; when they enhance the person's sense of belonging, self-esteem, and unique identity, I perceive them as manifestations of healthy family interaction (Kaslow, 1981d; Lewis, Beavers, Gossett, & Phillips, 1976; Olson, Russell, &

Sprenkle, 1983). To me, the gift of love without the contingency of a "payback" is the best gift parents can bestow on their children. In this area of life, my parents bestowed great riches, even though the love contained the wish that I fulfill their longings for achievement and recognition. It was a positive life script.

Of the several inexpensive housing options available at Ohio State University, I decided I wanted to live at Zonta International House on campus. The House accepted 16 residents per year—12 women from other countries and 4 from the United States who were to help orient the foreign students and make them feel welcome. To me it seemed the logical place to reside and expand the international family that I had begun years earlier. During the 15 months that I was a "Zonta Girl," most of the other residents were from Latin America. I spoke Spanish daily and found that I was *muy simpático* with many aspects of their culture. When there was a reception or party for the Latin students, I was often included. Because of my dark hair and eyes, as well as my demeanor, I was often taken for Latin and so I had many opportunities to share wonderful activities with my Latin sisters. We dated male foreign students from everywhere and I found the differences intriguing and captivating. Probably I learned more from my life at Zonta House than in graduate school and this reinforced my commitment to being involved eventually in "the world scene" although I had no vision of quite what that would mean or how I would "make it happen."

The two professors who most influenced my thinking and whetted my appetite for much more were Leontyne Young—who taught intensive casework from a psychodynamic perspective and whose major areas of research included the unconscious motivation of unwed mothers, and William Schwartz, a group worker deeply steeped in the thinking and writing of Karen Horney and in the understanding of group processes and leader interventions. I was awed by the fact that each had had books published and were considered seminal thinkers in their respective areas.

My block internship placement was at Jewish Family Service in Cincinnati. It was considered a fine agency and the staff liked having eager, inquisitive graduate students in their midst. My supervisor, Lotte Lotheim, was brilliant, talented, and willing to share her knowledge. She permitted me maximum leeway to experiment; her lucid explanations and her encouragement of my sometimes unconventional strategies were a perfect fit with my modus operandi.

Three incidents from this period remain indelibly etched in my memory and are marker occurrences along the next part of the pathway leading toward my ultimately becoming a family psychologist. Many of the agency's clients were immigrants newly arrived from Hungary. They had fled from their homeland as soon as they could get permission and make arrangements to emigrate after the German and Russian invasions of their country. Victims of the Holocaust and other forms of anti-Semitism, many arrived here beaten, bewildered, and totally dislocated; they were truly displaced persons. My anxiety about seeing my very first patient alone was heightened when I learned he was a recently arrived Hungarian refugee. I sought to learn as much as I could about the characteristics of this group in the two days between case assignment and his appointment. I was still ill prepared for his depressed and downtrodden appearance coupled with his many demands; he believed we all owed him something to make up for his myriad losses and great suffering. I had no frame of reference to help me form a therapeutic alliance; in addition, he only knew a few dozen words of English so I had to conduct the session in Yiddish. There were many words I didn't understand and he yelled at me for my stupidity. Given the number of Hungarians I was to see in the next months, I brushed up on my Yiddish, learned more German, and tried to acquire as much knowledge as I could about the culture and political system they came from, about the impact of the multiple losses suffered in wide-scale disasters such as the Holocaust, and about becoming a displaced person who is dependent on the compassion and generosity of strangers. This became another milestone in my quest for understanding of other lands and other people. But I had little idea then where this quest would ultimately lead.

The JFS building was a large, old, stately home converted into an agency facility. Staff mostly saw couples or, in cases where children were the concern, most of the treatment took place with the mothers. This agency used the then fairly typical child guidance model: The psychiatrist treated the child, if absolutely necessary, and social workers saw the parent(s). Since many of our clients couldn't afford baby-sitters, they brought the children along and left them relatively unattended in the waiting room. Because I found children running up and down the hallway and barging into therapy distracting, I decided to ask them to stay with their parents in the session. It rapidly became apparent to me that how parents said they related to and cared for their children usually did not match what they did. I also found it useful to see and work with the children directly. With my supervisor's permission, I began to see the family members together (before Satir popularized the word *conjoint* [Satir, 1964]), and to incorporate play therapy with the children—particularly with doll families and "let's pretend" stories. Allowed to be creative, I was delighted with the catharsis achieved and the progress made. So was my supervisor. By the mid-1950s I was treating families, using my prior casework and group work training as a springboard, learning through trial and error and following intuitive hunches. What a challenging and rewarding experience my internship year turned out to be!

CREATING A NEW FAMILY

Upon receiving my master's from Ohio State, I returned to Philadelphia and my parents' home. I immediately began to work at the Association for Jewish Children (AJC) as a caseworker in adoption and foster placement work. I was in my early twenties and shocked by the "irresponsible" behavior of young unwed mothers who deposited their unwanted children on the agency's doorstep in the middle of the night. It seemed patently unfair that several months after a child was settled into a "good" foster home, the natural mother could assert her claim to the child, even if she had had no treatment and was still evidencing a great deal of psychopathology. I was distressed that the child's needs and rights did not take precedence and vowed to become the child's advocate in all work that I undertook. I found it hard to comprehend why adolescents who did not yet want children became pregnant easily and many wonderful couples who desperately wanted a child could not conceive and resorted uneasily to adoption. I pondered what then seemed imponderable and realized there was so much I did not know.

Six months after I graduated, I was invited to return to BBYO with a promotion to Assistant Director of the Philadelphia Region. During my time at AJC, I had become engaged to Sol Kaslow, a young man I had dated prior to leaving for Ohio. Our wedding date was rapidly approaching and I decided that working at BBYO would provide a livelier and happier environment more compatible with the joy I was experiencing as a bride-to-be. I did not want the troubling aspects of my responsibilities and thoughts at AJC to spill over into my forthcoming marriage.

It was wonderful to return to my "BBYO family" for the next three years. When our first child, Nadine, was born I worked there part time for an additional three years until our son, Howard, came along. During these years I learned how to be an agency executive; much more about the vicissitudes of adolescents and the tremendous accomplishments healthy, bright young people can make; a great deal about mass programming and marketing; about effective and inspirational speaking; and about group and organizational dynamics. It was a heady environment, conducive to great productivity and much optimism about the meaning of life.

The BBYO experience paralleled the exuberance shared in our marriage. My parents and my husband got along extremely well. In him they acquired the son they had never had; he was a kind, respectful, attentive, and caring son-in-law throughout the balance of their lives. He truly joined my family of origin at the same time we were creating our own nuclear family.

A guiding principle of my own life has been a biblical precept from Ecclesiastes—for everything there is a season. It was our season to start a family. Natural childbirth was still a rarity but I knew it was what I wanted. After reading *Childbirth Without Fear* (Read, 1953), I searched for an obstetrician who was knowledgeable about this approach and finally located one obstetrics group and hospital that was willing to permit it. They even had the requisite breathing and exercise class. Sol was with me in the labor and delivery rooms—much to the shock and consternation of friends and relatives. From the first he has been an involved and loving father—enjoying the fathering role enormously.

There was no question about my priorities. My family was of utmost importance and I felt lucky to have two attractive, responsive, lively children. During their early childhood and latency years, we all had a wonderful time together—hiking, reading, playing, biking, riding horses, exploring the universe, going to children's theatre and concerts, baking, and traveling. Nadine took all kinds of dancing lessons, plus violin and piano lessons. Howard played little league softball and the drums. Both attended Hebrew and Sunday School and I taught at the Temple (Synagogue) they attended. Our family musical ensemble often consisted of Nadine playing violin, Howard on the drums, Mom (me) at the piano, and Sol, an appreciator of music but not a participant in the creative end, with tamborine in hand. We availed ourselves fully of the joys of a beautiful suburban community outside Philadelphia and of the cultural plentitude easily accessible in the city. Chauffeuring provided a chance to chat, minus interruptions, and was not perceived as a chore; everyone pitched in to keep the household and family running smoothly. We often look back nostalgically at those magical years. It did not occur to me that to be a devoted mother/wife was a sacrifice; rather I felt privileged to have been able to have had children.

What I had learned about childbirth, child development, and family life in graduate school and in practice was augmented and sometimes supplanted by what I was learning experientially in my own life and through observations of the lives of friends at the same stage in their family life cycle. Being home and confined for a few days with preschoolers when they had measles, chicken pox, mumps, and other normal childhood diseases in rapid succession was neither fun nor stimulating. It became clear that if a mother didn't have money for domestic help or baby-sitters, and had no relatives available in the vicinity, she could soon feel like a resentful caged animal. If her husband came home wanting attention and companionship and had little compassion for her plight, or refused to take over for a while so she could "escape" into the outer world to regain her equilibrium, both her ire and the level of marital discord increased. But this scenario and perspective didn't appear in Spock's books or those of other important authors for our generation. My friends and I pondered how strange it was that so many of the child development and other psychology books were written by men or unmarried women who had never raised a family. Perhaps I made an unconscious mental note then to someday write a much more inclusive treatise on typical problems of normal families; much of what germinated then came to fruition later in some of my writings on healthy couples (Kaslow, 1982b), healthy families (Kaslow, 1981d), and the family life of psychotherapists (Kaslow, 1987b; Kaslow & Schulman, 1987). The research I was doing during the "at home" years was of the participant-observer genre; I was living closely in the community of the families I was studying. It proved a vast laboratory full of rich data.

There was a large and active International House on the campus of the University of Pennsylvania. Because my prior contacts with foreign students had been so rewarding, because I recognized the enormity of the adjustment problems confronted by students studying in a strange land, and because I knew how much the women of Zonta House had appreciated receptive families in the community, Sol and I decided to become a "host family" for our local International House when Nadine was only two years old. We increasingly wanted to become "citizens of the world" who viewed people and events from a multicultural perspective. Over the next 15 years we hosted students from such countries as Japan, the Philippines, Mexico, Thailand, Korea, and India. The Indian student we were assigned, Inderjit Jaipaul, was a graduate student with a husband and two children. Our families were very compatible and we all became close friends; we spent many holidays together and shared our different worlds and religions. When they applied for U.S. citizenship, we became their sponsors. Today they are valued members of our family.

In serving as a "host family" we attended ethnic food and folk festivals, concerts of music from many lands, and sometimes served as parent surrogates. These experiences broadened our horizons immeasurably and helped us ensure that our children were not provincial in orientation.

PATHWAYS CHOSEN: UNIVERSITY TEACHING

Shortly after Howard was born and I was a full-time mom, I received a call from Temple University. I was asked to teach a course in marriage and the family two afternoons a week at a branch near my home. I was delighted as the hours coincided with his nap schedule. I had begun to feel intellectually stultified and was interested in a very part-time position. From the first day I entered a college classroom to teach I knew "this is what I want to do professionally." Immediately and ever since I have enjoyed the reading and lecture preparation, the questions from and comments by eager and curious students, their energy and optimism, the challenge of remaining vital and abreast of developments in the field, and the best of what academe represents.

It soon became evident that I couldn't progress beyond part-time instructor without a doctorate and I began to dream about enrolling in a doctoral program one day.

The decision to pursue my doctorate crystallized the following summer when I (taking the children along) went to Camp B'nai Brith in an administrative staff position. There were several brilliant Rabbis on staff, including Ira Eisenstein, with whom I worked very closely writing sermons and speeches, and with whom I had dialogues long into the night. The Rabbis encouraged me to pursue my dreams and clearly expressed their belief that I had the vitality, intelligence, tenacity, and level-headedness to handle the rigorous pressures of a compartmentalized life.

Sol and I talked it over and agreed I would start back with one course a semester until both children were in school full time. Geographically, my choices were limited to the Philadelphia area. It was almost 10 years since I had gotten my master's degree and the few top-of-the-line schools I was interested in applying to all required GRE's and/or the Miller Analogies Test. My parents and friends discouraged my planned new venture with statements such as, "Why do you need it? You have enough degrees", and "What about the children?"

THE DOCTORAL YEARS

Fortunately, my inner voice was stronger. I learned I could cram for the examinations after the children went to sleep. I did, and came through remarkably well—on the first try. In my application interviews I faced enormous prejudice against women with families; we were not considered good prospects or investments for a department. One chairman was tactless enough to say his program did not cater to "bored suburban housewives," a pejorative view I was to hear many times in the next few years. And, of course, no one had assistantships available to part-time students. I had passed Go and entered the obstacle course. There was no "sisterhood" or National Organization for Women to turn to—it was go it alone or stop. Lessons in persistence and determination abounded.

Since our personal funds were still limited, I took a part-time teaching position at the Ogontz Campus of Pennsylvania State University near our home and used my salary to cover tuition and other educational expenses. One of my colleagues there was Lita Linzer Schwartz, who had begun and completed her doctorate several years before I did. We often discussed how to juggle the multiple roles of mother, wife, chauffeur, professor, student, and friend without guilt or total exhaustion and provided support and solace to each other during turbulent periods (see Schwartz, Chapter 7, Volume 2 of this work). Our friendship ripened into a productive collaboration also. We later shared our concern about cults and their devastating effect on families (Kaslow & Schwartz, 1983; Schwartz & Kaslow, 1979, 1982). During the 1980s when both of us became involved in the area of divorce as teachers, therapists, and mediators, we coauthored a book, *Dynamics of Divorce: A Life Cycle Perspective* (Kaslow & Schwartz, 1987a) and reported on our research on older children of divorce (Kaslow & Schwartz, 1987b).

I selected Bryn Mawr College, a beautiful institution located in Philadelphia's Main Line, for my doctoral studies. They were willing to have me begin on a part-time basis. The entire atmosphere of Bryn Mawr, one of the Seven Sisters Women's Colleges (coed at the graduate level), was "upper class" and regal. It was quiet, dignified, and intellectually rigorous. What a contrast to the noisy, huge, urban universities I had previously attended! The superficial gentility was deceptive. The faculty was erudite and demanding; the other students ultra bright and highly competitive. I read voraciously and was glad I had only taken one course.

The hardest days were when I had to go to class and I had a sick child at home. I learned that fears of this produce many working women's greatest nightmares. Fortunately, my mom had become supportive of my return to college and was "on call" for such emergencies. The special ties between grandchildren and grandparents became apparent and treasured. I have embodied respect for these in my work, which seeks to ensure in the families I treat and the trainees I teach that grandparents and grandchildren have easy and loving access to one another. Later I came to value and incorporate work with multigenerational families when it appears necessary (Boszormenyi-Nagy & Spark, 1973; Framo, 1981) and to encourage people to reconnect with estranged members of their families of origin and/or to resolve unfinished issues from the past with them whenever feasible (Bowen, 1978). These aspects of the work of Framo, Boszormenyi-Nagy and Spark, and Bowen are particularly compatible with my own theoretical predilections, and so I gravitated toward them when I became conversant with them.

Toward the end of my first year at Bryn Mawr I was informed that my grace period for part-time work had expired and I now had to matriculate full time. I did. Fortunately, the children were rarely sick and they were in school a full day. The first two years my schedule consisted of teaching at Penn State or going to classes from 9 a.m. to 3 p.m. I chauffeured, handled dinner, helped with homework, and shared activities with the family. When the children went to bed at 9 p.m., I studied and wrote term papers. During the last two years, dissertation writing and seeing patients supplanted attending classes during school hours. The children recall falling asleep to the hum of the typewriter and often waking to the same clicking. They thought I never slept; sometimes I didn't.

Sol's cooperation was a steady force. While he was building his business, he also shared the parenting and household tasks and was my greatest cheerleader when I felt overwhelmed. The children accepted the reality of our way of life as having benefits for all, even though it was markedly different from that of our neighbors. They didn't find it strange that I studied while watching Howard's Little League games—only paying attention closely to the action when he was at bat or in the catcher's box. Later when I heard married male graduate students complain about the load they were carrying (especially if their wives typed papers and did all of the child care), I wasn't fully sympathetic. To those who say they cannot get advanced degrees because of family and financial constraints, I ask, why not? My experience and that of my ambitious, determined friends is that it can be done. Being well organized and able to concentrate on several things at once helps.

My favorite courses were theories of personality, psychoanalytic theory and practice, psychopathology, and family therapy. During my doctoral years, I saw some long-term patients in psychodynamic treatment and resumed seeing patients in marital and family therapy. Life was busy, exciting, and expansive.

In one psychoanalytic theory course I was asked to discuss Norman Brown's (1959) *Life Against Death* the following week. The particular portion assigned focused on the differences between the Apollonian and Dionysian ego types. Tired of all the excessive verbiage, I decided to write a free-verse narration (which one of my classmates read) depicting these personality types and to attempt to portray vividly the differences by means of modern dance rather than words. This medium seemed so much more expressive and alive. And since I had become imbued with holistic concepts (Angyal, 1965; Goldstein, 1959) it enabled me to find a channel for integrating body-mind, psyche-soma, id-ego, and self-other. The presentation was invigorating.

At that moment, many themes converged for me and my dissertation topic flashed into consciousness. It seemed imperative that dance, as one of my major vehicles for communication, self-expression, joyousness, and release, should become intertwined in my life as a therapist. This was essential for me to feel whole and not fragmented. I sought and gained permission to pursue an investigation of dance and movement therapies as nonverbal adjunctive treatment to verbal psychotherapy for my dissertation (Kaslow, 1969). I found that many dance and movement techniques had come to the fore in the "growth" environment of the 1960s and I explored bioenergetics, the human potential and encounter movements, sensitivity training, and hatha yoga—experientially, through observation, and through a literature search. In addition, I investigated art, music, and drama therapy—all in relation to traditional verbal psychotherapies—and concluded these all merited a place in the armamentarium of therapeutic approaches and that they clearly were valid in reaching and treating frightened, uncommunicative, and nonverbal patients. In coming to a greater understanding of unconscious processes and nonverbal body language, I found my ability to enter and touch the lives of hard-to-reach patients improved. Later, this background soil made me very receptive to transplanting and adapting techniques of sculpting (Duhl, Kantor, & Duhl, 1973; Satir, 1972) into my own work. One needs to be comfortable in and with one's own body to utilize these effectively. It also meant that later I intuitively resonated to the symbolic-experiential philosophy and practice of Whitaker and his colleagues (Neill & Kniskern, 1982; Whitaker, 1976; Whitaker & Bumberry, 1988) and was influenced by Whitaker's ideas and way of engaging and connecting to patients.

My tendency to incorporate seemingly disparate fields of knowledge and practice with ways of being in the world was no doubt multidetermined. I had never been a conformist or a purist and doctrinaire orthodoxies seemed too rigid to be defensible. Thus the eclecticism of my doctoral years, which led me to seek new integrations within a holistic paradigm and to avoid dichotomous thinking, became a continuing hallmark of my work.

Graduation was a long-awaited occasion. It was thrilling to have both my family of origin and my family of creation at the ceremony. The children wanted to know which came first—Doctor-Mommy or Mommy-Doctor? At the graduation party that my husband made for me—one of our male guests, an engineer, said to Nadine—"Your Mom is the first attractive, family-oriented woman I know to become a doctor." Incredulous, she took him by the hand and walked him into the family room saying, "Here's a whole roomful of them" since by then, some of my friends had also become M.D.s, Ph.D.s, and J.D.s. His comment was a sign of the social mores and expectations of the times; my daughter's response was the view of the future. For her it was also prophetic; she was then only 12 years old, yet her goals included getting a doctorate. Thirteen years later she became the second Dr. Kaslow in the family (see Chapter 11, Volume 2 of this work). Rather than resenting her mother's career, she identified with it and designed one for herself. This is part of the changing saga of the relationship of career mothers and daughters (Kaslow & Kaslow, 1981, 1985). It is no wonder that the family life of psychotherapists evolved as a major arena of professional interest for me and is one of the areas in which I have attempted to make a major contribution (Kaslow, 1984c, 1984e, 1987b; Kaslow & Schulman, 1987). It is my contention that although there must be some boundaries between our personal and professional lives, the two are inextricably intertwined and should be mutually enhancing and compatible. When this is not the case, severe role conflict and guilt encroach on one's functioning and become debilitating.

BECOMING IDENTIFIED AS A FAMILY PSYCHOLOGIST

My job search was circumscribed by geographic limitations; we liked living in the Philadelphia area and my husband's position as a manager of a brokerage firm precluded relocation. The best teaching position I could obtain was as an Assistant Professor at the Graduate School of Social Work at the University of Pennsylvania. I did not agree with the principles that undergirded their pedagogical and practice philosophy—most notably the adherence to the maxim that "growth through pain" is to be fostered. I believe the greatest growth occurs from encouragement, positive reinforcement, and the elimination of obstacles. Nonetheless, I was able to introduce and teach a family therapy course for two years (1970-1972) and I really liked the theory and practice of family treatment approaches. Although I also taught growth and development and individual casework practice, the family therapy course was my favorite and was very popular with the students.

Immersion in Family Therapy

Philadelphia at that time was a hub of family therapy activity. Initially when I applied to become a member of the high profile Philadelphia Family Institute, they asked, "Who did you train with," assuming it had to be one of their prestigious members. Their list included Ivan Boszormenyi-Nagy, Geraldine Spark, Ross Speck, Geraldine Lincoln Grossman, Gerald Zuk, Pirooz Sholevar, David Rubenstein, and numerous other leaders in the field. I indicated that I had taken a course at Bryn Mawr with Greta Zybon and, for the rest, had learned by trial and error and reading. I got accepted and avidly utilized the opportunity to observe several of these luminaries teach and do therapy—particularly Nagy, Rubenstein, and Framo.

I found David Rubenstein's work exhilarating and validating. I was still very much a novice when I first observed him treating a family through a one-way mirror. When I heard his warm and compassionate responses and interpretations and saw him changing patients' seating arrangements to modify the alliance and schism patterns and to facilitate more functional and rewarding transactions, my internal monologue said "that's exactly what I do." This provided support for me to continue combining existential, psychodynamic, and structural elements in my family systems work—despite criticisms from others that I wasn't a disciple of any one specific school of thought (see Rubenstein & Timmens, 1978, for more on his work).

I gravitated toward utilizing Boszormenyi-Nagy and Spark's interpretations on invisible loyalties and multidirectional partiality (1973) and experimented with Framo's model of couples group therapy (1973). The latter I adapted to a five-couple closed-end group model that suited my style as a therapist better than his three-couple open-ended model. I retained his ideas about why it is important to utilize a heterosexual cotherapy pair as the treatment team (Kaslow, 1981c; Kaslow & Lieberman, 1981). I continue to employ this treatment methodology, particularly with couples contemplating divorce, and often demonstrate it with simulated groups at workshops. It is predicated on principles of dynamics of both group therapy and couples therapy—representing another area in which I integrate approaches drawn from different but related fields.

By 1971 I knew that family therapy and what it entailed would be a major part of my teaching, practice, research, and writing. It was a relatively young field, receptive to innovation and expansion. I believed then, as now, that all treatment must occur in the context of the patient in relation to his/her significant others and the larger relevant ecosystem as life encompasses an ongoing undulating movement of the self toward and away from the system. This made much more sense to me than the "hard line" psychoanalytic approach. I had learned in my master's program that if one were treating a child and the parents called for information, that one was to interpret this as an effort to control the therapy and the therapist. For me it also signified the impact of one's therapy on other family members and was an expression of worry and concern as well. A family systems framework was clearly what I had been searching for to anchor my teaching and clinical work.

Supervision and Consultation

Within our doctoral program the students were clamoring for a course in supervision and consultation. Like psychology doctoral students, they were being asked to supervise master's students and provide consultation to community mental health centers, school systems, and social agencies. When approached to create and teach such a course, I gladly accepted the challenge. It grew into a mission. I could find no textbook that adequately addressed the material I thought should be covered. When several of my favorite colleagues hurled the gauntlet, saying, "If it doesn't exist, write it," I wrote my first book, *Issues in Human Services: A Sourcebook for Supervision and Staff Development* (Kaslow, 1972b). I believe that the quality of supervision, consultation, and staff training one receives as a graduate student, intern, or resident, and staff member or private practitioner is a critical element in one's continuous learning process. My commitment to expanding and refining this area of knowledge has remained constant and has resulted in two additional books

(Kaslow, 1977b; 1986c). In addition, there have been numerous articles and chapters concerned with administrative supervision (1980b) and how this is to be distinguished from and separated from clinical supervision of mental health professionals; on treating military families (1984d) and consultation to the military system (1985); on a model for an intensive six-day postgraduate training experience (1986a); and on specific supervision of couples and family therapy (1977, in press).

In the past 10 years I have spent a large portion of my time in private practice; part of this time was allocated to serving as a consultant to other private practitioners involved in doing marital and family therapy, sex therapy, and divorce mediation as well as individual psychotherapy. (I am an AAMFT-approved supervisor, an AASECT-approved supervisor, and an Academy of Family Mediators-approved consultant.)

Several key points have emerged from my study and practice of consultation to other therapists (Kaslow, 1986) that bear mention here.

- The consultation contract must be carefully negotiated and very clear before consultation is begun.
- In this litigious era, one must specify whether one is rendering supervision or consultation. If supervision, one carries a direct responsibility for the quality of the supervisee's work and therefore can be sued by the supervisee's patients under the doctrine of vicarious liability (Slovenko, 1980). Conversely, a consultee is free to accept or reject a consultant's ideas and recommendations, as the consultant bears no authority over him or her. Therefore, it is unlikely that a consultant would get entangled in vicarious liability lawsuits.
- Even senior practitioners sometimes become perplexed or stuck by a given case. Having an expert and trusted consultant to turn to is an important link; here one can explore countertransference issues, other reasons for blocking, and alternative ways of conceptualizing and intervening, as well as be stimulated to expand knowledge and augment skills.
- Solo private practice can be lonely. Having a valued consultant can alleviate some of the sense of professional isolation.

After leaving the faculty of the Graduate School at the University of Pennsylvania, I spent a year precepting residents in the Medical School's Department of Psychiatry. I was primarily engaged to precept in group therapy for therapy conducted in an inpatient setting. I was struck by the lack of involvement required of the patients' significant others. Families were considered more of a nuisance than a support system or essential part of the treatment team who would again be major players in the patient's life drama after release. My efforts to rectify this by introducing family systems concepts were of no avail. The resistance of old-liners was enormous and it took more than one lone voice to penetrate it.

Correctional and Forensic Psychology and Family Law: A New Pathway and Career Phase

During that same year (1972-1973) I was hired as a consultant to the Pennsylvania Law and Justice Institute. The Institute was dedicated to promoting justice for suspects prior to their being tried, and for inmates after incarceration. The Board of Directors was comprised of judges, attorneys, sociologists and criminologists, liberal lay citizens, and some former and current prisoners. I remember the astonishment of some when a guard brought a prisoner board member to a meeting in handcuffs. It was strange for many of the "respectable law-abiding citizens" to sit at the same table as equals with offenders and ex-offenders. My role as the "expert" in group dynamics and human relations was to facilitate their communication and understanding so they could forge and implement their agenda of improving the critical justice system.

At one of the training retreats run by the Law and Justice Institute, I met then Associate Commissioner of Corrections for Pennsylvania, Stewart Werner, MSW. We found that we shared the same philosophy regarding the correctional system—that rehabilitation was part of its mission and that treatment services, delivered by well-qualified professionals, had to become part of prison life. When Mr. Werner was promoted to Commissioner of Corrections (1973), he invited and urged me to establish a doctoral level component in correctional psychology and, as part of my faculty responsibility, to serve as Consultant in training and treatment services to the Bureau of Corrections.

Jules C. Abrams, Ph.D., Director of the Psychology Doctoral (Psy.D.) program at Hahnemann Medical College (now University) in Philadelphia was a farsighted and innovative individual. When I presented the idea for this program to him he liked it and I was hired as an Associate Professor of Psychology in Hahnemann's interdisciplinary department of Mental Health Sciences. We established an internship at Graterford Prison, one of Pennsylvania's maximum security facilities, and I supervised the interns who were placed there. Some students disliked the idea of an internship in a prison; others found it definitely challenging and worthwhile. I also taught a course at Hahnemann in Correctional Psychology. Periodically I went to Harrisburg to meet with the superintendents of all of the facilities about augmenting and expanding their treatment and rehabilitation services and implementing staff training programs for clinical staff. This became a model program (for details, see Kaslow, 1974b, 1975a; Kaslow & Abrams, 1976; Kaslow & De Cato,

1974; Kaslow & Fenster, 1976) that received a great deal of publicity. It also raised many questions about whether and how to treat in adult correctional settings (Kaslow, 1980b), and about ethical problems in the practice of prison psychology (Kaslow, 1980a). These were crucial, socially relevant issues in a milieu open to exploration and critical self-feedback.

My special interest was on the impact of the long-term, antisocial, illicit behavior of individuals on their significant others. Since those incarcerated in maximum security facilities are usually repeat offenders and "hardened" criminals, their families have lived with frequent arrests, days in court, convictions, and imprisonment. We investigated what kinds of families they came from and were likely to return to. We urged the Bureau of Corrections to permit contact visits for most and conjugal visits for "trustees" and others who had earned privileges for good behavior. We encouraged setting up play space for children in the visitation area so that they could visit with their incarcerated parents in the best environment possible under the circumstances. We attempted to convince our interns and other staff about the importance of occasional marital and/or family therapy sessions for prisoners and their significant others—particularly as part of discharge planning (Kaslow, 1978, 1987f; Kaslow & Zwerling, 1974). When this was instituted, it was noted that the partners had an opportunity to express their hopes and fears about their reunion after the prisoner's release and to grapple with the problems they could begin to anticipate.

Unfortunately, in 1975 the state decided to retrench on its commitment to rehabilitation programs and return to gearing its thrust toward punishment and warehousing, or so it appeared to us. We phased out this part of the Hahnemann correctional psychology activity. It was replaced by a much more broadly conceived program. Dr. Israel Zwerling, then chairman of the larger Department of Mental Health Sciences, created the Section of Forensic Psychology and Psychiatry and appointed me to serve as chief of the section. The section rapidly took hold and grew—its membership encompassed psychologists, psychiatrists, attorneys, and judges. The courses and community programs we ran reflected my growing interest in the areas of family law and mental health law and the interfaces and conflicts between the fields of law and psychology. One program that I generated as chief of this section was the Ph.D.-J.D. program cosponsored by Hahnemann and Villanova Law School. I served as this program's Co-Director with the Associate Dean of the Law School and received a wonderful exposure to the ethos, values, and content of law school education. I guest lectured in family law and law and psychiatry courses at Villanova, the University of Pennsylvania, and other neighboring law schools.

This led to my joining the American Psychology-Law Society and ultimately becoming involved in establishing the American Board of Forensic

Psychology (ABFP) and The American Academy of Forensic Psychologists (AAFP). I believed that we had staked out an area of competence and needed to publicize it to the profession and the community at large. It appeared imperative that we not lose ground to psychiatry and this profession was rapidly moving toward certification. I was elected to serve as the first president of both organizations (1977-1980). The ABFP established credentialing and examination procedures for the diplomate in forensic psychology. I was pleased to pass the rigorous exam and receive my (first) diplomate or board certification.

Military Families

Meanwhile, I taught family therapy courses in Hahnemann's psychology, psychiatry, and mental health technology programs and supervised interns and residents. One of the psychiatric residents I supervised was Richard Ridenour, M.D., a lieutenant in the U.S. Navy. He was doing his child psychiatry rotation at Hahnemann's Peberdy Clinic and began to do some cotherapy on family cases with a psychology intern, Janice Goldman. He was extremely astute and sensitive and really "turned on" to family therapy. He believed that the other residents at the Philadelphia Naval Hospital should also receive training in family therapy and recommended that I teach a 12-week course there. They interviewed several other local family therapists: all were male M.D.s. When they tentatively decided that they wanted to hire me, they were confronted with the fact that they had never before had a Ph.D. or a woman as a consultant/trainer. Because of the administrator's ambivalence about breaking out of the usual mold and the slowness of government bureaucracies, it took several months until it all gelled in 1974. Once it did, it was a superb fit from the very first session. I found then Captain James Sears, the chair of the Department of Psychiatry at the Philadelphia Naval Hospital, to be open-minded, highly intelligent, and very responsive to his residents and the patient population they served. To my surprise, because I held many stereotypes about "Navy Docs," I found these residents were curious, bright, eager to learn, and talented.

The first session I did a didactic lecture. They decided that they had so many families that should be treated, that the next session I should do a live demonstration with a high-ranking officer and his family and one of them would serve as cotherapist. It quickly became obvious that the officer-physician patient had some strong reservations about being referred to see a petite female psychologist who was a civilian. Since he was due to ship out in six weeks and the family was experiencing severe stress, it did not seem prudent to make his attitude toward the consultant the focus of the session. Thus, I chose to literally and figuratively go "one down" to make my cotherapist, those viewing over a one-way mirror, and the patients comfortable enough to proceed with the session. I sat on the floor and played with the youngest child. From this nonthreatening position I was able to guide my neophyte cotherapist and be discreetly confrontational with the commander-father. The family thought they had derived so much from the hour that they set another appointment with my cotherapist. I had learned a valuable lesson in the effective use of one's power with an authoritarian personality and with fledgling family therapists.

We continued utilizing this cotherapy format for several weeks. These lieutenant commander residents were avid learners and began to add families to their caseloads as quickly as they could. They were doing cotherapy and found that when they worked together in male/male pairs, since all of the residents were men, that it was not nearly as effective as when I served as cotherapist. They attributed this to the importance of the presence and input of a female therapist. Consequently, they asked if they could invite two of the department's female social workers to join in the course and to become cotherapists. They were pleased with how well this worked out and it markedly changed the intergroup relationships within the department—with the women gaining more stature and status.

As these residents and their superior officers were transferred out to different duty stations, they wanted to take family therapy with them. For several years I continued teaching annual courses at the Philadelphia Naval Hospital and also became a frequent guest lecturer and presenter at Grand Rounds at Portsmouth, San Diego, and Long Beach Naval Hospitals. At the Long Beach facility, long recognized for its flagship treatment of service personnel who have severe substance abuse problems, I consulted on marital, sexual, and family issues in the lives of the chemically addicted when Ted Williams, M.D., was director. I was also privileged to take their excellent course for doctors in substance abuse treatment. Subsequently, I have consulted with inpatient facilities in Florida for substance abusers and have done some writing on this topic (Kaslow & Mountz, 1985). In our practice we treat many chemically addicted patients, so this training has proven to be of lasting value.

After he finished his residency, Captain (now Admiral) Ridenour and I often guest-lectured and presented workshops together on the military family. This led to our being invited to write a book on *The Military Family: Dynamics and Treatment* (Kaslow & Ridenour, 1984), which covers issues ranging from the various meanings of "the military family" to the adaptability of children in military families to the increased complexities of life for military families due to the increasing number of dual career couples. Therapists who treat military families must be aware of how they are different from and similar to their civilian counterparts. They must be able to function within the constraints posed by working with the military such as having to terminate therapy quickly if someone is "shipped out" unexpectedly during a mobilization action and receiving orders to be on duty after a treatment session has been scheduled.

As my work with military families became known and recognized I was invited to serve as a Distinguished Visiting Professor at Lackland Air Force Base in San Antonio, Texas, for several years, and to do workshops on understanding and treating military families throughout the United States. *Duty, honor, country, patriotism,* and *"the right stuff"* (Wolfe, 1979) are words and ideas that have been infused with new meaning for me. In my writings on the military I have attempted to convey a sense of humility and awe about being privileged to train others to treat military families and to consult with systems in the military on a variety of issues about personnel.

One of the most unexpected and momentous experiences of this aspect of my career was an invitation I received in the spring of 1986 from Lt. Colonel Itamar Barnea of the Israeli Ministry of Defense. He had heard from other Israelis about my presentations at International Family Therapy Congresses there (in 1979 and 1983), as a guest lecturer at Tel Aviv University (1983), and at numerous institutes, agencies, and universities throughout Israel. He had also read *The Military Family* (Kaslow & Ridenour, 1984) and translated much of it into Hebrew. Because it contained much that was relevant to Israeli military families (almost all families in Israel but the most orthodox have or have had a member in the military). Upon learning I was due to return for the 1986 Family Therapy Congress, Dr. Barnea, in his position as Chief of Psychological and Psychiatric Services for the Air Force, invited me to consult and guest-lecture.

Although I had already taught in Israel during a period of turbulence when graduate students came to class in uniform and parked their guns at the door in case their unit was mobilized and they were summoned from class, I was unprepared for the barbed-wire fences and other tight security measures I found at the Air Force installation. In Israel, families live daily with the threat of war, loved ones being killed and maimed, frequent separations, the horror of sometimes being aggressors, the blood stains on their dream of peace and freedom in the land of milk and honey. The tough young men bemoaned fighting at the front when their babies were born, being away unexpectedly when their reserve unit was reactivated and again having to miss important family events—and never knowing when it will really end. Working with men and women in Israeli military families during war (the strife with Lebanon and Arab communities in Israel) has a compelling urgency about it that is absent when we deal with American military families in an era of relative peace.

I tried to provide (1) a conceptual framework in which to view the military family in its specific sociopolitical, economic, and religious context; (2) a highlighting of specific concerns which characterize many military families; (3) a familiarization with those intervention strategies likely to prove most quickly efficacious under the prevailing circumstances, and (4) a foundation for understanding the impact on the professional of being in the military and helping military families cope with daily life-threatening events and other disturbing exigencies in addition to the more usual vicissitudes of living. This work with the military has always seemed to have much more profound consequences than my treatment of the outpatient population I see at my office.

Families With a Learning Disabled Child

At Hahnemann, Dr. Abrams, a psychoanalytically oriented psychologist, treated many exceptional, learning disabled children. I shared with him my ideas about the importance of involving families. We had numerous dialogues about this as we sought to evolve a continuum of treatment strategies ranging from tutoring only, through tutoring plus child therapy, to concurrent parent-child therapy, to parent education groups, to family therapy plus educational interventions. We also evolved a schema for matching which interventions to use with which types of presenting problems and family dynamics (Abrams and Kaslow, 1976, 1977; Kaslow & Abrams, 1977).

Prior to that there had been a dearth of literature on this topic; our articles and presentations generated a great deal of interest. Part of this paucity was no doubt attributable to the fact that much of the family therapy field had evolved generically—looking at universals which seemed to characterize all family systems—like hierarchy and boundary issues and difficulties in communication and in separation-individuation. Many seemed to posit, overtly or covertly, that differential diagnosis and systems concepts were inherently incompatible and so the former receded in importance. Yet it seemed obvious as we worked with families with a learning disabled member that unless a correct diagnosis—formulated using psychological, neurological, and neuropsychological as well as family assessment techniques—was conducted, that one could not intervene utilizing the most effective treatment plan.

I served as a consultant to several special education schools in the Philadelphia vicinity from 1971-1980 and conducted programs utilizing dance, movement, and other creative arts therapy approaches adapted for learning disabled children who often need exposure to techniques that improve their eye-hand coordination and their overall body coordination (Kaslow, 1972a). By incorporating the use of art materials, music, and movement experiences into the cognitive learning environment, these children are enabled to achieve heightened sensory, tactile, and kinesthetic learning. These approaches can be employed to reinforce and extend their visual, mental learning. (Kaslow, 1974a, 1975b/1978, 1978).

We also trained parents in way of working with their children physically to maximum utilization of their existing capabilities. I was pleased to be able to adapt the work I had done for my dissertation for use with this underserved population and to see the enthusiasm and happiness it generated in these often troubled and rejected children. This dovetailed with my family therapy approach in treating these families and in training staff and faculty for treatment roles with families at special schools. One crucial point is that before many parents can accept the handicapped child they have, they must first "bury" the image of the ideal perfect child they had fantasized. Other salient ideas are that the parents must work through their guilt about their part in having a disabled child and stop blaming their partner. They must be helped not to let the child become a tyrannical despot who plays on their guilt and sympathy and often gets out of control. And they must be guided not to let the entire family life revolve around or the major part of its resources be allocated to the handicapped child—to the detriment and resentment of other family members (Kaslow, 1978; Kaslow & Cooper, 1978). Many of these points are also pertinent in treating families with children with other kinds of chronic physical, emotional, and educational disabilities.

An Official Family Therapy Training Program

There was so much interest in Philadelphia in formal and specific family therapy training within a university context that a Master's in Family Therapy Program was created at Hahnemann under the leadership of Ivan Boszormenyi-Nagy and with Robert Garfield as its first director. I was a member of the founding and core faculty that formulated the curriculum and standards. Although the program reflected Nagy's relational-contextual approach, it also incorporated other theoretical schools. I taught an overview course in comparative theories of family therapy, as I believe students should be exposed to the breadth of the field at the outset. Later, when they have some grounding in the broad spectrum, they can choose to become more proficient in one or several approaches. One is much less likely to become doctrinaire if one's education follows this route rather than if one learns one approach in depth as if it is the best and only right way and then learns that there are other, lesser schools of thought that can easily be disparaged and dismissed. It was probably out of these courses that the integrative, "diaclectic model" emerged more fully (Kaslow, 1981a). I continue to be interested in the various paradigms that are being generated and refined and in analyzing across theories to see how each addresses key variables such as time dimension of focus, what brings about change, length of treatment, and role of therapist (Kaslow, 1987a; Kaslow & Aradi, 1987). After comparing and contrasting from the extant literature and from conversations with and observations of leading theoreticians and practitioners, I return to my drawing board to attempt a new integration and synthesis, culling out what works and discarding what doesn't and trying to ascertain what approaches are most efficacious for what patients and problems. Since 1987, each year at the APA Convention, I have been giving a special seminar – an in-depth review of the major theories and techniques – for candidates applying for diplomate status in family psychology to the American Board of Family Psychology. Since the participants are all senior-level practitioners, this is an advanced and up-to-the-minute refresher course for which I prepare anew each time.

All of the faculty in the MFT program wanted to teach practice-oriented courses. I avoided competition and conflict by creating a unique course flowing from my special areas of "expertise" and containing information of vital import to the students. What evolved was an amalgamation of my forensic and family therapy involvements. This course, entitled "Legal Aspects of Family Therapy Practice," was taught from 1976 to 1980. It dealt with the different times during the family life cycle when the family may come in contact with the legal system and what the therapist should know to be optimally useful at these junctures. It also contained information on privilege, confidentiality, duty to warn, responding to subpoenas, and serving as an expert witness. Much time was spent on abortion, adoption, divorce and custody, mental health commitment, privacy rights of minors, and euthanasia. Many faculty took the course to fill in gaps in their knowledge reservoir. Student evaluations deemed it a wise, practical, somewhat "scary," essential course.

Now, a decade later, there is a mounting interest in the ethical and legal issues surrounding practice. This, as a personal stream of my interest, has found expression in the section of *The American Journal of Family Therapy* titled: "Family Law Issues in Family Therapy Practice" that I was asked to create by Richard Sauber, Ph.D. I have edited it for the past five years. Its goal is to bring these areas of overlap and interface to the attention of practitioners in "cutting edge" articles.

Recently, invitations to write and lecture about this topic have increased and my activity level in this potential mine field is bubbling again. Clearly we can no longer think in terms of a semisacred, confidential relationship between patients and therapists. The myriad legal and ethical issues surrounding practice makes the therapy room much less of a safe sanctuary for all. By imparting knowledge of these issues, I am part of the vanguard attempting to help therapists to practice ethically and avoid the pitfalls that lead to dreaded malpractice suits.

BECOMING AN EDITOR: JOURNALS AND MORE JOURNALS

In 1975 I was invited to become the second editor of the *Journal of Marriage and Family Counseling,* the fledgling journal of AAMFT. Its founding editor, William C. Nichols, had done a yeoman job of launching this publication and I realized being his successor would be a mammoth undertaking. Thrilled and honored to be selected, I agreed; I had little idea of what was entailed.

From 1976 to 1981 I served as editor; during this time the name of the journal was changed to *Journal of Marital and Family Therapy* to more accurately reflect its thrust. As the first female editor of a major family therapy journal, I endeavored to include more women on the editorial board. I also encouraged female acquaintances to begin to contribute to the literature. Our journal rapidly became the journal in the family therapy field with the largest circulation in the world. At that time the post of editor carried no financial remuneration; for me it was a labor of love that took countless hours a week. I personally edited and proofread every article that was accepted.

Being an editor is a weighty responsibility. The editor makes the final decision on what will and won't be published. If the journal is influential, these decisions shape the evolving literature of the field and impact on its direction and flow. I perceived this responsibility as a marvelous challenge and learned to live with the anger authors display when their articles are rejected. In reading everything that came across my desk in this field, I managed to keep abreast of what was transpiring in research and practice and to be among the avant-garde shaping the future. During my term as editor, I did one special international issue that was published simultaneously in English in *JMFT* and in Italian in *Terapia Familiare* by its editor, Maurizio Andolfi.

Since the mid-1970s I've served on about 18 editorial boards—mainly of journals devoted to the family, general psychology topics, and divorce mediation. I am still editing the section of *AJFT* alluded to earlier. In keeping with my international involvements, I am on the editorial boards of two Argentinian journals published in Spanish and of *Terapia Familiare,* published in Italian. My own articles have been translated and published in German, Hebrew, Polish, Norwegian, Spanish, and other languages.

I feel strongly about there being no barriers to the free dissemination of ideas in the field across cultures and languages. Thus, in 1979, as *JMFT* Editor, I hosted and chaired the first meeting of editors of journals in the family field throughout the world. I also chaired the second meeting in Israel in 1983. One action was to see that the editors made a verbal agreement to ask that their publishers not charge copyright reprint fees if an article is translated into another language with permission and with full citations included. There has been good compliance with this accord. I co-convened the meetings of the International Editors Group in Czechoslovakia in 1987 and in Ireland in 1989 with Jurgen Hargens of Germany. This group is comprised of an elite corps of people who influence what is destined to become the pace-setting literature.

The International Book of Family Therapy was published in 1982 (Kaslow, 1982a). It contains reprints of articles selected as outstanding by other editors as well as original articles. My lead chapter represented an effort to pull together the mainstreams in the field and to celebrate the pioneers.

Other offshoots of the editing activity have been invitations to conduct workshops on writing for publication and chairing and serving on search committees for journal editors. This seems important, as they become key players in fashioning our professional world. I'm often queried if I'd accept another editorship and I think the answer is still no. While I was *JMFT* Editor I completed one book of my own; since then I have been able to author and/or edit-write nine. I finally realized that there is a finite number of balls I can juggle simultaneously. And there are more books waiting to be written.

In 1986 I was approached by Bernie Mazel, then president of Brunner/Mazel, Inc., about becoming a series editor. Pleased with this opportunity to influence what was to be published in a different way, I accepted. The series, "New Frontiers in Couples and Family Therapy," is now off to a good start and, it is hoped, will expand considerably in the 1990s.

From 1982 to 1988 I served as Book Review Editor of the *AFTA Newsletter*. In selecting books to be reviewed, one plays a pivotal role in what books are brought to the attention of a wide readership. I resigned when it seemed time to move on.

OTHER HIGHWAYS, OTHER BYWAYS

My Hahnemann years were busy and eventful; I had become a full professor (1978) and had been engaged in many fruitful endeavors. But by 1980 I was restless. Thus I accepted an enticing offer to become Dean of the Florida School of Professional Psychology in Miami. The salary was excellent and I was the first woman to be appointed Dean of a Professional Psychology School.

My parents headed south in June 1980; Sol and I relocated in November. He was able to transfer to the Miami office of his firm and took on new responsibilities as a Vice President for Financial Planning. We thought all of the pieces of the puzzle would fit together well.

One of the projects I immediately got under way was to establish the Carl Whitaker Chair in Family Psychology. Carl came to do a workshop as our first fund-raising event. His admirers sent contributions and we were enthusiastic about this development and its potential.

Unfortunately, the school's policies and standards did not concur with my highly academic and professional orientation. All the faculty and other administrative staff were part-time. No one was engaged in research. Classes were large and the operating budget was almost 100% tuition-based, leaving the students (children) with enormous power over the faculty and administration (adults/parents). I quickly realized that I hadn't known the right questions to ask before accepting the position, and the school and I were incompatible. Disillusioned by what I found and could not change, I resigned after 10 months.

As the rest of the family had settled in well, no one else wanted to move back to Philadelphia. I missed my friends, colleagues, and the intellectual and cultural stimulation of a great metropolitan area. But, I was not ready to leave my family, nor was it fair to ask them to make a second move to accommodate me so soon after the first major transition. We decided we preferred Palm Beach over Miami, so Sol and I moved: he transferred within the same firm and I set up a full-time private practice under the name of Kaslow Associates, P.A., in 1982. It has flourished and I now have three associates. I also established the Florida Couples and Family Institute. The Institute, of which I am Director, provides the channel for our training and consulting activities.

Our son, Howard, graduated from Ithaca College and joined us in Florida. He likes the life-style and has become a stock broker in the same firm as his father. Nadine completed her Ph.D. at the University of Houston, did her internship and postdoctoral residency at the University of Wisconsin Medical School and has been on the faculty at Yale University Department of Psychiatry for the past six years (see Kaslow & Racusin, Chapter 11, Volume 2 of this work). We miss seeing her frequently but respect her need to be mistress of her own fate.

INDEPENDENT PRACTICE AND ITS MANY FACETS

My practice is quite general. I now see individuals, couples, and families—all within a family systems perspective. Many of my patients fall in the categories of talented, beautiful, and wealthy. Substance abuse is rampant. Divorce abounds. I use an individual and family life cycle model as a basis for the time perspective (Kaslow, 1979/1980, 1981b, 1983, 1984a, 1987d; Kaslow & Schwartz, 1987a; Kaslow & Steinberg, 1982). I have been concerned about the impact of divorce on children and on the extended family and with the havoc often wrought when couples proceed with an adversarial divorce.

After seeing the anguish and bitterness that was often stirred up during litigated divorces, I sought and found a "better way"for many in divorce meditation. When I first read Coogler's book (1978) in 1979, I knew this alternative dispute resolution strategy encompassed what I was searching for. I employed his methods until I took mediation training from Will Neville in 1981. I incorporated mediation into my practice, became an active board member of the Academy of Family Mediators (1983-1988) and served as its treasurer for several years. I have come to value the strategies utilized in mediation and sometimes adapt them for use in therapy, although I keep a clear demarcation between therapy cases and mediation cases. I helped establish and served as first president of the Florida Association of Professional Family Mediators. Because I believe that divorce is one of the most traumatic experiences a family can go through, I think divorce mediators should be well educated in graduate and professional schools and have a solid grounding in family psychology. Since 1983 I have conducted a minimum of three 40-hour basic mediation trainings per year—with an attorney or judge as a cotrainer. As a trainer I have helped to increase the size of the pool of qualified personnel available (Saposnek, Kaslow, & Haynes, 1988). We are working on licensure for mediators in Florida to ensure that they are well trained and experienced. I hope that the qualifications do not get watered down in trade-offs during the legislative process.

My own writings about divorce mediation have focused on the emotional impact of mediation on the couple and their children (Kaslow, 1984b) and on the psychological dimension of divorce mediation (Kaslow, 1988c). Divorce mediation is not a panacea or the best pathway for all, but for those who utilize it, both the short-term and long-term psychological benefits far outweigh those accrued from the adversarial system. These benefits include increased self-respect, a heightened sense of participation in decisions that affect one's life, and a more cooperative attitude toward coparenting that continues into the postdivorce family.

I have remained intrigued by couples—from premarriage through remarriage—and have reported on remarried couples (1988) and sexuality in May-December marriages (1989). One of my recent books has focused totally on couples therapy in a family context (Kaslow, 1988a).

In August 1989 I embarked on a study of couples married more than 25 years who consider themselves happy and choose to stay together because they value and enjoy their relationship. This builds on my long-standing interest in healthy couples (Kaslow, 1982b) and healthy families (Kaslow,

1981d). But my earlier work, like that in much of the field, has explored families in the beginning and early middle years of their being together. I'd like to ascertain what factors are conducive to satisfying, long-lasting marriages. Personally, I need to balance the pessimism and unhappiness I hear from my patients day after day with a continuing look at those who are optimistic about and fulfilled in their most intimate relationships; this is one of the main reasons I first decided to investigate and do consults with healthy families.

My interest in therapy with therapists (Kaslow, 1984c) and with the family life of psychotherapists (Kaslow, 1987b; Kaslow & Schulman, 1987) has continued. Probably one third of my patients are therapists or members of therapists' families. This poses many boundary issues regarding dual relationships. Palm Beach is a relatively small community and it is almost impossible, in treating therapist-patients (TP's) (see Fay & Lazarus, 1984) to keep the relationship totally "untainted." My TP's often emerge as participants in my workshops or seminars, on boards or committees on which I am also a member, at the same professional meetings, and sometimes at the same dinner parties, for they are also colleagues outside of the office! I have written and spoken to people in APA Governance about lessening the prohibition on dual relationships—realistically they are unavoidable—and the prohibition raising the specter of ethics violations. Since many therapists do want and need therapy, it would be infinitely more useful if APA promulgated guidelines for the inevitable instead of trying to outlaw it. And that's the subject for a future position paper.

I, like other therapists' therapists, have seen an increasing number of impaired or highly distressed therapists—for example, colleagues with debilitating physical or emotional illnesses, substance abuse problems, disorders manifested in sexual acting out, or severe burnout syndrome. Being their therapist presents myriad problems beyond the customary ones—such as the ethical dilemma of balancing the responsibility to the patient to maintain confidentiality against the professional responsibility to report allegations or suspicions of incompetency to state licensing boards and the APA Ethics Office. And what of the vicarious responsibility to protect the TP's patients—if he or she is too impaired to be practicing? I was pleased to be asked to contribute to an APA-published volume on the topic of distressed TP's (Kaslow, 1986d) and to help build the fund of data on this topic (Kilburg, Kaslow, & VandenBos, 1988d). For me, the privilege of being selected as a therapist's therapist and all of its compelling challenges continue to outweigh the thorny extra pressures.

An area of expanding activity in my practice during the past four years has been family business consultation. It seemed a natural progression to integrate my interest in family dynamics with my work in organization development and team building. I found that patients involved in family businesses often used a good deal of their therapy time discussing the way one aspect of their life impinged on and circumscribed the other. Other concerns are line of succession and power and authority issues and the financial web. When we formally launched this part of our Kaslow Associates activities in 1987, my husband and son joined me and my therapy associates in this endeavor. They are available to discuss financial planning, corporate and/or family investing, buy ins and buy outs, and other relevant fiscal issues. Working together, we all model the respectful and cooperative attitudes we promote. This leaves me free to deal with such matters as intergenerational conflict and sibling rivalry as they are played out in the workplace, marital strife as it invades the corporate boardroom, and why certain members of the family receive financial remuneration and others don't. My crystal ball says I will be shifting gears and doing much more family business consultation in the 1990s. Several articles are already in the planning stages to coincide with this shift.

GIVING PSYCHOLOGY AWAY

In the 1970s I often made guest appearances on radio and television in Philadelphia. This led to my having my own weekly television series on Family Problems for a year on the local Group W affiliate. We had two professional actors role-play typical problem scenarios. Then I would suggest ways to modify their behaviors that might lead to better outcomes and they would improvise to make it come out differently. The ratings were good but the series came to an end when I left to move to Florida.

Since then, I have gladly accepted invitations to be on radio and television programs. I am convinced that these are two of the best mediums for interpreting what we do to potential funders and consumers of psychological services. Highlights in the United States have been being on the Oprah Winfrey Show as the only guest talking about divorce therapy and divorce mediation; and being on the Phil Donahue Show twice on the subject of "Children Who Sue Parents." Overseas I have made tapes on family-related topics that have been translated and broadcast on radio in Hungary and in Germany. For me, this truly represents "taking it to the people."

Because of my commitment to publicizing psychology through the media, I became a charter member of the APA's Division of Media Psychology (#46) and a member-at-large of its board in 1989. One of my secret ambitions is to again host a TV series on family and other mental health topics. Any time in the early 1990s would be great.

OTHER ACTIVITIES IN THE 1980s: BEACONS FOR THE 1990s

After a few months in full-time independent practice, I knew I needed to supplement this new mainstay of my career. I felt isolated and alone. Soon thereafter I was invited to guest-lecture at Duke University's Department of Psychiatry. Out of that visit we were able to get a Foundation Grant for my becoming a Visiting Professor of Medical Psychology in Psychiatry. I helped create the family psychiatry rotation, have often done Grand Rounds, precepted interns and residents, and run family therapy seminars for staff. I look forward to my teaching there and at Florida Institute of Technology, where I have also served as a Visiting Professor of Psychology since 1985. Preparation for lectures is always refreshing as is the dialogue with students. Mentoring is a role I now find quite gratifying.

Many of my organizational involvements have been mentioned earlier. There are two more that have been particularly significant in the past decade. Sequentially, first comes APA's Division of Family Psychology (#43). As secretary of the predecessor organization, the Academy of Psychologists in Marital, Family, and Sex Therapy, I agreed with the other leaders that a Division was necessary to give us a real home in APA and to provide us with the opportunity to influence non-family psychologists to think more systematically and to recognize the specialty of family psychology. Along with Richard Mikesell, George Nixon, Don David Lusterman, Larry Vogel, Gloria Gottsegan, and numerous others, I was instrumental in piloting the formation of the division. I served as its third president and have been actively involved in division activities as a board member since its inception in 1984. Later I was overwhelmed by their nomination of me to APA for its Distinguished Contribution to Applied Psychology Award for my publications and leadership in the fields of family and forensic psychology. I was the 1989 recipient of this award and feel motivated anew by this occurrence.

Currently I am cochairing, with David Olson, the Division's Task Force on Family Diagnosis and Classification. I created this task force several years ago because I think we must develop standardized diagnostic terminology and criteria for making determinations. We cautiously hope that our schema will be accepted by the DSM IV Committee for field testing. We have been in contact with The Group for Advancement of Psychiatry's Task Force on the Family and are now part of an Interorganizational Coalition. Completion of this task looms important on the family psychology horizon and I am doing my utmost to ensure that it is successful. Perhaps in the 1990s our American Psychological Association will publish a special manual on Family Diagnosis and Classification and insurance companies will reimburse for family assessment and treatment. These are some of the goals of the Task Force.

Since 1971 when I "made my debut" on the speaking circuit, I have been fortunate to be invited to speak or lead workshops at many conferences, agencies, institutions, and universities. I have presented in more than half of our states and in Argentina, Australia, Canada, Chile, Czechoslovakia, England and Wales, Finland, Germany, Greece, Hungary, Iceland, Ireland, Israel, Japan, Mexico, Norway, Poland, and South Africa. Each day on the road is hectic, challenging, and exhilarating. I try to be informative, stimulating, and thought-provoking. As a result of these trips, I feel I am a part of a huge international family of family therapists and that we have an enormous amount to share with one another across space, languages, and time. These experiences have led to my always expecting the unexpected and to endeavoring to adapt a multicultural perspective that simultaneously responds to the universals that characterize people in all lands, such as feelings of loss, shame, guilt, sadness, joy, love, passion, and hatred, and cultural specifics—such as the regulating of distance and closeness, the way men and women are expected to interact, and prescribed roles in the family system. Questions that simply aren't part of our at-home reality are provocative. I've been asked such questions as, should the live-in nanny be included in the family therapy sessions (South Africa); how would one depict a healthy family with multiple wives and how should they be involved in therapy (Yemenite Jewish immigrant families in Israel); and do you know what to do if your books and videotapes are confiscated by customs officials at the airport (Chile)? The truly precarious situations have been few, the jet lag quickly subsides, and these negative aspects pale in comparison with the benefits derived from sharing in training experiences with colleagues from many countries and acquiring dear friends in many places.

In 1987 I decided to attend and present at the International Family Therapy Congress in Prague, Czechoslovakia. My presentation was on "The Self of the Therapist" and I thought it would draw a small audience. The topic apparently has widespread appeal; more than 250 people came. I particularly remember two women, one from Hungary and one from Yugoslavia, coming up afterward and remarking that I had so accurately described their life experiences in talking about ours and how surprised they were at the similarities. The Polish Journal reprinted one of my articles on this topic (Kaslow & Schulman, 1987) and I was asked to lecture on this topic in Finland in the fall of 1989. Therapists everywhere struggle with finding the vital balance between their personal and professional lives and commitments.

The Prague Conference was exhilarating—a blend of East and West, old and new, the past and the future. The evening before the conference closed, several people approached me about forming an international association to further the collaborative spirit that had been generated. We gathered together a dozen leaders from different countries and in June 1987 the International Family Therapy Association was born. We announced our formation at the final conference plenary. The Steering Committee met and I was elected first president. It is difficult to try to build an international organization with a meager budget derived, so far, only from dues and a few small contributions. Everything has been done by mail, as overseas conference calls are prohibitive in cost. As in establishing ABFP and the FAPFM, I wrote the Articles of Incorporation and Bylaws myself to save money and had them reviewed by our legal counsel, Stuart Klein. I didn't anticipate the facts that many members in socialist countries couldn't afford our modest dues because salaries are so low and that some currencies have no value outside of their countries. But we continued undaunted and our first full board meeting took place at the First World Conference of Family Therapy in Dublin in June 1989. Our dream of an organization whose policies are transnational and transpolitical and whose membership is open to all who are interested in the well-being of families has come to fruition. I will retain the stewardship until our next meeting in Krakow, Poland, in September 1990. By then the organization will be solid; its survival ensured. Many well-known family therapists are already clamoring to serve on the board.

My personal odyssey into the international sphere has far exceeded even my wildest speculation. I hope it will continue for at least another decade.

WHITHER THE FUTURE?

Many of my thoughts on the future I've already addressed—particularly regarding my personal aspirations for the next decade. By continuing to refine and expand my "diaclectic model" (Kaslow, 1981a) to include self and system, individual and family, and what sound research validates as the theories that have the best explanatory power and the intervention strategies that are optimally effective, I hope my work will remain vital and even trend-setting.

Family psychology is destined to expand and become more influential nationally and internationally in the fields of family therapy and psychology. We bring a scientific rigor, a desire to substantiate through research the validity of our clinical practice and even our intuitive hunches. We will increasingly incorporate individual developmental psychology with family life cycle concepts. The fellows of Division 43 and our Diplomates in family psychology will assume more leadership roles and be accorded greater recognition by virtue of their expertise—especially now that the American Board of Family Psychology has officially become one of the boards of the

American Board of Professional Psychology. We will continue to acknowledge our dual heritage (Kaslow, 1987e) and be involved in interdisciplinary collaboration and multidisciplinary family therapy organizations. A standardized family diagnosis and classification schema will be promulgated and published. More and more family psychology courses, tracts, and sequences will flourish in psychology doctoral programs and there will be more internships and postdoctoral residencies with a family psychology component or specialization. We will make our voices heard in academe, in the clinical arenas, in books and journals, and in APA boards and task forces, particularly regarding education and training of psychologists.

EPILOGUE

In writing this kind of chapter one faces the question of what to disclose, and why. It becomes an autobiographical treatise as well as a highlighting of one's contributions to the field. One seeks to be appropriately selective, modest, honest, and reasonably objective. It is difficult to write lucidly amidst the flood of memories seen now through a new lens—sometimes more critical, sometimes more mellow. It has been a deeply personal experience of reconstructing and reevaluating, and has provided a fine opportunity for sharpening future goals and directions.

Early in this chapter I mentioned the free verse narration I wrote for presentation as the background for my dance portrayal contrasting the Apollonian and the Dionysian personalities (Brown, 1959). Twenty years after my dissertation was accepted, I returned to this theme once again. I was asked to speak on a two-day panel on "The Dance of Self and System" by the Seattle Family Institute. I found this verse still encapsulates a portion of my worldview as I continue the quest for wholeness and to share this value with patients, trainees, friends, and colleagues. I'd like to close by sharing it with our readers.

Throughout the history of civilization a duality appears in the conception of humanity epitomized in dichotomous phrases such as Soul-Body, Mind-Body, Psyche-Soma, Ego-Id, and Conscious-Unconscious. A section in Norman Brown's *Life Against Death* vividly uses the symbolism of the Apollonian and the Dionysian to depict two very different kinds of orientation to life: the Apollonian pursuing knowledge on a cerebral plane divorced from body pleasures contrasted to the sensuous Dionysian who finds his place in the world by experiencing and sharing love, joy, and exuberance. Brown's book dramatizes the body-mind dualism and the problems that such a split reflects and causes. The following free verse contrasts and summarizes my interpretation of his concepts on the two ego orientations of the personality as manifested through the body and provides a backdrop against which to view current efforts geared to revitalizing and expanding the diminished role of the body in the total living experience.

The Apollonian

Born to be restricted, inhibited
To have energy desexualized
Displacement from below
Lifting the life force from pelvis and genitals upward
To heaven and sunlight
The dreamworld of fantasy, hallucinations.
Intellectualization, contemplation.

Repression, Aggression, Denial, Identification, and
Projection
Life held at a distance.
Sublimination of instinct, libido
Arise a "higher nature"!

Seeking, searching—being thwarted, unsatisfied,
pushed back.
Think—but don't feel. Look—but don't touch.
Negation of life, of body sensation.
Thought supreme, omnipotent, magical.

Symbolism. Hysteria. Abstraction. Self-consciousness.

The system tight, constricted, soon closed.
Aggression, guilt mount, bubble, explode—anger,
hostility, sterility, destruction.

PAIN

Sexuality atrophies, *intellect triumphs.*

DEATH IN LIFE.

The Dionysian

Created through love, wanted.
Born to feel, to experience, to enjoy, to remember.
To reach out and be met. Response, Recognition,
Affection, Touch, Taste.
To play, dance, laugh
To revel in joy.
To express bodily urges sensuously, completely,
rhythmically, actively

Energy flowing freely in self and to others.

Erotic union with another.
Both an artist and a work of art.
Impulse, spontaneity, abandon.
Limitless mobility, fluidity, radiation.
Affirmation, Consciousness.

Reunification of male-female, self-other, body-soul, ego-id, life-death.

Orgasmic ecstasy.
Eros

FREEDOM

The self alone and whole; the person full, in a relationship.

REFERENCES

Abrams, J. C., & Kaslow, F. W., (1976, Spring). Learning disability and family dynamics: A mutual interaction. *Journal of Clinical Child Psychology, V*(1), 35-40.

Abrams, J. C., & Kaslow, F. W., (1977). Family systems and the learning disabled child: Intervention and treatment. *Journal of Learning Disabilities, 10*(2), 27-31.

Angyal, A. (1965). *Neurosis and treatment: A holistic theory.* New York: John Wiley.

Boszormenyi-Nagy, I., & Spark, G., (1973). *Invisible loyalties.* New York: Harper & Row. (Reprinted 1984, New York: Brunner/Mazel.)

Bowen, M. (1978). *Family therapy in clinical practice.* New York: Jason Aronson.

Brown, N. O. (1959). *Life against death: The psychoanalytic meaning of history.* New York: Vintage.

Coogler, O. J. (1978). *Structured mediation in divorce settlement.* Lexington, MA: D. C. Heath.

Duhl, F. J., Kantor, D., & Duhl, B. S. (1973). Learning, space and action in family therapy: A primer of sculpture. In D. Bloch (Ed.), *Techniques of family psychotherapy.* New York: Grune & Stratton.

Fay, A., & Lazarus, A. A. (1984). The therapist in behavioral and multi-modal therapy. In F. W. Kaslow (Ed.), *Psychotherapy with psychotherapists* (pp. 1-18). New York: Haworth.

Foulks, E., Freeman, D.M.A., Kaslow, F. W., & Madow, L. (1977). The Italian evil eye: Mal occhio. *Journal of Operational Psychiatry, VIII*(2), 28-34.

Framo, J. L. (1973). Marriage therapy in a couples group. In D. A. Bloch (Ed.), *Techniques of family psychotherapy: A primer.* New York: Grune & Stratton.

Framo, J. L. (1981). The integration of marital therapy with sessions with the family of origin. In A. S. Gurman & D. P. Kniskern (Eds.), *Handbook of family therapy* (pp. 133-158). New York: Brunner/Mazel.

Goldstein, K. (1959). Organismic approach. In S. Arieti (Ed.), *American handbook of psychiatry II* (pp. 1333-1347). New York: Basic Books.

Kaslow, F. W. (1969). *Dance and movement therapies: A study in theory and applicability.* Doctoral dissertation, Bryn Mawr College, PA.

Kaslow, F. W. (1972a). A therapeutic creative arts unit at a school for children with learning disabilities. *Academic Therapy Quarterly, VII*(3), 297-306.

Kaslow, F. W. (1972b). *Issues in human services: A sourcebook for supervision and staff development.* San Francisco: Jossey-Bass.

Kaslow, F. W. (1974a). Movement, music and art therapy techniques adapted for special education. In R. Hyatt & N. Rolnick (Eds.), *Teaching the mentally handicapped child.* New York: Behavioral Publications.

Kaslow, F. W. (1974b). The Hahnemann correctional psychology program – Educating professionals for evolving roles in criminal justice. *The Quarterly* (Journal of Pennsylvania Probation and Parole Department), *XXXI*(3), 18-25.

Kaslow, F. W. (1975a). Practice trends in corrections and their implications for graduate and professional education. *The Quarterly, XXXII*(4).

Kaslow, F. W. (1975b/1978). The use of creative arts therapy in special education. In L. Schwartz (Ed.), *Stress their abilities: A primer in special education.* Belmont, CA: Wadsworth.

Kaslow, F. W. (1977a). Marital and family therapy supervision: Challenges and opportunities. In F. W. Kaslow (Ed.), *Supervision, consultation and staff training in the helping professions.* San Francisco: Jossey-Bass.

Kaslow, F. W. (Ed.), (1977b). *Supervision, consultation and staff training in the helping professions.* San Francisco: Jossey-Bass.

Kaslow, F. W. (1978). Therapy within the family constellation. In W. C. Adamson & K. Adamson (Eds.), *Specific learning disabilities: A handbook for bridging the gap.* New York: Gardner.

Kaslow, F. W. (1979/1980). Stages in the divorce process: A psycholegal perspective. *Villanova Law Review, 25,* 4-5, 718-751.

Kaslow, F. W. (1980a). Ethical problems in prison psychology. *Criminal Justice and Behavior, 7*(1), 3-9.

Kaslow, F. W. (1980b). Dilemma in adult correctional settings: To treat or not to treat and if so, how? In G. Cooke (Ed.), *The role of the forensic psychologist.* Springfield, IL: Charles C Thomas.

Kaslow, F. W. (1981a). A "diaclectic" approach to family therapy and practice: Selectivity and synthesis. *Journal of Marital and Family Therapy, 7*(3), 345-351.

Kaslow, F. W. (1981b). Divorce and divorce therapy. In A. Gurman & D. Kniskern (Eds.), *Handbook of Family Therapy* (pp. 662-696). New York: Brunner/Mazel.

Kaslow, F. W. (1981c). Group therapy with couples in conflict: Is more better? *Psychotherapy: Theory, Research, and Practice, 18*(4), 516-524.

Kaslow, F. W. (1981d). Profile of the healthy family. *Interaction, 4*(½), 1-15, and in *The Relationship* (1982), *8*(1), 9-24.

Kaslow, F. W. (1982a). History of family therapy in the United States: A kaleidoscopic overview. In F. W. Kaslow (Ed.), *The international book of family therapy* (pp. 5-40). New York: Brunner/Mazel.

Kaslow, F. W. (1982b). Portrait of a healthy couple. *Psychiatric Clinics of North America, 5*(3), 519-527.

Kaslow, F. W. (Ed.), (1982c). *The international book of family therapy.* New York: Brunner/Mazel.

Kaslow, F. W. (1983). Stages and techniques of divorce therapy. In P. A. Keller & L. G. Ritt (Eds.), *Innovations in clinical practice: A sourcebook* (Vol. 2, pp. 5-16). Sarasota, FL: Professional Resource Exchange, Inc.

Kaslow, F. W. (1984a). Divorce: An evolutionary process of change in the family system. *Journal of Divorce, 7*(3), 21-39.

Kaslow, F. W. (1984b). Divorce mediation and its emotional impact on the couple and their children. *American Journal of Family Therapy, 12*(3), 58-66.

Kaslow, F. W. (Ed.), (1984c). *Psychotherapy with psychotherapists.* New York: Haworth.

Kaslow, F. W. (1984d). Training and supervision of mental health professionals to understand and treat military families. In F. W. Kaslow & R. I. Ridenour (Eds.), *The military family: Dynamics, structure, and treatment* (pp. 269-305). New York: Guilford.

Kaslow, F. W. (1984e). Treatment of marital and family therapists. In F. W. Kaslow (Ed.), *Psychotherapy with psychotherapists* (pp. 79-100). New York: Haworth.

Kaslow, F. W. (1985). Consultation with the military: A complex role. In L. W. Wynne, T. Weber, & S. McDaniel (Eds.), *The family therapist as consultant.* New York: Guilford.

Kaslow, F. W. (1986a). An intensive training experience: A six day post graduate institute model. *Journal of Psychotherapy and the Family, 1*(4), 73-82.

Kaslow, F. W. (1986b). Seeking and providing supervision in private practice. In F. W. Kaslow (Ed.), *Supervision and training: Models, dilemmas and challenges* (pp. 143-158). New York: Haworth.

Kaslow, F. W. (Ed.), (1986c). *Supervision and training: Models, dilemmas, and challenges.* New York: Haworth. Also published in 1986 as monograph in *Clinical Supervision, 4*(½).

Kaslow, F. W. (1986d). Therapy with distressed psychotherapists: Special problems and challenges. In R. R. Kilburg, P. E. Nathan, & R. W. Thorenson, (Eds.), *Professionals in distress: Issues, syndromes and solutions in psychology* (pp. 187-210). Washington, DC: American Psychological Association.

Kaslow, F. W. (1987a). Marital and family therapy. In M. B. Sussman & S. K. Steinmetz (Eds.), *Handbook of marriage and the family* (pp. 835-859). New York: Plenum.

Kaslow, F. W. (Ed.), (1987b). *The family life of psychotherapists.* New York: Haworth.

Kaslow, F. W. (1987c). The military family: A kaleidoscopic overview. *Family Therapy Today,* pp. 1-7.

Kaslow, F. W. (1987d). Stages in the Divorce Process: Dynamics and Treatment. In F. W. Kaslow & L. L. Schwartz (Eds.), *The dynamics of divorce: A life cycle perspective* (pp. 23-37). New York: Brunner/Mazel.

Kaslow, F. W. (1987e). Trends in family psychology. *Journal of Family Psychology, 1*(1), 77-90.

Kaslow, F. W. (1987f). Couples or family therapy for prisoners and their significant others. *American Journal of Family Therapy, 15*(4), 352-360.

Kaslow, F. W. (Ed.), (1988a). *Couples therapy in a family context: Perspective and retrospective.* Rockville, MD: Aspen Systems Corporation.

Kaslow, F. W. (1988b). Remarried couples: The architects of stepfamilies. In F. W. Kaslow (Ed.), *Couples therapy in a family context: Perspective and retrospective* (pp. 33-48). Rockville, MD: Aspen Systems Corporation.

Kaslow, F. W. (1988c). The psychological dimension of divorce mediation. In J. Folberg & A. Milne (Eds.), *Divorce mediation: Theory and practice.* (pp. 83-108). New York: Guilford.

Kaslow, F. W. (1989). Sexuality in May-December marriages. In D. Kantor & B. F. Okun, *Intimate environments* (pp. 321-345). New York: Guilford.

Kaslow, F. W. (in press). Marital therapy supervision. In A. Hess (Ed.), *Psychotherapy supervision: Theory, research & practice* (Vol. II). New York: John Wiley.

Kaslow, F. W., & Abrams, J. C. (1976). Forensic psychology and criminal justice: An evolving subspecialty at Hahnemann Medical College. *Journal of Professional Psychology, 7*(4), 445-452.

Kaslow, F. W., & Abrams, J. C. (1977). Differential diagnosis and treatment of the learning disabled child and his/her family. *Journal of Pediatric Psychology, 4*(3), 253-264.

Kaslow, F. W., & Aradi, N. S. (1987). Theory integration in family therapy: Definition, rationale, content and process. *Psychotherapy, 24*(35), 77-90.

Kaslow, F. W., & Cooper, B. (1978). Family therapy with the learning disabled child and his/her family. *Journal of Marriage and Family Counseling, 3*(1), 41-49.

Kaslow, F. W., & De Cato, C. (1974). Psychology training and the correctional system. *The Prison Journal, LIV*(2), 57-68.

Kaslow, F. W., & Fenster, A. (1980b). Careers in forensic psychology. In P. Woods (Ed.), *Career opportunities for psychologists.* Washington, DC: American Psychological Association.

Kaslow, F. W., & Hyatt, R. (1982). Divorce: A potential growth experience for the extended family. *Journal of Divorce, 5*(½), 115-126.

Kaslow, F. W., & Kaslow, N. J. (1981). Dynamics of relationships between career mothers and young adult daughters. In A. Gurman (Ed.), *Questions and answers in the practice of family therapy* (Vol. I). New York: Brunner/Mazel.

Kaslow, F. W., & Kaslow, N. J. (1985). Career mothers and career daughters: A mutual interaction. *American Family Therapy Association Proceedings.* Washington, DC: American Family Therapy Association.

Kaslow, F. W., & Lieberman, E. J. (1981). *Couples group therapy: Rationale, dynamics, and process.* In G. P. Sholevar (Ed.), *The handbook of marriage and marital therapy* (pp. 347-362). New York: SP Medical and Scientific Books.

Kaslow, F. W., & Mountz, T. (1984). Ethical and legal issues in the treatment of alcoholics and substance abusers. In T. Bratter & G. Forest (Eds.), *Current treatment of substance abuse and alcoholism.* New York: Free Press.

Kaslow, F. W., & Ridenour, R. I. (1984). *The military family: Dynamics and treatment.* New York: Guilford.

Kaslow, F. W., & Schulman, N. (1987). How to be sane and happy as a family therapist or the reciprocal impact of family therapy teaching and practice and therapists personal lives and mental health. In F. W. Kaslow (Ed.), *The family life of psychotherapists* (pp. 79-96). New York: Haworth. Reprinted (1988) in *Psychoterapia* (Polish Journal), *2*(65), 5-24.

Kaslow, F. W., & Schwartz, L. L. (1983). Vulnerability and invulnerability to the cults: An assessment of family dynamics, functioning and values. In D. Bagarozzsi, A. Jurich, & R. W. Jackson (Eds.), *Marital and family therapy: New perspectives in theory, research and practice.* New York: Human Sciences Press.

Kaslow, F. W., & Schwartz, L. L. (1987a). *Dynamics of divorce: A life cycle perspective.* New York: Brunner/Mazel.

Kaslow, F. W., & Schwartz, L. L. (1987b). Older children of divorce: A neglected family segment. In J. Vincent (Ed.), *Advances in family intervention.* Greenwich, CT: JAI.

Kaslow, F. W., & Soehner, G. (1980). *Administrative supervision.* In S. L. White (Ed.), *Middle management in mental health.* San Francisco: Jossey-Bass.

Kaslow, F. W., & Steinberg, J. L. (1982). Ethical divorce therapy and divorce proceedings: A psychological perspective. In J. Hansen & R. L'Abate (Eds.), *Values, ethics, legalities, and the family therapist.* Rockville, MD: Aspen Systems Corporation.

Kilburg, R., Kaslow, F. W., & VandenBos, G. (1988d). Interdisciplinary update: Professionals in distress. *Hospital and Community Psychiatry, 39*(7), 723-725.

Lewis, J., Beavers, W. R., Gossett, J. T., & Phillips, V. A. (1976). *No single thread: Psychological health and the family system.* New York: Brunner/Mazel.

Neill, J. R., & Kniskern, D. R. (1982). *From psyche to system: The evolving therapy of Carl Whitaker.* New York: Guilford.

Olson, D. H., Russell, L. S., & Sprenkle, D. H. (1983). Circumplex model VI: Theoretical update. *Family Process, 22,* 69-83.

Read, G. D. (1953). *Childbirth without fear: The principles and practice of natural childbirth.* New York: Harper and Brothers.

Rubenstein, D., & Timmens, J. F. (1978). Depressive diadic and triadic relationships. *Journal of Marriage and Family Counseling, 4,* 13-24.

Satir, V. A. (1964). *Conjoint family therapy.* Palo Alto, CA: Science and Behavior Books.

Satir, V. A. (1972). *People-making*. Palo Alto, CA: Science and Behavior Books.

Schwartz, L. L., & Kaslow, F. W. (1979). Religious cults, the individual and the family. *Journal of Marital and Family Therapy, 5,* 15-26.

Schwartz, L. L., & Kaslow, F. W. (1982). The cult phenomenon: Historical, sociological, and familial factors contributing to their development and appeal. In F. W. Kaslow & M. Sussman (Eds.), *Cults and the family*. New York: Haworth.

Slovenko, R. (1980). Legal issues in psychotherapy supervision. In A. K. Hess (Ed.), *Psychotherapy supervision*. New York: John Wiley.

Whitaker, C. (1976). Hindrance of theory in clinical work. In P. J. Guerin (Ed.), *Family therapy: Theory and practice*. New York: Gardner Press.

Whitaker, C. A., & Bumberry, W. M. (1988). *Dancing with the family: A symbolic-experiential approach*. New York: Brunner/Mazel.

Wolfe, T. (1979). *The right stuff*. New York: Farrar, Straus, & Giroux.

Videotapes

Kaslow, F. W. (1988). *Divorce consultation/Divorce ceremony*. Farmington: University of Connecticut Medical School.

Kaslow, F. W., & Zwerling, I. (1974). *Treating a prisoner and his family*. Philadelphia: Hahnemann Medical College.

Saposnek, D., Kaslow, F. W., & Haynes, J. (1988). *The case of Willie: Three mediation approaches*. Eugene, OR: The Academy of Family Mediators.

15

The Bumpy Road from Child to Adult Aggression

K. DANIEL O'LEARY

My travels in psychology have not been clear trajectories from one thing to another. Instead, I have set some general travel plans, and I have had some fitful starts and some occasional flat tires. I will outline some of the plans and describe a few of those fitful starts and flat tires. In accordance with the book's dual focus, I will try to provide a sense of my research travels from a personal as well as a developmental perspective.

In the past, I have worked in the area of child hyperactivity/aggression. I now work in the area of adult aggression, and I have been looking at the interface between adult conflict and childhood problems for a number of years. The first ten years (1967-1977) of my professional life I spent developing intervention programs for aggressive/hyperactive children in homes and schools; the second ten years (1978-1988), I have been attempting to understand adult aggression, especially marital violence. Three issues will be delineated: (1) the research problems that I addressed, (2) what I feel we learned as a research group about childhood and adult aggression, and (3) what I think the field has learned about dealing with the problems of child and marital aggression. I will also try to convey why I did what I did and why I moved from one research area to another.

THE FIRST TEN YEARS (1967-1977)

When I entered graduate school, I had no idea how to deal with children. I was not from a big family, I had not been a camp counselor, I didn't spend time with little ones, and I had no idea that I would ever enter the child area. I have one brother who is three years younger than I. My mother was a high school choral director and my father was a biochemist and later a professor. None of these factors prompted me to have an interest in children. However, I had a convincing research adviser, Wesley Becker, who said: "O'Leary, there's a classroom of aggressive kids out there, they really need help and we know how to give it to them." I don't know if we really knew how to help them in 1966, but I went to a classroom of 17 children, mostly boys, who were then described as "emotionally disturbed". The DSM diagnoses of Unsocialized Aggressive Reaction or Attention Deficit Disorder with Hyperactivity were not used, but I saw the same mixed bag of symptoms or problems that we see today in classrooms for children with serious behavioral and emotional problems. They had one teacher who had quit and another was about to quit if something was not done. We implemented a token reinforcement program with these children (O'Leary & Becker, 1967).

Basically, we showed that if you can build a token reinforcement program in a classroom for emotionally disturbed children, you can get them to work hard and pay attention. We followed the lead of the laboratory group headed by Sidney Bijou and colleagues at the University of Washington where they had implemented a token reinforcement program with retarded children in Rainier School (Birnbrauer, Wolf, Kidder, & Tague, 1965). We found that with a significant number of variations from the program for retarded children, especially of a cognitive nature, we could facilitate the behavior of children in these classrooms (See Figure 15.1—from O'Leary & Becker, 1967). For example, rules for classroom conduct were posted on the blackboard daily and reviewed by the teacher once in the morning and once in the afternoon. In addition, the time period between the deliveries of the token reinforcement (in the form of a teacher rating from 1 to 10) ranged from 20 to 30 minutes. With variations and systematic replications, we were able to increase on-task behavior and reduce the disruptive behavior (O'Leary, Becker, Evans, & Saudargas, 1969). These programs certainly seemed to be reasonably successful in reducing off-task behavior (O'Leary & Drabman, 1971).

At about the time we had established reasonably successful token reinforcement programs in the classrooms, however, a visiting professor, Robin Winkler, came to the State University of Stony Brook at Stony Brook, New York, from Australia. Winkler and a Stony Brook graduate student, Richard Winnett (Winnett & Winkler, 1972), wrote an article entitled, "Behavior Modification in the Classroom: Be Still, Be Quiet, Be Docile". As a result of the symposium Winkler and I were in together, he wrote this article with Dick

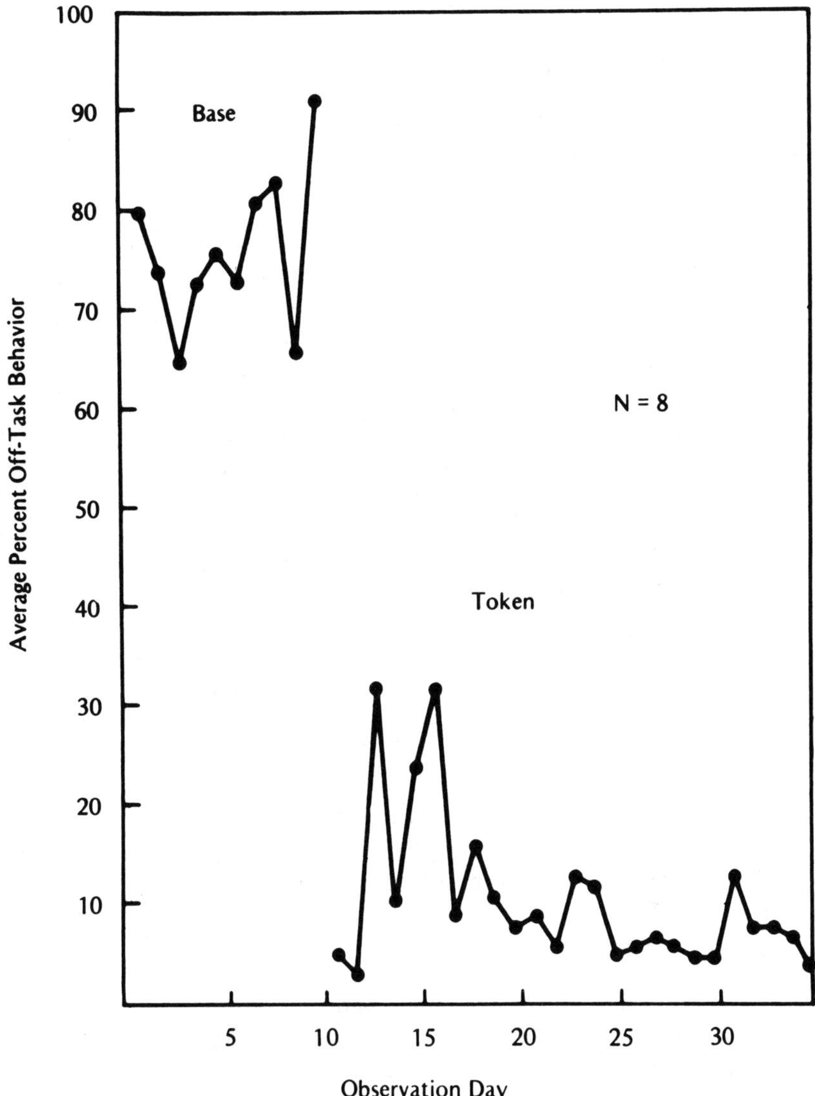

Figure 15.1. Average Percentages of Deviant Behavior During the Base and Token Periods

SOURCE: O'Leary, & Becker, 1967.

Winnett and challenged me. Basically, he was saying: Yes, you people who engage in behavior modification in the classroom and in the home can reduce the disruptive behavior of these children, but in essence, who cares? The issue is not whether they sit in their seats more often, or whether they raise their hands before they speak, but rather *whether they are producing academically.* This attack was a knife right in my back, which I did not take lightly. I wrote a rejoinder to that article because I felt there was some misrepresentation in it. While we chose to increase both on-task and academic behavior, we had not targeted increases in academic production per se.

I respected Winkler a great deal. Unfortunately, he died an early death in Australia in 1986 after a long bout with a debilitating disease. He was an excellent teacher and critic for any of us who attempted to help change behaviors for he seriously challenged us to focus on what the most functional behaviors were. I think he also emphasized, and in turn got us to emphasize, the moment-to-moment interaction with these children and their parents and teachers that in the long run is most crucial in producing both the academic and social change we desired. It is not the big back-up reinforcer but *the moment-to-moment teacher-child interactions.* It is the soft reprimands, the praise, the prompts, the encouragement, and the instructional format that makes the difference. It embodies some demonstration of caring in the context of a good instructional program.

What have I learned from my behavior modification research in the classroom? There are some significant successes and some failures that I will mention as well. One major success is probably best exemplified in something that many psychologists have not read about, the effectiveness of behavioral intervention in Head Start programs. The Head Start program was funded by the government, and it is probably the largest evaluation of university-based programs to change people's behavior that has ever existed in the United States. Two behavioral programs, one at the University of Oregon designed by Siegfried Engelmann and Wesley Becker, and one at the University of Kansas designed by Donald Buschell, emphasized instructional formats to shape behavior: praise, token reinforcement and soft reprimands. Those programs represented two of approximately twenty programs in the United States that were evaluated by the government. They now have been in existence for over fifteen years and they have been shown to be the most effective programs in producing academic achievement of these children (Becker, 1973).

Thus, we can straightforwardly address an issue raised by Winkler: Behavioral programs are not only producing increases in the children's on-task behavior in the classroom, the youngsters are achieving better, as well. I also think the research we did has had a lasting impact on the activities of classroom teachers, especially teachers of children with behavioral and emotional problems. There are thousands of classrooms today for children with special problems that use some variant of a token reinforcement program, such as a daily note-home system for an individual child or a token reinforcement program for the whole class.

Something else prompted me to partly change my research direction. The psychostimulant medications, dextroamphetamine and methylphenidate, were beginning to receive quite wide-spread use in the early 1970s. A physician, Rolf Jacob, came to visit me from Sweden, because in Sweden they had outlawed the use of psychostimulant medication with hyperactive kids, except in unusual cases (and then the use had to be approved by central boards). Dr. Jacob asked me if children who are hyperactive could be treated with the same kind of program I had been using with emotionally disturbed children. I really didn't know. I wasn't sure what a hyperactive kid was; the label then in use for children with serious behavioral and emotional problems was "Emotionally Disturbed Children". However, I said that I would be glad to try to find out if we could change the behavior of hyperactive children, and we wrote a proposal to the Swedish government to have Jacob come to study in the United States. We wanted to see if we could change the hyperactive behavior of the children in the classroom using a variant of a token reinforcement program with natural reinforcers in the classrooms, soft reprimands, prompts, praise, and shaping. We wanted to show that we could increase their attention, decrease their disruptive behavior, and increase their productivity. We knew from previous work by Conners (1969) that ratings of disruptive and hyperkinetic behavior decreased from approximately 2.5 to approximately 1.0 when the hyperactive children received psychostimulant medication. The challenge was to see if we could develop programs that would be as successful as psychostimulant medication.

I believe that we've had some clear success in reaching that objective. In addition, a number of other researchers have also shown that behavioral interventions are reasonable alternatives to psychostimulant medication (e.g., Gittelman-Klein et al., 1976; O'Leary, 1980, 1985) though they do not reduce the behavior of hyperactive children as quickly or quite as well. Unfortunately, with few exceptions behavioral researchers have not implemented classroom programs for a long enough period (e.g., one year with fading across the second year) to allow us to answer how well such programs fare in the long run. While both behavior therapy and psychostimulants are effective in the short run (i.e., for a period of eight weeks to 16 weeks) there are almost no studies showing long-range effectiveness. Furthermore, research by Weiss, Kluger, Danielson, and Elman (1975) indicates that psychostimulants *alone* are clearly not very helpful in the long run. In brief, behavioral interventions with hyperactive children are now seen by respected professionals as a major therapeutic intervention, though not the only one, to be used with hyperactive children (Conners & Wells, 1987).

These partial successes or partial failures, however you wish to view the results, inspired me to begin to look at alternatives or supplements to token reinforcement programs. We learned through token reinforcement programs that there was too little focus on those moment-to-moment interactions of the teachers and their children. But I learned some other practical things such as the potential impact of the presence of the observers on the children. With minor exceptions during the first few days of the observations, the children's behavior was not highly reactive to the observers' presence (Dubey, Kent, O'Leary, Broderick, & O'Leary, 1977).

Ron Kent and I, along with four excellent therapists, Ken Kaufman, Lisa Serbin, Sue O'Leary and Mary Stark, also found that we could help very aggressive children through parent-school consultation programs (Kent & O'Leary, 1976, 1977). We showed significant change in teacher ratings of aggressive behavior in the classroom and even changes in academic achievement. But we also observed that the youngsters who seemed to regress were those who came from highly discordant families and highly stressed families and our ability to try to provide behavior management consultation was just not enough. In essence, I believe that the model by which I was trained to conceptualize children's behavior was a limiting model. I was trained in a model based on Ullmann and Krasner (1965) where it was posited, as a basic tenet, that you could treat behavior in a situation and since behavior was situationally specific you could change the behavior in the particular situation and not worry about the larger environment. The model helped us in that it prompted us to go into classrooms—but it did not always fit. One child in a classroom where I was implementing a token reinforcement program came in the morning after his father—subsequent to a fight with his wife—had been shot in a barroom. What did we do? With the exception of a small discussion with the boy, we didn't delve into the situation. I wouldn't avoid that anymore. That, and other family incidents, stimulated me to look at a different aspect of child behavior; we decided to consider the interaction between marital and childhood problems.

THE SECOND TEN YEARS (1978-1988)

My transition out of the child treatment area was an abrupt one. My wife, Sue O'Leary, was being evaluated in a tenure-track position at Stony Brook. At that time, I had published two pieces of literature with her. One was a home-study done while we were both graduate students in psychology at the University of Illinois in Urbana working with Wes Becker (O'Leary, O'Leary,

& Becker, 1967). The other was a book called *Classroom Management: The Successful Use of Behavior Modification* (O'Leary & O'Leary, 1972). This book grew out of our joint experiences with Wes Becker, Susan's experience with Sidney Bijou's Child Behavior Laboratory at Illinois, and my classroom laboratory, Point Of Woods, at Stony Brook. When Sue came up for her first three-year evaluation, one of our professors at Stony Brook said, "How do we know what portion of that work is Susan O'Leary's?" Little did they know how much of it was mine! However, they gave her a one year renewal to evaluate whether they could have two people from the same family on the same faculty. This was at the time when there were nepotism rules at many universities, but not in our state system. I said a few angry things to myself and quickly exited the field of child behavior therapy. In short, my behavior would say to our faculty overtly, "You will not see me in that area and you can evaluate Susan O'Leary on the basis of her own efforts!" Indeed, they did evaluate her on her own, and she is now the Director of Clinical Psychology Training at Stony Brook.

After my fast exit from the classroom area, I began to work in the area of childhood problems as they related to marital problems. Based on a clinic sample, we found an association between marital and childhood problems, particularly for boys, and especially for conduct problems (Oltmanns, Broderick, & O'Leary, 1977). However, Robert Emery and I later performed a study in a public school and with 200 children. The correlations of marital discord and childhood problems were significant, but they were so small that they were practically nonsignificant (Emery & O'Leary, 1984).

Probably, my own background affected some of what I did next because I was from a divorced family. My mother, a high school choral director, came home one day and said to me, "Dan, I hate to hear the comments in the teachers' faculty room that, 'It's the divorced family that always produce the bad kids'." To be sure, in studies even today the research still indicates that more children from divorced families will fare less well socially and academically than children from intact families (Hetherington, Cox, & Cox, 1982; Kaslow & Schwartz, 1987; Wallerstein & Kelly, 1980). Here, too, we need be concerned about not only showing these significant differences, but we need also to be concerned about practical differences in the percentages of variance accounted for by variables such as marital discord and divorce.

While I have continued to research the relationship between childhood and marital problems, I have tried to be much more focused in my effort because I don't believe that parent problems per se necessarily adversely affect their children that markedly. The data simply do not support the view that marital discord per se is highly associated with child problems (O'Leary & Emery, 1983). We began to look at more specific aspects of marital discord, such as spouse abuse or punitiveness toward the child. We have found that the mother's direct physical aggression toward the child is more associated with conduct problems of the boys than is the parents' physical aggression toward each other (Jouriles, Barling, & O'Leary, 1989). However, we are not able to say that the parents' aggression toward each other has no impact. I believe that our models of parent-child interaction are today generally limiting in that while we talk about bidirectional variables, with few exceptions, we have not been that successful in looking at bidirectionality. Generally, we have not been able to place the behavior of children and their parents in a stream of events that really conceptualizes what many of the family systems people are talking about. There are a few exceptions that go beyond static associations. The Patterson (1982) coercion control model and the associated conditional probability analyses is one exception. Barkley's work with medication, showing that when the children are medicated the parents do not remain as controlling, is another exception (Barkley, Karlsson, Pollard, & Murphy, 1985). If it were really parental control that produces the problems of the children, you would expect the behavior of the parents to remain constant even when the children receive medication. Emery's research, where he has noticed that children will intervene when they see their parents engaging in aggressive interchanges, begins to show how children can operate in a larger system and how they can influence their parents (Vuchinich, Emery, & Cassidy, in press). But even when the bidirectionality is assessed, the models do not go far enough.

It is true that the witnessing of marital aggression is associated with a wide variety of child problems. However, parent-child aggression appears to be more important in the prediction of child deviance within maritally aggressive families (Jouriles et al., 1987; Jouriles, Murphy, & O'Leary, 1989).

It is unclear what impact the observation of physical aggression between parents has. First of all, the child does not see the father as many hours as he or she sees the mother. Sometimes, it is a chain of events where the father doesn't support the mother; when he hits her frequently but not in the presence of the child. Maybe he withholds a paycheck from her which, in turn, gets her in such an angry mood that she can no longer control her behavior to the child and she becomes particularly punitive. The complexity of such variables is clearly not in our models; therefore, we need to move to models of greater complexity which allows us to examine the parent-child processes more clearly.

Next came the transition of my interest to interspousal aggression. Alan Rosenbaum and I did a study relating to the characteristics of physically aggressive men and women (Rosenbaum & O'Leary, 1981). That work has prompted a line of research on characteristics of aggressive individuals and couples (e.g., O'Leary & Curley, 1986; Rosenbaum & O'Leary, 1981). More recently, we have been completing a study of engaged and, later, newly married people. In that work, we found that the prevalence of aggression toward a partner is quite high (O'Leary et al., in press). If asked, 44% of the women and 31% of the men reported that they engaged in physical aggression toward their partner in the year prior to marriage. Interspousal aggression is a highly prevalent problem. Individual variables that characterize abusive couples from nonabusive couples are related to general aggressive tendencies and, for men, to exposure to interparental violence in their families of origin. More significantly related to spousal violence was age and education. Further, both men and women who were in repeatedly physically aggressive relationships were more likely to be dissatisfied at 30 months than were nonaggressive couples.

In taking the stably aggressive people and looking at them from time one to time two (18 months after marriage), and then predicting their aggression at time three (30 months after marriage), we found that the predictability of these people's behavior increases markedly. We know that if a woman slaps her husband at premarriage and also slaps or hits him at eighteen months after marriage, the likelihood of hitting him on the third occasion is .72. If a man slaps or hits at premarriage and at 18 months post marriage, the likelihood of slapping or hitting his wife at 30 months past marriage is .59 (See O'Leary et al., in press).

In clinical interviews with approximately 100 of these 400 couples at the various assessment times, we found many of these people minimized the aggression a great deal. Both men and women regarded the aggressive behavior as undesirable and not justified, but they discounted its significance nonetheless. On the other hand, marital satisfaction of the partners of stably aggressive men and women decreased across time. That is, if you are a stably aggressive person and engage in pushing, shoving, or slapping, the marital satisfaction of your partner, on the average, indeed does go down. But to our surprise, two-thirds of the partners of the stably aggressive men and women are still not in what we called the clinically discordant range of marital satisfaction at 30 months past marriage. Thus, in a reasonably representative sample of young couples in New York State, we have found this surprising phenomenon that many people can engage in repeated forms of pushing, slapping, and shoving and still not report highly discordant marriages. To be sure, on the average, their marital satisfaction is clearly less than nonaggressive partners, and we predict that they will become more and more discordant if they continue to engage in this behavior. I also believe that the aggression of the men eventually will get more intense and have more serious physical consequence than it will for women. I should emphasize that while the rates of aggression for men and women might even be equal at any particular point, all of us who work in this field are almost uniformly of the opinion that the aggressive behavior of men has a much more significant physical impact than the aggressive behavior of women (e.g., Straus, Gelles, & Steinmetz, 1980). I do not mean to make light of the aggressive behavior of the female because I believe it also has its impact, but in terms of the perspective of spouse abuse it is the man's aggressive behavior that is generally more powerful and more physically debilitating.

THE NEXT TEN YEARS

The next ten years will lead to model testing: evaluating the contributions of various aspects of a person's past to predict whether they will engage in interspousal aggression (See Figure 15.2 – from O'Leary, 1988). Those predictors include such variables as violence in the family of origin, aggression as a personality style, stress, marital discord, alcohol use and abuse, and finally, a negative interchange between the partners. Thus far we've found all of these variables have some significance for the prediction of aggression (O'Leary, 1988) but the crucial aspect for us as clinicians is to learn what is most practically important. With these married couples, we have had to change our model of predicting physical aggression from the model that Alan Rosenbaum and I had developed where we thought that marital discord was the critical variable in terms of either producing or somehow prompting an aggressive interchange.

As I mentioned above, young married people are largely maritally concordant, *not discordant,* even if they repeatedly engage in physical aggression against one another. What we have been led to believe so far is that it is the specific negative interchanges between the partners that is, for most of them, the final common pathway leading to physical aggression (Murphy & O'Leary, 1988). To be more specific, if one uses a causal analysis, as we have to evaluate this model, the spouse-specific aggression is most highly predictable of whether the individuals or partners will engage in physical aggression. Furthermore, if we do follow-back studies, as have been done by a graduate student, Chris Murphy (Murphy & O'Leary, 1987), we show that if you look at people who are aggressive at 30 months but were not physically aggressive at an earlier time, you can predict their subsequent physical aggression from their verbal aggression. As I see it now, our task over the next decade is to develop an evaluation of our models and try to find out to what extent these variables interact with one another in fairly complex ways.

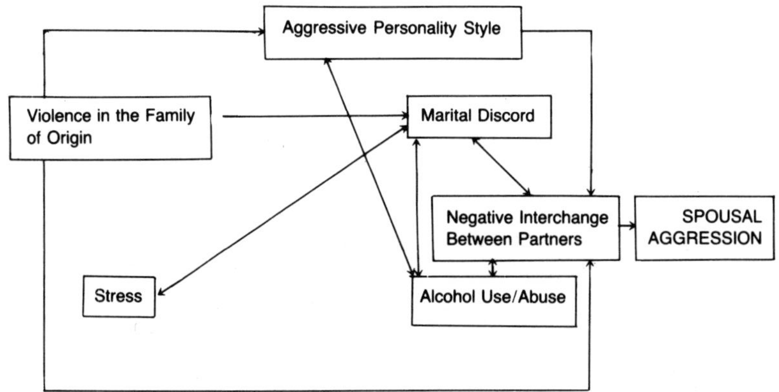

Figure 15.2. A Social Learning Model of Spousal Aggression
SOURCE: O'Leary, 1988.

A BROADER PERSPECTIVE ON AGGRESSION

Aggression can be viewed from very different perspectives. I recently presented my own work on aggression at the New York Academy of Medicine (November, 1987) where the Distinguished Einstein Prize was given to Robert Hind, a developmental psychologist from Cambridge. In his presentation, he depicted how aggression can be viewed from an ecological point of view, to a biological point of view, to an interpersonal view, and so on, and showed in rather interesting ways how aggression can be predicted in various species from proximity of the predator to the other partner whether one is viewing small animals, large animals or even interpersonal situations with humans. The second speaker was Dr. Frank Ervin, who has done classic work on surgical interventions for severely aggressive men. Ervin first described the range of aggressive behavior from aggressive behavior in child interactions of a nonaversive nature to the extremely violent homicidal behavior of men (and occasionally women). He showed in a fairly convincing way that when people engage in repeated homicidal behavior, 80% of them presented themselves for treatment repeatedly, asking for help, and said that they felt an aura coming on them before they engaged in this homicidal behavior. Many of these men had brain lesions (e.g., in the amygdala area of the brain that in turn influenced lower brain stem function (Mark, Sweet, & Ervin, 1975). For me, it showed the broad range of aggressive behavior and how we need to be alerted to the fact that others have been looking at aggressive behavior for generations before behavior therapy even got started. Drs. Hind and Ervin were at least twenty years my senior and had been working their whole lives in the area of aggression. For me, it emphasized the need to place aggression in a much larger context. Aggression is caused by many different factors and single variable models of aggression should clearly become a thing of the past.

I would now like to mention one other foray into the area of aggression and hyperactivity from a cultural standpoint. If you look at the combination of hyperactive and aggressive behavior in different cultural contexts, there appears to be some definite influence of the cultural context upon the children (Barling, O'Leary, & Taffinder, 1983; O'Leary, Vivian, & Nisi, 1985). Indian children in South Africa have almost no aggression/hyperactivity, and children in Germany also have relatively low rates of such behavior. The South African example produces for us a very interesting cultural comparison because there are Indians, Blacks, and Whites in a small geographical area where people generally are exposed to the same lighting conditions, the same water, and even much of the same food. Yet the Indians in South Africa, in classes of approximately the same size as those of the Whites, have rates of hyperactivity and aggression that are one-third of what we have seen in almost any other cultural situation. The Indians who walk the streets of Johannesburg, as Ghandi stated, "know their place." They don't talk back to their elders and they certainly don't talk back to others in public situations. This is just one example of how the larger cultural context impacts upon the portrayal of aggression.

AN EVALUATION OF THE TRIP

Now to summarize this bumpy road. Professor Richard Hackman of Harvard, former graduate school classmate with whom I have spent every Thanksgiving since graduate school, gave me a quotation of Sigmund Koch when we finished graduate school, which is on my office wall. The general thrust of that quotation is that in the long run when one evaluates your research and your scholarship twenty or fifty years from now there likely will be a totally different conceptual interpretation to account for all the data that you select. The bottom line of the quotation is that the ultimate criterion for you as a researcher, and is whether you've had fun doing what you did. Fortunately, I had fun along the bumpy path.

Further, I'd like to recount one research area on that road from child to adult aggression that was fun, but that others might call a bust. Rosenbaum and I went down a partly-blind alley when we looked at the potential influence of fluorescent lighting on irritability and hyperactivity for General

Electric. The Russians now give fifteen minutes off to people who work in a factory because they believe fluorescent lighting adversely affects people if they don't get enough near ultraviolet radiance from the sun. However, in our own research we didn't see any real effect of fluorescent lighting on hyperactivity or aggression (O'Leary, Rosenbaum, & Hughes, 1978). We had General Electric engineers rig our system and control the near ultraviolet at the end of the cathode ray tube. We had the lights turned on at six o'clock in the morning and we measured the ambient light and heat level on every child's desk. In short, we never found any effect of the fluorescent lights on the children. But we took a few trips to G.E. in Cleveland. We talked with some people that were investigating the bilirubin problem and did learn that the near ultraviolet component of sunlight can influence the health of young children.

I believe that researchers and clinicians with a behavioral orientation have no corner on the market in terms of changing behavior. I believe that insight oriented therapists, as exemplified by a recent study by Emmelkamp et al., (1988), may be able to effect significant changes in marital problems much the same as we have. Medication seems to do about as well as behavior therapy whether we're talking about hyperactivity or depression, the latter area being one in which I spent a fair amount of time over the past few years (Beach & O'Leary, 1985; O'Leary & Beach, 1988). There is not only one effective way to get to a clinically significant change. However, I think we have offered some significant therapeutic approaches to changing clinically significant behaviors and it's been fun doing it.

I received support from many people. My students and colleagues were as important to me as the research products. In addition to colleagues and collaborators mentioned earlier, others included Frank Fincham, Sharon Foster, Rolf Jacob (the physician who prompted me to get into hyperactivity), Ernie Jouriles, Susan Geiss, Al Israel, Ronald Prince, Evelyn Sandeen, Lisa Serbin, and Dina Vivian. There are others: Ken Kaufman, my first Ph.D. student, sets an example par excellence of a clinician. I received important intellectual support from my students and from post-doctoral colleagues, such as Ileana Arias, Julian Barling, Steve Beach, Joan Broderick, Ronald Kent, and Hillary Turkewitz. They shaped our research directions and they were critical in implementing our research programs.

Finally, one needs to be challenged in life in travels on the road to wherever they are going. I was challenged by Robin Winkler, and by my advisor, Wesley Becker, who said, "Dan, go out there and show that a token program can be implemented in a classroom for emotionally disturbed kids." We were challenged in the sixties and early seventies to show that an intervention, namely behavior therapy, could work. We can provide behavioral treatments that work. And if others can, too, what I need now is a challenge of some other nature. For me, it's going to be the challenge of evaluating models of etiology of physical aggression in couples. I want to check my ability to predict how people interact with one another in more complex ways that lead to spousal aggression.

Have I learned anything from my students? There is a game played at Stony Brook called "Diagnose the Faculty." I'm sure they won't tell me all the diagnoses I've had, but Evelyn Sandeen told me a few weeks ago that my diagnosis is 'Pathologically Optimistic'. What that meant was that I think I can do anything of a family or an academic nature despite all odds of time and space. Those who observed me while I was Chairman of Psychology, and later chairman of the Dean's Council, particularly during the time around the late seventies and early eighties, saw me running hither and yon like crazy. I was chairing a department, editing the Journal of Applied Behavior Analysis, and coaching a soccer team that I eventually took to Belgium. I remember meeting with our dean, Sydney Gelber, who would only schedule appointments on the hour. He never met with me for an hour. What happened to the last fifteen or twenty minutes? I finally found out that Dr. Gelber had had a heart attack and was protecting himself.

I've learned that maybe the "down-time" of people like Gelber is to return the phone calls, to get a drink of water, to unwind. And, if there is anything else that I have learned, it is that I should be more assertive about saying "NO". I've learned that a mark of some maturity should be the number of things that you refuse to do, not that you accept. I'm sure that my family who know that I have been a rose grower for many years hopes that I will take more time to smell those roses. I do spend every weekend on them, but it's probably fair to say that I don't take enough time to smell them. I hope to smell the fragrances more often.

WHITHER THE FIELD OF FAMILY PSYCHOLOGY?

In my opinion, one of the most pressing issues of family psychology is whether the concepts that exist and will be formulated about families can be translated into terms and propositions that can be empirically evaluated reasonably. As we moved from the individual to the dyad or marriage, we found that the issues addressed became much more complex, and often we did not have statistical methodologies that were readily available to us. Methods that take into account complex interdependencies and bidirectional influences are just beginning to be applied to dyads, and as the number of members in the family unit that we observe enlarges, the issues become even more complicated. Consequently, I believe that we will see more and more interdisciplinary research with sociologists and epidemiologists who are trained to use complex statistical models and who have some interest in families. If the biopsychosocial view of human behavior is taken seriously, as I believe that it should, interdisciplinary research with psychiatry, genetics, and biochemistry will also take place as researchers try to unravel the influence of family, biological, and social factors on human behavior. Such unraveling will require complex model evaluation that will allow us to examine causative factors in marital and family interaction (see Fincham & Bradbury, 1987, 1988; Markman, Floyd, Stanley, & Storaasli, 1988; O'Leary et al., in press; Vivian, Smith, & O'Leary, 1988). The aforementioned studies involving longitudinal and cross sectional analyses illustrate how cognitive processes such as assignment of blame can serve as initiators or maintainers of marital dissatisfaction, and how communication problems and emotional and negative escalation cycles early in marriage predict later marital dissatisfaction and physical aggression in marriage. In addition, complex statistical models are necessary to begin to illustrate the separate and interactive roles of heredity and environment on clinical phenomena like depression (Kendler, Heath, Martin, & Eaves, 1987). Finally, varied statistical methodologies for analyzing complex sequential patterns in marital relationships have just begun to receive necessary comparative evaluations (Mayer, Vivian, & Sandeen, 1987).

The influence of pressures to integrate various conceptualizations of behavior are increasing, especially to integrate the psychodynamic and behavioral conceptualizations (Goldfried & Newman, 1986). There is even an organization and a newsletter designed to promote the rapprochement of these two views of human behavior. Interestingly, while there have been a few conceptualizations that integrate some systems concepts with other approaches, the pressure is to integrate family systems approaches with behavioral and/or psychodynamic approaches. I do not believe that we currently have any overarching view of behavior that can easily integrate any of the major conceptualizations of behavior. Consequently, it seems best to empirically buttress our current approaches by borrowing those concepts that appear most likely to aid in the therapy change process. If the concepts aid an individual or a research team in changing behavior, the concepts can then be integrated within one's own theoretical framework. As more and more concepts get borrowed, the whole conceptual framework may have to be altered, or at minimum, our models will have to be much more complex. In the former case, there will be integration; in the latter, we may have the new general conceptualization of human behavior.

REFERENCES

Barkley, R. A., Karlsson, J., Pollard, S., & Murphy, J. V. (1985). Developmental changes in the mother-child interactions of hyperactive boys: Effects of two dose levels of Ritalin. *Child Psychology & Psychiatry, 26,* 705-715.

Barling, J., O'Leary, K. D., & Taffinder, A. (1983). *Hyperactivity in South Africa.* Unpublished manuscript, University of Witwatersrand.

Beach, S.R.H., & O'Leary, K. D. (1985). Treatment of depression with cognitive therapy or marital therapy. *Behavior Therapy, 17,* 43-49.

Becker, W. C. (1973). Some effects of direct instruction methods in teaching disadvantaged children in Project Follow-Through. *Proceedings of the International Symposium on Behavior Therapy.* Minneapolis, MN: Appleton-Century-Crofts.

Birnbrauer, J. S., Wolf, M. M., Kidder, J. D., & Tague, C. C. (1965). Classroom behavior of retarded pupils with token reinforcement. *Journal of Experimental Child Psychology, 2,* 219-235.

Conners, C. K. (1969). A teacher rating scale for use in drug studies with children. *American Journal of Psychiatry, 126,* 6.

Conners, C. K., & Wells, K. C. (1987). *Hyperkinetic children.* Newbury Park, CA: Sage.

Diagnostic and Statistical Manual of Mental Disorders, DSM-III-R. (3rd. ed.). (1987). Washington, DC: American Psychiatric Association.

Dubey, D. R., Kent, R. N., O'Leary, S. G., Broderick, J. E., & O'Leary, K. D. (1977). Reactions of children and teachers to classroom observers: A series of controlled investigations. *Behavior Therapy, 8,* 887-897.

Emery, R. E., & O'Leary, K. D. (1984). Marital discord and child behavior problems in a nonclinic sample. *Journal of Abnormal Child Psychology, 12,* 411-420.

Emmelkamp, P.M.G., Van Linden Van Den Heuvell, C., Ruphan, M., Sanderman, R., Scholing, A., & Stroink, F. (1988). Cognitive and behavioral interventions with distressed couples. *Journal of Family Psychology, 1,* 365-377.

Fincham, F. D., & Bradbury, T. N. (1987). The impact of attributions in marriage: A longitudinal analysis. *Journal of Personality and Social Psychology, 53,* 510-517.

Fincham, F. D., & Bradbury, T. N. (1988). The impact of attributions in marriage: Empirical and conceptual foundations. *British Journal of Clinical Psychology, 27,* 77-90.

Gittelman-Klein, R., Klein, D. F., Abikoff, H., Katz, S., Gloisten, A. C., & Kates, W. (1976). Relative efficacy of methylphenidate and behavior modification in hyperkinetic children: An interim report. *Journal of Abnormal Child Psychology, 4,* 361-379.

Goldfried, M. R., & Newman, C. (1986). Psychotherapy integration: An historical perspective. In J. V. Norcross (Ed.), *Handbook of eclectic psychotherapy.* New York: Brunner/Mazel.

Hetherington, E. M., Cox, M., & Cox, R. (1982). Effects of divorce on parents and children. In M. Lamb (Ed.), *Nontraditional families.* Hillsdale, NJ: Lawrence Erlbaum.

Jouriles, E., Barling, J., & O'Leary, K. D. (1987). Predicting child behavior problems in maritally violent families. *Journal of Abnormal Child Psychology, 15,* 165-173.

Jouriles, E., Murphy, C., & O'Leary, K. D. (1989). Interspousal aggression, marital discord, and child problems. *Journal of Consulting & Clinical Psychology, 57,* 453-455.

Kaslow, F., & Schwartz, L. L. (1987). *The dynamics of divorce.* New York: Brunner/Mazel.

Kendler, K. S., Heath, A. C., Martin, N. G., & Eaves, L. J. (1987). Symptoms of anxiety and depression: Same genes, different environments. *Archives of General Psychiatry, 44,* 451-459.

Kent, R. N., & O'Leary, K. D. (1976). A behavioral consultation program for parents and teachers of disruptive children. In D. Klein & R. Spitzer (Eds.), *Evaluation of psychotherapies* (pp. 89-95). Baltimore: Johns Hopkins University Press.

Kent, R. N., & O'Leary, K. D. (1977). Treatment of conduct problem children: BA and/or Ph.D. therapists. *Behavior Therapy, 8,* 653-658.

Mark, V. H., Sweet, W., & Ervin, F. (1975). Deep temporal lobe stimulation and destructive lesions in episodically violent temporal lobe epileptics. In W. S. Fields & W. Sweet (Eds.), *Neural bases of violence and aggression.* St. Louis, MO.: Warren H. Green, Inc.

Markman, H. J., Floyd, F. J., Stanley, S. M., & Storaasli, R. D. (1988). Prediction of marital distress: A longitudinal analysis. *Journal of Consulting and Clinical Psychology, 56,* 210-217.

Mayer, F. J., Vivian, D., & Sandeen, E. (1987, November). *A comparison of methods for statistical inference regarding sequential strategies.* Paper presented at Association for Advancement of Behavior Therapy, Boston, MA.

Murphy, C., & O'Leary, K. D. (1987). *Verbal aggression as a predictor of physical aggression in early marriage.* Paper presented at the National Conference for Family Violence Researchers, Durham, NH.

Murphy, C., & O'Leary, K. D. (1988). *Psychological aggression as a predictor of physical aggression in early marriage.* Manuscript submitted for publication.

O'Leary, K. D. (1978, June). *The etiology of hyperactivity.* Paper presented at the Second Annual Italian Behavior Therapy Association Meeting, Venice, Italy.

O'Leary, K. D. (1980). Pills or skills for hyperactive children. *Journal of Applied Behavior Analysis, 13,* 191-204.

O'Leary, K. D. (1983). Marital discord and childhood behavior problems. In M. D. Levine & P. Satz (Eds.), *Middle childhood: Development and dysfunction* (pp. 345-364). Baltimore: University Park Press.

O'Leary, K. D. (1985). Il bambino iperativo: perche. (The etiology of hyperactivity.) *Handicap e Disabilite, 6*(2), 27-32.

O'Leary, K. D. (1988). Physical aggression between spouses: A social learning theory perspective. In V. B. van Hasselt, R. L. Morrison, A. S. Bellack, & M. Hersen (Eds.), *Handbook of family violence.* New York: Plenum.

O'Leary, K. D., Barling, J., Arias, I., Rosenbaum, A., Malone, J., & Tyree, A. (in press). Prevalence and stability of spousal aggression. *Journal of Consulting & Clinical Psychology.*

O'Leary, K. D., & Beach, S.R.H. (1988). *Marital therapy: A viable treatment for depression and marital discord.* Unpublished manuscript, SUNY, Stony Brook, NY.

O'Leary, K. D., & Becker, W. C. (1967). Behavior modification of an adjustment class: A token reinforcement program. *Exceptional Children, 33,* 639-642.

O'Leary, K. D., Becker, W. C., Evans, M. B., & Saudargas, R. (1969). A token reinforcement program in a public school: A replication and systematic analysis. *Journal of Applied Behavior Analysis, 2,* 3-13.

O'Leary, K. D., & Curley, A. D. (1986). Assertion and family violence: Correlates of spouse abuse. *Journal of Marital and Family Therapy, 12,* 281-289.

O'Leary, K. D., & Drabman, R. S. (1971). Token reinforcement programs in the classroom. A review. *Psychological Bulletin, 75,* 379-398.

O'Leary, K. D., & Emery, R. E. (1983). Marital discord and childhood behavior problems. In M. D. Levine & P. Satz (Eds.), *Middle childhood: Development and dysfunction* (pp. 345-364). Baltimore: University Park Press.

O'Leary, K. D., & O'Leary, S. G. (1972). *Classroom management: The successful use of behavior modification.* Elsmford, NY: Pergamon.

O'Leary, K. D., O'Leary, S. G., & Becker, W. C. (1967). Behavior modification of a deviant sibling interaction pattern in the home. *Behavior Research and Therapy, 5,* 113-120.

O'Leary, K. D., Rosenbaum, A., & Hughes, P. C. (1978). Fluorescent lighting: A purported source of hyperactive behavior. *Journal of Abnormal Child Psychology, 6,* 285-289.

O'Leary, K. D., Vivian, D., & Nisi, A. (1985). Hyperactivity in Italy. *Journal of Abnormal Child Psychology, 13,* 165-173.

Oltmanns, T. F., Broderick, J. E., & O'Leary, K. D. (1977). Marital adjustment and the efficacy of behavior therapy with children. *Journal of Consulting and Clinical Psychology, 45,* 724-729.

Patterson, G. R. (1982). *Coercive family process.* Eugene, OR: Castalia.

Rosenbaum, A., & O'Leary, K. D. (1981). Marital violence: Characteristics of abusive couples. *Journal of Consulting and Clinical Psychology, 49,* 63-71.

Straus, M. A., Gelles, R. J., & Steinmetz, S. K. (1980). *Behind closed doors.* New York: Anchor Books.

Ullmann, L. P., & Krasner, L. (1965). (Eds.) *Case studies in behavior modification.* New York: Holt, Rinehart & Winston.

Vivian, D., Smith, D. A., & O'Leary, K. D. (1988, November). *Emotional expression at premarriage as a predictor of discord at 18 and 30 months postmarriage.* Paper presented at Association for Advancement of Behavior Therapy, New York.

Vuchinich, S., Emery, R., & Cassidy, J. (in press). Family members as third parties in dyadic family conflict: Tragedies, alliances, and outcomes. *Child Development.*

Wallerstein, J. S., & Kelly, J. B. (1980). *Surviving the breakup: How children and parents cope with divorce.* New York: Basic Books.

Weiss, G., Kluger, E., Danielson, E., & Elman, M. (1975). Effect of long-term treatment of hyperactive children with methylphenidate. *Canadian Medical Association Journal, 112,* 159-165.

Winnett, R. W., & Winkler, R. (1972). Behavior modification in the classroom: Be still, be quiet, be docile. *Journal of Applied Behavior Analysis, 5,* 499-504.

16

The Missing Link in Marital Therapy

AUGUSTUS Y. NAPIER

I undoubtedly share with every other family psychologist a curiosity about the intricacy of family life, an interest which in my case originates in the muffled and obscure tensions in my extended family; and while my exaggerated sense of responsibility for helping families certainly originates in my grandiose fantasies surrounding my father's timely disappearance (during the Oedipal years) into the army in World War II, my decision to become a family therapist occurred in a "conversion" experience. While visiting the University of Wisconsin during my search for an internship site at the completion of my psychology doctoral training at the University of North Carolina in Chapel Hill, I saw Carl Whitaker, who had been my individual therapist several years earlier when we both lived in Atlanta, interview a family on the other side of a one-way mirror; and that was it. Seeing the transformation in a suicidal adolescent as Carl confronted her parents about their marital problems convinced me. "I want to be able to do that," I said to myself. Fortunately, I didn't understand then how long and difficult the road to becoming a family therapist would be.

FAMILY ORIGINS

Having grown up in Lumber City, a small town in southern Georgia, where both of my parents' families were respected and admired—my paternal grandfather was a beloved physician, my maternal grandfather a successful farmer and businessman – I was surrounded by family history and family politics. I cannot remember a time when I was not intrigued by the relationships that swirled around me. My father was sometimes harsh, sometimes gentle, brilliant, and troubled. The youngest child of a workaholic doctor and an overinvolved mother who had been orphaned in childhood, he never succeeded occupationally and later in his life was alcoholic. The vicissitudes of his career took us to several towns and cities, but we always came back to Lumber City. Throughout my childhood, my younger (by four years) sister and I leaned heavily on our strong, resilient mother, who as the eldest of four children – she also had a depressed mother and a hardworking father – became the mainstay of our family.

I was a shy, well-behaved boy, and in high school I did everything I could to make my mother proud of me, at the same time attempting to keep a low profile with my jealous father. A turning point occurred when I won a scholarship to Connecticut Wesleyan, where I was offered a first-rate liberal education, and where I met my wife-to-be, Margaret, who was a student at Mt. Holyoke. Our meeting remains the most significant event in my life, and it has been central to my professional as well as my personal history.

In 1961, only days before Margaret and I were to have been married, following her graduation from college, I lost my nerve and canceled our wedding. I was then plunged into an identity crisis. Returning to Atlanta, where my parents had moved, I was led by my resourceful mother to Carl Whitaker, M.D., who was then in private practice there. Margaret went into therapy in New York City with Asya Kadis, an Adlerian therapist; at the same time she enrolled in the master's program in French literature at Columbia. For two years we struggled to be "individuated," and coped with our personal demons. It is time and effort we have always been grateful to have spent on our separate selves.

By the time we had decided to try marriage again, I had become intrigued by the turbulent complexity of psychotherapy and had decided to become a therapist. I chose psychology (instead of psychiatry or social work) because its emphasis on research, on learning theory, and on normal behavior made it seem more rational and more optimistic than the other mental health fields; and perhaps because a nomadic teacher had at one time drifted through my south Georgia high school and taught an interesting psychology course. His course had introduced at least one unconfident, troubled teen to the possibility of insight into, and help with, his difficulties.

At about the time Carl closed his practice and left to teach in the Department of Psychiatry at the University of Wisconsin, Margaret and I married and moved to Chapel Hill, where I had a generous NIMH research fellowship. The experience of being in therapy had also interested Margaret in the possibility of working with disturbed children. Those were traditional days, and Margaret, whose undergraduate major was political science and who had by then gotten the master's degree in French literature from Columbia, heroically earned a master's degree in education and psychology from Duke University while helping me through my Ph.D. program.

When we moved to Wisconsin for my internship, and while I apprenticed myself to Whitaker, Margaret had the major responsibility for our children. Concurrently she founded and directed a progressive school, Wingra, which is still thriving.

Margaret's and my interest in working together began as an experiment, a kind of marital hobby. I was seeing a couple in which the wife was anxious about the impending delivery of their first child, and I could not seem to help her calm down. Since Margaret had just had a marvelous experience with the birth of our third child, I said to the wife, "I know someone who can help you." Margaret joined the therapy, and the couple did so well that we decided to add another couple, and then later a family.

Our work together began in earnest as I wound down my long training with Whitaker, which continued as I joined the faculty at the University of Wisconsin; and as we began to talk of leaving Madison. Carl had said that becoming a family therapist was a 10-year project, and it took almost exactly that much time for me. Along the way Margaret began to go to workshops and to get supervision herself, a process which she has continued.

The Family Crucible is a portrait of my dedication to learning at Carl Whitaker's side, and I wrote it in part to express my gratitude to him for the help he gave me (and so many others as well) in learning to confront, understand, and love families. Not until 10 years later did I write, in the recently published *The Fragile Bond,* (Napier, 1988) of the difficulties of trying to individuate from the mentor relationship, problems I was pleased to learn, through a belated reading of Levinson's (1978) *The Seasons of a Man's Life,* were not uniquely mine.

DEFINING A PROFESSIONAL STANCE

Just as Robert Frost reserved the term *poet* as a praise-word, I have a similar reverence for the appellation *family therapist.* Having recently turned 50, surely I can finally claim to be a family therapist; and with a firm grip on self-definition, surely I possess a sense of professional competence. Whatever hesitance I feel in the face of these imperatives, and I do feel some, I can blame on the formidable challenge of working with families, and on the incredible speed of "time's chariot." I did not begin graduate study at UNC until my mid-twenties, and my effort to become a family therapist did not become clearly focused until I was nearly 30 and in the internship at Wisconsin. I spent most of my thirties learning to work competently with families within a relatively protected relationship with Whitaker in Madison; following a "becoming one's own man" crisis (Levinson, 1978) I dedicated my forties to developing my own style as a family therapist. Only at 50 do I finally feel spontaneous and creative; and I now look forward to seeing what emerges in my work.

Somewhere along the way I fell in love with marriage: as an intellectual puzzle; as embodying a set of problems that need solutions; and, because my own marriage has become more and more satisfying, as a way of living. Not only do I enjoy working with couples, but I often work with Margaret, with whom I see at least half my clients. Together, we seem to be hopelessly entangled in marriage, in each other, and in working with couples.

MARITAL CHOICE

In nearly 20 years of work with couples and families, I have also come to believe in the inherent wisdom of marital choice. It took me a while to realize that not all couples "fall in love" with each other as people, the way Margaret and I did. Some choices are "underdetermined," made casually, intellectually, or out of a need to do the right thing at the right time. Still other marriages are "overdetermined," or made in the midst of a storm of emotional need: she needs a father and marries her high school teacher, or he is in a fight with his mother over his right to be separate and marries a girl his mother can't stand. These marriages, contracted with indifference or desperation, are indeed held by a fragile bond.

When the intuitive mechanism of choice is not overridden by anxiety or stress, we are extremely skillful in choosing a mate. While no choice protects us from incredible amounts of distress, or excuses us from having to work terribly hard at marriage, this kind of "integrated" marital choice offers us a unique opportunity to grow. In *The Fragile Bond* I outline some ideas about marital choice, though they fall far short of being a coherent theory. I believe that our mate is, in ways that are usually not obvious at first, a kind of *psychological twin.* Though our respective approaches to the world may be very different, *shared core experiences from childhood allow us to identify with each other's fundamental views of the world.* Our mate also confronts us with aspects of ourselves that are hidden, denied, or undeveloped. We have plenty of opportunities to project our own problems into our mate; we also have a powerful incentive to reach into our untapped potential in order to deal with this often maddening Other who may be like us in areas of functioning in which we approve of ourselves, and different from us in areas where we dislike ourselves (Fowler, 1859).

Our choice of a partner also represents an attempt to gain security. We marry someone who reminds us of the person in childhood who made us feel the most loved and safe. While that person is often, for both men and women, mother (Aron, 1974), it might be older sister, grandfather, or a favorite aunt or uncle. But our mate is also a good role-player, and can often imitate, and allow us to replicate in his or her uniquely confusing person, all the key players in our family of origin. But since we are never simply interested in replication alone, our mate also presents us with unique and different aspects of the Protective Other (parent, surrogate parent) that are in the direction, at least, of Ideal Parent.

We are also drawn to aspects of our mate's family that are strategically similar to, and different from, our family of origin (Napier, 1971). Ideally, we will be able to identify with our mate's family of origin in the areas of experience in which we derived comfort and pleasure from our own family; and find them mercifully different in ways where we found our family deficient. In a simple example, my family had difficulty with anger, and Margaret's with closeness; I was drawn to her family's capacity to fight openly, she to my family's capacity for togetherness. I believe these choices include an attraction to specific role patterns in our mate's family of origin. I learned from her father's career success; she learned from my mother's having had a satisfying career.

Not only do we unconsciously "plan" to marry someone who will force us to face ourselves and our family of origin, but we are confronted with powerful "levers" of change. In marriage, the only way to avoid a frightening regression into our core childhood dilemmas may be to alter our vulnerability to these dynamics. Our mate threatens to recapitulate our "worst case dilemmas," and in the bilateral reenactment of both our childhood scripts, we both seem to be compelled to change if the relationship is to survive. Our mate not only provides the stimulus that reactivates our sense of self as a child, but also challenges us to move beyond those strictures.

Just as there is a constant tension between our needs to repeat the past (and thus gain the security that comes from familiarity) and our needs to change and grow, there is a tension between the temptation to sink into the despair of perpetual reenactment, versus the imperative to break out of the past and create new structures and life-possibilities. This struggle is never resolved, and on the largest scale it represents the tension between the impulse toward life and the wish for death that Freud described in his later writings (Freud, 1922).

STAGES OF MARITAL WORK

What follows in the next section is a description of my current "theory" and practice in couples treatment.

All marital therapy, then, takes place in the midst of a struggle between the temptations of stasis and the imperatives of change. It also plays itself out against a background in which both partners function as amateur therapists to each other. Even though this amateur self-help within marriage is unintended and often misguided, "professional" therapy often has great difficulty competing with it. A major question in the early stages of treatment is whether the partners will risk being "unfaithful" to each other by working with the temporary foster parents, their cotherapists.

Forming a Diagnostic Framework

As Margaret and I begin work with a couple—and their children are usually included in the meetings—we look at their system from six perspectives (see Figure 16.1).

1. The depth dimension includes an assessment regarding the level of commitment in the marriage: the solidity of the emotional "glue" with which the marriage began, and the current state of that binding force.
2. The power dimension describes symmetrical or asymmetrical power arrangements, with the assumption that covert trends are at least as significant as overt patterns (the one-up partner is protected from knowing about his "child" self, for example). Parental dominance models, sibling order patterns, and family of origin roles often determine these arrangements.
3. The horizontal dimension portrays the pursuit-distance dance (Fogarty, 1979), or rejection-intrusion pattern (Napier, 1978). Patterns may be symmetrical or asymmetrical. Symmetrical distancers are disengaged; symmetrical pursuers are enmeshed.
4. We insist on evaluating the degree of interpersonal equity within the marriage: that is, whose feelings seem to command the most attention; and how is the work/obligation quotient apportioned? In many instances, we still find women at an unfair disadvantage in relation to their husbands. Even though women's power may have increased in marriage, women still give more emotionally than their partners do.
5. Flexibility is a key ingredient in marriage, and couples are often polarized in this dimension, with one partner a "yea-sayer" (to change), the other an emotional conservative, or "naysayer." Looking at this area gives us a way of examining the couple's approach to the prospects of change in the therapy process.

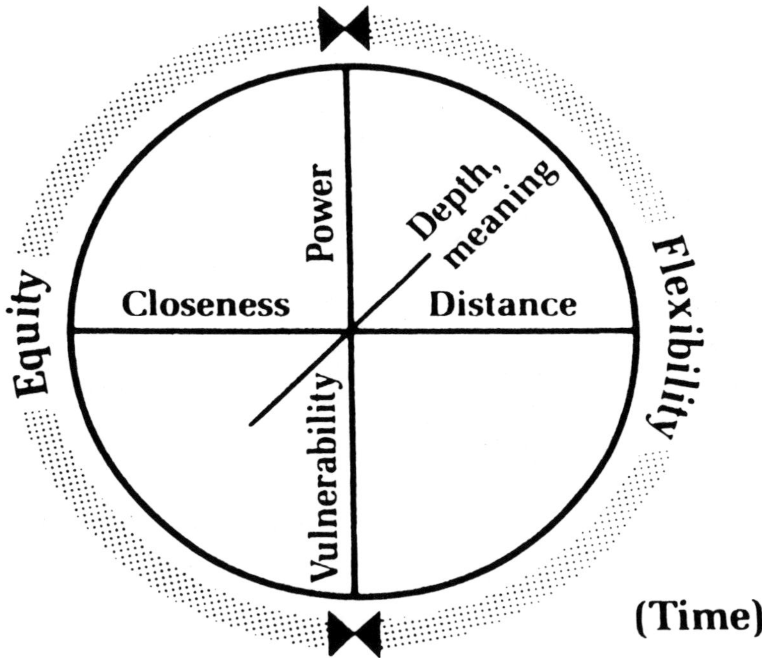

Figure 16.1.

6. Time is a global, pervasive consideration. We place the couple on a developmental continuum as to chronological age and stage of family development, but we also assume that all serious marital conflicts reactivate the "deep time" of childhood trauma.

Engagement Phase

The initial stages of experiential marital therapy are similar to other approaches (Napier, 1987a, 1987b). The opening session (which is usually a double session) of necessity includes a component of assessment. The battle for structure (Napier & Whitaker, 1978) preceding this session often revolves around whether to include the children, and I usually insist on their coming. We will not begin without one of the spouses or begin with undisclosed secrets communicated to the therapist over the telephone. These initial requirements for inclusion and disclosure sometimes result in the loss of couples who are manipulative or uncommitted to therapy.

The essential tasks of early therapy are to challenge the scapegoating process within the family, including the family's tendency to identify marital issues as being in one spouse; and to define the family's problems, and the work that arises from them, as systemic in nature. In therapy, the scapegoat is promoted upward, the righteous partner is demoted. The couple's communication process is held up to scrutiny, and a dominant theme in their struggle is also defined (power, closeness, commitment, flexibility, equity). Bilateral responsibility for these patterns is tied to family of origin scripting, issues that we feel obliged to point out early in therapy but that we do not expect to be embraced heartily by the couple. Before this engagement phase is complete, however, the couple should have experienced a new insight into themselves as a couple, and they should have a clear sense of the therapists' capacities for leadership, fairness, and caring.

Process Phase

The next work leads to the process phase of therapy, in which communication style is the focus. The couple is required to take initiative in "staging" their own conflicts in the presence of the therapists, and they receive feedback about the problematic aspects of their communication. "Dirty fighting," double-binding messages, indirect communication, and denial are confronted; and hierarchical messages in particular are pointed out. At first these problematic behaviors are described by the therapists, but soon the couple is pressured to change their communication pattern in the immediate present. A special point is made of one-up or one-down stances, and the couple's childhood training in taking these positions is explored.

Behavioral Phase

Most spouses are fixated on a projective, blaming focus on the partner, and the next phase of therapy involves getting both mates to take responsibility for the self, and to contract for making carefully negotiated changes that are in the direction of fair, empathic peer teaming. As we ask each person to alter his/her scripting, we encounter powerful resistance; but most couples are able to push through to a certain amount of deliberate, behavioral change. She makes herself be less directive; he pushes himself to be more assertive. They both agree to take more time for their relationship. I have termed this phase *behavioral* in that the marriage clearly benefits from the partners' realization that they can make consciously chosen changes in their behavior.

I do not expect these behavioral changes to last, though some couples who are frightened by deeper levels of therapy are content to stop here. They may drop out of treatment as soon as they gain some insight into the origins of their problems and make improvements in their communication.

Resistance

In attempting to disrupt the couple's implicit caretaking of each other and in engaging them in a cooperative peer endeavor, we have challenged vital security mechanisms in the marriage; and if the couple continues in therapy, we can expect entrenched resistance. Soon, the partners are again complaining of the same patterns, and we are likely to begin to repeat our advice to them. The problem is that we have asked them to stop using each other as "therapists," but they have as yet no trusted replacement figures. The question at hand is whether the couple can be "unfaithful" to each other by linking up in a more involved way with the cotherapists; and while they may not trust each other either, they are certain to project onto the therapists many of the fears and uncertainties that rightfully belong to their parents.

Therapist Challenge

This uncertainty about whether they can trust the therapists must be resolved, and it is usually addressed in what I have termed the *therapist challenge*. A member of the family is unconsciously chosen to defy or provoke the therapists. The overtly powerful spouse, for example, may confront the therapists or attempt to manipulate them, or the one-down spouse may insist tenaciously on being the "patient." Depending on their particular areas of anxiety, the couple may challenge the therapists' intelligence (do we see their dynamics clearly?), caring (can we be empathic?), or self-assurance (can they push us around?).

The therapists must not only respond to the challenge with calm, firm, professional resolve; but we must indicate in our response a clear sense of counter-challenge. There is a palpable question about who in the therapist-client relationship is going to regress; and we should make it clear that it must be the clients.

Not only must we be unswerving in our refusal to give up our professional position, but since we anticipate that the opportunity to enter the marital system on a deeper level will take place through an individual regression of one of the spouses, we should indicate the direction in which we expect regression to take place in the couple. Often we must move in opposition to the couple's invitation for involvement. Thus we will dodge the pursuer's request to get the distancer to be more intimate, moving instead to engage the pursuer around his or her driven need for acceptance. Essentially, we are pushing one spouse to be in "individual therapy" within the couple's therapy context; and the invitation is a strategic one. In the same vein, we begin to push the one-up, overfunctioning partner to look at his or her hidden needs, and we search for a therapeutic vector in relationship with this client. This invitation for individual involvement must come after the couple has made a firm commitment to bilateral responsibility for their problems. Regressive work marks the beginning of the mid-phase of therapy; it is rarely appropriate at the beginning of treatment, when an individual focus is often evidence of the couple's resistance to facing conflict issues.

Individuation-Regression

As we enter the mid-phase, then, the couple is saying implicitly, "We insist that you accept our system as it is," and we counter by saying, "You must change this pattern, and you must change it in this direction."

If the therapists pass the couple's "test," and if the couple can gather the courage, one partner in the marriage usually regresses. I have termed this shift the *individuation-regression,* in that the "elected" individual comes to a session overburdened with feeling, often at the verge of tears. This person then collapses into strong, primary feeling in the session, reaching out to the therapists in what is essentially an act of marital infidelity. The implicit message is, "I give up on getting what I need from my spouse; please help me." Our response should convey support, empathy, and permission to "let down." Insight into the origins of the individual's distress may be useful after the affective catharsis, but we should be careful not to inhibit this person's emotional response by being overly interpretive.

If this individual feels supported by this exchange, it marks the beginning of a new level of trust in the therapeutic relationship. A rejection-phobic pursuer, for example, may not only find a new kind of acceptance from the therapists, but this experience may also provide an impetus to begin to depend less heavily on the partner, and to begin to look critically at his or her own history in the family of origin.

The therapeutic "leverage" acquired through this new therapist-client coalition destabilizes the marriage. The nonaligned partner feels threatened, and vaguely jealous of the spouse's new alliance. For example, if the pursuer uses the therapist's support to stop pursuing, the distancer becomes acutely aware of the pursuer's failure to seek closeness; and the distancer's covert rejection issues, which have been hidden to this point, become obvious. The distancer may thus be thrown into crisis.

Individuation-Accommodation

The stage is then set for a second regressive move, which I term *individuation-accommodation.* The second spouse is precipitated into movement as an accommodation to the first spouse's change, though the outcome is similar: in a moment of panic or despair, this partner too finds a new alliance with the therapists.

Existential Shift

Because both partners now have more trusting therapeutic alliances with the therapists — and each partner may be aligned with a particular therapist — the stage is set for more active confrontation between the spouses. Aware of new sources of support, one or both may be less cautious, and may break with old patterns. The usual outcome is a "big fight," with long-suppressed angers ventilated. Sometimes one partner becomes exasperated with the marriage itself, questioning the entire relationship. This reevaluation of the marriage prompts an existential shift, in which the old caretaking arrangements break down. A few couples may move toward divorce at this point, but most proceed to try to make new agreements within the marriage.

This pattern, in which first one and then the other partner aligns with the therapists, followed then by a new level of honesty and openness in the relationship itself, becomes the dominant sequence as work continues; and it may be repeated many times. With each individual's successive alignment with the therapists, the opportunity to explore family of origin issues increases. Greater awareness of these background problems can then be used cognitively to interrupt old patterns of attack and defense; and the therapists' empathy for these historical problems provides an implicit "reparenting" experience.

Family of Origin Phase

With both partners having greater awareness of historical issues, and with both assuming more self-responsibility, blaming is less problematic; but increased attention to family of origin issues brings a new kind of distress. It is easier to imagine one's partner to be "the problem" than to know that one's own history, and one's response to that history, must be addressed. Depressed about having to face themselves, and guilty at realizing how angry they are at their parents, both partners approach the late stages of couples work with trepidation. "Things seem to be getting worse rather than better," they may complain.

Since it is aimed at helping both partners "re-script" the powerful roles and injunctions of childhood, the family of origin stage of marital therapy is the most ambitious, and some couples are discouraged by its challenges. When they discover that they will need to examine their unquestioning loyalty to their parents, and that they will need to break with deeply familiar roles in many of their relationships, some decide to opt for a negotiated truce in the marital war. Very few couples enter this phase without at least a brief hiatus in treatment. To the request that they bring in their parents they may say, "You must be kidding!"

For a number of years, I approached this stage of couples work with excitement as I eagerly anticipated bringing in both partners' parents, and perhaps their entire families of origin—as I had learned to do at Whitaker's side. I still feel that excitement, though it is tempered by experience. One of the most appealing aspects of family of origin work is its drama. Most families have waited so long to address their problems, and the hour is so late, that the scenes we witness are indeed powerful and moving. A young professional weeps as he talks to his father about what it was like for him to feel emotionally responsible for his dying mother while the father was pursuing his workaholic law practice; and the retired father then cries as he describes how his father had died when he was seven, and how he went to work full time at 14. "I thought working hard was all I could do," he laments, attempting to apologize to his neglected son. He also promises to try to change the pattern; and later he begins to invite his son to ski with him.

THE MISSING LINK

Just as insight into historical issues is not sufficient for real change, there are also limitations in direct family-of-origin work. Parents often live at a distance from their adult children and cannot participate frequently in therapy; they may be powerfully resistant to the therapy process; some may be deteriorated alcoholics, seriously depressed, or in some other way psychologically vulnerable; they may have died. In almost every instance, the adult child has more accumulated anger, and more primitive anger, than he or she can safely direct at elderly parents. Our client's parents probably still have many of the emotional problems that caused our client so much difficulty in childhood. So while some long-denied angers can be expressed, and apologies offered, and while parents mellowed by time can tender compensations to their adult children, there still remain haunting intimations of what could have been. This missing affective experience is invariably what our adult clients really deserved in childhood: love, attentiveness, understanding, discipline, support.

It is tempting for us to assume that we must provide what our clients' parents did not; that the therapeutic relationship is the only alternative for our clients. In effect, we offer ourselves as parent surrogates. Given the numbers of clients we see, and the severity of many of their problems, this can be an unrealistic offer to make, and it may not be very effective. We too are likely to become ambivalent figures to our clients, and the mixture of caring and frustration that inevitably develops in the client-therapist relationship may leave our clients feeling at an impasse with us as well. In time, we may become targets for their displaced anger at their parents.

What is needed is a way of addressing the primitive anger and grief that our clients feel about their parents, and particularly a way that allows a cathartic discharge of these threatening emotions—without their having to traumatize their parents; and without their directing these feelings at us. A further and most important need is a series of reparative experiences that address specific deficits in childhood. Often these deficits are symbolized by charged memories of scenes that portray the injustice of the client's childhood: hurtful remarks, abusive incidents, solitary scenes of neglect, traumatic memories of conflicts between others. Often there is a yearning for these specific scenes to be changed or reenacted.

The main requirement for this "missing link" in couples work (or work with any adult client in a family) is a method that allows control in staging and restaging key family dramas—without requiring that the family of origin change dramatically. The work of Albert and Diane Pesso offers exciting potential to this latter stage of family of origin work.

SYMBOLIC RESTRUCTURING

Several family therapists have addressed the need for symbolic resolution of family-of-origin dilemmas, with the best known approach being Satir's "family reconstruction," described by Nerin (1985). Combining a variety of techniques, including body sculpting, guided fantasy, role playing, and psychodrama, Satir's approach involves both staging patterns in the extended family, and rescripting those patterns in a more positive direction.

In *Family Interfaces: Transgenerational Patterns,* Jeannette Kramer (1985) describes a number of techniques that she has adapted from others' work with individuals and nonfamily groups, and that attempt to bring focus and resolution to the adult client's childhood experiences. These include gestalt methods, such as the use of an "empty chair" to symbolize a parent figure and to facilitate dialogue with that parent; family sculpture (Duhl, Kantor, & Duhl, 1973), in which role-players are positioned to indicate the individual's perception of family dynamics; and a regression-integration technique called "redecision therapy" (Goulding & Goulding, 1979) in which the adult client is encouraged to retrace a painful present dilemma backward in time to an original decision in childhood, a "decision" that was made in an effort to survive a seemingly impossible situation.

In these approaches, techniques developed by individual or group therapists are incorporated into family or couples work. Using symbols to represent childhood figures and relying on a kind of hypnotic induction to recreate the "aura" of the original situation, the therapist provides both a set of stimuli for recreating a childhood situation, and emotional support for reexperiencing it more fully than was possible in childhood. The therapist also suggests a more positive and more empowering outcome for the adult client.

While I see all these adjuncts to family work as useful, my own exploration has led me to an approach that addresses family-of-origin dilemmas on a more primitive, and more physical, level.

THE PESSO SYSTEM

Albert and Diane Pesso (Pesso, 1969, 1971), who together created the "psychomotor" approach to therapy, were both teachers of dance at Emerson College. Their earliest "experiments" were designed to help their students who were emotionally blocked find ways of dancing more freely. Realizing that family-of-origin conflicts were at the root of their dancers' problems, they evolved a system of motoric expression of feeling toward role-players who were stand-ins for family figures. Staging these pivotal family scenes often provoked strong emotion, and the Pessos concentrated on motoric as well as verbal discharge of negative emotion toward these figures.

After moving into a psychiatric setting (first at Boston Veterans Administration Hospital, then later at McLean Hospital in Boston, where the Pessos directed a special treatment unit for a number of years), they incorporated concepts from ego psychology, sometimes splitting positive and negative attributes of ambivalent figures. They also developed a sophisticated system of providing physical boundaries for patients, which facilitated a sense of safety in the expression of powerful affect. Concerned that the intense expression of negative affect often left their patients feeling that they had "blown away" their parents, they began to design enactments that also presented ideal, reparative figures who behaved in the ways their clients wished their parents had acted. These positive, healing dramas formed new images that began to compete with the negative patterns of childhood, often opening patients to new possibilities in current relationships.

The Pessos' system is a complex one with its own training and certification process, and it has been used principally with ad hoc groups of therapists who work on their own issues while being trained. The Pesso system bears some similarity to gestalt and psychodrama approaches, but it is unique in combining a sophisticated "externalization" (through role-playing) of the individual's intrapsychic conflicts, which are expressed in extremely powerful "body language." The most appealing aspect of this system is its emphasis on emotional "truth," as revealed in bodily states.

The Pessos' sensitivity to body tension and expression allows them to bypass intellectual defenses, while the therapist's tight control of the work, including the creation of physical restraints, facilitates a sense of emotional safety. In this work, the client often makes startling discoveries about his or her feelings, and is usually able to accomplish discharge of primitive negative emotion, and to risk vulnerable healing experiences with ideal figures.

I have incorporated certain of these techniques into the couples treatment format, and I have found them extremely useful. Not only do they permit an expression of primitive affect related to childhood experience, but they also help both partners develop the beginnings of more positive parental images, which can then shape anticipation of more positive responses from each other. These internal shifts can also pave the way for more constructive resolution of conflicts with the actual parents. Rage and the desire for reprisal are thus handled in a symbolic experience, while the actual relationships with the parents are approached with the hope of rebuilding them as adult-to-adult relationships. Discharge of negative affect toward the parents may also improve both spouses' parenting of their own children. An example may illuminate the process for the reader.

Case Study Using the Pesso System

Jim and Elise came to therapy following an incident in which Jim had lost his temper and hit Elise. This was only the latest of several such occurrences, and Jim had also verbally abused Elise and was beginning to yell loudly at their two-year-old son, Jerry. Initial work consisted in getting firm agreements from Jim that he would refrain from the physical use of force; and on helping Elise set firm limits with him. Having lost her mother at an early age, Elise was timid and deferential with Jim, and she required substantial support in learning to take a stronger stand with him. Later work in therapy dealt with some of her deficits, but the initial focus was on the forces in Jim's life that led him to be abusive.

The older of two children, Jim had grown up in a conflictual household that included Jim's paternal grandmother, whose favorite he had been. Jim had been physically and verbally abused by his father, who had in turn been abused by his father. These facts came to light in an early session with Jim's family of origin, which included all the members of his nuclear family except his grandmother, who had been dead for several years. As the abuse was discussed, Jim's father became agitated and defensive, and the family refused to return after one interview.

In several couples sessions, Margaret and I began to help Jim work on his anger at his father. As he talked about the father, Jim also became agitated, and his face flushed. We suggested that he imagine his father in an empty chair, and when he looked frightened at that possibility, we recommended that he place beside this chair another chair that symbolized a "restraining figure" such as a policeman who would prevent the father from hurting him. With this symbolic "security," Jim began to verbalize his hurt and anger, saying to the father, "You should never have done what you did," and "I'm very angry at you for hitting me and my brother."

As he recalled a particularly frightening scene in which the father had grabbed him by the throat, I noticed that Jim's throat was flushed and red and that his hands were opening and closing spasmodically. Careful attention to the client's body state is central to the Pessos' approach, and cathartic motoric discharge related to areas of physical tension is seen as necessary to "clear" such long-stored traumatic experience. Since Jim's hands seemed to be the part of his body in which his anger was focused, I moved to allow him a controlled physical way of expressing this affect. I helped him choose a tough, spongy cushion and to imagine that it represented the part of his father that he was angriest at. Emphasizing that this was only a cushion, and that it symbolized only one aspect of his father—the abusive part—I encouraged him to express whatever he felt like doing toward this object. I also reassured him that the protective figure would prevent the father from retaliating.

At first Jim only spoke to the cushion, expressing the anger he had addressed to the empty chair. With our encouragement he grasped the pillow and squeezed it gently, then more firmly. Suddenly his face became flushed, and he began a more intense confrontation with the pillow. He squeezed it hard, then twisted it violently, shouting, "You bastard, you son-of-a-bitch." For the next several minutes, he abused the cushion, twisting it, hitting it in his lap, throwing it on the floor and stepping on it, shouting obscenities at it. "I'm going to kill you," he yelled loudly, "the way you tried to kill me!" Finally he picked up a foam bat and began pounding the pillow violently until he was exhausted. Throughout this encounter, I used the Pessos' technique of "accommodating" to Jim's expression of anger by emitting agonized groans, sounds which allowed him to feel that his efforts were having an effect.

After many minutes of strenuous exertion, Jim sank exhausted into his chair and began weeping. Margaret and I then sat on either side of him and offered him support. Sadness is often the sequel to such expression of anger, as the deeper hurt which has been masked by anger begins to emerge; and in this moment emotional support by the therapists is crucial.

In a subsequent session in which he seemed both relieved and somewhat depressed, we helped Jim work on developing an image of an "ideal father." Again we had Jim imagine an ideal father in an empty chair, and I spoke for this idealized image. "What would an ideal father be like?" I asked.

"He would never hit his children," he said sadly. "He would find other ways of disciplining them."

"If I had been your father," I said warmly, glancing at the empty chair to emphasize that the voice was representing that figure, "I would never hit you. I would find other ways of disciplining my children." As I spoke these reassuring words, Jim visibly relaxed. Then I asked, "What else would the ideal father say to you?"

"He would take an interest in me and help me learn to do the things I needed to know, like how to work on cars," he said.

"I would take an interest in you and help you learn to do the things you need to know, like how to work on cars," I again said positively and supportively; and once more Jim seemed obviously touched by my tone of voice and by the image of fatherhood that it conveyed. As the session progressed, he visualized other aspects of the ideal father: his interest, his compassion, his ability to hear his feelings, his emotional strength. Several times during this session he began to cry softly as he implicitly contrasted this image with his childhood father. But the predominant emotion was one of relief and gratitude as he experienced the tone of voice, the words, the concern of a more loving "father." While the empty chair symbolized this father figure, the fact that I was speaking for this figure caused Jim to look increasingly at me.

At the end of the session I "de-roled" the chair, and said that I was no longer role-playing the voice of the ideal father, just as in the previous session I had done with the symbolism of the cushion which represented the negative aspects of the father. In such semihypnotic exercises, it is important to mark the transition between the hypnotic experience and the "reality" of the therapy interview.

While we helped Jim fashion other exercises in which he expressed anger at his father, and in which he visualized ideal images of several members of his family of origin, he obtained immediate and lasting relief from that first cathartic session in which he assaulted a cushion with some of the murderous intensity that had been directed at him when he was a child. As we worked further, Jim leaned more heavily on me for support, a relationship that was probably enhanced by my playing the role of the voice of the ideal father.

Nearly a year after the first session with his family of origin, Jim brought his father—alone—for several sessions. He felt that his father would be less defensive if he did not need to bolster his image with the rest of the family, and that intuition proved correct. The father, who had just retired, was much more relaxed and vulnerable, and discussed his own childhood abuse with a great deal of feeling. The sessions were cathartic for the father, and he began to reach out to his alienated son. Jim felt extremely grateful for the father's interest, and since these interviews the two of them have had a much more positive relationship. Jim and Elise were, in fact, somewhat concerned recently to discover that Jim's parents—at the father's initiative—were thinking of moving from Arizona to the younger couple's city in their retirement.

Pesso Techniques in Conjoint Therapy

This kind of symbolic work is ideally done in a group setting where individuals can be chosen to play both negative and positive roles, and where the entire family of origin pattern can be staged, and then re-staged. Group members can also provide physical limits and restraints that allow extremely intense work on anger. In my experience, a couple's group is an ideal format for these exercises, as it allows couples the opportunity to focus on their relationship issues, or to shift and work symbolically on family-of-origin conflicts. But as I have tried to show, the Pessos' techniques can be a valuable adjunct to conjoint therapy with couples, especially in instances where a male-female cotherapy team works together.

Though they must be done carefully, these symbolic "structures" can also be useful in building therapeutic bridges within the client-therapist relationship. For example, a woman who mistrusts her husband and all males (including the male cotherapist) because of an abusive experience with her father may begin by being led by the woman cotherapist in expressing anger at an empty chair or pillow. As the client begins to feel the sadness of the absence of healthy fathering, the woman therapist might suggest that the male therapist be enrolled as first the voice of the ideal father, and then eventually to role-play the ideal father directly. Approached skillfully (and the use of psychomotor techniques in therapy requires extensive training), such delimited but charged experiences may allow the client to shift internal decisions made in childhood and to begin to lean for the first time on a male (or female, in other instances) support figure.

The decision to use these powerful tools in regressive work must be approached cautiously, and an obvious complication for the therapist in volunteering to be associated with an ideal image is the possibility of creating a supercharged transference relationship in the client. For this reason, it is preferable to use symbolic referents; and the group context allows the therapist to work on a very intense level without being so direct a target of positive expectations. The group can also become a more loving, stronger, therapeutic "family" than its members experienced in childhood.

Pesso speaks of the psychomotor group as forming a "sphere of possibilities," possibilities that go beyond the members' prior experience. While his system has not been derived from or tailor-made for work with families, it deals with historic family issues in a way that I find extremely exciting. This approach allows the therapist to recreate for the adult client a version of the original family in which the client is empowered to seek a primitive and cathartic "revenge" for prior wrongs. The client is then given the opportunity to refashion in a supportive, symbolic "family" the world as it could have been. With this healing vision held firmly in view, the chances of the client's finding in the present some version of this world are substantially enhanced.

These techniques cannot substitute for the intricate work of assembling and working with the present-day, as well as the historic, family; but they do allow us a degree of control in creating a new and hopeful sphere of possibilities in our work with families. In the latter stages of marital and family therapy, these techniques may indeed provide the missing link in moving from a painful past to a more hopeful future.

TOWARD THE FUTURE

In recent years, family psychologists have been pulled between two contrasting approaches in their work with families. One group, which might be termed "systems purists," has focused on defining the family as a system, and has posited a variety of increasingly technical and preplanned interventions that are designed to change the dynamics of the system. These therapists might be seen as "emotional distancers," in that they work removed from the family, often interposing a one-way mirror between them and the family.

The "psychodynamic" approach is more traditional, emphasizing the relationship with the family, and drawing on a background of concepts that are closely linked with the history of individual therapy. These therapists may be more or less confrontive or nondirective, but they all value long-term involvement between family and therapist; and they emphasize traditional values such as insight, caring, and the commitment to hard work. This group might be called "emotional pursuers," and we could be seen as codependent.

For a number of years, we traditionalists have been out of favor, and the glitzy systems purists have been in vogue. I believe that our field's affair with technical wizardry is losing its intensity, and that a reexamination of our relationship with the history of psychotherapy is in order. Family therapy is well established enough to begin to incorporate some previously shunned concepts and values that have been developed in work with individual clients; and we can do so without relinquishing our commitment to working with entire families. Like many others, I believe that greater integration of systemic and individual therapies will occur; and I believe that the work of therapists like the Pessos will contribute to this bridging of approaches.

In the next few years, I plan to become more skilled in the use of techniques of symbolic resolution of family of origin conflicts, and I hope to apply these skills to work with couples groups, and perhaps to groups of families as well.

I am also keenly aware of the limited ability of psychotherapy to help families cope with societal injustices. We therapists must address the larger social system that victimizes all of us; ultimately, we must become political activists, using our experiences with families to help bring about social change. We must learn to speak and write to progressively larger audiences.

Just as we become convinced that technical intervention does not substitute for the long-term investment of caring and effort in the lives of our clients, we need to recognize the fundamental efficacy of prevention, and of the involvement of the larger society in concerns which have heretofore belonged to the client-therapist relationship.

The other frontier for family therapists is in the person of the therapist. We have too long neglected the mental health of the helpers. We must give more formal attention to the emotional needs of family therapists, providing support and therapy for all students, and building in routine procedures and safeguards for the working professional (Kaslow, 1984, 1987). We cannot give to others concern and caring that we have neglected to seek for ourselves, and our professional societies must provide focus on and support for the person of the therapist.

REFERENCES

Aron, A. (1974). Relationships with opposite-sex parents and mate choice. *Human Relations, 27,* 17-24.

Duhl, F., Kantor, D., & Duhl, B. (1973). *From the inside out and other metaphors.* New York: Brunner/Mazel.

Fogarty, T. F. (1979). The distancer and the pursuer. *The Family, 7,* 11-16.

Fowler, O. S. (1859). *Matrimony.* Boston: O. S. Fowler.

Freud, S. (1922). *Beyond the pleasure principle.* London: International Psychoanalytic Press.

Goulding, M. M., & Goulding, R. L. (1979). *Changing lives through redecision therapy.* New York: Brunner/Mazel.

Kaslow, F. W. (1984). *Psychotherapy with psychotherapists.* New York: Haworth.

Kaslow, F. W. (1987). *The family life of psychotherapy: Clinical implications.* New York: Haworth.

Kramer, J. (1985). *Family interfaces: Transgenerational patterns.* New York: Brunner/Mazel.

Levinson, D. J. (1978). *The seasons of man's life.* New York: Knopf.

Napier, A. Y. (1971). The marriage of families: Cross-generational complementarity. *Family Process, 9,* 373-395.

Napier, A. Y. (1978). The rejection-intrusion pattern: A central family dynamic. *Journal of Marriage and Family Counseling, 4*(1), 5-12.

Napier, A. Y. (1987a). Early stages in experiential marital therapy. *Contemporary Family Therapy, 9,* 23-41.

Napier, A. Y. (1987b). Later stages in experiential marital therapy. *Contemporary Family Therapy, 9,* 42-57.

Napier, A. Y. (1988). *The fragile bond.* New York: Harper & Row.

Napier, A. Y., & Whitaker, C. A. (1978). *The family crucible.* New York: Harper & Row.

Nerin, W. (1985). *Reconstruction: Long day's journey into light.* New York: W W. Norton.

Pesso, A. (1969). *Movement in psychotherapy.* New York: New York University Press.

Pesso, A. (1971). *Experience in action.* New York: New York University Press.

17

The Triple Threat of Bridging Research, Theory, and Practice

DAVID H. OLSON

It is both an honor and a privilege to write a short autobiography about how I became a family psychologist. First of all, it is interesting that only in the years since APA established Division 43 of Family Psychology have I felt comfortable using that as my professional label. Being a Family Psychologist enables me to bridge the two areas that I feel most comfortable with professionally, that is, the family profession and psychology. Previous to this time, I had often called myself a psychologist, a family specialist, a marriage and family therapist, and Professor of Family Studies. Now that I am finally comfortable with a professional identification, let me begin by describing the paths that I took to becoming a family psychologist.

BECOMING A FAMILY PSYCHOLOGIST

Although I was interested in psychology as an undergraduate, I never knew where that discipline would take me. I always attempted to follow my interests, which have pulled me in the direction of trying to better understand intimate relationships.

Roots in Family of Origin

I grew up in a traditional Norwegian family that was Lutheran and lived by the Protestant work ethic. Both of my parents were very supportive of me emotionally and also helped me financially when I needed resources to finish school, even though it meant a sacrifice for them. They were loving parents and were extremely hardworking, always willing to sacrifice for both their sons. My father was an engineer by training but he and my mother ran a hardware store together during most of my years in elementary school through high school.

Although my parents valued education, they did not pressure me to go to college; nonetheless, they were always happy with whatever my achievements were. In their concern for us fitting into the American culture, they were unwilling for us to learn Norwegian, even though they spoke it in private with relatives and friends. All in all, they were extremely supportive of me and were always pleasantly surprised when I achieved in anything, including sports or education.

I grew up surrounded by most of my father's and mother's family and relatives. At times, I felt like I could not "get away with" anything because relatives were always emotionally and/or physically present. Being the oldest child in my family, and also the oldest male in my generation in my father's family (and he was also the oldest child), I often felt responsible for doing well in whatever I did so as not to embarrass my parents or relatives. This feeling was often a guiding force even though the pressure was often self-imposed and more implicit than explicit.

Concept of Balance

As I was born a Libra, it might seem logical that the concept of balance would play an important part in my life. I didn't realize how important balance was until the last few years. First of all, balance is a critical concept in bridging research, theory, and practice. It is impossible to be effective at integrating these domains unless you have competence and interest in all three domains and are willing to balance your time between them. It means, therefore, that I cannot be a full-time researcher, a full-time teacher, or a full-time therapist. It has also helped me to constantly balance time and energy between these domains.

The concept of balance also is important in my daily life, in which I try to balance work, my couple and family relationships, and time for myself. Here, too, balance is a critical concept because it emphasizes the need to juggle multiple tasks and demands and to realize that balance is a dynamic process that must always be a part of one's awareness. Balance also is a major concept in the Circumplex Model of Marital and Family Systems, which will be described later.

Professional Heritage

Training in Psychology

I received my bachelor's degree in psychology from St. Olaf College (1962) and my master's in psychology from Wichita State University (1964). Then I went on to complete my doctorate at Pennsylvania State University (1967) and took postdoctoral training in marriage and family therapy at the University of Minnesota (1968). At each stage in this process, I was not sure where exactly the next stage would lead. In fact, when I started my bachelor's degree, I assumed I would become an M.D., until I realized how squeamish I was about dissecting animals and how much I disliked chemistry. A real turning point in my goals came when I worked at a residential treatment center for severely emotionally disturbed children.

Learning a Systems Perspective at a Resident Treatment Center for Children

After my bachelor's and master's degrees, I spent the two summers of 1962 and 1964 at a residential treatment center called Hathaway Home for Children in Pasadena, California. Working at that home with extremely emotionally disturbed children convinced me of the importance of a systems perspective. After working with some of these disturbed children for a few weeks, the staff could see considerable change and progress in their development. After sending these children home for just a day visit with their parents, however, we frequently saw the children regress.

The new staff were often surprised by this dramatic change but the ongoing staff assured them that regression after a home visit was very typical. However, they never developed any interventions with the parents to change their system, but simply saw this as one of the natural outcomes of the child's visit home. From that experience, I became increasingly convinced that in order to be effective in the long run with these children, one needed to also work with the home environment where the children were to live after the treatment was completed.

Another significant learning experience from that Center was about systems and the importance of a team approach where all staff worked together to help the children. All the staff worked as a "cooperative team." This included the cooks, groundkeepers, the recreation workers, the teachers, houseparents, social workers, and psychiatrists. Daily and weekly staff meetings focused specifically on how to treat particular children that week. This "team approach" impressed me in terms of its effectiveness, and also in the mutual respect and support that this approach generated among the staff. Since that time, I have often tried to develop a "team approach" in the projects I have directed.

Bridging Family and Psychology

At Penn State, I was involved in both the Family Relations program and the Clinical Psychology program (1964-1967); at that time, I was one of the few students who tried to bridge the two areas. After completing the Clinical Psychology sequence and having worked with Carlfred Broderick in learning about family theory and research, I tried to encourage the Psychology Clinic to allow me to see couples and families. This initial request was refused, but ultimately a strategic move enabled this to happen.

My first marriage counseling (now called marital therapy) case was quite important in my professional development. No couples had at that time (1965) been seen at the Psychology Clinic on campus. My first clinical case was a male exhibitionist who had been caught three previous times on campus and was required to come to the clinic. As we were trained in the Rogerian approach, I did my best to be an understanding and empathic listener.

At about the same time a colleague in my class, Craig Messersmith, began seeing a woman who had phobic reactions to snakes. Although he was a better Rogerian therapist than I because this approach was compatible with his personal style, he had great difficulty getting this woman to discuss anything, whereas my client was very happy to come to all of the sessions and talked incessantly, even about feelings.

One day after our supervision class, it became obvious that these two people were husband and wife. I thought it would be ideal to see them together, even though I didn't know much about marriage counseling. When we recommended to our clinical supervisor that we see these people as a couple, he denied our initial request. Knowing that he had done his dissertation on Rogerian group therapy, we then proposed that we establish a small group with two therapists and this couple. The supervisor was willing to try this idea as long as it was videotaped and supervised.

In brief, the outcome of the case was quite dramatic. Even though we were both inexperienced therapists, we found the dynamics in the couple very interesting and revealing. Whenever the husband would try to talk, his wife would interrupt and become generally disruptive. After several sessions of focusing on their communication style and working primarily on their relationship, the individual symptoms that they had exhibited seemed to "magically disappear." It seemed magical because we did not focus specifically on the individual symptoms and yet they seemed to become less frequent and less problematic. More specifically, he no longer had the urge to be an exhibitionist and her phobic reaction to and fantasies about snakes disappeared. This case helped to crystallize in my mind the importance of working with a couple as a system.

Postdoctoral Training in Marital and Family Therapy

After completing my doctorate in 1967, I had to decide between doing a traditional psychology internship or a postdoctoral program in marriage and family. Because I did not feel adequately trained to work with couples or families, I chose the latter. I was fortunate to be accepted into the postdoctoral training program in marital and family therapy at the University of Minnesota. This unique program was directed by Dr. Gerry Neubeck and Dr. Richard Hey who were pioneers in marriage counseling. From that experience, I had the opportunity to work with all types of couples and families in a variety of settings. That year's experience increased my commitment to the field of marriage and family therapy.

At that time (1967), marriage counseling was still in its infancy and very little was even known about family therapy. A few mavericks were starting to discuss seeing families together. In 1961, Don Jackson and a few colleagues launched *Family Process* as a professional journal. During that time, Virginia Satir, Jay Haley, Lyman Wynne, Murray Bowen, and Nathan Ackerman were among the most visible family therapists.

Spirit of Creativity

In many ways, I felt like a maverick in trying to bridge psychology and the family field both in my doctoral training and my postdoctoral work. It was often difficult for many in traditional academic departments to see the need to pursue the integration of these fields. Frequently this occurs because most academic departments reward professors for work that will directly advance their own discipline and typically it is easier to publish and work within one specific discipline than to bridge or integrate perspectives. I was convinced, however, of the value of integrating these disciplines even though I was not sure how this could be accomplished.

MAJOR THEMES AS A FAMILY PSYCHOLOGIST

Most of my contributions to the field would never have occurred if I had not teamed up with exceptional colleagues and doctoral students. Much of my work has been done in teams, which I believe facilitates collaboration and cooperation versus competition. Working with teams continues to be a gratifying and effective way of developing ideas, projects, and inventories for me. The following are some of the major themes and projects that I have worked on over the last 20 years.

Bridging Research, Theory, and Practice

If there is one theme that has been characteristic of my work, it is the attempt to bridge the domains of research, theory, and practice (Olson, 1976, Chapter 23). When I wrote my first paper elaborating on this approach, I described the advantages of working collaboratively to therapists and researchers. I called this the *triple threat approach* because this integrative idea enhances each of these separate domains in a way that cannot be done if each domain is focused on independently. The term *triple threat* comes from a situation in football where a quarterback has an option to do three things: run with the ball, lateral the ball, or pass.

One of my secretaries mistyped triple threat as triple *treat.* This fortuitous typing error helped to clarify for me that this approach is also a treat in that it is more enjoyable and exciting for me than working in any of these three areas separately. One of the ways that I have endeavored to integrate these three domains is through the development of marriage and family inventories.

Even my first published article focused on developing a *Premarital Attitude Scale* (Olson, 1967) and illustrating how it could be integrated into teaching the class and also be used to assess the attitude change resulting from the class (Olson & Gravatt, 1968). Another example of this integrative approach was an attempt to describe how the SIMFAM family interaction game (developed by Murray Straus, who was then at the University of Minnesota) could be used for research and theory building and as a diagnostic tool for marital and family therapy (Olson & Straus, 1972).

Treating Relationships

My first book, called *Treating Relationships* (Olson, 1976), focused on another theme that has been central to my professional career. Having worked with individuals exhibiting all types of symptoms, it became more and more clear that their problems also affected other people and were linked in causal ways to the relationship with these "significant others," whether parents, spouses, or close friends. Therefore, it seemed increasingly obvious that these people could be helpful in the treatment process.

At that time, many of the therapists who were also doing research on couple and family therapy were psychologists. In fact, *Treating Relationships* contained chapters by many of the leading family psychologists: James Alexander on "Behavioral Systems Therapy for Families," Gerald Patterson on "Parents and Teachers as Change Agents," Richard Stuart on "An Operant Interpersonal Program for Couples," Elaine Bleckman on the "Family Contract Game," Bernard Guerney on "Conjugal Relationships Enhancement Program," Louise Guerney on "Filial Therapy Program," and David Fournier on "Diagnosis and Evaluation in Marital and Family Therapy." (See Chapters 5 and 10, respectively, in this volume for long contributions by B. Guerney and Alexander).

Marriage and Family Inventories

I have greatly enjoyed both the process and outcome of developing more than 15 different marriage and family inventories. These are increasingly being used nationally and internationally by people in various disciplines for research and clinical work with couples and families. My interest in developing them comes from my background in psychology, where I was trained to be concerned about reliability, validity, and clinical utility. It also fits with the "dust bowl empiricism" which I apparently acquired from living and being educated at the University of Minnesota.

I began developing inventories when I was a doctoral student; my first inventory was the "Premarital Attitude Scale" (PMAS) (Olson, 1968). The PMAS eventually led to the development of PREPARE and ENRICH, premarital and marital inventories that are now computerized (Olson, Fournier, & Druckman, 1980). Both of these inventories are extensively used and have achieved high levels of reliability, validity, and clinical utility (Fowers & Olson, 1986). PREPARE has now been taken by over 250,000 premarital couples and ENRICH has been taken by at least 100,000 married couples.

The most comprehensive series of self-report inventories was developed by a team that included Hamilton McCubbin, Howard Barnes, Andrea Larsen, Marla Muxen, and Marc Wilson. They are published in a volume entitled *Family Inventories* (Olson et al., 1982); it includes FACES, Parent-Adolescent Communication, Family Strengths, and several other self-report scales. These scales were all used in a national survey of 1,000 nonclinical families and the results of that survey are published in the book *Families: What Makes Them Work,* completed by the same collaborative team (Olson et al., 1983).

Insider Versus Outsider Perspectives

When I initially wrote the paper entitled "Insiders' and Outsiders' View of Relationships" (Olson, 1977), I did not realize how much of my work and ideas would build on this theme and how many theoretical and assessment issues are raised by this distinction. In both clinical and research work, the insider's perspective focuses on feelings and thoughts and is often measured by self-report methods. The outsider's perspective includes observing behavior and rating it either subjectively or with some objective rating scale.

Therapists and researchers are now increasingly aware of the different types of information these two perspectives and methods provide. The fact that the two approaches do not tend to correlate has raised some important questions about validity. While some maintain that one approach is most valid, I maintain that both are valid and each is different and important.

Because of their differences, it is essential that in clinical work and in research that both perspectives be utilized. More specifically, self-report and observational approaches must be used together to capture the complexity of family systems.

Not only did we discover that self-report and observational methods do not correlate very highly, but family members do not agree with each other on how they each see their own family. In our study of 1,000 nonclinical couples across the family life cycle (Olson et al., 1983), the average correlation between family members on all the self-report scales was moderate (r = .35-.45). Because of this low correlation between family members, we have developed a variety of couple and family scores which can be used to help capture the complexity of the family system (Larsen & Olson, 1990; Olson et al., 1983).

The Circumplex Model of Marital and Family Systems

One of the major ways I have found of integrating my knowledge about couple and family systems is with the Circumplex Model. It has also enabled me to bridge research, theory, and practice and this has been facilitated by developing both self-report and observational inventories. The self-report inventories include *Family Adaptability and Cohesion Evaluation Scales* (FACES), and the *Clinical Rating Scale* (CRS) that can be used by observers or therapists (Olson & Killorin, 1985). FACES (Versions I, II, and III) has been used in more than 500 studies since the first version was introduced in 1979; more than 150 of these studies are now completed.

The Circumplex Model was developed in the late 1970s with Douglas Sprenkle and Candyce Russell who were then doctoral students in Family Social Science at the University of Minnesota. It was an attempt to conceptually integrate a diverse set of clinical concepts that were emerging from the fields of family therapy and family sociology, and from studies of small groups. The three dimensions that consistently seem to emerge as underlined dimensions were *cohesion, adaptability,* and *communication.*

Since the initial work on the Circumplex Model (Olson, Sprenkle, & Russell, 1979), we have collaborated on more than 10 articles that have reviewed the growing research on the Model and the value of the Model in clinical assessment, treatment planning, and intervention. The most recent publication that brings together some of the clinical applications of this Model is in the book, *Circumplex Model: Systemic Assessment and Intervention* (Olson, Russell, & Sprenkle, 1989).

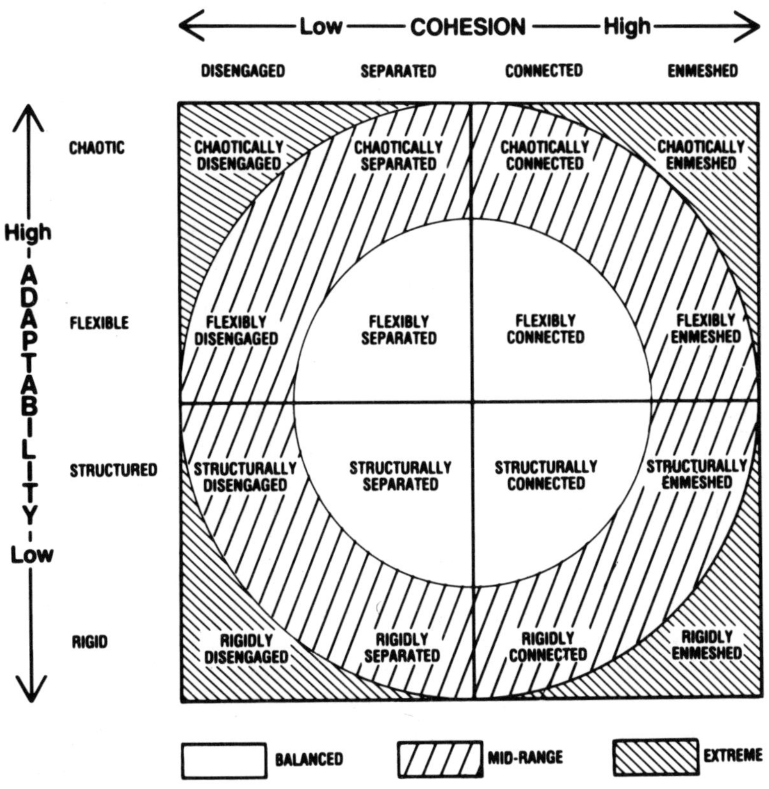

Figure 17.1. Circumplex Model: Sixteen Types of Marital and Family Systems

The Circumplex Model is a systemic model (see Figure 17.1). It was initially developed for understanding couple and family systems, but it is also being used for understanding other organizational systems, that is, departments or small working groups, or larger systems. It has also been expanded for use at the ecosystemic level to describe how organizations work together as a system.

More specifically, Don-David Lusterman (1989) has recently written a paper illustrating how, in working with a problem child, it is important to involve a collaborative team that includes representatives from other system levels, that is, school administrators, teachers, the juvenile officer, the school psychologist, the therapist in a community, and the parent(s). He uses the Circumplex Model to understand and describe how well these people work as an effective system, which determines how effective they will be in helping the child. (See Lusterman, Chapter 12, Volume 2 of this work.) In other words, this systemic model can be used from the dyadic level to a macrolevel in understanding and changing dynamics within these systems.

Other professionals have built on the Circumplex Model and integrated it with family-based and interdisciplinary programs. It has been used as the core of a family enrichment program (Carnes, 1981); as the base for a "System Map" for describing couple, family, and work relationships (Miller, 1988); and in the field of speech and communication (Galvin & Brommel, 1986).

Multisystem Assessment of Stress and Health (MASH) Model

My most current work builds upon my interest in individual and system level perspectives and my work on stress and coping in couple and family systems. Combining these two perspectives has enabled me to develop a new model called the *Multisystem Assessment of Stress and Health* (MASH) model. The MASH model theoretically builds on the assumption that stress impacts a system, which then triggers coping resources; the effectiveness of these resources determines the final level of adaptation. This basic model is multisystem because it can be applied at the individual, couple, family, and work level. The model provides a way to look at stress, coping, and adaptation across multisystem levels. This enables one to have a more comprehensive perspective on a person's life and assess the total impact of these various components on a person's life and well-being.

A new inventory called *Health and Stress Profile* (HSP) was developed to assess the four major dimensions of stress, system, coping resources, and adaptation at the four system levels of individual, couple, family, and work. These self-report scales have been integrated into the HSP. The HSP is computerized and designed so that a computer report summarizing the data and providing recommendations can be given to the individual. The computerized approach also enables us to conduct ongoing and systematic studies of the theoretical model and the effectiveness of programs which might build upon this assessment procedure.

THE FUTURE OF FAMILY PSYCHOLOGY

I will briefly describe what I see as some of the critical issues confronting the field of family psychology today and in the next two decades.

Integration of Theoretical Models and Therapeutic Approaches

While conceptual and therapeutic diversity is important, there is increasing need and interest for the field to explore ways of integrating the theoretical models and therapeutic approaches that have been developed over the last three decades. Theoretically, it is clear that the three central dimensions of many of the models developed to date include family cohesion, adaptability, and communication. How these are integrated and utilized for research and clinical work represents a major challenge for the field to continue developing.

Many of the gurus of family therapy have developed major intervention approaches, yet it is increasingly obvious that *no one approach can be used for treating all types of couple and family problems.* I perceive the major therapeutic orientations to be strategic therapy, structural therapy, systemic therapy, communication approaches, behavioral therapy, and cognitive therapy. Each of these approaches has its unique clinical interventions and all are at times useful.

Much could be gained from considering these therapeutic approaches and their specific techniques as simply "tools of the trade" that should be in the repertoire of all marriage and family therapists. In that way, therapists could select the most appropriate techniques for the kind of presenting symptoms experienced by their clients. We must hope that what type of interventions works best for what type of problems will also become more clear.

One of the major gaps in the field is the lack of adequate linkage between family assessment and family intervention techniques. Part of this is a consequence of the lack of systematic use of family assessment tools for doing diagnosis. Too often today, family therapists base their assessments exclusively on their own subjective evaluations and they rarely use objective family assessment tools. The use of self-report methods is particularly compatible with the orientation and training of psychologists.

Comprehensive assessment is critical in order to determine what type of interventions with what type of family system with what type of presenting symptom(s) are likely to be most effective. In that regard, the Circumplex Model is particularly useful because it enables one to do a multimethod assessment using both self-report assessments from various family members and a therapist rating using the Clinical Rating Scale.

Linking Family Assessment with DSM IV

In order for marital and family therapy and systemic perspectives to be more integrated for treating individuals, it is critical that the assessment link individual symptomatology (physical and emotional) with significant others in their lives, which is typically their couple and family relationships. At the present time, Florence Kaslow and myself are cochairing a Task Force within APA's Division 43 to explore ways in which family assessment, diagnosis, and classification can be integrated into DSM IV and ICD X. Within the American Psychiatric Association, Dr. Hurta Gutman and colleagues are working on a GAP (Group for the Advancement of Psychiatry) Report that is also addressing this major topic within psychiatry.

It is hoped that, as assessment of individual symptoms, both psychological and physical, also includes significant others in the person's life, it will become obvious that these people should also be included in the treatment process. Hence, marital and family intervention will, thereby, become the treatment of choice for an increasingly broader range of individual and relationship problems.

Although this integration is partially driven by marriage and family therapists who want third-party payments for their services, it also has a potential for making a significant contribution and impact, both theoretically and therapeutically.

Collaborative Projects

There needs to be increasing efforts to integrate the three domains of research, theory, and practice. This integration can do much to facilitate the development of each of the areas. This cannot be accomplished, however, unless researchers, theorists, and therapists collaborate as teams rather than work in isolation from each other.

One critical problem that can be addressed in these collaborative projects is the relationship between self-report and observational approaches. This question is important conceptually, methodologically, and clinically. Because most past research has indicated a lack of congruence between a family member's perspective and a therapist's perspective, this raises the issue of which approach is most valid. I believe each approach is appropriate and valid in its own right. Until we have a clearer understanding of when these discrepancies occur and do not occur, however, we will not be able to clearly understand the dynamics within the "family-therapist system."

SUMMARY AND EPILOGUE

Having been a part of the process of seeing the field of marriage and family therapy grow from its infancy, it is gratifying to see the dramatic progress that has been made in just 25 years. While the excitement and enthusiasm of this approach has created much vigor among both academicians and practitioners, it is critical that increasing scientific rigor be used to improve and expand our theoretical basis, our clinical assessments, and our therapeutic interventions.

Personally, I am committed to further developing the Circumplex Model as a theoretical model and as a tool for clinical assessment, treatment planning, and intervention. I am also planning to continue to develop and refine a range of couple and family inventories that have high reliability, validity, and clinical utility. I am increasingly moving toward a multisystem perspective of bridging individual, couple, family, and work systems, particularly regarding how they cope with stress. As Churchill once said, "This is not the end. It is not even the beginning of the end. Let us hope it is the end of the beginning."

REFERENCES

Carnes, P. (1981). *Understanding us.* Denver, CO: Interpersonal Communications Programs.

Fowers, D. J., & Olson, D. H. (1986). Predicting marital success with PREPARE: A predictive validity study. *Journal of Marital and Family Therapy, 12,* 403-413.

Galvin, K., & Brommel, B. (1986). *Family communication: Cohesion and Change.* Chicago, IL: Scott, Foresman.

Larsen, A., & Olson, D. H. (1990). Capturing the complexity of family systems: Integrating family therapy, family scores, and family analysis. In T. W. Draper & A. C. Marcos (Eds.), *Family variables: Conceptualization, measurement, and use* (pp. 19-47). Newbury Park, CA: Sage.

Lusterman, D. D. (1989). School-family intervention and the circumplex model. In D. H. Olson, C. S. Russell, & D. H. Sprenkle (Eds.), *Circumplex model: Systemic assessment and intervention.* New York: Haworth.

Miller, S. (1988). *Connecting.* Denver, CO: Interpersonal Communications Programs.

Olson, D. H. (1968). Student attitudes toward marriage. *College Student Survey, 1,* 71-78.

Olson, D. H. (Ed.). (1976). *Treating Relationships.* Lake Mills, IA: Graphic Press.

Olson, D. H. (1977). Insiders' and outsiders' view of relationships: Research strategies. In G. Levinger & H. Raush (Eds.), *Close relationships.* Amherst: University of Massachusetts Press.

Olson, D. H. (1986). Circumplex Model VII: Validation studies and FACES III. *Family Process, 25,* 337-351.

Olson, D. H., Fournier, D. G., & Druckman, J. M. (1980). *PREPARE/ENRICH counselor manual.* Minneapolis, MN: PREPARE/ENRICH, Inc.

Olson, D. H., & Gravatt, A. G. (1968). Attitude change in a functional marriage course. *Family Coordinator, 17,* 99-104.

Olson, D. H., & Killorin, E. (1985). *Clinical rating scale for the circumplex model of marital and family systems.* St. Paul, MN: Family Social Science, University of Minnesota.

Olson, D. H., McCubbin, H. I., Barnes, H., Larsen, A., Muxen, M., & Wilson, M. (1982). *Family inventories.* St. Paul, MN: Family Social Science, University of Minnesota.

Olson, D. H., McCubbin, H. I., Barnes, H., Larsen, A., Muxen, M., & Wilson, M. (1983). *Families: What makes them work.* Beverly Hills, CA: Sage.

Olson, D. H., Russell, C. S., & Sprenkle, D. H. (Eds.), (1989). *Circumplex model: Systematic assessment and intervention.* New York: Haworth. (Also published in two volume special issue of *Journal of Psychotherapy and the Family.*)

Olson, D. H., Sprenkle, D. H., & Russell, C. S. (1979). Circumplex model of marital and family systems I: Cohesion and adaptability dimensions, family types, and clinical applications. *Family Process, 18,* 3-28.

Olson, D. H., & Stewart, K. L. (in press). Family systems and health behaviors. In H. Schroeder (Ed.), *New directions in health psychology: Assessment.* New York: Hemisphere.

Olson, D. H., & Straus, M. A. (1972). A diagnostic tool for marital and family therapy: The SIMFAM technique. *Family Coordinator, 21,* 251-258.

18

An Individual Psychotherapist Discovers Marital Therapy

DAVID G. RICE

BECOMING A FAMILY PSYCHOLOGIST

I consider myself a clinical psychologist first: a marital and family therapist second. This mirrors my training and my age. My contributions to the field reflect a background in both disciplines.

Roots in My Family of Origin

My background is hopelessly middle-class. I was born in Charleston, West Virginia (population circa 90,000), in 1938, and grew up there, except for a year and a half when I lived in Lewisburg, West Virginia, a small town 100 miles east of Charleston, in the mountains near Virginia. My family was conventional, religious (American Baptist), and relatively free of pathology, though with several neurotic strains I still joust on occasion. My father was an accountant for a large oil company; my mother was a teacher (eight grades in a one-room school) who gave up her profession once she had children. I am the oldest of three and share the pleasures/handicaps of being a first-born. I have a brother (three years younger) in Charleston, who is an artist and Montessori teacher, and a sister (six years younger) who has a Ph.D. in marriage and family therapy and is on the social science faculty of a small college in south-central Kentucky. Both are married and have children.

My parents were encouraging academically, though apart from competitive games of Scrabble, which Mother always won, the domestic atmosphere was not particularly intellectual. They were accepting of individual differences and choices—perhaps because they had difficulty setting limits—and the freedom to do pretty much what one wanted paradoxically minimized rebellion. They were devoted to one another, had shared values, and worked hard to contain anger and minimize conflict, at some cost to each parent's health. Mother was sensitive to Dad's feelings, could analyze his behavior and explain it to us. "You know, he was the youngest in his family by far; he never grew up around kids and he doesn't always remember what they are like." Her sensitivity seemed to help; it was shared lovingly and it's the only thing I know about my family that specifically pointed me toward being a therapist.

One important experience taught me change is possible. I was reunited with my friends and classmates in Charleston for my sophomore year in high school after having left them in the middle of junior high school to move to Lewisburg while my father worked "in the field." Upon returning to Charleston, there was no transfer credit socially; I had to reestablish myself in the face of changed alliances. I could not complete athletically in the larger school as I had in the smaller one. It was a time of change and challenge; I felt I had to be a different person than I had become in Lewisburg. This experience taught me about stress, about plasticity of personality, and about having to fall back on one's own resources. It eventually led to a fascination with psychology.

Professional Heritage: Theoretical and Clinical

I went to the College of William and Mary in Williamsburg, Virginia. My father was happy; it was located in his native state. He told me the best jobs (1955) were in engineering. William and Mary had a 3:2 plan with MIT to produce "liberal" engineers; no one ever said how many actually made it. Physics was my worst subject in high school; it was my only "D" in college. After one year, I told my adviser (the chair of the physics department) that I was switching my major from pre-engineering to psychology. He said: "Oh, it's too bad you're leaving science."

My undergraduate psychology professors were strongly experimental, vigorously trained (Yale and Brown) and generally seemed to care. In many courses there was only one "A" awarded; I had to go for it. They tolerated my interest in clinical psychology, as well as my participation in a campus religious group that basically served as a social outlet. They encouraged me to aim high for graduate school. My adviser said "Yale," I said "Stanford," and Wisconsin said "Yes." Carl Rogers was there, it was cold, and it wasn't California.

Graduate school was difficult, competitive, and intimidating. It was very experimental/clinical. I learned how to criticize research better than I learned how to do it. Rogers nurtured creativity, an openness to individuality, and a respect for attempting to anchor one's clinical understandings via scientific grounding (Rogers, 1959). He struggled to integrate his beliefs about psychology and his background in religion; he was a good role model. He was also my first therapist. I longed for a more personal relationship with him, but then so did everybody else. He had his own struggles at Wisconsin and rarely expressed his anger directly, a modeling I could have used. I had a fine major professor (Bob Martin, now at the University of North Carolina), who let me find my own way and worked hard to get me through.

I met my wife, Joy, in graduate school in a Theories of Counseling class. She came from the middle-class suburbs of Chicago, had a background in art, and a good deal more social savoir faire. She switched to clinical psychology and we helped each other through graduate school. We shared strong family and educational values and were moving away from the religious beliefs of our parents.

I took my internship during 1962-1963 in the Department of Psychiatry at Wisconsin. I'm still there. During my internship, I didn't have to be defensive about clinical psychology, and I learned a general respect for physicians. Joe Kepecs, a psychoanalyst, and Norm Greenfield, then Director of Psychology, taught me to think psychodynamically while not abandoning the psychologist's critical eye. They helped me see that individuals change slowly, that they resist meaningful and lasting change and that the therapist must be patient, something with which I still struggle. They taught me a healthy skepticism about fads in psychotherapy, the need for a sense of humor, and the critical role of life experience (and clinical experience) in truly understanding people.

There was a psychophysiology laboratory in Psychiatry. The basic work that eventually led to biofeedback treatment techniques was just beginning in psychophysiology labs across the country. I did my dissertation on autonomic self-control in the laboratory, and Psychiatry subsequently offered Joy an internship and me a faculty position. I worked in collaborative psychophysiological research, supervised interns and residents, ran the psychological testing service (still do), began a clinical practice, and did enough science to earn tenure in 1970.

Carl Whitaker joined the Wisconsin faculty around 1963. He brought new ways of thinking that fascinated everyone but, I'm convinced, were truly understood by no one. Carl Rogers and the new chairman, Milt Miller, had established a phenomenological theory and practice base in the department. They thought Whitaker's work fell within this framework; the "psychodynamic" faculty members were not so sure. The 1960s were upon the University of Wisconsin and it was a time of excitement, turmoil, and change. I miss it.

My first attempt at couple therapy came in 1964 when Joy and I tried doing cotherapy. Carl Whitaker said that was the way to do it and cotherapy dyads were popping up all over the department. For us and most everybody else who had been trained exclusively in individual therapy, it was a disaster. We saw an unsuspecting young couple; I did almost all the talking and thought things went great. The couple left, Joy was livid, and approximately 10 years of work on ourselves and our relationship ensued before we attempted cotherapy again. Fortunately, things went much better then and Joy remains my preferred cotherapist.

I entered a short psychoanalysis in 1967, with Joe Kepecs. Three years as an assistant professor had taken its toll. I wasn't sure I was going to make it, as there had been little feedback about how I was doing. My colleagues assumed I knew that things were fine. I could not believe I was that out of touch with the world around me and the feelings of others. Joe told me: "Look, if you don't want to be a professor, don't be a professor." It was the first time I realized I *truly* had a choice and it helped me decide to stay in academia.

Pathways Chosen:
Professional Life Cycle Development and Choices

I tried hard to do analytic therapy, but I could not be patient and just listen. My interventions gave new meaning to the phrase "premature interpretation." Personally I needed to be active and feel in control, and I felt guilty about both these aspects of my personality. Being able to treat the "patient's" system was like a breath of fresh air. I began to see a lot of couples and some families. Clinically, it was a *much better fit of who I am with what I do best,* a meshing I've told countless numbers of student therapists to strive for.

At least one key ingredient was still missing. Perhaps, like my father, I did not truly understand the behavior of children. I was lost without verbal cues and marveled at my internship supervisors' ability to make sense out of what felt like random interventions I made during play therapy. Having children (two boys, born in 1968 and 1971) eventually made it possible for me to feel comfortable treating families.

Joy accepted a position on the faculty in the Department of Educational Policy Studies in 1974. She was a professor half-time, in clinical practice half-time, director of a counseling center for returning adult students, and a near full-time mother and homemaker. Some things had to change, and most of them had to do with me. It was not easy and I was not programmed for it, although countless times I had watched my father wash the dishes even when he was exhausted from being on the road.

I began to appreciate that often people, let's say men, change in a marriage only when their backs are up against the wall. I learned about why the perception of equity is so important to a relationship, some sense of what truly endures and how not to "sweat the small stuff" (something I have to learn over and over). And I learned a bit of humility; some of my colleagues would say "not enough."

In 1976, Joy and I went to Nairobi, Kenya, to explain the parameters of marriage and marital therapy as done in the West. We had read earnestly and respectfully about the kinship system and African family forms. Anthropology had been my minor in college. At the end of the talk we asked if there were questions. A tall, distinguished African professor at the University of Nairobi stood up and said: "That's all well and good, Drs. Rice, but in my country we work these things out in the family." His one sentence put us in our place and ended the question session.

I've had the privilege of working with good interns and post-docs. As Director of Psychology Training since 1974, I've also had a hand in selecting them. Among those who have gone on (and achieved stature) in family psychology, Alan Entin, Alan Gurman, Nadine Kaslow, David Kniskern, and Augustus Napier were interns and/or post-docs in our program. Al Gurman joined the Psychiatry faculty in 1972; along with Joy, he has been my closest professional collaborator. Since 1976 Al and I have codirected the Couples/Family Therapy Clinic and taught marital and family therapy seminars together. We published a book of readings in 1975 entitled *Couples in Conflict: New Directions in Marital Therapy.* I recall that the deadline was past and every chapter was in except one: Whitaker's. Getting it was one problem; understanding it was another. Al had an idea that worked: We drew up a crisp set of questions, interviewed Carl at my house over a carafe of wine and recorded everything. The transcript was edited, the manuscript was done, and everyone was happy.

Over time Al and I have diverged in our thinking. The trainees enjoy having us comment on and critique each other's clinical performance: me from an object relations viewpoint, Al from a structural/strategic one. He tells me I'm more of a cognitive therapist than I think I am. I tell him he's more of a cognitive therapist than he thinks he is. The roots of psychology run deep in both of us. Sharing clinical matters regularly with Joy and Al has so far prevented early burnout for me.

In 1979 I wrote *Dual-Career Marriage: Conflict and Treatment.* It grew out of both personal experience in my marriage and the problems brought to me in clinical practice by an increasing number of couples. Elaine Walster, a social psychologist at Wisconsin, had written about the concept of equity in interpersonal relationships (Walster, Walster, & Berscheid, 1978). Sager's 1976 book, *Marriage Contracts and Couple Therapy,* had greatly influenced my understanding of marital dynamics. The two concepts of equity and the marital contract formed the theoretical background for the book and I focused on particular applications for two-career couples.

Writing the book brought home again the importance of life experience in understanding clients. I became aware of this factor early in graduate school, in my beginning courses and practica in psychotherapy, where the women students far outdistanced the men in generic therapy skills, particularly the capacity for empathy. I often feel I can help someone more effectively if I have had a similar set of experiences to what they are describing. This was my first, naive theory of therapy in graduate school. It was influenced obviously by Rogers's (1959) concept of congruence. I still believe it contains a kernel of truth.

Joy and I wrote *Living Through Divorce: A Developmental Approach to Divorce Therapy,* published in 1986. We had written articles together, starting in 1971, when "Implications of the Women's Liberation Movement for Psychotherapy" was (surprisingly) accepted by the *American Journal of Psychiatry.* Neither of us was quite sure what writing a book together would entail for our relationship. We were troubled by the pro-marriage bias of much of the marriage counseling field and how therapists often would "give up" on couples when divorce was imminent. The body of psychological knowledge on the developmental life span seemed a useful framework for understanding the parameters of divorce.

In the book, we state our belief that divorce has come to be a common, almost predictable developmental life stage. As such, going through the divorce process for many individuals leads to a crisis in identity and self-esteem. Identity issues at this life stage revolve around the loss of marital roles. No longer being someone's "husband" or "wife" can reactivate basic questions of "Who am I?" with accompanying anxiety and a sense of deep loss. Self-esteem issues primarily relate to the experience of narcissistic injury that can follow marital separation and divorce. Such perceived injury often raises for the individual the basic question, "Am I a lovable person?" The question is painful at a time when one may feel like a failure at a major endeavor in one's life, i.e., marriage. Our experience is that divorce therapy can help one grow through the crisis of marital separation and divorce to achieve a stronger sense of identity and an enhancement of self-esteem.

The book was basically Joy's; I wrote several chapters and did the editing (I had the mother who taught English). We worked well together and the boys cooperated; perhaps they were apprehensive when we told them we were writing a book about divorce and decided to be on their best behavior. They made up for it later, quickly submerging us in the many facets of parenting adolescents.

It is more difficult to identify any *enduring* research contributions (journal articles) I have made to the field of marital and family therapy. Periodic royalty checks have a way of reminding me that at least someone may be reading the *books* I've published. I did several studies attempting to discern which types of therapist personalities work well together in cotherapy. Will Fey, a colleague in the department, had devised a self-report questionnaire about therapist in-session behavior and preferences. Will and I collaborated in a series of cotherapist studies with Joe Kepecs, Al Gurman, and Andy Razin. We found significant differences in the preferred "style" of a cotherapist, related to how one described his or her *own* in-therapy behavior (Rice, Fey, & Kepecs, 1972; Rice, Gurman, & Razin, 1974). We also found that therapy was subjectively rated as going better when therapists of comparable experience levels worked together. And we learned that female therapists were more self-disclosing than male therapists, though with experience males also "opened up" in therapy.

Another study looked at the question of whether spouse cotherapists had any particular advantages over cotherapists not married to each other (Rice, Razin, & Gurman, 1976). We did not find clear advantages for spouse cotherapists, although there have been several clinical papers on this topic in the marital and family therapy literature.

I remain interested in the dynamics of cotherapy and recently published a chapter on supervising therapist dyads (Rice, 1986). Practical considerations, particularly economic factors, have limited the available patient and therapist populations for doing further research. Insurance companies increasingly are restrictive in paying for one therapist, let alone two. Along these lines, I have just completed a year's service as faculty coordinator of the department's HMO. I am tired. I have been through several philosophical struggles in the long-standing battle to make psychotherapy cost-effective. I have needed to justify marital and family therapy as treating "psychopathology," certainly as more than just dealing with "problems in living." I feel I made the case well, but the battle will continue.

IDENTIFICATION AS A FAMILY PSYCHOLOGIST

Focus: Treatment Strategies

When asked about my theoretical stance, I refer to myself as "hopelessly eclectic." I believe strongly in certain constructs, e.g., that individuals and families have an inherent tendency toward growth and self-actualization, that dysfunctional couples engage in neurotic collusion and projective identification and that a multilevel contract made up of expectations governs marital interaction and needs to be revised over time. I do have clear preferences about how to conduct therapy and some of these are elaborated in this section.

These beliefs (hypotheses) do not fit a coherent theory and, as a family psychologist, that makes me feel unscientific. I know I have company.

My practice is about half individual therapy and half family therapy, the latter mostly with couples. I have spent a good deal of time and effort comparing these two modalities. I have a healthy respect for the therapeutic power of both types of treatment and an appreciation of some important differences. For example, I am frequently reminded how an individual's personality structure sets limits on the degree of adaptability and change in relationships.

The individual therapist generally has more leverage in producing change. The main reason is that the transferential relationship is stronger and the therapist comes to be seen as a more central figure in the client's life. *Because of the power of individual therapy, increasingly I have taken the position of not treating couples where one or both members are concurrently in individual therapy.* I ask couples to either delay marital therapy until the individual therapy is over, or to suspend individual therapy until marital therapy is completed. Usually they comply; if they do not wish to accede to my request, I refer them to another therapist who is more flexible in this regard.

In my experience, when someone already in individual therapy requests marital therapy, there are usually nefarious motivations. Often the spouse not in therapy is feeling threatened by perceived changes in the partner. There is a competition between the spouse not in treatment and the individual therapy that might have been avoided if both husband and wife had met with the therapist at some point. If both spouses are seen at least once, and both agree that individual therapy with one partner is the treatment of choice, future competitive struggles and potential acting out behaviors usually can be avoided. If someone is married or in a serious significant relationship, I will almost always see both individuals for at least part of the treatment period. Few psychological problems are the sole domain of an individual in a family system. This idea is "old hat" to family therapists; it is less likely to be seen as necessary by individual therapists, often to the potential detriment of both therapist and client(s).

The above modus operandi is modified for couples who are separated. I prefer to see such dyads in a structured separation with counseling format (Toomin, 1972). Individual sessions with each spouse alternate with couple sessions. The therapy format mirrors the reality of the relationship: these individuals are still together (not yet divorced) but are apart (no longer living together). My experiences with the structured separation with counseling procedure are elaborated in a recent chapter (Rice & Rice, 1986b).

I have been impressed by other important differences between individual and marital therapy. Most of these differences follow from the fact that the relationship between the spouses is and remains stronger than that between either partner and the therapist. This is almost always true, even when the marriage is very dysfunctional. Despite a couple presenting their relationship as being at great odds, it is important for the therapist to remember that *the partners have a long history of getting together to resist outside influences,* for example, parents, in-laws, or landlords. Families simply work that way. A brother can criticize his sister unmercifully on a daily basis, but let someone outside the family make disparaging remarks and he will quickly jump to her defense. Families and couples are thus experts at resisting outside interventions, including those of the therapist. My experience has been that resistance to change, in general, is greater when one is treating a system than when one is doing individual therapy, and this follows from the above reasoning.

The combination of greater resistance and less therapist power has several implications for the couples and family therapist. First, he or she must work actively to become an integrated part of the system. Carl Whitaker called this "the battle for structure." It is only after this battle is won that treatment can begin and the next phase, "the battle for initiative" can commence (Whitaker, in Neill & Kniskern, 1982). The route for the therapist into a family system is a highly individualized one. Carl enters by relating in a grandfatherly way to the children. That is why he insists on seeing the whole family right from the first session. Until he explained this, many of us were puzzled as to why he wanted very young children to be present, as their behavior seemed distracting and usually they showed no obvious signs of psychopathology. Carl explained his rationale and it made sense, for him.

I find two intangibles helpful for getting integrated into the family system: (1) a sense of humor, including not taking myself too seriously; and (2) indications that I believe marriage can work over the long haul to bring fulfillment. I rarely state the latter, as it would seem like I'm forcing my beliefs onto clients. But they seem to know of my belief in this regard and to take reassurance from it, even when their main purpose in seeing me is to help "dissolve" the relationship.

I have learned that couples and families want a therapist who can be active, take charge at times and set limits, particularly in the case of nonproductive fighting. My doing these things has seemed to help build the therapeutic alliance.

Even before short-term therapy was in vogue, I realized that it was unusual to see couples and families for long stretches of continuous therapy. This differed from my experience with individual treatment. I came to see how this variation in treatment length reflected some differences between the two modalities. The combination of greater system resistance and less therapist leverage often added up to shorter treatment of couples and families. From a more positive perspective, couples and families come, through treatment, to be better therapists for one another. Much therapeutic work with such cases revolves around learning to listen, being empathic, and accepting others, i.e., good generic therapy skills. When individuals in the family can do this for one another, they may no longer feel as much need for a therapist.

Since marital/family therapy typically is short-term, an active intervention style that helps the therapist become a meaningful part of the family system is necessary. Sometimes I do see couples and families over a long period of time (greater than two years) but it almost always involves a series of several short-term therapies. The "patients" try things on their own and then feel free to come back again for a new phase when they need help. Increasingly, individual therapy is moving in this direction, given reduced third-party coverage and the growth of managed health-care systems.

A final difference between marital/family and individual therapy follows from this variation in treatment duration, i.e., the need to take seriously the couple's or family's presenting complaint. Even when I believe that the dysfunctional behaviors that brought a couple to therapy (e.g., sexual difficulties) are symptomatic of other problems (e.g., a breakdown in communication), I will address and start to work on the presenting problem. Once there is some positive change, treatment can be extended to the underlying problem, and other related concerns. I also believe in a "consumer" model; the couple or family needs to believe that the problem as they see it is being taken seriously by the therapist. Otherwise, the system resists and therapy usually ends prematurely. This dynamic has been less true in individual therapy, where the greater perceived power of and stronger transference toward the therapist may lead the patient to accept the "doctor's" characterization of what is wrong. External pressures to make therapy short-term increasingly seem likely to blur duration differences between the two therapeutic modalities.

Areas of Major Concern

Training and experience doing individual therapy has taught me to respect an individual's psychological defenses and their adaptive nature. It has made me realize that change often is frightening and therefore will likely be resisted. I do not believe there is a "quick" way, even in the face of much psychic pain, to overcome defenses and resistances and I am skeptical of therapeutic techniques that claim this ability. Along these lines, I have difficulty with much that is written about and practiced under the label of "strategic therapy." I do not believe the techniques proferred (e.g., paradoxical intervention) lead to lasting change. In reading some of the burgeoning literature in this area, I am reminded frequently of why Freud abandoned hypnosis. Although hypnotic treatment produced dramatic symptomatic change, e.g., removing leg paralysis in patients with conversion hysteria, it did not resolve basic problems (e.g., sexual guilt due to social/religious indoctrination) and did not lead to lasting change. I'm still looking for long-term follow-up studies demonstrating the efficacy of strategic therapy. I will try to keep an open mind.

Most of my other concerns about the field of family psychology and therapy have to do with education and training. I worry that the discipline lacks vigor and is moving away from a scientific base. I also am concerned about the fragmentation of psychology and the other mental health disciplines. These and other issues are discussed in the next section.

THE FUTURE OF FAMILY PSYCHOLOGY

I do not know with certainty where the field is heading, but certain trends disturb me a great deal.

At a national conference on psychology internship training two years ago I described myself as a "charter member of the Society for Anachronistic Clinical Psychologists." For example, I am troubled by what seems like a decrease in the quality of training of psychologists. Perhaps unfairly, I blame some of this on the professional school movement. At the risk of being labeled an "elitist," I feel we are training too many psychologists and not training them well, particularly in science. I can see the results as a consulting editor for two family therapy journals. Carefully designed and statistically well analyzed studies by psychologists researching marital and family therapy are few and far between.

I am hopeful that the 1990s will lead to stringent efforts to standardize the training and experience requirements necessary for psychologists to practice marital and family therapy. My preference is for a Ph.D. in clinical psychology and a clinical internship, followed by one or two years of postdoctoral specialization in marital/family treatment. This training sequence would prepare therapists to assess underlying psychopathology in couples and families and to treat such disorders effectively. Standardization of training would also improve chances for continued national recognition and reimbursement by third-party payers.

I am disturbed by psychologists (and psychiatrists) who want to escalate the conflicts with organized psychiatry. I still feel the two professions (and their clients) have much to gain by working together and a great deal to lose by fighting one another. I'd like to believe that cooperation could lead, for example, to the inclusion of marital and family psychopathology as a meaningful part of DSM IV or V, i.e., not as a V code but as legitimate Axis I and II disorders. Not only would this help with third-party coverage, but it could pave the way for increased research funding to study such disorders. The disease model is not popular with many psychologists, but it is realistically the model that seems most likely to be supported with generous research funds.

Perhaps the biggest change in the field since I have been a practitioner is the need to prepare individuals and families for discontinuous developmental change. The nuclear family that remains intact over the development life span is becoming rarer (Ahrons & Rodgers, 1987). Increasingly, individuals are likely to be part of more than one nuclear family and will need to develop adaptive skills to cope with these experiences. Family psychologists can help educate the general public about expected family changes. Reduced economic circumstances place a hardship on many divorced, widowed, and single-parent families. Family therapists need to make sure they do not increase the stress on such families through discrimination and stigmatization.

Given economic realities, the trend toward short-term therapy seems likely to continue. For efficient treatment, family psychologists need to have good assessment skills. Setting realistic short-term treatment goals requires an appreciation of the limits on potential change of each spouse's personality organization. As strategic therapists have indicated, sometimes it can be more effective to work with rather than against the individual's resistance. The therapist's relationship skills are critical in short-term therapy; one does not have long to build a therapeutic alliance. Pressure on therapists to work efficiently and to document their results will increase in the next decade.

In regard to my own future contributions to the field of family psychology, I am compelled to be modest. Assumption of increased administrative duties in recent years has curtailed my research efforts. I do expect to continue writing chapters and maybe a book or two. The field of family psychology could use a good, empirically grounded introductory clinical text for graduate students and psychiatry residents who are learning marital and family therapy. Do I want to take one to two years out of my life to undertake such a project? Perhaps the muse will provide an answer.

SUMMARY AND CONCLUSIONS

Friends and clients have asked me: "What does it take to make a good marriage?" I usually answer with one word: *flexibility.* I see many couples and families who are prisoners of their own rigidity. Often the roots of inflexibility are historical. "We've always done it this way," or "That's just the way men (women) are," or "That's the way I was brought up and it was good enough for me." To have difficulty accepting change is to be poorly prepared for the ebb and flow of marriage. My terse answer to the above question is obviously too simplistic, however.

In addition to the standard building blocks of trust and respect, another key ingredient in a good marriage is the perception of choice. The behaviorist in me still debates the existentialist. Without a perceived choice, "holy wedlock" becomes "holy deadlock." Some of the most miserable couples I have seen are "stuck" with one another. An early pregnancy may have precluded a sense of truly choosing to love one another. Family, financial, social, and/or religious pressures lock individuals into relationships. Participation in an affair may give one or both spouses the illusion of choice. Many of these couples can only break the paralyzing status quo by separating. As Toomin (1972) argues, *a structured separation can reintroduce choice into the relationship.* Some couples separate, reconcile, and are happier. Others separate, reconcile, and are still miserable. Many go on to divorce but the majority of these individuals, partly through therapy, appear to choose more wisely the second time around. *The feeling that one continues to choose to be married to this particular person throughout the marital life span is important to personal fulfillment.* A little serendipity in selecting a partner never hurts.

In summary, my training and experience as an individual therapist has helped me to do better marital and family therapy, has given me an appreciation of how much attitudinal and behavioral change is possible when one can apply maximal therapeutic resources, and has taught me the adaptive nature of defenses and resistances that each individual brings to family relationships. These coping behaviors usually are not surrendered easily or quickly in order that new growth potentially can take place.

My own marriage and nuclear family, as well as my family of origin, provided many life experiences necessary to empathize with others' struggles. Personal therapy was useful in untangling the helpful messages of significant others from the unhelpful. I sometimes think about what other career I might have chosen. Nothing else seems to mesh as well who I am with what I do.

REFERENCES

Ahrons, C. R., & Rodgers, R. H. (1987). *Divorced families: A multi-disciplinary developmental view.* New York: W. W. Norton.

Gurman, A. S., & Rice, D. G. (1975). *Couples in conflict: New directions in marital therapy.* New York: Jason Aronson.

Neill, J. R., & Kniskern, D. P. (1982). *From psyche to system: The evolving therapy of Carl Whitaker.* New York: Guilford.

Rice, D. G. (1979). *Dual-career marriage: Conflict and treatment.* New York: Free Press.

Rice, D. G. (1986). Supervision of co-therapy. In F. Kaslow (Ed.), *Supervision and training: Models, dilemmas and challenges* (pp. 119-142). New York: Haworth.

Rice, D. G., Fey, W. F., & Kepecs, J. G. (1972). Therapist experience and "style" as factors in co-therapy. *Family Process, 11,* 1-12.

Rice, D. G., Gurman, A. S., & Razin, A. M. (1974). Therapist sex, "style" and theoretical orientation. *Journal of Nervous and Mental Disease, 159,* 413-421.

Rice, D. G., Razin, A. M., & Gurman, A. S. (1976). Spouses as co-therapists: "Style" variables and implications for patient-therapist matching. *Journal of Marriage and Family Counseling, 2,* 55-62.

Rice, D. G., & Rice, J. K. (1986b). Separation and divorce therapy. In N. S. Jacobson & A. S. Gurman (Eds.), *Clinical handbook of marital therapy* (pp. 279-299). New York: Guilford.

Rice, J. K., & Rice, D. G. (1975). Implications of the "Women's Liberation Movement" for psychotherapy. *American Journal of Psychiatry, 130,* 191-196.

Rice, J. K., & Rice, D. G. (1986a). *Living through divorce: A developmental approach to divorce therapy.* New York: Guilford.

Rogers, C. R. (1959). A theory of therapy, personality and interpersonal relationships as developed in the client-centered framework. In S. Koch (Ed.), *Psychology: A study of a science* (pp. 184-256). New York: McGraw-Hill.

Sager, C. J. (1976). *Marriage contracts and couple therapy.* New York: Brunner/Mazel.

Toomin, M. K. (1972). Structured separation with counseling: A therapeutic approach for couples in conflict. *Family Process, 11,* 299-310.

Walster, E., Walster, G. W., & Berscheid, E. (1978). *Equity: Theory and research.* Boston: Allyn & Bacon.

19

Up the Downer Staircase and Other Perturbations

M. DUNCAN STANTON

When I was about 10 years old, my Sunday school teacher gave our class an assignment: to draw a picture of our projected adult vocational situation. Because my aspirations included being an explorer, missionary, scientist, physician, and artist all at the same time, this task posed no minor problem. But I gave it a shot. The grand creature that emerged from my crayons stood in a primitive, probably African, culture. He wore an artist's smock as he touched a paintbrush to an easel. He had on jungle boots, riding pants, a clergyman's collar, and a physician's head mirror. Looking back on it, he probably needed only a clown's nose and some face paint to complete the mosaic.

Though I now joke about this pictorial pastiche, it was actually a fairly accurate amalgam of a number of themes that had carried down through my family. On my mother's side, the ascribed roles were those of clergyman, physician, or artist, with an occasional musician or educator thrown in for seasoning. My father's side tended toward science, engineering, law, and adventure. The harlequinesque Albert Schweitzer was simply an attempt to honor them all.

During the middle years of high school, I leaned toward becoming a jet pilot. This would have been the culmination of an intense and long-held interest in aviation. It might very well have happened had my eyes been good enough to have secured for me an Air Force or Naval ROTC scholarship. They were not, however, so that idea eventually had to be left in the hangar.

As I approached college, my aspirations distilled to a more realistic mix. My mother was an outgoing, people-type person who spent a lot of time with benevolent causes and organizations. My father had been a science and math teacher who later joined industry as a science educator. It made implicit sense, therefore, for me to join these two in the study of psychology—the "science of people." This gave me somewhat of an edge relative to my peers when, in 1958, I started my college freshman year at Alfred University in upstate New York. While many of them struggled to find direction and select a major, I knew from the start that psychology was to be my field.

This tendency to assimilate was part of a family ethic. We were from "mongrelia," having roots in England, Scotland, Wales, Holland, France, Ireland, and Germany.[1] Although most branches of the family tree had floated to the New World in the early or middle 1600s, a few had drifted onto the beach later, in the 18th and 19th centuries. Like so many Americans, we were hardly a pure strain, and our family's preference was to try to keep the better parts of each culture. Consequently, the notion also held to try to retain characteristics from each side when it came time to choose a vocation.

In addition, my position in my family of origin had bearing. I was the middle of three children, having an older brother and younger sister. The odd thing was that although my brother was just as intelligent and competent as I, I seemed to be granted more prerogatives. In some ways, I was treated as the oldest son. I also frequently felt that I had inordinate power in my family—when I took a stand, everybody backed off. It was never clear to me how much of this so-called power was bestowed and how much of it I demanded based on my genetic, constitutional makeup, or even upon some sort of spiritual force. I do know that as far back as I can remember, I felt destined to make a mark on the world—to bring about a positive and significant contribution.

THE GRADUATE YEARS

Upon entering graduate school at George Washington University in 1962, I intended to become a school psychologist. The faculty there—particularly Eva Johnson, Bernard I. Levy, and Thelma Hunt—soon, however, turned my head toward clinical psychology.[2] This shift of interest was fortified by clinical experiences in 1963-1964 at St. Elizabeth's Hospital under the tutelage of Margaret Ives, Katherine Beardsley, Lourdes Ortega, and Arnold Peterson.

A parallel interest that developed was to become a researcher, particularly of clinical problems. The seeds of this were sown in many conversations I had into the night with Willard Caldwell, a developmental and comparative psychology professor at GWU who was open to offbeat ideas and unusual research. I began to see myself as fitting into the mold of such noted psychopathologists as Jules Masserman and Howard Liddell, whose work on experimental neuroses by then had garnered considerable attention. This direction was given considerable impetus by Margaret Mercer and Richard Chase at St. Elizabeth's. In 1963, they took me under their wing as a research assistant and shared with joy their vast and diverse knowledge in research and human behavior. I was hooked.

Whereas I had gained a firm grounding in clinical and theoretical psychology at GWU, I felt my experimental training needed bolstering. Therefore, upon completing my master's degree in 1964, I moved to the University of Maryland where I had been granted a fellowship.[3] The Maryland program was known to be strong in experimental psychology, being at the time a bastion of behaviorism. This was fine because it exposed me to methods and ways of thinking with which I had been only tangentially familiar. The professors were demanding and in some cases impatient, but the teaching was superb. I dove into the experimental pool and within two years had enough courses to have qualified for a master's degree in experimental psychology. From 1965 to 1966 I also worked part-time in sensory-deprivation research under Thomas I. Myers and Seward Smith at the Naval Medical Research Institute in Bethesda.

The negative side of the Maryland experience was that the department was adding new experimental faculty all the time, each with a particular specialty area. Consequently, a student who was majoring—or, like me, minoring—in that track was having constantly to master whole new areas (e.g., vision, verbal learning, psycholinguistics, brain stimulation, operant conditioning, stimulus generalization, taste) in order to pass the experimental comprehensive exams. It became clear to me that at the present rate, my minor probably was going to consume more time than my major. So I decided to switch. I had obtained enough coursework in experimental psychology to satisfy my personal requirements, and choosing a new minor that held great fascination for me—social psychology—seemed a logical alternative.

It turned out to be a wise and fortunate choice. I greatly enjoyed social psychology, and the things I learned from its faculty (Charles Ward, Theodore Higgs, Harold Vetter, and Elliott McGinnies) provided me with a breadth and depth that I still find useful.

On the clinical end, Maryland's program was eclectic. Although strongly behavioral, it recently had expanded into the community mental health area. Leopold Walder, my advisor, was doing innovative things with parents—teaching them how to handle their children better. His spiritual brother from the experimental faculty, Roger McIntire, also was applying learning techniques to real-life situations. Although these were not "family therapy" approaches in the usual sense of the words, they did contribute to an expansion of consciousness and gave me a better sense of what could actually be done, interactively, with clinical problems.

Considering the way that I now work, clinically, I have sometimes said that very little of my graduate training translated directly into the specific operations of treating families and systems. This probably holds for most other psychology graduate programs of that era (1960s) as well. There just were not many psychology faculty members or departments with expertise or interest in treating families or family systems. For me, the two influences that came closest were the aforementioned application of behavioral techniques with children and the community mental health coursework and experience I had at Maryland (Stanton & Vetter, 1968) under Robert Waldrop and, most particularly, Stuart Golann—two excellent teachers with a view of the whole.

Another person who began to influence me during that period was Mark Kane Goldstein. He had entered Maryland as a graduate student after obtaining a master's degree at Columbia and spending two years as a naval psychologist with the Marines. He had been influenced strongly by his brother-in-law, Ogden R. Lindsley, a noted Skinnerian who had been applying operant principles with humans. Goldstein had taken this notion further and had developed an innovative approach in which he used behavioral principles with couples. He expanded and refined this work later, at Cornell, and then at the University of Florida. We became close friends and to this day he has remained both personally and professionally important to me.

A note about my military status is appropriate here. While in college I had taken four years of ROTC, which secured for me a commission and a two-year obligation for active duty in the U.S. Army. I had chosen this option because I did not want to be drafted and spend the time as an enlisted man, with lower pay and responsibilities. (My brother had been drafted in 1959 and essentially wasted two years of his life as a post statistician at Ft. Dix. The barrenness of that experience was not lost on me.) Besides, there was no war going on at the time, so the possibility of combat duty seemed remote. So, upon graduation from college, I deferred my military obligation in order to attend graduate school. While in graduate school, the Army Surgeon General's Office approached me about enrolling in their Graduate Psychology Training Program. Under this arrangement, I would continue my schooling for two or three years while drawing full pay and allowances, and also would take an APA-approved internship at one of the Army's major hospitals. My part of the bargain was to increase my active-duty commitment from two to four years following completion of my degree. Of particular appeal was the possibility of drawing an officer's pay while attending graduate school. This would allow me to marry my first wife, Toni Harshberger, and not have to subsist on the kind of near-starvation income that most of the other graduate students endured. I bought it.

In 1966, after completing my coursework, I began an internship at Walter Reed General Hospital. There I learned psychodynamically oriented psychotherapy from Earl Janda, Mark Lewin, and Carl Lauterbach. With Vincent Sweeney and Mark Lewin as mentors, I began doing group therapy. I also got supervision in treating children and their parents from Edmund Phillips in the Child Psychiatry Clinic. Virginia Satir came to town and words like "family therapy" and "family process" could be overheard occasionally in the halls and offices. I gave presentations to the psychology staff and interns on Lyman Wynne and Margaret Singer's research and on marital therapy, and attended a similar presentation given by another intern specifically on family therapy. Things were starting to coalesce.

THE REAL WORLD

It was in my first post-Ph.D. position that I might truly be considered to have "broken out of the mold." I had been put in charge of a child clinic at Fort Dix, New Jersey, and initially began seeing children individually, in line with the ethos of that facility. This proved ineffective and futile, so I soon started to see their parents concurrently. As I found myself getting caught in the middle, however, I shifted to convening them together, in a bunch. My results improved markedly. I began voraciously reading the available family therapy literature and sought training with Satir.

Less than a year later, my family work was put on hold, as I was reassigned to an Army psychiatric team in Vietnam. A month before my arrival, this team had established the first systematic program in that country for treating drug problems among servicemen. Whereas I had gained some earlier experience in treating alcoholism, including couples therapy for drinking problems, drug abuse was a new world. Drugs were rampant by then and their treatment fascinating. I supplemented my clinical work (only part of which was with drug problems) by undertaking research on the extent of drug abuse among soldiers both entering and leaving Vietnam (Stanton, 1972). When I later returned home, I began to be called upon to advise on policy and to assist in the establishment of numerous drug treatment programs within the Army medical system. In addition, my Vietnam research on drug abuse prevalence received considerable attention; my testimony regarding it before a U.S. Senate subcommittee was covered widely by the national press and aired for almost a full minute on Cronkite's *CBS Evening News*. And that's how (professionally) I got "into drugs." Whereas this work was not particularly family oriented, it had become almost inadvertently an area of expertise that I had neither foreseen nor originally intended. Later, I was to find ways of merging it with my systems interests.

Back in the States, I was assigned to Ft. Meade, Maryland for a little over a year. While there, I saw families under the supervision of Fred Fisher (who had been trained by Ross Speck), took additional training with Satir, conducted research on both race relations and drug abuse prevalence, and also engaged in two other activities that deserve mention. First, I continued my community mental health work involving consultation to schools and interfacing with other community systems. Second, I devoted a good deal of my energies to group work within what came to be known as the Human Potential Movement. I took training in Gestalt groups, T groups, and organizational development, even spending two weeks in Bethel, Maine, at a program of the National Training Laboratories. Whereas I later shifted away from this second activity, this experience proved invaluable in helping me relax inhibitions about (1) being "exposed" in public, (2) conducting multiperson sessions such as one encounters with family therapy, and (3) having to take almost complete charge of a session, even if briefly, as a situation might sometimes demand.

From Ft. Meade I moved back to Walter Reed to become assistant chief of the psychology service and run the psychology internship. While there, I took a family therapy seminar with Donald Ray Bardill, also teaching a couple of the sessions myself. By then, I was seeing families and couples almost exclusively and began to include in my caseload some families with drug abuse as the presenting problem.

TO PHILADELPHIA

As my obligation to the military drew to a close, I began to scout around for jobs in late 1971. I was interested in obtaining a faculty position in the East or Midwest, with particular preference for the metropolitan areas of Boston, Hartford, and Philadelphia. I decided to accept a position, starting in the summer of 1972, as assistant professor of psychology in psychiatry at the University of Pennsylvania, with primary duties as associate director of Penn's inpatient service at Philadelphia General Hospital. There were four primary reasons for this choice: First was the quality of the faculty and facilities at Penn, with its unequaled reputation for psychotherapy research under such leaders as Lester Luborsky, Aaron T. Beck, and Martin Orne. Second, if there was a mecca for family therapy at that time, it was Philadelphia; no other city had the number and density of family therapy pioneers that Philadelphia had. Third, Ivan Boszormenyi-Nagy was a consultant to the unit I would join and I found his work intriguing. Finally, the Penn job might allow me a chance to get exposure to, and possibly work with, the Philadelphia Child Guidance Clinic (PCGC), which was affiliated with the Penn Department of Psychiatry. Jay Haley, Salvador Minuchin, and Braulio Montalvo were at PCGC then and all had appeal. I enjoyed Haley's writings—his no-nonsense, exceedingly funny, and clear approach to working with families attracted me. Minuchin, Montalvo, and their colleagues were treating lower-income, primarily black families and this was a population to which I, too, felt a commitment. I also was impressed by their resolve to gather outcome data on their therapy, because I felt strongly that if the field of family therapy was to gain a firm foothold in the mental health establishment, it would have to subject itself to the scrutiny of well-designed research.

The Philadelphia General Hospital job had strong pros and cons. The weekly consultations with Ivan Nagy and the regular cotherapy experiences with our mutual colleague, Nobu Miyoshi, were high points. Nagy's thinking, particularly his ideas about family loyalty, influenced me profoundly and still color my theoretical formulations and clinical operations. It was also during this period that I wrote two papers for *Professional Psychology* that (1) pointed out some of the implications of systems thinking for psychological practice, (2) noted how the two were compatible, and (3) encouraged the field of psychology to embrace family therapy (Stanton, 1975a, 1975b).

My direct work on the Penn psychiatric unit was less rewarding. I was responsible for a kind of modified therapeutic community within an acute inpatient service. Although I enjoyed the patient contact, I actually had very little authority. I was not happy with the almost mechanical diagnosis and disposition process, feeling it to be too depersonalized, as if we were dealing with cattle rather than people. Around that time I saw the movie *One Flew Over the Cuckoo's Nest* and became both shaken and depressed; I could see that I had become part of an oppressive system, like the one McMurphy had challenged, and that I had very little power to do anything about it. In particular, one incident during my second year there stands out: We had put on a talent show and party in which patients read poems and performed interpretive dances to music played by other patients. It was both creative and moving. Following the talent show, we had a dance in which patients, many staff, and most of the psychiatric residents danced together and had a tremendous time, filled with smiles, jokes, and laughs. Patients and staff had been transformed into people. I felt uplifted. *This* was the kind of atmosphere I was trying to promote. It wasn't until later that evening that the crash came. The ward staff, threatened by the closeness and freedom of the afternoon activities, lowered the boom. They tightened up all privileges and did whatever they could to disparage the patients and put them in their place. A recalibration had occurred. It had been too much for them because, as one staff member had put it some months before, "the only difference between us and them [the patients] is that we have the keys." The staff needed to reestablish the patient-staff boundary more firmly than ever and regain control. And I was crushed. I decided I had paid my dues; I had to get out.

One of my goals upon discharge from the Army had been to apply for a grant to study the family patterns and the effectiveness of family treatment with drug abusers. Toward this end, I had drawn up a research design and had made some initial inquiries at the National Institute on Drug Abuse (NIDA). When Byron Fiman—a colleague with whom I had been conducting race-relations research—heard I was going to Philadelphia, he suggested I get in touch with Thomas Todd, who was doing psychotherapy and family therapy research at PCGC. About a month after my arrival, I followed this recommendation and contacted Todd. He was interested and we began to collaborate. At the recommendation of the chairman of the Department of Psychiatry, Albert Stunkard, we linked up with the nearby Penn-affiliated Drug Dependence Treatment Center of the Philadelphia VA Hospital, which was being run by Charles P. O'Brien and George Woody. In late 1972, we began to gather data on frequency of family contact of the VA drug patients. Whereas it had been my experience that such people were commonly in touch with their families of origin, we needed to know the extent to which it actually occurred among these particular patients in order to design properly an intake process for the proposed research.

During this period, my informal affiliation with PCGC began to increase. I attended several seminars there and took a one-week course with Harry Aponte and Lynn Hoffman. I also arranged for Jay Haley and Braulio Montalvo to conduct a few consultations to my inpatient service at Philadelphia General. All the while, Todd and I were working on the drug-abuse study, eventually submitting a grant proposal to NIDA in early 1973. The proposal was deferred once—following a site visit—and eventually funded in 1974.

The original plan for the drug-abuse grant was that it be conducted at Philadelphia General, with Todd and the therapists—who would be located primarily at PCGC—being hired part-time. During the period between notification that it would be funded and the date that funding was slated actually to begin, Salvador Minuchin, the PCGC director, proposed that we bring the whole grant under PCGC's roof rather than have it straddle the two institutions. PCGC was about to move to its new location adjoining Penn and close to the VA Hospital. By housing the grant in the new quarters, we would overcome a number of logistical problems, lose nothing in terms of proximity to the patient population, and the overhead could then go to PCGC and help cover the heavy costs of its new building. I was most open to this arrangement, as long as certain conditions were met. First, because the grant covered only 50% of my salary, I desired that the other half of my time be spent as a senior therapist and supervisor in the PCGC outpatient department, seeing a broad spectrum of cases. (By that time I had been supervising trainees in family therapy, had run an internship, and had become a diplomate in clinical psychology of the American Board of Professional Psychology.) Second, I requested ongoing supervision by one of the four prominent family therapists at PCGC—Aponte, Haley, Minuchin, or Montalvo (Hoffman had since moved to New York). Minuchin had no problem with these terms, so the agreement was consummated. I moved to PCGC full-time in July of 1974.

The clinic was an exciting place to be at that time. There was considerable energy and much innovation. Of course, the most well-known activities were Minuchin's program with psychosomatic families (which also included Bernice Rosman and Ronald Liebman, among others), Haley's project with families of first-break schizophrenics, and Montalvo's and Aponte's work with lower-income families and community systems. In addition, there was a program for training paraprofessionals led by Marianne Walters, Sam Scott's project with families of the retarded, Kalman Flomenhaft's program for training mental health workers around the state, and the new inpatient service run by Lee Combrinck-Graham and Wayne Higley. After 1974, programs that emerged included Jody Shor's and Marianne Walter's foster-parent project, the single-parent project conducted by Marion Lindblad-Goldberg and Joyce Dukes, Marla Isaac's program with families of divorce, Jay Jemails's research on pregnant adolescents, and a number of psychosomatic projects overseen by Bernice Rosman. I found the ferment and the atmosphere both challenging and exhilarating. I also improved and expanded my therapeutic skills immeasurably, particularly through the personal supervision and cotherapy experiences I had with Harry Aponte, Avner Barcai, Henry Berger, Susan Freeman, and Braulio Montalvo, plus multiple consultations with Jay Haley and Salvador Minuchin.

Our own program, soon named the Addicts and Families Program, fit right into PCGC, eventually developing an identity, visibility, and momentum of its own. It had two major thrusts. One of these was to study the interaction patterns of families of 20- to 35-year-old addicts, comparing them with normals and also in response to symptomatic change (refer to Stanton, 1981c; Stanton et al., 1978, 1980; Steier, Stanton, & Todd, 1982a, 1982b). The other major activity was both to develop and to measure the effectiveness of a family treatment approach with such cases. In this second endeavor, we were influenced strongly by the model Haley had developed in working with young schizophrenics (Haley, 1980), and he served briefly as a supervisor and later as a consultant to our program. We also borrowed from Minuchin and Montalvo's therapeutic approach, particularly regarding structural theory, the use of in-session enactment, and many of the "micro-moves" that occur during therapy (Minuchin, 1974; Minuchin, Rosman, & Baker, 1978).

As we progressed, however, we found we had to tap our own creativity in order to develop methods and ways of thinking that were pegged more closely to families of addicts and to the complex process of addiction and its treatment. For instance, we developed what we called "noble ascriptions" for positively interpreting actions—frequently destructive ones—by family members. We found we could not always avoid dealing with the kinds of death, bereavement, and martyrdom issues that so frequently consumed these families. Case-management issues also loomed large, and we ended up by securing major input by the therapist *and* the family on such questions as whether methadone should be increased or decreased, when detoxification should occur, and so on. Related to this, we had to develop methods for working with other treatment systems so that the addict did not triangulate among us and compromise the therapy.

The Addicts and Families Program ran from 1974 to 1983. It included a series of different grants and projects over the years, and involved more than 80 clinicians, researchers, consultants, and administrative staff. There is not room here to recount the wealth of findings and principles that emerged from that effort, most of which have already been disseminated fairly widely in the literature.[4] It is probably fair to say, however, that this work has had a major impact, both as to practice and policy, at both the local and national levels. In addition, publications from the program have been translated into at least five languages other than English, and the treatment model has been applied in at least a dozen countries outside North America. In 1980, the work received the award for Outstanding Research Contribution in Marital and Family Therapy from the American Association for Marriage and Family Therapy (AAMFT).

Partly as a result of my work in the Addicts and Families Program, in the mid-1970s I began to receive solicitations from a number of federal agencies in Washington, DC. I was asked to review grants, consult on programs, and present at symposia sponsored by NIDA and by the National Institute of Alcohol Abuse and Alcoholism (NIAAA). In 1977, this culminated in my being invited to serve as a consultant for four years to the White House Office on Drug Abuse Policy. I prepared a report for that office that reviewed the literature on the family and addiction (Stanton, 1979c). That review led to further searches, resulting in my digging into many obscure corners to locate both historic and relatively unknown publications that previously had not been collected under one title. The fruit of these efforts was the publication of a bibliography and several overviews of the family aspects of substance abuse (Stanton, 1978a, 1979a, 1979b, 1980, 1985). I became almost a professional reviewer. Although such a responsibility had its high points, the amount of work it required was daunting. Once I moved on, I left that chapter of my life with little ambivalence.

One activity that differentiated me from most of my colleagues at PCGC was the time I devoted to the Family Institute of Philadelphia (FIP). The FIP had been founded in 1962-1963 by a group of Philadelphia's finest—Ivan Boszormenyi-Nagy, James Framo, Alfred Friedman, Geraldine Grossman, Jerry Jungreis, Leon Robinson, David Rubenstein, John Sonne, Geraldine Spark, Ross Speck, and Oscar Weiner. When I arrived in town, the institute had an active training program and sponsored a large annual conference. Of the staff at PCGC, only Braulio Montalvo, Bernice Rosman, Marion Lindblad, John Rosenberg, and I were members. Of these five, only Rosenberg and I remained active, once I succeeded Montalvo in giving the structural lectures in 1976. The low representation from PCGC had arisen years before, when Sal Minuchin had elected to break with the FIP. Although tension still existed from that schism, I decided that those were not my battles. I figured there was too much rich stimulation and enjoyable colleagueship close to my doorstep to pass up. I joined in 1973, eventually becoming a member of the training committee, and I profited immensely from my ten years of membership. When I eventually departed Philadelphia, I left the FIP with both sadness and fond memories.

Early in my work with families with an addicted member, I became struck by the preponderance of death themes and unresolved grief experiences they commonly manifested. A tie-in between these themes and the self-destructive, suicidal behavior of the addicted member began to make itself clear. In October of 1973, at the FIP annual conference, I had an experience in which these ideas crystallized and I eventually put them down in a paper entitled "The Addict as Savior: Heroin, Death and the Family" (Stanton, 1977). At around the same time, I met Sandra Coleman, a fellow FIP member who also was delving into addiction and these kinds of family processes. We began a collaboration, and a shared admiration for the work of Norman Paul, that resulted in several publications and joint research efforts over the ensuing years (Coleman & Stanton, 1978a, 1978b; Stanton & Coleman, 1980).

In the mid-1970s, as I became more familiar and comfortable with both structural and strategic approaches, I began to wonder whether they couldn't be combined, both conceptually and operationally. Indeed, Tom Todd and I often seemed to be doing just that in our everyday clinical work. I began to try to define some rules for such an integration. By 1978, I had coined the term *structural/strategic* therapy. In the spring of 1979, Howard Liddle brought a class of his Temple University graduate students to PCGC to sit in on part of one of our drug-abuse workshops and to meet afterwards with me. At that gathering, I also described this new structural/strategic work. Howard grew quite enthused and urged me to write it up. Consequently, I took pen in hand and the rules and methods eventually came out in a set of publications in 1981 (Stanton, 1981a, 1981b, 1981c). Apparently these writings filled a gap, as the reception within the field has been quite positive and gratifying.

At around the same time that I was trying to come to grips with the structural/strategic approach, I was also grappling with issues of a theoretical nature. In particular, it puzzled me that various groups in the field who were basically sympathetic to each other's work also were divided when it came to the application of certain types of interventions. On one side there were the structurally oriented groups, whose efforts derived to some extent from Nathan Ackerman, psychodrama, and behavior therapy, and who were most visibly represented by the PCGC contingent. I could see many similarities between structural therapy and the methods applied by a number of other therapists, some of whom worked with individuals. On the other side were the more strategic groups, with a historical lineage that started at least with Milton Erickson and included those in the Palo Alto Brief Therapy Project. The overlap between their paradoxical approach and some other therapists (such as Victor Frankl) was also evident, but as Dell (1981) had pointed out, paradoxical therapy still stood as "a set of techniques in search of a theory." It seemed to me that there had to be some way of conceptualizing people, systems, and therapy — some sort of paradigm — that could subsume these two general approaches and that could also incorporate developmental and historical data. I also wondered whether clues for resolution might be found in theories and phenomena arising from the natural sciences.

I wrestled with this problem for some time — reading extensively across a number of fields, observing cases, and cogitating. Then, one evening in early 1979, it started to come to me. Ideas, words, even images began popping into my mind. I started to write and the process took on an almost automatic quality. It was like a semitrance, in that I was perfectly aware of my whereabouts and actions, but the text kept tumbling out almost on its own. When I finished, I had the seeds of what I was later to term a *geodynamic balance* theory of systems and systemic change. To those notes I began to add periodically as new inspirations occurred and new readings or experiences brought light. Several of the concepts were presented in a 1981 chapter (Stanton, 1981c), and in 1982 I began to compose a paper that would attempt to pull it all together. I first presented these ideas publicly in 1983, and the paper published in 1984 was entitled "Fusion, Compression, Diversion and the Workings of Paradox: A Theory of Therapeutic/Systemic Change" (Stanton, 1984). It had taken over five years to reach fruition.

The geodynamic-balance paper proposed two major change processes in family and human systems: diversion approaches, which challenge and block an interaction pattern directly; and compression methods, which push a process further along its path to the point of repulsion or rebound. Families and system members are portrayed in interpersonal fields within which they traverse "orbits" that bring them toward and away from each other. Life-cycle events are regarded as to the way, and the extent to which, they alter these fields and orbits.

Reaction to the geodynamic paper has been interesting. Some of my colleagues have hailed it; others have been noncommittal. My impression is that it is not understood easily. Perhaps this is because I have not explained it clearly enough, or perhaps it is because the theory requires a thinking cap that is too "unusual." I do know that when I am working clinically with this paradigm in mind, I am operating on a different conceptual plane. It is pitched at a sort of abstract metalevel that allows me to see patterns I would not otherwise discern. I also know that when I have taught it to our trainees at Rochester, using diagrams and videotapes for explication, most of them seem to grasp at least the rudiments without a great deal of difficulty. In any event, I consider it to be by far my most important contribution to the field.

In October of 1980, a significant event took place in my life. Florence Kaslow, an FIP colleague, called and asked if I would be willing to host a visitor to PCGC. The person was one of the founders of family therapy in South Africa and the first president of the South African Institute of Marital and Family Therapy. She was on a lecture tour in the United States that Florence had helped arrange and wanted to see what was going on at PCGC. I agreed, and a few days later Judith Landau arrived at the clinic. I arranged for her to sit in on several lectures and sessions and introduced her to my friend and neighbor, Ross Speck, who also was visiting that morning. As the day progressed, we began to talk about her work and her theories. She had created a developmental theory of family change that, to my amazement, put together the pieces in a problem I had been puzzling over: how addiction rates could be greater among immigrant families with small (or yet unborn) children than among families who emigrated when the children were adolescents or adults. Her work with families in cultural transition, and her innovative techniques for treating extended family systems and networks, were the most exciting revelations I had encountered in years. I had no choice but to marry her.

In 1982, Judith joined me in Philadelphia for a multilevel collaboration that has continued unabated. She took a position at the Fairmont Institute directing an adolescent psychiatric unit (in which 72% of the patients had substance-abuse problems and 90% had at least one alcoholic parent) while also teaching in the Family Therapy Training Center at PCGC. We also started to do some team work at PCGC and found it to be a very creative and synergistic experience (Landau & Stanton, 1983; Landau-Stanton & Stanton, 1986). Our therapy approaches, theories, and experiences meshed to create a much more complete and effective model of treatment.

A year later we were contacted by the University of Rochester. Lyman Wynne was planning to shift his activities within the Department of Psychiatry to include more writing and travel, and less administration. This would free up the directorship of the Division of Family Programs, which he headed, and we were asked if we were interested in taking over the operation. A joint package was being offered, with promotions for both of us and the latitude and support to initiate several programs we had in mind. It was one of those offers you don't refuse. We didn't.

AT ROCHESTER

Upon arrival in Rochester we had two primary charges, in addition to continuing the existing activities of the division. The first was to establish a postdegree training program, including clinical externships, practica, seminars, and the construction of training videotapes. The second was to put the Family and Marriage Clinic, which had fallen on tough times, on solid footing once again. These activities certainly were made easier by the long-standing influence of Wynne and, from 1969, Rodney Shapiro (who had departed a few years before for San Francisco). There already were six video rooms in place, and a medical center and community that were generally open and receptive. In other words, major groundwork had been laid over the years prior to our arrival, so we did not have to devote undue energy to the basics.

The Family Therapy Training Program got off the ground in the fall of 1984 with 39 trainees. It has not looked back since. It has drawn trainees from around the United States and a dozen foreign countries. Presently, it includes approximately 150 trainees of whom 70 are involved in some kind of externship. Of particular note is that trainees may obtain university credit for any or all of their courses and externships—rather unusual for a postdegree institute and a palpable indication of the kind of support we obtained from the University of Rochester.

The Family and Marriage Clinic is also flourishing. The patient flow is good, the administrative process has been smoothed out, and it is peopled by a highly competent and energetic staff. It has reached out to the community and is viewed as an important resource, getting referrals not only locally but regionally.

Finally, Judith and I, in conjunction with our colleagues and trainees at Rochester, have set out to refine and expand the therapy model we began to develop in 1982, and to undergird it with a theory of family, systems, and therapy that is comprehensive, understandable, and unique. Although a few of the rudiments have been published (e.g., Landau, 1982; Landau & Stanton, 1983; Landau-Stanton, 1990; Landau-Stanton & Stanton, 1985; Stanton,

1984; Stanton & Landau-Stanton, 1990), as of this writing we are preparing a book on this work. Following that, we will return to the research world to investigate the utility and predictive potential of the theory and the methods.

THE LARGER CONTEXT AND THE FIELD

In terms of my place in the worlds of family psychology and family therapy, several thoughts occur. Apparently my abilities as an editor have been appreciated by peers and colleagues, as I presently serve on 10 editorial boards and have had to decline invitations to several others because of competing time commitments. A particular privilege has been the opportunity to succeed Salvador Minuchin on the board of directors of *Family Process.* As Broderick and Schrader (1981) note, the *Family Process* board of directors represents a kind of zenith among leaders in the field. The invitation came in 1982 as a complete surprise, especially because I had joined the journal's board of advisory editors only the year before.[5]

Another set of honors has arisen from the American Psychological Association, where I have been elected a fellow in four divisions—those of Clinical Psychology (Div. 12), Psychopharmacology (Div. 28), Psychotherapy (Div. 29), and Family Psychology (Div. 43). In addition, I have been privileged to have been elected to the board of directors of Division 43 and have been made a fellow by the AAMFT. It has also been my good fortune to have been invited to speak or teach in over two dozen countries across five continents, thereby having direct contact with 25,000 to 35,000 professionals. Were I to hazard a guess as to how I might be perceived in the field, perhaps it would be as an "all-rounder" who has published (Thomas & McKenzie, 1986) and made contributions (Textor, 1983) in the several areas of clinical method, research, theory, and teaching.

EPILOGUE

As I look back over these pages, there is an inclination to summarize what I think have been my major areas of contribution to family psychology and family systems. Four come to mind. In chronological order, first is the work in the area of substance abuse, in its various facets; second is the structural/strategic theory approach; third is geodynamic balance theory; and last is the work we are engaged in presently at Rochester. This work is still "becoming," but I wouldn't be surprised if it were to have the greatest impact of all. In the end, you, the reader, will have to decide.

NOTES

1. I am reminded of a workshop I gave in England a few years ago to a group from various countries in the United Kingdom.. Near the end, a participant asked me what the "M" in "M. Duncan Stanton" stood for. I replied, "The name is Morris. It's Welsh. And Duncan is Scotch. And Stanton is English. And I also have some Irish blood. You're all covered and next month I intend to run for Mayor of London." The audience burst into laughter and then applauded. I was tickled. The next morning I visited the local court house to see about changing my name to Duke Whittington.

2. In Hunt's abnormal psychology course, incidentally, I read Don D. Jackson's (1960) book, *The Etiology of Schizophrenia,* which included chapters by Theodore Lidz and Stephen Fleck, Murray Bowen and John Weakland, but the significance of their work did not take hold for me until several years later.

3. Richard Chase had encouraged me to go to Columbia to study under his former colleagues, Howard Hunt and Joseph Zubin. But the idea came up too late for me to obtain an assistantship there, and I knew I could not survive financially in New York City without some sort of stipend.

4. In addition to the references mentioned above pertaining to our research on patterns in families of addicts, the following are suggested: for information on the evolution and management of the project itself, see Stanton, Todd, and associates (1982) and Todd and Stanton (1983); regarding treatment methods, see Stanton and Todd (1979, 1981), Stanton et al. (1982), and Van Deusen, Stanton, Scott, and Todd (1980); for results and outcome data, see Stanton (1978b), Stanton, Steier, and Todd (1982), Stanton and Todd (1981), and Stanton et al. (1982).

5. The other members of the *Family Process* Board of Directors currently are Edgar H. Auerswald, Michael Goldstein, Peggy Papp, Robert Ryder, Margaret Thaler Singer, Carlos Sluzki (Editor), Helm Stierlin, Carl Whitaker, and Lyman Wynne (President). During my first year, Donald Bloch served as Editor, and Reuben Hill and Arthur Rosenthal (the Director of Harvard University Press) served as members.

REFERENCES

Broderick, C. B., & Schrader, S. S. (1981). The history of professional marriage and family therapy. In A. S. Gurman & D. P. Kniskern (Eds.), *Handbook of family therapy.* New York: Brunner/Mazel.

Coleman, S. B., & Stanton, M. D. (1978a). An index for measuring agency involvement in family therapy. *Family Process, 17,* 479-483.

Coleman, S. B., & Stanton, M. D. (1978b). The role of death in the addict family. *Journal of Marriage and Family Counseling, 4,* 79-91.

Dell, P. (1981). Some irreverent thoughts on paradox. *Family Process, 20,* 37-41.

Haley, J. (1980). *Leaving home.* New York: McGraw-Hill.

Jackson, D. D. (Ed.). (1960). *The etiology of schizophrenia.* New York: Basic Books.

Landau, J. (1982). Therapy with families in cultural transition. In M. McGoldrick, J. Pearce, & J. Giordano (Eds.), *Ethnicity and family therapy.* New York: Guilford.

Landau, J., & Stanton, M. D. (1983). Aspects of supervision with the "Pick-a-Dali Circus" model. *Journal of Strategic and Systemic Therapies, 2,* 31-39.

Landau-Stanton, J. (1990). Issues and methods of treatment for families in cultural transition. In M. P. Mirkin (Ed.), *The social and political contexts of family therapy.* Needham Heights, MA: Allyn & Bacon.

Landau-Stanton, J., & Stanton, M. D. (1985). Treating suicidal adolescents and their families. In M. P. Mirkin & S. L. Koman (Eds.), *Handbook of adolescents and family therapy.* New York: Gardner.

Landau-Stanton, J., & Stanton, M. D. (1986). Family therapy and systems supervision with the "Pick-a-Dali Circus" model. In F. W. Kaslow (Ed.), *Supervision and training: Models, dilemmas and challenges.* New York: Haworth.

Minuchin, S. (1974). *Families and family therapy.* Cambridge, MA: Harvard University Press.

Minuchin, S., Rosman, B. L., & Baker, L. (1978), *Psychosomatic families.* Cambridge, MA: Harvard University Press.

Stanton, M. D. (1972). Drug use in Vietnam: A survey among Army personnel in the two northern corps. *Archives of General Psychiatry, 26,* 279-286.

Stanton, M. D. (1975a). A neglected facet of second-order effects in mental health treatment. *Professional Psychology, 6,* 237-238.

Stanton, M. D. (1975b). Psychology and family therapy. *Professional Psychology, 6,* 45-49.

Stanton, M. D. (1977). The addict as savior: Heroin, death and the family. *Family Process, 16,* 191-197.

Stanton, M. D. (1978a). The family and drug abuse: A bibliography. *American Journal of Drug and Alcohol Abuse, 5,* 151-170.

Stanton, M. D. (1978b). Some outcome results and aspects of structural family therapy with drug addicts. In D. Smith, S. Anderson, M. Buxton, T. Chung, N. Gottlieb, & W. Harvey (Eds.), *A multicultural view of drug abuse: The selected proceedings of the National Drug Abuse Conference—1977.* Cambridge, MA: Schenkman.

Stanton, M. D. (1979a). Drugs and the family: A review of the recent literature. *Marriage and Family Review, 2*(1), 1-10.

Stanton, M. D. (1979b). Family treatment approaches to drug abuse problems: A review. *Family Process, 18,* 251-280.

Stanton, M. D. (1979c). Family treatment of drug problems: A review. In R. L. Dupont, A. Goldstein, & J. O'Donnell (Eds.), *Handbook on drug abuse.* (National Institute on Drug Abuse publication). Washington, DC: U.S. Government Printing Office.

Stanton, M. D. (1980). Some overlooked aspects of the family and drug abuse. In B. Ellis (Ed.), *Drug abuse from the family perspective: Coping is a family affair* (National Institute on Drug Abuse publication; DHHS: ADM 80-910). Washington, DC: U.S. Government Printing Office.

Stanton, M. D. (1981a). An integrated structural/strategic approach to family therapy. *Journal of Marital and Family Therapy, 7,* 427-439.

Stanton, M. D. (1981b). Marital therapy from a structural/strategic viewpoint. In G. P. Sholevar (Ed.), *The handbook of marriage and marital therapy.* Jamaica, NY: SP Medical and Scientific Books.

Stanton, M. D. (1981c). Strategic approaches to family therapy. In A. Gurman & D. Kniskern (Eds.), *Handbook of family therapy.* New York: Brunner/Mazel.

Stanton, M. D. (1984). Fusion, compression, diversion and the workings of paradox: A theory of therapeutic/systemic change. *Family Process, 23,* 135-167.

Stanton, M. D. (1985). The family and drug abuse: Concepts and rationale. In T. E. Bratter & G. G. Forrest (Eds.), *Alcoholism and substance abuse: Strategies for clinical intervention.* New York: Free Press.

Stanton, M. D., & Coleman, S. B. (1980). The participatory aspects of indirect self-destructive behavior: The addict family as a model. In N. Farberow (Ed.), *The many faces of suicide.* New York: McGraw-Hill.

Stanton, M. D., & Landau-Stanton, J. (1990). Therapy with families of adolescent substance abusers. In H. Milkman & L. Sederer (Eds.), *Treatment choices for alcoholism and substance abuse.* Lexington, MA: Lexington.

Stanton, M. D., Steier, F., & Todd, T. C. (1982). Paying families for attending sessions: Counteracting the dropout problem. *Journal of Marital and Family Therapy, 8,* 371-373.

Stanton, M. D., & Todd, T. C. (1979). Structural family therapy with drugs addicts. In E. Kaufman & P. Kaufman (Eds.), *The family therapy of drug and alcohol abuse.* New York: Gardner.

Stanton, M. D., & Todd, T. C. (1981). Engaging "resistant" families in treatment: II. Principles and techniques in recruitment; III. Factors in success and cost effectiveness. *Family Process, 20,* 261-293.

Stanton, M. D., Todd, T. C., & Associates (1982). *The family therapy of drug abuse and addiction.* New York: Guilford.

Stanton, M. D., Todd, T. C., Heard, D. B., Kirschner, S., Kleiman, J. I., Mowatt, D. T., Riley, P., Scott, S. M., & Van Deusen, J. M. (1978). Heroin addiction as a family phenomenon: A new conceptual model. *American Journal of Drug and Alcohol Abuse, 5,* 125-150.

Stanton, M. D., Todd, T. C., Steier, F., Van Deusen, J. M., Marder, L. R., Rosoff, R. J., Seaman, S. F., & Skibinski, E. (1980). *Family characteristics and family therapy of heroin addicts: Final report 1974-1978.* Report prepared for the Psychosocial Branch, National Institute on Drug Abuse, 1979 (Revised 1980) (Grant No. R01 DA 01119).

Stanton, D., & Vetter, H. J. (1968). The mental health specialist as consultant in a chronic disease hospital. *Psychiatric Quarterly* (Supplement), *42,* 282-296.

Steier, F., Stanton, M. D., & Todd, T. C. (1982a). Normal and dysfunctional families: A study of quantitative distinctions in organization. In L. Troncale (Ed.), *A general survey of systems methodology: Proceedings of the twenty-sixth annual meeting, Society for General Systems Research.* Washington, DC.

Steier, F., Stanton, M. D., & Todd, T. C. (1982b). Patterns of turn-taking and alliance formation in family communication. *Journal of Communication, 32,* 148-160.

Textor, M. R. (1983). An assessment of prominence in the family therapy field. *Journal of Marital and Family Therapy, 9,* 317-320.

Thomas, F. N., & McKenzie, P. N. (1986). Prolific writers in marital and family therapy. *Journal of Marital and Family Therapy, 12,* 175-180.

Todd, T. C., & Stanton, M. D. (1983). Research on marital and family therapy: Answers, issues, and recommendations for the future. In B. Wolman & G. Stricker (Eds.), *Handbook of family and marital therapy.* New York: Plenum.

Van Deusen, J. M., Stanton, M. D., Scott, S. M., & Todd, T. C. (1980). Engaging "resistant" families in treatment. I. Getting the drug addict to recruit his family members. *International Journal of the Addictions, 15,* 1069-1089.

20

The Family Psychologist as Scientist-Practitioner: Conflicts and Compromises

JOHN P. VINCENT

Much of my work has addressed families who are in the process of transition—initially couples who were expecting their first child, and most recently families affected by separation or divorce. Using these interest areas as a backdrop, in this chapter I explore some issues with which I've struggled in arriving at my own conception of what it means to be a family psychologist. I address how I acquired my own voice through facing some inevitable conflicts and forging my own compromises between different professional roles, theoretical paradigms, and clinical goals. Although my work has been characterized by an ever-broadening conceptual base through which to view both normal and problematic family interaction, a central theme has revolved around the optimal balance of research versus clinical work. The scientist-practitioner model in clinical psychology has had a long and rather tattered history. In looking back over my own career, I would like to trace the various approximations to this model that I have attempted in my own work, and consider the viability of the scientist-practitioner perspective for family psychologists.

ROOTS

Growing up in Salt Lake City, Utah, amidst the strong family ethic that prevails within the Mormon community no doubt influenced my choice of profession. My own family is a study in contrasts. My father was the eldest and only son of three children from second-generation Welsh immigrants. His father, a railroad worker and sometime blacksmith, was a delightful man, a tinkerer of sorts, and had a keen sense of humor. My father's mother died the year I was born. I don't know much about her, but from stories I learned that she was a hard-working woman, a bit short-tempered, but devoted to her children. From all accounts my father's major ambition was to rise from his humble beginnings. He was the first in his family to finish college, later earned a master's degree, and tried his hand at college teaching. His experience as a college teacher never seemed of much real significance to me, except for the fact that my mother was one of his students, and for some unknown coincidence I have spent the past 16 years behind the ivy-covered walls of academia. Even though drive and a sound mind were among my father's assets, early onset of coronary heart disease and an array of other problems kept him from realizing very much of his considerable potential.

My mother was the third of four children and only daughter of a socially prominent and relatively affluent family. Her father, who died many years before my birth, assumed a rather godlike quality in her memory. He was the first student-body president of Stanford University, a personal friend of Leland Stanford, and something of a folk hero to those who knew him. Why he passed up a lucrative law practice in San Francisco to return to Provo, Utah, has always baffled me, but he became a very big fish in a minuscule pond as circuit judge, entrepreneur, and city father. Upon his death, he left behind my grandmother (a feisty little woman with a fabulous wit), my mother, and her three brothers (all of whom became successful physicians and settled in California). It was always my mother's dream that both my brother—Robert, who is six years my senior—and I would follow in her brothers' footsteps, but alas, we both ended up in the mental health profession—he with a doctorate in social work, and I as a clinical psychologist. This was a profound disappointment to her, and it took several years before she finally accepted the fact that neither of her sons would become a "real doctor".

In my own case, undergraduate work at the University of Utah in Salt Lake City between 1964 and 1968 provided the first opportunity to define a direction. After proving to everyone that my academic interests fell outside the domain of pre-med, I decided on a major in psychology. Good fortune followed that decision. Donna Gelfand, who was then an assistant professor in the psychology department (she is now chair), and Don Hartmann invited me to participate in their ongoing research. Both had been students of Albert Bandura at Stanford and were and still are striking examples of the gifted, ambitious clinical scientist that I soon tried to emulate. Furthermore, both had been smitten by the burgeoning behavior-modification movement, and I was quick to count myself among the legion who sought to slay the mighty psychoanalytic dragon on a sword of learning theory-based interventions. When it came time to pick graduate schools, it was imperative that I find one that was aligned strongly with the "new truth".

The University of Oregon, where I studied from 1968 to 1972, proved to be an excellent choice. I was assigned to Bob Weiss as my advisor, and began what was one of the most exciting eras of my life. Oregon was a fascinating place at that time. Weiss had been hired to rebuild the clinical program in line with the Boulder model conception of clinical psychology (see Raimy, 1950; Shakow, 1947), colored with a distinctly behavioral wash. The faculty and students were organized in clinical-research teams around projects that involved an integration of research and service with specific target populations. My interest in families was clear at the onset. I see the family as the fundamental building block of all human development and the wellspring from which all human enterprise is born. How could anyone not find it an interesting and a worthy topic for study? I had a cursory introduction to family therapy, which at Oregon involved teaching parents of problem children how to implement programs of contingency management. Much of the approach was patterned after Gerry Patterson's work (e.g., Patterson, 1986; Patterson & Reid, 1970), and at the time, I could think of no other treatment model that had so much promise.

My first real exposure to families, however, grew out of some other fortuitous circumstances. Bob Weiss, Gerry Patterson, and Robert Ziller—a social psychologist—had been awarded funding by the Office of Naval Research to study small-group conflict (Patterson & Weiss, 1971). Since landlocked Eugene, Oregon, was noticeably short of submarine crews, Patterson, Weiss, and Ziller convinced the Navy that married couples provided appropriate and readily available small groups through which new principles and techniques of conflict management could be developed. It was out of this slight-of-hand maneuver that the Oregon Marital Studies program was launched in the early 1970s and much of the early work in articulating behavioral marital therapy was conducted (see Weiss, Hops, & Patterson, 1973). Buoyed by the optimism that behavioral principles could be successfully applied to marital conflict, the marital therapy team began its work.

Although I don't want to belittle the important contributions that came from these humble beginnings, I should make a couple of points. First, our work occurred largely in a vacuum. Save a few digressions in the growing literature on marital and family therapy, most of which was considered irrelevant, the bulk of concepts and techniques were elaborated from the extant literature on behavior therapy. Second, few of us who actually implemented behavioral marital therapy had any prior clinical experience with couples, and precious little psychotherapy experience of any sort. Call it naïveté, arrogance, or whatever, but we really believed that helping couples pinpoint problems in behavioral terms and conducting short-term problem-solving therapy through negotiation of behavioral contracts was sufficient to resolve long-standing relationship problems. The clients, on the other hand, seemed invested far more in humiliating each other in front of witnesses than in deciding how many times hubby had to take out the trash in order to earn a back rub from his wife. The use of contingency contracts to help resolve marital conflicts was first suggested in the late 1960s (see Stuart, 1969). The notion evolved from social exchange theory (Thibault & Kelley, 1959) and was thought to help restore positive reciprocity in marital dyads where some form of aversive control had become the principal means of promoting behavior change. Distinctions were made between "good faith" and "quid pro quo" contracts. The good-faith variety was thought to be preferable because one spouse's agreed-upon behavior change was not linked directly to that of his or her partner (see Weiss, Birchler, & Vincent, 1974). Unfortunately, there is no evidence that supports the efficacy of contingency contracts per se in behavioral marital therapy (see Jacobson, 1981), and close tracking of spousal behavior—which is encouraged by use of behavioral contracts—was shown to be a property of distressed as opposed to healthy relationships and therefore a questionable goal for couples therapy (Jacobson & Moore, 1981).

Although I am forever disappointed that the problems of marriage are not solved so easily, the experience at Oregon left another mark that took a long time to fade. Implicit in the early Boulder model/behavioral zeitgeist was an important assumption—if you can't specify it and measure it, it isn't real. A corollary was that most traditionally trained clinicians are muddleheaded charlatans who invent abstractions that can never be studied systematically, and are of limited therapeutic value anyway. It was this apparent disdain of the practitioner side of the scientist-practitioner model that led me for several years to restrict my vision to those phenomena that one could ostensibly see and measure.

A doctoral internship at the VA in Palo Alto during 1971-1972 was the next important step in my training. Given my newfound interest in couples and families, I believed that a rotation in the family-studies unit would help round out my clinical expertise. Shelly Starr (then chief of the unit), Jay Mann, and guest appearances by Paul Watzlavick, Richard Fisch, and their cohorts from the Mental Research Institute placed a near-fatal dent in my once impregnable behavioral armor. This was my first intensive exposure to the angst associated with having my colleagues observe my work from behind a one-way mirror. Furthermore, I was surrounded by people whom I respected that looked at the world very differently than I. Further shocking my developing identity was the cognizance that clinical work was valuable in its own right, and that clinicians could actually be rather brilliant, even though many of the concepts they used could neither be observed nor measured easily. Despite the fact that my clinical horizons had been opened somewhat, my future as an academic already had been well laid. After my internship, I joined the faculty at the University of Houston in 1972 as an assistant professor in the clinical psychology training program.

In looking back over the past 16 years, it is clear that the tension between the scientist-researcher and clinician was ever present and that I have forged at least three different compromises: the scientist, the practitioner, and the scientist-practitioner. I will try to capture the important elements of each compromise in the context of discussing my efforts to become a family psychologist.

THE SCIENTIST

The momentum established during graduate school as a behaviorally oriented clinician clearly dominated my early years at Houston. I replicated the working model under which I had been trained, and began doing research on various facets of the behavioral view of marriage. All of my early work had a strong observational-assessment flavor, which I extended to a follow-up of my dissertation research contrasting the verbal and nonverbal behavior of happily and not-so-happily married couples (e.g., Vincent, Weiss, & Birchler, 1975). This line of research led to a strong interest in methodological issues associated with research on marital interaction. The final study out of this thrust involved an investigation of experimental demand effects in observations of couples' conflict resolution. It is perhaps of no real surprise to anyone who has watched couples fight, but we demonstrated that observational assessments of verbal behavior, but not nonverbal behavior, could be faked easily (Vincent, Friedman, Nugent, & Messerly, 1979). Beyond my interest in validity issues with observational assessment, it is obvious to me now that I was looking for some forum to challenge the underpinnings of behavioral research with couples and express my growing belief that the approach was naive and shortsighted.

In addition to research with couples, I also pursued an interest, developed during graduate school, in hyperactive children. Along with Ben Williams at Baylor College of Medicine in Houston, I developed a classroom-based observational assessment system to monitor the behavior of hyperactive children, their peers, and their teachers. The assumptions behind the assessment system were influenced strongly by my behavioral proclivities, and the system was designed with hopes of demonstrating subtle contingency control over behavioral excesses in children (Vincent, Williams, Harris, & Duval,

1980). The project also provided me with an initial exposure to behavioral ecology, a systems perspective that addresses the contextual determinants of behavior as well as the intended and unintended impact of various interventions strategies (see Willems & Stuart, 1980). Even though my research activity in the area of childhood hyperactivity was short-lived, my interest in understanding how seemingly well-intentioned interventions can trigger a variety of desirable and undesirable systemic forces has continued. These effects are well illustrated in Wahler's work with oppositional children (see Wahler, 1975). For example, in one case a child's general behavioral improvement at school was associated simultaneously with some negative changes at school as evidenced by greater oppositionality, and with some other positive changes at home in the form of increased peer interaction. Kazdin (1982) has provided an excellent discussion of the assessment and treatment implications of these phenomena, which he describes as "response covariation".

I also became involved in another collaborative research project around 1978 with Paul Baer, chief psychologist at Baylor College of Medicine. The project involved the study of conflict resolution among families with a hypertensive father. This endeavor had a theoretical attraction to me, in that it permitted study of how aspects of the family system are linked with chronic medical problems. Specifically, we were interested in whether or not the physical health status of fathers is related to particular family conflict-resolution strategies. Ever since the work of Franz Alexander (1950), individuals who developed essential hypertension were suspected of having problems dealing with anger. The "anger in" or "suppressed rage" hypothesis coupled with the fact that hypertension tends to run in families led us to speculate that perhaps the family of a hypertensive patient provides an environment that teaches maladaptive ways of managing conflict. I am also sure that my interest in families with hypertensive fathers was stimulated by personal issues, because my own father had suffered from the disease most of his adult life, and his illness and death when I was 22 years of age had a profound effect on my own life.

Using an observational-assessment procedure adapted from the Marital Interaction Coding System (Hops, Wills, Patterson, & Weiss, 1971), we studied family interaction patterns around attempts to resolve experimentally induced conflicts. There was rather clear evidence of differences between families with a hypertensive father compared with those with a normotensive father in expression of nonverbal negative behavior (Baer, Reed, Bartlett, Vincent, Williams, & Bourianoff, 1983; Baer, Vincent, Williams, Bourianoff, & Bartlett, 1980). In this instance, nonverbal negative behavior consisted primarily of "not tracking" (gaze aversion). Family scores on nonverbal negative behavior also included a few instances of "no response" (a category that is coded when a family member fails to respond to an overture from someone else in the family), and "turn off" (a facial grimace indicating displeasure). The two groups of family did not differ in frequencies of positive verbal behavior, positive nonverbal behavior, or negative verbal behavior.

In the context of an experimentally induced family conflict, gaze aversion is one means of regulating affect in the interaction. As Baer (1983) noted, this behavior in family members would indicate an "unreadiness to communicate, submission, or means of reducing aversive emotional arousal". This conflict-avoidant interaction pattern in hypertensive families may thus promote learning of arousal-inhibiting or internalizing affect-management styles that correspond to the psychological correlates of hypertension (Baer, 1983). Although speculative at best, this finding provided some impetus to further exploration of conflict resolution and anger management in family members who are at risk for later development of hypertension.

Although I was busy and reasonably productive during the middle to late 1970s, I did not feel that I had staked out an area that was truly mine. I'm not quite sure what steps led to it, but at some point I became intrigued with the prospect of integrating my work with couples with my interest in families. Eventually this evolved into a short-term longitudinal study of couples who were expecting their first child. I was struck by the well-replicated finding from the family sociology literature that couples experience a precipitous decline in marital satisfaction following birth of the first child (Rollins & Cannon, 1974). Birth of a first child represents for most young couples a major developmental task. It was an easy extrapolation from my earlier work in behavioral marital therapy to postulate that couples with faulty problem-solving skills would have greater than average difficulty in managing the transition from dyad to triad (see Vincent, Harris, Cook, & Brady, 1980). I teamed up with Nancy Cook, who at that time was in the department of human development at the University of Houston, and Patrick Brady, who was at the Houston Child Guidance Center. We convinced NIMH that the project deserved funding, and what followed may forever dissuade me from taking on another large-scale research project. In addition to developing yet another observational coding system for marital interaction, a companion observational system to capture attentional synchrony and facial expression between parents and their newborn infants, and a host of other assessment devices, we started collecting longitudinal data on three waves of expectant parents during their third trimester of pregnancy, at birth, one month, two months, and 18 months postnatally. The project provided a fascinating opportunity to study the transition from couple to family as well as to think through the adaptive ways that new parents accommodate to this critical developmental task. (Some of the details of this work are discussed in Vincent, Cook, & Brady, 1981).

The final arena during my so-called scientist era involved my editorship of *Advances in Family Intervention, Assessment and Theory.* Bob Sprague, whom I first knew through our mutual interest in childhood hyperactivity, approached me about my interest in developing a series to showcase good examples of a clinical-research approach to the study of families. At that time I was enamored with the possibility of promoting what I thought was the optimal approach to family psychology—the thoughtful integration of hard science and clinical acumen in addressing particular family problems (see Vincent, 1980b). It is by now obvious that at several points in my career I have questioned whether or not I would be able to achieve such an integration in my own work. In editing the four volumes of the series (Vincent, 1980a, 1981, 1983, 1987), however, I am delighted to have found individuals who indeed have been able to pull it off. I will come back to this subject in the last section of the chapter.

THE PRACTITIONER

My growing disenchantment with research is probably not clear from the previous section. Starting in 1974, I began a small private practice, partly to keep a hand in active clinical work and also to continue exploring some of the ideas that I had been exposed to during the clinical part of my graduate training. For years I denied that my clinical activity was of much significance to my professional identity, yet I found myself spending more and more time seeing clients. Houston provided a stimulating environment for anyone interested in family therapy. Don Williamson, Morris Taggert, and their colleagues had become quite visible in promoting marital and family therapy, and Walt DeLange at the Houston Child Guidance Center and Harry Goolishian at the Galveston Family Institute had made major inroads in providing training opportunities in family therapy at local mental health agencies. It was also clear that my graduate training had equipped me rather poorly to be an effective clinician. The all-purpose behavioral model that seemed so attractive in earlier years did not prove very useful with many of the clients whom I had begun to see.

In my role as professor and clinical supervisor at the university, I found myself pushing into heretofore uncharted territory—reading very carefully the work of the major family therapists, and even the classics in psychoanalysis. As I continued to sharpen my clinical skills, a curious schizophrenia developed. As a researcher I was the rational, logical positivist trying to operationalize phenomena through objective, observable measures and plotting methodologically sound research studies that sought to elucidate the relationships among those variables. As a clinician, I was content to think in a language of metaphor, grappling with unseen and unmeasurable phenomena and tuned in to the quality of the relationship that I had forged with another human being. Finally, sometime around 1981, I stopped doing research.

In retrospect, a variety of factors led to this decision. I had grown weary of the work involved in trying to execute research that satisfied my standards as a methodologist. For some reason, I was attracted to projects that required an inordinate amount of effort to answer what, at the outset, seemed like straightforward questions. In fact, I was overwhelmed by the complexities involved in doing methodologically adequate family research, but was unwilling to take shortcuts that would be more expedient. The more manageable questions all seemed trivial and failed to satisfy my self-imposed requirement that the answer should have some demonstrable impact on how we work with families clinically. It had also become clear that I did not know very much about how families really operated. The decision to immerse myself in clinical work until I had a better sense of the right questions seemed like the logical course of action.

My practitioner era was truly a time of tremendous learning, both clinically and personally. I credit the input of Harry Goolishian (a family psychologist), George Taylor (a psychoanalyst), and Glenn Cambor (a psychoanalyst/family therapist) for their help in shaping my development as a clinician. I also owe a debt of gratitude to the individuals and families who sought my help during our mutual education. There is something very compelling and affirming about the partnerships we strike with our clients. I am still unsure whether it is our teachers and mentors who teach us about human behavior, or our clients.

The theoretical model that has evolved out of my practitioner era may sound like a bad stereotype of "the eclectic who does a little bit of everything". For anxiety problems and those stemming from a self-defeating dialogue with oneself I still look very much like the cognitive-behaviorist. Even so, for cases that fit nicely within a behavioral model, and for those that do not, I try to evolve a working formulation of the individual's role in his or her family and the values and themes that characterize recent generations of the family. Out of my struggle to understand better the interplay of individual, dyadic, and family forces, the power of intergenerational influences has become abundantly clear. I also incorporate some of the contributions from the ego analysts and self-psychologists in tracing the major ingredients to an individual's sense of identity (see Blanck & Blanck, 1974, 1979; Kernberg, 1975; Kohut, 1971, 1977; Stolorow & Lachman, 1980). Like many of my colleagues who work with families today, I have found value in using aspects of object-relations theory in exploring the underlying relationship contracts and frustrated transference wishes that frequently arise in both a client's choice of marital partner and the reciprocal interactions between parents and children (Dicks, 1967; Gill, 1982; Meisner, 1978; Sager, 1981; Scharff & Scharff, 1987). Concepts from self-psychology also have figured prominently in my views about the therapeutic relationship (Gedo, 1979, 1981; Gedo & Goldberg, 1973; Schafer, 1983). The transference themes that emerge in the context of treatment present rich material diagnostically, and are frequently very useful in helping clients understand and resolve relational artifacts from the past that hamper current adjustment.

By contrast, for couples and families who are suited well to brief therapy, I frequently begin with relatively straightforward behavioral interventions. If these techniques seem inappropriate, I generally shift to a strategic approach and use various forms of reframing and symptom prescription. The behavioral and strategic approaches are actually quite compatible: the main differences involve the rationale one gives the client and whether or not one leverages client resistance in the delivery of therapeutic directives. I am hard-pressed to explain how I weave together these seemingly incompatible theoretical threads, but judging from the results the fabric is quite pleasing. In looking over how I conceptualize my work as a therapist, I am struck by the irony that I sound like one of those muddleheaded clinicians that I was warned about as a graduate student!

THE SCIENTIST-PRACTITIONER

Even though my disenchantment with research led me to abandon it for several years, I still harbored the conviction that a workable integration of the clinician and researcher was a worthy and perhaps even achievable goal. I would therefore like to discuss my most recent attempt at this integration in the mid-1980s.

Following my interest in how families manage important life transitions, I cultivated a strong interest in work with families who are at some stage in the process of divorce. My interest in the area evolved very naturally from my clinical work. Perhaps because Houston has one of the highest divorce rates in the country, I found that for a great number of my clients, divorce—either their own or their parents—was a major theme in their lives. To a systems theorist, divorce represents a fascinating issue. In the context of studying the metamorphosis that occurs within the divorcing family system, we frequently see extreme emotional symptoms and striking examples of outrageous behavior. The impact on the participants as well as their children can be utterly devastating. This is a problem that really got my attention, and rekindled my wish to make substantive contributions to an important area of family psychology.

In addition to my strong clinical interest in divorce, the area presented some fascinating opportunities for research. Though there have been some landmark studies of divorce (e.g., Hetherington, Cox, & Cox, 1982; Wallerstein & Kelly, 1980), it was obvious to me, the scientist, that most of the research in the area was flawed seriously, and the state of our expertise—in terms of understanding the process of divorce recovery theoretically, as well as in designing effective treatments—was woefully inadequate. Assuming that I was finally willing to make the compromises necessary to conduct research in an incredibly complex and methodologically challenging area, there were attractive opportunities for a satisfying integration of the scientist and practitioner.

Beginning in 1985, along with a former student and valued colleague (Gerry Harris), I established Divorce Adjustment Services, a nonprofit, university-based clinical research project. Given my belief that a strong community perspective was important, our first step was to secure the support of several judges in the Harris County and Fort Bend County family courts. Thanks to funding from the Meadows Foundation, we then conducted a thorough survey of all mental-health service providers in the Houston metropolitan area and established a comprehensive referral network of those with expertise in treating families of divorce. Until we could develop our own service-delivery program, I believed that an important place to start was to steer families who were in need of help to qualified and affordable professionals.

In 1987, we moved to step two, development of time-limited cost-effective services for families affected by divorce. It is at this current step that the integration of research and clinical work is now possible. Based on the available literature and on our own clinical experience with families who had undergone divorce, we began articulating an ecosystemic model for understanding the process of divorce from the standpoint of each family member. The model specifies the common pathways in the divorce recovery process and helps identify systemic forces that either augment or impede the recovery process. Developing the ecosystemic model has occurred in concert with careful assessment of each family member that we serve and ongoing refinement of our intervention programs.

The need for low-cost programs to service a potentially large number of families led us to concentrate on development of complementary time-limited, group-based programs for parents and children. The programs had to incorporate a number of goals: The interventions needed to attend to emotional issues associated with loss, abandonment, and assaults to one's self-esteem. We also had the pragmatic objective of teaching parents better problem-solving and coping skills designed to help them function better as individuals and restore equilibrium to the parent-child relationship. Improving their social problem-solving skills in concert with age-appropriate therapeutic experiences was a major goal for the children of divorce.

The work of Pedro-Carroll and Cowen (1985) provided a great starting point for our child program, and we feel that we have made a few additions that improve this already excellent program. It is with the parents, however, that most of the innovation took place. Vestiges of my early exposure to parent training can still be seen, but with a new twist. It became increasingly obvious that we needed a two-stage program for parents. Many adults experience a profound sense of loss associated with trying to disentangle the bonds of attachment. It is also clear that most adults are ambivalent about the impending loss and act in ways that simultaneously reinforce and sever those bonds. Emotional attachments can be reinforced by how former spouses behave (frequent, unnecessary phone calls), how they think ("I can't bear a life without him or her"), and how they feel. At the emotional level, friendly, positive emotions accompany this process as well as hostile, vengeful ones that seem to say, "I must really love someone toward whom I feel so hatefully."

Once a divorce is inevitable, these efforts to maintain emotional involvement with the former spouse soon become destructive, and clinically the first order of business is to help clients gradually resolve these lingering attachments. In this first stage of treatment, intense emotions typically are encountered, and a combination of powerful evocative techniques, group support, and behavioral exercises like role-playing, self-monitoring, and cognitive restructuring are helpful. We are not clear at this stage in our thinking whether these powerful attachment themes are simply part of the transition process for virtually all divorcing adults, whether particular individuals with fragile identities are susceptible to extreme disturbances in this area, or both. *It is clear, however, that if attachment to the former spouse is not resolved within a reasonable amount of time, the individual's life remains at a standstill, their emotional resources for effective parenting are compromised seriously, and other therapeutic efforts to teach coping skills and parenting techniques will fall "like water off a duck's back."* Once accomplished it appears that the more straightforward psychoeducational format associated with parent training and problem-solving therapy works quite well. We are in the midst of designing research that will test some of these assumptions, specifically the relative impact of child intervention and therapy for parents directed toward resolving attachment issues and enhancing parental competence and problem-solving skills.

I would like to discuss why this new endeavor represents a better integration of the scientist and practitioner than my earlier approximations. This is first evident in my choice of problem. Much of my interest in the area grew out of a wealth of clinical experience in working with families of divorce. Not all intuition must derive from clinical work, but in this instance it was fertile ground for developing new ideas. Second, the interventions per se are based on a hybrid of theoretical models and techniques that follow directly from my own clinical work. This notable absence of theoretical purity mirrors my own views that good family therapy must address intra- and interpersonal processes, which can be conceptualized from multiple perspectives. For me to feel comfortable with our interventions, they must ring true and satisfy my clinical instincts that they make sense. Interventions designed in an earlier era would have been decidedly more cerebral in both their derivation and focus. Finally, the whole enterprise has explicitly clinical goals achieved through application of research methods. The clinician generates the ideas and ultimately benefits from the products; the researcher sharpens the ideas and tests their veracity. Although there are numerous examples of this partnership in psychology, this is the closest that I have come in my own work to actually achieving it.

WHITHER FAMILY PSYCHOLOGY?

In looking at the field of family psychology from my particular vantage point, how do I believe the field should proceed? I would like to address the question from the perspective of research and practice, and return to the question of whether the scientist-practitioner model is viable and achievable for family psychologists.

Research

I believe that it is the psychologist's commitment to research and accountability that distinguishes his or her contribution to family psychology from the other disciplines. It is also our commitment to research that has relegated us to among the least heralded in the family field. A great deal of the literature in family therapy has been unencumbered by the need to present convincing data—either research on the assumptions that underlie therapeutic methods or evaluations of the methods themselves. The Ph.D. continues to be a research degree, and no self-respecting psychologist can abandon totally the tenets of science in promoting a particular world view. This value bias may appear as a liability in the short run, especially if we look at the popularity of our workshops and the number of our disciples. *I believe that in the long run, however, it is exactly this commitment to verifiability that will prevail.* Continually trying to answer the questions "Does it work?" and "Why does it work?" should keep the field from embarking on too many unpromising tangents. This pronouncement comes, of course, from someone who has questioned seriously the value of research in his own career. The logical-positivist scientific approach has its limits, and the fact that we can't see a phenomenon and measure it doesn't mean that it doesn't exist. I also believe, however, that competent, clinically relevant research is essential for progress in understanding human behavior. Our challenge is to continue to make diligent progress using our intuition as clinicians and our hard-nosed skepticism as researchers to unravel the mysteries involved with family life.

The principal challenges for research in family psychology continue to be in the areas of assessment and methodology. Many of the assessment issues—like the unit of analysis, decisions regarding the relevant dimensions, signs versus samples, and the paucity of psychometrically adequate instruments—have been spelled out (Gurman & Kniskern, 1981; Vincent & Carter, 1988). As complicated as these issues are, the problems associated with experimental design and data analysis in family research present even more formidable challenges.

Advocates of the "new epistemology" have argued against the relevancy of traditional research methodology for study of families. The researcher in me is not convinced, however, that wholesale dismissal of empirical methods represents an acceptable or appealing solution. Rather, I believe that the next generation of family psychologists have their work cut out in rendering dynamic systemic processes to more penetrating scientific scrutiny.

Clinical Innovation

Underneath it all, we have to rely on the ingenuity and creativity of the clinician to help the field progress. *We are all committed to discovering what works for which families.* To that end, we must support the efforts of the front-line clinician in trying to impact favorably the lives of those within a given family. Family therapy was founded in rebellion—a kind of reaction formation against the prevailing psychodynamic treatment model and the associated assumption that the individual was the proper unit of focus. Many of us have discovered that we may have thrown out the baby with the bath water. For many family members, their individual psychodynamics are extremely important, and working with individuals using the family as a backdrop is sometimes the best kind of family therapy. Families are infinitely complex entities, and we all struggle for concepts that work and allow us to simplify the chaos in order to intervene effectively. In striving for new innovations in the future, I hope that the next generation does not compound an original error among family therapists, and fail to realize that a great deal of very useful and effective clinical lore comes from outside the ranks of family psychology.

When discussing the creative process involved in clinical innovation, it is tempting to think along the lines of technique. New ways of conceptualizing family interaction typically stimulate new strategies for intervention. I would be the last to argue against technical innovation, but my exposure to psychodynamic methods leads to an important caveat. I believe that family therapists frequently have been remiss in downplaying the importance of the therapeutic relationship as well as the contribution of the therapist's personal issues to that relationship. Many of our colleagues, especially those who think along strategic lines, are inclined to promote a therapeutic model that places the therapist conveniently outside the family system (e.g., Fisch, Weakland, & Segal, 1982; Haley, 1976; Stanton, 1981; Watzlavick, Weakland, & Fisch, 1974). Although this is sometimes an effective short-term ploy, a family psychology that fails to consider how the therapist's psychological dynamics impact the course of family therapy is destined to miss the boat.

Scientist and Practitioner: One Person or Two?

Does the integrated scientist-practitioner model have much appeal to family psychology? Goldfried and Padawer (1982) have suggested that scientists and practitioners tend to be different types of people, and that it is unlikely that high-level accomplishment in both areas can be expected from the same individual. Although I tend to agree with their position, I still believe that with sufficient maturity and adequate opportunities for learning both sets of skills, it is possible to have both the scientist and practitioner live in harmony within the same person. I could wax on about the interlocking domains of the context of discovery (clinical realm) and the context of verification (scientific realm), but it still begs the question as to why these two activities must be housed within the same individual. For want of a better answer, it keeps us honest. Clinicians do indeed have a propensity for looking at their work in a self-serving way. We don't always know what we are doing, a topic that was addressed refreshingly in Coleman's book *Failures in Family Therapy* (1985). On the other hand, when researchers are given free reign, they often confuse the trivial with the profound. The tension between these two parts of one's professional identity is healthy. It represents a fundamental conflict within our view of ourselves as family psychologists that will not simply go away by exclusive focus on one half over the other. Tolerance of contradiction and ambiguity has been suggested as one indication of the mature personality. It is my conviction that striving for workable compromises between these often-disparate professional selves will have the most favorable impact on the maturing field of family psychology.

REFERENCES

Alexander, F. (1950). *Psychosomatic medicine.* New York: W. W. Norton.

Baer, P. E. (1983). Conflict management in the family. In J. P. Vincent (Ed.), *Advances in family intervention, assessment and theory, Vol. III.* Greenwich, CT: JAI Press.

Baer, P. E., Reed, J., Bartlett, P. C., Vincent, J. P., Williams, B. J., & Bourianoff, G. G. (1983). Studies of gaze during induced conflict in families with a hypertensive father. *Psychosomatic Medicine, 45,* 232-242.

Baer, P. E., Vincent, J. P., Williams, B. J., Bourianoff, G. G., & Bartlett, P. C. (1980). Behavioral response to conflict and children's blood pressure in families with hypertensive fathers. *Hypertension, 2,* 70-77.

Blanck, G., & Blanck, R. (1974). *Ego psychology: Theory and practice.* New York: Columbia University Press.

Blanck, G., & Blanck, R. (1979). *Ego psychology II. Psychoanalytic developmental psychology.* New York: Columbia University Press.

Coleman, S. B. (1985). *Failures in family therapy.* New York: Guilford.

Dicks, H. V. (1967). *Marital tensions.* New York: Basic Books.

Fisch, R., Weakland, J. H., & Segal, L. (1982). *The tactics of change: Doing therapy briefly.* San Francisco: Jossey-Bass.

Gedo, J. E. (1979). *Beyond interpretation: Toward a revised theory for psychoanalysis.* New York: International Universities Press.

Gedo, J. E. (1981). *Advances in clinical psychoanalysis.* New York: International Universities Press.

Gedo, J. E., & Goldberg, A. (1973). *Models of the mind: A psychoanalytic theory.* Chicago: University of Chicago Press.

Gill, M. (1982). *The analysis of transference.* New York: International Universities Press.

Goldfried, M. R., & Padawer, W. (1982). Current status and future directions in psychotherapy. In M. R. Goldfried (Ed.), *Converging themes in psychotherapy: Trends in psychodynamic, humanistic, and behavioral practice.* New York: Springer.

Gurman, A. S., & Kniskern, D. P. (1981). Family therapy outcomes research: Knowns and unknowns. In A. S. Gurman & D. P. Kniskern (Eds.), *Handbook of family therapy.* New York: Brunner/Mazel.

Haley, J. (1976). *Problem solving therapy.* San Francisco: Jossey-Bass.

Hetherington, E. M., Cox, M., & Cox, R. (1982). Effects of divorce on parents and children. In M. E. Lamb (Ed.) *Nontraditional families: Parenting and child development.* Hillsdale, NJ: Lawrence Erlbaum.

Hops, H., Wills, T. A., Patterson, G. R., & Weiss, R. L. (1971). *Marital interaction coding system,* Eugene: University of Oregon and Oregon Research Institute. (Order from ASIS/MAPS c/o Microfiche Publications, 305 E. 46th Street, New York, New York, 10017.)

Jacobson, N. S. (1981). Behavioral marital therapy. In A. S. Gurman & D. P. Kniskern (Eds.) *Handbook of family therapy.* New York: Brunner/Mazel.

Jacobson, N. S., & Moore, D. (1981). Behavior exchange theory of marriage: Reconnaisance and reconsideration. In J. P. Vincent (Ed.) *Advances in family intervention, assessment and theory, Vol. II.* Greenwich, CT: JAI Press.

Kazdin, A. E. (1982). Symptom substitution, generalization, and response covariation: Implications for psychotherapy outcome. *Psychological Bulletin, 91,* 349-365.

Kernberg, O. (1975). *Borderline conditions and pathological narcissism.* New York: Jason Aronson.

Kohut, H. (1971). *The analysis of self: A systematic approach to the psychoanalytic treatment of narcissistic personality disorders.* New York: International Universities Press.

Kohut, H. (1977). *The restoration of the self.* New York: International Universities Press.

Meisner, W. W. (1978). The conceptualization of marriage and family dynamics from a psychoanalytic perspective. In T. J. Paolino & B. S. McCrady (Eds.), *Marital therapy: Psychoanalytic, behavioral and systems theory perspectives.* New York: Brunner/Mazel.

Patterson, G. R. (1986). Performance models for antisocial boys. *American Psychologist, 41,* 432-444.

Patterson, G. R., & Reid, J. B. (1970). Reciprocity and coercion: Two facets of social systems. In C. Neuringer & J. D. Michael (Eds.), *Behavior modification in clinical psychology.* New York: Appelton-Century-Crofts.

Patterson, G. R., & Weiss, R. L. (1971). A behavioral approach to small group conflict. Office of Naval Research Contract No. N000014-67-A-0446-0003.

Pedro-Carroll, J. L., & Cowen, E. L. (1985). The children of divorce intervention program: An investigation of the efficacy of a school-based prevention program. *Journal of Consulting and Clinical Psychology, 53,* 603-611.

Raimy, V. C. (1950). *Training in clinical psychology.* Englewood Cliffs, NJ: Prentice-Hall.

Rollins, C., & Cannon, K. L. (1974). Marital satisfaction over the family life cycle: A reevaluation. *Journal of Marriage and the Family, 36,* 271-282.

Sager, C. J. (1981). Couple's therapy and marriage contract. In A. S. Gurman & D. P. Kniskern (Eds.) *Handbook of family therapy.* New York: Brunner/Mazel.

Schafer, R. (1983). *The analytic attitude.* New York: Basic Books.

Scharff, D. E., & Scharff, J. S. (1987). *Object relations family therapy.* Northvale, NJ: Jason Aronson.

Shakow, D. (1947). Recommended graduate training in clinical psychology. *American Psychologist, 2,* 539-548.

Stanton, M. D. (1981). Strategic approaches to family therapy. In A. S. Gurman & D. P. Kniskern (Eds.), *Handbook of family therapy.* New York: Brunner/Mazel.

Stolorow, R. D., & Lachman, F. M. (1980). *Psychoanalysis of developmental arrests: Theory and treatment.* New York: International Universities Press.

Stuart, R. B. (1969). Operant interpersonal treatment for marital discord. *Journal of Consulting and Clinical Psychology, 33,* 675-682.

Thibault, J. W., & Kelley, H. H. (1959). *The social psychology of groups.* New York: John Wiley.

Vincent, J. P. (1980a). *Advances in family intervention, assessment and theory, Vol. I.* Greenwich, CT: JAI Press.

Vincent, J. P. (1980b). Empirical clinical study of families: Social learning theory as a point of departure. In J. P. Vincent (Ed.), *Advances in family intervention, assessment and theory, Vol. I.* Greenwich, CT: JAI Press.

Vincent, J. P. (1981). *Advances in family intervention, assessment and theory, Vol. II.* Greenwich, CT: JAI Press.

Vincent, J. P. (1983). *Advances in family intervention, assessment and theory, Vol. III.* Greenwich, CT: JAI Press.

Vincent, J. P. (1987). *Advances in family intervention, assessment and theory. Vol. IV.* Greenwich, CT: JAI Press.

Vincent, J. P., & Carter, A. (1988). Assessment of family functioning. In K. D. O'Leary (Ed.), *Assessment of marital discord,* New York: Lawrence Erlbaum.

Vincent, J. P., Cook, N. I., & Brady, C. P. (1981). The emerging family: Integration of a social learning and developmental perspective. In J. P. Vincent (Ed.), *Advances in family intervention, assessment and theory, Vol. II.* Greenwich, CT: JAI Press.

Vincent, J. P., Friedman, L. C., Nugent, M. S., & Messerly, L. (1979). *Journal of Consulting and Clinical Psychology, 47,* 557-566.

Vincent, J. P., Harris, G. E., Cook, N. I., & Brady, C. P. (1980). Learning to be a family: A behavioral-systems model of family development. In D. Rathjen & J. P. Foreyt (Eds.), *Social competence: Interventions with adults and children,* New York: Plenum.

Vincent, J. P., Weiss, R. L., & Birchler, G. R. (1975). A behavioral analysis of problem-solving among distressed and nondistressed married and stranger dyads. *Behavior Therapy, 6,* 475-487.

Vincent, J. P., Williams, B. J., Harris, G. E., & Duval, G. (1981). Observations of hyperactive children: A multiple validation strategy. In K. Gadow & J. Loney (Eds.), *Psychosocial aspects of drug treatment for hyperactivity,* New York: AAAS Publications.

Wahler, R. G. (1975). Some structural aspects of deviant child behavior. *Journal of Applied Behavior Analysis, 8,* 27-42.

Wallerstein, J. S., & Kelly, J. B. (1980). *Surviving the breakup: How children and parents cope with divorce.* New York: Basic Books.

Watzlavick, P., Weakland, J. H., & Fisch, R. (1974). *Change: Principles of problem formation and resolution.* New York: W. W. Norton.

Weiss, R. L., Birchler, G. R., & Vincent, J. P. (1974). Contractual models for negotiation training in marital dyads. *Journal of Marriage and the Family, 36,* 321-330.

Weiss, R. L., Hops, H., & Patterson, G. R. (1973). A framework for conceptualizing marital conflicts, a technology for altering it, some data for evaluating it. In F. W. Clark & L. A. Hamerlynck (Eds.), *Critical issues in research and practice: Proceedings of the fourth Banff International Conference on Behavior Modification.* Champaign, IL: Research Press.

Willems, E. P., & Stuart, D. G. (1980). Behavioral ecology as a perspective on marriages and families. In J. P. Vincent (Ed.), *Advances in family intervention, assessment and theory, Vol. I.* Greenwich, CT: JAI Press.

Epilogue

Because the history of the field has been a rich and variegated tapestry, it became necessary to divide this into two volumes to include the numerous individuals who have made major contributions to the evolution and substance of family psychology. In Volume 1 we have featured the work of the first generation pioneers and renegades—those whose ideas began to be disseminated orally to their colleagues, students, and conference attendees and in print through book chapters and articles before 1969. We deeply regret that individuals such as John Bell, James Framo, Gerald Zuk, and Rachel Hare Mustin were not able to participate because of prior commitments. Their important substantive contributions are hereby acknowledged as are those of others who were invited but had to decline because of pressing earlier obligations.

As is clear in the chapters, this was an exciting and heady time of charting new pathways, of experimentation, of throwing off old shackles while trying to build on the validated foundations from the past. Those who "succeeded" were courageous and able to withstand immense and intense criticism from their more traditional colleagues. They derived enormous gratification from the results of their work in extending the horizons of theory about family system dynamics and functioning and from seeing the improvements their new interventions helped foster in the treatment of families.

The innovators and expanders of the second generation added new energy, concepts and techniques to the field that by 1969 had begun to be perceived as serious and vigorous. Many brought solid research backgrounds to their work and were concerned about the validity of the ideas being espoused; they stressed the urgency of utilizing well-designed research studies to determine the critical variables and their interrelationships. They also pressed for and conducted replication studies so that change attributable to therapist style and not transmissible in training might be identified. Originally most of them (us) were considered rebellious upstarts; today all are acknowledged and respected members of the established family therapy community. Interestingly, we all continue to share a common bond in remaining challengers who traverse new highways and byways—never content to remain in a static stance.

Volume 1 introduced the first two generations of leading theorists, researchers, and clinicians. In addition, it follows their work through to the present and projects it into the future. For what else came to the forefront between 1977 and 1990, see Volume 2.

Author Index

Subject Index

About the Contributors

James F. Alexander, Ph.D., received his Ph.D. in Clinical Psychology from Michigan State University in 1967. He joined the faculty of the University of Utah Department of Psychology, and has remained there to the present. Jim became a full professor in 1978, was Director of Clinical Training for eight years, and has received the College of Social-Behavioral Science Superior Teaching Award. Nationally, he has presented over 100 colloquia and workshops, and is or has been on eight editorial boards. He has been a consultant to several branches of the National Institute of Mental Health, Veterans Administration Facilities, family therapy training institutes, and state and local juvenile justice and community mental health systems. Recently, he received the AFTA award for distinguished contribution to family therapy research. He has also presented three consecutive preconference institutes at the Association for the Advancement of Behavior Therapy Annual Convention, another for the American Family Therapy Association, and was a "live master" presenter at the convention of the American Association for Marital and Family Therapy. He is Fellow and a past President of Division 43, Family Psychology, of the American Psychological Association (1989).

Harlene Anderson, Ph.D., joined the Family Study Project in the early 1970s as a member of the teaching team. At the Medical Branch in Galveston, she was originally an Associate in Psychology in the Department of Pediatrics and later became a Faculty Associate in Psychiatry and the Behavioral Sciences. In 1978, along with George Pulliam and Paul Dell, Anderson and

Goolishian formed the Galveston Family Institute, a nonprofit educational, research, and clinical center devoted to the study and practice of systems theory in clinical work. She was the Institute's first full-time faculty member and is currently its Co-Director. Drs. Anderson and Goolishian's writings have centered around the concept of the problem-determined system, alternative clinical theory, hermeneutics and interpretation in the social sciences, and human systems as meaning generating systems situated in language. At the practice level they have been concerned with the role of language, the codetermination of meaning, and the place of the interpretive sciences as they are applied to the therapy session, problems of supervision and teaching in psychotherapy, and to issues involved in agency and larger systems consultation.

Carolyn L. Attneave, Ph.D., lived from earliest years in at least two cultures: The American Indian world of her maternal grandparents, and the upwardly mobile, migratory mainstream world of her parents. These experiences imprinted a deep appreciation for the variety of family forms and traditions, which carried over into work with troubled children and adults. Graduate work at Stanford before and after World War II included first-hand explorations of the emerging interdisciplinary General Systems Theory, which had great relevance for understanding families and cultures. This focus is reflected in professional work in settings as varied as elementary and preschools to university teaching, and from applied public health settings to research and consultation in cross-cultural and family situations. Experience in rural settings allowed many family and network concepts—not always considered orthodox—to develop and be practically applied. Chance discovery of an independently developing field of family therapy led her to the East Coast where she became acquainted with the leaders in family therapy of the 1970s, and gained insight into urban applications.

Cole Barton, Ph.D., read Watzlawick, Beavin, and Jackson's *Pragmatics of Human Communication* as an antidote for intellectual ennui. Compelled by the ideas in this book, he then sought out Jim Alexander and the graduate students at the University of Utah as the theoretical, research, and clinical laboratory for developing family therapy in the intermountain West. In participating in this research group, he experienced a felicitous blend of exciting theory development, rigorous research training, extremely rewarding and supportive clinical experience, and extraordinary friendships. He has pursued an academic career that blends teaching, training of family therapists in community service programs, and research. In addition to continuing to help develop Functional Family Therapy, he is currently working with Chris Hatcher and Jim Alexander to understand the needs of families of missing children. He is grateful to clients who have taught him about the power and pain in families. He is even more grateful to his wife, parents, children, and good friends who have become as family, all of whom have shown him how magnificent families can be.

Arthur M. Bodin, Ph.D., basically in private practice, is also a Senior Research Fellow at the Mental Research Institute, Palo Alto, CA; an Associate Clinical Professor of Psychology, Department of Psychiatry, University of California, San Francisco School of Medicine; and Co-Founder and President of the Board of the Emergency Treatment Center. He is a Past President of the Division of Family Psychology of the American Psychological Association and a Past President of the California State Psychological Association. He is on the Editorial Board of the *Journal of Family Psychology, Family Therapy Today,* and the *Journal of Psychotherapy in Private Practice.* He served on the Board of Advisory Editors of *Family Process* and on the Editorial Advisory Board of the *Journal of Marital and Family Therapy.* He also served on the Western Regional Board of the American Board of Professional Psychology and was a Founding Director of the American Board of Forensic Psychology. After two terms on APA's Council of Representatives, he now serves on the APA Publications and Communications Board. In 1983 he received the Award for Distinguished Contribution to New Directions in Family Therapy from the American Family Therapy Association. His was one of the first psychology dissertations to apply social psychological methods to research on family interaction. He designed three exploratory family measurement instruments: the Bodin Family Agreement Measure (BFAM), the Self-Disclosure Questionnaire (SDQ), and the Bodin Family Life Space Diagrams (BFLSD). His two dozen publications are largely on family psychology.

Israel W. Charny, Ph.D., is Associate Professor of Psychology at the Bob Shapell School of Social Work at Tel Aviv University, where he is Director of the Postgraduate Interdisciplinary Program in Family Therapy and the Graduate Social Work Program in Family Therapy. He was the Founding and First President of the Israel Family Therapy Association, and has been honored by the American Association of Marriage and Family Therapy as an International Fellow and as a "Master" in family therapy. He is also Executive Director of the Institute of the International Conference on the Holocaust and Genocide in Jerusalem. Prior to moving to Israel in 1973, he was Professor of Psychology at the Reconstructionist Rabbinical College in Philadelphia and Director of a psychological group practice, in the Philadelphia area. He received his Ph.D. in clinical psychology from the University of Rochester in 1957 and his A.B. in psychology from Temple University in 1952.

Sandra B. Coleman, Ph.D., is a family psychologist whose career has been a blend of both clinical and research interests. Widely published, she is perhaps best known for her recent book, *Failures in Family Therapy.* During the 1970s as director of a national study on the role of family therapy in the drug abuse field, she did ground-breaking work in discovering the degree to which families were essential to the recovery process. During the next decade she was a frequent consultant and Task Force member on national drug abuse projects. She also served a four-year term as a member of a research subcommittee for the National Institute on Drug Abuse (NIDA). Her own NIDA-funded research included a major investigation of the role of unresolved deaths, multiple loss, and separation patterns in multigenerational family life cycle. This research clearly established the heroin addict family as significantly different from both psychiatric and normal subjects and gave solid support to her many theoretical publications on the role of death and loss in addict families. Currently she is working on a drug abuse handbook for parents based on her findings in the field of addiction. She is also presently completing a study on the role of gender in family therapy training institutes. In her clinical role she serves as Executive Director of the Family Guidance Center, a private family therapy program in Bucks County, PA. She is also a faculty member of both Hahnemann University and the Family Institute of Philadelphia and is on the editorial board of several major family therapy journals, including the *Journal of Family Psychology.*

Harold A. Goolishian, Ph.D., dates his beginnings in marriage and family therapy to the early 1950s. He received his Ph.D. in Clinical Psychology from the University of Houston in 1953. He is a Diplomate in Clinical Psychology and in Marital and Family Therapy. His tenure at the University of Texas Medical Branch at Galveston began with a faculty appointment in 1951 and ended with retirement as a Professor in 1981. He holds clinical appointments at several medical schools and universities.

Bernard G. Guerney, Jr., Ph.D., is a Professor of Human Development and Family Studies, and Director of the Individual and Family Consultation Center at Pennsylvania State University. He is an AAMFT Approved Supervisor, and holds diplomates in Clinical Psychology, Counseling and Psychotherapy, Behavioral Medicine, and Marital and Family Therapy. Alone or with others, he has written or edited four books, over 80 articles and chapters, and has produced numerous manuals, training tapes, and films in the areas of individual, marital, and family therapy. He is on the editorial boards of many marital and family therapy journals. For their work in developing marital and family Relationship Enhancement therapy and enrichment programs, Dr.

Guerney and his wife, Louise, have won national awards from the Association of Couples for Marriage Enrichment, the Pennsylvania Psychological Association, the Celebrate the Family Symposium, and the National Council on Family Relations. He has conducted scores of workshops here and abroad, training professionals in his method of marital/family therapy and conducting live case demonstrations.

Alan S. Gurman, Ph.D., is a Professor of Psychiatry at the University of Wisconsin Medical School, where he is the Director of the Psychiatric Outpatient Clinic and Co-Director of the Couples/Family Clinic. He is a graduate of the Boston Latin School (1963), Boston University (B.A., 1967), and Columbia University (Ph.D., 1971). The recipient of distinguished career awards in family therapy research from both the American Association for Marriage and Family Therapy (AAMFT) and the American Family Therapy Association (AFTA), he is a Fellow of the American Psychological Association (Division 43) and the AAMFT. He has served as President of the Society for Psychotherapy Research, a member of the AFTA Board of Directors, and a member of the Advisory Board of the Society for the Exploration of Psychotherapy Integration. The author of over 100 publications, he has edited or written eight books, including the *Handbook of Family Therapy* and *Theory and Practice of Brief Therapy,* and was the Editor of the *Journal of Marital and Family Therapy* from 1982 to 1990. In 1983, he was identified as the fifth most frequently cited author in family therapy. He maintains an active practice of marital, family, and individual psychotherapy, and is a Diplomate of the American Board of Family Psychology. He and his wife and two sons live in Madison, Wisconsin, where he is an avid gardener and the coach of one of the top-rated youth soccer teams in the state.

Dale L. Johnson, Ph.D., is a professor at the University of Houston where he directs the Parent-Child Research Center and teaches courses in both the developmental and clinical psychology programs. A native of North Dakota, he was educated at the University of North Dakota and the University of Kansas. His Ph.D. was from Kansas in 1957 in clinical psychology. He has been a staff psychologist at the Houston VA Hospital and was director of the small-group research program there. He has done cross-cultural work with the Mazahua, Navajo, Zuni, Sioux, and Makah American Indians. He was a Fulbright Senior Lecturer in Bergen, Norway. For the past two decades his work has focused on the development and evaluation of family support programs for low-income Mexican American families, and for families of persons with serious mental illness. He is an active member of the National Alliance for the Mentally Ill.

Florence W. Kaslow, Ph.D., is currently in independent practice as a psychologist/therapist and mediator in West Palm Beach, Florida. She is President of Kaslow Associates, P.A., and Director of the Florida Couples and Family Institute. She is an Adjunct Professor of Medical Psychology, Department of Psychiatry at Duke University Medical Center in Durham, North Carolina, and a Visiting Professor of Psychology at Florida Institute of Technology in Melbourne, Florida. She is a Past President of APA Division 43 (Family Psychology), and has served as a Board Member of APA Division 41 (Law and Psychology) and Division 46 (Media Psychology). Dr. Kaslow is past Editor of the *Journal of Marital and Family Therapy* (1976-1981) and is currently on the editorial board of *JMFT* as well as numerous other journals. She is editor of the Family Law Issues in Family Therapy Practice section of the *American Journal of Family Therapy.* She has edited and/or coauthored twelve books and has contributed chapters to many others. Her books include *Dynamics of Divorce: A Life Cycle Perspective* (coauthored with Lita L. Schwartz) and *Couples Therapy in a Family Context: Perspective and Retrospective.* Over 90 of her articles have been published in professional journals. She holds Diplomates in Clinical and in Forensic Psychology, a Diplomate in Family Psychology, and is a Fellow of APA, AAMFT, and other organizations. She serves as a site visitor for APA and AAMFT and has travelled throughout the United States and other countries including Norway, Japan, South Africa, Canada, Israel, England, Argentina, Chile, Hungary, Germany, and Czechoslovakia, doing workshops and guest lecturing. She received The Family Psychologist of the Year Award (APA) in 1986. In May 1987, she became the First President of the International Family Therapy Association. In 1987, she was elected to the National Academies of Practice as a Distinguished Practitioner in Psychology. In 1989 she was the recipient of the APA *Distinguished Contribution to Applied Psychology Award.*

Luciano L'Abate, Ph.D., came to the USA as an exchange student after World War II to attend Tabor College. He also attended Wichita University for his M.A. and Duke University from which he received his Ph.D. After a two-year postdoctoral fellowship in child psychotherapy at Michael Reese Hospital in Chicago, he moved to Washington University School of Medicine for four years and then to Emory University School of Medicine for one year and a half. From there, he moved to Georgia State University where he has spent the remainder of his academic career. He is a Diplomate and Examiner of the American Board of Examiners in Professional Psychology and Approved Supervisor of the American Association for Marriage and Family Therapy. He is a Fellow of Division 12 in the American Psychological Association and a Life Member of the American Orthopsychiatric Association. He is also a Charter Member of the American Family Therapy Association and a member of the National Council for Family Relations. He has been in part-time private clinical practice for 33 years.

Robert MacGregor, Ph.D., ABPP, was the full-time family therapy consultant for the State of Illinois Department of Mental Health for ten years. The Team-Family Method and its diagnostic approach to therapy, which he was teaching throughout the state, is an expression of the Multiple Impact Therapy, which was developed years earlier in Galveston, Texas. The method reflects a combination of MacGregor's interpersonal training with Harry Stack Sullivan, M.D.; his group psychotherapy research with Jerome D. Frank, Ph.D., M.D.; his training at the Veteran's Administration, Washington, DC; and a diagnostic typology that he developed as part of his doctoral dissertation at New York University (1954). The types were translated into levels of developmental arrest with the help of Mary H. MacGregor, M.A., his wife and developmental psychology colleague from the University of Michigan. At Michigan, he gained an understanding of family support systems from his task as part of the University's extramural services. Working with Drs. Alvin Zander, Fritz Redl, William Morse, and Vice President Howard Y. McClusky, he taught community organization in small towns all over the State of Michigan.

Augustus Y. Napier, Ph.D., is currently Director of The Family Workshop, a treatment and training institute in Atlanta, where he works frequently with his wife, Margaret, who is a family therapist and an educator. Formerly on the psychiatry faculty of the University of Wisconsin—Madison, he is the author, with Carl Whitaker, M.D., of *The Family Crucible,* as well as numerous other publications. He is a frequent consultant and workshop leader in family therapy and is active in The American Family Therapy Association and The American Association of Marriage and Family Therapy. He is a Fellow and Approved Supervisor in AAMFT and has served on The Commission of Accreditation for Marriage and Family Therapy Education. He is an advisory editor of *Contemporary Family Therapy,* and *The Journal of Divorce.* His recent book, *The Fragile Bond* (1988), addresses changing patterns in marriage, with a special focus on men's roles.

William C. Nichols, Ed.D., ABPP, a Diplomate in Clinical Psychology, decided to concentrate on the family in the late 1950s. Long concerned with integrating individual and social/group emphases, he defined family therapy as "treating the individual in context." His career has included teaching and supervising masters, doctoral, and postdoctoral students in individual, marital, and family therapy. A former president of both the American Association for Marriage and Family Therapy and the National Council on Family Relations, he founded the *Journal of Marital and Family Therapy,* has edited two other family journals, and has made significant contributions in the areas of licensure and accreditation, as well as in practice. He is author of *Marital Therapy: An Integrative Approach* (1988) and senior author of *Systemic Family Therapy* (1986). After many years of full-time independent practice, he is currently executive director of the Governor's Constituency for Children in Florida, and continues editing and writing in professional and popular areas.

K. Daniel O'Leary, Ph.D., is a Distinguished Professor of Psychology and past Chairman of the Psychology Department of the State University of New York at Stony Brook. He is a clinical psychologist who received his Ph.D. from the University of Illinois at Urbana in 1967. After Illinois, he went directly to Stony Brook and became a Professor there in 1973 and Chairman in 1978. He was editor of the *Journal of Applied Behavior Analysis* (1978-1980) and he is Associate Editor of the *Journal of Abnormal Psychology.* He is, or has been, on numerous other editorial boards. He is Past President of Division 12, Section III, of the American Psychological Association, and he is a Fellow of the American Psychological Association (Divisions 7, 12, and 25). He was president of the American Association for Advancement of Behavior Therapy. He wrote *Mommy I Can't Sit Still: Coping with the Aggressive and Hyperactive Child* (1984) and *Assessment of Marital Discord* (1987). He is coauthor of *Behavior Therapy: Application and Outcome* (1975, 1987 with G. T. Wilson), *Classroom Management* (1972, 1977 with Susan O'Leary), *Principles of Behavior Therapy* (1980, with G. T. Wilson), and *Marital Therapy Treatment for Depression* (1990, with Beach and Sandeen). He received the Distinguished Scientist Award from the Clinical Division (12, Section III) of the American Psychological Association in 1985 and was installed to the National Academies of Practice in Psychology, 1986. During the first portion of his research career, his research focused on token reinforcement, self-control, hyperactivity, and observational methodology. During the past ten years, his research has been on marital therapy, the relationship between marital and child problems, and spouse abuse. In addition to numerous colloquia at universities across the United States, he has given invited addresses in Australia, Canada, China, Columbia, England, Germany, Italy, Mexico, Peru, Scotland, South Africa, Spain, Sweden, and Wales.

David H. Olson, Ph.D., is Professor of Family Social Science at the University of Minnesota. He is currently President of the National Council on Family Relations (NCFR). He is a Licensed Consulting Psychologist (State of Minnesota) and Fellow in both the American Association of Marriage and Family Therapy (AAMFT) and the American Psychological Association

(APA). He is Associate Editor on the Advisory Board of eight family journals. He received the award for Distinguished Contribution to Family Therapy Research from the American Family Therapy Association (AFTA). His books include *Treating Relationships, Power in Families,* 10 volumes of the *Inventory of Marriage and Family Literature, Family Perspectives in Child and Youth Series,* and *Circumplex Model: Systemic Assessment and Treatment of Families.* He has developed 10 inventories that are used extensively for research and clinical work with couples and families. His best known self-report instruments include FACES, Pair, PREPARE, and ENRICH.

David G. Rice, Ph.D., was born in Charleston, West Virginia. He received his B.S. (1959) from the College of William and Mary in Virginia, and his M.S. (1961) and Ph.D. (1964) from the University of Wisconsin—Madison. Currently, he is Professor, Director of Psychology Training, and Chief Psychologist in the Department of Psychiatry at the University of Wisconsin Medical School. He is a Fellow of the American Association for Marriage and Family Therapy. He has been active in clinical psychology internship training, serving on the Executive Committee and as Secretary-Treasurer of the Association of Psychology Internship Centers. He maintains an active practice of individual and family therapy in Madison, Wisconsin, where he lives with his wife and two sons.

M. Duncan Stanton, Ph.D., is Professor and Director of the Division of Family Programs in the Department of Psychiatry at the University of Rochester School of Medicine. From 1974-1983 he was on the staff of the Philadelphia Child Guidance Clinic, serving both as Director of Research and as Director of the Addicts and Families Program. He was on the Psychiatry faculty of the University of Pennsylvania School of Medicine from 1972 to 1983 and from 1974 to 1979 was Director of Family Therapy at the Philadelphia VA Drug Dependence Treatment Center. From 1973 to 1983 he was active in the Family Institute of Philadelphia, serving on its Training Committee for five years. He is a Diplomate in Clinical Psychology and in Marital and Family Therapy. He is a founding member of AFTA, a Fellow and Approved Supervisor of AAMFT, and a Fellow in APA Divisions 12, 28, 29 and 43. He has over 100 professional and scientific publications and has given over 175 workshops and presentations on four continents. He is particularly known for his approach to integrating structural and strategic theory and practice in family therapy. His work with substance abuse dates from the mid-1960s when, as an Army psychologist, he was involved in treating alcohol problems. He is a consultant to the National Institute on Drug Abuse and has frequently consulted to the National Institute of Mental Health and the National Institute on Alcohol Abuse and Alcoholism. From 1977 to 1981 he was the family consultant to the White House Office of Drug Abuse Policy. He is on the editorial boards of ten scientific/professional journals, including *Family Process,* the *Journal of Marital and Family Therapy,* and the *American Journal of Drug and Alcohol Abuse.* In 1980 he was presented the "Award for Outstanding Research Contribution in Marital and Family Therapy" by the American Association for Marriage and Family Therapy and in 1988 he received an "Award of Appreciation" from the National Council on Family Relations.

Margaret Thaler Singer, Ph.D., is currently an adjunct professor in the Department of Psychology at the University of California, Berkeley, and in private practice. She has been affiliated with the University of Colorado School of Medicine, Walter Reed Army Institute of Research, the Adult Psychiatry Branch of the National Institute of Mental Health, the University of Rochester, and the University of California at San Francisco and at Berkeley. She has received national awards from the American Psychiatric Association, the American College of Psychiatrists, the National Mental Health Association, and the American Family Therapy Association. She is the recipient of the National Institute of Mental Health Research Scientist Award, and for her research on cults, the Leo J. Ryan Memorial Award. She was the first woman and first Ph.D. to be president of the American Psychosomatic Society. Her interests and research have been broad, ranging from studies of aging, stress, schizophrenia, prisoners of war, communication in families, hypnosis, cults, and group influence techniques, to forensic psychology. She has lectured widely in the United States and abroad, including in the House of Lords. Her long-term interest has centered on the role of language as it influences persons toward individuality, creativity, and freedom or toward constriction and compliance. Her future plans are to write about the myriad of fascinating individuals and families she has followed across time.

John P. Vincent, Ph.D., received his doctorate in clinical psychology from the University of Oregon in 1972. After an internship at the Veterans Administration Hospital, Palo Alto, California, he joined the faculty in the Department of Psychology, University of Houston. He is now Associate Professor of Psychology and Director of the Clinical Psychology Training Program. He also holds a faculty appointment in the Department of Psychiatry, Baylor College of Medicine, and is cofounder of the Institute for Family Treatment. He has edited a four volume series, *Advances in Family Intervention, Assessment and Theory,* and serves on the editorial boards of the *Journal of Marital and Family Therapy* and the *American Journal of Family Therapy.* He has authored numerous articles, book chapters, and conference presentations on assessment and treatment of marital and family problems, childhood hyperactivity, health psychology, and methodological issues in clinical research. He is a frequent guest on radio and television programs and has been featured in both regional and national publications. He maintains a private practice in Houston and has had extensive clinical experience with couples, families, and individuals. He is also a certified sex therapist. At present, he is interested in development and evaluation of low-cost, group-based interventions for children and their parents following divorce. He is married and resides with his wife in Houston.